T0301512

WILEY

Handbook of Anti Money Laundering

WILEY

Handbook of Anti Money Laundering

Dennis Cox

This edition first published 2014

Registered office
John Wiley & Sons Ltd, The Atrium, Southern Gate, Chichester, West Sussex, PO19 8SQ, United Kingdom

For details of our global editorial offices, for customer services and for information about how to apply for permission to reuse the copyright material in this book please visit our website at www.wiley.com.

Library of Congress Cataloging-in-Publication Data is available

A catalogue record for this book is available from the British Library.

ISBN 978-0-470-06574-7 (hbk) ISBN 978-0-470-68527-3 (ebk)
ISBN 978-1-118-94050-1 (ebk)

Cover Design: Wiley
Cover Image: © iStock.com/burwellphotography

Set in 10/11pt Sabon LT Std by Laserwords Private Limited, Chennai, India
Printed in Great Britain by TJ International Ltd, Padstow, Cornwall, UK

CONTENTS

INTRODUCTION

This book sets out to be a handbook for financial crime experts within companies. It seeks to provide them with sufficient information to enable them to understand the key issues that relate to two of the largest problems faced by financial institutions today: money laundering and terrorist financing.

This is an intermediate text, providing detailed information to enable the key issues to be understood and the regulatory framework appreciated. Since the market for money laundering and terrorist financing is, by its nature, global, so is this text. Consequently, whilst different rules and regulations are implemented into local legislation, it is the global standards which underpin all of these local requirements. Therefore, such global standards as exist at the time of writing this text are included within the book.

We have also provided summary guidance on the financial crime and terrorist finance rules and regulations operating in all of the major global financial centres. In the case of Europe, due to the similarity of the regulations based upon the relevant directives, which are discussed in this work, we have not provided an analysis for every country. As always, this material can only be up to date as at the date that the book has gone to print. If you require detailed rules and regulations regarding a specific market, then you should refer to the actual rule book or local legal advice to provide final guidance. This book will, however, provide you with the outline information that you will require for the majority of issues you face on a day-to-day basis.

Money laundering is one of the few growth industries that seem to be prospering at present. As a consequence of this, the regulatory structures have been developing globally and the quality of investigation improving. Offshore financial centres have been under the spotlight not just due to their data secrecy requirements but also since they have historically been used by the unscrupulous to hide income from local taxation authorities, thereby avoiding tax.

As a consequence of the increased investigation of these areas, the number of prosecutions has increased. Throughout this book we do provide examples of cases where prosecutions have been successful, and indeed these are included within the country profiles which form the majority of this book. Since it is clearly important that any case referred to has completed its legal pathway, cases can only be used after their conclusion, which can take a number of years.

The following are some examples of recent prosecutions:

Example 1: Wisconsin (USA) Restaurant Owner Sentenced to 48 Months for Structuring Financial Transactions (2009)

In Madison, Wisconsin, the owner of a restaurant was sentenced to 48 months in prison for money-laundering offences related to the structuring of financial transactions.

According to court documents, the restaurant owner borrowed $616,726 from a regular customer of his restaurant. He instructed the customer to write the cheques in small amounts so that he could use them to pay food distributors. However, in practice, rather than using these funds to pay suppliers, he actually negotiated the cheques for cash. To reduce the chance of being detected, the restaurant owner drove to multiple banks and multiple branches of the same bank to deposit the cash. This was undertaken to avoid US regulatory reporting, since if a cash transaction of more than $10,000 was received, the bank would have been required to generate a transaction report.

This demonstrates one of the key issues with money-laundering detection. The rules are designed to attempt to identify inappropriate transactions, but the unscrupulous then identify ways to avoid detection. Another approach taken by the restaurant owner was to make use of associates to cash cheques on his behalf and then return the funds to him.

In this case, the criminal activity is actually fraud. The restaurant owner is seeking to use the financial systems to enable him to make full use of the monies. In money laundering there is always some form of criminal activity – who would need to disguise legitimate funds? Often it is the nature of the funds which determines the approach that is likely to be adopted. Here, we have a fraudster using multiple bank accounts to attempt to disguise the source of funds. As we shall see in subsequent chapters, this is but one of many possible criminal activities, and there are also many forms of money laundering, although they all do have similar properties.

(*Source:* http://www.fbi.gov/milwaukee/press-releases/2009/mw092209-1.htm)

Sometimes the investigations undertaken by the crime agencies can result in successful prosecution, as shown by the following press release from the United Kingdom's Serious Organised Crime Agency (SOCA), which, in 2013, became the National Crime Agency (NCA):

Example 2: Suspected Heroin Trafficker Captured in the Netherlands (2009)

SOCA reported that a forty-four-year-old had been arrested by Amsterdam Regional Police at a petrol station in Almere on the outskirts of Amsterdam. He was believed to have been the head of an organised crime gang responsible for the importation of hundreds of kilos of heroin into the UK. He was captured following an operation involving both SOCA and the Dutch police.

Details of his status as a wanted fugitive had been publicised through Crimestoppers "Operation Captura", something which the suspected trafficker alluded to when arrested. He commented that he had felt unsafe in Spain knowing that he was wanted there, and so had moved to the Netherlands. He added that, now that he had been arrested, he was glad that it was all over. The case highlights a number of matters. Firstly, that organised crime is often involved with money laundering, since there are funds whose source will need to be disguised. Secondly, there is the importance of international cooperation. A single investigator in a single jurisdiction is unlikely to see the totality of the criminal activity, since this will often use multiple jurisdictions and financial institutions. Finally, in this case publicity caused the fugitive to change his pattern of behaviour and ultimately resulted in his being apprehended.

A SOCA spokesman said: "This arrest is a massive endorsement for Crimestoppers Operation Captura and its reputation in the criminal community. SOCA and our international partners, working together with Crimestoppers and the general public, are having a real impact on UK fugitives abroad – making sure they realise that, at any moment, there could be a knock on the door followed by the clink of handcuffs."

Clearly, international contacts are also required to detect major money-laundering rings. Another press release from the UK's Serious Organised Crime Agency highlights this clearly:

Example 3: International Money Launderer Arrested (2009)

NJ, the subject of a long-term investigation by SOCA and international partners, was arrested in New Delhi, India. NJ is alleged to have controlled a worldwide money-laundering system that, at its height, was capable of moving $2.2 billion a year.

NJ, who is banned from entering the UK, was originally arrested in Dubai in 2007 by Dubai police as part of a year-long joint investigation between SOCA, the Dubai police and the Italian Guardia di Finanza, but fled to India while awaiting trial. SOCA subsequently worked closely with the Dubai and Indian authorities to assist with their enquiries. NJ is currently in custody in India and SOCA is liaising with both Indian and Dubai police on the next steps.

Commenting on the arrest, SOCA Deputy Director Ian Cruxton said:

> *"This operation is part of SOCA's long-term strategy targeting specialist money launderers based overseas. The illegal money transfer systems they use provide the infrastructure to launder cash for organised crime groups whose activities directly impact on the United Kingdom.*
>
> *These networks pay no attention to cultural or geographical barriers. They launder money for organised crime groups from any ethnic background or criminal business, particularly UK, Pakistani and Turkish nationals based in the UK and mainland Europe involved in drugs trafficking.*
>
> *SOCA continues to share intelligence and work with international partners to create a hostile environment for criminals both domestically and internationally."*

This book aims to provide all bank employees with the basic information that they need to be part of the global attempt to identify and prosecute those involved in money laundering or terrorist financing, whilst explaining the key terms and associated risks. It should be part of an education and awareness campaign conducted throughout the financial institution to raise people's knowledge of key requirements and expectations, ensuring that each firm complies with the local rules and regulations promulgated in their jurisdiction by their relevant authority. In the course of the following chapters we shall explain some of the approaches that a bank needs to adopt to deter money laundering and to enable terrorist financing to be identified.

Where possible or appropriate we have included references to relevant rules and regulations within the body of the book, where the reader may find additional information if required.

In writing any book the author needs a good team around them. In this case, my colleagues at Risk Reward Limited and, in particular, Gurmeet Rathor and Grant Duranti have provided both content and assistance throughout the development of this book. Without their help this book would never have been completed.

Rules in this area do, of course, change and while every attempt has been made to ensure that everything included herein is fully up to date at the time of printing, additional research (or additions to this never-ending book) may be required in the future.

I do hope that you find this book helpful and comprehensive, and remember that if you are working for a bank and money laundering or terrorist financing have not yet been identified, it does not mean that they are not around – it just means that you have not found them yet.

Dennis Cox
Risk Reward Limited
London
October 2013

1 WHAT IS MONEY LAUNDERING?

1.1 THE INITIAL CONCERNS

The growth industry which we refer to as money laundering has developed significantly over recent years. The industry really started with what might be considered a key public concern over organised crime and the negative impact that this was having on people. The governing authorities surmised that, by tracking the movement of cash, they would then be able to detect unusual patterns of behaviour. This led to a series of rules being put in place, originally locally but increasingly globally, to enable relevant authorities to identify organised crime through its use of the financial sector.

The key element that underpins the regulation is that inappropriate funds were being moved within the banking system to disguise the original source of the funds, enabling organised crime to make free use of funds that may have originated from tainted sources, including drug trafficking. Essentially, the plan was to use the movement of the gains to identify the criminal, since the original criminal activity was so hard to detect.

The impetus behind money-laundering legislation in any country always comes from some form of issue which is considered to be of such magnitude that it actually gets onto the political agenda. The legislation is then generally developed in a hurry to meet these perceived and specific needs. We are seeing this at present with the revised banking regulations, designed to try to prevent a financial crisis yet actually creating one of their own.

The initial drive to combat money laundering derived from the wish to reduce narcotic-related criminal activity. Much of the original legislation concentrated on narcotic-related issues, since this area was seen as being the primary concern. This initial legislation has now been extended in most countries to include terrorist financing and, more recently, to incorporate funds resulting from any form of illegal act. The definition of what is an illegal act does vary between countries and is likely to be broader than you might initially expect.

To take one area where there may be concerns, taxation-related matters are a particularly complex area for financial crime regulation. Tax avoidance is generally not illegal unless it is deemed abusive, whereas tax evasion is illegal. In cases where tax evasion has taken place, criminals have the use of the funds that should have been paid over as taxation and therefore these are funds relating to criminal activity. Any transaction relating to these funds will now be considered as money laundering. Changes in regulation and legislation that are currently being implemented are often designed to capture different elements of the abuse of the taxation system of the relevant jurisdiction and this has led to much of the recent growth in financial crime regulation.

As discussed, the consequence of the manner in which legislation has been enacted globally is that what are considered to be money-laundering predicate offences do vary considerably between countries. More recently there has been a significant effort to achieve a level of international standardisation within the money-laundering deterrence arena, led by groups such as the Financial Action Task Force (FATF) as discussed in Chapter 3, although they, of course, do not have any statutory responsibility. It remains the responsibility of the local legislature to implement the requirements into local law – and they will often take into account specific local issues and other existing legislation in doing so. This is particularly the case in respect of the USA, as discussed in Chapter 9, and is addressed in more detail in the various country profiles which conclude this text.

1.2 WHAT IS MONEY LAUNDERING?

The idea of money laundering is simple in principle. The person who has received some form of ill-gotten gains will seek to ensure that they can use these funds without people realising that they are the result of inappropriate behaviour. To do this they will need to disguise the proceeds such that the original source of the proceeds is hidden and therefore the funds themselves appear to be legitimate. Given that it is often cash that needs to be disguised, the criminal will often seek out legitimate cash-based businesses to enable them to disguise the source of their illegitimate cash.

When you are discussing the laundering of money, there are generally two different connotations to consider. Money laundering refers both to the use of a cash business such as a launderette to facilitate the mingling of legal and illegal funds and also to the generic process of disguising the original proceeds of the funds, a process more normally referred to as layering. By mixing legitimate and illegitimate funds, the entire amount could potentially appear to be legitimate, and would therefore have been laundered, achieving the objectives of the money launderer. The funds will appear to have come from the legitimate business whereas some of the funds actually have arisen from criminal activity of some type. Indeed, coin-operated launderettes, which are generally cash-based businesses, would represent an ideal opportunity to achieve this, and much early money laundering did make use of legitimate cash-based activity to disguise and transform ill-gotten gains.

If a business normally takes in cash of, say, £20,000 per week, would anyone notice if this increased to £25,000? The original £20,000 is clearly legitimate business that is being conducted, whereas the next £5,000 may represent funds from an inappropriate source that is being laundered through the medium of the legitimate business. It is hard for any financial institution to identify that a firm should have only banked £20,000 when in fact it banked £25,000, so this type of money laundering is actually very difficult to identify. The only approaches to addressing such issues are due diligence on the part of bank employees and modelling approaches which serve to select specific accounts warranting additional investigation. Of course, any investigation work must be undertaken without notifying the customer that they are under suspicion, as we shall discuss later.

It is important to recognise that there are two main styles of money laundering – professional and amateur. The professional money launderer will take advantage of any perceived weakness in the systems of control operated by a financial institution or regulatory structure. Amateur money laundering takes an opportunity and does not really cover its tracks very well, leaving obvious causes for concern which are easy to identify either by employees being diligent or through the use of modelling systems. It is normally the latter type of money laundering that is detected by law-enforcement agencies. The professional is always much harder, and therefore more expensive, to identify.

As discussed above, initially cash-based businesses were one of the key areas on which money launderers would concentrate to launder their funds. Returning to the business of a launderette, this is an obvious example of such a suitable vehicle for the money launderer. Anyone can walk into a coin-operated launderette and put their coins into the machine or pay the attendant for laundry services. The payments will predominantly be in cash and there can be very little control to ensure that the funds that would be banked by the launderette business are actually the same as those that are received by the launderette. This therefore achieves the objectives of money laundering – the use of the launderette business will enable a criminal to disguise the source of their funds so that they appear to be from legitimate sources and can be used freely.

Clearly, organised criminals are able to take advantage of any number of cash-based businesses to disguise illegal proceeds. The following are just a few of the types of business which have been subject to abuse by money launderers:

- Launderettes
- Newspaper sales
- Taxis
- Bars and fast food restaurants
- Casinos
- Insurance
- Asset management
- Antiques
- Property.

Some of the vehicles will not be used for the primary placement of cash but will become part of the layering process which is considered in more depth in the next chapter. Of course, as detection of money laundering has become more sophisticated, then so has the skill of the money launderer, giving rise to more complex ways of making use of the financial markets.

1.3 THE PROCESS OF MONEY LAUNDERING

Money laundering is essentially a three-stage process, as discussed in Chapter 2. It starts with the criminal activity that gives rise to the illegal funds. We have mentioned drug-trafficking offences, but everything from tax evasion to bribery and corruption results in funds being produced which the criminal will seek to disguise. The funds need first to be received and then introduced into the system. It is often at this first introduction phase that the detection authorities have their best chance of identifying the funds as being inappropriate, leading to potential criminal prosecution. This stage is then followed by the layering and integration phases.

Clearly, a series of fees and costs will need to be incurred by the launderer to achieve their objective of disguising the original source of the funds. It is the combination of the level of criminal activity in the world with the level of fees that may be earned that results in money laundering being such a lucrative industry. Of course, as the money launderer becomes more sophisticated, it is also incumbent on the financial intermediaries (banks, brokers, insurers, casinos and other entities) together with law-enforcement agencies to become more sophisticated and vigilant in their deliberations. This tends to result in new legislation being implemented to deal with what is the last problem that has been identified – whether it actually reduces money laundering is, of course, another matter. While we still have activities that we consider to be criminal, we will have criminal proceeds and consequently money laundering to contend with.

1.4 THE PRIMARY OFFENCES

Initially, the drive of the money-laundering-deterrence legislation was to restrict and identify the activities of organised criminals and gangs. This was then extended to the area of narcotics and drug trafficking – indeed much of the current legislation has drug-trafficking prosecution at its heart. The idea is that by making it difficult for the syndicate that is producing the narcotics and then distributing them around the world to make use of the funds generated, there will be a reduction in the level of narcotics that are available and therefore drug taking will reduce. Of course, for this to be the case the penalties under the legislation and the likelihood of being detected must be higher than the expected benefits from the narcotics trade. Whether this is actually the case is open to debate and could be one of the reasons why the narcotics trade does not appear to be diminishing.

In more recent years terrorist financing has also become a major cause for concern, and again money-laundering deterrence has been targeted as one of the ways in which the authorities within a country can be seen to be acting to attempt to reduce the ability of such organisations to act within a specific jurisdiction.

So, the three original key areas where money-laundering-deterrence legislation and regulation were intended to be effective were:

- Organised crime
- Drug trafficking
- Terrorist financing.

Each of these is a clearly illegal activity in most countries, although they are not always easy to define completely or accurately. More recently in many countries the scope of such rules and regulations has broadened significantly, effectively becoming what might be considered "all crimes" legislation. This clearly results in a broadening of the areas of criminal activity being covered by such legislation, which would include some or all of the following:

- Robbery or theft
- Blackmail or extortion
- Bribery and corruption
- Piracy of various types
- Illegal pornography or issues related to sexual matters
- People trafficking
- Tax evasion.

1.5 DUE DILIGENCE

The role of the financial institution is to be diligent and to act when it becomes suspicious. Whilst in the case of tax evasion the suspicion may not immediately be obvious to people involved with managing the account at the financial institution, in other cases it will be. It is therefore important for financial institutions and other relevant entities to identify their customers and associates properly, undertaking what are referred to as due diligence procedures, or, if they are relationships that are identified as having a high perceived risk, undertaking enhanced due diligence procedures.

Such a due diligence process begins with procedures whose objective is the identification of the customer or associate as an appropriate person for the firm to do business with. This will involve obtaining information on both people and companies and their source of funds as required by local regulation and the policies and procedures of the firm.

This, of course, relies on the staff of the financial institution undertaking their roles with care and this can be difficult. Banks want to sell financial service products to their clients. If a client comes to a bank and wants to open a bank account, the bank needs to obtain the information it requires to comply with the regulations while at the same time selling to the customer. If staff begin to see the financial crime regulatory requirements as little more than a regulatory construct, they will not remain as vigilant as should be the case and the money launderer will become a customer.

Continual training is required to constantly emphasise the importance of the controls applied by the bank. Only through the first line of defence of the bank, the front-office staff, exercising careful due diligence can a firm really be protected.

After taking on the initial relationship, the requirement to undertake due diligence does not end. The financial institution will still be required to undertake monitoring of the customer to see that the activities undertaken appear to be consistent with their understanding of the customer and are not suspicious. This ongoing due diligence obligation will continue throughout the customer relationship and will again be enshrined in local regulation and the policies and procedures of the firm.

If a suspicion has been identified, it needs to be investigated by the financial institution to ensure that there are real grounds for suspicion. The requirements in this respect are generally included in local regulation, transposed into the rules of the firm. Only once the transaction has been investigated should the suspicion be reported to the relevant authorities by the relevant officer at the financial institution, a role normally referred to as the Money Laundering Reporting Officer (or MLRO). The suspicious activity report (or SAR) submitted to the relevant authority will potentially document that the financial institution has met its obligations under the relevant legislation, providing a safe harbour from prosecution. It will also provide the enforcement authorities with another link in what might be a lengthy chain of reports which could lead to a successful prosecution.

1.6 THE EVASION OF TAXATION

There are few things more certain in life than taxation, unless you are lucky enough to be based in a jurisdiction where no taxes are, in fact, payable – certain countries in the Middle East, for example.

In most countries, some or all of the following taxes apply:

- Income tax
- Corporation tax
- Sales tax or Value Added Tax
- Inheritance tax
- Capital gains tax
- Local sales tax
- Car tax
- Petroleum revenue tax
- Gaming duty
- Alcohol duties
- National insurance
- Property taxes.

With such a range of possible taxes available that both individuals and businesses could be subject to, it is hardly surprising that an industry has emerged to assist individuals and corporations in minimising the amount of taxation that they are required to pay.

When you are organising your affairs to minimise the taxation that will be levied, this is clearly a legal process unless you are based in a country that has implemented abusive taxation avoidance legislation. Generally, the failure to pay taxation that is due and payable is clearly a criminal offence and therefore would be covered by "all crimes" money-laundering-deterrence rules and regulations. The problem is that taxation statutes and their legal interpretation are generally far from certain and therefore court action is often required to enable the legal position to be clarified with any degree of certainty.

To illustrate the problem, consider the following. A company is seeking to acquire another business. At the time when a transaction was entered into to buy the company, the acquired business may have thought that what it was doing was legal, and therefore that it was paying the correct sums of taxation to the relevant collecting authority. It may only be after the case has been resolved in favour of the taxation authorities that the firm would have been guilty of money laundering, since it would have failed to pay the appropriate amount of taxation on the due date. The firm that has purchased the business then has concerns in that it may have overpaid for the company it has acquired.

Of course, such a case would tend to focus on the economic reality of the situation as opposed to money laundering, which is really not a concern, since there was no such intention in the activity. It is cases where there is a lack of clarity in taxation legislation that tend to prove problematic and it is when the company is taking actions to minimise taxation which are perhaps pushing the boundaries that problems occur.

Tax havens are financial centres which offer a range of services to international businesses and individuals to reduce or eliminate their home country taxation liability. For some time now, and particularly since the economic crash of 2008, there has been significant global financial and political impetus to clamp down on tax havens. With the objectives of both preventing financial crime and ensuring the full amount of revenue is received by the exchequer, countries such as Switzerland and Luxembourg have come under increased scrutiny as their financial privacy laws are being eroded. This is likely to lead to the discovery of a number of questionable, if not illegal, schemes which were previously protected by the renowned privacy laws of the havens, while encouraging criminals to devise new and more advanced schemes to evade the uncovering of their frauds once again.

Difficulties arise when a scheme which was thought to have been legal becomes illegal, something that can easily occur where there is tax planning taking place. In such cases, the funds which were once legal have now become illegal and therefore will be subject to the financial crime regime.

1.7 SUSPICION AND REPORTING

The key issue is that actions taken by firms to attempt to reduce the level of their taxation may eventually be seen as being too extreme and therefore could potentially be considered as being illegal. If a country adopts an "all crimes" approach to money-laundering deterrence, then there may be a requirement for such matters to be reported immediately to the reporting authorities in cases where there clearly is a suspicion. Of course, the point at which the suspicion occurs may itself be unclear.

A suspicious activity report (or SAR) will typically then be provided to the relevant in-country authority for them to consider whether action should be taken. In many cases, the authorities will not have sufficient information to take action, in which case nothing will happen. In other cases, they will link information from the single SAR with other SARs that they receive, leading to information linking investigations and ultimately to criminal prosecution.

1.8 THE LOCAL SERVICE PROVIDER

Do you personally have any local service providers that you pay in cash? This might include plumbers, carpenters, gardeners, taxi drivers, builders and similar parties. Would you expect that person to disclose all of their income to the relevant taxation authorities? Is it possible that they may choose to show a lower amount of revenue than is actually the case to reduce the amount of taxation that would be due and payable? This is clearly a plausible scenario, but is it sufficient to result in the money-laundering-deterrence regime applying and a SAR being produced?

Generally, such activities are, to some extent, not included within this form of legislation. Basically it would not be helpful for financial institutions and others to report cash-based businesses to the relevant authorities purely because they were cash-based businesses. Just because it is possible for the activity to permit tax evasion, does not mean that there actually will be tax evasion and therefore, generally, this cannot be sufficient to result in a suspicion of money laundering and consequent reporting to the approved party. However, if there is a clear suspicion, then such reporting should still take place.

Could there also be obligations on a financial institution regarding the under reporting of income or some other form of tax evasion? The answer is clearly yes. If the firm should have been aware that the firm was under reporting its income or in some other way evading taxation unlawfully, then this would be a reason to report the firm to the relevant authorities and for the money-laundering-deterrence legislation to apply.

However, since the financial institution may not be the only firm with which the customer is undertaking banking activity, the ability of the single firm to identify such cases is limited.

1.9 LICENCE PAYMENTS

In some countries it will be illegal to drive without a driving licence, or to operate a specific car without the vehicle having been approved, or to have a television without the relevant approval. Such areas are generally seen as being too minor to warrant investigation by relevant authorities and are therefore generally seen as more minor offences. Accordingly, retaining the funds that you should have paid for the licence will not, in itself, mean that you are guilty of money-laundering offences in addition to the original offence resulting from failure to have the licence.

What this means is that, as you move from one jurisdiction to another, it is always important to make sure that you are fully aware of what the predicate offences are within the specific jurisdiction that you are involved with. It is also important to stress that some jurisdictions include an element of extraterritorial provisions, enabling the regulator in one country to take an interest in payments in another country, with the USA being one obvious such case, as set out in Chapter 9.

Of course, tax evasion is not at the heart of the money-laundering-deterrence regime, yet it is increasingly one of the major areas where such legislation is applied. Understanding the local regulatory requirements for due diligence, monitoring and reporting, training staff adequately and rigorously applying relevant procedures is always the best protection for any firm in any jurisdiction.

2 THE PROCESS OF MONEY LAUNDERING

2.1 THE MONEY-LAUNDERING CYCLE

Money laundering is generally seen as a three-stage process, as shown in Figure 2.1.

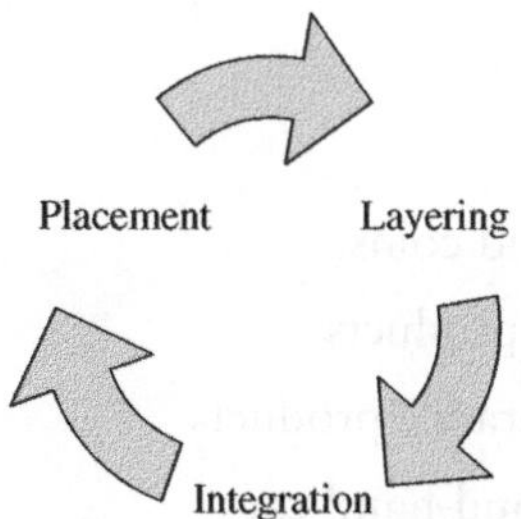

Figure 2.1 The three-stage money-laundering process

The idea is that the initial proceeds enter the banking system at a perceived point of weakness (the placement phase) and then the funds are moved around such that the initial source of the funds is disguised (the layering phase). The funds are eventually reintegrated into the mainstream banking system as clean funds (the integration phase).

These three stages shall be considered separately.

2.1.1 The Placement Phase

The placement is the initial stage of the process. The illegitimate funds have been obtained in some way, perhaps as a result of extortion, theft or drug trafficking, or any other form of predicate crime. These funds will need to be placed initially into the banking system to commence the money-laundering process.

Placement is not just the movement of cash into a bank account, even though this is the process that is most frequently considered. The initial placement purely means moving the funds from their original cash source into some other form which will enable the money launderer to undertake further layering and therefore disguise these amounts.

For example, were a money launderer to purchase a physical asset, say a painting or another asset of value, then this asset could be subsequently sold and this would then release funds which would appear to be legitimate. Consequently, the acquisition of the painting at an auction for cash would represent money laundering. So, it is not just the placement of cash into a bank account that represents the first stage in the layering process, rather it is the initial transfer of the questionable asset into another form.

Money launderers will typically focus on areas in the financial system where there appears to be the least obvious control. Consequently, if the money launderer has particular knowledge that an individual or company is in particular need of cash, then this will probably be an indicator as to an opportunity to be selected for the original placement of illegitimate funds. This is because the individual or company need is such that the level of due diligence that it conducts may be reduced, enabling the money launderer to profit.

All of the following could be used for the placement process:

- The purchase of paintings
- The purchase of antiques
- Buying things in a market
- The acquisition of stamps and coins
- The purchase of investment products
- Taking out unnecessary insurance products
- The purchase of new or second-hand cars
- The purchase of boats
- Buying chips at a casino
- Purchasing lottery tickets
- Purchasing premium bonds
- Acquiring shares in private companies
- Providing cash loans to companies
- Purchasing commodities or precious metals.

Effectively, the placement is limited only by the vision of the money launderer.

If there is a branch of a bank that is known to be under pressure to increase its deposit base, then the money launderers will actively seek it out. If there is a bank that is struggling to maintain liquidity, then it may also become an obvious target. If a salesman is given a target to achieve a bonus, then he may also become an opportunity for the money launderer, since he will potentially be liable to lower his money-laundering-deterrence guard while seeking to achieve sales. It is the person or business that most needs the cash or sales that is most likely to be targeted by the unscrupulous.

From the position of the firm, this highlights where additional controls are required. If a firm implements a bonus regime that requires a target of deposit to be achieved, then it has created an incentive that may run contrarian to the objective of a financial crime deterrence programme. By creating bias in the system, encouraging staff to seek out depositors, the message will be sent out to the market that this firm is actively seeking deposits. In trying to achieve the sales targets set, the employees of the firm may choose to ignore warning signals which at other times might have caused them to question the depositor.

However, given the nature of the current financial market, many firms are actively seeking to grow their deposit books. The additional reputational risks that are consequent to this route of action need to be addressed. This should be achieved through a combination of additional controls including the following:

- **Secret shopping:** A series of staff should seek to deposit funds at your branches, particularly those that are not currently achieving their targets. The secret shopper is, of course, an employee of the firm. They will pose a series of scenarios to the branch or other staff which, under normal circumstances, would have been expected to raise concerns. If the relevant employee fails to take the action intended, then the firm will be aware that its financial crime deterrence programme has ceased to operate effectively.
- **Increased supervision:** For a sample of accounts opened, the central management team should undertake a series of specific additional reviews to ensure that the risk profile identified for the customer is consistent with the information actually gathered.

2.1.2 *The Layering Phase*

Once the funds have initially been placed, the next phase of the money-laundering programme is the layering phase. As stated above, the objective of the layering phase is to disguise the proceeds of crime such that the original source and the current position of the funds are unclear. This can typically be as easy as using the illegitimate funds to invest in something legitimate, so that the funds now appear to be "clean". In other cases, a far more complex series of transactions will be entered into.

In more complex schemes, the money launderer will move the funds between a number of accounts in a number of different jurisdictions and through a series of companies to ensure that the trail is as complicated as possible. This will essentially obscure the audit trail and sever the link with the original criminal proceeds. In the most professional cases of money laundering identified, the funds can actually "spin" up to ten times prior to being integrated into the banking system.

Money launderers will face varying levels of difficulty during the layering phase depending on the chosen method of investment. For example, antiques, paintings and stamps can all be legitimately acquired privately, and thus have a low level of risk for the money launderer. You can purchase them at antique markets, shops, auctions or even car boot sales or flea markets. They can be inherited, found or gifted. Some of these routes maintain formal records of the purchase or sale, whereas others do not.

That legitimate activity may not have records provides a good cover for the money launderer, since there can be little proof of where the asset came from. They could say it was inherited when, in fact, it was purchased from a flea market. If no questions are asked, then the money launderer is clearly at a significant advantage.

A more risky method of layering would be the purchase of property. This is because lawyers or solicitors will become involved. Lawyers generally are also under money-laundering obligations and need to conduct various due diligence of their own to meet the standards placed upon them. Accordingly, the lawyers may be alerted to concerns as a result of conducting their own due diligence. They may also be under an obligation to report inappropriate activity, but again this will depend on the rules of the jurisdiction and, of course, the scruples of the lawyer.

2.1.3 The Integration Phase

Integration is the final stage of the money-laundering process. It is the stage where illegal proceeds are re-integrated into a legitimate financial system to be assimilated with other assets in the system. This is where the disguised criminal proceeds can be returned to and used by the money launderer and they will now appear to be legitimate funds. Money launderers will typically put the "cleaned" money into the normal economy to make it appear to have been earned legitimately. The main aim of the money launderer is to integrate funds successfully so that it becomes difficult for anyone to distinguish between legitimate and illegitimate (criminal proceeds) funds and they will then be free to use them for any purpose they require.

There are many ways in which laundered money can be integrated back into the normal economy. With the money launderer, however, the main objective of money laundering at this stage is to reunite themselves with the criminal proceeds in a manner that does not draw attention or suspicion. More about suspicion later, but it is often by the money launderer abusing successful schemes of money laundering through greed that the financial institution subsequently becomes suspicious and the criminal is identified.

For example, the purchases of property, sports cars, art work, jewellery, etc. are common ways for the launderer to enjoy their laundered money without necessarily drawing attention to them. The risk is that conspicuous displays of wealth could either cause suspicion or result in envy, resulting in identification of inappropriate actions. However, money launderers will use more and more creative and unique ways to achieve their objectives.

Common methods of integration used by money launderers include the following:

- One of the simplest methods of integrating funds was to transfer money to a legitimate bank from a shell bank owned by the launderers. Shell banks, which have little legitimate business, are now generally addressed in jurisdictional rules and therefore this is becoming a more complex area to manage.
- Money launderers can send embellished invoices overvaluing goods or services which allow them to move funds from one country to another. The invoices act as verification for the origins of the funds placed with financial institutions.
- Money launderers can establish anonymous companies in countries where the right to secrecy is guaranteed. They are then able to grant themselves loans out of the laundered money in the event of a future legal transaction. Furthermore, they may increase their profits, they will also claim tax relief on the loan repayments and charge themselves interest on the loan.

- The use of trading accounts with financial institutions is another obvious example. The money launderer transfers funds into an open brokerage account, allowing the financial institution to trade on their behalf. At some later stage they take the funds, which have then been laundered, from the account.
- The money launderer can cancel an insurance policy after the premium has been paid. The premium returned by the insurance company is, of course, laundered funds.
- Assets acquired can be sold either in an open market or as a private sale, with funds being received ideally electronically into a legitimate bank account, perfectly laundered of course.

These are but a few of the ways in which the assets can be integrated back into the normal economy. The launderer's objective is normally to obtain cash payment from a legitimate bank that they can pay into their account at another legitimate bank. Once this has been achieved, the laundering cycle is normally complete and the criminal is free to use the funds for any purpose they require without any expectation of being detected.

3 INTERNATIONAL MONEY-LAUNDERING REGULATION – THE ROLE OF THE FINANCIAL ACTION TASK FORCE[1]

3.1 WHO ARE THE FINANCIAL ACTION TASK FORCE?

The Financial Action Task Force (FATF) is an inter-governmental body established in 1989 by the Ministers of its member jurisdictions. The objectives of the FATF are to set standards and promote effective implementation of legal, regulatory and operational measures for combating money laundering, terrorist financing and other related threats to the integrity of the international financial system. The FATF is, therefore, a "policy-making body" which works to generate the necessary political will to bring about national legislative and regulatory reforms in these areas.

The FATF has developed a series of recommendations that are recognised as the international standard for combating money laundering and the financing of terrorism and proliferation of weapons of mass destruction. They form the basis for a coordinated response to these threats to the integrity of the financial system and help ensure a level playing field. First issued in 1990, the FATF Recommendations were revised in 1996, 2001, 2003 and, most recently, in 2012 to ensure that they remain up to date and relevant, and they are intended to be for universal application.

The FATF monitors the progress of its members in implementing necessary measures, reviews money-laundering and terrorist-financing techniques and countermeasures, and promotes the adoption and implementation of appropriate measures globally. In collaboration with other international stakeholders, the FATF works to identify national-level vulnerabilities with the aim of protecting the international financial system from misuse.

The FATF's decision-making body, the FATF Plenary, meets three times per year.

3.2 FATF RECOMMENDATIONS

In response to mounting concern over money laundering, the Financial Action Task Force on Money Laundering (FATF) was established by the G-7 Summit that was held in Paris in 1989. Recognising the threat money laundering posed to the banking system and to financial institutions, the G-7 Heads of State or Government and the President of the European Commission convened the Task Force from the G-7 member states, the European Commission and eight other countries.

[1] Extracts from the FATF Recommendations and relevant FATF guidance and best practices are reproduced with kind permission of the Financial Action Task Force.

The FATF was given the responsibility of examining money-laundering techniques and trends, reviewing the action which had already been taken at a national or international level and setting out the measures that still needed to be taken to combat money laundering. In April 1990, less than one year after its creation, the FATF issued a report containing a set of forty recommendations, which were intended to provide a comprehensive plan of action needed to fight money laundering. They still form the real basis for all money-laundering regulations worldwide and while they have now been updated, these original recommendations largely remain the key requirements.

In 2001, the development of standards in the fight against terrorist financing was added to the mission of the FATF, extending its role beyond pure money-laundering deterrence. As a consequence, in October 2001, the FATF issued eight special recommendations to deal with the issue of terrorist financing. The continued evolution of money-laundering techniques led the FATF to revise the FATF standards comprehensively in June 2003. In October 2004, the FATF published a ninth special recommendation, further strengthening the agreed international standards for combating money laundering and terrorist financing, resulting in the production of what came to be known as the 40+9 Recommendations.

In February 2012, the FATF completed a thorough review of its standards and published the revised FATF 40 Recommendations. The objective of this revision was to further strengthen global safeguards and also to protect the integrity of the financial system by providing governments with stronger tools to take action against financial crime. Of course, since the FATF does not have any legal standing in any country, this is really attempting to create a global level playing field in financial crime and terrorist-financing deterrence by creating international best practice, hoping that this will exert pressure for compliance. The recommendations have been expanded to deal with perceived new threats such as the financing of the proliferation of weapons of mass destruction, and to be clearer on transparency and tougher on corruption. The nine special recommendations on terrorist financing have now been fully integrated with the measures against money laundering. This has resulted in a stronger and clearer set of standards, albeit substantially unchanged in many areas.

The FATF, of course, has no global jurisdiction and consequently it is incumbent upon local rules and regulations to be implemented. As referred to above, the FATF does, however, conduct reviews of the level of compliance within jurisdictions to the FATF recommendations and this does provide some level of impetus for their implementation. These reports are publicly available on the FATF website. In this chapter we also identify whether these recommendations are new in 2012 or whether these are the existing recommendations from the 40+9 set.

The 40 current FATF recommendations are outlined below.

Recommendations

1. **Assessing risks and applying a risk-based approach (*New recommendation*)**
   - Countries should identify, assess and understand the money-laundering and terrorist-financing risks for the country, and should take action, including designating an authority or mechanism to coordinate actions to assess risks, and apply resources, aimed at ensuring the risks are mitigated effectively.

- Based on that assessment, countries should apply a risk-based approach (RBA) to ensure that measures to prevent or mitigate money laundering and terrorist financing are commensurate with the risks identified. This approach should be an essential foundation to efficient allocation of resources across the anti-money-laundering and countering the financing of terrorism (AML/CFT) regime and the implementation of risk-based measures throughout the FATF Recommendations.
- Where countries identify higher risks, they should ensure that their AML/CFT regime adequately addresses such risks. Where countries identify lower risks, they may decide to allow simplified measures for some of the FATF Recommendations under certain conditions.
- Countries should require financial institutions and designated non-financial businesses and professions (DNFBPs) to identify, assess and take effective action to mitigate their money-laundering and terrorist-financing risks.

This is a new, explicit recommendation, which perpetuates the principle of taking a risk-based approach. The FATF is keen for its members to adopt risk-based strategies to its AML regimes, which is further highlighted by the fact that this recommendation appears before the criminalisation of the money-laundering offence, which has been relegated to Recommendation 3.

By bringing this in as the first recommendation, the FATF is outing the onus on firms to implement such a risk-based regime and, as we shall discuss later, this may require the implementation of some form of money-laundering-deterrence monitoring software. The risk-based approach to implementation is, however, not without some measure of risk. If a risk-based approach results in less work being conducted in one area to enable more work to be conducted in another, then the risk exists that the initial analysis will be proven to be incorrect. In such cases, the firm will need to show that its procedures are not only compliant with local rules and regulations but also meet expectations that are likely to be developed with the benefit of hindsight.

The consequence of this is that while it is important to implement a risk-based approach, as we shall discuss again later, firms must ensure that their procedural and transactional documentation is adequate to provide a defence against an accusation that the risk-based approach was being used to enable a firm to "turn a blind eye" to potential money laundering.

2. **National cooperation and coordination (*Previously addressed in Recommendation 31*)**
   - Countries should have national AML/CFT policies, informed by the risks identified, which should be reviewed regularly, and should designate an authority or have a coordination or other mechanism that is responsible for such policies.
   - Countries should ensure that policy-makers, the financial intelligence unit (FIU), law-enforcement authorities, supervisors and other relevant competent authorities, at the policy-making and operational levels, have effective mechanisms in place which enable them to cooperate, and, where appropriate, coordinate domestically with each other concerning the development and implementation of policies and activities to combat money laundering, terrorist financing and the financing of proliferation of weapons of mass destruction.

This is more expansive than the 2003 recommendation. It does suggest that the local regime should be based on local risk analysis so that it is necessary for FIUs (or other appropriate bodies) to undertake a review of the risks that both financial crime and terrorist financing pose to their local markets. Of course, it would be helpful were this to be made public so that firms could then apply this within their implementation of the risk-based approach, but at present few countries have clearly set this out publicly.

3. **Money-laundering offence (*Previously addressed in Recommendations 1 and 2*)**
   - Countries should criminalise money laundering on the basis of the Vienna Convention and the Palermo Convention.
   - Countries should apply the crime of money laundering to all serious offences, with a view to including the widest range of predicate offences.

The United Nations Conference for the Adoption of a Convention against Illicit Traffic in Narcotic Drugs and Psychotropic Substances met at the Neue Hofburg in Vienna from 25th November to 20th December, 1988 and this resulted in what is now known as the Vienna Convention. This was published as the *United Nations Convention against Illicit Traffic in Narcotic Drugs and Psychotropic Substances 1988*, highlighting the limited focus of the convention. 106 countries participated in the convention. The convention itself consists of 34 articles including consideration of the labelling of exports and commercial documents. As such, this convention is for a wider audience than purely the financial community.

This particular article does warrant additional review. It states:

> *"Each party shall require that lawful exports of narcotic drugs and psychotropic substances be properly documented. In addition there is a requirement to document the quantity being exported, and the name and address of the exporter, the importer and, when available, the consignee. Each party is required to ensure that consignments of narcotic drugs and psychotropic substances being exported are not mislabelled."*

So the objective is to separate legal drug import and export from illegal trafficking through a labelling system.

The Palermo Convention dates from 8th January, 2001 and was again published by the United Nations. The United Nations were "deeply concerned by the negative economic and social implications related to organised criminal activities, and convinced of the urgent need to strengthen cooperation to prevent and combat such activities more effectively at the national, regional and international levels". They also noted with deep concern the growing links between transnational organised crime and terrorist crimes. They sought to broaden the previous treaty to include other areas including terrorist financing and corruption and were seeking bilateral agreements between parties to enable better detection and investigation to occur. The organisation even went so far as to state the information that a cross-jurisdictional information request should include, as well as including the requirements for training of law-enforcement officers.

By including these conventions within this recommendation the FATF is seeking to highlight the importance of cooperation and also to reflect much of the work that has been conducted which should be included within local jurisdictional law. This FATF recommendation is considerably more succinct than the 2003 recommendations, even though the two conventions mentioned were passed prior to 2003. This, therefore, affords countries more freedom in the manner in which they criminalise money laundering.

4. Confiscation and provisional measures (*Previously addressed in Recommendation 3*)
Countries should adopt measures similar to those set forth in the Vienna Convention, the Palermo Convention and the Terrorist Financing Convention, including legislative measures, to enable their competent authorities to freeze or seize and confiscate the following, without prejudicing the rights of bona fide third parties:

(a) property laundered;
(b) proceeds from, or instrumentalities used in or intended for use in, money laundering or predicate offences;
(c) property that is the proceeds of, or used in, or intended or allocated for use in, the financing of terrorism, terrorist acts or terrorist organisations; or
(d) property of corresponding value.

Such measures should include the authority to:

(a) identify, trace and evaluate property that is subject to confiscation;
(b) carry out provisional measures, such as freezing and seizing, to prevent any dealing, transfer or disposal of such property;
(c) take steps that will prevent or void actions that prejudice the country's ability to freeze or seize or recover property that is subject to confiscation; and
(d) take any appropriate investigative measures.

Countries should consider adopting measures that allow such proceeds or instrumentalities to be confiscated without requiring a criminal conviction (non-conviction-based confiscation), or which require an offender to demonstrate the lawful origin of the property alleged to be liable to confiscation, to the extent that such a requirement is consistent with the principles of their domestic law.

The International Convention on the Suppression of the Financing of Terrorism was adopted by the United Nations on 5th December, 1999. Focussing on legal definitions and penalties, the requirement for international cooperation and customer information requirements, it led to the development of the nine additional FATF terrorist-financing principles.

This recommendation requires legislation to be implemented to enable the competent authorities to seize the assets of money launderers or assets used in terrorist financing. Of course, there is normally different legislation regarding such matters, which usually covers all crime, not just money laundering. For example, direct theft of an asset (e.g. a car) would already typically be caught by such legislation. What this recommendation achieves is to extend this to all areas of money laundering and terrorist financing. It tends to result in competent authorities having the ability to seize physical property and bank accounts, as well as the high-profile cars.

In terms of development from the 2003 recommendations, this recommendation widens the scope of the previous recommendation by including the Terrorist Financing Convention (even though this was passed in 1999), expanding the freezing and seizing power to three instances rather than one, and including property involved in terrorist financing.

The peculiarity of this recommendation, which also appears in Recommendation 38, is the use of the word "instrumentalities" – in English, this word would not be used in this scenario. The Encarta English Dictionary defines instrumentalities as the plural of instrumentality, which is defined as "the quality or state of being instrumental". The word "instruments" would appear to fit with the context of this recommendation and would make much more sense than "instrumentalities", so we take "instrumentalities" to mean "instruments" here.

Terrorist Financing and Financing of Proliferation

5. **Terrorist financing offence (*Previously addressed in Special Recommendation II*)**

   – Countries should criminalise terrorist financing on the basis of the Terrorist Financing Convention, and should criminalise not only the financing of terrorist acts but also the financing of terrorist organisations and individual terrorists even in the absence of a link to a specific terrorist act or acts. Countries should ensure that such offences are designated as money-laundering predicate offences.

This recommendation widens the scope of the previous special recommendation to include the financing of individual terrorists, whereas the 2003 recommendation only suggested that "each country should criminalise the financing of terrorism, terrorist acts and terrorist organisations". This gives countries a wider scope to apply pre-emptive measures before a terrorist act has been committed, and gives countries the power to intervene even if they are unaware who a suspected terrorist is cooperating with. Of course, this recommendation is not binding – it is up to individual countries to pass legislation to make this effective. Without this, the recommendation is just an idea with no legal force.

6. **Targeted financial sanctions related to terrorism and terrorist financing (*Previously addressed in Special Recommendation III*)**

   – Countries should implement targeted financial sanction regimes to comply with United Nations Security Council resolutions relating to the prevention and suppression of terrorism and terrorist financing. The resolutions require countries to freeze, without delay, the funds or other assets of, and to ensure that no funds or other assets are made available, directly or indirectly, to or for the benefit of, any person or entity either

   (a) designated by, or under the authority of, the United Nations Security Council under Chapter VII of the Charter of the United Nations, including in accordance with Resolution 1267 (1999) and its successor resolutions; or

   (b) designated by that country pursuant to Resolution 1373 (2001).

This recommendation expands on the previous special recommendation by specifying "targeted financial sanctions" in addition to the freezing requirements imposed by the resolutions.

The requirement to freeze assets without delay poses some logistical problems. The regulator is unlikely to have the authority to freeze the assets of a customer of a bank, whereas the FIU or some other appropriately authorised body probably will have. However, this is entirely dependent on the laws of the country. In any case, a court application will still generally be required. Furthermore, an FIU will be dealing with all of the legal issues arising throughout a country, so some delay is inevitable. It will take time for the FIU to receive, assess and approve a freezing order, by which time the funds may have been moved freely by the customer.

Another issue this recommendation poses is the willingness of banks to freeze the assets of its customers. Where this is done and it turns out that the customer was not involved in criminal activity, there will inevitably be complaints, compensation and probably a loss of business for the bank. Financial institutions will understandably be unwilling to expose themselves to this risk, and any reluctance will cause further delay, contrary to the objectives of this recommendation.

A nineteen-page best practice paper accompanies this recommendation, outlining identification procedures, access to and freezing of prohibited funds. Example provisions appear below, but please refer to the guidance for the full text.

The best practice provides that "Recommendation 6 is intended to assist countries in implementing the targeted financial sanctions contained in the UN resolutions relating to the prevention and suppression of terrorism and terrorist financing. These resolutions require countries to freeze, without delay, the funds or other assets of, and to ensure that no funds or other assets are made available, directly or indirectly, to or for the benefit of, any person or entity either (a) designated by, or under the authority of, the United Nations Security Council (the Security Council) under Chapter VII of the Charter of the United Nations, including in accordance with the Al-Qaida/Taliban sanctions regimes; or (b) designated by that country or by a supra-national jurisdiction pursuant to UNSCR 1373. Such measures may be either judicial or administrative in nature."

In terms of practical application, the guidance calls for "institutional arrangements allowing for close co-ordination among financial, intelligence and law enforcement authorities and the incorporation of the measures into the country's broader counter-terrorism policy. Countries should also have in place procedures to protect all sources of information, including intelligence and closed-source materials, used in the designation of persons and entities as being subject to the asset freeze measures."

With regards to legal process, "measures to freeze terrorist funds or other assets may complement criminal proceedings against a designated person or entity, but are not conditional upon the existence of such proceedings. The measures serve as a preventive or disruptive tool when criminal proceedings are either not possible or not practical. This does not, of course, prevent freezing procedures as such forming a part of criminal procedures."

For the effective implementation of an asset freeze, robust identifying information is essential. At the extreme end of the scale, poor quality identifiers are an obstacle to the enforcement of an asset freeze. Single-name identifiers, in particular, represent problems for enforcement. Best efforts should therefore be made to ensure as much identifying information as possible is provided upon designation, and that such information is updated as more identifying data become available. Where operational imperatives allow, jurisdictions may consider postponing a designation in situations where there is insufficient identifying information, until further information is available.

In order to implement the targeted financial sanction regimes required under Recommendation 6, including initiating, or making proposals for, designations, there will be a need to engage with a range of authorities (for example, Foreign Affairs, Justice, Treasury, Finance, Central Bank, Interior or Public Safety) and agencies (for example, security, intelligence, law enforcement, the FIU). Countries should have appropriate structures and procedures to ensure the effective implementation of the asset-freeze mechanism.

In order to comply with requirements to grant exemptions for access to frozen funds or other assets for basic or extraordinary expenses as set out in Resolution 1452 (2002) whilst still ensuring that the asset freeze is maintained, strong relationships and robust cross-government processes should be built and maintained.

In the UK, the Treasury's Asset Freezing Unit is responsible for designating terrorist freezing targets under Resolution 1373 (2001). More information on the Asset Freezing Unit and a consolidated list of asset freeze targets designated by the United Nations, European Union and United Kingdom under legislation relating to current financial sanction regimes are available in the relevant chapters of this book.

7. **Targeted financial sanctions related to proliferation (*New recommendation*)**

   - Countries should implement targeted financial sanctions to comply with United Nations Security Council resolutions relating to the prevention, suppression and disruption of proliferation of weapons of mass destruction and its financing. These resolutions require countries to freeze, without delay, the funds or other assets of, and to ensure that no funds and other assets are made available, directly or indirectly, to or for the benefit of, any person or entity designated by, or under the authority of, the United Nations Security Council under Chapter VII of the Charter of the United Nations.

This recommendation is similar to Recommendation 6, and poses the same problems regarding freezing assets without delay. While this idea is desirable in theory, the logistics required may cause problems in practice.

8. **Non-profit organisations (*Previously addressed in Special Recommendation VIII*)**

   - Countries should review the adequacy of laws and regulations that relate to entities that can be abused for the financing of terrorism. Non-profit organisations are particularly vulnerable, and countries should ensure that they cannot be misused:

   (a) by terrorist organisations posing as legitimate entities;

(b) to exploit legitimate entities as conduits for terrorist financing, including for the purpose of escaping asset-freezing measures; and

(c) to conceal or obscure the clandestine diversion of funds intended for legitimate purposes to terrorist organisations.

This recommendation has not changed since the 2003 version, when it was completely new. It requires reviews to be conducted into not-for-profit organisations which could potentially be used for money laundering. The level of work required varies considerably between jurisdictions.

Linguistically, this recommendation refers to "non-profit organisations". This is unusual, as the usual terms would be "charities" or "not-for-profit organisations". Strictly speaking, any business which makes a loss is a non-profit organisation, although this is clearly not the intended meaning in this recommendation.

The recommendation also requires countries to think through the nature of the structures available within their legal jurisdiction, identifying non-profit organisations as an example. It may well be that there are other constructs within a specific jurisdiction that are particularly suitable for money laundering which would then be caught by this recommendation.

The interpretive notes to the recommendation define a non-profit organisation as "a legal person or arrangement or organisation that primarily engages in raising or disbursing funds for purposes such as charitable, religious, cultural, educational, social or fraternal purposes, or for the carrying out of other types of 'good works'". There is no further definition of the subjective term "good works", but it is clear from this definition that "non-profit organisation" is intended to mean the same thing as the more standard "not-for-profit organisation". As with a number of instances in these recommendations, the language is perhaps not as clear as it could be.

An updated best practice was introduced in June 2013 in conjunction with the non-profit organisation sector; it aimed to prevent misuse of non-profit organisations for the financing of terrorism while, at the same time, respecting legitimate actions of NPOs.

Recommendation 8 should be implemented in line with Recommendation 1; that is, on the basis of a risk assessment. The interpretive note to Recommendation 8 requires countries to identify, prevent and combat terrorist misuse of non-profit organisations (NPOs) through a four-pronged approach involving:

(a) outreach to the NPO sector concerning terrorist-financing issues;

(b) supervision or monitoring of the NPO sector;

(c) effective information gathering and investigation; and

(d) effective capacity to respond to international requests for information about an NPO of concern.

These four elements (outreach, supervision, information gathering and investigation, and capacity to respond to international requests) apply to all NPOs, which are defined as a legal person or arrangement or organisation that primarily engages in raising or disbursing funds for purposes such as charitable, religious, cultural, educational, social or fraternal purposes, or for the carrying out of other types of "good works".

Regarding element (b) (supervision or monitoring), countries should take steps to promote effective supervision or monitoring of their NPO sector as a whole based on their domestic NPO sector review and risk assessment. In practice, countries should be able to demonstrate that the requirements of paragraph 5(b) of the INR8 apply to NPOs which account for (1) a significant portion of the financial resources under control of the sector, and (2) a substantial share of the sector's international activities. Countries should also take into account the work that is undertaken by NPOs in line with the oversight references outlined in the best practice paper.

Additionally, countries should ensure that any NPO falling within the FATF definition of a legal person or legal arrangement is also subject to the requirements of FATF Recommendation 24 or 25 respectively, on the transparency and beneficial ownership of legal persons and legal arrangements.

The guidance also provides specific best practice examples in areas including the monitoring and use of payments and activities, and the identification of beneficiaries.

Preventive Measures

9. **Financial institution secrecy laws (*Previously addressed in Recommendation 4*)**
   - Countries should ensure that financial institution secrecy laws do not inhibit implementation of the FATF Recommendations.

This is perhaps one of the more contentious recommendations, and has not changed since 2003. Clearly, offshore and other financial centres have, for many years, taken advantage of data secrecy regulations to prevent disclosure of confidential information to enquiring regulatory agents. This recommendation sought to reduce the incidence of such approaches and more recent political pressure has resulted in greater relaxation of such secrecy rules in money-laundering or tax-evasion enquiries.

Its application has been fraught, with some disclosures by financial institutions in some countries actually being challenged by the courts and in some cases being found to be illegal. The offshore centres market their secrecy credentials to attract the business that they are seeking. This requirement begins to put all of this business activity potentially at risk.

The purposes of this regulation include the detection of tax evasion and the prevention of tax avoidance. Tax evasion means the illegal evasion of tax which is legitimately owed to the State, whereas tax avoidance is legally organising your affairs so that you owe the minimum amount of tax possible. Jurisdictions with stringent secrecy laws, such as Switzerland, are seen as particularly attractive to those who are employing either of these techniques, as being able to keep your affairs secret makes it difficult to detect any discrepancy in the amount of tax due. In addition to this, the recommendation also serves a more literal purpose. Being able to trace funds without being inhibited by secrecy laws will enable the authorities to find the source of any questionable assets, and in turn prevent money laundering.

Customer Due Diligence and Record-keeping

10. Customer due diligence (*Previously addressed in Recommendation 5*)

- Financial institutions should be prohibited from keeping anonymous accounts or accounts in obviously fictitious names.
- Financial institutions should be required to undertake customer due diligence (CDD) measures when:

  (a) establishing business relations;

  (b) carrying out occasional transactions:

    (i) above the applicable designated threshold (US$/EUR 15,000); or

    (ii) that are wire transfers in the circumstances covered by the Interpretive Note to Recommendation 16;

  (c) there is a suspicion of money laundering or terrorist financing; or

  (d) the financial institution has doubts about the veracity or adequacy of previously obtained customer identification data.

- The principle that financial institutions should conduct CDD should be set out in law. Each country may determine how it imposes specific CDD obligations, either through law or enforceable means.
- The CDD measures to be taken are as follows:

  (a) Identifying the customer and verifying that customer's identity using reliable, independent source documents, data or information.

  (b) Identifying the beneficial owner, and taking reasonable measures to verify the identity of the beneficial owner, such that the financial institution is satisfied that it knows who the beneficial owner is. For legal persons and arrangements this should include financial institutions understanding the ownership and control structure of the customer.

  (c) Understanding and, as appropriate, obtaining information on the purpose and intended nature of the business relationship.

  (d) Conducting ongoing due diligence on the business relationship and scrutiny of transactions undertaken throughout the course of that relationship to ensure that the transactions being conducted are consistent with the institution's knowledge of the customer, their business and risk profile, including, where necessary, the source of funds.

- Financial institutions should be required to apply each of the CDD measures under (a) to (d) above, but should determine the extent of such measures using a risk-based approach (RBA) in accordance with the Interpretive Notes to this recommendation and to Recommendation 1. Financial institutions should be required to verify the identity of the customer and beneficial owner before, or during the course of, establishing a business relationship or conducting transactions for occasional customers. Countries may permit financial institutions to complete the verification as soon as reasonably practicable following the establishment of the relationship, where the money-laundering and terrorist-financing risks are effectively managed and where this is essential not to interrupt the normal conduct of business. Where the financial institution is unable to comply with the applicable requirements under paragraphs (a) to (d) above (subject to appropriate modification of the extent of the measures on a risk-based approach), it should be required not to open the account, commence business relations or perform the transaction; or should be required to terminate the business relationship; and should consider making a suspicious transaction report in relation to the customer.

- These requirements should apply to all new customers, although financial institutions should also apply this recommendation to existing customers on the basis of materiality and risk, and should conduct due diligence on such existing relationships at appropriate times.

The section regarding high-risk customers from the 2003 recommendation does not appear in the main body of the 2012 version, but is addressed in the interpretive notes. This new version of this recommendation obliges countries to set CDD obligations in law, whether this is through legislation or legally binding regulations. The requirement to understand the nature and purpose of a business relationship expands on the prior requirement to merely collect information, which is reflective of the advanced corporate and financial structures utilised today. The obligation not to open an account or commence business relations when CDD cannot be completed is also an extension of the 2003 recommendations.

The interpretive notes to this recommendation provide a large amount of additional guidance. For example, they give examples of potentially higher-risk situations (in addition to those set out in Recommendations 12 to 16):

(a) Customer risk factors:

  (i) The business relationship is conducted in unusual circumstances (e.g. significant unexplained geographic distance between the financial institution and the customer).

  (ii) Non-resident customers.

  (iii) Legal persons or arrangements that are personal asset-holding vehicles.

  (iv) Companies that have nominee shareholders or shares in bearer form.

  (v) Businesses that are cash-intensive.

  (vi) The ownership structure of the company appears unusual or excessively complex given the nature of the company's business.

(b) Country or geographic risk factors:

  (i) Countries identified by credible sources, such as mutual evaluation or detailed assessment reports or published follow-up reports, as not having adequate AML/CFT systems.

(ii) Countries subject to sanctions, embargos or similar measures issued by, for example, the United Nations.

(iii) Countries identified by credible sources as having significant levels of corruption or other criminal activity.

(iv) Countries or geographic areas identified by credible sources as providing funding or support for terrorist activities, or that have designated terrorist organisations operating within their country.

(c) Product, service, transaction or delivery channel risk factors:

(i) Private banking.

(ii) Anonymous transactions (which may include cash).

(iii) Non-face-to-face business relationships or transactions.

(iv) Payments received from unknown or un-associated third parties.

Guidance of this nature is essential to the success of the principle of taking a risk-based approach. There is an inevitable amount of perception and subjective opinion when assessing the risk posed by a particular customer, so standard risk indicators provide vital guidance. However, as these are only given as guidance, it would seem that they may fall short of standardising the risk-based approach. Their lack of legal force means that if a country does not agree with them, it is free to ignore them. However, were it to do so, this would appear within the country review conducted by the FATF. Generally, the approach is to achieve these requirements or to implement regulations that achieve the same objectives.

One question which remains unanswered in both the recommendation and the interpretive note is the extent to which compliance is required before it is satisfactory. For example, if a financial institution is unable to find one comparatively small piece of information but has a fairly comprehensive due diligence file, would this still be classed as incomplete? What if the institution chooses not to conduct adequate CDD, citing the fact that it is satisfied that the customer does not pose a serious risk and is therefore complying with its obligation to take a risk-based approach?

Regulators normally take a "reasonable man" approach to such circumstances, such that if the approach adopted by the firm is reasonable in the circumstances, this would not be seen as a breach of local regulations. However, if the omission was wilful with the intention of undermining the objectives of the regulations, then this would be considered a breach locally. In any case, where it is not possible or cost effective to obtain specific information, this should be documented by the firm together with the actions taken to mitigate the risk of abuse.

It should be noted that these are not the PEP rules, which are addressed in Recommendation 12.

11. Record-keeping (*Previously addressed in Recommendation 10*)

– Financial institutions should be required to maintain, for at least five years, all necessary records on transactions, both domestic and international, to enable them to comply swiftly with information requests from the competent authorities. Such records must be sufficient to permit reconstruction of individual transactions (including the amounts and types of currency involved, if any) so as to provide, if necessary, evidence for prosecution of criminal activity. Financial institutions should be required to keep all records obtained through CDD measures (e.g. copies or records of official identification documents like passports, identity cards, driving licences or similar documents), account files and business correspondence, including the results of any analysis undertaken (e.g. inquiries to establish the background and purpose of complex, unusual, large transactions), for at least five years after the business relationship is ended, or after the date of the occasional transaction.

- Financial institutions should be required by law to maintain records on transactions and information obtained through the CDD measures.
- The CDD information and the transaction records should be available to domestic competent authorities.

This regulation has undergone subtle but important changes. The phrase "should be required", which appears twice, was simply "should" in the 2003 recommendation, and the new version obliges countries to incorporate these principles into domestic legislation, thereby increasing their enforceability. The obligation to keep all records has been strengthened from just an obligation to keep records, and the express inclusion of any analysis undertaken is coherent, with the emphasis on taking a risk-based approach. Furthermore, the reference to occasional transactions reflects the way modern business is done, and the obligation by law to maintain records further affirms the subtle strengthening of this provision.

This recommendation does not come with interpretive notes. For this reason, it seems particularly strange that no reference is made in the recommendation to enhanced due diligence (EDD), only to customer due diligence (CDD). While there are obligations to conduct enhanced due diligence in other recommendations (see Recommendation 12, for example), these instances do not make explicit reference to record-keeping.

Taken literally, this would seem to suggest that there are no record-keeping requirements for enhanced due diligence, which is, of course, incorrect. It would be logical to have the most stringent record-keeping requirements for the customers who pose the greatest risks, or at the very least equivalent record-keeping requirements to those imposed on standard customers, so we can only assume that "CDD" in this recommendation is to be taken as an umbrella term for all due diligence and therefore also includes EDD.

Additional Measures for Specific Customers and Activities

12. Politically exposed persons (*Previously addressed in Recommendation* 6)

- Financial institutions should be required, in relation to foreign politically exposed persons (PEPs) (whether as customer or beneficial owner), in addition to performing normal customer due diligence measures, to:

  (a) have appropriate risk-management systems to determine whether the customer or the beneficial owner is a politically exposed person;

(b) obtain senior management approval for establishing (or continuing, for existing customers) such business relationships;

(c) take reasonable measures to establish the source of wealth and source of funds; and

(d) conduct enhanced ongoing monitoring of the business relationship.

- Financial institutions should be required to take reasonable measures to determine whether a customer or beneficial owner is a domestic PEP or a person who is in, or has been entrusted with, a prominent function by an international organisation. In cases of a higher risk business relationship with such persons, financial institutions should be required to apply the measures referred to in paragraphs (b), (c) and (d).
- The requirements for all types of PEP should also apply to family members or close associates of such PEPs.

The differentiation between foreign and domestic PEPs is a new addition to the recommendations, as is the extension of the PEP rules to beneficial ownership and to family members and close associates of PEPs. This narrows the scope for abuse of PEPs. The problem is, of course, in identifying family members and close associates. A brother-in-law, for example, might be difficult to identify, yet is a close family member by marriage.

Additional guidance on PEPs was released in June 2013. Key to the effective implementation of Recommendation 12 is the effective implementation of customer due diligence requirements: for financial institutions to know who their customers are. External sources of information for determining PEPs exist, such as commercial and other databases, and the paper provides some guidance on the use of these and other, external sources of information. However, these databases are not sufficient to comply with the PEP requirements, nor does the FATF require the use of such databases. PEPs are specifically addressed in Chapter 17.

When considering whether to establish or continue a business relationship with a PEP, the focus should be on the level of ML/TF risk associated with the particular PEP, and whether the financial institution or DNFBP has adequate controls in place to mitigate that ML/TF risk so as to avoid the institution being abused for illicit purposes should the PEP be involved in criminal activity. This decision should be taken on the basis of the customer due diligence process and with an understanding of the particular characteristics of the public functions that the PEP has been entrusted with. The decision to establish or continue a customer relationship with a PEP should be guided primarily by an assessment of ML/TF risks, even if other considerations, such as regulatory risk, reputational risk or commercial interests, are taken into account.

Financial institutions and DNFBPs should consider whether they may be more vulnerable to domestic PEPs compared to foreign PEPs. For example, small financial institutions, with little or no exposure to foreign financial markets, which determine that they are dealing with a foreign PEP, should consider in detail the reasons why such a relationship is being started. Financial institutions which operate in domestic markets where there are known issues relating to corruption should consider whether their exposure to domestic PEPs may be higher than to foreign PEPs.

In all cases, where a financial institution or DNFBP suspects, or has reasonable grounds to suspect, that funds are the proceeds of criminal activity, an STR (suspicious transaction report) should be filed with the FIU.

A financial institution or DNFBP may perform the steps that are required for the implementation of the domestic/international organisation PEP requirements in concert as part of their procedures implementing Recommendation 10. Pursuant to Recommendation 12, financial institutions and DNFBPs are required to take reasonable measures as part of their internal controls to determine if a customer or beneficial owner is a domestic/international organisation PEP. To do this, financial institutions and DNFBPs should review, according to relevant risk factors, the CDD data collected pursuant to Recommendation 10.

In cases where the customer is determined to be a domestic/international organisation PEP, then financial institutions or DNFBPs should undertake a risk assessment of the PEP's business relationship. To this effect, they should notably gather sufficient information to understand the particular characteristics of the public functions that the PEP has been entrusted with and, in the case of an international organisation, the business model of that organisation. Information on international organisations, for example, may be found on their respective websites. The risk assessment should be a composite assessment of all the risk factors and needs to be done to determine if the business relationship with the PEP involves a higher risk. This assessment of the business relationship may take into account, among other factors (i) customer risk factors, (ii) country risk factors and (iii) product, service, transaction or delivery channel risks.

Additional factors to be taken into account should include the nature of the prominent public function that the PEP has, such as his or her level of seniority, access to or control over public funds and the nature of the position held.

13. Correspondent banking (*Previously addressed in Recommendation 7*)

- Financial institutions should be required, in relation to cross-border correspondent banking and other similar relationships, in addition to performing normal customer due diligence measures, to:

  (a) gather sufficient information about a respondent institution to understand fully the nature of the respondent's business and to determine from publicly available information the reputation of the institution and the quality of supervision, including whether it has been subject to a money-laundering or terrorist-financing investigation or regulatory action;

  (b) assess the respondent institution's AML/CFT controls;

  (c) obtain approval from senior management before establishing new correspondent relationships;

  (d) clearly understand the respective responsibilities of each institution; and

  (e) with respect to "payable-through accounts", be satisfied that the respondent bank has conducted CDD on the customers having direct access to accounts of the correspondent bank, and that it is able to provide relevant CDD information upon request to the correspondent bank.

- Financial institutions should be prohibited from entering into, or continuing, a correspondent banking relationship with shell banks. Financial institutions should be required to satisfy themselves that respondent institutions do not permit their accounts to be used by shell banks.

"Clearly understand", under point (d), has replaced the requirement to document that appeared in the 2003 recommendations. While this is more beneficial in a practical sense, it does not suggest that there is any relaxation in the requirement to document everything under the record-keeping recommendation. Previously it would have been possible to have documented matters without considering whether they were appropriate and therefore suspicious. The change in the recommendation makes it clear that this is no longer the case.

The prohibition on entering a relationship with a shell bank is essentially a new requirement for the 2012 recommendations, although such rules had already been implemented by many jurisdictions.

14. Money or value transfer services (*Previously addressed in Special Recommendation VI*)

- Countries should take measures to ensure that natural or legal persons that provide money or value transfer services (MVTS) are licensed or registered, and subject to effective systems for monitoring and ensuring compliance with the relevant measures called for in the FATF Recommendations. Countries should take action to identify natural or legal persons that carry out MVTS without a licence or registration, and to apply appropriate sanctions. Any natural or legal person working as an agent should also be licensed or registered by a competent authority, or the MVTS provider should maintain a current list of its agents accessible by competent authorities in the countries in which the MVTS provider and its agents operate. Countries should take measures to ensure that MVTS providers that use agents include them in their AML/CFT programmes and monitor them for compliance with these programmes.

This is more expansive than the 2003 recommendation, although not largely different substantively. The requirement to maintain a current list of agents is new, as is the express requirement to include agents in AML/CFT programmes. Western Union would be an example of an international MVTS.

In the UK, the requirement for MVTS to be licensed or registered by the FSA is implemented by the Payment Services Regulations 2009 (last updated in October 2012), which implemented the EU Payment Services Directive. Therefore, the UK was compliant with this recommendation before it was introduced. The FSA register can be found at http://www.fsa.gov.uk/register/psdFirmSearchForm.do.

15. New technologies (*Previously addressed in Recommendation 8*)

- Countries and financial institutions should identify and assess the money-laundering or terrorist-financing risks that may arise in relation to:

  (a) the development of new products and new business practices, including new delivery mechanisms; and

(b) the use of new or developing technologies for both new and pre-existing products.

- In the case of financial institutions, such a risk assessment should take place prior to the launch of the new products, business practices or the use of new or developing technologies. They should take appropriate measures to manage and mitigate those risks.

The 2003 recommendation was mainly concerned with anonymity, whereas this recommendation is considerably more thorough and wide-ranging. This reflects the technological era and the rise of cyber crime, as well as reiterating the need for a risk-based approach. It should be noted that this recommendation is very similar to a recommendation given by the Bank for International Settlements (BIS), which, in turn, reflected the pre-emptive part of the so-called Basel II rules which are in the process of being replaced by Basel III.

16. Wire transfers (*Previously addressed in Special Recommendation VII*)

- Countries should ensure that financial institutions include required and accurate originator information, and required beneficiary information, on wire transfers and related messages, and that the information remains with the wire transfer or related message throughout the payment chain.
- Countries should ensure that financial institutions monitor wire transfers for the purpose of detecting those which lack required originator and/or beneficiary information, and take appropriate measures.
- Countries should ensure that, in the context of processing wire transfers, financial institutions take freezing action and should prohibit conducting transactions with designated persons and entities, as per the obligations set out in the relevant United Nations Security Council resolutions, such as Resolution 1267 (1999) and its successor resolutions, and Resolution 1373 (2001), relating to the prevention and suppression of terrorism and terrorist financing.

The requirement to include meaningful information from the 2003 recommendations has been removed, as have the examples of information. This reduces the stringency of the recommendation, but was due to practical problems found in the nature of business conducted. However, the requirement to monitor for any missing beneficiary information has been added, as has the obligation to take freezing action and to follow the UN resolutions.

The requirement for basic information is set out in this recommendation, even though it would be impossible to transfer money without identifying a beneficiary. Without some identification it would be difficult to see how the MVTS would know where to send the money. The information required here is essential for money to be transferred, and without it the transaction would automatically fail, so this recommendation is really only of limited use. In many countries more stringent requirements are either implemented or are being planned.

Reliance, Controls and Financial Groups

17. Reliance on third parties (*Previously addressed in Recommendation 9*)

- Countries may permit financial institutions to rely on third parties to perform elements (a)–(c) of the CDD measures set out in Recommendation 10 or to introduce business, provided that the criteria set out below are met. Where such reliance is permitted, the ultimate responsibility for CDD measures remains with the financial institution relying on the third party.

- The criteria that should be met are as follows:
  - (a) A financial institution relying upon a third party should immediately obtain the necessary information concerning elements (a)–(c) of the CDD measures set out in Recommendation 10.
  - (b) Financial institutions should take adequate steps to satisfy themselves that copies of identification data and other relevant documentation relating to the CDD requirements will be made available from the third party upon request without delay.
  - (c) The financial institution should satisfy itself that the third party is regulated, supervised or monitored, and has measures in place for compliance with CDD and record-keeping requirements in line with Recommendations 10 and 11.
  - (d) When determining in which countries the third party that meets the conditions can be based, countries should have regard to information available on the level of country risk.
- When a financial institution relies on a third party that is part of the same financial group, and
  - (a) that group applies CDD and record-keeping requirements, in line with Recommendations 10, 11 and 12, and programmes against money laundering and terrorist financing, in accordance with Recommendation 18; and
  - (b) where the effective implementation of those CDD and record-keeping requirements and AML/CFT programmes is supervised at a group level by a competent authority, then

  relevant competent authorities may consider that the financial institution applies measures under (b) and (c) above through its group programme, and may decide that (d) is not a necessary precondition to reliance when higher country risk is adequately mitigated by the group AML/CFT policies.

The obligation to regard the level of country risk replaces an obligation to consider whether a country adequately applies the FATF Recommendations. While this is slightly more expansive in a substantive sense, this only really affirms the impetus on taking a risk-based approach. The financial group section is new for the 2012 recommendations, and reflects the importance of the large corporate structures that are now employed.

This recommendation raises two important points, the first of which relates to the ultimate responsibility for a CDD failure remaining with the financial institution that is relying on a third party. Regardless of how responsibility is delegated, it cannot be abrogated.

Any bank which fails to comply with its CDD responsibilities is likely to suffer reputational damage, particularly if financial penalties are imposed; HSBC is a recent example of this. With this in mind, a bank, when applying a risk-based approach, must implement the necessary controls prior to delegating work conducted in this respect, since it retains the risk should anything go wrong. The approach to be conducted is essentially the same as with any other outsourcing relationship entered into by the financial institution and we would recommend the *Risk in Outsourcing* paper promulgated by the Bank for International Settlements (BIS) as representing best practice in this regard.

The other important point arising from this recommendation relates to a major change, since there is now the ability to rely on other CDD from your own group. This is extremely helpful for international corporate due diligence, and will streamline the process during international transactions and the formation of business relationships. However, to obtain approval under this exemption, the firm would have to prove that it meets standards set by the host regulator and that compliance with this exemption does not prejudice the home regulator.

18. Internal controls and foreign branches and subsidiaries (*Previously addressed in Recommendations 15 and 22*)

- Financial institutions should be required to implement programmes against money laundering and terrorist financing. Financial groups should be required to implement group-wide programmes against money laundering and terrorist financing, including policies and procedures for sharing information within the group for AML/CFT purposes. Financial institutions should be required to ensure that their foreign branches and majority-owned subsidiaries apply AML/CFT measures consistent with the home country requirements implementing the FATF Recommendations through the financial groups' programmes against money laundering and terrorist financing.

The specifications regarding what should be included in the requisite programme appeared in the 2003 recommendations, but have now been removed and included in the interpretive notes only. This recommendation is considerably more succinct than the two it replaces, but is largely similar from a substantive perspective.

19. Higher-risk countries (*Previously addressed in Recommendation 21*)

- Financial institutions should be required to apply enhanced due diligence measures to business relationships and transactions with natural and legal persons, and financial institutions, from countries for which this is called for by the FATF. The type of enhanced due diligence measures applied should be effective and proportionate to the risks. Countries should be able to apply appropriate countermeasures when called upon to do so by the FATF. Countries should also be able to apply countermeasures independently of any call by the FATF to do so. Such countermeasures should be effective and proportionate to the risks.

The obligation to take a risk-based approach has been specifically included in the 2012 recommendations, and the details regarding the nature of the enhanced customer due diligence (EDD) to be undertaken are included in the interpretive notes. The 2003 recommendations expressly referred to transactions that have no apparent purpose, but this has now been removed from the body of the recommendation and is instead included in the interpretive notes.

It is interesting to note that the FATF equates higher risk to non-compliance with FATF Recommendations. This takes no account of the country's financial crime record, political stability or any other circumstances which would make the country a high-risk jurisdiction with which to do business. As far as the FATF is concerned, if they comply with its recommendations, they're safe. It is difficult to see how this is consistent with the impetus on taking a risk-based approach.

The list of higher-risk countries, according to FATF compliance, appears at the end of this chapter. There are a number of other sources of what might best be described as higher-risk countries and we would refer you to Transparency International as being one primary source for such information. Its current list is included as an appendix to this book.

Reporting of Suspicious Transactions

20. Reporting of suspicious transactions (*Previously addressed in Recommendation 13 and Special Recommendation IV*)

- If a financial institution suspects or has reasonable grounds to suspect that funds are the proceeds of a criminal activity, or are related to terrorist financing, it should be required, by law, to report promptly its suspicions to the FIU.

This recommendation amalgamates the two previous recommendations by incorporating both criminal activity and terrorist financing, which is used as an umbrella that is then expanded on in the interpretive notes.

The term "promptly" is not defined in the interpretive notes to this provision, which is unhelpful. In theory, it could mean immediately, by the end of the business day, within 48 hours or within five, seven or ten working days. Accordingly, it is for the firm to be able to justify that it undertook the reporting once it was in a position to do so without obvious delay.

This recommendation also fails to address the amount of information required to be supplied with a report. For example, if you have suspicions without formal information to back this up, then this recommendation could be taken to suggest that you are still obliged to report. Generally, without information there would not be sufficient data to support a suspicion and no report would therefore be made.

However, if you are in the process of collating information, it is unclear when the ideal time to report would be – i.e. immediately, when you have some information or when you have all of the relevant information. The local FIU would normally provide guidance in such cases and helplines are normally available to the MLRO in cases of concern.

21. Tipping off and confidentiality (*Previously addressed in Recommendation 14*)

- Financial institutions, their directors, officers and employees should be:

(a) protected by law from criminal and civil liability for breach of any restriction on disclosure of information imposed by contract or by any legislative, regulatory or administrative provision, if they report their suspicions in good faith to the FIU, even if they did not know precisely what the underlying criminal activity was, and regardless of whether illegal activity actually occurred; and

(b) prohibited by law from disclosing ("tipping off") the fact that a suspicious transaction report (STR) or related information is being filed with the FIU.

This recommendation has not changed since the 2003 recommendations, apart from its number. Paragraph (a) provides the protection that the officers require. Of course, paragraph (b) could become a problem were allegations made against a firm that had actually reported its suspicion. It would be in the position of being unable to respond to allegations and newspaper stories without breaching legal provisions and this could result in unfortunate consequences.

It is important for information services, such as newspapers and information providers, to appreciate this issue and consider the implications when they are making allegations.

Designated Non-financial Businesses and Professions

22. DNFBPs: customer due diligence (*Previously addressed in Recommendation 12*)

- The customer due diligence and record-keeping requirements set out in Recommendations 10, 11, 12, 15 and 17 apply to designated non-financial businesses and professions (DNFBPs) in the following situations:

  (a) Casinos – when customers engage in financial transactions equal to or above the applicable designated threshold.

  (b) Real estate agents – when they are involved in transactions for their client concerning the buying and selling of real estate.

  (c) Dealers in precious metals and dealers in precious stones – when they engage in any cash transaction with a customer equal to or above the applicable designated threshold.

  (d) Lawyers, notaries, other independent legal professionals and accountants – when they prepare for or carry out transactions for their client concerning the following activities:

    (i) buying and selling of real estate;

    (ii) management of client money, securities or other assets;

    (iii) management of bank, savings or securities accounts;

    (iv) organisation of contributions for the creation, operation or management of companies;

    (v) creation, operation or management of legal persons or arrangements, and buying and selling of business entities.

  (e) Trust and company service providers – when they prepare for or carry out transactions for a client concerning the following activities:

    (i) acting as a formation agent of legal persons;

    (ii) acting as (or arranging for another person to act as) a director or secretary of a company, a partner of a partnership, or a similar position in relation to other legal persons;

(iii) providing a registered office, business address or accommodation, correspondence or administrative address for a company, a partnership or any other legal person or arrangement;

(iv) acting as (or arranging for another person to act as) a trustee of an express trust or performing the equivalent function for another form of legal arrangement;

(v) acting as (or arranging for another person to act as) a nominee shareholder for another person.

This recommendation has not changed since 2003, apart from the numbering.

This composite recommendation seeks to broaden the money-laundering requirements beyond the financial services sector, picking up accountants, lawyers, casinos, estate agents and trust providers, amongst others. This then leads to an interesting issue as to who within the relevant jurisdiction actually takes ownership of the regulation in such areas. Sometimes it is obvious, as may be the case for chartered accountancy or legal practices, whereas in other cases the business area may actually be unregulated. Are casinos and real estate agents regulated in all countries? Accordingly, it will be important for the financial institution to verify the legal regulatory structure that is in place in all such cases.

Many countries have actually taken these provisions further. In the UK, for example, chartered accountants and auditing firms are subject to these provisions. Regulatory bodies tend to have their own rules which are much more detailed than the ones provided by this recommendation, despite being a subset of the FATF rules.

23. DNFBPs: Other measures (*Previously addressed in Recommendation 16*)

- The requirements set out in Recommendations 18 to 21 apply to all designated non-financial businesses and professions, subject to the following qualifications:

  (a) Lawyers, notaries, other independent legal professionals and accountants should be required to report suspicious transactions when, on behalf of or for a client, they engage in a financial transaction in relation to the activities described in paragraph (d) of Recommendation 22. Countries are strongly encouraged to extend the reporting requirement to the rest of the professional activities of accountants, including auditing.

  (b) Dealers in precious metals and dealers in precious stones should be required to report suspicious transactions when they engage in any cash transaction with a customer equal to or above the applicable designated threshold.

  (c) Trust and company service providers should be required to report suspicious transactions for a client when, on behalf of or for a client, they engage in a transaction in relation to the activities referred to in paragraph (e) of Recommendation 22.

The exemption when legal or professional privilege applies has been moved to the interpretive notes. Other than that, there has been no change to this recommendation from those appearing in 2003.

Transparency and Beneficial Ownership of Legal Persons and Arrangements

24. **Transparency and beneficial ownership of legal persons (*Previously addressed in Recommendation 33*)**

    - Countries should take measures to prevent the misuse of legal persons for money laundering or terrorist financing. Countries should ensure that there is adequate, accurate and timely information on the beneficial ownership and control of legal persons that can be obtained or accessed in a timely fashion by competent authorities. In particular, countries that have legal persons that are able to issue bearer shares or bearer share warrants, or which allow nominee shareholders or nominee directors, should take effective measures to ensure that they are not misused for money laundering or terrorist financing. Countries should consider measures to facilitate access to beneficial ownership and control information by financial institutions and DNFBPs undertaking the requirements set out in Recommendations 10 and 22.

This recommendation has been expanded since 2003. Terrorist financing has been included with the requirement to prevent the misuse of companies for money laundering, which is a continuous theme of expansion throughout the recommendations. Furthermore, the specification that companies able to issue bearer shares should be subject to effective money-laundering-deterrence measures has been expanded, to specifically include companies able to issue bearer share warrants or those which allow nominee shareholders or nominee directors. Although this highlights areas where the FATF has identified a need for enhanced monitoring, there is a risk that, by implication, it could exclude companies not mentioned here.

The requirement for financial institutions to identify beneficial ownership has been extended to DNFBPs by this recommendation. Furthermore, in the 2003 recommendation countries "could" consider measures to facilitate access to beneficial ownership, which has now been replaced by the obligatory "should". This marks a slight expansion and the expectation of increased enforceability of this recommendation.

25. **Transparency and beneficial ownership of legal arrangements (*Previously addressed in Recommendation 34*)**

    - Countries should take measures to prevent the misuse of legal arrangements for money laundering or terrorist financing. In particular, countries should ensure that there is adequate, accurate and timely information on express trusts, including information on the settlor, trustee and beneficiaries, that can be obtained or accessed in a timely fashion by competent authorities. Countries should consider measures to facilitate access to beneficial ownership and control information by financial institutions and DNFBPs undertaking the requirements set out in Recommendations 10 and 22.

This recommendation has only added the references to terrorist financing and DNFBPs to the 2003 recommendation. Furthermore, the requirement to consider measures to facilitate access to beneficial ownership and control information has been strengthened from "could" in 2003; the word "should" in 2012 now makes this an obligation.

Powers and Responsibilities of Competent Authorities, and Other Institutional Measures

26. Regulation and supervision of financial institutions (*Previously addressed in Recommendation 23*)

– Countries should ensure that financial institutions are subject to adequate regulation and supervision and are effectively implementing the FATF Recommendations. Competent authorities or financial supervisors should take the necessary legal or regulatory measures to prevent criminals or their associates from holding, or being the beneficial owner of, a significant or controlling interest, or holding a management function in, a financial institution. Countries should not approve the establishment, or continued operation, of shell banks. For financial institutions subject to the Core Principles, the regulatory and supervisory measures that apply for prudential purposes, and which are also relevant to money laundering and terrorist financing, should apply in a similar manner for AML/CFT purposes. This should include applying consolidated group supervision for AML/CFT purposes. Other financial institutions should be licensed or registered and adequately regulated, and subject to supervision or monitoring for AML/CFT purposes, having regard to the risk of money laundering or terrorist financing in that sector. At a minimum, where financial institutions provide a service of money or value transfer, or of money or currency changing, they should be licensed or registered, and subject to effective systems for monitoring and ensuring compliance with national AML/CFT requirements.

Financial supervisors should be able to impose the necessary legal or regulatory requirements under this recommendation, as well as competent authorities. This affords countries more freedom in implementing this recommendation, and suggests an acceptance that the end result (the implementation) is more important than the method (which body implements it).

The prohibition on terrorist financing, as well as money laundering, has been included in this recommendation, which is a standard change. There is also a prohibition on the establishment or operation of shell banks, which complements the prohibition on entering into a correspondent banking relationship with a shell bank from Recommendation 13. However, it does seem strange that the shell bank recommendations appear in two different recommendations, 13 recommendations apart.

27. Powers of supervisors (*Previously addressed in Recommendation 29*)

– Supervisors should have adequate powers to supervise or monitor, and ensure compliance by, financial institutions with requirements to combat money laundering and terrorist financing, including the authority to conduct inspections. They should be authorised to compel production of any information from financial institutions that is relevant to monitoring such compliance, and to impose sanctions, in line with Recommendation 35, for failure to comply with such requirements. Supervisors should have powers to impose a range of disciplinary and financial sanctions, including the power to withdraw, restrict or suspend the financial institution's licence, where applicable.

This recommendation has been expanded, but not substantively changed since 2003. There is more detail regarding sanctions – dealt with further in the subsequent recommendations – which highlights the importance of compliance with this provision.

28. **Regulation and supervision of DNFBPs** (*Previously addressed in Recommendation 24*)

   – Designated non-financial businesses and professions should be subject to regulatory and supervisory measures as set out below:

   (a) Casinos should be subject to a comprehensive regulatory and supervisory regime that ensures that they have effectively implemented the necessary AML/CFT measures. At a minimum:

      (i) casinos should be licensed;

      (ii) competent authorities should take the necessary legal or regulatory measures to prevent criminals or their associates from holding, or being the beneficial owner of, a significant or controlling interest, holding a management function in, or being an operator of, a casino; and

      (iii) competent authorities should ensure that casinos are effectively supervised for compliance with AML/CFT requirements.

   (b) Countries should ensure that the other categories of DNFBPs are subject to effective systems for monitoring and ensuring compliance with AML/CFT requirements. This should be performed on a risk-sensitive basis. This may be performed by:

      (i) a supervisor, or

      (ii) an appropriate self-regulatory body (SRB), provided that such a body can ensure that its members comply with their obligations to combat money laundering and terrorist financing.

   – The supervisor or SRB should also:

   (a) take the necessary measures to prevent criminals or their associates from being professionally accredited, or holding or being the beneficial owner of a significant or controlling interest or holding a management function, e.g. through evaluating persons on the basis of a "fit and proper" test; and

   (b) have effective, proportionate and dissuasive sanctions in line with Recommendation 35 available to deal with failure to comply with AML/CFT requirements.

The final section outlining the sanctions available to the supervisor or SRB has been added to the recommendation. As with the previous recommendation, this strengthens the regulation and, in theory, deters non-compliance. However, in practice, there could be local practical problems here if some of the areas are not currently regulated.

Operational and Law Enforcement

29. FIUs (*Previously addressed in Recommendation* 26)

- Countries should establish an FIU that serves as a national centre for the receipt and analysis of:
  (a) suspicious transaction reports; and
  (b) other information relevant to money laundering, associated predicate offences and terrorist financing, and for the dissemination of the results of that analysis.
- The FIU should be able to obtain additional information from reporting entities, and should have access on a timely basis to the financial, administrative and law-enforcement information that it requires to undertake its functions properly.

This recommendation has been reworded, but not substantively changed since 2003.

30. Responsibilities of law-enforcement and investigative authorities (*Previously addressed in Recommendation* 27)

- Countries should ensure that designated law-enforcement authorities have responsibility for money-laundering and terrorist-financing investigations within the framework of national AML/CFT policies. At least in all cases related to major proceeds-generating offences, these designated law-enforcement authorities should develop a proactive parallel financial investigation when pursuing money laundering, associated predicate offences and terrorist financing. This should include cases where the associated predicate offence occurs outside their jurisdictions. Countries should ensure that competent authorities have responsibility for expeditiously identifying, tracing and initiating actions to freeze and seize property that is, or may become, subject to confiscation, or is suspected of being proceeds of crime. Countries should also make use, when necessary, of permanent or temporary multi-disciplinary groups specialised in financial or asset investigations. Countries should ensure that, when necessary, cooperative investigations with appropriate competent authorities in other countries take place.

This recommendation has been expanded considerably, with law-enforcement agencies now being required to take proactive action and have wider and more comprehensive powers than existed under the previous recommendation. While there has been no substantive change as such, the scope of this recommendation has been expanded.

31. Powers of law-enforcement and investigative authorities (*Previously addressed in Recommendation* 28)

- When conducting investigations of money laundering, associated predicate offences and terrorist financing, competent authorities should be able to obtain access to all necessary documents and information for use in those investigations, and in prosecutions and related actions. This should include powers to use compulsory measures for the production of records held by financial institutions, DNFBPs and other natural or legal persons, for the search of persons and premises, for taking witness statements and for the seizure and obtaining of evidence.

- Countries should ensure that competent authorities conducting investigations are able to use a wide range of investigative techniques suitable for the investigation of money laundering, associated predicate offences and terrorist financing. These investigative techniques include: undercover operations, intercepting communications, accessing computer systems and controlled delivery. In addition, countries should have effective mechanisms in place to identify, in a timely manner, whether natural or legal persons hold or control accounts. They should also have mechanisms to ensure that competent authorities have a process to identify assets without prior notification to the owner. When conducting investigations of money laundering, associated predicate offences and terrorist financing, competent authorities should be able to ask for all relevant information held by the FIU.

The second section of this recommendation is new, and significantly expands the powers of competent authorities to combat money laundering and terrorist financing. The first section has also undergone minor alterations, expanding the scope of the 2003 recommendation.

32. Cash couriers (*Previously addressed in Special Recommendation IX*)
    - Countries should have measures in place to detect the physical cross-border transportation of currency and bearer negotiable instruments, including through a declaration system and/or disclosure system.
    - Countries should ensure that their competent authorities have the legal authority to stop or restrain currency or bearer negotiable instruments that are suspected to be related to terrorist financing, money laundering or predicate offences, or that are falsely declared or disclosed.
    - Countries should ensure that effective, proportionate and dissuasive sanctions are available to deal with persons who make false declaration(s) or disclosure(s). In cases where the currency or bearer negotiable instruments are related to terrorist financing, money laundering or predicate offences, countries should also adopt measures, including legislative ones consistent with Recommendation 4, which would enable the confiscation of such currency or instruments.

Obviously, monies moving across borders could be inappropriate, therefore the FATF has introduced these requirements which are broader than the requirements in the original recommendations.

The placing of this recommendation seems strange. It does not make sense to have this recommendation in the middle of the recommendations about sanctions. Instead, it would seem much more logical to place this recommendation much earlier, with the correspondent banking or other payment system provisions.

Additionally, the idea that a country can have measures to detect bearer negotiable instruments is fanciful, which is reinforced by the suggestion that this could be done through a declaration or disclosure system. Large amounts of currency will inevitably take up space in a suitcase, and would be possible, albeit potentially difficult, to find. Bearer negotiable instruments, however, can be single pieces of paper, which would be easy to hide in a suitcase or large file. If, for example, a corporate trainer was giving a presentation in another country and was shipping handouts of his 600 PowerPoint slides for 20 delegates, that could easily generate 3,000 pieces of paper. It would be entirely impractical for a customs official to check every side of every page to ensure that no bearer negotiable instruments had been hidden in one of the packs.

It also seems strange that this recommendation seeks to restrain bearer negotiable instruments. Even if they were previously used to launder illegitimate funds, the instrument could have been purchased legitimately on the market for value by an innocent purchaser. Restraining the instrument in this instance would be shutting the stable door long after the horse had bolted with a saddlebag full of the proceeds of crime.

Further on this point, no courier would ever agree to these recommendations, in case a bearer negotiable instrument is included in documents they are shipping. A courier is a transporter with no involvement in the business of its clients, and would not agree to take the risk of having legitimate documents confiscated, which would place itself in breach of contract.

To comply with these requirements a firm should implement a series of policies and procedures which provide a programme that should be conducted in such cases. This would highlight such instruments as requiring a higher level of due diligence due to the ease of transfer; but the same is also true of other assets including coins and paintings, for example.

General Requirements

33. **Statistics (*Previously addressed in Recommendation* 32)**

- Countries should maintain comprehensive statistics on matters relevant to the effectiveness and efficiency of their AML/CFT systems. This should include statistics on the STRs received and disseminated; on money-laundering and terrorist-financing investigations, prosecutions and convictions; on property frozen, seized and confiscated; and on mutual legal assistance or other international requests for cooperation.

This recommendation has undergone minor reductions, but no substantive changes have been made since 2003. The reference to reviewing the effectiveness of the systems using the statistics no longer appears in this recommendation, but the same obligation is imposed by Recommendation 2.

34. **Guidance and feedback (*Previously addressed in Recommendation* 25)**

- The competent authorities, supervisors and SRBs should establish guidelines, and provide feedback, which will assist financial institutions and designated non-financial businesses and professions in applying national measures to combat money laundering and terrorist financing, and, in particular, in detecting and reporting suspicious transactions.

In 2012 this obligation has been extended to supervisors and SRBs, but this is the only change which has been made to this recommendation.

Of course, in designing such guidelines some authorities will add additional requirements of which the international bank must be aware. Clearly, different authorities respond in differing ways with varying levels of information, but at least this recommendation sets the objective clearly. In some countries, by the time a response is received from the regulatory agency the money launderer will be long gone, effectively undermining the entire process.

Sanctions

35. Sanctions (*Previously addressed in Recommendation 17*)

- Countries should ensure that there is a range of effective, proportionate and dissuasive sanctions, whether criminal, civil or administrative, available to deal with natural or legal persons covered by Recommendations 6, and 8 to 23 that fail to comply with AML/CFT requirements. Sanctions should be applicable not only to financial institutions and DNFBPs, but also to their directors and senior management.

The scope of this provision has been extended, as directors and senior management were not specifically covered by the 2003 recommendation. This is consistent with the strengthening of various other recommendations, and making management personally liable for non-compliance will inevitably make the recommendations more effective. The reference to a "range" of sanctions is also new, and enhances this point.

International Cooperation

36. International instruments (*Previously addressed in Recommendation 35 and Special Recommendation I*)

- Countries should take immediate steps to become party to and implement fully the Vienna Convention, 1988; the Palermo Convention, 2000; the United Nations Convention against Corruption, 2003; and the Terrorist Financing Convention, 1999. Where applicable, countries are also encouraged to ratify and implement other relevant international conventions, such as the Council of Europe Convention on Cybercrime, 2001; the Inter-American Convention against Terrorism, 2002; and the Council of Europe Convention on Laundering, Search, Seizure and Confiscation of the Proceeds from Crime and on the Financing of Terrorism, 2005.

The scope of the legislation countries are required to implement has been expanded, but this is inevitable given that some of these conventions were passed after the 2003 recommendations were released. In principle, however, this recommendation has not changed since 2003.

37. Mutual legal assistance (*Previously addressed in Recommendation 36 and Special Recommendation V*)

- Countries should rapidly, constructively and effectively provide the widest possible range of mutual legal assistance in relation to money-laundering, associated predicate offences and terrorist-financing investigations, prosecutions and related proceedings. Countries should have an adequate legal basis for providing assistance and, where appropriate, should have in place treaties, arrangements or other mechanisms to enhance cooperation. In particular, countries should:

(a) Not prohibit, or place unreasonable or unduly restrictive conditions on, the provision of mutual legal assistance.

(b) Ensure that they have clear and efficient processes for the timely prioritisation and execution of mutual legal assistance requests. Countries should use a central authority, or another established official mechanism, for effective transmission and execution of requests. To monitor progress on requests, a case management system should be maintained.

(c) Not refuse to execute a request for mutual legal assistance on the sole ground that the offence is also considered to involve fiscal matters.

(d) Not refuse to execute a request for mutual legal assistance on the grounds that laws require financial institutions to maintain secrecy or confidentiality.

(e) Maintain the confidentiality of mutual legal assistance requests they receive and the information contained in them, subject to fundamental principles of domestic law, in order to protect the integrity of the investigation or inquiry. If the requested country cannot comply with the requirement of confidentiality, it should promptly inform the requesting country.

- Countries should render mutual legal assistance, notwithstanding the absence of dual criminality, if the assistance does not involve coercive actions. Countries should consider adopting such measures as may be necessary to enable them to provide a wide scope of assistance in the absence of dual criminality.
- Where dual criminality is required for mutual legal assistance, that requirement should be deemed to be satisfied regardless of whether both countries place the offence within the same category of offence, or denominate the offence by the same terminology, provided that both countries criminalise the conduct underlying the offence.
- Countries should ensure that, of the powers and investigative techniques required under Recommendation 31, and any other powers and investigative techniques available to their competent authorities:

  (a) all those relating to the production, search and seizure of information, documents or evidence (including financial records) from financial institutions or other persons, and the taking of witness statements; and

  (b) a broad range of other powers and investigative techniques

  are also available for use in response to requests for mutual legal assistance, and, if consistent with their domestic framework, in response to direct requests from foreign judicial or law-enforcement authorities to domestic counterparts.
- To avoid conflicts of jurisdiction, consideration should be given to devising and applying mechanisms for determining the best venue for prosecution of defendants in the interests of justice in cases that are subject to prosecution in more than one country.
- Countries should, when making mutual legal assistance requests, make best efforts to provide complete factual and legal information that will allow for timely and efficient execution of requests, including any need for urgency, and

should send requests using expeditious means. Countries should, before sending requests, make best efforts to ascertain the legal requirements and formalities to obtain assistance.

- The authorities responsible for mutual legal assistance (e.g. a Central Authority) should be provided with adequate financial, human and technical resources. Countries should have in place processes to ensure that the staff of such authorities maintain high professional standards, including standards concerning confidentiality, and should be of high integrity and be appropriately skilled.

The requirements relating to mutual legal assistance have been expanded considerably since 2003. Mutual legal assistance was covered in the 2003 recommendations, but not in this level of detail and not with this level of force. This reflects the worldwide, cross-jurisdictional and cross-border nature of modern money laundering, and that mutual legal assistance is vital to an effective AML regime.

38. Mutual legal assistance: freezing and confiscation (*Previously addressed in Recommendation 38*)

- Countries should ensure that they have the authority to take expeditious action in response to requests by foreign countries to identify, freeze, seize and confiscate property laundered; proceeds from money laundering, predicate offences and terrorist financing; instrumentalities used in, or intended for use in, the commission of these offences; or property of corresponding value. This authority should include being able to respond to requests made on the basis of non-conviction-based confiscation proceedings and related provisional measures, unless this is inconsistent with fundamental principles of their domestic law. Countries should also have effective mechanisms for managing such property, instrumentalities or property of corresponding value, and arrangements for coordinating seizure and confiscation proceedings, which should include the sharing of confiscated assets.

The requirements relating to non-conviction-based confiscation proceedings are new to the FATF Recommendations, and are also introduced in Recommendation 4. Developing the previous recommendation, this expands the scope of the mutual legal assistance.

39. Extradition (*Previously addressed in Recommendation 39*)

- Countries should constructively and effectively execute extradition requests in relation to money laundering and terrorist financing, without undue delay. Countries should also take all possible measures to ensure that they do not provide safe havens for individuals charged with the financing of terrorism, terrorist acts or terrorist organisations. In particular, countries should:

  (a) ensure money laundering and terrorist financing are extraditable offences;

  (b) ensure that they have clear and efficient processes for the timely execution of extradition requests including prioritisation where appropriate. To monitor progress of requests, a case management system should be maintained;

  (c) not place unreasonable or unduly restrictive conditions on the execution of requests; and

  (d) ensure they have an adequate legal framework for extradition.

- Each country should either extradite its own nationals, or, where a country does not do so solely on the grounds of nationality, that country should, at the request of the country seeking extradition, submit the case, without undue delay, to its competent authorities for the purpose of prosecution of the offences set forth in the request. Those authorities should take their decision and conduct their proceedings in the same manner as in the case of any other offence of a serious nature under the domestic law of that country. The countries concerned should cooperate with each other, in particular on procedural and evidentiary aspects, to ensure the efficiency of such prosecutions.
- Where dual criminality is required for extradition, that requirement should be deemed to be satisfied regardless of whether both countries place the offence within the same category of offence, or denominate the offence by the same terminology, provided that both countries criminalise the conduct underlying the offence.
- Consistent with fundamental principles of domestic law, countries should have simplified extradition mechanisms, such as allowing direct transmission of requests for provisional arrests between appropriate authorities, extraditing persons based only on warrants of arrests or judgments, or introducing a simplified extradition of consenting persons who waive formal extradition proceedings. The authorities responsible for extradition should be provided with adequate financial, human and technical resources. Countries should have in place processes to ensure that the staff of such authorities maintain high professional standards, including standards concerning confidentiality, and should be of high integrity and be appropriately skilled.

The scope of this recommendation has been expanded by introducing numerous procedural requirements, which will enhance the efficiency and the overall effectiveness of extradition requests. This is an essential part of AML sanctions, and is complicit with the strengthening of this area highlighted in the previous recommendations.

The phrase "without undue delay", in relation to countries dealing with extradition requests, may not be practical. An example of this was the recent case involving five terrorism suspects including Abu Hamza, where one of the suspects, Babar Ahmad, was charged with money laundering. The extradition process from the UK took eight years, as there were many legal and human rights issues to be tried. Given the nature of the legal system, with various domestic and European appeal courts including the Court of Appeal, the Supreme Court and the European Court of Human Rights, there will be cases where it is simply impossible to extradite a suspect "without undue delay".

40. Other forms of international cooperation (*Previously addressed in Recommendation 40*)

- Countries should ensure that their competent authorities can rapidly, constructively and effectively provide the widest range of international cooperation in relation to money laundering, associated predicate offences and terrorist financing. Countries should do so both spontaneously and upon request, and there should be a lawful basis for providing cooperation. Countries should authorise their competent authorities to use the most efficient means to cooperate. Should a competent authority need bilateral or multilateral agreements or arrangements, such as a Memorandum of Understanding

(MOU), these should be negotiated and signed in a timely way with the widest range of foreign counterparts. Competent authorities should use clear channels or mechanisms for the effective transmission and execution of requests for information or other types of assistance. Competent authorities should have clear and efficient processes for the prioritisation and timely execution of requests, and for safeguarding the information received.

Parts of this recommendation have been incorporated into other recommendations on sanctions, so this recommendation now appears shorter. However, as with the previous sanctions recommendations, it has been enhanced. The references to MOUs are new, and there are various minor linguistic alterations making this recommendation more forceful.

3.3 FATF HIGH-RISK COUNTRIES

The following lists outline the jurisdictions which the FATF considers to be high risk, in accordance with their level of compliance with AML procedures. The lists were correct as of May 2014.

The FATF calls on its members and other jurisdictions to apply countermeasures to protect the international financial system from the ongoing and substantial money-laundering and terrorist-financing (ML/TF) risks emanating from the jurisdictions.

- Iran
- Democratic People's Republic of Korea (DPRK).

Jurisdictions with strategic AML/CFT deficiencies that have not made sufficient progress in addressing the deficiencies or have not committed to an action plan developed with the FATF to address the deficiencies. The FATF calls on its members to consider the risks arising from the deficiencies associated with each jurisdiction, as described below.

- Algeria
- Ecuador
- Ethiopia
- Indonesia
- Kenya*
- Myanmar
- Pakistan
- Syria
- Tanzania*
- Turkey
- Yemen.

* Kenya and Tanzania are now identified in the FATF document *Improving Global AML/CFT Compliance: On-going Process* due to their progress in substantially addressing their action plan agreed upon with the FATF.

3.4 SOUND MANAGEMENT OF RISKS RELATED TO MONEY LAUNDERING AND FINANCING OF TERRORISM

The Basel Committee on Banking Supervision, sitting within the Bank for International Settlements, is the leading global standard-setter for worldwide banking regulation and supervision. Its mandate is to strengthen the regulation, supervision and practices of banks worldwide, with the purpose of enhancing financial stability. In full support of the Financial Action Task Force Recommendations, the Committee issued a paper entitled *Sound management of risks related to money laundering and financing of terrorism* in January 2014, which provides a framework of regulatory best practice broadly based on the FATF Recommendations.

The paper divides its recommendations across three lines of defence against money laundering.

3.4.1 The First Line of Defence

The paper states that the front-office staff acting in a client-facing role should be considered the first line of defence against financial crime. They are in charge of identifying, assessing and controlling the risks of their business, and should know and carry out the policies and procedures and be allotted sufficient resources to do this effectively. The obligations fall both on the staff, who should remain vigilant at all times to apply the principles without alerting the clients, and the senior management, to select appropriate staff and ensure that adequate guidance and training to fulfil the role bestowed on them is available.

3.4.2 The Second Line of Defence

The senior management and compliance team form the second line of defence against money laundering. The chief officer in charge of AML/CFT should have the responsibility for ongoing monitoring of the fulfilment of all AML/CFT duties by the bank. This implies sample testing of compliance and review of exception reports to alert senior management or the board of directors if it is believed management is failing to address AML/CFT procedures in a responsible manner. The chief AML/CFT officer should be the contact point regarding all AML/CFT issues for internal and external authorities, including supervisory authorities or FIUs.

While this may be a good idea in principle, its application will inevitably vary depending on the size of the institution. The chief AML officer of a major organisation will find it particularly difficult to monitor all AML obligations, and so this will usually be delegated to staff working closer to the front-office operation.

3.4.3 The Third Line of Defence

The internal audit function provides the third line of defence, and plays an important role in independently evaluating the risk management and controls. It discharges its responsibility to the audit committee of the board of directors or a similar oversight body through periodic evaluations of the effectiveness of compliance with AML/CFT policies and procedures. The guidance provides that a bank should establish policies for conducting audits of (a) the adequacy of the bank's AML/CFT policies and procedures in addressing identified risks; (b) the effectiveness of bank staff in implementing the bank's policies and procedures; (c) the effectiveness of compliance oversight and quality control including parameters of criteria for automatic alerts; and (d) the effectiveness of the bank's training of relevant personnel. Senior management should ensure that audit functions are allocated staff who are knowledgeable and have the appropriate expertise to conduct such audits. Management should also ensure that the audit scope and methodology are appropriate for the bank's risk profile and that the frequency of such audits is also based on risk. Periodically, internal auditors should conduct AML/CFT audits on a bank-wide basis. In addition, internal auditors should be proactive in following up their findings and recommendations. As a general rule, the processes used in auditing should be consistent with the internal audit's broader audit mandate, subject to any prescribed auditing requirements applicable to AML/CFT measures.

While this is an important part of the AML deterrence regime, the hands-off, reactive and intermittent nature of internal audit means that by the time any suspicious activity is found, it may be too late. Instead, this line of defence serves to plug any gaps in the front-line first and second lines of defence.

The sound practices paper largely follows the FATF proposals. There are, however, a couple of sections which do provide some useful additional guidance.

3.4.4 Risk Assessment and Management

Under the above heading the BIS states:

> *"The bank should have a thorough understanding of all the risks associated with its customers across the group, either individually or as a category, and should document and update these on a regular basis, commensurate with the level and nature of risk in the group. In assessing customer risk, a bank should identify all relevant risk factors such as geographical location and patterns of transaction activity (declared or self-stated) and usage of bank products and services and establish criteria for identifying higher-risk customers. These criteria should be applied across the bank, its branches and its subsidiaries and through outsourced activities. Customers that pose a higher risk of ML/FT to the bank should be identified across the group using these criteria. Customer risk assessments should be applied on a group-wide basis or at least be*

> *consistent with the group-wide risk assessment. Taking into account differences in risks associated with customer categories, group policy should recognise that customers in the same category may pose different risks in different jurisdictions. The information collected in the assessment process should then be used to determine the level and nature of overall group risk and support the design of appropriate group controls to mitigate these risks. The mitigating factors can comprise additional information from the customer, tighter monitoring, more frequent updating of personal data and visits by bank staff to the customer location."*

Again, the risk-based approach is emphasised, but I would particularly highlight the mention made of outsourced activities. It needs to be recognised that such activities are still the responsibility of the bank even if not conducted by the bank. Accordingly, the same standards of risk management and due diligence should be applied.

3.4.5 Policies and Procedures

Within this section the following paragraphs appear:

> *"Regardless of its location, each office should establish and maintain effective monitoring policies and procedures that are appropriate to the risks present in the jurisdiction and in the bank. This local monitoring should be complemented by a robust process of information-sharing with the head office, and if appropriate with other branches and subsidiaries regarding accounts and activity that may represent heightened risk."*

> *"To effectively manage the ML and FT risks arising from such accounts, a bank should integrate this information based not only on the customer but also on its knowledge of both the beneficial owners of the customer and the funds involved. A bank should monitor significant customer relationships, balances and activity on a consolidated basis, regardless of whether the accounts are held on-balance sheet, off-balance sheet, as assets under management or on a fiduciary basis, and regardless of where they are held. The FATF standards have now also set out more details relating to banks' head office oversight of group compliance, audit and/or AML/CFT functions. Moreover, if these guidelines have been conceived primarily for banks, they might be of interest for conglomerates (including banks)."*

Again, the risk-based approach is emphasised, an approach the BIS takes in most of its pronouncements. The issue of monitoring on a consolidated basis can cause difficulties for a bank. Many banks do not have identical computer systems operating in every jurisdiction, and consequently account-naming conventions can vary. This could result in complexities in appreciating global consolidated exposures. Accordingly, financial institutions do need to have a clear data strategy and account-naming convention to deal with such matters; a task which should not be underestimated.

The remaining matters in this paper essentially repeat matters that have already been referred to in this book.

4 THE EC MONEY LAUNDERING DIRECTIVES

At the time of writing, the European Commission is proposing to introduce the Fourth Money Laundering Directive, while the Third Money Laundering Directive is currently in force. The proposed changes do not appear to be particularly radical. Instead, they are focussed on streamlining, clarifying and harmonising the current Directive. The proposals include expanding the scope of the risk-based approach, and harmonising the criminalisation of the money-laundering and terrorist-financing offences. There are also proposals to harmonise the CDD requirements across Member States, and to introduce clearer rules on reporting obligations.

The new package has two main elements which are intended to complement other actions taken or planned by the Commission in respect of the fight against financial crime, corruption and tax evasion; these consist of:

- A directive on the prevention of the use of the financial system for the purpose of money laundering and terrorist financing;
- A regulation on information accompanying transfers of funds to secure "due traceability" of these transfers.

Both proposals fully take into account the latest recommendations of the Financial Action Task Force (FATF), the world anti-money-laundering body, and go further in a number of fields to promote the highest standards for combating money laundering and countering terrorism financing.

In the press release the EU states that the new Directive:

- Improves clarity and consistency of the rules across the Member States
  - by providing a clear mechanism for identification of beneficial owners. In addition, companies will be required to maintain records as to the identity of those who stand behind the company in reality.
  - by improving clarity and transparency of the rules on customer due diligence in order to have in place adequate controls and procedures, which ensure a better knowledge of customers and a better understanding of the nature of their business. In particular, it is important to make sure that simplified procedures are not wrongly perceived as full exemptions from customer due diligence.
  - and by expanding the provisions dealing with politically exposed persons (i.e. people who may represent higher risk by virtue of the political positions they hold) to now also include "domestic" (those residing in EU Member States) in

addition to "foreign" politically exposed persons and those in international organisations. This includes, among others, Heads of State, members of government, members of parliament and supreme court judges.

- Extends its scope to address new threats and vulnerabilities
  - by ensuring, for instance, a coverage of the gambling sector (the former Directive covered only casinos) and by including an explicit reference to tax crimes.
- Promotes high standards for anti-money laundering
  - by going beyond the FATF requirements in bringing within its scope all persons dealing in goods or providing services for cash payments of EUR7,500 or more, as there have been indications from certain stakeholders that the current EUR15,000 threshold was not sufficient. Such persons will now be covered by the provisions of the Directive including the need to carry out customer due diligence, maintain records, have internal controls and file suspicious transaction reports. That said, the Directive provides for minimum harmonisation and Member States may decide to go below this threshold.
- Strengthens the cooperation between the different national financial intelligence units (FIUs) whose tasks are to receive, analyse and disseminate to competent authorities reports about suspicions of money laundering or terrorist financing.

The two proposals foresee a reinforcement of the sanctioning powers of the competent authorities by introducing, for instance, a set of minimum principle-based rules to strengthen administrative sanctions and a requirement for them to coordinate actions when dealing with cross-border cases.

One proposal sums up the whole of the proposed changes – "*The Commission is considering improving co-operation between national FIUs*". Of course, this was highlighted as a major issue within the revised FATF Recommendations (see Chapter 3). Rather than implementing radical changes, the European Commission appears to be reasonably happy with the existing AML framework. Therefore, the impetus is on organisation and harmonisation rather than overhauling the Directive substantively.

This chapter will outline both the current Third and the proposed Fourth Money Laundering Directives.

4.1 THE THIRD MONEY LAUNDERING DIRECTIVE

4.1.1 Background to the Directive

The escalation of money laundering and terrorist financing together with tax evasion and national austerity programmes has had the effect of pushing combating money laundering and financial crime onto the European Union (EU) political agenda. This has prompted a wave of directives to be passed through the European Commission. The general aim of all these directives was protecting the global financial system from being used for illegal purposes. The various EU money-laundering directives are the way in which the EU incorporates the FATF's international standards in order to provide consolidated money-laundering legislation, while at the same time highlighting specific additional concerns which are of interest to EU lawmakers. As with all EU directives, the requirement is on national governments to transform these requirements into local law.

The First EU Money Laundering Directive (1991) focused on combating the laundering of drug proceeds through the financial sector. Specific obligations were placed on firms in the financial sector and the Directive introduced requirements relating to the maintenance of systems for customer identification, staff training, record-keeping and the reporting of suspicious transactions.

The Second Money Laundering Directive (2001) amended the First Money Laundering Directive by introducing changes in two main areas. Firstly, it expanded the scope of predicate offences for which suspicious transaction reporting was mandatory from drug trafficking (the First Directive) to all serious offences. Secondly, it also extended the scope of the Directive to include a number of non-financial activities and professions including lawyers, notaries, accountants, estate agents, art dealers, jewellers, auctioneers and casinos.

The final text of the Third EC Directive was published in the official journal of the European Union on 25th November, 2005. Member States had until 15th December, 2007 to implement the Directive. Many countries have already implemented the Directive whilst some are yet to fully implement it. The text of the Directive may be found on the European law website: http://eur-lex.europa.eu/

The Money Laundering Regulations 2007, which implement the Directive in the UK, came into force on 15th December, 2007.

4.1.2 Aims of the Directive

The Third Directive notes that money laundering, by its very nature, is an international problem and therefore must be addressed at an international level. It recognises that measures adopted on a national level can never fully counter money-laundering activity. Consequently, international coordination and cooperation is needed so that consistent action taken at an international level can effectively combat money laundering and terrorist financing. The European Community has taken particular account of the FATF Recommendations to provide a base in order to achieve their objectives.

The Third Directive provided a common basis for implementing the FATF Recommendations which were introduced in June 2003, although these have subsequently been revised in 2012 (see Chapter 3). The 2003 recommendations took into account the risks and practices which had developed since the previous Directive (the Second Directive). It was also the aim of the UK's then regulatory body, the Financial Services Authority, and other international regulatory bodies to implement a risk-based approach to combating money laundering. The Third Directive also aimed to ensure that these new requirements were feasible, proportionate and justified by conducting cost–benefit analysis.

4.1.3 The UK Implementation of the Directive

The Third Directive on Money Laundering was implemented into UK law on the 15th December, 2007 by the Money Laundering Regulations 2007. The Joint Money

Laundering Steering Group (JMLSG) produced guidance to reflect the changes to the UK's legal framework as a result of the implementation of the Directive, as these were now legally binding. In many cases financial firms were already adopting the measures the Money Laundering Regulations 2007 had made mandatory. This is addressed in further detail in Chapter 6.

4.1.4 Key Provisions of the Directive

The new Directive recommended a number of changes. Some of the changes were new, whilst others developed and amended previous provisions. In this chapter we will look at key provisions which brought about substantial change and also the main provisions that the Third Directive recommends Member States to implement. These key provisions will, therefore, either be incorporated into domestic legislation of EU Member States directly, as seen with most of the relevant EU country legislation, or used as guidance.

For countries outside of the EU, the Third Directive can, to some extent, be considered international best practice and therefore it remains of interest. It also provides information relevant for financial institutions in overseas jurisdictions that are dealing with institutions and customers based within the EU.

4.1.5 Overview of the Directive

The Third Directive is actually Directive 2005/60/EC of the European Parliament and of the Council of 26th October, 2005 ("the Directive") on the prevention and use of the financial system for the purposes of money laundering and terrorist financing. The Third EC Money Laundering Directive sets out guidance which consolidates previous EU treaties and legislation. As discussed above, the Directive is fundamentally based on the FATF Recommendations. The EU has adopted a risk-based approach to addressing money-laundering deterrence, which is encouraged throughout various provisions of the Directive, particularly within due diligence requirements. In this chapter we provide some brief details of the Directive, but for full information you will still need to refer to the Directive itself.

Scope of the Third Directive

Paragraph 8 of the guidance in the Directive extends the scope of the Directive to also combat the financing of terrorism. As such, it is picking up the nine special recommendations that the FATF issued in the aftermath of 11th September, 2001. As with any EU directive, there is a clear political element and in this case the Directive states that the misuse of the financial system to channel criminal or even clean money to terrorist purposes represents a clear risk to the integrity, proper functioning, reputation and stability of the financial system. Accordingly, the preventative measures in the Directive should cover not only the manipulation of money derived from crime but also the collection of money for terrorist purposes.

As we shall see later, the Directive creates a broad definition of terrorist financing. Of course, again we have the problem that a terrorist in one country might be considered a freedom fighter in another and, of course, such organisations do change over time.

Accordingly, it will always be worth checking whether a particular body is considered a terrorist organisation at a particular point in time.

What is Considered to be Money Laundering by the Third Directive?

The Directive has the requirement that Member States must essentially ensure that money laundering and terrorist financing are prohibited to the maximum extent feasible. Of course, this sounds fine in principle, but in practice would be difficult to comply with. The maximum extent feasible might be so onerous as to impact legitimate activity. Indeed, it is the legitimate customer that is often put at a disadvantage by such regulation.

The Directive states that the following, when committed intentionally, shall be regarded as "money laundering":

1. The conversion or transfer of property, knowing that such property is derived from criminal activity or from an act of participation in such activity, for the purpose of concealing or disguising the illicit origin of the property or of assisting any person who is involved in the commission of such activity to evade the legal consequences of his action.

   Consequently, it is clear that failing to provide information or assisting a family member to enable them to escape prosecution would be considered money laundering. Likewise, assisting a firm to provide financial statements that are inaccurate might also be caught by such rules.

2. The concealment or disguising of the true nature, source, location, disposition, movement, rights with respect to, or ownership of property, knowing that such property is derived from criminal activity or an act of participation in such activity.

   While this requirement is quite broad, there is, in this case, still the requirement for knowledge, although in some jurisdictions there is the assumption that there should have been knowledge which impacts the "ignorance" defence. What this would mean in practice is that it would not be possible to claim that you tried to ignore the concerns which a reasonable man would have had.

3. The acquisition, possession or use of property, knowing at the time of receipt that such property was derived from criminal activity or an act of participation in such activity.

   Consequently, if you did not know that an item had been purchased using laundered money, then you would not be guilty of an offence. For example, if someone sells you a stolen car without you being suspicious and you then sell it on to a third party, you would not be guilty of money laundering if you did not know at the time that the car had been stolen. This can be a useful "get out of jail" card since it would require the enforcement agencies to prove knowledge beyond reasonable doubt to get a prosecution.

4. Participation in, association to commit, attempt to commit and aiding, abetting, facilitating and counselling the commission of any of the actions mentioned in the foregoing points.

   The implication of this is that you do not actually need to be successful in money laundering to have committed an offence. Even if you tried to commit the crime but failed to complete the transaction, you would still clearly be guilty.

Terrorist financing means the provision or collection of funds, by any means, directly or indirectly, with the intention that they should be used, or in the knowledge that they are to be used, in full or in part, in order to carry out any of the offences within the meanings of Articles 1–4 of Council Framework Decision 2002/474/JHA of 13th June, 2002 on combating terrorism. This has the effect of drawing the rules extremely broadly and you might notice it includes indirect means. For example, if you allowed your name to be used to encourage a person to provide funds to a terrorist organisation, then you would clearly still be guilty of an offence even though you might not know the person approached.

The Directive states that knowledge, intent or purpose, for the purposes of the above definitions, may be inferred from objective factual circumstances. This puts the onus onto the local agencies and financial institutions to undertake such work as they consider appropriate to build up a case based on the balance of probability. It does say objective factual information is required and therefore rumour and supposition would not be considered sufficient.

The Directive does include some useful definitions for each of the following:

- Credit institutions
- Financial institutions
- Property
- Criminal activity
- Serious crime
- Beneficial owners, including corporate entities
- Trust and company service providers
- Politically exposed persons
- Business relationship
- Shell bank.

However, there is no requirement for anyone to actually use these definitions and, in practice, many jurisdictions use their own definitions which are consistent with local rules and regulations.

Application of the Third Directive

The Third Directive has widened the application of the Second Directive to include all of the following:

1. Credit institutions.
2. Financial institutions.
3. Legal and natural persons exercising professional activities including:
    (a) Auditors, external accountants and tax advisors.
    (b) Notaries and other independent legal professionals when they participate in acting on behalf of and for their client in any financial or real estate

transaction, or by assisting in the planning and execution of transactions for their clients concerning:

(i) Buying and selling of real estate, property or business entities;

(ii) Managing of client money, securities or other assets;

(iii) Opening or management of bank, savings or securities accounts;

(iv) Organisation of contributions necessary for the creating, operation or management of trusts, companies or similar structures.

(c) Trust or company service providers.

(d) Real estate agents.

(e) Other natural or legal persons trading in goods where payments are made in cash in the amount of EUR 15,000 or more, whether in a single or linked transaction.

(f) Casinos.

This is a major broadening of the types of business that are now caught by the rules and in particular catches quite a few consultancy and accounting firms. The managing client money rules will, in many cases, broaden the net to include fund management firms that might have been left out of the regime within some jurisdictions. The objectives are clear in that the Third Directive is seeking to ensure that anyone moving significant sums is now to be identified and reviewed. Whether such bodies have actually been involved with money-laundering identification is not an issue with which to concern ourselves. They are now part of the regime and will need to comply. The only question remaining is who is the relevant authority in such cases?

There is an even wider "catch-all" provision. Member States can extend the provisions of the Directive in whole to professions and to any category of undertaking which engages in activities likely to be used for money-laundering or terrorist-financing purposes.

The Third Directive also includes a range of more specific guidance which firms will be required to comply with once these have been transcribed into national law.

Customer Due Diligence

When should a firm carry out due diligence?

The general requirement to conduct due diligence applies in the following cases:

1. When establishing a business relationship.
2. When carrying out occasional transactions amounting to EUR 15,000 or more, whether the transaction is carried out in a single operation or several operations which appear to be linked.
3. When there is suspicion of money laundering or terrorist financing regardless of any derogation, exemption or threshold.
4. When there are doubts about the adequacy of previously obtained customer identification.

We shall consider this in more detail later (Chapters 13 and 22). Notice that the primary responsibility is at the start of the relationship, but continues throughout the relationship. Of course, money launderers and terrorist financers will know this and accordingly will attempt to appear legitimate at the start of the relationship, undertaking inappropriate activity at a later stage. As we will see, there are also ongoing monitoring requirements.

What due diligence measures are required?

There is a list of required due diligence procedures in the Directive which do tend to form the basis for requirements in European States. These are as follows:

1. Identifying the customer and verifying the customer's identification on the basis of documents, data or information obtained from a reliable and independent source.

   Notice the requirement here is for independent sources, so you should not just accept documents provided to you by the customer – if they are undertaking criminal activity, they are likely to have perfect documents which are, in all probability, forged. Some form of independent confirmation should, where possible, be obtained. If it is not available then the firm will need to judge, using the risk-based approach, whether it has sufficient data to commence the relationship.

2. Identifying, where applicable, the beneficial owner of the account and using risk-based measures to verify identity so that the institution is satisfied that it knows who the beneficial owner is, including trusts and similar legal arrangements.

   This will include taking risk-based measures to understand the ownership and control structure of the customer. The importance of beneficial ownership is that the person appearing as the owner may, in reality, just be acting on behalf of the actual owner. As such, they may be partners in law firms or similar service providers appointed purely to act on the instructions of the actual controller. The information required is who is really behind the transactions, since they are more likely to be the criminal elements.

   This due diligence should take place before the establishment of a business relationship or the carrying out of any transaction. To fulfil this requirement a firm or person can decide whether they make use of public records of beneficial owners, or whether they ask their clients for relevant data or information, or how else they obtain sufficient information to provide themselves with adequate due diligence information. In other words, they can almost do whatever they like. However, in all cases the procedures adopted should be specified by the rules and regulations of the firm and should also be consistent with the requirements of local law, which could be to a higher standard than that applied by the Directive.

3. Obtaining information on the purpose and intended nature of the business relationship.

   This is required to enable the firm to subsequently identify transactions which are inconsistent with the purpose of the relationship to enable suspicious transactions to be identified. Without knowing what the account is to be used for, it will not be possible to identify transactions which are not consistent with the expectations for such a customer.

4. Conducting ongoing monitoring of the business relationship including scrutiny of transactions undertaken to ensure that they are consistent with the institution's or person's knowledge of the customer, the business and risk profile.

   This review should include obtaining information, where necessary, of the source of funds and ensuring that documents, data or information held are kept up to date. There is actually no requirement to obtain independent evidence of the source of funds, just to record the source of funds. For example, if the customer says they sold a car and received cash, there is no requirement to see that they actually ever had a car and whether it could have been worth the amount of funds received. All the firm would need to do is record that they received cash from the sale of a car.

   Of course, that is all that is required to comply with the Directive. A firm will always seek to protect its reputation and, accordingly, may choose to undertake additional verification work. If funds were left to a customer in the will of a relative, for example a grandparent, were there to be subsequent grandparents that also provided such legacies, then at some stage you would expect the firm to identify that this might be suspicious.

The issue of legal confidentiality

Where notaries, independent legal professionals, auditors, external accountants and tax advisors are in the course of ascertaining the legal position for their client or defending or representing their client in judicial proceedings or advice on instituting or avoiding proceedings, they do not need to comply with these requirements. This is to make sure that the legal process is not prejudiced and also to enable the "expert" to discuss matters with their client appropriately. If they had to make a report every time their client said something that might be considered illegal, then the whole process under which the legal profession operates could be undermined.

Under the Directive, basic due diligence requirements are mandatory for the categories of customers listed below. The requirements are distinguished between the different types of customer as the Directive recognises the different levels of risk which different types of customers represent. Accordingly, the requirements on the various customers must vary in order for firms to fully protect themselves against ML/TF.

Personal customers: Personal customers represent a lower level of risk to firms than that of other categories of customers. As a result, the due diligence requirements are not as onerous. In the first part of this section we set out the basic due diligence requirements as set out in Article 8.

Corporate customers: Corporate customers represent a slightly higher level of risk than personal customers, as transactions involve larger amounts of money and can become quite complex. Again, these have been set out in the first part of this section which includes the basic due diligence requirements as set out in Article 8.

Beneficial owners: The Directive places emphasis on the identification of beneficial owners, and verification of the beneficial owner's identity, as this category of customer is recognised as being a high-risk entity. The Directive advises Member States to introduce more specific and detailed provisions relating to the identification of the customer and of any beneficial owner and the verification of their identity. To that end, a precise definition of "beneficial owner" is essential. The Directive defines a "beneficial owner" as the natural person who ultimately owns or controls the customer and/or the natural person on whose behalf a transaction or activity is being conducted.

Where applicable, the institution should identify the intended beneficial owner and take risk-based measures to verify their identity. Such work will include investigation into legal persons, trusts and similar legal arrangements, and the firm then taking risk-based measures to understand the ownership and control structure of the customer.

Article 9 requires that the identification of the customer and the beneficial owner should take place before the establishment of a business relationship or the carrying out of a transaction. To fulfil this requirement, it is left to those institutions and persons whether they make use of public records of beneficial owners, or whether they ask their clients for relevant data or information, or how else they obtain sufficient information to provide themselves with adequate due diligence information.

Enhanced due diligence

Enhanced due diligence is required in all cases where the situation represents a higher money-laundering or terrorist-financing risk. Such procedures will apply particularly for non-face-to-face business, politically exposed persons and international correspondent banking relationships.

The Directive does provide some basic guidance, but we expand on this further in the relevant chapters of this book.

Problems associated with non-face-to-face customers

Where the customer has not been physically present for identification purposes, firms should apply one or more of the following measures:

1. Ensure that the customer's identity is established beyond reasonable doubt by obtaining additional documents, data or information.
2. Undertake supplementary measures to verify or certify the documents supplied.
3. Ensure that the first payment is carried out through an account opened in the customer's name with a credit institution.

Whilst the Directive states "one or more", in most cases we are finding that the expectation is that all three measures will be adopted unless there is a good reason why one or other is unsuitable in the circumstances. Even this is not ideal. Identification documents that show a picture cannot be compared to the actual customer themselves, since they are never met.

Problems associated with international correspondent banking

In respect of cross-frontier correspondent banking relationships with respondent institutions from third countries, the requirements are for credit institutions to:

1. Gather sufficient information about a respondent institution to understand fully the nature of the respondent's business and to determine, from publicly available information, the reputation of the institution and the quality of supervision applied locally.

   This information is generally available in the market, and regulatory structures are even ranked by independent bodies to provide additional third party analysis.

2. Assess the respondent institution's anti-money-laundering and anti-terrorist-financing controls.

   This is rather harder to obtain other than directly from the firm itself. Even then it will not be clear which of the policies and procedures presented are actually being complied with. However, firms may be required to complete a report to their regulators in respect of what is known as the Pillar 2 capital assessment (or ICAAP). This document is required for most banks, with a similar document also being required for insurance companies in Europe (the ORCA from the Solvency 2 Directive). Such documents will provide information on how the financial institution operates its control environment and will therefore be of benefit.

3. Obtain approval from senior management before establishing new correspondent banking relationships.

   This will at least ensure that someone within the business has considered whether the relationship really is appropriate and consistent with the brand values of the firm.

4. Document the respective responsibilities of each institution with regard to money-laundering deterrence.

   As a general rule, firms are now rarely relying directly on work being conducted by a third party and are often repeating such work for themselves. However, it should be noted that the revised FATF Recommendations (Chapter 3) do allow reliance to be placed on another member of the same group's identification procedures so long as they are consistent with those that would have been undertaken within your own jurisdiction.

5. With respect to payable-through accounts, the firm needs to be satisfied that the respondent credit institution has verified the identity of, and performed ongoing due diligence on, customers having direct access to accounts of the correspondent and that it is able to provide relevant customer due diligence data to the correspondent institution upon request.

   This is to deal with cases where the customer is only passing through the correspondent relationship and not known in any other way, clearly an area of potentially heightened risk of money laundering. Whether it is actually even legal to provide the due diligence materials maintained will depend on the individual jurisdictional laws and rules which could inhibit the effectiveness of this rule.

Of course, trying to apply these rules within Europe where all countries in principle have implemented the same rules is rather different from applying them in non-European markets where different standards apply.

Problems associated with politically exposed persons

A "politically exposed person" (PEP) is defined as someone who is, or has been, entrusted with prominent public functions and their immediate family members, together with persons known to be their close associates.

In respect of transactions or business relationships with politically exposed persons residing in another Member State or in a third country, the requirement is for a firm to:

1. Have appropriate risk-based procedures to determine whether the customer is a politically exposed person.
2. Have senior management approval for establishing business relationships with such customers.
3. Take adequate measures to establish the source of wealth and source of funds that are involved in a business relationship or transaction.
4. Conduct enhanced ongoing monitoring of the business relationship.

As you will see, the definition applies to people that have been, or are in, office, therefore someone who has run for office, but not been elected, is not a PEP. Whilst this is what is stated in the Directive and is normally what has been transcribed into national law, it may well not be sufficient to provide the level of protection that a firm requires. Accordingly, many firms are adopting a wider definition that provides for additional investigation of a broader group of customers. The level of confirmation of wealth is clearly an issue, and in such cases just asking the customer cannot be sufficient. You know what the concerns are: the firm is concerned that the politically exposed person may have taken advantage of their position to increase their personal wealth. Additional enquiries independent of the customer will therefore be required to meet these demands.

Problems associated with anonymous accounts

There is particular concern over products or transactions that might favour anonymity. Effectively, the requirements have the aim of trying to prevent firms using numbered accounts or other secrecy approaches which may inhibit the identification of the actual or beneficial owner of an account. Basically, any firm should know the identity of the beneficial owners of all accounts that they are involved with.

Problems associated with casinos

Everything we have looked at so far in the Directive is related to banks and other types of financial institution. This section is rather different. There is a requirement that all casino customers should be identified and their identity verified if they purchase or exchange gambling chips with a value of EUR 2,000 or more. Casinos subject to State intervention shall be deemed, in any event, to have satisfied the customer due diligence requirements, if they register, identify and verify the identity of their customers immediately on or before entry, regardless of the amount of gambling chips purchased.

The requirement is easy to put into place, but the level of actual monitoring will be dependent upon the agencies that verify compliance by the casino. Of course, casinos are perfect for money laundering. You take cash in to the casino and there is no reason for you to have to say where the funds are from. You then provide some required identification documentation, but there is no need to provide any form of secondary identification. You purchase your chips and then go for a meal. Then you cash in your chips and receive laundered money. Perhaps this is a true case of having your chips and eating them. At least this regulation represents the starting point for effective regulation of the casino industry, although such regulation does vary considerably between jurisdictions.

What is simplified due diligence?

Simplified due diligence was introduced as an exemption to full due diligence where the customer is a credit or financial institution covered by the Directive or a credit or financial institution situated in a third country which imposes equivalent requirements and is appropriately supervised.

No requirement for due diligence at all

The Directive does not require customer due diligence to be conducted (at Member State discretion) in respect of:

1. Listed companies whose securities have been admitted to be traded on a regulated market which are subject to disclosure requirements consistent with Community legislation.

   This is because they will have been verified by the listing authority. Of course, the firm will still need to confirm that the company is that listed firm and not a firm trying to steal the identity of that listed firm.

   In practice, rather than pretending to be the listed firm, the unscrupulous will take the identity of a subsidiary of the listed firm. The subsidiary is, of course, not listed and in such cases it is incumbent upon the firm to conduct due diligence procedures to establish that the listed firm does indeed have such a subsidiary and that the officers approaching the financial institution are who they say they are. They also need to have the required levels of authority to bind the firm.
2. Beneficial owners of pooled accounts held by notaries and other independent legal professionals provided that they are subject to requirements to combat money laundering or terrorist financing consistent with international standards and are supervised for compliance.

   There is also a requirement that they will provide information on the identity of the beneficial owner, on request, to the institution that acts as the depository institution for the pooled accounts. Again, this exception is because the notary is under essentially the same identification obligation and has been reviewed in this regard by their regulator.
3. Domestic public authorities.

   The reason for this is because they clearly could never be guilty of money laundering. However, I would still expect any firm to wish to identify the public authority if only to ensure that there are no political issues which they need to be aware of. The politically exposed person rules will still probably require some form of due diligence to be conducted.

4. Customers representing a low risk of money laundering or terrorist financing.

   This is a consequence of the risk-based approach being applied and is purely because the regulators would wish the financial institution to concentrate on areas which are more likely to represent a significant risk. Such an example of a low-risk transaction or relationship might include payments taken directly from a salary by an employer. The financial institution would know exactly where the funds were from and who they were held by, which means the transaction clearly represents a very low risk of money laundering.

5. Life insurance policies where the annual premium is no more than EUR 1,000 or the single premium is no more than EUR 2,500.

   While cancelled life insurance policies could be used for money laundering, the view is generally taken that the level of funds laundered would render this cumbersome and expensive for the launderer to manage, and accordingly the risk posed to the system is low. Furthermore, cancelled life insurance policies are always reviewed by the insurance company so that they can understand what has caused the cancellation, since such cancellations are essentially expensive to the insurance company.

6. Insurance policies of pension schemes if there is no surrender clause and the policy cannot be used as collateral.

   This is because it is considered difficult to launder through such instruments. The absence of a surrender clause is an important consideration in coming to such a decision. In looking at such matters a distinction might be drawn between the pension scheme of a large or listed company and that of an SME or personally controlled company where the pension fund is only part of the real assets of the proprietor.

7. A pension, superannuation or similar scheme that provides retirement benefits to employees, where contributions are made by way of deduction from wages and the scheme rules do not permit the assignment of a member's interest under the scheme.

Really this is all about applying the risk-based approach to supervision and investigation. What the Directive is really saying is that these types of product or service are not really suitable for money laundering or terrorist financing and therefore it would be onerous to impose the same level of regulation on them. Notice, for example, the references to surrender clauses or value. Surrender clauses can be used by money launderers, but in the absence of such a clause it is difficult to see how the product could be a suitable money-laundering vehicle for the criminal fraternity.

Reporting Obligations

The main obligation here is to create a financial intelligence unit (FIU). Reporting should concentrate on transactions which are particularly likely, by their nature, to be related to money laundering or terrorist financing, together with particularly complex or unusually large transactions and any unusual patterns of transactions which have no apparent economic or visible purpose.

Such suspicious transactions must be reported to the relevant FIU. The unit will be responsible for receiving, requesting, analysing and disseminating to the competent authorities and the disclosure of information which concerns potential money laundering, potential terrorist financing or is otherwise required. The Third Directive requires that the FIU must have access to the financial administrative and law-enforcement information that it requires to fulfil its tasks properly.

There is a safe harbour here for the reporting employee at the financial institution. The disclosure of information by an employee or director of an institution does not constitute a breach of any restriction on the disclosure of information imposed by contract or by any legislative, regulatory or administrative provision, and shall not involve the institution or person or its directors or employees in liability of any kind. This protects the whistleblower and enables (indeed perhaps even encourages) reporting of relevant information.

Tipping Off

There is an important prohibition from disclosing to customers or third persons (other than regulators) the fact that information has been transmitted to the relevant FIU or that a money-laundering or terrorist-financing investigation is being, or may be, carried out. Disclosure of information may also be made between institutions of different Member States, provided these countries meet the conditions laid down in Article 11(1).

This effectively enshrines the principle of tipping off, which therefore becomes an offence. Clearly, tipping off, as we discuss in Chapter 23, is a significant risk for any investigator and limits both the questions that may be asked and also the way in which they are posed.

Record-keeping

In terms of record-keeping, the requirements of the Third Directive are as follows:

1. **Customer due diligence:** A copy of, or the references requested of, the evidence required for a period of at least five years after the business relationship with their customer has ended.
2. **Business relationships and transactions:** The supporting evidence and records, consisting of the original documents or copies admissible in court proceedings under the applicable national legislation, for a period of at least five years following the carrying out of the transactions or the end of the business relationship.

There is a requirement that Member States must review the effectiveness of their systems to combat money laundering by maintaining comprehensive statistics on matters relevant to the effectiveness of such systems.

Such statistics shall, at a minimum, cover the following:

1. The number of suspicious transaction reports made to the FIU.
2. The follow-up given to these reports.
3. On an annual basis, the number of cases investigated.
4. The number of persons prosecuted.

5. The number of persons convicted for money-laundering or terrorist-financing offences.
6. How much property has been frozen, seized or confiscated.

Reporting is only a small part of the issue and can surely not really judge effectiveness, since the size of the sampled population will not be known. If a country improves its money-laundering procedures it will probably identify more money laundering, but it will never know what has not been discovered. Regardless of this, Member States are required to ensure that a consolidated review of these statistical reports is published.

As you can see, much of the Directive actually relates to the operation of the relevant FIU, with much of this being of interest, but of limited direct relevance to, the MLRO.

Internal Procedures, Training and Feedback (Articles 34–35)

Institutions and persons covered by the Directive must establish adequate and appropriate policies and procedures for the following:

- Customer due diligence
- Reporting
- Record-keeping
- Internal control
- Risk assessment
- Risk management
- Compliance management
- Communication in order to prevent operations related to money laundering or terrorist financing.

They must also communicate relevant policies and procedures to branches and majority-owned subsidiaries in third countries. There is also a requirement that relevant training must be provided for relevant employees. This may involve participation in special ongoing training programmes to help them recognise which operations may be related to money laundering and terrorist financing and instruct them as to how to proceed with such cases.

The requirements regarding training and understanding money laundering and terrorist financing are clearly crucial. By emphasising the importance of understanding how the criminal operates, the Directive is seeking to improve the quality both of skills within the deterrence industry and also perhaps the introduction of more thoughtful detection of inappropriate activity.

The Broadening of Supervision in the Third Directive

In broadening the nature of firms caught by the regulations, there is now a requirement for currency exchange offices, money transmission or remittance offices and trust and company service providers and casinos to be licensed or registered and licensed to operate their business legally.

The key issues here relate to the extension of the regime to additional types of organisation. The trust and company services are the major area where approaches differ between countries. Clearly, an organisation has to be designated to monitor adherence to these obligations and then have the skills and staff necessary to undertake such work.

If you are a trust or company service company then you will need to see if you fall within the structure of your local rules and regulations and, if so, identify the body with which you are required to register. With such registration there is likely to be a series of additional responsibilities and requirements with which you will be required to comply. These will then need to be expressly transferred into the policies and procedures of your firm and notified as appropriate to your relevant employees and, where relevant, clients.

Penalties Under the Third Directive

Article 39 concerns itself with penalties and whilst not being too specific provides guidance which local jurisdiction legislatures have been taking into account. It states that natural and legal persons must be held liable for infringement of national provisions adopted pursuant to the Directive and that the penalties must be effective, proportionate and dissuasive.

Article 39 further provides that in addition to a Member State's right to impose criminal penalties, they must also have appropriate administrative measures or administrative sanctions which can be imposed against credit and financial institutions for infringement of national provisions adopted pursuant to the Directive. However, such measures or sanctions must be effective, proportionate and dissuasive.

Risk-based Approach

As set out earlier, the Third Directive recognises the concept of a risk-based/risk-sensitive approach to combating money laundering. Accordingly, the implementation of a risk-based approach is encouraged throughout various provisions of the Directive, particularly, as we have seen, in the due diligence requirements. This is to ensure that institutions direct their attention and resources to those areas where they are most likely to identify cases of inappropriate activity.

The principle is that actual customer due diligence requirements may be determined on a risk-sensitive basis depending on the type of customer, business relationship, product or transaction. However, there is the requirement for the firm to be able to demonstrate that the extent of the measures taken by it is appropriate in view of the risks posed by money laundering and terrorist financing.

The effect of the clarifying requirements is to apply the risk-based approach more carefully in practice. Institutions will be required to document their approaches in clear guidance notes and policies and procedures within their organisation. Such procedures will then need to be followed rigorously in practice, without bias, to justify the appropriateness requirement.

Reliance on Third Parties

The Third Directive also allows Member States to permit institutions and persons covered under the Directive to rely on third parties to meet certain requirements such as customer due diligence. Where a Member State permits currency exchange offices and money transmission or remittance offices situated in its authority to be relied on as third parties domestically, that Member State shall permit them to recognise and accept the outcome of the customer due diligence requirements outlined in the Directive by the same category of institution in another Member State. However, as discussed earlier, this has been restricted in the revised FATF Recommendations issued in 2012 (see Chapter 3).

Conclusions

The Third Directive provides Member States with the regulatory framework that they require for dealing with money-laundering deterrence and terrorist financing. The individual Member State then needs to develop specific approaches to be applied locally to implement these requirements. As such, any international jurisdiction could use the Directive as a basis for framing their own rules and regulations. Consequently, you may well consider the Directive to be international best practice even if you are not based in one of the Member States.

It is important for any jurisdiction to recognise that the Directive only provides outline guidance and will always need to be supplemented by additional local guidance, together with being transcribed into local law. As such, while it provides the framework, it cannot provide the details due to the differences inherent in local rules, regulations and structures. In the detailed chapters of this book we look at some of the specific areas where additional guidance is required and set out the key issues that will need to be considered.

4.2 THE FOURTH MONEY LAUNDERING DIRECTIVE

The Commission planned to bring forward a proposal for a fourth Anti-Money Laundering Directive (AMLD) in Autumn 2012, which was released in February 2013 and is not expected to be implemented in the UK until 2015/16. Some of the key changes are outlined below:

Transactions greater than EUR 7,500: The threshold for traders in high-value goods dealing with cash payments and traders carrying out occasional transactions to carry out due diligence will be reduced from EUR 15,000 to EUR 7,500. This is in response to reports by Member States that the EUR 15,000 threshold was being abused by criminals, and it is intended that by halving it, the opportunity for criminals will be significantly reduced.

Information on the beneficial owner: The revised Directive proposes new measures in order to provide enhanced clarity and accessibility of beneficial ownership information. It requires legal persons to hold information on their own beneficial ownership. This information should be made available to both competent authorities and obliged entities. For legal arrangements, trustees are required to declare their status when becoming a customer and information on beneficial ownership is similarly required to be made available to competent authorities and obliged entities. This requirement represents a crackdown on the use of corporate structures to disguise financial crime, and is introduced at a time when piercing the corporate veil is frequently being tested in the courts.

Risk-based approach: The concept of the risk-based approach is introduced in the Fourth Money Laundering Directive, as a balance between financial crime deterrence and economic stability. While this has been the UK position since the introduction of the Money Laundering Regulations 2007, taking a risk-based approach brings the Directive into line with the FATF Recommendations.

Simplified and enhanced due diligence: In the proposal, obliged entities would be required to take enhanced measures where risks are greater and may be permitted to take simplified measures where risks are demonstrated to be lower.

Politically exposed persons: The definition of PEPs will be expanded to include domestic PEPs – in recognition of the risk involved with dealing with PEPs.

The gambling sector: The requirements for customer due diligence are extended to the entire gambling sector, broadening from merely casinos. Given the rapid growth of the mobile/in-play gambling market, this is not surprising.

The proposed update of the legal rules will have to be adopted by the European Parliament and the Council of Ministers under the ordinary legislative procedure. However, it is not anticipated that there will be any significant changes proposed during this process.

5 UN RESOLUTIONS

A number of UN resolutions are referred to in the FATF Recommendations, as discussed in Chapter 3. Further information on these resolutions can be found in this chapter.

5.1 CHAPTER VII OF THE CHARTER OF THE UNITED NATIONS

This chapter, containing thirteen articles, outlines the ability of the Security Council to determine threats to world peace and take appropriate action. In particular, Article 39 provides that "the Security Council shall determine the existence of any threat to the peace, breach of the peace, or act of aggression and shall make recommendations, or decide what measures shall be taken ... to maintain or restore international peace and security".

5.2 RESOLUTION 1267 (1999)

As well as imposing a freezing order and condemning the Taliban, this resolution provides for the formation of a Committee of the Security Council consisting of all the members of the Council to report on the effectiveness of the fight against the Taliban.

The sanctions have since been modified and strengthened by subsequent resolutions, including Resolutions 1333 (2000), 1390 (2002), 1455 (2003), 1526 (2004), 1617 (2005), 1735 (2006), 1822 (2008), 1904 (2009) and Resolution 1989 (2011), so that the sanctions measures now apply to designated individuals and entities associated with Al-Qaida, wherever located. The names of the targeted individuals and entities are placed on the Al-Qaida Sanctions List. Narrative summaries of reasons for listing the individuals, groups, undertakings and entities included in the Consolidated List (where available) can be found at the following URL: www.un.org/sc/committees/1267/narrative.shtml.

The Al-Qaida Sanctions List consists of two sections:

1. Individuals associated with Al-Qaida.
2. Entities and other groups and undertakings associated with Al-Qaida.

Currently the list includes 224 individuals and 64 entities, although this is subject to regular change. Examples from the Al-Qaida Sanctions List appear below. The full list is available at http://www.un.org/sc/committees/1267/aq_sanctions_list.shtml, and was last updated on 11th July, 2013 (correct at the time of writing).

Individuals associated with Al-Qaida

QI.A.163.04. Name: 1: MOUSTAFA 2: ABBES 3: na 4: na

Name (original script): 23456 01/س

Title: na

Designation: na

DOB: 5 Feb. 1962

POB: Osniers, Algeria

Good quality a.k.a.: (a) Mostafa Abbes (b) Mostafa Abbas born in France on 5 Feb. 1962 (c) Mustafa Abbas (d) Moustapha Abbes

Low quality a.k.a.: na

Nationality: Algerian

Passport no.: na

National identification no.: na

Address: Algeria

Listed on: 17 Mar. 2004 (amended on 26 Nov. 2004, 21 Dec. 2007, 2 Dec. 2008, 25 Jan. 2010, 16 May 2011)

Other information: Brother of Youcef Abbes (QI.A.166.04). Review pursuant to Security Council Resolution 1822 (2008) was concluded on 28 Sep. 2009.

QI.A.166.04. Name: 1: YOUCEF 2: ABBES 3: na 4: na

Entities and other groups and undertakings associated with Al-Qaida

QE.R.128.08.

Name: RAJAH SOLAIMAN MOVEMENT

A.k.a.: (a) Rajah Solaiman Islamic Movement (b) Rajah Solaiman Revolutionary Movement

F.k.a.: na

Address: (a) Barangay Mal-Ong, Anda, Pangasinan Province, Philippines (b) Sitio Dueg, Barangay Maasin, San Clemente, Tarlac Province, Philippines (c) Number 50, Purdue Street, Cubao, Quezon City, Philippines.

Listed on: 4 Jun. 2008 (amended on 13 Dec. 2011)

Other information: Founded and headed by Hilarion Del Rosario Santos III (QI.S.244.08). Associated with the Abu Sayyaf Group (QE.A.1.01) and Jemaah Islamiyah (QE.J.92.02) the International Islamic Relief Organization, Philippines, branch offices (QE.I.126.06) and Khadafi Abubakar Janjalani (QI.J.180.04). Review pursuant to Security Council Resolution 1822 (2008) was concluded on 13 May 2010.

5.3 RESOLUTION 1373 (2001)

Resolution 1373 is more wide-ranging than Resolution 1267, in that it covers all acts of terrorism and terrorist financing. It requires all states to:

- Prevent and suppress the financing of terrorist acts;
- Criminalise the funding of terrorism;
- Freeze, without delay, funds and other financial assets or economic resources of any persons connected with terrorism;
- Refrain from providing any form of support to entities or persons involved in terrorist acts;
- Take the necessary steps to prevent the commission of terrorist acts;
- Deny safe haven to those who finance, plan, support or commit terrorist acts, or provide safe havens;
- Prevent those who finance, plan, facilitate or commit terrorist acts from using their respective territories for those purposes against other states or their citizens;
- Ensure that any person who participates in the financing, planning, preparation or perpetration of terrorist acts or in supporting terrorist acts is brought to justice;
- Afford one another the greatest measure of assistance in connection with criminal investigations or criminal proceedings relating to the financing or support of terrorist acts, including assistance in obtaining evidence in their possession necessary for the proceedings;
- Prevent the movement of terrorists or terrorist groups by effective border controls and controls on issuance of identity papers and travel documents, and through measures for preventing counterfeiting, forgery or fraudulent use of identity papers and travel documents.

It also calls upon states to increase cooperation and communication to prevent the financing of terrorism. Of course, the detailed rules with respect to the financial community are promulgated by the Financial Action Task Force (FATF), as discussed in Chapter 3.

6 THE UK REGULATORY FRAMEWORK

6.1 BACKGROUND

In the UK, financial services regulation has travelled through a series of routes to arrive at the current position, which itself is in a period of change. Initially, regulation in the UK for banking was the clear responsibility of the Bank of England, with its powers being enshrined in a series of banking laws and guidance published in various regulations.

This changed with the development of broader financial services regulation as a result of the implementation of the Financial Services Act 1986. This did not really change the responsibilities of the Bank of England, which remained a full central bank with responsibility for the regulation of banks, but introduced the Securities and Investments Board. The Board carried out very little direct regulation, but did ensure that a series of industry-based regulators achieved the standards of regulation required. Effectively, this enshrined the principle of self-regulation which became a driver for UK financial services regulation for a decade. The Securities and Investments Board was eventually replaced by the Financial Services Authority (FSA), which also took over the responsibilities for the majority of the self-regulatory bodies that previously existed (for example, the Personal Investment Authority (PIA) and the Investment Managers Regulatory Organisation (IMRO)).

6.2 THE FINANCIAL SERVICES ACT 2012

The most recent development came on 1st April, 2013, when the Financial Services Act 2012 divided the FSA into two new entities: the Financial Conduct Authority (FCA) and the Prudential Regulation Authority (PRA). The FCA regulates the financial services industry with a focus on consumers and stability within the industry, while the PRA, which is a part of the Bank of England, is responsible for the prudential regulation of banks, building societies, credit unions, insurers and major investment firms.

The Financial Services Act 2012 made significant amendments to the Financial Services and Markets Act 2002 (FSMA), which had previously set out the structure of financial service regulation in the UK.

The Financial Services Act imposes both definitive and aspirational objectives on both the FCA and the PRA.

6.3 THE FINANCIAL CONDUCT AUTHORITY OBJECTIVES

The single definitive objective of the FCA is "ensuring that the relevant markets function well". The relevant markets are defined as the financial markets, the markets for regulated financial services and the markets for services that are provided by persons other than authorised persons in carrying on regulated activities but are provided without contravening the general prohibition (see Section 6.6, "Fit and Proper Person Rules" below), and the FCA must take the following aspirational objectives into account when fulfilling this strategic objective.

6.3.1 *The Integrity Objective*

The integrity objective means protecting and enhancing the integrity of the UK financial system, including its soundness, stability and resilience, its not being used for a purpose connected with financial crime, its not being affected by behaviour that amounts to market abuse, the orderly operation of the financial markets and the transparency of the price-formation process in those markets.

This is similar to the "market confidence" objective which was imposed on the FSA by FSMA, although this objective was only written in very vague terms. The "integrity" objective is a direct response to the substantial negative publicity received by the banking sector during the 2008 crash and subsequent recession, and so the new regulatory requirements have a political as well as fiscal side to them.

The reduction of financial crime was a specified objective under the previous FSMA regime, but has now been reduced to the status of only a consideration as part of a wider objective. This could be seen to weaken the level of attention that is given to this area by regulators, although there is no evidence that this is actually the case. By focussing the regulation on systemic system maintenance and the customer, as the two regulators are now primarily tasked with achieving, the criminal law issues with respect to money laundering and terrorist financing become, to some extent, of secondary importance.

6.3.2 *The Protection of Consumers Objective*

The protection of consumers objective means securing the appropriate degree of protection for consumers, and was originally imposed on the Financial Services Authority under FSMA. In considering what degree of protection may be appropriate, the Authority must have regard to the differing degrees of risk involved in different kinds of investment or other transaction; the differing degrees of experience and expertise that different consumers may have in relation to different kinds of regulated activity; any information which the consumer financial education body has provided to the Authority in the exercise of the consumer financial education function; the needs that consumers may have for advice and accurate information; and the general principle that consumers should take responsibility for their decisions.

In addition to these considerations, the 2012 Act adds three extra factors which were not imposed on the FSA: the general principle that those providing regulated financial services should be expected to provide consumers with a level of care that is appropriate having regard to the degree of risk involved in relation to the investment or other transaction and the capabilities of the consumers in question; the differing expectations that consumers may have in relation to different kinds of investment or other transaction; and any information which the operator of the ombudsman scheme has provided to the FCA. These considerations have a protective nature to them, and are likely to have been implemented in response to the financial crisis and the negative publicity which followed.

6.3.3 *The Competition Objective*

The competition objective refers to the regulator promoting effective competition in the interests of consumers in the markets for regulated financial services. The matters to which the FCA may have regard include the needs of different consumers who use or may use those services, including their need for information that enables them to make informed choices; the ease with which consumers who may wish to use those services, including consumers in areas affected by social or economic deprivation, can access them; the ease with which consumers who obtain those services can change the person from whom they obtain them; the ease with which new entrants can enter the market; and how far competition is encouraging innovation.

The goal of this is to have a broader offering of services available to the customer, which are easy to understand and cost-effective. Of course, the impact of regulation is often to limit the choice available, as fewer firms are able to earn a return adequate to support their cost and capital structures, so the objective, while laudable, may be difficult to achieve in practice. The competition objective did not feature in the previous FSMA regime.

6.4 THE PRUDENTIAL REGULATION AUTHORITY (PRA) OBJECTIVES

The Financial Services Act imposes strategic objectives and an aspirational objective on the PRA in the same way as it does on the FCA. The PRA's main objective is to promote the safety and soundness of PRA-authorised persons, which it must do by seeking to ensure that the business of PRA-authorised persons is carried on in a way which avoids any adverse effect on the stability of the UK financial system, and seeking to minimise the adverse effect that the failure of a PRA-authorised person could be expected to have on the stability of the UK financial system.

6.4.1 *Insurance Objective*

The only aspirational objective imposed on the PRA is related to the insurance sector. In discharging its general functions so far as relating to a PRA-regulated activity relating to the effecting or carrying out of contracts of insurance or PRA-authorised persons carrying on that activity, the PRA must contribute to the securing of an appropriate degree of protection for those who are, or may become, policyholders. This section applies only if the effecting or carrying out of contracts of insurance as principal is, to any extent, a PRA-regulated activity.

6.5 ENHANCING PUBLIC UNDERSTANDING OF FINANCIAL MATTERS

The FSMA created the Consumer Financial Education Body to enhance the understanding and knowledge of members of the public of financial matters (including the UK financial system), and the ability of members of the public to manage their own financial affairs. The consumer financial education function included, in particular, promoting awareness of:

- The benefits of financial planning;
- The financial advantages and disadvantages in relation to the supply of particular kinds of goods or services;
- The benefits and risks associated with different kinds of financial dealing (which includes informing the FCA and other bodies of those benefits and risks);
- The publication of educational materials or the carrying out of other educational activities;
- The provision of information and advice to members of the public;
- Assisting members of the public with the management of debt; and
- Working with other organisations which provide debt services, with a view to improving the availability to the public of those services, the quality of the services provided and consistency in the services available, in the way in which they are provided and in the advice given.

Although the provisions for its creation are repealed by the Financial Services Act 2012, there are new provisions to continue its existence. Furthermore, the final two parts of its remit – both relating to debt – have been added, in response to the heightened public awareness and political implications of debt since 2008.

6.6 FIT AND PROPER PERSON RULES

The FSMA introduced the regulatory framework through the General Prohibition in 2000, and is unaltered by the recent legislative changes. The General Prohibition states that "no person may carry out a regulated activity in the UK unless they are an authorised or an exempt person". Therefore, firms and individuals who work for firms must be approved by the FCA. In order to be approved by the FCA individuals responsible must be "fit and proper", which means that they are considered appropriate people to be involved with such a significant role.

Individuals will be considered to be "fit and proper" by the FCA in relation to the following:

- Honesty, integrity and reputation;
- Competence and capacity;
- Financial soundness.

Within the rule book of the Financial Conduct Authority the regulations promulgated by the Joint Money Laundering Steering Group (see Chapter 7) are adopted as best practice. No separate detailed guidance regarding money-laundering deterrence and terrorist financing appears within the FCA handbook, although the FCA has released a separate guide to minimising the risk of money laundering, which is not binding.

6.7 FCA REGULATION AND MONEY-LAUNDERING DETERRENCE

With regard to discharging its general functions, both the FCA and the PRA are obliged, under the Financial Services Act, to have regard to:

1. The need to use the resources of each regulator in the most efficient and economic way.
2. The principle that a burden or restriction which is imposed on a person, or on the carrying on of an activity, should be proportionate to the benefits, considered in general terms, which are expected to result from the imposition of that burden or restriction.
3. The desirability of sustainable growth in the economy of the United Kingdom in the medium or long term.
4. The general principle that consumers should take responsibility for their decisions.
5. The responsibilities of the senior management of persons subject to requirements imposed by or under this Act, including those affecting consumers, in relation to compliance with those requirements.
6. The desirability, where appropriate, of each regulator exercising its functions in a way that recognises differences in the nature of, and objectives of, businesses carried on by different persons subject to requirements imposed by or under this Act.
7. The desirability in appropriate cases of each regulator publishing information relating to persons on whom requirements are imposed by or under this Act, or requiring such persons to publish information, as a means of contributing to the advancement by each regulator of its objectives.
8. The principle that the regulators should exercise their functions as transparently as possible.

The FCA's outline requirements relating to money laundering are contained in the FCA rulebook, under the Senior Management Arrangements, Systems and Controls (SYSC) rules. Having comparatively limited "rules" supplemented by a non-binding guidebook has enabled firms to have more discretion when choosing to adopt anti-money-laundering practices. Guidelines relating to money laundering contained in SYSC include the following:

- A firm must take reasonable care to establish and maintain effective systems and controls for compliance with applicable requirements and standards under the regulatory system and for countering the risk that the firm might be used to further financial crime.
- A firm must ensure that these systems and controls enable it to identify, assess, monitor and manage money-laundering risk, and are comprehensive and proportionate to the nature, scale and complexity of its activities.
- A firm must carry out regular assessments of the adequacy of these systems and controls to ensure that it continues to comply with the requirements.
- The FCA, when considering whether a breach of its rules on systems and controls against money laundering has occurred, will have regard to whether a firm has

followed relevant provisions in the guidance for the UK financial sector issued by the Joint Money Laundering Steering Group.

- In identifying its money-laundering risk and in establishing the nature of these systems and controls, a firm should consider a range of factors, including its customer, product and activity profiles, its distribution channels, the complexity and volume of its transactions, its processes and systems and its operating environment.

The rulebook also provides that a firm should ensure that the systems and controls include:

- Appropriate training for its employees in relation to money laundering.
- Appropriate provision of information to its governing body and senior management, including a report at least annually by that firm's Money Laundering Reporting Officer (MLRO) on the operation and effectiveness of those systems and controls.
- Appropriate documentation of its risk-management policies and risk profile in relation to money laundering, including documentation of its application of those policies.
- Appropriate measures to ensure that money-laundering risk is taken into account in its day-to-day operation, including in relation to the development of new products, the taking on of new customers and changes in its business profile.
- Appropriate measures to ensure that procedures for identification of new customers do not unreasonably deny access to its services to potential customers who cannot reasonably be expected to produce detailed evidence of identity.

A firm must allocate to a director or senior manager (who may also be the Money Laundering Reporting Officer) overall responsibility within the firm for the establishment and maintenance of effective anti-money-laundering systems and controls.

Additionally, a firm must appoint an individual as MLRO, with responsibility for oversight of its compliance with the FCA's rules on systems and controls against money laundering, and ensure that its MLRO has a level of authority and independence within the firm and access to resources and information sufficient to enable him to carry out that responsibility. The job of the MLRO within a firm is to act as the focal point for all activity within the firm relating to combating money laundering. The FCA expects that a firm's MLRO will be based in the United Kingdom.

The regulatory structure under which UK money-laundering deterrence and terrorist-financing legislation operates is considered in the following sections.

6.8 THE PROCEEDS OF CRIME ACT 2002

The Proceeds of Crime Act 2002 (POCA) consolidates and extends the existing UK legislation regarding money laundering. The legislation covers all crimes and any dealing in criminal property, with no exceptions and unusually no de minimis. The effect of this is that any theft or other criminal offence regardless of value is, in principle, subject to these rules. The POCA has three main objectives:

1. It establishes the Assets Recovery Agency to conduct an investigation to discover whether a person holds criminal assets and to recover the assets in question.

2. It creates five investigative powers for the law-enforcement agencies:
   - A production order;
   - A search and seizure order;
   - A disclosure order;
   - A customer information order;
   - An account-monitoring order.
3. It establishes the following criminal offences:
   - Acquiring, using, possessing, concealing, disguising, converting, transferring or removing criminal property from the jurisdiction, or entering into or becoming involved in an arrangement to facilitate the acquisition, retention, use or control of criminal property by another person.
   - For persons working in the regulated sector, of failing to make a report where they have knowledge or suspicion of money laundering or reasonable grounds for having knowledge or suspicion that another person is laundering the proceeds of any criminal conduct, as soon as is reasonably practical after the information came to their attention in the course of their regulated business activities.
   - For anyone taking any action likely to prejudice an investigation by informing (tipping off) the person who is the subject of a suspicious report, that a report has been made to a nominated officer or to the Serious Organised Crime Agency (SOCA),[1] or that the police or customs authorities are carrying out, or intend to carry out, a money-laundering investigation.
   - Destroying or disposing of documents which are relevant to an investigation.
   - Failing to comply with a requirement imposed under a customer information order, or knowingly or recklessly making a statement in purported compliance with a customer information order that is false or misleading in a material particular.

POCA also sets out the maximum penalties as follows:

- For the offence of money laundering, 14 years' imprisonment and/or an unlimited fine. However, an offence is not committed if the offence was reported to SOCA as soon as was reasonably practical.
- For failing to make a report of suspected money laundering or for "tipping off", five years' imprisonment and/or an unlimited fine.
- For destroying or disposing of relevant documents, five years' imprisonment and/or an unlimited fine.

The Proceeds of Crime Act is just one of the many laws which impacts on money laundering and terrorist financing. It needs to be considered in terms of its impact on other

[1] Note that on the 7th October, 2013, the Serious Organised Crime Agency (SOCA) became the National Crime Agency (NCA).

relevant regulation, including the Policing and Crime Act 2009, Coroners and Justice Act 2009, UK Borders Act 2007 and, most recently, the Crime and Courts Act 2013, as well as the four codes of practice which supplemented this legislation.

6.9 TERRORISM ACT 2000, AND THE ANTI-TERRORISM CRIME AND SECURITY ACT 2001

The Terrorism Act 2000 establishes a series of offences related to the involvement of persons or organisations in arrangements for facilitating, raising or using funds for terrorist purposes.

The Terrorism Act sets out the following criminal offences:

- For any person not to report the existence of terrorist property where there are reasonable grounds for knowing or suspecting the existence of terrorist property.
- For anyone taking any action likely to prejudice an investigation by informing (i.e. tipping off) the person who is the subject of a suspicion report, or anybody else that a disclosure has been made to a nominated officer or to the SOCA, or that the police or customs authorities are carrying out, or intending to carry out, a terrorist-financing investigation.
- For anyone entering into or becoming concerned in an arrangement which facilitates the retention or control by, or on behalf of, another person of terrorist property by concealment, by removal from the jurisdiction, by transfer to nominees or in any other way.

Other counter-terrorism legislation was passed in 2005 (Prevention of Terrorism Act 2005), 2006 (Terrorism Act 2006), 2008 (Counter-Terrorism Act 2008) and 2010 (the Terrorist Asset-Freezing etc. Act 2010), all of which state the prevention of terrorism as one of their purposes in their introductory text. This repeated strengthening of the counter-terrorism framework highlights the UK's dedication to preventing this area of financial crime. Under the Terrorist Asset-Freezing etc. Act 2010, the Treasury is required to publish a quarterly report to Parliament on its operation of the UK's asset-freezing regime.

The parallels to the POCA can be seen clearly, with the general wording being both consistent and similar.

The Terrorism Act then sets out the following penalties:

- The maximum penalty for failure to report under the circumstances set out above is five years' imprisonment and/or an unlimited fine.
- The maximum penalty for the offence of actual money laundering is 14 years' imprisonment and/or a unlimited fine.

Again, these are consistent with the approach adopted by the POCA.

The Anti-terrorism Crime and Security Act 2001 gives the authorities power to seize terrorist cash, to freeze terrorist assets and to direct firms in the regulated sector to provide the authorities with specified information on customers and their (terrorism-related) activities. As such, it implements those of the nine special recommendations of the Financial Action Task Force (FATF) not already incorporated into UK legislation.

6.10 MONEY LAUNDERING REGULATIONS 2007

The Money Laundering Regulations 2007 specify arrangements which must be in place within firms within the scope of the regulations, in order to prevent operations relating to money laundering or terrorist financing.

6.10.1 The Scope of the Regulations

In terms of their scope, the Money Laundering Regulations apply, *inter alia*, to:

- The regulated activities of all financial sector firms which include:
  - banks, building societies and other credit institutions;
  - individuals and firms engaged in regulated investment activities under the Financial Services and Markets Act 2000 (FSMA);
  - issuers of electronic money;
  - insurance companies undertaking long-term life business, including the life business of Lloyds of London;
  - Bureaux de change, cheque-encashment centres and money-transmission services;
  - Trust and company service providers;
  - Casinos;
  - Dealers in high-value goods (including auctioneers) who accept payment in cash of EUR 15,000 or more, whether this is a single or linked transaction;
  - Lawyers and accountants when undertaking relevant business.

6.10.2 The Key Requirements

Persons who are subject to the Money Laundering Regulations are required to establish adequate and appropriate policies and procedures in order to prevent operations relating to money laundering or terrorist financing, covering:

- Customer due diligence
- Reporting
- Record-keeping
- Internal control
- Risk assessment and management
- Compliance management
- Communications.

The FCA institutes proceedings for offences committed under the regulations against both regulated and non-regulated firms. A breach of the money-laundering regulations is not dependent on whether money laundering has actually taken place. Firms can be sanctioned for not having adequate anti-money laundering/counter-terrorist-funding systems. Failure to comply with any of the Money Laundering Regulations constitutes a punishable offence by a maximum of two years' imprisonment, a fine or both.

As you can see, these broadly address the issues set out in the EU's Third Directive, as discussed in Chapter 4.

7 HOW MONEY-LAUNDERING-DETERRENCE REGULATIONS ARE APPLIED IN THE UK – THE JOINT MONEY LAUNDERING STEERING GROUP

In the UK, the main regulatory guidance with regard to money-laundering deterrence and terrorist financing is produced by the Joint Money Laundering Steering Group (JMLSG), which is made up of the leading UK trade associations in the financial services industry, including the British Bankers' Association. Its existence actually pre-dated the creation of the UK's original unitary regulator, the Financial Services Authority. The aim of the JMLSG is to encourage good practice in countering money laundering and to give practical assistance in interpreting the statutory UK Money Laundering Regulations. This is primarily achieved by the publication of industry guidance which offers advice on suitable ways to comply with laws and regulations on financial crime. It also highlights areas of concern and suggests processes and procedures that should be considered.

It is important to note that the UK has statutory provisions and therefore any breach of the regulations represents a criminal, rather than a civil, matter.

The rules themselves have been through many changes over the years and have both increased and decreased in their depth and scope. Initially drafted by experts in each individual field of financial services (the so-called coloured books), the rules have now been consolidated and reflect the UK's interpretation of relevant EU legislation as implemented into UK law incorporating FATF guidance.

Guidance is only issued by the JMLSG after it has been approved by HM Treasury and, as such, UK courts must take the guidance into account in the event of any legal proceedings. Adherence to the guidance is also regarded by the FCA and the PRA as demonstrating compliance with their relevant systems and controls rules. As such, the regulators have effectively taken the totality of the JMLSG guidance and incorporated it into their own rule books.

7.1 MEMBERSHIP

The JMLSG is made up of the leading UK trade associations in the financial services industry. As of July 2013, these consisted of the following organisations:

- Asset Based Finance Association (ABSA);
- Association of British Credit Unions Ltd (ABCUL);

- Association of British Insurers (ABI);
- Association of Foreign Banks (AFB);
- Association of Financial Mutuals (AFM);
- Association for Financial Markets in Europe (AFME);
- Association of Independent Financial Advisers (AIFA);
- Association of Private Client Investment Managers and Stockbrokers (APCIMS);
- British Bankers' Association (BBA);
- British Venture Capital Association (BVCA);
- Building Societies Association (BSA);
- Council of Mortgage Lenders (CML);
- Electronic Money Association (EMA);
- Finance & Leasing Association (FLA);
- Futures and Options Association (FOA);
- Investment Management Association (IMA);
- Tax Incentivised Savings Association (TISA);
- Wholesale Market Brokers' Association (WMBA).

The breadth of the organisations represented provides a warning as to the scope of money-laundering regulation in the UK. In addition, other organisations, whilst not being direct members, have attendance rights, including bodies such as the Institute of Chartered Accountants in England and Wales, the equivalent bodies in Scotland and in Ireland and both the Institute and Faculties of Actuaries. The JMLSG has been producing money laundering guidance for the financial sector since 1990, initially in conjunction with the Bank of England, and then with the FSA to provide regularly updated guidance on the various money-laundering regulations in force – those set in 1993, 2001, 2003 and 2007. In June 2013, HMRC released three short factsheets summarising and offering advice and best practice on the money-laundering regulations. The factsheets cover an introduction to the regulations, visits by HMRC under the regulations and a guide to complying with obligations, including risk-management and reporting procedures. The factsheets are available from the HMRC website.

Given that the new regulators (FCA and PRA) do not have money-laundering deterrence as a primary objective, it will be interesting to see how new guidance is developed in future and the role that these new regulators will choose to adopt.

7.2 THE RISK-BASED APPROACH

A major revision of JMLSG's guidance was published in January 2006 (and has been amended subsequently), based on a number of fundamental principles – including that of senior management accountability and the adoption of a risk-based approach. The risk-based approach allows firms to focus their money-laundering deterrence and counter-terrorist-financing resources on areas where the risk of money laundering and/or terrorist financing is considered highest. As we saw in Chapter 4, this had specifically been recommended by the Third Directive. The guidance therefore embodies what are considered to be proportionate and cost-effective approaches to managing these risks.

Text from the guidance is reproduced with the kind permission of the Joint Money Laundering Steering Group.

A risk-based approach essentially includes the following:

- Senior management roles should include the identification of a Money Laundering Reporting Officer (or MLRO, see Chapter 12), responsible for the supervision of internal anti-money-laundering policies, procedures and investigations, together with measures implemented to combat the financing of terrorism.
- Such policies and procedures must be formally documented. The documentation maintained must include a named employee as being responsible for implementing and assessing the risks faced by the firm.
- All firms must identify what they consider to be low-risk and high-risk clients. Low-risk clients are normally seen as those with a regular income which have a long-term active relationship with the firm. High-risk clients are generally the rest.

7.3 THE REGULATORY FRAMEWORK

The JMLSG has periodically reviewed its guidance, and has made changes and additions as required. As mentioned above, an important revision took place in 2006 to reflect the implementation of the Proceeds of Crime Act 2002, and there were then subsequent revisions that implemented the Money Laundering Regulations 2007, which, in turn, implemented the EU Third Money Laundering Directive in the UK.

The JMLSG states that the purpose of the guidance is to:

- Outline the legal and regulatory framework for anti-money laundering/countering terrorist financing (AML/CTF) requirements and systems across the financial services sector;
- Interpret the requirements of the relevant law and regulations, and how they may be implemented in practice;
- Indicate good industry practice in AML/CTF procedures through a proportionate, risk-based approach; and
- Assist firms to design and implement the systems and controls necessary to mitigate the risks of the firm being used in connection with money laundering and the financing of terrorism.

The actual guidance is available for you to download for free from the following website: www.jmlsg.org.uk. The guidance is over 500 pages long, spanning three parts, and includes the following sections:

Part I:

Senior management responsibility;

Internal controls;

Nominated officer/MLRO;

Risk-based approach;

Customer due diligence;

Suspicious activities, reporting and data protection;

Staff awareness, training and alertness;

Record-keeping.

These general rules have been used and are consistent with the guidance produced in the relevant chapters of this book and therefore are not reproduced here.

Part II (sector-specific guidance):

Retail banking;

Credit cards, etc;

Electronic money;

Credit unions;

Wealth management;

Financial advisers;

Life assurance, and life-related pensions and investment products;

General insurers;

Non-life providers of investment fund products;

Discretionary and advisory investment management;

Execution-only stockbrokers;

Motor finance;

Asset finance;

Private equity;

Corporate finance;

Trade finance;

Correspondent banking;

Syndicated lending;

Wholesale markets;

Name-passing brokers in inter-professional markets;

Brokerage services to funds;

Invoice finance.

We have incorporated certain key elements of the guidance in this chapter.

Part III (specialist guidance):

Transparency in electronic payments (wire transfers);

Equivalent jurisdictions;

Equivalent markets;

Compliance with the UK financial sanctions regime;

Directions under the Counter-Terrorism Act 2008, Schedule 7.

From this website, all of the rules can be seen in detail and they do form a useful reference set for money-laundering deterrence specialists in any country. The guidance is detailed and consistent with the FATF principles, together with relevant EU legislation, but actually goes much further, providing guidance in areas of specific concern. In the remainder of this book we provide such guidance as is appropriate for the global reader. If you wish to look at specific UK guidance, reference needs to be made to the specific UK rules as set out on the above website. Of course, if you do require detailed local guidance, reference will need to be made to your local relevant authority and the rules that they have promulgated which achieve the same objectives.

Much of the content of the JMLSG guidance is consistent with the guidance that is offered throughout this book, so has not been reproduced here. However, as stated above, some of the Part II guidance information is worthy of your additional attention, and certain aspects are provided here in summary form for reference.

7.3.1 Credit Cards

Credit cards are a way of obtaining unsecured borrowing. As such, the initial risks are more related to fraud than to "classic" money laundering, but handling the criminal property arising as a result of fraud is also money laundering. Card issuers will, therefore, generally carry out some degree of credit check before accepting applications.

The money-laundering risk relates largely to the source and means by which repayment of the borrowing on the card is made. Payments may also be made by third parties. Such third party payments, especially if they are in cash or by debit cards from different locations or accounts, represent a higher level of money-laundering risk than when they come from the cardholder's bank account by means of cheque or direct debit.

Balances on cards may move into credit if cardholders repay too much, or where merchants pass credits/refunds across an account. Customers may ask for a refund of their credit balance. Issuance of a cheque by a card issuer can facilitate money laundering.

Cash may be withdrawn in another jurisdiction. This is, in any event, the case in respect of an amount up to the credit limit on the card. Where there is a credit balance, the amount that may be moved is correspondingly greater; it is possible for a cardholder to overpay substantially, and then to take the card abroad to be used. However, most card issuers limit the amount of cash that may be withdrawn.

Where several holders are able to use a card account, the card issuer may open itself to a money-laundering or terrorist-financing risk in providing a payment token to an individual in respect of whom it holds no information. The issuer would not know to whom it is advancing money, unless it has taken some steps in relation to the identity of all those entitled to use the card. Such steps might include ascertaining whether the primary or any secondary cardholder is resident in a high-risk jurisdiction or whether any primary or secondary cardholder is a politically exposed person.

Measures that a firm might consider for mitigating the risk associated with a credit card customer base include the following:

- Deciding whether to disallow persons so identified in the above two categories, or to subject them to enhanced due diligence, including full verification of identity of any secondary cardholder.
- Requiring the application process to include a statement of the relationship of a secondary cardholder to the primary cardholder based on defined alternatives (e.g. family member, carer, none).
- Deciding whether to disallow as a secondary cardholder on a personal account any relationship deemed unacceptable according to internal policy parameters, or where the address of the secondary cardholder differs from that of the primary cardholder, or to subject the application to additional enquiry, including verification of the secondary cardholder.
- Becoming a member of closed user groups sharing information to identify fraudulent applications, and checking both primary and secondary cardholder names and/or addresses against such databases.
- Deciding whether to decline to accept, or to undertake additional or enhanced due diligence on, corporate cardholders associated with an entity which is engaged in a high-risk activity, or is resident in a high-risk jurisdiction, or has been the subject of (responsible) negative publicity.
- Implementing ongoing transaction monitoring of accounts, periodic review and refinement of the parameters used for the purpose.
- In the event that monitoring or suspicious reporting identifies that a secondary cardholder has provided significant funds for credit to the account, either regularly or on a one-off basis, giving consideration to verifying the identity of that secondary cardholder where it has not already been undertaken.
- Deciding whether the cardholder should be able to withdraw cash from his card account.
- Deciding whether the card may be used abroad (and monitoring whether it is used abroad).

7.3.2 *Electronic Money*

Under the Electronic Money Regulations 2011 (Reg. 2(1)), electronic money is defined as:

> "Electronically (including magnetically) stored monetary value as represented by a claim on the electronic money issuer which:
>
> (a) is issued on receipt of funds for the purpose of making payment transactions;
>
> (b) is accepted by a person other than the electronic money issuer; and
>
> (c) is not excluded by Regulation 3."

Regulation 3 of the Electronic Money Regulations 2011 states that electronic money does not include:

1. Monetary value stored on instruments that can be used to acquire goods or services only:
   (a) in or on the electronic money issuer's premises; or
   (b) under a commercial agreement with the electronic money issuer, either within a limited network of service providers or for a limited range of goods or services.
2. Monetary value that is used to make payment transactions executed by means of any telecommunication, digital or IT device, where the goods or services purchased are delivered to, and are to be used through, a telecommunication, digital or IT device, provided that the telecommunication, digital or IT operator does not act only as an intermediary between the payment service user and the supplier of the goods and services.

Electronic money is a retail payment product that is used predominantly for making small-value payments and is currently growing in many jurisdictions. That the JMLSG has already included guidance in this area will be of interest to many international regulators seeking to develop their own regulations.

Electronic money is susceptible to the same risks of money laundering and terrorist financing as other retail payment products. Furthermore, where electronic money is limited to small-value payments, its use is less attractive to would-be launderers. For terrorist financing and other financial crime, electronic money offers a more accountable, and therefore less attractive, means of transferring money compared to cash.

The electronic money products in commercial use today do not provide the privacy or anonymity of cash, nor its utility. This is due to a number of factors. Products may, for example, be funded by payments from bank accounts or credit cards and therefore reveal the identity of the customer at the outset. The use of most electronic money products also tends to leave an electronic trail.

As issuers of electronic money usually occupy the position of intermediaries in the payment process, situated between two financial or credit institutions, they are often able to provide additional transaction information to law enforcement that complements identity data provided by other financial institutions. This may be equally or more valuable evidence than a repetition of the verification of identity process.

Fraud prevention and consumer protection concerns led to the placement of transaction, turnover and purse limits on products, limiting the risk to both issuer and consumer. These limits act to restrict the usefulness of the product for money laundering, and make unusual transactions more detectable.

The following factors will increase the risk of electronic money products being used for money laundering or terrorist financing:

- High, or no, transaction or purse limits. The higher the value and frequency of transactions, and the higher the purse limit, the greater the risk, particularly where customers are permitted to hold multiple purses; the EUR 15,000 [£12,500] threshold for occasional transactions provided in the Money Laundering Regulations 2007 may, in this context, provide a convenient comparator when assessing such risk.
- Frequent cross-border transactions, unless within a single scheme, can give rise to difficulties with information sharing. Dependence on counterparty systems increases the risk.
- Some merchant activity, such as betting and gaming, poses a higher risk of money laundering. This is because of the higher amounts of funds that are transacted and because of the opportunities presented within the merchant environment.
- Funding of purses by unverified parties presents a higher risk of money laundering, whether it is the customer who is unverified or a third party.
- Funding of purses using cash offers little or no audit trail of the source of the funds and hence presents a higher risk of money laundering.
- Funding of purses using electronic money products that have not been verified may present a higher risk of money laundering.
- The non-face-to-face nature of many products gives rise to increased risk.
- Segmentation of the business value chain, including use of multiple agents and outsourcing, in particular to overseas locations, may give rise to a higher risk.
- The technology adopted by the product may give rise to specific risks that should be assessed.

The systems and controls issuers put in place must be commensurate with the money-laundering and terrorist-financing risk they are exposed to. The detail of issuers' systems and controls will, therefore, vary. Examples include those that:

- Place limits on purse storage values, cumulative turnover or amounts transacted;
- Can detect money-laundering transaction patterns;
- Can identify multiple purses held by a single individual or group of individuals, such as the holding of multiple accounts or the "stockpiling" of pre-paid cards;
- Can look for indicators of accounts being opened with different issuers as well as attempts to pool funds from different sources;

- Can identify discrepancies between submitted and detected information;
- Restrict funding of electronic money products to funds drawn on accounts held at credit and financial institutions in the UK, the EU or a comparable jurisdiction, and allow redemption of electronic money only into accounts held at such institutions.

7.3.3 Wealth Management

Wealth management is the provision of banking and investment services in a closely managed relationship to high-net-worth clients. Such services will include bespoke product features tailored to a client's particular needs and may be provided from a wide range of facilities available to the client, including:

- Current account banking;
- High-value transactions;
- Use of sophisticated products;
- Non-standard investment solutions;
- Business conducted across different jurisdictions;
- Offshore and overseas companies, trusts or personal investment vehicles.

Money launderers are attracted by the availability of complex products and services that operate internationally within a reputable and secure wealth management environment that is familiar with high-value transactions. The following factors contribute to the increased vulnerability of wealth management:

- Wealthy and powerful clients: Such clients may be reluctant or unwilling to provide adequate documents, details and explanations. The situation is exacerbated where the client enjoys a high public profile, and where they wield, or have recently wielded, political or economic power or influence.
- Multiple and complex accounts: Clients often have many accounts in more than one jurisdiction, impacting the firm's ability to identify true purpose.
- Cultures of confidentiality: Wealth management clients often seek reassurance that their confidential business will be conducted discreetly.
- Concealment: The misuse of services such as offshore trusts and the availability of structures such as shell companies helps to maintain an element of secrecy about beneficial ownership of funds.
- Countries with statutory banking secrecy and countries where corruption is known, or perceived, to be a common source of wealth.
- Movement of funds: The transmission of funds and other assets by private clients often involves high-value transactions, requiring rapid transfers to be made across accounts in different countries and regions of the world.
- The use of concentration accounts (i.e. multi-client pooled/omnibus-type accounts) to collect together funds from a variety of sources for onward transmission is seen as a potential major risk.

- Credit: The extension of credit to clients who use their assets as collateral also poses a money-laundering risk unless the lender is satisfied that the origin and source of the underlying asset is legitimate.
- Commercial activity conducted through a personal account, or personal activity conducted through a business account, so as to deceive the firm or its staff.

In addition to the standard identification requirement, as a minimum requirement to counter the perceived and actual risks, the firm, and those acting in support of the business, must exercise a greater degree of diligence throughout the relationship which will be beyond that needed for normal retail banking purposes. The firm must endeavour to understand the nature of the client's business and consider whether it is consistent and reasonable, including:

- The origins of the client's wealth;
- Where possible and appropriate, documentary evidence relating to the economic activity that gave rise to the wealth;
- The nature and type of transactions;
- The client's business and legitimate business structures;
- For corporate and trust structures, the chain of title, authority or control leading to the ultimate beneficial owner, settler and beneficiaries, if relevant and known;
- Where appropriate, the reasons a client is using complex structures;
- The use made by the client of products and services;
- The nature and level of business to be expected over the account.

The firm must be satisfied that a client's use of complex business structures and/or the use of trust and private investment vehicles has a genuine and legitimate purpose.

Visiting clients can be an important part of the overall customer due diligence process. In wealth management, relationship managers should generally visit their clients at their place of business in order to substantiate the type and volume of their business activity and income, or at their home if the business factor is not so relevant. The relationship manager who undertakes the visit should make a record by documenting:

- The date and time of the visit;
- The address or addresses visited;
- A summary of both the discussions and assessments;
- Any commitments or agreements;
- Any changes in client profile;
- The expectations for product usage, volumes and turnover going forward;
- Any international dimension to the client's activities and the risk status of the jurisdictions involved.

The relationship manager should then update the client's profile where appropriate.

7.3.4 *General Insurers*

General insurers should consider the following:

- Development of internal policies and procedures;
- Communication of those policies and procedures to all staff;
- Clear and written procedures in place to help staff identify the kinds of activities or customers that might arouse suspicion;
- Clear guidance to be given to all staff on the risk and implications of alerting potential or actual customers (or agents thereof) to the fact that a SAR has been submitted, i.e. the "tipping off" provision of POCA;
- Clear guidance to be given to all staff on the risk and implications of failing to report their suspicions;
- Short reporting lines between front-line staff and a nominated officer;
- Record-keeping, both of decisions made in the event of a suspicious claim being reported to evidence the making of the report and, in the event of a SAR not being made, the reasons why no notification was made;
- Screening procedures to ensure high standards on recruitment;
- Ongoing employee training to ensure employees recognise suspicious activities and understand the procedure in place internally to record suspicious activities;
- A system of testing compliance: this should be both independent and adequately resourced.

7.3.5 *Execution-only Stockbrokers (ExOs)*

Some ExO stockbrokers deal with high volumes of low-value customer transactions, whereas others direct their services towards higher net worth customers, and thus have fewer customers. Stockbroking customers may adopt a variety of trading patterns; the firm may be offering no advice and may have little or no knowledge of a particular customer's motives.

ExO customers are also free to spread their activities across a variety of brokers for perfectly valid reasons, and often do. Each broker may therefore actually have little in terms of transaction history from which to identify unusual behaviour. Many firms provide ExO stockbroking services on a non-face-to-face basis, including via the internet.

In view of the above, whilst stockbroking might be regarded as being of *lower* risk compared to many financial products and services, the risk is not as low as in providing investment management services to the same types of customer from similar jurisdictions.

7.3.6 *Asset Finance*

Generally with asset finance, no monies are advanced to the customer, but are paid into a supplier's bank account to fund the purchase of an asset which is made available under contract to the customer. Repayments by the customer are usually made from other bank accounts by direct debit. Risk is also associated with hire purchase and lease products, as they could be used for layering.

Given that a loan does not result in the borrower receiving funds from the lender, but the use of assets, the initial transaction is not very susceptible to money laundering. The main money-laundering risk arises through the acceleration of an agreed repayment schedule.

Asset finance products, therefore, generally carry a low inherent money-laundering risk. An asset finance company will normally only accept payment of instalments from the customer named on the agreement, and in the case of overpayment will only make repayment to the customer named on the agreement.

All asset finance providers should carry out full credit searches on the businesses they transact with. Additional steps to verify identity will vary across the three markets, as set out below. Note that this may well go beyond what is required by the current money-laundering regulations, certainly in relation to low-risk areas which can now rely on simplified due diligence (SDD). However, these additional measures will still be important for fraud purposes.

7.3.7 Corporate Finance

As with any financial service activity, corporate finance business can be used to launder money.

Money-laundering activity through corporate finance will not usually involve the placement stage of money laundering, as the transaction will involve funds or assets already within the financial system. However, corporate finance could be involved in the layering or integration stages of money laundering. It could also involve the concealment, use and possession of criminal property and arrangements to do so, or terrorist funding.

The money-laundering risks associated with corporate finance relate to the transfer of assets between parties, in exchange for cash or other assets. The assets can take the form of securities or other corporate instruments.

Where there is less transparency over the ownership of the customer, for example, where ownership or control is vested in other entities such as trusts or special purpose vehicles (SPVs), or less of an industry profile or less independent means of verification of the customer, a firm should consider how this affects the ML/TF risk presented. It will, in certain circumstances, be appropriate to conduct additional due diligence, over and above the firm's standard evidence.

Firms have an obligation to verify the identity of all beneficial owners. They should also know and understand any associations the customer may have with other jurisdictions, and may also consider whether they should verify the identity of other owners or controllers.

Firms should maintain file notes setting out the basis on which they are able to confirm the structure and the identity of the customer and individuals concerned.

7.3.8 Trade Finance

A key risk around trade finance business is that seemingly legitimate transactions and associated documents can be constructed simply to justify the movement of funds between parties, or to show a paper trail for non-existent or fraudulent goods. In particular, the level and type of documentation received by a firm is dictated principally by the applicant or instructing party, and, because of the diversity of documentation, firms may not be expert in many types of the documents received as a result of trade finance business when standard forms are not used.

Such a risk is probably greatest where the parties to an underlying commercial trade transaction are in league to disguise the true nature of a transaction. In such instances, methods used by criminals to transfer funds illegally range from over and under invoicing, to the presentation of false documents or spurious calls under default instruments. In more complex situations, for example where asset securitisation is used, trade receivables can be generated from fictitious parties or fabricated transactions (albeit the use of asset securitisation in trade finance is a very limited activity). The use of copy documents, particularly documents of title, should be discouraged.

The Financial Action Task Force (FATF), regulators and others have identified misuse of the trade system as one of the methods by which criminal organisations and terrorist financiers move money for the purpose of disguising its origins and integrating it into the legitimate economy. FATF typology studies indicate that criminal organisations and terrorist groups exploit vulnerabilities in the international trade system to move value for illegal purposes. Cases identified include: illicit trafficking in narcotic drugs; illicit trafficking in stolen or other goods; corruption and bribery; fraud; counterfeiting/piracy of products; and smuggling. More complicated schemes integrate these fraudulent practices into a complex web of transactions and movements of goods and money.

The FATF's June 2006 study notes that the basic techniques of trade-based money laundering include:

- **Over invoicing:** By misrepresenting the price of the goods in the invoice and other documentation (stating it at above the true value) the seller gains excess value as a result of the payment.
- **Under invoicing:** By misrepresenting the price of the goods in the invoice and other documentation (stating it at below the true value) the buyer gains excess value when the payment is made.
- **Multiple invoicing:** By issuing more than one invoice for the same goods, a seller can justify the receipt of multiple payments. This will be harder to detect if the colluding parties use more than one financial institution to facilitate the payments/transactions.
- **Short shipping:** The seller ships less than the invoiced quantity or quality of goods, thereby misrepresenting the true value of goods in the documents. The effect is similar to over invoicing.
- **Over shipping:** The seller ships more than the invoiced quantity or quality of goods, thereby misrepresenting the true value of goods in the documents. The effect is similar to under invoicing.

- **Deliberate obfuscation of the type of goods:** Parties may structure a transaction in a way to avoid alerting any suspicion to financial institutions or to other third parties which become involved. This may simply involve omitting information from the relevant documentation or deliberately disguising or falsifying it. This activity may or may not involve a degree of collusion between the parties involved and may be for a variety of reasons or purposes.
- **Phantom shipping:** No goods are shipped and all documentation is completely falsified.

Generally, these techniques involve fraud by one party against another, but may also depend upon collusion between the seller and buyer, since the intended outcome of the trade is to obtain value in excess of what would be expected from an arm's length transaction, or to move funds from point A to point B without being detected or accounted for by the authorities. The collusion may arise, for example, because the parties are controlled by the same persons, or because the parties are attempting to evade taxes on some part of the transaction.

Where the nature of a transaction displays higher risk characteristics than normal business undertaken for the customer (instructing party), for example, the buyer falls into a higher risk category, then the firm should consider undertaking additional due diligence in line with its risk policies. Some of the checks firms could undertake (not all of which may be applicable or available in each case) include:

- Making enquiries, as appropriate, into the ownership and background of the other parties to the transaction, e.g. the beneficiary(ies), agents, shipping lines, and taking further steps to verify information or the identity of key individuals as the case demands.
- Seeking information from the instructing party about the frequency of trade and the quality of the business relationships existing between the parties to the transaction. This should be documented to assist future due diligence.
- Checking the transaction against warning notices from external public sources, for example the ICC's International Maritime Bureau.
- Referring the transaction to external agencies specialising in search and validation services in respect of bills of lading, shipping services and commodity prices, for example the ICC Commercial Crime Services.
- Checking details of the source of goods.
- Checking public source information for prices of goods such as commodities – where the contract price is significantly different from the market (say 25%) then consider further investigation.
- Attending and recording relationship meetings with the instructing party; visiting them by arrangement.
- For export letters of credit, referring details to other group resources on the ground in the country of origin, to seek corroboration.
- Checks into the verification of shipments after the UCP operation is over, drawn at random from a sample of transactions, across a cross-section of the bank's trade finance clients. This may help to identify spurious transactions where buyers and sellers act in collusion.

The enhanced due diligence should be designed to understand the nature of the transaction, the related trade cycle for the goods involved, the appropriateness of the transaction structure, the legitimacy of the payment flows and what control mechanisms exist.

7.3.9 Correspondent Banking

The correspondent often has no direct relationship with the underlying parties to a transaction and is therefore not in a position to verify their identities. Correspondents often have limited information regarding the nature or purpose of the underlying transactions, particularly when processing electronic payments or clearing cheques. For these reasons, correspondent banking is, in the main, non-face-to-face business and must be regarded as high risk from a money-laundering and/or terrorist-financing perspective. Firms undertaking such business are required by the ML Regulations "to apply on a risk-sensitive basis enhanced customer due diligence measures".

Correspondent banking relationships, if poorly controlled, can allow other financial service firms with inadequate AML/CFT systems and controls, and customers of those firms, direct access to international banking systems.

The following risk indicators should be considered both when initiating a relationship, and on a continuing basis thereafter, to determine the levels of risk-based due diligence that should be undertaken:

- **The respondent's domicile:** The jurisdiction where the respondent is based and/or where its ultimate parent is headquartered may present greater risk (or may mitigate the risk, depending on the circumstances). Certain jurisdictions are recognised internationally as having inadequate anti-money-laundering standards, insufficient regulatory supervision, or presenting greater risk for crime, corruption or terrorist financing. Other jurisdictions, however, such as many members of the Financial Action Task Force (FATF), have more robust regulatory environments, representing lower risks.
- **The respondent's ownership and management structures:** The location of owners, their corporate legal form and/or a lack of transparency of the ultimate beneficial ownership are indicative of the risk the respondent presents. Account should be taken of whether the respondent is publicly or privately owned; if publicly held, whether its shares are traded on a recognised market or exchange in a jurisdiction with a satisfactory regulatory regime, or, if privately owned, the identity of any beneficial owners and controllers. Similarly, the location and experience of management may indicate additional concerns, as would unduly frequent management turnover. The involvement of PEPs in the management or ownership of certain respondents may also increase the risk.
- **The respondent's business and customer base:** The type of business the respondent engages in, as well as the type of markets it serves, is indicative of the risk the respondent presents.
- **Downstream correspondent clearing:** A downstream correspondent clearer is a respondent that receives correspondent banking services from a correspondent and itself provides correspondent banking services to other financial institutions in the same currency as the account it maintains with its correspondent. When these services are offered to a respondent that is itself a downstream correspondent

clearer, a correspondent should, on a risk-based approach, take reasonable steps to understand the types and risks of financial institutions to whom the respondent offers such services, special care being taken to ensure there are no shell bank customers, and consider the degree to which the respondent examines the anti-money-laundering/terrorist-financing controls of those financial institutions.

All correspondent banking relationships with respondents from non-EEA States must be subject to an appropriate level of due diligence, which, at a minimum, meets the requirements laid down in Regulation 14(3) of the ML Regulations and additionally will ensure that a correspondent is comfortable conducting business with/for a particular respondent (and hence its underlying customers) given the respondent's risk profile.

In assessing the level of due diligence to be carried out in respect of a particular respondent, the correspondent must consider:

- **Regulatory status and history:** The primary regulatory body responsible for overseeing or supervising the respondent and the quality of that supervision. If circumstances warrant, a correspondent should also consider publicly available materials to ascertain whether the respondent has been the subject of any criminal case or adverse regulatory action in the recent past.
- **AML/CFT controls:** A correspondent should establish whether the respondent is itself regulated for money-laundering/terrorist-financing prevention and, if so, whether the respondent is required to verify the identity of its customers and apply other AML/CFT controls to FATF standards/equivalent to those laid down in the Money Laundering Directive. Where this is not the case, additional due diligence should be undertaken to ascertain and assess the effectiveness of the respondent's internal policy on money-laundering/terrorist-financing prevention and its Know Your Customer and activity monitoring controls and procedures.
- **Shell banks:** Whether the respondent has confirmed that it will not provide banking services to, or engage in business with, shell banks.

Prior to establishing a new correspondent relationship, a person from senior management and independent from the officer sponsoring the relationship must approve the setting up of the respondent's account. For higher risk relationships, the correspondent's compliance (or MLRO) function should also satisfy itself that the risks are acceptable.

Correspondents are required by Regulation 14(3) of the ML Regulations to subject respondents from non-EEA States to enhanced customer due diligence, but should consider doing so whenever the respondent has been considered to present a greater money-laundering/terrorist-financing risk. The enhanced due diligence process should involve further consideration of the following elements designed to ensure that the correspondent has secured a greater level of understanding:

- **Respondent's ownership and management:** For all beneficial owners and controllers, the sources of wealth and background, including their reputation in the marketplace, as well as recent material ownership changes (e.g. in the last three years). Similarly, a more detailed understanding of the experience of each member of executive management as well as recent material changes in the executive management structure (e.g. within the last three years).

- **Respondent's business:** Gather sufficient information about the respondent to understand fully the nature of its business. In addition, determine from publicly available information the reputation of the respondent and the quality of its supervision.
- **PEP involvement:** If a PEP appears to have a material interest or management role in a respondent, then the correspondent should ensure it has an understanding of that person's role in the respondent.
- **Respondent's anti-money-laundering/terrorist-financing controls:** An assessment of the quality of the respondent's AML/CFT and customer identification controls, including whether these controls meet internationally recognised standards. The extent to which a correspondent should enquire will depend upon the perceived risks.
- **Document the relationship:** Document the respective responsibilities of the respondent and correspondent.

7.3.10 Wholesale Markets

Traded products are usually traded on regulated markets, or between regulated parties, or with regulated parties acting as agent or principal. However, the characteristics of products, which facilitate the rapid and sometimes opaque transfer of ownership, the ability to change the nature of an asset and market mechanisms that potentially extend the audit trail, together with a diverse international customer base, have specific money-laundering risks that need to be addressed and managed appropriately.

One of the most significant risks associated with the wholesale markets and traded products is where a transaction involves payment in cash and/or third party payments.

Given the global flows of funds in the wholesale financial markets, it is important to recognise that although customers may remit funds from credit institutions, a firm could still be used to launder money. Traded products might, for example, be used as a means of changing assets rapidly into a different form, possibly using multiple brokers to disguise total wealth and ultimate origin of the funds or assets, or as savings and investment vehicles for money launderers and other criminals.

Firms dealing in traded products in the wholesale markets do not generally accept cash deposits or provide personal accounts that facilitate money transmission and/or third-party funding that is not related to specific underlying investment transactions. In the money markets, however, customers may request payments to third parties (e.g. FX payments to suppliers) and the associated ML risks need to be considered by the firm. There may also be third party funding of transactions in the commodities markets. Also, where a bank is lending funds to a customer to purchase a physical commodity and the customer hedges the risks associated with the transaction in the derivatives market through a broker, the bank may guarantee the payment of margin to that broker; this results in a flow of money between the broker and bank on the customer's behalf.

The extent to which certain products are subject to margin or option premium payment arrangements will affect the level of risk. The nature and form of any margin will need to be taken into account by the firm, through its risk-based approach, when identifying the customer and determining appropriate payment procedures.

OTC and exchange-based trading can also present very different money-laundering risk profiles. Exchanges that are regulated in equivalent jurisdictions, are transparent and have a central counterparty to clear trades can largely be seen as carrying a lower generic money-laundering risk. OTC business may, generally, be less well regulated and it is not possible to make the same generalisations concerning the money-laundering risk as with exchange-traded products. For example, trades that are executed as OTC but then are cleared centrally have a different risk profile to trades that are executed and settled OTC.

Therefore, from an AML/CFT perspective:

- If the firm is acting as principal with another exchange member, the exchange member is the firm's customer.
- Where an exchange-based trade is randomly and automatically matched with an equal and opposite exchange-based trade, it is recognised that, due to market mechanisms, the name of the other exchange member(s) may not be known. In these situations, where all the parties are members of the exchange and there is a CCP to match and settle the trades, the firm cannot know and therefore does not need to verify the identity of the other exchange member.
- Where a firm is acting as principal with a non-exchange member, the non-exchange member is the firm's customer.
- Where a firm is acting as agent for another party, the party for whom the firm is acting will be the firm's customer.
- Where the firm is acting for another party who is an intermediary for underlying third parties, the intermediary will be the customer of the firm, provided simplified due diligence can be applied.

8 THE WOLFSBERG PRINCIPLES[2]

The Wolfsberg Group is an association of eleven global banks which aims to develop financial service industry standards and related products for Know Your Customer, Anti-Money-Laundering and Counter-Terrorist-Financing policies.

The Group came together in 2000, at Château Wolfsberg in north-eastern Switzerland, in the company of representatives from Transparency International, including Stanley Morris, and Professor Mark Pieth of the University of Basel, to work on drafting anti-money-laundering guidelines for private banking. *The Wolfsberg Anti-Money-Laundering Principles for Private Banking* were subsequently published in October 2000, revised in May 2002 and again most recently in June 2012.

The Group then published a *Statement on the Financing of Terrorism* in January 2002, and also released the *Wolfsberg Anti-Money-Laundering Principles for Correspondent Banking* in November 2002 with the *Wolfsberg Statement on Monitoring Screening and Searching* being issued in September 2003. In 2004, the Wolfsberg Group focused on the development of a due diligence model for financial institutions, in cooperation with Banker's Almanac, thereby fulfilling one of the recommendations made in the Correspondent Banking Principles.

During 2005 and early 2006, the Wolfsberg Group of banks actively worked on four separate papers, all of which aimed to provide guidance with regard to a number of areas of banking activity where standards had yet to be fully articulated by lawmakers or regulators. It was hoped that these papers would provide general assistance to industry participants and regulatory bodies when shaping their own policies and guidance, as well as making a valuable contribution to the fight against money laundering. The papers were all published in June 2006, and consisted of two sets of guidance: *Guidance on a Risk Based Approach for Managing Money Laundering Risks* and *AML Guidance for Mutual Funds and Other Pooled Investment Vehicles.* Also published were *FAQs on AML issues in the Context of Investment and Commercial Banking* and *FAQs on Correspondent Banking*, which complement the other sets of FAQs available on the site: on Beneficial Ownership, Politically Exposed Persons and Intermediaries.

In early 2007, the Wolfsberg Group issued its *Statement against Corruption*, in close association with Transparency International and the Basel Institute on Governance. It describes the role of the Wolfsberg Group and financial institutions more generally in support of international efforts to combat corruption. The *Statement against Corruption* identifies some of the measures financial institutions may consider in order to prevent corruption in their own operations and protect themselves against the misuse of their operations in relation to corruption. Shortly thereafter, the Wolfsberg Group and The Clearing House Association LLC issued a statement endorsing measures to enhance the transparency of international wire transfers to promote the effectiveness of global anti-money-laundering and anti-terrorist-financing programmes.

---

[2] Excerpts from the Wolfsberg Principles reproduced with kind permission of the Wolfsberg Group.

In 2008, the Group decided to refresh its 2003 *FAQs on PEPs*, followed by a reissued *Statement on Monitoring, Screening and Searching* in 2009. 2009 also saw the publication of the first *Trade Finance Principles* and *Guidance on Credit/Charge Card Issuing and Merchant Acquiring Activities*. The *Trade Finance Principles* were expanded upon in 2011 and the Wolfsberg Group also replaced its 2007 *Wolfsberg Statement against Corruption* with a revised, expanded and renamed version of the paper: *Wolfsberg Anti-Corruption Guidance*. This Guidance takes into account a number of recent developments and gives tailored advice to international financial institutions in support of their efforts to develop appropriate anti-corruption programmes, to combat and mitigate bribery risks associated with clients or transactions and also to prevent internal bribery.

More recently, focus has expanded to the emergence of new payment methods and the Group published *Guidance on Prepaid and Stored Value Cards*, which considers the money-laundering risks and mitigants of physical prepaid and stored value card issuing and merchant acquiring activities, and supplements the Wolfsberg Group *Guidance on Credit/Charge Card Issuing and Merchant Acquiring Activities* of 2009.

In 2014 the Group issued *Guidance on Mobile and Internet Payment Services (MIPS)* and reissued the *Principles for Correspondent Banking* first issued in November 2002.

8.1 WOLFSBERG STANDARDS

The Wolfsberg Standards consist of the various sets of AML Principles, as well as related statements, issued by the Group since its inception:

- *Wolfsberg Principles for Correspondent Banking* (2014)
- *Wolfsberg Statement - Guidance on Mobile and Internet Payment Services (MIPS)* (2014)
- *Wolfsberg Private Banking Principles* (*May* 2012)
- *Wolfsberg Guidance on Prepaid and Stored Value Cards* (14th October, 2011)
- *Wolfsberg Anti-Corruption Guidance* (2011)
- *Statement on the publication of the Wolfsberg Anti-Corruption Guidance* (August 2011)
- *The Wolfsberg Trade Finance Principles* (2011)
- *Wolfsberg Monitoring Screening Searching Paper* (9th November, 2009)
- *Wolfsberg AML Guidance on Credit/Charge Card Issuing and Merchant Acquiring Activities* (May 2009)
- *The Wolfsberg Trade Finance Principles* (January 2009)
- Wolfsberg Group, *Clearing House Statement on Payment Message Standards* (April 2007)
- Wolfsberg Group, *Notification for Correspondent Bank Customers* (April 2007)
- *The Wolfsberg Statement against Corruption* (February 2007)
- Wolfsberg Statement – *Guidance on a Risk Based Approach for Managing Money Laundering Risks* (March 2006)
- Wolfsberg Statement – *Anti-Money Laundering Guidance for Mutual Funds and Other Pooled Investment Vehicles* (March 2006)
- *Wolfsberg Statement on Monitoring Screening and Searching* (September 2003)
- *Wolfsberg Statement on The Suppression of the Financing of Terrorism* (January 2002).

In the following sections we consider key elements of certain of these statements. Further information on individual elements of the statements appears in the relevant chapters of this book. If you do need full details of all or any of the statements, then reference should be made to the original statements. The principles are reproduced with the kind permission of the Wolfsberg Group.

8.1.1 *Wolfsberg Anti Money Laundering Principles for Correspondent Banking (2014)*

These principles update those originally issued in November 2002 and reiterate the requirements set out by FATF. The principles are also intended to be applied to SWIFT Relationship Management Application (RMA) relationships in part, or in totality, using a risk based approach.

Responsibility and Oversight

Apart from the normal requirements regarding policies and procedures and governance there is also a requirement that at least one person, senior to or independent from, the officer sponsoring the relationship, should approve the correspondent banking relationship. There is also a requirement for independent review.

Risk Based Due Diligence

Again the risk based approach is adopted taking into account the nature of the supervisory environment in which the firm operates. The particular risks of the relationship do need to be considered with information being updated on a risk basis including the use of trigger events. These include relevant money-laundering-deterrence-related adverse media or adverse client behaviour that results in a material change in the client and this should prompt a review of the relevant documentation and information.

Elements that should be used to address specific risk indicators include the following, if appropriate:

- The correspondent banking client's geographic risk
- Branches, subsidiaries and affiliates of correspondent banking clients
- Branches, subsidiaries and affiliates of the institution
- The correspondent banking client's ownership and management structures
- The correspondent banking client's business
- The correspondent banking client's customer base
- Products or services offered to the correspondent bank client
- Regulatory status and history
- Anti money laundering controls
    - The correspondent banking client's AML procedures should be assessed
- No business arrangements with shell banks
    - This should be confirmed by the institution
- Client visit
    - Unless other measures suffice, a representative should visit the correspondent banking client prior to, or within a reasonable period of time after, the establishment of the relationship.

Enhanced Due Diligence

Three issues are identified:

- PEP involvement
  - This is where a PEP is involved with the correspondent banking client. A normal PEP review should be conducted taking into account the risk to the relationship.
- Downstream correspondents
  - These are also referred to as "nested" relationships and are where facilities are provided to other banks. The additional monitoring is similar to the initial indicators above.
- Approval
  - Again a higher level of approval is required with a review of high risk relationships on at least an annual basis.

The remaining sections refer to monitoring and integration with the anti money laundering programme.

8.1.2 *Wolfsberg Private Banking Principles – May 2012*

This recently updated guideline provides general principles for banks, particularly in relation to KYC and due diligence.

The guideline provides that banks will endeavour to accept only those clients whose source of wealth and funds can be reasonably established to be legitimate. The primary responsibility for this lies with the private banker who sponsors the client for acceptance. Mere fulfilment of internal review procedures does not relieve the private banker of this basic responsibility. Bank policy will specify what such responsibility and sponsorship entail. The use of the word "endeavour" is due to the rules of Wolfsberg not strictly being obligatory.

Identification

The bank will establish the identity of its clients and beneficial owners prior to establishing business relationships with such persons. Identity is generally established by obtaining the name, date of birth (in the case of individuals), address and such further information as may be required by the laws of the relevant jurisdictions.

The requirement is for the bank to take reasonable measures to verify identity when establishing a business relationship as noted below, subject to applicable local requirements.

Natural persons: Identity will be verified to the bank's satisfaction on the basis of official identity papers or other reliable, independent source documents, data or information as may be appropriate under the circumstances.

Corporations, partnerships, foundations: Identity will be verified on the basis of documentary evidence of due organisation and existence.

Trusts: Identity will be verified on the basis of appropriate evidence of formation and existence or similar documentation. The identity of the trustees will be established and verified.

Identification documents, if used for verification purposes, must be current at the time of opening and copies of such documents should be obtained.

Beneficial Ownership

Beneficial ownership, for AML purposes, must be established for all accounts. The guideline sets out various situations in which beneficial ownership should be ascertained:

Natural persons: When the account is in the name of an individual, the private banker must establish whether the client is acting on his/her own behalf. If doubt exists, the bank will establish the capacity in which, and on whose behalf, the account holder is acting.

Legal entities: Where the client is a private investment company, the private banker will understand the structure of the company sufficiently to determine the provider of funds, the beneficial owner(s) of the assets held by the company and those with the power to give direction to the directors of the company. This principle applies regardless of whether the share capital is in registered or bearer form.

Trusts: Where the client is a trust, the private banker will understand the structure of the trust sufficiently to determine:

(a) the provider of funds (e.g. settlor);

(b) those who have control over the funds (e.g. trustees);

(c) any persons or entities who have the power to remove the trustees; and

(d) the persons for whose benefit the trust is established.

Partnerships: Where the client is a partnership, the private banker will understand the structure of the partnership sufficiently to determine the provider of funds and the general partners.

Foundations: Where the client is a foundation, the private banker will understand the structure of the foundation sufficiently to determine the provider(s) of funds and how the foundation is managed.

In each of the above cases, the private banker will make a reasonable judgment as to the need for further due diligence.

Intermediaries

The nature of the relationship of the bank with an intermediary depends on the type of intermediary involved.

Introducing intermediary

An introducing intermediary introduces clients to the bank, whereupon the introducing intermediary's clients become clients of the bank. The bank will generally obtain the same type of information with respect to an introduced client that would otherwise be obtained by the bank, absent the involvement of an introducing intermediary. The bank's policies will address the circumstances in, and the extent to which, the bank may rely on the introducing intermediary in obtaining this information.

Managing intermediary

A managing intermediary acts as a professional asset manager for another person and either:

1. Is authorised to act in connection with an account that such person has with the bank (in which case the considerations noted above with respect to introducing intermediaries would apply); or
2. Is itself the account holder with the bank, to be treated as the client of the bank.

The private banker will perform due diligence on the introducing or managing intermediary and establish, as appropriate, that the intermediary has relevant due diligence procedures for its clients, or a regulatory obligation to conduct such due diligence, that is satisfactory to the bank.

Powers of Attorney/Authorised Signers

The relationship between the holder of a power of attorney or another authorised signer, the account holder and, if different, the beneficial owner of the account, must be understood.

The identity of a holder of general powers over an account (such as the power to act as a signatory for the account) will be established and, as appropriate, verified.

Practices for Walk-In Clients and Electronic Banking Relationships

The guideline obliges banks to determine whether walk-in clients or relationships initiated through electronic channels require a higher degree of due diligence prior to account opening. The bank is also obliged specifically to address measures to establish and verify satisfactorily the identity of non-face-to-face customers.

Due Diligence

In addition to the information contemplated above, the guideline states that it is essential to collect and record the following information for clients and beneficial owners:

- Source of wealth;
- Net worth;
- Source of initial funding of account;
- Account information;
- Purpose for account;
- Expected account size;
- Expected account activity;
- Occupation;
- Nature of client's (or beneficial owner's) business;
- Role/relationship of powers of attorney or authorised third parties;
- Other pertinent information (e.g. source of referral).

Applying a risk-based approach, the bank will corroborate the information above on the basis of documentary evidence or reliable sources. Unless other measures reasonably suffice to conduct the due diligence on a client (e.g. favourable and reliable references), a client will be met prior to account opening, at which time, if identity is verified on the basis of official identity documents, such documents will be reviewed.

Numbered or Alternate Name Accounts

The guideline only permits numbered or alternate name accounts if the bank has established the identity of the client and the beneficial owner. These accounts must be open to a level of scrutiny by the bank's appropriate control layers equal to the level of scrutiny applicable to other client accounts. Furthermore, wire transfers from these accounts must reflect the true name of the account holder.

Concentration Accounts

Under the guideline, the bank is not allowed to permit the use of its internal non-client accounts (sometimes referred to as "concentration accounts") to prevent association of the identity of a client with the movement of funds on the client's behalf, i.e. the bank will not permit the use of such internal accounts in a manner that would prevent the bank from appropriately monitoring the client's account activity.

Oversight Responsibility

New clients, subject to a risk-based approach, must be approved by at least one person other than the private banker.

Client Acceptance: Situations Requiring Additional Diligence/Attention; Prohibited Customers

Prohibited customers

The bank will specify categories of customers that it will not accept or maintain.

General

In its internal policies, the bank must define categories of persons whose circumstances warrant enhanced due diligence. This will typically be the case where the circumstances are likely to pose a higher than average risk to a bank.

Indicators

The circumstances of the following categories of persons are indicators for defining them as requiring enhanced due diligence:

- Persons residing in and/or having funds sourced from countries identified by credible sources as having inadequate AML standards or representing a high risk for crime and corruption.
- Persons engaged in types of economic or business activities or sectors known to be susceptible to money laundering.
- "Politically exposed persons," frequently abbreviated as "PEPs".

Clients who are not deemed to warrant enhanced due diligence may be subjected to greater scrutiny as a result of:

- Monitoring of their activities;
- External inquiries;
- Derogatory information (e.g. negative media reports);
- Other factors which may expose the bank to reputational risk.

Senior management approval

The bank's internal policies should indicate whether, for any one or more among these categories, senior management must approve entering into new relationships.

Relationships with PEPs may only be entered into with the approval of senior management.

Cash handling

The bank's policies and procedures will address client cash transactions, including specifically the receipt and withdrawal of large amounts of cash.

Updating Client Files

The private banker is responsible for updating the client file on a defined basis and/or when there are major changes. The private banker's supervisor or an independent control person will review relevant portions of client files on a regular basis to ensure consistency and completeness. The frequency of the reviews depends on the size, complexity and risk posed by the relationship.

With respect to clients classified under any category of persons mentioned above as requiring enhanced due diligence or being prohibited, the bank's internal policies will indicate whether senior management must be involved in these reviews and what management information must be provided to management and/or other control layers. The policies and/or procedures should also address the frequency of these information flows.

Reviews of PEPs must require senior management's involvement.

Practices when Identifying Unusual or Suspicious Activities

Definition of unusual or suspicious activities

The bank will have a written policy on the identification of, and follow-up on, unusual or suspicious activities. This policy and/or related procedures will include a definition of what is considered to be suspicious or unusual and give examples thereof. The guideline provides examples of potentially suspicious activities and how to spot them, including:

- Account transactions or other activities which are not consistent with the due diligence file;
- Cash transactions over a certain amount;
- Pass-through/in-and-out transactions.

Unusual or suspicious activities can be identified through:

- Monitoring of transactions;
- Client contacts (meetings, discussions, in-country visits, etc.);
- Third party information (e.g. newspapers, other media sources, internet);
- Private banker's internal knowledge of the client's environment (e.g. political situation in his/her country).

Follow-up on unusual or suspicious activities

The private banker, management and/or the control function will carry out an analysis of the background of any unusual or suspicious activity. If there is no plausible explanation, a decision involving the control function will be made to:

- Continue the business relationship with increased monitoring;
- Cancel the business relationship;
- Report the business relationship to the authorities.

The report to the authorities is made by the control function and senior management may need to be notified (e.g. Senior Compliance Officer, CEO, Chief Auditor, General Counsel). As required by local laws and regulations, the assets may be blocked and transactions may be subject to approval by the control function.

Monitoring and screening

The primary responsibility for reviewing account activities lies with the private banker. The private banker will be familiar with significant transactions and increased activity in the account and will be especially aware of unusual or suspicious activities. In addition, a sufficient monitoring programme must be in place. The bank will decide to what extent fulfilment of this responsibility will need to be supported through the use of automated systems or other means.

With respect to clients classified as high risk, the bank's internal policies will indicate how the account activities will be subject to monitoring.

A sufficient sanctions programme must be in place, and no bank or employee may provide any assistance to a client trying to deceive the authorities.

The guideline obliges banks to include standard controls to be undertaken by the various "control layers" (private banker, line management, independent operations unit, Compliance, Internal Audit) in its policies and procedures. These controls will cover issues of frequency, degree of control, areas to be controlled, responsibilities and follow-up, compliance testing, etc.

An independent audit function (which may be internal to the bank) will test the programmes contemplated by these controls.

Reporting

There will be regular management reporting established on money-laundering issues (e.g. number of reports to authorities, monitoring tools, changes in applicable laws and regulations and the number and scope of training sessions provided to employees).

Education, training and information

The bank will establish a training programme on the identification and prevention of money laundering for employees who have client contact and for Compliance personnel. Regular training (e.g. annually) will also include how to identify and follow up on unusual or suspicious activities. In addition, employees will be informed about any major changes in AML laws and regulations.

All new employees will be provided with guidelines on the AML procedures.

Record retention requirements

The bank will establish record retention requirements for all AML-related documents. The documents must be kept for a minimum of five years, or longer, as may be required by local law and regulation.

Exceptions and deviations

The bank will establish an exception and deviation procedure that requires risk assessment and approval by an independent unit.

AML organisation

The bank will establish an adequately staffed and independent department responsible for the prevention of money laundering (e.g. Compliance, independent control unit, Legal).

8.1.3 Statement on Anti-Corruption

In August 2011, the Wolfsberg Group replaced its 2007 *Wolfsberg Statement against Corruption* with a revised, expanded and renamed version of the paper: *Wolfsberg Anti-Corruption Guidance*. This Guidance takes into account a number of recent developments and gives tailored advice to international financial institutions in support of their efforts to develop appropriate anti-corruption programmes, to combat and mitigate bribery risks associated with clients or transactions and also to prevent internal bribery.

Bribery is commonly described as involving the promise, offer/acceptance or transfer of an advantage, either directly or indirectly, in order to induce or reward the improper performance of a function or an activity. It may occur in a commercial arrangement (so-called commercial bribery) or involve the misuse of public office or public power for private gain in order to obtain, retain or direct business or to secure any other improper advantage in the conduct of business.

Financial Institutions' Internal Measures/Anti-corruption Programme

The statement provides guidance on anti-corruption programmes. It states that financial institutions should risk assess their own acuities, products and services, as appropriate, to develop and implement effective anti-corruption policies, procedures and measures, which are proportionate to the corruption risks identified. The following internal measures are important mitigants that a financial institution should consider implementing to prevent bribery and to protect employees, as well as the organisation itself, in the event that an allegation of direct or indirect bribery or corruption is raised:

- Senior management commitment;
- Risk assessment;
- Clear, practical and proportionate policies;
- Monitoring and review.

Misuse of the Financial System through Corruption

Financial institutions may be misused to further acts of corruption or to launder the proceeds of bribery. For example:

- A customer directing or collecting funds for the purpose of paying a bribe;
- A recipient of a bribe placing proceeds of the illicit bribe payment into the financial system;
- The deposit of misappropriated state assets;
- The clearing of transactions in any of the above cases.

In many instances, and without further information (for example, absent red flags), it may not be apparent from account activity that misuse is occurring and, therefore, it is hardly possible for financial institutions to make a distinction between accounts and transactions associated with corruption and those accounts and transactions that have a legal and sound commercial basis. This is particularly, but by no means exclusively, the case when dealing with substantial companies with complex business operations. The primary responsibility to ensure that funds are neither collected nor used for illicit operations, including bribery, must rest with a financial institution's customer or that customer's representatives. This is particularly true since a financial institution will seldom have a complete overview of its customers' financial activity.

Transactions involving the proceeds of corruption often follow patterns of behaviour common to money laundering associated with other criminal activities. Adherence to existing anti-money-laundering policies, procedures and controls is therefore important in the fight against corruption. By the same token, the standards and guidance set out in existing Wolfsberg papers are similarly relevant to determine and manage money-laundering risks related to corruption.

Risk-based Approach

The anti-corruption programme addressing internal bribery risks should be based upon the financial institution's wider risk-management strategy which will encompass a risk-based approach. There is an appendix to the guideline providing further guidance based on the following criteria:

- Services risk
- Country risk
- Customer risk
- Industry risk
- Transaction risk indicators ("red flags").

Services risk

The payment and receipt of bribes may be effected through a variety of services provided by financial institutions. However, in considering and assessing exposure to this risk, there are certain services that may be considered more vulnerable to abuse than others. The risks and possible mitigating measures are highlighted below, together (where appropriate) with any particularly relevant red flags.

Private banking

Risks: Private banking, particularly international private banking services, is vulnerable for a variety of reasons, including the high-net-worth characteristics of the customer base, the offshore nature of the facilities offered and the type of products and services available (e.g. asset protection and investment vehicles such as trusts, foundations, personal investment companies, cross-border wire transfers, etc.). In particular, recipients of bribes may seek international private banking services to launder the proceeds of the bribes.

Mitigating measures: Important mitigating measures include acceptance procedures for customers including the identification of beneficial ownership, the verification of identity and due diligence, notably establishing the source of wealth and source of funds deposited. These measures should also take into account risk indicators such as countries identified as representing higher risk for corruption, whether the customer is categorised as a PEP, or whether the customer is involved in a higher risk industry (e.g. arms dealing, or acting as an agent or intermediary for the arms trade, or other industry sector identified as posing increased corruption risks). Various risk attributes and red flags should be taken into account by an institution's policies to identify when enhanced due diligence should be applied to a prospective or existing client relationship. Adherence to the *Wolfsberg AML Principles on Private Banking* should constitute effective risk management in this area.

Red flags: Substantial cash or wire transfers to or from an account of a private banking customer where such activity is not consistent with legitimate or expected activity. In particular, substantial activity over a relatively short time period and/or the improper use of corporate vehicles to obscure ownership and/or the involvement of industries and/or countries posing increased corruption risk may also raise suspicions that require further due diligence and investigation.

Project finance/export credits

Risks: The provision of finance to customers of a financial institution and/or involvement in transactions linked to major project finance initiatives, such as those to support public sector infrastructure/construction projects or the exploitation of natural resources, is particularly vulnerable to the payment of bribes or other corrupt activity, not least because of the size and complexity of projects of this nature, in combination with the generally large number of participants involved, including government export credit agencies, private companies and banks. The responsibilities of financial institutions will generally be limited to their direct involvement in the financial advisory services, arranging or financing process such as with the borrower, exporter of record or sponsor and then only as regards disbursement of funds to, or for and on behalf of, the direct customer.

Mitigating measures: Where governments, international organisations or multilateral lending organisations are involved in loans, donations or other arrangements or in facilitating trade through export credits, financial institutions may have an involvement in these arrangements. In these circumstances, financial institutions can reasonably expect such governments or organisations to conduct appropriate assessments (diligence) on the parties involved and to take other appropriate measures to ensure that funds are not siphoned off to pay bribes. Financial institutions will, however, need to complete their own due diligence as appropriate to their customers.

Red flags:

(a) Projects located in countries where corruption risks are regarded as being high;

(b) A project structure involving legal entities in offshore jurisdictions where the ownership and role of the entity is not clear and purpose of the payment is not transparent;

(c) A project involving the use of intermediaries;

(d) Project payments to third parties, whose role in the transaction is unclear or who request unusually opaque methods of payment.

Factors that could be considered by a financial institution whose customers are directly involved in project finance or related activities might include country, industry and political risk (see the sections on Country risk and Customer risk below) as well as due diligence or enhanced due diligence on the customer. For example, it might be appropriate to consider a customer's record in relation to convictions or other sanctions for corruption, if known. It would not be reasonable to extend due diligence beyond the direct customer to sub-contractors, suppliers, agents, consultants or other intermediaries. However, if the financial institution discerns something sufficiently unusual about the transaction, it should seek clarification about the matter, so as to dispel concerns it may have with regard to the transaction.

Retail banking

Risks: The diversity of products and services offered through a retail banking operation results in a huge variety of customers. This factor, together with the nature and scale of transactions executed through retail banks, means that it is virtually impossible to identify specific transactions that may be linked to corrupt activities, particularly petty corruption, unless such transactions are sufficiently unusual and are identified in the course of monitoring designed to detect money laundering.

Mitigating measures: In general, a retail bank's AML policies and procedures should be applied, adopting a risk-based approach.

Country risk

Countries having been identified by credible sources as having significant levels of corruption; for further information see the *Wolfsberg Guidance on a Risk Based Approach*.

Customer risk

Certain customers identified during due diligence or enhanced due diligence (initial and ongoing) may potentially represent a greater degree of risk. Such due diligence or enhanced due diligence may include identification of negative publicly available information from credible sources that calls into question a customer's activities regarding corruption, or, indeed, that indicates that prosecutions or actions have been taken by governmental authorities and/or law enforcement. The risks and possible mitigating measures are highlighted below, together with any particularly relevant red flags.

Politically exposed persons

PEPs potentially represent higher risk either because they are in a position to exert undue influence on decisions regarding the conduct of business by private sector parties, or they have access to state accounts and funds.

Red flags: Substantial cash or wire transfers into, or from, an account of a customer identified as a PEP, where such activity is not consistent with legitimate or expected activity. In particular, substantial activity over a relatively short time period and/or the improper use of corporate or other vehicles to obscure ownership may also raise suspicions.

Intermediaries/agents

In certain industries, the services of intermediaries or agents are used by companies to help secure or retain business abroad. Commissions paid to agents have sometimes been used to pay bribes to government officials on behalf of a company. Intermediaries and/or agents are often difficult to identify.

Mitigating measures: If a financial institution is able to identify a private banking prospect or client as an intermediary and/or agent, particularly in industries and/or sectors identified as posing increased corruption risk, it may determine that enhanced due diligence would be appropriate because, for example, the services (private banking), industry, country and/or transactional risk indicators are present which could increase the risks posed for the financial institution in dealing with the customer. Under these circumstances, the financial institution might consider one or more of the following as part of that enhanced due diligence exercise, for example whether the customer:

(a) Has a family member in a government position, especially if the family member works in a procurement or decision-making position or is a high-ranking official in the department with which the intermediary is known to have dealings and that is the target of the intermediary's efforts.

(b) Has failed upon request (or has been suspiciously reluctant) to disclose owners, partners or principals; uses shell or holding companies or equivalent structures that obscure ownership without credible explanation.

(c) Has little or no expertise in the industry or the country in connection with which he acts as an intermediary.

(d) Anticipates substantial commission payments as an intermediary, either in absolute terms or as a percentage of the main contract sum, which cannot plausibly be verified vis-à-vis the role undertaken.

(e) Is retained by a company whose reputation in relation to the payments of such commissions is questionable by reference to prior convictions or governmental actions, or that is reputed otherwise to engage in improper payments to governmental organisations.

Red flags: Substantial cash or wire transfers into or from an account of a customer identified as an agent or intermediary where such activity is not consistent with legitimate or expected activity. In particular, substantial activity over a relatively short time period and/or the improper use of corporate vehicles to obscure ownership and/or the involvement of industries and/or countries posing increased corruption risk may also raise suspicions.

Correspondents

Correspondent customers potentially represent higher risks because the bank typically has no direct relationship with the customers of the correspondent bank. The bank is, therefore, unable as a matter of course to verify the identity of these underlying customers or understand the nature of the business and transactions (e.g. wire transfers, clearing cheques) it processes on their behalf.

Industry risk

Certain business sectors and industries have historically been identified with high perceived levels of corruption. Financial institutions therefore need to assess, based on their own criteria, whether the activity of a customer in a particular industry poses a higher risk of corruption.

Where risk factors are identified, an assessment should be made as to whether the customer should be the subject of enhanced due diligence, transaction monitoring, senior management approval and/or other measures, including review and oversight of their financial operations, as may be appropriate. In some circumstances, the filing of a suspicious activity report (SAR) or other notification to the authorities may be required by local law or regulations.

A Multi-stakeholder Approach

The international community recognises the need for States to cooperate with one another in order to prevent and eradicate corruption. Organisations like the OECD and the UN also recognise that if efforts are to be effective, the involvement and support of individuals and groups outside the public sector are required, including civil society, non-governmental organisations and community-based organisations. Private sector companies and their related industry organisations, Chambers of Commerce and other industry organisations also have an important role to play in this regard in apprising financial institutions of developments to prevent corruption by industrial sectors or individual firms.

The Wolfsberg Group supports the publicly led multi-stakeholder approach to addressing the following important areas where further dialogue and cooperation may lead to improvements in preventing and deterring bribery and other corrupt activity as it affects the financial sector:

Governments and international institutions (IMP, World Bank): Where governments, through their diplomatic services or political analysts, have evidence of corruption in foreign countries or have evidence that foreign officials and their families have acquired assets through corruption, they should take appropriate action such as sharing this assessment with civil society and the private sector in an appropriate manner.

Governments and their agencies: Export credit agencies, development aid, lending and trade departments should carry out coordinated due diligence and monitoring so that an appropriate audit trail in respect of money transfers and credits may be established by them.

Governments and international bodies: A more coordinated and harmonised approach should be developed between governments as to the recovery and repatriation of assets held by financial institutions and identified as connected to corruption.

Law enforcement and financial intelligence units: Should identify new techniques used by money launderers in relation to bribery and other corrupt activity, communicate typologies to the financial community and develop appropriate countermeasures.

Regulators and supervisors: In relation to the development of policies and procedures that are consistent with regard to the definition and identification of politically exposed persons as well as the initial and ongoing management of relationships with customers who fall into this category.

Civil society and non-governmental organisations: Should identify trends, patterns and mechanisms used by bribe payers and recipients, thereby gaining a better understanding of the causes and effects of bribery and other corrupt activity, in order to prevent the misuse of financial institutions and support the development of appropriate standards and controls.

The Wolfsberg Group believes that constructive dialogue in this area will help to increase the knowledge and ability of such agencies and institutions to identify trends, patterns, money-laundering techniques and mechanisms used in the furtherance of acts of bribery and corruption and, with an effective public/private partnership, financial institutions will be better placed to assist in the fight to prevent and/or detect and disclose incidents of corruption.

8.1.4 Wolfsberg Guidance on Mobile and Internet Payment Services (MIPS)

This guidance supplements the guidance issued on credit/charge card issuing and merchant acquiring activities and on prepaid and stored value cards. It discusses the roles and operations of MIPS and also discusses Non-Bank Service Providers (NBSPs).

MIPS Risk Factors

The concerns over MIPS are where the following services are included within their product offering:

- Ability to transfer funds (domestically and/or internationally)
- Speed of transfer of funds
- Lack of, or difficulty in providing, an audit trail
- Lack of, or difficulty in compiling, an aggregate view of multiple transactions
- Lack of face to face contact
- Identification means either not taken, or taken and not verified
- The ability to reload
- The ability to load/reload with cash
- The ability to withdraw cash
- The ability to load/transfer from alternative funding sources.

The analysis of these features will enable a firm to assess the money laundering risks posed and the controls that can be applied to mitigate these risks.

The following factors should be considered when assessing the risk:

- Intended geographical scope of the MIPS
- Intended usages of the MIPS
- Knowledge about MIPS users
- Intended scope of MIPS (open/closed loop)
- Source of funding
- Value limits
- Cash withdrawal via automated teller machines (ATM)/cash redemption of monetary value
- Value term limit
- MIPS KYC/CDD requirements for service activation.

AML Framework

Again a risk based approach is adopted. For low risk propositions no identification and verification is required so long as patterns do not change over time. For higher risk propositions the identification of the MIPS user is required as well as verification of name and address.

In terms of screening for low risk propositions no sanctions screening is required, whereas for higher risk propositions it is required before the account or service is opened and during the lifetime of the relationship.

All partners in the service should be subject to appropriate risk based due diligence.

In terms of transaction monitoring the following are identified as being worthy of note:

- Unusual level and frequency of ATM usage
- Unusually high value/volume payment service activity
- Unusually high velocity payment service activity
- Identifying patterns of high cash activity
- MIPS usage in unexpected or high risk countries
- Identifying patterns related to typologies.

Conclusion

In conclusion the Wolfsburg Group believes that:

- NBSPs involved in money transmission should be subject to AML regulation/oversight
- Unregulated NBSPs should be considered as high risk
- Financial institutions need to consider their regulatory/reputational position when dealing with unregulated NBSPs if money transmission is involved
- Increased harmonisation of mobile, internet and prepaid-related terminology is desirable to aid discussion and guidelines.

9 THE US REGULATORY FRAMEWORK

This chapter provides an overview of the USA regulatory framework. Additional information on the specific rules applied in the USA is included in the USA country profile in Chapter 27 of this book (Section 27.36). This chapter provides more detailed information about the current American AML regulations.

9.1 THE US PATRIOT ACT

The 342-page US Patriot Act forms the current cornerstone of US anti-money-laundering legislation. Passed in 2001, the actual title of the legislation is:

> *"Uniting and Strengthening America by Providing Appropriate Tools Required to Intercept and Obstruct Terrorism (USA PATRIOT ACT) Act of 2001."*

As you will notice from the title, the Patriot Act is not actually an "all crimes" piece of legislation and restricts itself to detecting and preventing terrorist financing only. Perhaps, given the date that this legislation was passed by the House of Representatives (24th October, 2001) and signed by the then President George W. Bush (26th October, 2001), this is not surprising.

This Act adds to the existing US legislation on anti-money-laundering by extending the Bank Secrecy Act across the entire financial services industry. However, different institutions will find that the Act impacts them in different ways, since there are additional criteria that relate to the size and complexity of an institution and the nature of their operations.

9.2 THE OTHER KEY US REGULATIONS

US banks were already subject to money-laundering regulations prior to the enactment of the Patriot Act, as shown in Table 9.1.

Table 9.1 Key US regulations relating to money laundering prior to the Patriot Act

Act	*Year*
Bank Secrecy Act	1970
Money Laundering Control Act	1986
Annunzio Wiley	1992
Money Laundering Suppression Act	1994
Funds Transfer Rules	1996

It is from the 1970 Bank Secrecy Act that the rules related to record retention and the requirement to report transactions of $10,000+ emanate, and these rules continue to apply. The 1986 Act introduced the key offences resulting from money laundering.

Suspicious transaction reporting emanates from Annunzio Wiley, whereas suspicious activity reporting comes from the 1994 Money Laundering Suppression Act. While you might hope that all of this regulation might be consolidated into a single Act, there is no suggestion that such consolidation is likely in the near future.

The US is the only country we have identified which appears to have adopted such a piecemeal approach to money-laundering deterrence and terrorist financing.

9.3 KEY ISSUES IN THE US PATRIOT ACT

As we have noted, the US Patriot Act is lengthy, perhaps too lengthy, and, as discussed above, it is predicated on the existing legislation. Its focus is on the requirements with respect to terrorist financing and therefore the obligations of the Patriot Act do not apply in respect of other offences.

This is, to an extent, a complication for the Money Laundering Reporting Officer (MLRO) operating in the US, since the rules relating to general money laundering and those applying to terrorist financing will essentially be different. There are a lot of clauses which relate to the role and authority of relevant agencies and courts to authorise or undertake surveillance or prosecution. These are not discussed here. However, other clauses are of interest to financial institutions and are worthy of review.

9.3.1 Civil Rights and Safety

By making safety a paramount consideration, the general stance of the Act is set within certain bounds which do differ from legislation enacted in other countries. Remember that reference will still need to be made to the Bank Secrecy Act in respect of other issues.

9.3.2 Asset Seizure

Section 106 of the Patriot Act modifies provisions relating to presidential authority under the International Emergency Powers Act to authorise the President, when the United States is engaged in armed hostilities or has been attacked by a foreign country or foreign nationals, to confiscate any property subject to US jurisdiction of a foreign person, organisation or country that he determines has planned, authorised, aided or engaged in such hostilities or attacks.

This actually provides an interesting challenge for a firm. It will clearly need to undertake enhanced due diligence in such cases and to provide data to agencies as required. The key question is whether such jurisdictions and nationals can be identified prior to their appearing on such a list to enable enhanced due diligence to take place. To some extent you would expect US banks to identify jurisdictions that the US might become engaged in hostilities with in advance, undertaking enhanced due diligence in all such cases.

Clearly, what is required is to know the jurisdiction of all customers, and this, of course, is required by general due diligence requirements. We would expect any US bank to maintain clear records in this regard.

9.3.3 Enhanced Surveillance Procedures

The clauses here amend the Federal criminal code to authorise the interception of wire, oral and electronic communications for the production of evidence of:

1. Specified chemical weapons or terrorism offences.
2. Computer fraud and abuse.

Why are chemical weapons specifically referred to and not, for example, nuclear weapons? Again, this really relates to the way in which the legislation was enacted. The rules set out the way that the authorities can legally undertake investigation procedures and also set out the various extraterritorial implications. Interestingly, the legislation permits the seizure of voice-mail messages under a warrant.

It also expands the scope of subpoenas for records of electronic communications to include the length and types of service utilised, temporarily assigned network addresses and the means and source of payment (including any credit card or bank account number).

In terms of the logistical issues, there is a statement that nothing in the Act shall impose any additional technical obligation or requirement on a provider of a wire or electronic communication service or other person to furnish facilities or technical assistance. Furthermore, a provider of this type of service, and a landlord, custodian or other person who furnishes these facilities or technical assistance, shall be reasonably compensated for such reasonable expenditures incurred in providing such facilities or assistance.

This means that there is nothing additional that such firms are required to do; but if they are required to do anything then they will, in principle, be adequately compensated. In this, the regulations do not actually go as far as the regulations implemented in other countries where they are requiring electronic communication service providers to maintain records for a specified time period to facilitate investigations that might be required. Of course, whether there is any real compensation is another matter.

9.3.4 International Counter Money Laundering and Related Measures

This part of the Patriot Act amends Federal law governing monetary transactions to prescribe procedural guidelines under which the Secretary of the Treasury (the Secretary) may require domestic financial institutions and agencies to take specified measures if the Secretary finds that reasonable grounds exist for concluding that jurisdictions, financial institutions, types of accounts or transactions operating outside or within the United States are of primary money-laundering concern. The requirements include mandatory disclosure of specified information relating to certain correspondent accounts. It is these sections which actually impose the greatest burden on a financial institution.

The Act mandates the establishment of due diligence mechanisms to detect and report money-laundering transactions through private banking accounts and correspondent accounts, issues already dealt with by the Wolfsberg Principles (Chapter 8). The Act essentially makes these principles mandatory, with the obligation on detection and subsequent reporting, although this is only in relation to terrorist financing.

The systems that will be implemented in practice clearly fall into two categories – systems that look for specific attributes (or scenarios) and those that look for unusual transactions (based on some system-defined inference process). Given the level of data that is maintained by a financial institution, most financial institutions will implement software to assist such suspicion recognition. This is further considered in Chapter 26. In the absence of such software, the responsibility will be on the financial institution to justify to its regulators that it is undertaking sufficient due diligence in this respect. This will require both significant Know Your Customer-style documentation and an audit trail which addresses cases that have been identified as a result of the investigative work conducted.

The Act prohibits US banks from maintaining correspondent accounts with foreign shell banks, one of the Financial Action Task Force (FATF) requirements which also appears within the Wolfsberg Principles.

Any bank needs to recognise that the extraterritorial arrangements can become a problem, since the Act establishes Federal jurisdiction over:

1. Foreign money launderers (including their assets held in the United States); and
2. Money that is laundered through a foreign bank.

In cases involving a US bank subsidiary, or a foreign bank with a branch in the US, the MLRO will need to be aware of these extraterritorial provisions and take such actions as are necessary to meet these requirements.

9.3.5 Forfeiture Rules

Section 319 of the Patriot Act authorises the forfeiture of money-laundering funds from interbank accounts. It also requires a financial institution, upon request of the appropriate Federal banking agency, to make available within 120 hours all pertinent information related to anti-money-laundering compliance by the institution or its customer.

Firms need to have regard to this 120-hour rule and ensure that their systems have the capability to provide information in the form required on a timely basis. In practice, this means having the major documents available that would need to be supplemented by the relevant information concerning a particular transaction or relationship. Information regarding the structure of reporting, approval procedures, the role of the MLRO, reporting procedures and other policies and procedures can easily be available at any time, so it is only information concerning a specific investigation which should cause any problem with the 120-hour limit.

Section 319 further grants the Secretary summons and subpoena powers over foreign banks that maintain a correspondent bank in the United States. This type of regulation will cause banks to consider what activities they carry out in the USA and why, perhaps resulting in less business being conducted within that jurisdiction.

Finally, there is also a requirement that a financial institution that is subject to these rules must terminate within ten business days any correspondent relationship with a foreign bank after receipt of written notice that the foreign bank has failed to comply with certain judicial proceedings. The civil penalties for failure to terminate such a relationship are also set out.

Clearly, correspondent banking relationships should be under regular review such that the firm can satisfy itself that it is being operated in accordance with international best practice and local jurisdictional regulation. We would direct you to the guidance from the FATF (Chapter 3) and also the JMLSG (Chapter 7) in this regard.

9.3.6 Identification, Record and Reporting Requirements

The record and reporting requirements appear within Section 321 of the Patriot Act. It subjects to recording and reporting requirements monetary instrument transactions conducted by:

1. Any credit union; and
2. Any futures commission merchant, commodity trading advisor or commodity pool operator registered, or required to register, under the Commodity Exchange Act.

Section 325 then authorises the Secretary to issue regulations to ensure that concentration accounts of financial institutions are not used to prevent association of the identity of an individual customer with the movement of funds of which the customer is the direct or beneficial owner.

In addition, Section 326 directs the Secretary to issue regulations prescribing minimum standards for financial institutions regarding customer identity in connection with the opening of accounts.

9.3.7 Bank Holding Company Act

Section 327 of the Patriot Act amends the Bank Holding Company Act of 1956 and the Federal Deposit Insurance Act to require consideration of the effectiveness of a company or companies in combating money laundering during reviews of proposed bank shares, acquisitions or mergers.

Section 328 then implements another of the FATF special recommendations by directing the Secretary to take reasonable steps to encourage foreign governments to require the inclusion of the name of the originator in wire transfer instructions sent to the United States and other countries, with the information to remain with the transfer from its origination until the point of disbursement.

9.3.8 Bank Secrecy Act Amendments and Related Improvements

Among the various Acts that the Patriot Act amended, one was the Bank Secrecy Act, which was amended to revise requirements for civil liability immunity for voluntary financial institution disclosure of suspicious activities. For example, it authorises the inclusion of suspicions of illegal activity in written employment references. Of course, were there to be such a suspicion then a formal report would have been made by the firm, which would normally require total secrecy. Whether anyone has actually included any such information in a reference we somewhat doubt, and suggest that the firm would instead choose to make a report to the relevant agency.

Section 356 of the Patriot Act instructs the Secretary to:

1. Promulgate regulations requiring registered securities brokers and dealers, futures commission merchants, commodity trading advisors and commodity pool operators to file reports of suspicious financial transactions.
2. Report to Congress on the role of the Internal Revenue Service in the administration of the Bank Secrecy Act.
3. Share monetary instrument transaction records upon a request from a US intelligence agency for use in the conduct of intelligence or counterintelligence activities, including analysis, to protect against international terrorism.

Section 359 then further extends these requirements to cover any licensed sender of money or any other person who engages as a business in the transmission of funds, including through an informal value transfer banking system or network (e.g. hawala).

9.3.9 Penalties

The Patriot Act also increases the penalties that may be levied in respect of terrorist financing. Section 363 increases to $1 million the maximum civil penalties (from the rather dated $10,000) and criminal fines (currently $250,000) for money laundering. It also sets a minimum civil penalty and criminal fine of double the amount of the illegal transaction. Section 365 amends Federal law to require reports relating to coins and currency of more than $10,000 received in a non-financial trade or business.

You might well consider that the new penalty is still rather low given the seriousness of the potential issue.

9.3.10 Currency Crimes

The Patriot Act also establishes a bulk cash smuggling felony of the knowing concealment and attempted transport (or transfer) across US borders of currency and monetary instruments in excess of $10,000, with intent to evade specified currency-reporting requirements.

Further extraterritorial requirements sit in Section 377. This section grants the United States extraterritorial jurisdiction where:

1. An offence committed outside the United States involves an access device issued, owned, managed or controlled by a financial institution, account issuer, credit card system member or other entity within US jurisdiction; and
2. The person committing the offence transports, delivers, conveys, transfers to or through or otherwise stores, secretes or holds within US jurisdiction any article used to assist in the commission of the offence or the proceeds of such offence or property derived from it.

This is quite a broad requirement, but do notice the use of the word "and". If the article was not held within the USA, then this rule would not apply.

9.3.11 *Strengthening the Criminal Laws against Terrorism*

The Patriot Act also amends the Federal criminal code to prohibit specific terrorist acts or otherwise destructive, disruptive or violent acts against mass-transportation vehicles, ferries, providers, employees, passengers or operating systems. Section 803 prohibits harbouring any person knowing, or having reasonable grounds to believe, that such person has committed, or is about to commit, a terrorism offence, while Section 804 establishes Federal jurisdiction over crimes committed at US facilities abroad.

Much of this, in effect, duplicates existing regulation.

9.4 THE BANK SECRECY ACT 1970

Remember that the Patriot Act is purely focussed on terrorist financing. It is the Bank Secrecy Act that addresses the main money-laundering deterrence regulation in the USA.

The Currency and Foreign Transactions Reporting Act, also known as the Bank Secrecy Act (BSA), and its implementing regulation, 31 CFR 103, is a tool the US government uses to fight drug trafficking, money laundering and other crimes. Congress enacted the BSA to prevent banks and other financial service providers from being used as intermediaries for, or to hide the transfer or deposit of money derived from, criminal activity. The Office of the Comptroller of the Currency (OCC) monitors national bank compliance with the BSA and 31 CFR 103.

More than 170 crimes are listed in the Federal money-laundering statutes. They include drug trafficking, gunrunning, murder for hire, fraud, acts of terrorism and the illegal use of wetlands. The list also includes certain foreign crimes. Therefore, a financial institution must educate its employees, understand its customers and their businesses and have systems and procedures in place to distinguish routine transactions from ones that potentially give rise to a level of suspicious activity.

US penalties for money laundering can be severe. Individuals, including bank employees, convicted of money laundering face up to 20 years in prison for each money-laundering transaction conducted. Businesses, including banks and individuals, face fines up to the greater of $500,000 or twice the value of the transaction. Any property involved in the transaction or traceable to the proceeds of the criminal activity, including loan collateral, personal property and, under certain conditions, entire bank accounts (even if some of the money in the account is legitimate) may be subject to forfeiture. In addition, banks risk losing their charter, and bank employees risk being removed and barred from the industry.

Under the provisions of the Controlled Substances Act of 1978, the Money Laundering Control Act of 1986 and the Anti-Drug Abuse Act of 1988, real or personal property traceable to illegal drug sales or purchased with laundered money is subject to government seizure and forfeiture. Occasionally, seized property is collateral for bank loans.

Therefore, a bank must obtain and confirm enough information about its customers to protect its loan collateral from loss due to government forfeiture.

9.4.1 Independent Testing of Compliance

The bank's internal or external auditors should be able to:

- Attest to the overall integrity and effectiveness of management systems and controls, and BSA technical compliance.
- Test transactions in all areas of the bank, with emphasis on high-risk areas, products and services to ensure the bank is following prescribed regulations.
- Assess employees' knowledge of regulations and procedures.
- Assess adequacy, accuracy and completeness of training programmes.
- Assess adequacy of the bank's process for identifying suspicious activity.

Internal review or audit findings should be incorporated into a board and senior management report and reviewed promptly. There then needs to be appropriate follow-up. Of course, the guidance on internal audit is best found in the Bank for International Settlements paper *The Internal Audit Function in Banks* published in June 2012 and available at: http://www.bis.org/publ/bcbs223.pdf.

Of course, the Bank for International Settlements, just like the Financial Action Task Force and the Wolfsberg Group, does not have any direct legal status, meaning that its requirements do not need to be implemented into local law or regulation. It does, however, represent international best practice in this area and is a useful form of reference.

9.4.2 Compliance Officer

Under the BSA, a US national bank must designate a qualified bank employee as its BSA Compliance Officer, to have day-to-day responsibility for managing all aspects of the BSA compliance programme and compliance with all BSA regulations. The BSA Compliance Officer may delegate certain BSA compliance duties to other employees, but they must not delegate compliance responsibility.

The bank's board of directors and senior management must ensure that the BSA Compliance Officer has sufficient authority and resources to administer effectively a comprehensive BSA compliance programme.

Notice that the term used is Compliance Officer, not the more internationally recognised term Money Laundering Reporting Officer (or MLRO).

9.4.3 Training

The BSA requirement in this regard is that banks must ensure that appropriate bank personnel are trained in all aspects of the regulatory requirements of the BSA and the bank's internal BSA compliance and anti-money-laundering policies and procedures.

An effective training programme includes provisions to ensure that all bank personnel, including senior management, who have contact with customers (whether in person or by phone), who see customer transaction activity or who handle cash in any way, receive appropriate training.

Those employees include persons involved with:

- Branch administration
- Customer service
- Lending, private or personal banking
- Correspondent banking (international and domestic)
- Trusts
- Discount brokerage
- Funds transfer
- Safe deposit/custody
- Vault activities.

Training is required to be ongoing and must incorporate current developments and changes to relevant regulations. New and different types of money-laundering schemes that have evolved in the market and might involve customers and financial institutions should also be addressed in this training. It also should include examples of money-laundering schemes and cases, tailored to the audience, and the ways in which such activities can be detected or resolved.

Training should focus on the consequences of an employee's failure to comply with established policy and procedures (e.g. fines or termination). Programmes should provide personnel with guidance and direction in terms of bank policies and available resources.

There are, of course, online products available, but in our opinion they would need to be supported by documented examinations (perhaps also online) to formally document that the knowledge gained from the online training had been assimilated properly.

9.4.4 Reporting Requirements

The BSA regulations require all financial institutions to submit five types of report to the government:

1. **IRS Form 4789 Currency Transaction Report (CTR):** A CTR must be filed for each deposit, withdrawal, exchange of currency or other payment or transfer, by, through or to a financial institution, which involves a transaction in currency of more than \$10,000.

   Multiple currency transactions must be treated as a single transaction if the financial institution has knowledge that: (a) they are conducted by, or on behalf of, the same person; and, (b) they result in cash received or disbursed by the financial institution of more than $10,000 (31 CFR 1010.100(t), formerly 31 CFR 103.11(n)) (31 CFR 1010.311, formerly 31 CFR 103.22(b)(1)).

2. **US Customs Form 4790 Report of International Transportation of Currency or Monetary Instruments (CMIR):** Each person (including a bank) who physically transports, mails or ships, or causes to be physically transported, mailed, shipped or received, currency, traveller's cheques and certain other monetary instruments in an aggregate amount exceeding $10,000 into or out of the United States must file a CMIR (31 CFR 1010.340, formerly 31 CFR 103.23).
3. **Department of the Treasury Form 90-22.1 Report of Foreign Bank and Financial Accounts (FBAR):** Each person (including a bank) subject to the jurisdiction of the United States having an interest in, signature or other authority over, one or more bank, securities or other financial accounts in a foreign country must file an FBAR if the aggregate value of such accounts at any point in a calendar year exceeds $10,000 (31 CFR 1010.350, formerly 31 CFR 103.24).
4. **Treasury Department Form 90-22.47 and OCC Form 8010-9, 8010-1 Suspicious Activity Report (SAR):** Banks must file a SAR for any suspicious transaction relevant to a possible violation of law or regulation (31 CFR 1020, formerly 31 CFR 103.18) (12 CFR 12.11).
5. **Designation of Exempt Person Form TDF 90-22.53:** Banks must file this form to designate an exempt customer for the purpose of CTR reporting under the BSA (31 CFR 1020.315, formerly 31 CFR 103.22(d)). In addition, banks use this form annually to renew exemptions for eligible non-listed business and payroll customers (31 CFR 1020.315).

9.4.5 Record-keeping Requirements

The BSA regulations require banks to maintain a variety of records to ensure, among other things, that transactions can be reconstructed. Two of these record-keeping requirements are discussed below. Detailed descriptions of these and other record-keeping requirements for banks can be found in 31 CFR 103. The retention period for all records required to be kept under the BSA regulations is five years.

Monetary Instrument Sales Records

A bank must retain a record of each *cash* sale of bank cheques, drafts, cashier's cheques, money orders and traveller's cheques between $3,000 and $10,000 inclusive. These records must include evidence of verification of the identity of the purchaser and other information (§ 1010.415, formerly 31 CFR 103.29).

Funds Transfer Record-keeping and Travel Rule Requirements

A bank must maintain a record of each funds transfer of $10,000 or more which it originates, acts as an intermediary for or receives. The amount and type of information a bank must record and keep depends upon its role in the funds transfer process. Also, a bank that acts as an originator or intermediary for a funds transfer must pass certain information along to the next bank in the funds transfer chain (§ 1010.311, formerly 31 CFR 103.33 (e) and (g)).

Under the phase II rule, twelve months of account history must exist before the customer can be exempted. The months do not have to be consecutive, but should be recent.

- The customer must engage frequently in large currency transactions (eight or more a year).
- The customer must be incorporated or organised under the laws of the United States or a state, or registered or eligible to do business in the United States.
- Annually, banks must verify whether each exemption continues to meet the exemption eligibility requirements. Banks may develop their own methods and procedures for this annual review.
- Biennially, banks must file the "Designation of Exempt Person" form for each non-listed business and payroll customer.
- As part of the biennial filing of the "Designation of Exempt Person" form, the bank must certify that, as part of its BSA compliance programme, it has policies and procedures in place for identifying, reviewing and reporting suspicious activity in accordance with the SAR filing requirements (31 CFR 1020, formerly 31 CFR 103.18).

9.4.6 *Suspicious Activity Reporting Requirements*

An effective BSA compliance programme must also include controls and measures designed to identify and report suspicious transactions in a timely manner. A financial institution must apply due diligence to be able to make an informed decision about the suspicious nature of a particular transaction and whether to file a suspicious activity report (SAR).

SARs must be filed with the appropriate authority within prescribed time frames following the discovery of:

- Insider abuse involving any amount.
- Violations of Federal law aggregating $5,000 or more when a suspect can be identified.
- Violations of Federal law aggregating $25,000 or more regardless of a potential suspect.
- Transactions aggregating $5,000 or more that involve potential money laundering or violations of the BSA if the bank knows, suspects or has reason to suspect that the transaction:
  - involves funds from illegal activities or is intended or conducted to hide or disguise illicit funds or assets as part of a plan to violate or evade any law or regulation or to avoid any transaction reporting requirement under Federal law;
  - is designed to evade any of the BSA regulations; or
  - has no business or apparent lawful purpose or is not the sort in which the particular customer would normally be expected to engage, and the bank knows of no reasonable explanation for the transaction after examining the available facts, including the background and possible purpose of the transaction.

The rules continue to provide additional guidance regarding the identification of potential money laundering, repeating much of the material already included within this handbook.

Clearly, the policies and procedures implemented within a US bank need to comply with all of these rules and regulations. The complexity of the changing regulatory structures in the US and the lack of consolidated legislation does provide a higher level of complexity than occurs in other markets. A consequence of this is that it is more likely that a US bank will employ specialist legal resources in this arena than would be the case in other countries.

It is, of course, the board that remains responsible for the operation of the bank, regardless of the business area that it is involved with. Accordingly, the board should be trained with regard to these requirements, actively involved with the programme and, in particular, should approve the policies and procedures adopted.

At the time of writing there is discussion of new regulations being implemented in the UK to ensure that the FATF Recommendations are clearly and fully implemented into US legislation, but at present the legislative changes have not been drafted.

10 FINANCIAL SANCTIONS

10.1 WHAT ARE FINANCIAL SANCTIONS?

Financial sanctions are orders which prevent firms from dealing with individuals or organisations who can be linked to the financing of terrorism. They are issued by international bodies such as the United Nations and the European Union as well as by individual jurisdictions. This is not an area where risk-based regulation applies. The goals of the rules are clear – these are people and organisations that a firm should not deal with.

Individuals or organisations linked with the financing of terrorism or nuclear proliferation are known as "targets" and will be specifically referred to. This is an approach which operates within the international community through the provision of lists, as well as through individual governments acting unilaterally. For example, it is an offence under UK law to provide funds to those on the international list unless, in the case of financial institutions, a licence is obtained from Her Majesty's Treasury. Financial sanctions are mostly focused on international targets, and currently there are around 50 UK individuals and entities on the HM Treasury sanctions lists.

10.2 FAILING TO COMPLY

Firms which allow individuals connected with financing terrorism to maintain accounts or undertake transactions with them risk criminal penalties. In this case, the penalties would be enforced by the jurisdictional legal services against the firm, and in some cases also against the management directly. The legal consequences of failing to comply with the orders can be substantial.

In the US, the US Department of Justice levied fines on Lloyds of $350 million for breaches of US sanctions against Iran and Sudan on 9th January, 2009. In this case, more than $350 million moved from places such as Iran through locations around the world because Lloyds removed relevant stripped identifying information from international wire transfers that would have raised a red flag at US financial institutions and caused such payments to be scrutinised, according to the Department of Justice. This was, at that time, the largest ever penalty under US sanctions legislation.

The Department of Justice press release stated:

> *"Under the IEEPA, it is a crime to wilfully violate, or attempt to violate, any regulation issued under the Act, including the Iranian Transactions Regulations, which prohibit exportation of services*

> *from the United States to Iran, and the Sudanese Sanctions Regulations, which prohibit exportation of services from the United States to Sudan."*

Clearly, in this case there was the allegation that the firm was deliberately seeking to take action to enable inappropriate persons or firms to be assisted with their illegal activity. However, generally there are problems that need to be addressed. Of course, the costs to the firm greatly exceed the size of the penalty. In this case they would also include improving training, investigating thousands of transactions and changing systems and controls to meet regulatory expectations.

Aside from the financial penalties for firms, the reputational risk that a firm will suffer from being associated with the funding of terrorism will potentially be immense. Clearly, therefore, any firm needs to implement full and complete policies, processes, procedures and training to alert staff to these issues and minimise the risks as far as is possible.

10.3 SANCTIONS LISTS

Lists of targets with which firms must avoid dealings are generally published within individual jurisdictions, and in the UK can be found at HM Treasury's website at http://www.hm-treasury.gov.uk/d/sanctionsconlist.pdf

For each organisation listed, specific details of individuals associated with the organisation are set out in reasonable detail, the following being a historic example:

Name: BIN LADEN 1: USAMA 2: MUHAMMED 3: AWAD 4: n/a 5: n/a.

Title: Shaykh/Hajj

DOB: (1) 28/07/1957. (2) 30/07/1957. (3) 10/03/1957. (4) 01/01/1957. (5) --/--/1956. (6) --/--/1957.

POB: (1) – (2) Jeddah, (1) Yemen (2) Saudi Arabia

a.k.a: (1) ABD AL-HAKIM, Abu Abdallah (2) AWDH, Bin Laden, Osama, Mohamed (3) BIN LADEN, Usama (4) BIN LADIN, Osama (5) BIN LADIN, Osama, bin Muhammad, bin Awad (6) BIN LADIN, Shaykh, Usama (7) BIN LADIN, Usama (8) BIN LADIN, Usama, bin Muhammad, bin Awad (9) BIN LADIN, Usamah, Bin Muhammad (10) BIN MUHAMMAD, Bin Laden, Usamah (11) OSAMA, Ben Laden (12) OSSAMA, Ben Laden (13) USAMA, Ben Laden (14) USAMA BIN MUHAMMED BIN AWAD, Osama Bin Laden.

Other information: UN Ref QI.B.8.01. Saudi citizenship withdrawn. Afghan nationality given by the Taliban regime. Also referred to as Al Qaqa. Confirmed to have died in Pakistan in May 2011. Listed on: 23/02/2001. Last updated: 19/05/2011 Group ID: 6896.

The list literally goes from A to Z over 74 pages, or from Al-Qaida to:

Organisation name: ZIMBABWE MINING DEVELOPMENT CORPORATION

Address: 90 Mutare Road, PO Box 2628, Harare, Zimbabwe.

Other information: Associated with the ZANU-PF faction of Government. ZMDC falls under the responsibility of ZANU-PF Minister of Mines and Mining Development. Listed on: 27/01/2009. Last updated: 23/02/2012 Group ID: 10744.

A consolidated list of asset-freeze targets designated by the United Nations, European Union and United Kingdom under legislation relating to current financial sanctions regimes is available below. This list denotes the "regimes", which include organisations and jurisdictions. Each "regime" has associated individuals, in the same format as the Osama Bin Laden example above, which can be found on the website. The list of "regimes", as of July 2013, is as follows:

- Afghanistan
- Belarus
- Democratic Republic of the Congo
- Egypt
- Eritrea
- Federal Republic of Yugoslavia and Serbia
- Iran (Human Rights)
- Iran (Nuclear Proliferation)
- Iraq
- Ivory Coast
- Lebanon and Syria
- Liberia
- Libya
- North Korea (Democratic People's Republic of Korea)
- Republic of Guinea
- Republic of Guinea-Bissau
- Somalia
- Sudan
- Syria
- Tunisia
- Zimbabwe.

These rules do regularly change and firms move on and off the list. In the UK, for example, on 24th December, 2012, HM Treasury issued a financial sanctions notice on Iran regarding nuclear proliferation. The changes take the form of the addition of one individual and 18 entities to Annex IX to the 2012 Regulation, the removal of two entities from Annex IX and amendments to the identifying information of three existing entries in Annex IX.

The following were among those identified specifically in this notice (http://www.hm-treasury.gov.uk/d/fin_sanc_notice_iran_cir_241212.pdf).

10.3.1 *Individuals*

Name: ZANJANI, Babak

DOB: 12/03/1971

Other information: EU listing. Not UN. Key facilitator for Iranian oil deals and transferring oil-related money. Zanjani owns and operates the UAE-based Sorinet Group, and some of its companies are used by Zanjani to channel oil-related payments.

Group ID: 12824.

As you will note, many of the other bodies specifically identified in the notice are related to Mr Zanjani. On 23rd December, 2012 he issued a statement that denied any wrong-doing, saying his bank and other companies did not work for the Iranian government.

From the point of view of the firm, it must take note of the notice and not deal with the person. It is for the person to manage to get their name removed from the list, not for the firm to take a risk-based or value judgment. Whether the person is innocent or guilty is, with regret, of limited consequence to a firm. It is required to comply with the rules and that is the end of the matter. Consequently, firms need to have a system in place which allows them to update their records as the lists change to ensure that they are compliant.

10.3.2 *Entities*

Name: ALUMINAT

Address: (1) Parcham St, 13th Km of Qom Rd, 38135, Arak. (2) Unit 38, 5th Fl, Bldg No 60, Golfam St, Jordan, 19395-5716, Tehran, Iran.

Other information: EU listing. Not UN. Tel: 98 212049216/98 22049928/98 22045237. Fax: 98 21 22057127. Website: www.aluminat.com

Group ID: 12820.

This example highlights the care that needs to be taken. There is another firm named Nordisk Aluminat A/S, which is a legitimate Danish company established in 1981. It has a different website (www.aluminat.dk) and is not implicated in any way by this sanctions report. The financial institution needs to ensure that the sanctions are applied to precisely the right person in this regard and do not adversely affect a firm which has a similar name. No bank can assume that such firms are connected.

Name: CF SHARP AND COMPANY PRIVATE LIMITED

Other information: EU listing. Not UN.

Group ID: 12835.

In this case very little information is provided to assist the financial institution; we are not even provided with an address in Tehran. This is not to be mixed up with CF Sharp Group (www.cfsharp.com), which, again, is a legitimate business and a leader in the fields of crewing, travel, freight forwarding, brokerage, air cargo, airline GSA, land-based recruiting and training.

Name: FIRST ISLAMIC INVESTMENT BANK (FIIB)

Address: (1) 19A-31-3A, Level 31 Business Suite, Wisma UOA, Jalan Pinang 50450, Kuala Lumpur, Wilayah Persekutuan. (2) Investor Relations, Menara Prima 17th floor Jalan Lingkar, Mega Kuningan Blok 6.2, South Jakarta, Jakarta, Indonesia, 12950. (3) Unit 13 (C), Main Office Tower, Financial Park Labuan Complex, Jalan Merdeka, 87000 Federal Territory of Labuan, Labuan F.T; 87000, Malaysia.

Other information: EU listing. Not UN. Tel: 603 21620361/603 21620362/603 21620363/603 21620364/6087417049/6087417050/622157948110. FIIB is part of the Sorinet Group owned and operated by Babak Zanjani. It is being used to channel Iranian oil-related payments.

Group ID: 12825.

This case directly links to the individual identified in the first reference. Notice the bank operates in Malaysia and Indonesia and is on the list due to its ownership. This highlights the importance of following these rules rigorously. The Malaysian bank appears on a UK list because it is owned by a Group (Sorinet) which is owned and operated by a person on the list (Babak Zanjani).

Name: HONG KONG INTERTRADE COMPANY LTD (HKICO)

Address: Hong Kong

Other information: EU listing. Not UN. HKICO is a front company controlled by EU-designated National Iranian Oil Company (NIOC).

Group ID: 12822.

Name: MOALLEM INSURANCE COMPANY (MIC)

a.k.a: (1) Export and Investment Insurance Co. (2) Moallem Insurance (3) Moallem Insurance Co.

Address: (1) No. 56 Haghani Boulevard, Vanak Square, Tehran, 1517973511, Iran, PO Box 19395-6314. (2) 11/1 Sharif Ave, Vanaq Square, Tehran, 19699, Iran.

Other information: EU listing. Not UN. Tel: 98 21886776789/98 21887950512/98 21887791835. Fax: 98 2188771245. Website: www.mic-ir.com. Main insurer of IRISL.

Group ID: 12836.

Name: ORGANISATION OF DEFENSIVE INNOVATION AND RESEARCH (SPND)

Other information: EU listing. Not UN. Run by UN-designated Mohsen Fakhrizadeh and is part of the Ministry of Defence For Armed Forces Logistics (MODAFL). SPND's head of security is Davoud Babaei.

Group ID: 12821.

Name: PETRO SUISSE

Address: Avenue De la Tour-Halimand 6, 1009 Pully, Switzerland.

Other information: EU listing. Not UN. Assisting designated entities to violate the provisions of the EU Regulation on Iran.

Group ID: 12823.

Here you have a firm based in Switzerland directly implicated in sanctions violations.

Name: SHARIF UNIVERSITY OF TECHNOLOGY

Address: Azadi Ave, 11365-8639, Tehran, Iran.

Other information: EU listing. Not UN. Tel: 98 21 66022727. Fax: 98 2166036005. Website: www.sharif.ir. Assisting designated entities to violate the provisions of the EU Regulation on Iran.

Group ID: 12816.

You would generally not expect to see universities on such lists, so this example proves that any form of firm could be implicated and therefore included.

Name: SIMATEC DEVELOPMENT COMPANY

Other information: EU listing. Not UN. Assisting designated entities to violate the provisions of UN and EU sanctions on Iran. As of early 2010, Simatec was contracted by UN-designated Kalaye Electric Company (KEC) to procure Vacon inverters to power uranium enrichment centrifuges. As of mid-2012, Simatec was attempting to procure EU-controlled inverters.

Group ID: 12819.

In this example, the notice does provide a significant amount of additional information to explain, in some ways, why the firm appears on the list.

The issue for any bank is to ensure that it is receiving complete and accurate lists to apply in practice. If a money-laundering-deterrence solution is acquired by the firm, it will generally include such updating automatically. However, it is the bank that needs to ensure this.

10.4 ASSET FREEZING UNIT

Financial sanctions can be imposed by an independent body, or a subsidiary body of a larger financial government organisation. For example, as discussed in the UK, financial sanctions are actually imposed by the Treasury's Asset Freezing Unit (AFU). The AFU is responsible for the implementation and administration of domestic financial sanctions, for domestic designations under the Terrorist Asset-Freezing etc. Act 2010, for providing advice to Treasury Ministers on the basis of operational advice, on domestic designation decisions and for carrying out various other duties with regard to the implementation and administration of financial sanctions.

The AFU also issues notices and notifications advising of the introduction, amendment, suspension or lifting of financial sanctions regimes with a view to making bodies and individuals likely to be affected by financial sanctions aware of their obligations, and provides, on the financial sanctions home page of the Treasury website, a consolidated list of financial sanctions targets which consists of the names of individuals and entities that have been listed by the United Nations, European Union and/or the United Kingdom under legislation relating to a specific financial sanctions regime. Where there is a legal basis for an asset freeze in the UK, the name of the target will be included in the consolidated list.

In the event that a customer is found to be on a financial sanctions list, the obligation is on the firm to stop providing services or products to the target immediately and then to contact HM Treasury's Asset Freezing Unit.

These UK lists will potentially prove of assistance to any firms in designing procedures to identify what might be considered the highest risk customers. Of course, such firms, organisations and individuals regularly change their identities and so the historic nature of such information must always be a concern to a firm. However, any financial institution would be expected to have identified and acted upon what is, in effect, a public analysis of areas of concern. When this is combined with the information promulgated by Transparency International, it will prove to be of assistance if a firm is undertaking scenario modelling or is in the process of developing a risk-based approach.

10.5 COMPLIANCE WITH FINANCIAL SANCTIONS

Firms must ensure that they develop policies and procedures to ensure compliance with local financial sanctions legislation and guidance. In order to ensure compliance with financial sanctions regulations, the following actions are recommended:

- A firm should undertake and regularly review risk assessments, especially on clients involved in either the weapons or components industries, together with market counterparties from certain specified higher risk jurisdictions.
- A firm should also establish and regularly review a clear counter-terrorist-financing policy which has been tailored to its business profile.
- A firm should develop appropriate operating procedures which should be regularly reviewed and amended to ensure that they remain appropriate for the firm and are consistent with the policies and goals of the firm.
- Financial sanctions awareness and the importance of these rules should be included within training and awareness programmes for all staff to enable them to understand both their personal and their corporate obligations.
- Specific additional procedures should be implemented to address new and transferred clients or counterparties where these originate from high-risk countries.
- Generally, firms should evaluate the source and origin of funds, together with country risk leading to identification of high-priority relationships that should be subject to enhanced due diligence and monitoring as part of the implementation of the risk-based approach.

10.6 FINANCIAL SANCTIONS AS PART OF NORMAL MONEY-LAUNDERING-DETERRENCE PROCEDURES

In some firms, financial sanctions may not currently be checked as part of the existing anti-money-laundering procedures implemented as part of a general deterrence regime. Unlike the risk-based processes and procedures which are generally appropriate for money-laundering deterrence, the financial sanctions rules are different. In this case, the financial sanctions lists must be checked prior to carrying out any transaction and this is not dependent on the threshold amount of the transaction concerned. It is the nature of the transaction which breaches the rules, not its size.

Furthermore, while politically exposed persons form part of normal money-laundering-deterrence regulation, that monitoring should not be considered as being similar to monitoring for compliance with financial sanctions. The main difference here is that PEPs are classified as anyone who is, or is associated with, a high-profile political position, as discussed in Chapter 17. Being a PEP does not mean the person is guilty of money laundering or other illegal activity, rather it implies that enhanced due diligence should be conducted.

Financial sanctions are usually focused on targets known in the world of financial crime because of their illegal activities, which include the financing of terrorism and nuclear proliferation. As such, targets on these lists are aware that they are on a sanctions list, which is public. Since this is, therefore, public information, there can be no equivalent offence of "tipping off". The regulated firm needs to know whether it is dealing with such people and act accordingly – there is no choice in such cases.

10.7 DIFFICULTIES FACED BY FIRMS WHEN MONITORING FINANCIAL SANCTIONS

Firms which fail to have in place procedures, systems and controls to monitor financial sanctions can face heavy financial penalties as a result of either misconceptions or a general lack of understanding exhibited by their staff. It is vital for firms to remember that financial sanctions require additional attention, and are not monitored as part of general money-laundering-deterrence systems and controls. Some of the common misconceptions which firms have regarding financial sanctions are summarised below. Where a single jurisdiction is used, we have directly referred to the UK, whereas for international readers, you should have reference to the sanctions list promulgated locally by your relevant authority.

1. It is important to remember that financial sanctions apply to all firms, and not just banks or financial institutions.
2. Firms also have a common misconception that if they process only low-value transactions they are not subject to financial sanctions requirements. Remember that the targets on financial sanctions lists are on those lists irrespective of any financial limits.
3. There is a wide range of targets typically on such lists. In the UK, the list includes both UK-based targets and international targets. As demonstrated above, a UK firm, for example, cannot assume that all targets are only UK-based.
4. Financial sanctions regulations will apply to firms even if they do not hold client money.
5. The offence of "tipping off" is not an issue, since those on the sanctions list already know they are on the list, so at least that is one less thing to worry about.
6. Politically exposed persons (or PEPs) are not the same as sanctions targets, but some PEPs may also be on the sanctions list.
7. Financial sanctions regulations also apply to insurance companies.
8. Typical money-laundering-deterrence due diligence monitoring requirements are not the same as sanctions list screening, but they may be closely linked.
9. Sanctions compliance is a completely discrete legal regime and does not adopt a risk-based approach.

10. Sanctions checks carried out by third parties can only be relied on when the accepting firm has verified that the referring firm has completed recent sanctions screening.

So, for a firm operating in any jurisdiction, the obligation is to understand and comply with its local financial sanctions, both in its home country and in any host countries where it operates branches or subsidiaries. In most countries, ignorance of the fact that a person is on the sanctions list is not sufficient to avoid prosecution for the offence of assisting terrorist financing.

11 RISK MANAGEMENT AND MONEY-LAUNDERING DETERRENCE

11.1 THE RISKS WITHIN MONEY-LAUNDERING DETERRENCE

Financial crime represents a major source of risk to a firm and always has a high priority with both regulators and the board. This means that it is important for money-laundering deterrence and terrorist-financing avoidance to be included within any enterprise risk-management framework. It also requires major control and management programmes to be implemented effectively. At the heart of a successful enterprise risk-management programme are the key concepts of risk identification and risk appetite. In the case of financial crime deterrence, a key control must be effective training together with the Know Your Customer processes and procedures, as discussed in earlier chapters and reiterated later here.

A firm faces a series of risks when considering financial crime deterrence programmes and policies. Some of these follow from the nature of the illegal events themselves and others from the way that the firm deals with these events in practice. The risk management of financial crime deterrence comprises several layers of control that always need to be present within the daily operations of the firm. Firms also need to have the governance structures in place to ensure that prompt and effective action is taken when a case requiring either investigation or reporting is identified.

It is imperative that firms constantly review their corporate structures to see that their chosen approach to risk management of money-laundering deterrence remains appropriate, is consistent with local and international rules and regulations and accords with their business models.

Certain types of business which might be considered to be of higher risk will warrant a greater level of risk management control than would be the case for other businesses. Examples of high-risk businesses would be ones that regularly receive funds from individuals in what might be considered to be higher risk jurisdictions, ones that accept significant levels of cash or ones that only deal with their customers remotely. Each of these types of business would require a level of enhanced due diligence and additional, ongoing monitoring to be conducted.

According to the then UK regulator, the FSA, in June 2012, some of the most common problems being experienced by firms are:

- Failure to identify PEP accounts;
- Failure to conduct enhanced due diligence on high-risk accounts;
- Inadequate challenge from relevant staff when high-risk factors are clearly apparent; and
- The firm continuing to accept customers or continuing relationships when serious allegations about criminal activity have not been considered properly.

The requirement for staff to have a detailed understanding of their roles and obligations within a financial crime deterrence regime operates at all levels of the business, from the doorman to the Chairman. It also needs to take into account outsourced service providers, contractors and temporary staff. A well-equipped financial crime deterrence team will include senior management that possesses the necessary expertise to enable it to be authoritative in the implementation of a risk-based approach to money-laundering deterrence.

It is, however, a fallacy for any firm to believe that any level of monitoring will result in the risks relating to financial crime being totally eradicated. What a firm is seeking to do is to minimise the risks using a risk-based approach and to have the policies and procedures in place that meet the expectations of the regulator, market and society to act as a defence if risks actually crystallise.

The key risks that apply in this case might be categorised as follows:

- Regulatory risk
- Reputational risk
- Operational risk.

11.1.1 Regulatory Risk

Regulatory risk is generally part of operational risk, as set out within the Basel Accord as promulgated by the Bank for International Settlements, which we shall consider later in this chapter. However, it is generally managed separately, although often the ownership of this risk is unclear. It may seem appropriate for the Money Laundering Reporting Officer to own regulatory risk for financial crime deterrence. That would make that person responsible for ensuring that the firm has the policies and procedures in place to meet the expectations and demands of local regulators, and also those of international regulators where relevant.

What the MLRO cannot be made responsible for is any case of money laundering or terrorist financing that is actually found in practice. Their role is to ensure that the staff is trained and the procedures required by the local jurisdiction are implemented, including the investigation and reporting of complaints. This will, however, not entirely stop the firm being used by money launderers, due to the complexity and sophistication of the techniques applied which override banking controls. However, it may serve to reduce the incidence or severity of illegal activity.

In terms of the management of regulatory risk, it will be important for the firm to have access to the necessary lists and reports which highlight high-risk or inappropriate customers, including sanctions and politically exposed person (PEP) lists. Senior management will want to know that these lists have been received and promptly acted upon by the relevant bank officials.

There will also need to be a system to ensure that changes in applicable rules and regulations are identified promptly, and necessary changes to policies and operating procedures implemented. It may well be that the person responsible for regulatory risk may only provide the guidance to others who are then responsible for the implementation of necessary changes, but such delegation of responsibility does not come without an element of risk. We would always recommend that the person with the regulatory responsibility undertakes such monitoring as they consider to be adequate to ensure that necessary changes are made and tested prior to final implementation. They may also require an element of ongoing monitoring to be conducted together with commensurate reporting.

One additional matter that needs to be considered is whether any of the regulations actually operate extraterritorially and also how they are impacted by data secrecy laws applying in another jurisdiction. While it is an objective for data secrecy rules not to impede investigations, it is still worth checking what the actual position is in a jurisdiction and taking appropriate local legal guidance where necessary.

11.1.2 *Reputational Risk*

For any institution, maintenance of its reputation is central to long-term success. Without a reputation, a firm is really nothing, since there is little that one bank could do that another could not easily copy.

A significant failure to protect itself from dealing with unscrupulous individuals or companies can significantly impact the reputation of a firm. Indeed, as we shall see, even failing to maintain adequate operational controls can cause reputational impact. Ownership of reputational risk within a bank is often unclear and it is rarely identified as a separate risk class, since its occurrence is generally the consequence of the occurrence of another risk. However, this does not need to be the case, since a rumour concerning the nature of the customer environment of a bank can be created by anyone using electronic media, and this has the potential to severely impact reputation.

The recent case involving HSBC in December 2012 clearly highlights the importance of the issue. In a press release, HSBC confirmed that it will pay US authorities $1.9 billion in a settlement over money-laundering failures. In a statement, HSBC admitted having poor money-laundering controls.

The bank said it had subsequently spent $290 million on improving its systems to prevent money laundering and clawed back some bonuses paid to senior executives in the past.

The relevant US Senate report was heavily critical of HSBC's money-laundering controls. The report alleged that:

- HSBC in the US had not treated its Mexican affiliate as high risk when the Senate believed that it should have done so;
- The Mexican bank had transported $7 billion in US bank notes to HSBC in the US, but HSBC had not considered that to be suspicious;
- It had circumvented US safeguards designed to block inappropriate transactions, including allowing 25,000 transactions over seven years;
- In less than four years it had cleared $290 million in "obviously suspicious" US traveller's cheques for a Japanese bank.

Again, the issue relates to a jurisdiction considering certain activity as reasonable but being unable to defend it to a regulator. The key issue is that the firm is not only required to be avoiding money laundering and terrorist financing, but must clearly have the controls and procedures in place that the regulators expect.

Modelling and Managing Reputational Risk

Modelling reputational risk is still at an early stage of development in most firms, yet it is not difficult to model effectively. Using the simple metric based on the principle that an event has to occur, it has to become public and the public has to care, then it is relatively straightforward to design appropriate approaches. Of course, the frequency of the event does make a significant difference and would need to be factored in as well.

The management of reputational risk does need to be considered as a separate issue, if only to ensure that no matters are omitted. The reputational risk programme in this case will start with the senior management operating a tone from the top that is appropriate. It will then be important for the firm to consider the nature of the relationships that it maintains and the level of monitoring that it should conduct. This will be designed not only to meet the regulatory demands but also to ensure that, as far as possible, the firm is able to justify its actions in public to counter any reports made.

Know Your Customer (KYC) requirements will be a significant part of this, as considered in Chapter 13. The basic and most essential feature of all anti-money-laundering legislation and regulations all over the world is the need for detailed customer due diligence to be conducted. Companies must carry out additional due diligence requirements on relationships identified as being of heightened risk in order to gain in-depth knowledge of the customer they are dealing with.

Information which is provided by customers cannot be taken at face value, as the risk of not undertaking or investigating the validity of customer information can result in serious consequences. Due diligence requirements will typically impose requirements on firms to enable them to understand their clients. While the actual local requirements will vary between institutions and jurisdictions, the objectives will not vary. Indeed, the work conducted on a risk basis to actually confirm identity will need to be sufficient to effectively mitigate the perceived transaction and relationship risks.

KYC is essentially conducting background checks on clients and customers to enable the firm to acquire additional information regarding their customers, so that they can be assured that they are not conducting inappropriate activity. While there is always an attempt to identify the inappropriate, there can be no certainty that all such cases will be identified; so there will need to be an approach to adopt in cases where, regardless of the efforts of the firm, a case of money laundering or terrorist financing fails to be identified by the firm and is, instead, identified by enforcement agencies.

In such cases, the firm needs to have its communications team adequately briefed on the nature of the generic procedures that the firm always undertakes. Without discussing any specific case, they would need to disclose that the firm takes its obligations seriously and undertakes checks that go beyond those required by local legislation, and that there is no claim that the firm deliberately was involved in facilitating the activity. Highlighting that criminal elements are increasingly sophisticated and accordingly even the most prudent of firms can inadvertently be caught in the net will also be of assistance. It is paramount that the individuals providing information on behalf of the firm are appropriately trained, able to provide the information required with confidence and have the ability to reinforce the reputation of the firm.

As part of the KYC procedures, the firm should conduct such detailed enquiries as it considers necessary using the risk-based approach to validate documents and information provided by the customer. Even though this is generally not required by legislation, we would still recommend that a firm should attempt to substantiate claims regarding the source of funds. Thinking of the case of a firm that has been found to be harbouring a money launderer, trying to justify simply recording the source without verification would represent a difficult position to support.

Increasingly, regulatory authorities in sophisticated financial centres are taking the view that it is not enough merely to know your customer through obtaining identification documents. There is an increasing expectation that a firm should go behind the information provided by a customer to test its validity. Such checks should occur at the beginning of any financial relationship where the accepting business must satisfy itself that the new customer is an appropriate firm to do business with. No relationship should be worth the reputation of the firm, so the old mantra "If in doubt, throw it out" will remain valid.

The importance of carrying out KYC due diligence can never be underestimated, as inadequate KYC due diligence may make the difference between a transaction being carried out and not being carried out. If an entity cannot obtain sufficient detail to establish the customer's identity, or if there are any suspicions about the background of the customer, customer relations should generally not be established.

Why should firms carry out KYC requirements?

The UK regulations state:

> "The due diligence carried out on new customers is in two distinct parts. As well as verifying his identity, the risk-based approach will lead to a need, in appropriate cases, to obtain additional information in respect of some customers. KYC checks are designed to:
>
> 1. Understand the customer's circumstances and business – including, where appropriate, the source of funds, and in some cases the source of wealth.
> 2. Understand the purpose of specific transactions.
> 3. Understand the expected nature and level of transactions; and keeping such information current and valid."

The UK's approach to identification requires the firm to consider the risk of money laundering based on its client portfolio and range of services. It recommends a standard approach to identification, with additional information where the risk profile of a particular client or class of client and/or service requires it.

What does KYC involve?

Usually, this system of control involves taking identification in some prescribed form, as discussed in earlier chapters. Typically, documents such as national identity cards, passports and driving licences are recommended to be taken and the details contained on them recorded and kept for a designated number of years. Records are usually kept for up to five years from the date of the transaction. It is always necessary for the firm to look at the specific requirements within its country and at least to undertake the work required by these rules. However, we would also recommend that a risk-based approach should be applied to the level of work to be conducted to ensure that the work actually undertaken is commensurate with the level of reputational risk that the relationship poses to the firm.

KYC – What to look out for

There are always different types of transaction which might be considered to pose an additional risk of being inappropriate and therefore warrant additional investigation. The following list is in no way exhaustive, but it does represent a starting point for such investigation. Many of the software tools available will look at relationships in this way and highlight the accounts which are most likely to represent inappropriate activity and therefore will warrant additional investigation. These include the following:

- New business customers that are reluctant to provide information on their business activities, location and directors.
- New personal customers who supply incomplete, conflicting or incongruous information when establishing a relationship.
- Customers who do not provide phone or fax numbers or those for whom the numbers provided relate to serviced office/accommodation addresses.
- Diplomatic passports from what might be considered by the firm as being relatively obscure countries, or ones where it would be hard for the firm to recognise a legitimate passport. Any country where passports can easily be obtained by paying for them would also represent a higher risk. Such passports may be genuine (i.e. genuinely issued after payment), however this does not mean that the holder is genuine or the name shown on the passport is the real one. The firm should try and evaluate whether the other details given, together with the appearance/attitude of the person, match whatever diplomatic post he/she is claiming to hold.
- Residential addresses of applicants may be mail-drop addresses (beware of "Suite" numbers, home addresses in downtown business areas, PO Boxes and incomplete addresses). The firm should check for a telephone listing for the person at the given address and carry out a credit reference check on that address. The emergence of social media also provides the firm with other sources of information that might be used for confirmation of information.
- No firm should accept photocopies. Original sources are more reliable and less likely to have been tampered with.
- It is doubtful whether one organisation can rely on the due diligence/KYC checking conducted by another organisation. To avoid issues of liability, it is always best for a firm to carry out its own due diligence.

- The firm should be suspicious of businesses that present financial reporting that is at odds with similar-sized businesses in the same industry sector.
- It should also be suspicious if a group of accounts or relationships is opened by foreign nationals who visit the organisation together on the same day. A situation that is far more difficult to identify is where multiple accounts or relationships are opened on the same day by a group of foreign nationals at different banks/companies in the same city.
- Suspicions should also be aroused if multiple business relationships are opened by an individual using the same address, or different individuals using the same address. Additionally, definite suspicion should result if numerous accounts or relationships are established using variations of the same name.

11.1.3 *Operational Risk*

This is described by the Bank for International Settlements in its sound practices paper as:

> *"the risk of loss resulting from inadequate or failed internal processes, people, systems, or from external events."*

Essentially, it arises from the day-to-day running of a company's business functions. While a firm seeks to reduce the incidence of financial crime by implementing a robust series of policies and procedures, these still need to be adhered to. Failure to do so will, in extreme cases, result in both regulatory penalties and reputational damage. It is therefore important for two main areas of money-laundering-deterrence procedures to be monitored appropriately:

1. The process of KYC and monitoring of the relationships maintained by the firm.
2. The process leading to the reporting of concerns to the appropriate authorities.

In preceding paragraphs we have concentrated on the first of these risk areas and recommended the maintenance of robust controls. The second issue is rather different in that it relates to the operation of the financial crime reporting system itself. It is incumbent upon the relevant officers to maintain a detailed record of any relationship reported to them, highlighting clearly the work that has been undertaken either to confirm or reject the concerns.

The trail of investigation leading to reporting to the appropriate authority will be important, not just for the firm to show that it has acted diligently, but it will also support the safe harbour provisions included within the regulations.

Globally, penalties for failure to meet the expected demands are becoming increasingly prevalent. Another recent UK case clearly identifies both the problem and the views of the regulator.

On 5th May, 2010, the regulator reported that it had imposed a financial penalty of £140,000 on an online provider of foreign exchange services for speculative trading, for failing to have in place adequate anti-money-laundering systems and controls.

Its former Money Laundering Reporting Officer (MLRO) also received a financial penalty of £14,000, again highlighting the importance that the regulator places on this role.

The regulator emphasised that, amongst its many requirements, was a requirement that regulated firms should carry out risk assessments of the money-laundering and financial-crime risks that they are exposed to. However, they identified that the firm failed to carry out thorough assessments for in excess of two years, which, as a result, put the firm at risk of being used to further financial crime.

Specifically, they identified that the firm failed to carry out satisfactory customer due diligence procedures at the account-opening stage and failed to monitor accounts adequately. These failings were particularly serious as the firm's customer relationships did not operate on a face-to-face basis. They also noted that the firm failed to have in place adequate systems for screening customers against global sanctions lists and for determining whether customers were politically exposed persons (PEPs).

In terms of reporting suspicious activity reports, a further UK regulatory penalty both identifies the problem and clearly demonstrates the impact.

On 10th December, 2003, the FSA fined Abbey National (now Banco Santander) companies a total of £2,320,000 for serious compliance failings. Abbey National plc was fined £2 million for breaches of the FSA's Money Laundering Rules, while Abbey National Asset Managers Limited (ANAM) was fined £320,000 for systems and control breaches. Both cases reflected wider control failings, including inadequate monitoring of key regulatory risks across the Abbey National group over a prolonged period.

Regarding Abbey National plc, the regulator stated that:

> *"The failure by Abbey National to monitor compliance with FSA Money Laundering Rules demonstrated a marked lack of regard for its regulatory obligations. Abbey National failed to ensure that suspicious activity reports were promptly considered and reported to the National Criminal Intelligence Service and to identify customers adequately. Both these controls are fundamental to the UK's Anti-Money Laundering regime's effectiveness. Their failings also reflected the fact that the overall control environment, particularly compliance monitoring, has been weak across the group over a prolonged period."*

The regulator's investigation revealed weaknesses in Abbey National's anti-money-laundering controls across its retail banking division. The investigation found that from December 2001 until April 2003, Abbey National failed to adequately monitor anti-money-laundering (AML) compliance following the introduction of the FSA's Money Laundering Rules.

The failings included reliance on a system of self-certification of AML compliance by branches, the lack of AML compliance monitoring by a central function and the failure to provide key management information to the Money Laundering Reporting Officer (MLRO) function regarding this process. These failings contributed to high rates of non-compliance with Know Your Customer (KYC) requirements which persisted until April 2003.

The FSA's enquiries also revealed that, in respect of customer transactions carried out or attempted during 2002, Abbey National's MLRO function failed to ensure that internal suspicious activity reports (SARs) were promptly considered and reported as required. This breach extended from February 2002 to October 2003.

Money laundering is a global industry, and the controls that should be implemented are essentially the same regardless of the actual jurisdiction in which an institution is based. The rules and best practice standards are international, and the risk management function should ensure that they are built into a complete risk-management framework to ensure that the firm is properly protected.

12 THE ROLE OF THE MONEY LAUNDERING REPORTING OFFICER

12.1 WHAT IS A MONEY LAUNDERING REPORTING OFFICER?

International organisations such as the Financial Action Task Force and the Bank for International Settlements actually do not have the ability to impose rules or regulations. Instead, this is left to the local jurisdiction to implement according to the requirements of the local legal and regulatory framework. Consequently, global money-laundering regulations place the requirement to instigate local rules and regulations that set out responsibilities, accountabilities and procedures on individual countries.

In order to comply with what are often referred to as the systems and control function requirements regarding money-laundering deterrence, there is normally a requirement to appoint a responsible individual to take ownership of the process, who is referred to as a Money Laundering Reporting Officer (or MLRO). In the few jurisdictions where there is no specific requirement for a Money Laundering Reporting Officer to be appointed, there is still a requirement for an individual to take similar responsibilities.

Among the key responsibilities is the requirement that the MLRO should be the first point of contact within a firm for any issues which relate directly or indirectly to money-laundering deterrence or suspected terrorist-financing activity. They should be responsible for any strategic decisions made by the firm concerning money laundering and financial crime deterrence. The MLRO, therefore, has ultimate managerial responsibility for regulation of money laundering. Insufficient performance of this role can result in fines being issued by the appropriate regulatory authority, depending on the rules of the relevant jurisdiction. However, this does not, in any way, diminish the role of the board of the firm. Corporate governance principles state clearly that it is the governing body that has responsibility for the direction of the business, including its risk management and strategy. This clearly also includes money-laundering deterrence and the avoidance of assisting terrorists with financing. Accordingly, the MLRO responsibilities should be taken with this overall governance framework in mind. If the MLRO believes that there is a conflict between the way that the firm is being run by the executive management and the obligations that are placed upon them as MLRO, they are required to make this known to the appropriate authorities.

The regulators do place major importance on the firm's implementing appropriate controls in these areas, and failure to do so can put both the firm and the MLRO at risk. For example, in May 2012 the Financial Services Authority (FSA), which was at that time the UK's financial services regulator, penalised Habib Bank AG, Zurich in respect of money-laundering-deterrence failings. A penalty of £525,000 was placed on the firm, with an additional £17,500 on the MLRO for failing to establish and maintain adequate AML systems and controls.

In its public report, the FSA stated that during the period 15th December, 2007 to 15th November, 2010, the bank had failed to establish and maintain adequate controls for assessing the level of money-laundering risk posed by its customers. In particular, the bank had maintained a high-risk country list which excluded certain high-risk countries on the basis that it had group offices in them.

This is an important issue and one that deserves additional consideration in terms of the responsibility of the MLRO. The MLRO may believe that an area of the world is low risk, they may even emanate from that region themselves. This is actually of very little relevance to the situation. The obligations are clear. The MLRO should ensure that the level of due diligence conducted takes into account all the available evidence and also meets the expectations of the regulators. Failure to achieve this will be difficult to justify and can lead to regulatory difficulties.

So, in this case, the bank's local knowledge of what the FSA considered to be high-risk countries did not negate its requirement to treat them as posing a higher risk of money laundering, and consequently conducting enhanced due diligence.

However, for there to be a penalty on a firm there are normally a number of things that have gone wrong, and this case was no exception. The FSA also identified significant failings with regard to the bank's risk classification of customers and the rigour of procedures applied to identify and assess such customers. In particular, the bank was criticised for failing to conduct enhanced due diligence on higher risk customers. The FSA also found that the bank failed to conduct adequate enhanced due diligence in relation to higher risk customers.

Among the significant failings found were that, on a high percentage of files, high-risk accounts had been inappropriately classified as normal risk. They also found that the enhanced due diligence conducted was inadequate (in that insufficient information or supporting evidence had been gathered), and that, in some cases, the enhanced due diligence had not been conducted prior to transactions occurring on the account.

The penalty on the MLRO may appear to be small, but it is a clear message and it would be unlikely for such an MLRO to find alternative employment in a similar capacity subsequently.

12.2 WHO CAN BE APPOINTED AS AN MLRO?

An MLRO will normally be expected to hold a senior management position, and will need to be trained on both regulatory and compliance issues concerning money-laundering deterrence and terrorist financing. In terms of seniority, this is because the MLRO will be required to conduct investigations and these could involve very senior management and also sensitive subjects. The need for care and tact, supported by their seniority within the organisation, enables such a role to be undertaken successfully.

Clearly, the MLRO must also have sufficient resources, time and support staff to enable them to undertake their role effectively. The duty normally sits with the firm to ensure that the MLRO is able to monitor the day-to-day operation of its money-laundering and terrorist-financing-deterrence activities. However, if there are not adequate systems to enable this to be achieved, the responsibilities of the MLRO are not, in any way, diminished. It is they who must demand the systems and people that they require, commensurate with the level and complexity of the firm. The general requirement states that the MLRO must also be able to respond promptly to any reasonable request for information made by relevant regulatory authorities. To be able to achieve this, the MLRO needs to understand what information is held by the firm and how it can easily be accessed to meet such demands. Often this will require the use of specific software, although this need not necessarily be the case. As firms increasingly move towards data solutions which facilitate better use of data, as a consequence they also provide the MLRO with the additional tools that they require to achieve their roles.

The question then arises whether the role of the MLRO can easily be combined with another role within the firm. This is particularly an issue for the smaller firm. Combining the role of the MLRO with that of the Compliance Officer, who takes responsibility for ensuring that the business complies with all other rules and regulations, can be considered an appropriate solution. No other role actually provides the same level of independence that is required, and combination with the role of Head of Internal Audit would not appear to be ideal. Since internal audit reports essentially to the board and its subsidiary Audit Committee and undertakes work at their behest, they will also wish to conduct audits into the money-laundering and terrorist-financing-deterrence procedures that have been implemented within the firm.

If another role is to be selected to be combined with that of the MLRO, then the key issue to consider is to what extent the role is either client- or counterparty-facing, or able to influence the recording or processing of such transactions. If any role does exist without any of these responsibilities, then this may become the least worst alternative.

12.3 THE ROLE OF THE MONEY LAUNDERING REPORTING OFFICER

As mentioned earlier, the MLRO is responsible for the oversight of implementation of anti-money-laundering and terrorist-financing-deterrence strategies and policies.

The key elements of the MLRO role will usually consist of:

- Making strategic decisions concerning suspicious activity reports;
- Responsibility to deal with internal reporting of suspicious activity;
- Responsibility to report to and send notifications and disclosures to the appropriate regulatory authorities;
- Establishing and maintaining arrangements for awareness and training to all internal staff;
- Monitoring and controlling money-laundering policies and procedures;
- Producing an annual report covering the anti-money-laundering activity of the previous year;
- Liaising with regulatory authorities to deal with such matters as consent to proceed with a transaction and other disclosure issues, particularly with regards to clients or third parties.

One of the key elements resulting in the appointment of the MLRO is the protection normally afforded to them through locally implemented legislation. It is such legislation that protects the MLRO and enables them to override customer confidentiality in making reports to the relevant reporting agency. Such protection does not normally extend to any other parties within the regulated entity. The MLRO is also normally able to undertake their investigations, leading up to whether a case will or will not be reported, knowing that, in the absence of manifest negligence, they will actually also be protected.

Clearly, the exact legal protection afforded by local legislation will vary, and, again, reference should be made to local rules where detailed guidance is required.

12.3.1 *The Safe Harbour and its Limitations*

Global money-laundering regulations specify that any MLRO acting less than diligently will still be subject to certain sanctions. The extent of such a sanction will vary depending on the relevant regulation that has been implemented locally. There will generally be a defence within most money-laundering regulations to act as a safe harbour for the MLRO in respect of any action resulting from breaching data secrecy and confidentiality rules, as long as they act diligently.

The typical wording of most local regulation will state that the MLRO still needs to have demonstrated that they have maintained due care and attention in order to obtain protection from prosecution. To achieve this, there is clearly an obligation on the MLRO to maintain adequate documentation to support the decisions that they have made.

Again, the maintenance of detailed policies and procedures together with relevant documentation is always the best way for the MLRO to demonstrate that they have acted appropriately, so long as they are clearly complied with. To make sure that such processes and procedures are adequate, many MLROs will have their documentation reviewed by internationally recognised legal experts to confirm their compliance with best practice and local regulation.

12.3.2 *Matrix Management*

One of the MLRO's main roles is the reporting of suspicious activity and ensuring that sufficient procedures are in place to carry out the required reporting to the relevant authority. In some cases, the MLRO may delegate some of his/her role to a deputy MLRO. Generally speaking, it is not advisable to have too many people involved in the process of reporting suspicions, as the required confidentiality of the process may be compromised. The more direct the process of reporting a suspicion is, the less likely the risk of the client being alerted to a suspicion.

In large corporations, the sheer volume of suspicions which an MLRO receives means it will not always be practical for the MLRO to have sole responsibility for receiving notifications and suspicions. Therefore, larger, more complex corporations will have a system of dual notification in place, whereby notifications of suspicions can be reported either to the MLRO or another individual within the business unit. Such a role is generally separate from the delegated role that a deputy MLRO may have delegated to them. The idea is to have an alternative contact within the firm, who has a high level of training but operates in a different part of the business structure. This type of role tends to be allocated to Compliance Officers. Compliance Officers have a quasi-legal background and so they are able to contribute a high level of knowledge and expertise to the process.

However, the main criterion to have in mind when allocating this role is to appoint someone whose role is as minimally client-facing as possible. The analogy behind this is that limited client contact means the reporting officer is less likely to inadvertently alert clients to any suspicions. Once a suspicion has been raised, it is usually difficult for an employee who has knowledge of such reporting and deals directly with the reported client to remain independent and avoid instigating probing questions from a potentially wary client. For example, a client relationship manager who deals with a client under suspicion may need to continuously find reasons to delay completing a transaction which involves transferring funds. The client will clearly be alerted to the possibility of concerns if the client relationship manager is now suddenly always unavailable. There is also the possibility that employees who work closely with their clients may, in rare cases, themselves be involved in the fraud or money laundering. It is, therefore, advisable to maintain a degree of separation in order to dilute the degree of influence which such an employee might have.

While we have outlined the benefits of appointing an alternative notifying officer from a higher, non-client-facing level, we realise that this style of structure may be primarily limited to large corporations. Employees of small companies tend to have an overlap in functions and responsibilities, with it being possible that all functions may, in some sense, be client-facing. This may be addressed with the possibility of outsourcing some of the work of the MLRO, whilst not outsourcing the legal responsibilities. This clearly will help maintain an MLRO's independence and, as an outsourced resource will certainly not have any contact with clients, will maintain confidentiality.

12.3.3 What is an MLRO's Internal Reporting Procedure?

All suspicions identified within the business must be reported to the MLRO or to a deputy MLRO, if the MLRO has chosen to appoint one. Ideally, the process of reporting suspicions should be as direct and timely as possible. All suspicions which are reported to the MLRO should be fully documented, with the date and time together with the full name of the member of staff and position and role within the firm recorded.

An initial report should be prepared with details of the customer and a full statement detailing information giving rise to the suspicion. The MLRO will then acknowledge receipt of the report and inform the member of staff to do nothing which may prejudice any potential investigation or tip off the customer. All internal enquiries, including investigations conducted to confirm the suspicion and decisions made whether or not to submit the report to the relevant reporting agency, should be also be documented in full.

This is done as a matter of good practice to enable the MLRO to make reference to past suspicions, should an investigation subsequently arise and to provide some level of defence in case of reports not made after investigation, highlighting that appropriate actions were, in fact, taken. Reports should also include whether any transactions were actually prevented from proceeding any further as a result of a money-laundering suspicion being identified.

It is also good practice for the MLRO to maintain a register of suspicions received, investigated and reported to provide some monitoring of the process. This will, in particular, highlight any cases where the MLRO has been required by the relevant agency to take specific action, such as freezing an account. It will also highlight the number of cases where the MLRO has made a report, but there has been no direct response from the relevant agency of any kind.

12.3.4 *What is Contained in the MLRO's Annual Report?*

In order to maintain adequate systems and controls for compliance with its regulatory obligations, in many countries firms are required to commission an annual report from their MLRO. Such an annual report aims to focus on specific outcomes rather than just providing a list of various statistics. It should generally conclude on the effectiveness of the firm's money-laundering and terrorist-financing-deterrence systems and make recommendations for improvements.

Another benefit of producing such a report is that it is a helpful tool which enables the MLRO to document key money-laundering and terrorist-financing-deterrence policies and procedures, identifying key issues of relevance to senior management.

Recommendations made by the MLRO in the report should then be considered by the firm's senior management. It is the role of the senior management to assess whether internal reports are being made when required and to consider whether figures revealed in the report could, in fact, conceal inadequate reporting. Having considered the report, senior management will then need to take any necessary action to remedy any deficiencies identified by the report.

Annual reports made by the MLRO may cover all, or any, of the following information:

Nominated Officer (or MLRO)

The name of the nominated officer should be stated, together with a summary report on their activities.

Director/Senior Management

The report should outline the demarcation of responsibilities between the MLRO and senior management of the firm, providing additional clarity as to the protection provided to the MLRO by relevant legislation.

MLRO Functions

The responsibilities of the MLRO should be confirmed as well as highlighting any areas where the MLRO considers that they are restricted from carrying out their function. The report may also consider whether the MLRO has sufficient resources and access to information.

Staff Training

The report should include information concerning the training of staff, including who has been trained, methods of training and any difficulties faced in achieving a satisfactory level of training. Any recommendations or improvements to training should also be considered.

Information to Senior Management

A description of the reporting procedure to senior managers who receive reports should be included. The extent to which customer or counterparty names should be included in such reporting should also be considered, since additional disclosure could potentially increase the risk of tipping off.

Documentation of Policies and Risk Assessments

The report should describe arrangements for documentation of policies and risk assessments. The report may specifically describe how the firm uses local regulatory and statutory guidance. The report will typically identify deficiencies in current policies and reporting procedures, as well as outlining the seriousness of the issue and any recommendations for change. This part of the report may also comment on any new regulatory or legislative changes which will impact on the firm's risk-management processes.

New Products

As new products are introduced, it will be important for the MLRO to consider to what extent they may potentially be used by people engaged in money laundering and terrorist financing, such that appropriate policies and procedures can be adopted prior to the product launch. In the report, the MLRO will refer to the new products that either have been or are planned to be launched, consider the susceptibility to money laundering and terrorist financing and document the actions proposed or taken to mitigate such susceptibility.

Financial Exclusions

Many jurisdictions have specific rules requiring financial institutions to avoid excluding any specific customer grouping from the business conducted by the firm. Such rules can potentially run contrarian to the objectives of the MLRO. Accordingly, in the annual report the MLRO should describe the arrangements for dealing with customers who are financially excluded and their impact on the money-laundering and terrorist-financing regime adopted.

Arrangements for Monitoring Effectiveness of Systems and Controls

Normally, the report will set out how the MLRO is achieving all of their objectives, including the maintenance of effective systems and controls. In this respect, the contents of the report typically refer to the following in summary:

- The nature of the systems and controls operated by the business;
- Recommendations for the firm's systems and controls to ensure that they cover areas of:
  - the system for producing information provided to relevant agencies and to senior management;
  - the adequacy of relevant risk-management policies and risk profiles;
  - the processes adopted in respect of new products, the taking on of new customers and changes in business profile;
- Conclusions regarding the nature of employee acceptance and recruitment processes and procedures.

Summary of Business Areas

In their report, the MLRO will generally outline the business operations and activities of the firm, highlighting how susceptible these are to use by criminal elements and the implications these then have on the money-laundering and terrorist-financing controls that are applied.

Customers and Customer Due Diligence Processes

Clearly, the adequacy of customer due diligence remains at the heart of the work that the MLRO requires the business to undertake, and accordingly this is generally also included in their annual report. Key elements of such a report will generally include the following:

- Details of the firm's customer base, including information on size, area of business, country of origin, percentage increases/decreases and anything unusual;
- Information on the firm's politically exposed person (PEP) policies and procedures;
- The firm's arrangement for sanctions compliance, including information on procedures, checks, who is verified and the type of transactions that are checked;
- Details of arrangements where identification and due diligence are not carried out directly by the firm;
- The procedures which are used for identification verification, including any exceptions which may exist;
- Details as to how high-risk customers are dealt with;
- Information on how Know Your Customer (KYC) information is collected, together with information, if relevant, concerning the implementation and modelling of the risk-based approach;
- The firm's arrangements for monitoring transactions;
- Information summarising the firm's product range and the risk that this poses to the firm in terms of its susceptibility to being used by criminal elements;
- Normally there is also a discussion of the geographical areas of operation of the business and any additional risks that these pose.

Overall Assessment of Systems and Controls

While customer due diligence is a fundamental part of the deterrence policies, ongoing controls, policies and procedures are also of significant importance. It is incumbent upon the MLRO to ensure that senior management and the regulators have a full and comprehensive understanding of the nature of the control environment employed by the firm, together with the conclusions as to the adequacy of such procedures. Accordingly, the report normally will address the following issues:

- The nature of the systems and controls in place and whether they are comprehensive and proportionate;
- Whether such systems and controls have been regularly reviewed, by whom and the conclusions that have arisen;

- Whether there have been any control failures. Any such failures will generally be identified, as well as any rule breaches and remedial action taken.

Record-keeping

MLRO and firm record-keeping requirements do vary between jurisdictions, with many regulators undertaking reviews into both the adequacy of such records and their compliance with the relevant rules and regulations. Accordingly, in their report the MLRO will typically wish to refer to the following matters:

- The format and location of where records are kept, together with any changes that have been made to the way the information is recorded or stored;
- Whether there have been any failures in controlling the record-keeping procedures, as well as any recommendations for change.

Suspicious Transaction Reporting

This is also a fundamental part of the role of the MLRO; accordingly, reference to this will generally also be made in the annual report, without highlighting specific details of individual cases identified and whether they were, or were not, reported. Matters that will generally be referred to in the report will include:

- An outline of the methods used to identify suspicious transactions and any limitations to this process;
- Any improvements, enhancements or proposed systems changes which the MLRO feels are necessary.

Internal Reporting

- A summary of the number of internal reports made by each business area;
- The number of internal reports which were not forwarded to the relevant money-laundering authority. The report will also generally highlight whether this number has increased or decreased from previous years;
- Any circumstances which may have led to changes in reporting, and identification of possible trends;
- Any quality checks on reporting that are made by the MLRO.

External Reporting

A separate section of the annual report normally provides the senior management and regulators with information regarding reporting actually made by the MLRO. The contents of this section will typically include the following matters:

- Whether there were any cases of money laundering where a report was not made;
- A breakdown of the number of reports which were passed to money-laundering authorities per business area;
- Any changes/trends in reporting;

- Any feedback from the relevant money-laundering authority on reporting, whether individually or by sector;
- A review of the nature of actions taken concerning non-cooperative jurisdictions, including any measures implemented within the firm.

Recommendations for Action

This section should detail recommendations made by the MLRO to senior management. This should be described in order of priority areas of remedial and preventative action, as well as an expected timeframe for action. The MLRO should also comment on the adequacy of resources, as well as any recommendations for change.

13 KNOW YOUR CUSTOMER

13.1 WHAT IS KNOW YOUR CUSTOMER?

The basic and most essential feature of all anti-money-laundering legislation and regulations all over the world is the need for appropriate and adequate customer due diligence to be conducted, both when the relationship is entered into and subsequently during the lifetime of the relationship. Such due diligence is to enable the bank to really understand the customer and the risks they pose both to the firm and to society at large, not only in terms of the risk of money laundering or terrorist financing, but also in terms of their profitability to the firm.

The level and depth of the analysis that a firm will be required to conduct will need to be commensurate with the risks that the relationship poses. Clearly, it will not normally be sufficient for the firm just to accept information which is provided to them by customers at face value; however, as we shall see, often the local jurisdictional requirements translating FATF Recommendations into local rules may purely require recording rather than investigating or confirming information. We would always recommend that some level of investigation should generally be undertaken to establish that documents and information provided are indeed valid and that they may be used to confirm and support customer information and identification. Failure to do so could result in obviously fraudulent documents being accepted in error, with potentially serious consequences.

If a firm is purely relying on documents being provided to it by a single party, then that party may, of course, be conducting illegal activity – and criminals tend to have perfect documents. They know the rules just as much as the firm and its MLRO does, and consequently will take advantage of any perceived weakness in the processes and controls applied to enable them to launder or fund as they require.

Regulations that are implemented within individual jurisdictions are likely to specify individual due diligence requirements that should be conducted. We discuss these on a case-by-case basis in the various country profiles of Chapter 27. There are two approaches adopted globally: either there is a general requirement imposed on the firm that it should understand its clients; or there are more detailed rules and regulations specifying the precise work to be conducted in specific situations, known as "Know Your Customer" (KYC) requirements.

KYC is essentially the work conducted by a firm to undertake background checks on clients and customers to enable the firm both to obtain and confirm additional information regarding its customers. Detailed enquiries, if conducted, should be able to validate documents and information provided by the customer, together with substantiating claims regarding the source of funds. However, in many cases firms purely record the source of funds on the KYC rather than actually proving that the source is appropriate. In Chapters 15 and 16 we consider specific requirements with regard to both retail and corporate customers.

Increasingly, regulatory authorities in sophisticated financial centres are taking the view that it is not enough merely to know your customer through obtaining identification documents. They expect that the firm's investigations will critically examine the information provided to test its validity. Such checks will typically occur at the beginning of any financial relationship, where the accepting business must satisfy itself that the new customer entering into a financial transaction or business relationship is an appropriate customer to do business with.

This work is closely linked to both customer relationship management and the selling process. Firms need to undertake adequate work to confirm that the product being sold to the customer is appropriate to the customer's needs and requirements and that it is consistent with the risk profile of the firm. As such, every sale made by a firm should include some element of KYC completion. This information can also be used by a firm to identify products that would typically be purchased by customers with this specific profile, leading to additional income for the firm (customer relationship management).

Therefore, there are many reasons for a firm to maintain KYC information, and the requirements are to implement standard procedural requirements. Since the need for reliable KYC information is not just dependent on the regulations relating to money laundering and the financing of terrorism, firms are able to use selling compliance rules and customer relationship management requirements to enable them to obtain the information they may also require to meet money-laundering deterrence and terrorist-financing obligations.

As part of the battle against money laundering and terrorist financing, the importance of a firm carrying out adequate KYC due diligence procedures can never be underestimated. Inadequate KYC due diligence may make the difference between a transaction being carried out and not being carried out; and a firm being prosecuted or not prosecuted. If an entity cannot obtain sufficient details to adequately establish the customer's identity, or if there are any suspicions about the background of the customer, customer relations should generally not be established. However, the customer should not be notified that the relationship has not proceeded due to money-laundering concerns, since this would represent tipping off (see Chapter 23).

13.2 WHY SHOULD FIRMS CARRY OUT KYC REQUIREMENTS?

Generally, the due diligence carried out by a firm on new customers is in two distinct parts. As well as verifying their identity, the risk-based approach will lead to a need, in appropriate cases, to obtain additional information in respect of some customers. Clear policies and procedures are required to ensure that such requirements are rigorously complied with in all cases where such enhanced due diligence procedures (or EDD) are required. These KYC checks are designed to:

1. Understand the customer's circumstances and business, including, where appropriate, the source of funds, and in some cases the source of wealth.
2. Understand the purpose of specific transactions.
3. Understand the expected nature and level of transactions, and ensure that information maintained is both current and valid.

The firm should consider the risk of a relationship being related to money laundering based on its client portfolio and its range of services in determining the extent and nature of due diligence to be conducted. A standard approach should be adopted to deal with the identification of customers using a series of appropriate checklists, with additional information being required where the risk profile of a particular client or class of client and/or service requires it. All such checklists should be reviewed on a regular basis to ensure that they are up to date and complete.

13.3 WHAT DOES KYC INVOLVE?

Usually, this system of control involves taking identification in some prescribed form. Typically, documents such as national identity cards, passports and driving licences are recommended to be taken and the details contained on them recorded or copied, and kept for a designated number of years. Records are usually kept for up to five years from the date of the transaction (for a one-off transaction) and for a period after the end of the relationship with the client in the case of longer and multiple transactions.

Specific requirements in respect of retail customers are addressed in Chapter 15, and in respect of corporate customers in Chapter 16.

13.4 WHAT ARE THE GENERAL ISSUES?

13.4.1 Reluctance to Provide Information

Banks will find that, in practice, there is a pattern to the type of things that can go wrong, which needs to be included in awareness training for staff (see Chapter 14). Some of these things are included within this section. One example is any cases where new business or personal customers are reluctant to provide information on their normal activities, location and directors. It must be emphasised that this does not mean the customer is money laundering; they may just have inappropriate concerns about sharing their personal information. However, there have been cases of actual money laundering which would have been identified had the suspicion identified initially on the opening of the account been investigated thoroughly.

13.4.2 Conflicting Information

Another concern is new personal customers that supply incomplete, conflicting or incongruous information when establishing a relationship. Many customers will initially provide incomplete information; indeed, you have probably done so yourself. This would not be reason alone for enhanced due diligence to be conducted. However, if there are repeated problems, or information is regularly corrected, then this would raise additional awareness of the risks of inappropriate conduct.

Of course, the experienced money launderer will come prepared with all of the information that could possibly be requested, so it may be the customer who provides perfect information that actually becomes a cause for concern.

13.4.3 Provision of Key Data

Customers that do not provide addresses, phone or fax numbers, or those for whom the numbers provided relate to serviced office/accommodation addresses, are also high risk. The problem here is that the customer is not enabling the firm to make regular contact with them and may only be temporarily present where they are currently working. A firm can easily set up what appears to be an office in a serviced office suite or a pop-up office, then leave the following day. When the bank's officer arrives at the site they will see what appears to be a fully functioning business, not knowing that it will be closed the following day. The controls here are the same for money laundering and avoiding terrorist financing as the ones required by the firm to avoid fraud. The officer needs to think through the purpose of the process that they are conducting. If they are purely going through the motions, this will be known by the criminal fraternity and the firm will be targeted for the layering or placement of illegal funds.

Firms should always check phone numbers and addresses, making surprise visits where appropriate and reviewing phone listings which are publicly available. In many cases, firms will undertake credit reference agency searches to ensure that the customer has provided what appear to be consistent data sets.

13.4.4 Fraudulent Information

Firms need to be aware of the risks associated with identification documents, for example the problems caused by camouflage passports. A camouflage passport is a passport issued in the name of a non-existent country that is intended to look like a real country's passport. Such passports are also often sold with several matching documents, including an international driving licence and similar supporting identity papers.

Camouflage passports are generally issued in names of countries that no longer exist or have changed their name, for example Burma or Ceylon. Others use the names of places that exist but cannot issue passports, for example Zurich or New York. They can also be issued in the names of feasible but wholly fictitious countries, for example Koristan (which is a place in Turkey) or the Simon Islands (there is a St Simon's Island in the Caribbean).

It is important for the original passport to be seen, a photocopy is generally not enough. Of course, when you are subsequently checking documentation it will not be possible to know whether the officer of the bank actually received an original document or a copy, with observation and enquiry essentially being the only available true verification.

The firm may accept a copy of a passport or other identification document which has been duly authorised by a notary public and will always keep a copy of the passport on file. The date and time when the passport was received should ideally also be recorded to highlight that such procedures were undertaken prior to transactions actually being carried out.

You always need to be careful when checking passport or other documentation. Forged passports are, with regret, easily available and that enables the criminal to place their face onto a legitimate passport. The issue is always whether you can really link the face to the name. Just because you look like the passport does not mean that you actually have the true name as appearing on the passport. Of course, any other documents providing supporting evidence, for example utility or phone bills, can easily be forged as well. A recent example was reported in India in 2012, when it was alleged that a passport was obtained using a falsified birth certificate and was used to travel to 25 countries, including known tax havens. It is relatively easy to obtain a forged passport and indeed these may be actually cheaper to obtain than the real ones. There is a lot of evidence in a passport other than just the photograph page, including visas which may or may not include pictures. Forgers of passports are actually relatively predictable, so looking through at the work that would be required to produce a fake may also provide the firm with useful information.

It is also worthy of note that some countries allow their citizens to have more than one valid passport at a time. This is particularly common for businessmen who may need one passport to be held by an embassy to obtain a visa while they are travelling on another passport. If the firm considers this to be a relevant concern, a simple question on a questionnaire will elicit the information required.

As mentioned above, the passport may include other information of interest to the bank. In the case discussed above, the allegation includes the fact that the individual travelled to a number of what might be termed high-risk countries. Such information would appear clearly in the passport, yet it is generally only the identification page that is copied and the other information is often ignored. Forged passports do not, for example, include visas that are affixed to the passport, rather they tend to have stamps on them (and then generally no more than three and not on more than two pages). The presence of complex visas including a picture that is the same as that appearing on the passport provides the bank with significant additional evidence, which, surprisingly, they often fail to recognise.

13.4.5 *Diplomatic Passports*

Another concern is diplomats generally, and in particular diplomatic passports from relatively small or new countries. Such passports may be genuine (i.e. genuinely issued after payment), however this does not mean that the holder is genuine or the name shown on the passport is the real one. The firm may not even have an awareness of what a passport from that country actually looks like or whether a diplomatic passport differs from a standard passport from that country.

The firm should always attempt to evaluate whether the other details given, together with the appearance and attitude of the customer, appear to be consistent with the information being provided. In the case of a diplomat, the person's persona should match whatever diplomatic post he/she is claiming to hold.

There are even websites which still offer to provide fake passports, although these are described as being for entertainment only and are not government documents. One website offers 100% privacy guaranteed and states:

> *"Welcome to FalseDocuments.cc – the unique producer of quality fake documents. We offer only high-quality fake passports, driver's licenses, ID*

> *cards and other products for the following countries: Australia, Belgium, Brazil, Canada, Finland, France, Germany, Italy, Netherlands, UK, USA and some others."*

I am sure that at the time of reading this work, this website will have been removed, but others will always spring up to take its place, albeit without such an obvious and potentially high-risk claim. The firm states that these documents are only to be used for entertainment; however, when they have left the firm, the use to which they are put is outside of the control of the producer. The question for the regulated or other firm confronted by such a document is whether they would be able to recognise a forged entertainment-only passport from a real passport obtained validly.

Of course, diplomats can commit money laundering or undertake terrorist financing, and such cases have been found. One former Russian diplomat who served as a procurement officer at the United Nations was found guilty of laundering more than $300,000 from what prosecutors said were secret payments from foreign companies seeking contracts to provide goods and services to the UN. He admitted accepting more than $1 million in the scheme and was sentenced to four years and three months' imprisonment and ordered to pay $73,671.

13.4.6 *Financial Information*

In the course of receiving corporate due diligence materials the firm will receive financial information regarding the nature of the business to be conducted. As will be discussed further in Chapter 16, firms should review such material to identify whether the level of activity appears consistent with the size and scope of the firm's activities.

It may be hard to identify what is unusual. If a client starts to receive funds from a new country that might be a concern, or they may just have started to win customers there. As a bank customer, I tend to notify my bank if something that could potentially be considered as being unusual is likely to occur in the short term, for example a receipt from a country we have not done business with before. They then put a note on the file that I have called and explained the transaction. Of course, a money launderer would actually do exactly the same thing!

13.4.7 *Too Fast*

Another area of suspicion is the rushing customer. If a group of accounts or relationships is opened by foreign nationals who visit an organisation together on the same day, then this is potentially a process designed to put due diligence procedures under pressure. There should be enhanced due diligence in such cases, even if this does mean there will be a delay in opening the account. A situation that is far more difficult to identify is where multiple accounts or relationships are opened on the same day by a group of foreign nationals at different banks/companies in the same city.

Similar suspicions should be aroused if multiple business relationships are opened by an individual using the same address, or different individuals using the same address. Additionally, definite suspicion should result if numerous accounts or relationships are established using variations of the same name, for example Risky Reward Limited, Reward Risk Limited and Risk reward Limited. Such names could be used to try to take the identity of the reputable risk management, recruitment and training firm Risk Reward Limited (www.riskrewardlimited.com).

13.5 RELIANCE ON THIRD PARTIES

Historically, firms used to rely heavily on work conducted by other banks and also work conducted by their branches and subsidiaries. This is no longer considered appropriate and penalties have arisen where firms have relied for identification solely on this basis. Generally, each office should conduct its own due diligence, since without undertaking such analysis it will be difficult for it to have sufficient understanding of the nature of the customer to identify unusual transactions warranting investigation.

If there is a branch/head office relationship, it may be appropriate for the relevant work to be conducted once but provided to both offices. In all cases, the rules of the local jurisdiction should be reviewed and complied with in this respect.

In the UK, HM Treasury stated the following in July 2009:

> *"Certain third parties, meeting the appropriate standards, may be relied upon to carry out the work of obtaining documents and verifying identity etc., but the relevant person can only properly discharge the responsibilities placed on him by knowing the identify of his customer and (as appropriate) beneficial owner."*
>
> *Source:* http://www.hm-treasury.gov.uk/d/fin_banking_secrecy_cdd.pdf

This was, of course, based on the FATF recommendation extant at that time and pre-dates the 2012 revision of those recommendations.

13.6 THE THIRD EC DIRECTIVE – KYC REQUIREMENTS

The Third EC Directive provides consolidated guidance on anti-money-laundering procedures to be adopted by Member States of the European Community. As always with EC legislation, Member States are under an obligation to adopt these rules and implement them into their national laws and legislation. Article 8 of the Third EC Directive outlines the following basic KYC procedures and requirements:

(a) Identifying the customer and verifying the customer's identification should be undertaken on the basis of documents. Data or information should be obtained from a reliable and independent source.

(b) Financial institutions should identify, where applicable, the beneficial owner of an account. They should undertake risk-based adequate measures to verify their identity so that the institution or person covered by this Directive is satisfied that it knows who the beneficial owner is, including as regards legal persons, trusts and similar legal arrangements, taking risk-based and adequate measures to understand the ownership and control structure of the customer.

(c) They should obtain information regarding the purpose and intended nature of the business relationship.

(d) They should conduct ongoing monitoring of the business relationship including scrutiny of transactions undertaken throughout the course of that relationship to ensure that the transactions being conducted are consistent with the institution's or person's knowledge of the customer, the business and risk profile including, where necessary, the source of funds and ensuring that documents, data or information held are kept up to date.

Additional enhanced due diligence (EDD) requirements exist for particular circumstances relating to:

- Beneficial owners not clearly identified;
- Dealing with non-face-to-face customers;
- International correspondent banking;
- Politically exposed persons;
- Anonymous accounts;
- Casinos.

Generally, there is a requirement that Member States must ensure that institutions and persons covered under the Directive apply due diligence measures to existing and new customers on a risk-sensitive basis.

13.7 THE UK KYC REQUIREMENTS

The Joint Money Laundering Steering Group (JMLSG, see Chapter 7) Prevention of Money Laundering/Combating Terrorist Financing rules consolidate all UK AML legislation, including the Money Laundering Regulations 2007, to provide industry guidance to the UK financial sector.

The KYC requirements are referred to by the JMLSG in the guidance as CDD (customer due diligence) measures, and are essentially the same concept. The KYC/CDD requirements contained in this guidance aim to consolidate previous KYC requirements.

13.7.1 Required CDD

The guidance aims to help a firm to determine the extent of CDD measures which it must undertake. CDD measures which a firm wishes to carry out must be determined on a risk-sensitive basis, taking into account the type of customer, business relationship, product or transaction. Firms must be able to demonstrate that their CDD procedures are appropriate in view of the risks of money laundering and terrorist financing.

CDD measures must be carried out by firms when they:

- Establish a business relationship;
- Carry out an occasional transaction;
- Suspect money laundering or terrorist funding;
- Doubt the veracity of documents, data or information previously obtained for the purpose of identification or verification.

CDD procedures that must be conducted include:

Identifying the customer and verifying their identity: The firm identifies the customer by obtaining a range of information about them. The verification of the identity consists of the firm verifying some of this information against documents, data or information obtained from a reliable independent source.

Identifying the beneficial owner, where relevant, and verifying their identity: A beneficial owner is normally an individual who ultimately owns or controls the customer or on whose behalf a transaction or activity is being conducted. In respect of private individuals, the customer himself is the beneficial owner, unless there are features of the transaction or surrounding circumstances that indicate otherwise. Therefore, there is no requirement on firms to make proactive searches for beneficial owners in such cases, but they should make appropriate enquiries where it appears that the customer is not acting on his own behalf.

Where an individual is required to be identified as a beneficial owner or where a customer who is a private individual is fronting for another individual who is the beneficial owner, the firm should obtain the same information about that beneficial owner as it would for a customer. The identity of a customer must be verified on the basis of documents, data or information obtained from a reliable independent source. The obligation to verify the identity of a beneficial owner is for the firm to take risk-based and adequate measures so that it is satisfied that it knows who the beneficial owner is. It is up to each firm whether it makes use of records of beneficial owners in the public domain (if any exist), asks its customers for relevant data or obtains the information otherwise. There is no specific requirement to have regard to particular types of evidence.

In lower risk situations, therefore, it may be reasonable for firms to be satisfied as to the beneficial owner's identity based on information supplied by the customer. This includes information provided by the customer (including trustees or other representatives whose identities have been verified) as to their identity, and confirmation that they are known to the customer. While this may be provided orally or in writing, any information received orally should be recorded in written form by the firm.

Obtaining information on the purpose and intended nature of the business relationship: A firm must understand the purpose, and indeed the nature, of the business relationship or transaction. In some instances this will be self-evident, but in many cases the firm may have to obtain information in this regard. Depending on the firm's risk assessment of the situation, information that might be relevant includes some or all of the following:

(a) The nature and details of the business/occupation/employment;

(b) A record of changes of address;

(c) The expected source and origin of the funds to be used in the relationship;

(d) Initial and ongoing sources of wealth income (particularly within a private banking or wealth management relationship);

(e) Copies of recent and current financial statements;

(f) The various relationships between signatories and with underlying beneficial owners;

(g) The anticipated level and nature of the activity that is to be undertaken through the relationship.

13.7.2 Quality and Quantity of CDD

Evidence of identity can take a number of forms. In the UK rules in respect of individuals, much weight is placed on so-called "identity documents", such as passports and photo card driving licences, and these are often the easiest way of being reasonably satisfied as to someone's identity. It is also possible to be reasonably satisfied of a customer's identity based on other forms of confirmation, including written assurances from persons or organisations that have dealt with the customer for some time.

How much information to ask for, and what to verify, in order to be reasonably satisfied as to a customer's identity are matters of judgment for the firm. These must be exercised on a risk-based approach, taking into account the following factors:

- The nature of the product or service sought by the customer (are there any other products or services to which they can migrate without further identity verification?).
- The nature and length of any existing or previous relationship with the customer and the firm.
- The nature and extent of assurances from other regulated firms that may be relied on.
- Whether the customer is physically present.

13.7.3 Documentary Evidence Used as Part of KYC

Documentation purporting to offer evidence of identity may emanate from a number of sources, with differing levels of reliability and integrity. The broad hierarchy of documents includes:

- Certain documents issued by government departments and agencies or by a court;
- Certain documents issued by other public bodies or local authorities;
- Certain documents issued by regulated firms in the financial services sector;
- Certain documents issued by those subject to ML Regulations or equivalent legislation;
- Documents issued by other organisations.

Firms should recognise the fact that some documents are more easily forged than others. If suspicions are raised in relation to any document offered, firms should take practical and proportionate steps to establish whether the document has been lost or stolen. Thus, firms must also have in place procedures, and be prepared to accept a range of documents. They may also wish to employ electronic checks, either on their own or in tandem with documentary evidence.

Of course, the UK rules meet the requirements of the EU discussed previously and are also consistent with the FATF rules.

14 MONEY LAUNDERING TRAINING

14.1 THE IMPORTANCE OF STAFF AWARENESS AND TRAINING

Having staff that are fully trained and possess the required level of knowledge of the key financial crime regulatory requirements that exist within their jurisdiction, together with what constitutes money laundering and terrorist financing is absolutely critical. Accordingly, maintaining adequate staff awareness and appropriate relevant financial crime and terrorist-financing deterrence training is important to any financial institution in achieving its overall objective of combating money laundering and terrorist financing.

For any firm, just having a series of rules, regulations, checks and balances would have limited effect if the employees who must implement the measures were inadequately trained and therefore unaware of these obligations. One of the most important controls over the prevention and detection of money laundering is to have staff that are alert to the risks of money laundering and terrorist financing, and that are well trained in the identification of unusual or suspicious activities.

It is essential that firms implement a complete and structured policy of training that encompasses all relevant employees, so that, in particular, they are aware of their personal obligations with regard to money-laundering deterrence and terrorist financing. They also need to understand the role that they play in the overall achievement of the firm's objectives regarding money-laundering deterrence and preventing the firm being used for terrorist financing. This will be of particular importance to staff that are customer facing and/or who handle customer transactions and instructions, although all staff will require training. Generally, it is also sensible for such training to be extended to include temporary and contract staff carrying out similar customer-facing functions, since they will also be conducting the policies and procedures of the firm, and any failure by such contract staff would impact the reputation of the firm itself.

Clearly, if training is appropriate for a full-time employee, then a contractor that undertakes the same role should be trained to a similar standard.

14.2 THE CORE OBLIGATIONS OF TRAINING

The core obligations of training staff with regard to money-laundering deterrence and terrorist financing are that relevant employees are:

- Made aware of the risks posed by money laundering and terrorist financing, the relevant legislation and their obligations under that legislation.
- Made aware of the identity and responsibilities of the firm's nominated officer and Money Laundering Reporting Officer (MLRO).

- Trained in the firm's procedures and in how to deal with potential money-laundering or terrorist-financing transactions or activity.
- Made aware of how money-laundering crimes operate and how they might take place through the firm.
- Made aware of what actually might represent terrorist financing and how this would appear within their records.
- Understand the legal position of the firm and of individual members of staff and of how these legal positions might change based upon the actions actually taken.
- Understand how to operate a risk-based approach to combating money laundering and terrorist financing.

14.3 LEGAL AND REGULATORY OBLIGATIONS

In many jurisdictions, including the United Kingdom, individual members of staff may face criminal penalties if they become involved in money laundering or terrorist financing, or if they fail to report their knowledge or suspicions when they had reasonable grounds for knowing or suspecting money-laundering or terrorist-financing activity. It is important that staff are made aware of these obligations, and that they are provided with sufficient training in how to discharge these obligations.

Regulators in most countries will detail what they require in respect of money-laundering awareness and training. In the United Kingdom, the main obligation placed by the current regulator, the Financial Conduct Authority (FCA), rules on senior management is that they must take measures to ensure that employees are made aware of laws which relate to money laundering and terrorist financing, and given training on how to deal with transactions related to money laundering.

The FCA suggests that firms, when considering training and competence, ensure that:

- Their employees achieve the right level of competence;
- Their employees remain competent for the work they do;
- Their employees are appropriately supervised;
- Their employees' competence is regularly reviewed;
- The level of competence is appropriate to the nature of the business;
- An MLRO has been appointed with responsibility for oversight of the firm's anti-money-laundering systems and controls, including appropriate training for employees (see Chapter 12).

Whilst these are the UK requirements, they would appear to be appropriate for all institutions globally.

The FCA published *Financial Crime, A Guide for Firms* in April 2013, which replaces the previous guide issued by the FSA. It does include some helpful materials to enable a firm to consider whether it is meeting the training objectives of the firm's financial crime and terrorist-financing deterrence policies. It sets out a series of self-assessment questions together with providing what the FCA considers to be best and poor practice. Firms should have regard to this in the development of their own training programmes.

Self-assessment Questions:

(a) What is your approach to vetting staff? Do vetting and management of different staff reflect the financial crime risks to which they are exposed?

(b) How does your firm ensure that its employees are aware of financial crime risks and of their obligations in relation to those risks?

(c) Do staff have access to training on an appropriate range of financial crime risks?

(d) How does the firm ensure that training is of consistent quality and is kept up to date?

(e) Is training tailored to particular roles?

(f) How do you assess the effectiveness of your training on topics related to financial crime?

(g) Is training material relevant and up to date? When was it last reviewed?

Examples of Good Practice:

(a) Staff in higher-risk roles are subject to more thorough vetting.

(b) Tailored training is in place to ensure staff knowledge is adequate and up to date.

(c) New staff in customer-facing positions receive financial crime training tailored to their role before being able to interact with customers.

(d) Training has a strong practical dimension (e.g. case studies) and includes some form of testing.

(e) The firm satisfies itself that staff understand their responsibilities (e.g. computerised training contains a test).

(f) Whistleblowing procedures are clear and accessible, and respect staff confidentiality.

Examples of Poor Practice:

(a) Staff are not competent to carry out preventative functions effectively, exposing the firm to financial crime risk.

(b) Staff vetting is a one-off exercise.

(c) Training dwells unduly on legislation and regulations rather than practical examples.

(d) Training material is not kept up to date.

(e) The firm fails to identify training needs.

(f) There are no training logs or tracking of employees' training history.

(g) Training content lacks management sign-off.

(h) Training does not cover whistleblowing or escalation procedures.

Source: http://media.fshandbook.info/Handbook/FC2_20130401.pdf

There is much that is helpful in this analysis. In terms of the training programme, remember that it does need to be conducted regularly. The challenge to firms is to keep it both fresh and relevant. The approach we recommend is to design tailored programmes that meet the needs of specific groups. While this may be considered time-consuming, the benefits are clear. They will enable the staff to appreciate what the issues are within their actual roles rather than enduring generic training which focusses on principles and fails to achieve traction with the specific employee.

Notice that the FCA does have concerns over online training. The problem with much online training is that it is of limited benefit. The distractions of the day impact the ability of the employee to focus on the training, the benefit of which is subsequently reduced. The provision of a test at the end of the programme will enable the firm to assess whether key learning messages have been assimilated by the employee. But why restrict this to online training? We would recommend that such an approach should be extended to all training conducted, again with the objective of achieving an audit trail which demonstrates that key learning messages have been achieved.

In most countries, failure by a firm to provide adequate training can result in severe consequences. Typically, in the event that an employee fails to make a disclosure to its relevant agency when there were reasonable grounds for knowing or suspecting money laundering or terrorist financing, then there will be a liability on both the employee and the firm. The penalties can be significant and include fines, restriction of activity, retraining or, at worst, prison.

Timely investigations and proper documentation of the analysis need to be conducted by trained staff who have their key goal of complying with the required regulations of both their host and home jurisdiction. Failure to invest in such areas can prove costly.

If the employee that failed to make the report had not been provided with relevant and appropriate training suitable for their role, this will act as a defence for the employee involved, and an additional liability will then be imposed on the firm. A successful defence by the employee will leave the firm open to prosecution or regulatory sanction for failing to have adequate training. Consequently, the burden is on firms not only to obtain acknowledgement of training from individual employees, but also to take steps to ensure its effectiveness.

14.4 STAFF RESPONSIBILITIES

In order to comply with the overall obligations under the various money-laundering legislation and regulations, responsibilities are distributed amongst the various employment levels within the firm.

14.4.1 Senior Management

As we have discussed, it is the responsibility of senior management to ensure that it has in place appropriate systems to combat money laundering and terrorist financing, and therefore senior managers need to have sufficient monitoring and reporting to enable them to actually know that these obligations are being met.

The maintenance of effective training arrangements is also the responsibility of the relevant director or senior manager. However, it is normally the responsibility of the MLRO to ensure that the firm's compliance with money-laundering measures is appropriate. This is normally achieved through providing oversight in respect of training, including taking reasonable steps to ensure the firm's systems and controls include appropriate training for employees. Remember that the requirements for training are normally for all staff and therefore should also extend to awareness training for senior management, MLROs and nominated officers.

The key training responsibility of the MLRO, including training for senior management, can be summarised as providing the guidance necessary to ensure that relevant employees are aware of:

- Their responsibilities under the firm's arrangements for the prevention of money laundering and terrorist financing, including those for obtaining sufficient evidence of identity, recognising and reporting knowledge or suspicion of money laundering or terrorist financing.
- The identity and responsibilities for the nominated officer and the MLRO.
- The potential effect on the firm, on its employees personally and on its clients of any breach of that law.

14.4.2 *Staff*

As discussed above, it is the responsibility of senior management to ensure that all staff are aware of their personal responsibilities regarding anti-money-laundering procedures at the start of their employment. These responsibilities should be clearly documented for ease of reference for the duration of their employment. Some of the unusual patterns of behaviour, transactions and scenarios that staff are advised specifically to look out for are detailed in Chapter 19.

Failure to report suspicions, tipping off those suspected of money laundering and prejudicing an investigation into money laundering or terrorist financing are all generally offences under relevant local legislation. In many cases, the individual employee who tips off the client can be personally subject to some form of enforcement action. These offences would have an obvious application to those staff that engage in customer-facing activity, but would also apply to back-office staff. Accordingly, it is important that all employees are provided with sufficient training, whether in the regulated sector or not.

14.5 INTERNAL TRAINING PROCEDURES

The rules therefore require that specialised training must be provided to all of a firm's employees. This training should explain to employees how the products and services offered by the firm may be used as a vehicle for money laundering or terrorist financing. This is because unless the training appears to be applicable to the nature of the business being conducted, there will be little obvious relevance to the day-to-day work of the employees.

The training should also explain the firm's procedures and the methods it uses to manage these risks. The legal liabilities, both to the firm and to its employees, will need to be explained to highlight how important this training actually is. Employees should be informed how the firm itself may be at risk of prosecution if suspicious transactions are proceeded with in the absence of consent from the relevant authorities. As a starting point, employees should be informed of what they need to know in terms of their particular role and what they should do if they become suspicious regarding either a case of money laundering or terrorist financing. Depending on the level of interaction that employees have with customers and customer data, the different roles will require different training tailored to their particular function. Customers may need to be informed of Know Your Customer requirements as well as the importance of customer identification procedures and how to monitor customer activity.

Relevant employees should also be made aware of particular circumstances or customers who present a higher risk of money laundering or terrorist financing, or who are financially excluded. Training should, therefore, include information on the additional work to confirm identity that should be undertaken in such cases, and any additional local steps or reporting that should be made.

Staff must also be made aware of the changing behaviour and practices amongst money launderers and those financing terrorism. The FATF's *Guidance for Financial Institutions in Detecting Terrorist Financing* contains an in-depth analysis of the methods used in the financing of terrorism and the types of financial activities constituting potential indicators of such activities. These documents, which are continuously updated, are available at www.fatf-gafi.org. In the UK, information concerning risk profiles and threat assessments is published by the National Crime Agency (previously the Serious Organised Crime Agency), which can be found at www.nationalcrimeagency.gov.uk. Furthermore, in the UK, illustrations of real case studies of how individuals and organisations might raise funds and how financial products may be used by money launderers are published by the Joint Money Laundering Steering Group and can be found at www.jmlsg.org.uk. All of this material is suitable for inclusion in training materials.

14.6 TRAINING METHODS AND ASSESSMENT

There are various ways in which firms may decide to carry out staff training, and the approach adopted will, of course, depend on the method that best suits the firm while still achieving the objectives of local regulations. The approach adopted by a firm that has all of its employees at one site will be different to the approach adopted by a firm which has staff distributed over a range of sites.

Employees who work with high-risk customers or more specialist areas of finance may require more direct and tailored classroom-based learning than would be suitable for the generality of staff. Distributing training videos within a firm may stimulate interest, but continually showing the same video may produce diminishing returns. Furthermore, it becomes extremely difficult to know the level of attention that has been given by a specific employee to such training without some form of assessment procedures being conducted in addition to viewing the video.

As an alternative to such generic materials, specific training highlighting issues inherent within a firm's procedure manuals is useful in raising staff awareness and supplementing other forms of training. The main benefits of such a form of training are that it is tailored to the specific needs of a group of employees and will appear immediately relevant to the work being conducted on a day-to-day basis.

It is recommended that all training be ongoing and given at appropriate intervals to all relevant employees. Particularly in larger firms, this may take the form of a rolling programme. Once a method of training has been chosen, it is vital to establish comprehensive records in order to monitor who has been trained, when the training was received and the nature and effectiveness of training provided. As previously mentioned, this is also carried out by a firm to provide evidence of its compliance with AML legislation, as well as in the event that a firm is held liable when an employee's actions are called into question. Accordingly, the assessment process and its recording are also of paramount importance.

Providing an email update to staff, or allowing them to view a film at their own time, is unlikely to be adequate without some formal process of assessment. Typically, a short examination based on multiple choice questions being asked will be suitable – with ten questions being a typical length of an assessment. If a delegate fails twice on a multiple choice question, then you would expect that delegate to view the training materials again and then re-sit the examination.

15 RETAIL CUSTOMER IDENTIFICATION

15.1 WHO ARE RETAIL CUSTOMERS?

Retail customers are essentially private individuals who act in their own capacity. Customer identification procedures that are suitable for personal customers will inevitably be different from those that are applied to corporate customers. This is due to the nature of the relationship and also the nature of the documentation that is available to retail customers to provide to the financial institution.

Of course, in corporate relationships it may still be appropriate to identify some of the owners, controllers or stakeholders depending on the nature of the relationship. In such cases, the process that is undertaken is similar to that addressed in this chapter and will be in addition to the procedures to be adopted in respect of corporate customers, which are discussed in Chapter 16.

The procedures that will be adopted within a firm will need to meet the requirements of both their host (i.e. the jurisdiction where they are based) and home regulatory regime (i.e. the jurisdiction where their head office is based). The host requirement is obvious: since the firm is conducting business in that country it will need to comply with the rules of that country. In this chapter we discuss general requirements and provide UK-based rules as an example. In the country profiles included within Chapter 27, you will find summary specific requirements for specific countries.

We have also suggested that it would be wise to meet the higher requirements set by complying with both host and home regulations. Your home regulator is unlikely to be willing to accept that a lower level of identification is acceptable to a firm's overseas units. Accordingly, achieving the higher of home and host regulation would appear a prudent approach to be adopted by any firm.

While the distinction between a retail and a corporate customer might appear, on first consideration, to be straightforward, in practice this is not always clear cut. Consider the case of an individual that forms themselves into a company. Should the corporate customer rules be applied for identification, or should the firm continue to use the retail customer rules? What if the customer has one assistant? Would that make such a difference to the risk profile of the customer that a change in identification approach should be made?

In practice, you will find that firms do operate different approaches. What is most important for the firm to achieve is that, regardless of the approach adopted, sufficient information is obtained to enable the firm to really understand the nature of the customer's activity. The firm should have a clear policy which sets out the identification requirements in all such cases, with the objective always being to obtain sufficient reliable evidence to provide the firm with the protection it requires to demonstrate that appropriate procedures have been complied with. In making such an assessment, the firm should consider the nature of the financial crime risk that the relationship introduces, and conduct such analysis as appears appropriate in the circumstances.

15.2 BASIC RETAIL IDENTIFICATION EVIDENCE

Firms must generally initially identify private individuals by obtaining three key pieces of information:

- Full name
- Residential address
- Date of birth.

However, this information must be obtained from reliable and independent sources. It is not sensible just to ask the customer to provide the data to the firm, since that will not provide any evidence of independent review. Instead, reference should be made to reliable documents that are prepared by a third party (agency or government, for example). In particular, photocopies should not be accepted unless they have clearly been authorised by an appropriate legal resource.

Typical documents required include a passport, driving licence or identity card, together with some form of utility or other bill that will prove address. The key element is having at least one piece of evidence that includes the face of the customer, such that it can be confirmed by the financial institution by seeing the person actually being met. Of course, any of these documents could be forged, with a utility bill being capable of being forged on a photocopier.

In terms of specific requirements, reference will still need to be made to local rules, since these do vary. Clearly, firms should take particular care when dealing with customers that they do not meet face to face. The objective is always, where possible, to see originals of documents when verifying identity, but non-face-to-face customers are likely to be reluctant to send valuable original documentation through the post. This leads to the problems of dealing with non-face-to-face customers, as discussed in Chapter 18.

15.3 DOCUMENTARY VERIFICATION

Once retail customer documents have been produced by the customer on request, the firm is still generally under an obligation to conduct validation procedures to ensure that they are reliable. We would recommend that such validation should be conducted particularly in cases where the relationship has been identified as being of enhanced risk, requiring additional or enhanced due diligence procedures to be adopted.

The highest quality documentation which firms can place reliance on will be documentary evidence issued by a government department or agency. The logic for this is that government agencies can, in theory, be relied upon to have undertaken procedures to verify their own evidence, checking the existence and characteristics of the person concerned. However, relevant staff still need to be aware of the possibility that such documents might be forged and to know any specific signs that might alert them to such a fact.

The evidence obtained must give the firm reasonable confidence in the customer's identity, which the firm should weigh against the risks involved in relying on this evidence. Non-government-issued documentary evidence may be accepted if it originates from a public sector body or a firm regulated by the financial services. In other cases, this may be used to provide supporting evidence in addition to a primary government-issued document. Of course, the bodies that produce such documents and the specific documents available will vary between countries.

Government-issued documents which incorporate a full name, address, date of birth and photograph typically include the following:

- Valid passport;
- Valid driving licence including a photograph of the customer;
- National identity card, ideally also including a photograph of the customer.

There may be other documents acceptable to a firm for identification specified by the regulations, but these are normally only acceptable when two pieces of identification documentation are required, which is the position in some countries.

One of the concerns, as mentioned above, is forgery. A passport which has almost no stamps in it with a photograph that looks exactly like the customer is likely to carry a higher risk of forgery than a passport that looks like the customer on a bad day with a load of individual country stamps. Would you use your best photograph for your passport? What are you not allowed to do on a passport photo? The forger will not generally forge more than two country visa stamps and rarely on more than one page. It is just too much like hard work for them. So, a photograph that looks like the customer on a new-looking, fairly empty passport warrants a higher level of scepticism than one which is full of visas with a picture that is clearly pretty awful!

Government-issued documents without a photograph may also be used for customer identification, as long as they incorporate the customer's full name and are supported by a second document which is government-issued, or issued by judicial or public sector authority or a regulated firm which incorporates full name, address and date of birth. In the UK, statements or invoices from utility companies can be used to meet this requirement, but we would recommend caution. Any piece of evidence that can be forged on a photocopier must, by its very nature, be considered to provide limited evidence. Such documents are normally only used to verify address data, although this may be independently available in some form of electoral role documentation, in the telephone book or through the use of social media records of the individual.

Generally speaking, face-to-face verification can be achieved by the customer producing a valid passport or photocard licence and the firm confirming that the picture shown is a reasonable likeness of the customer. Remember that if the picture is a perfect likeness, this may provide cause for concern, since the money launderer always has perfect documents.

The objective of the provision of such documents is to enable the firm to show that the individual has met all of the required and procedurally driven identification requirements for money-laundering and terrorist-financing-deterrence purposes. However, they may not be sufficient in themselves, and consequently firms will need to apply a risk-based approach when determining the level of additional identification checks to be conducted, which is generally referred to as enhanced due diligence. Firms may wish to pay particular attention to managing fraud or credit risk, and so may restrict the use of certain identification documents. This will depend on the current status of forgery in their country. Indeed, it is the falling cost of forged documents which is such a concern at present.

In the UK, the obligations have moved towards really understanding your customer and away from simple, narrow requirements, which is clearly appropriate. It does, of course, raise additional problems for banks that are not dealing directly with their customers in person, for example internet banks and credit card vendors. Accordingly, a higher level of additional verification is required in such cases.

15.4 CUSTOMER EXCLUSION

In most countries there are specific rules on financial exclusion, and this can lead to some unusual cases. How would you identify the street vendor who does not have a permanent address and is perhaps illiterate? In practice, firms may be willing to accept a symbol made by the customer who is unable to sign their name and will also undertake and record additional procedures that need to be conducted in such cases.

If the firm has rules requiring a retail customer to possess a passport or driving licence and another form of identification, there will be some customers that will not have such documents. If you consider the case of a teenage child, they may have a passport, but no other documentation. Clearly, a letter of reference from the parent should be acceptable as additional identification, but this historically was not allowed in the UK. In one case, a teenage customer of a bank, who we will refer to as Robert, wanted to open another account at the same bank. He had a passport, but since he lived with his parents did not have either a utility bill or a driving licence. The bank rejected its own documents as evidence and told Robert to take £1 to another bank up the road. Using the first bank's bank statement and the passport, he would be able to open an account at the second bank. With the information from the second bank, he could return to the first bank and use this additional information to open an account. This is regulation that clearly is ineffective and has fortunately, in the case of the UK, been repealed.

15.5 ELECTRONIC VERIFICATION

Electronic verification of identity should be carried out by a firm using the customer's name, address and date of birth to carry out an electronic check directly or through a supplier (for example, a commercial agency such as Experian). Electronic verification provides additional independent assurance that the customer is who they say they are. Even electronic verification needs to meet a standard level of confirmation before it can be relied upon by a financial institution. To be acceptable there needs to be a match for the individual's name or current address, and a second match on an individual's name with their current address or date of birth. When firms use commercial agencies for electronic verification, they must ensure that they fully understand the systems and scoring mechanisms used by the firm when interpreting the results. There should always be a manual review of any such documents in case of manifest error by the agency.

Firms should remember that although outsourcing of a role to a commercial agency is permitted, they can delegate the work but not abrogate responsibility. Accordingly, a measure of oversight would still need to be maintained. There is a specific Bank for International Settlements paper entitled *Outsourcing in Financial Services* issued in February 2005 (http://www.bis.org/publ/joint12.pdf), to which reference should be made for specific guidance to be adopted in such cases, including the documentation to be maintained and the maintenance of suitable service level agreements (SLAs) which must be monitored effectively.

15.6 IMPERSONATION FRAUD

Impersonation fraud (or phishing) has become an increasing problem in recent years and is probably the fastest-growing area of fraud in the modern world. There are many reasons why a firm should manage the risk of impersonation fraud, only one of which relates to money-laundering deterrence. The greatest risk is, of course, fraud, and the disappearance of the customer with the funds of the firm, together with the reputational impact when this is discovered. There are greater risks in this respect when a firm is using electronic data to carry out additional anti-fraud checks as part of its routine procedures. In such cases, the firm should implement additional due diligence procedures which incorporate the following:

- Requiring the first payment to be carried out in an account in the customer's name with a locally regulated credit institution, or one from an equivalent jurisdiction.
- Verifying additional aspects of a customer's identity using independent third party sources.
- Making telephone contact with the customer prior to opening the account on a home or business number which has been verified electronically, or making what is referred to as a "welcome call" to the customer before transactions are permitted. This is used to verify additional aspects of personal identity information that have previously been provided by the customer during the process leading to the setting up of the account.
- Communicating with the customer at an address that has been independently verified, e.g. direct mailing. Firms should not rely solely on addresses provided by the customer, since this would increase the risk of fraud.
- Other card or account activation procedures, all of which should be clearly documented and understood by all staff. Firms need to make sure that all procedures are rigorously applied and that there is no ability for an employee to override the requirement to undertake a procedure. Such inappropriate activity would enable staff to assist in fraudulent activity being conducted.

As an individual there are things that you can do to reduce the chance that your identity will be stolen. The Metropolitan Police in the UK have issued the following guidance in this respect which includes the actions to be taken:

HOW IS YOUR IDENTITY USED?

Once a key piece of information, such as card details, has been obtained, other information may be gathered from other sources, depending on the intention of the fraudster. Put together, they can obtain sufficient information to impersonate somebody and make a payment using their financial information.

- Information that was given for another purpose may be used as a basis for ID fraud.
- Internet sites such as Facebook, other social networking sites and publicly available information such as the Voters' register are used to gather identifying personal information.
- The most common types of identity fraud involve the use of compromised credit and debit card details.
- Account takeover is a growing trend. Information is obtained to take over bank, card and loan accounts in order to make high-value purchases and take out loans.
- Genuine documents may be obtained such as passports and driving licences.

Be vigilant in providing and using your personal information. In particular:

Your address:

- If you start to receive post for someone you don't know at your address, find out why.
- Register to vote at your current address. Lenders use the electoral roll to check where you live.
- When registering to vote, tick the box to opt out of the "Edited" register to prevent unsolicited marketing mail. (This does not affect credit checks.)
- Sign up with the Mail Preference Service to prevent marketing letters.
- Protect mail left in communal areas of residential properties.
- Re-direct your mail when moving home.

Your accounts:

- Regularly check statements and chase up any that are not delivered when expected.
- Shred, using a cross-cut (confetti) shredder, anything containing personal information.
- Sign up with a credit reference agency for alerts.
- Regularly check your credit reports from a credit reference agency.
- Sign up to Mastercard secure code or Verified by Visa when you receive your cards, even if you do not intend to use your cards online – this protects you if your card or details are lost or stolen.

Your phones:

- Beware of unsolicited phone calls, letters and emails pretending to be your bank or other financial institution and asking you to confirm your personal details, passwords and security numbers.
- Sign up with the Telephone Preference Service to prevent marketing phone calls.
- If using a smartphone, install anti-virus software on it.

Your computer:

- Keep your computer security programs (anti-virus, anti-spam) up to date.
- Restrict the amount of personal information that you disclose on the web.
- Don't fall for online scams, phishing emails, advance fee or other internet-related frauds.
- Know how to verify secure websites if making financial transactions.
- When forwarding emails, delete other people's email addresses, and if sending an email to several people, "blind copy" their email addresses to guard against email scammers.

You should:

- Opt out where you can – companies may send you marketing mail or share your details in mailing lists with other companies.
- Don't divulge more information than you need to – why do they want so much personal information?
- Think very carefully before giving information to researchers or charity collectors.
- Have a secure place to store confidential documents at home. In a safe, for example.
- Don't carry what you don't need in your wallet, purse or bag, such as passports or credit cards.

If you think that you are a victim of identity fraud – act quickly:

- Do not ignore the problem – it might not be you that has ordered some goods or opened an account, but the debt falls to your name and address.
- Inform the card issuer or other financial institution concerned as soon as possible.
- Do not destroy the card if it is still in your possession – keep it as evidence.
- Identify fraudulent transactions as soon as possible. Inform the companies involved if possible.
- Inform the police if you have lost money directly or can identify a suspect. Card companies pass information relating to transactions on compromised cards directly to the police.
- Obtain a copy of your credit report from a credit reference agency.
- Credit reference agencies offer free advice services to victims of ID fraud.
- Sign up with the CIFAS Protective Registration Service: 0330 1000 180 (local rate) or email: protective.registration@cifas.org.uk.

Source: http://content.met.police.uk/Article/Identity-fraud--is-someone-using-your-identity/1400010760805/1400010760805

There is much good advice here. We are continually surprised that people provide so much detail on social media sites, which has the effect of making them more vulnerable to identity theft. Once your identity has been stolen, this is likely to haunt your financial reputation for many years to come.

15.7 FAMILY MEMBERS

In most jurisdictions there is generally no requirement to verify the identity of any other family members of the customer, or any requirement to obtain information on them. The rules tend to follow a simple legal view, in that it is the customer that is opening the account, not the family. Accordingly, information on family members is generally not recorded. In some countries, it would be illegal to even make such enquiries.

Of course, this does increase the risk that your firm will be used by the unscrupulous. If the spouse of the customer seeking a facility has been found guilty of money laundering, terrorist financing or fraud, this would clearly be relevant to a firm's assessment of the customer. In the notices published by the UN, EU and others you will note references being made to the stated person being an associate of a known terrorist financer.

That such enquiries cannot officially be made has the effect of increasing the opportunity for abuse of the system. Clearly, if a firm does undertake any such review then it must not be documented if such documentation would breach local rules. There can always be another reason to reject a customer.

If it is legal to conduct such additional investigation then the economic linkage test should be applied. Could the customer that the firm is seeking to identify actually have such a close relationship with another party that it would impact on the financial crime risk associated with this relationship? If such a relationship does exist then enhanced due diligence would suggest that the additional individual should be identified in addition to the primary customer. Again, this can only be undertaken if this is allowed within the regulations of your jurisdiction.

15.8 TRANSACTION MONITORING

In terms of accounts that are maintained with customers, the level of updating that is required to take place subsequent to the original account opening varies considerably between jurisdictions. In some countries, if a retail customer had taken out a property loan they would need to provide details of their current employer such that a deduction could be made from their salary. Changes in employer likewise must be reported immediately.

In other cases, all such loans are recorded on a central government database. The alternative is the situation in countries such as the UK where the customer is under no obligation whatsoever to provide up-to-date information to the firm. Accordingly, the firm will not even know who the customer is employed by, only who they were employed by when they took out the facility. Clearly, this severely impacts the ability of the firm to identify what might be considered inappropriate transactions.

What a firm should do is to consider the nature of the information available to it and undertake such monitoring as it considers appropriate in the circumstances to provide the assurance it believes it requires. This is often in addition to the requirements of local regulations.

There is also a requirement for the firm to conduct ongoing monitoring of the customer, and this is addressed in Chapter 22.

15.9 SOURCE OF FUNDS

Firms are generally required to record the source of funds for a deposit or repayment by a customer. However, the regulatory rules rarely specify that this has to be verified, which is perhaps rather unusual and could render the process pointless. If we take a case where a customer deposits $35,000, then they might say that the money was a gift from a friend, a legacy from a deceased relative or the proceeds from the sale of a car. The firm will record this, but it is not under any obligation to see if the customer actually had a friend, relative or car.

It is difficult to imagine that the money launderer will be caught out by this test. They are hardly likely to say either that they cannot remember or that they were drug trafficking, for example. The only thing that a firm can do is to remain vigilant and see if things appear to be inconsistent with their understanding of the customer. It is through investigation of an unusual pattern of behaviour that the firm should be able to identify, and therefore detect, inappropriate conduct.

Generally, this is an area where the rules are really only requiring a firm to conduct a process, rather than seeking to ensure that reliable evidence is obtained. The firm should still consider whether there is any evidence that might suggest that the funds may not be from the suggested source. The suspicion could result from the way that the funds are received, or from the illogicality of the information provided. If there are repeated legacies, for example, from the same parent, then this could be a cause for concern. You generally only die once.

16 CORPORATE CUSTOMER IDENTIFICATION

16.1 WHO IS A CORPORATE CUSTOMER?

There are many different forms of corporate customer, ranging from listed companies through private limited liability companies to partnerships, trusts and charities. Corporate customers that are public companies listed on stock exchanges will already be subject to market regulation and higher levels of public disclosure, in terms of their management, ownership and business activities. Their accounts will be subject to external audit by an independent firm and their results will be analysed by the media. Such corporate customers may be considered as potentially lower risk from a customer identification viewpoint due to the level of scrutiny that clearly exists, although such firms could still, of course, be involved in inappropriate activity.

In the UK, there are unlisted securities exchanges which appear to be listed but still have reasonably high levels of scrutiny. Larger, unlisted companies will also still be subject to higher levels of public disclosure and an external audit. They may have issued fixed-income securities which are themselves listed, increasing the independent level of scrutiny on the firm. It is this level of public exposure which makes corporate customers particularly concerned about money-laundering risks. Such firms will no more wish to be involved with money laundering or terrorist financing than would be the case for the bank.

The key problem is that detailed information concerning such companies, such as company accounts, is easily accessible public information. Clearly, companies can be particularly vulnerable to the criminal intentions of money launderers, since they can access such information to use to their advantage. It is, therefore, advisable for firms in their verification processes to take into account that public information may be manipulated by money launderers to disguise their illegitimate objectives, stealing the identity of a legitimate business to cover their activity.

There are different problems in respect of family-owned and smaller companies. In such cases, there is a limited level of independent verification and differing expectations on the role of the auditor. In the case of smaller corporates there might not even be a requirement for the firm to have external auditors, or for an audit to be conducted. The bank will need to consider this when taking documentation and consider whether additional procedures should be undertaken.

16.2 RISKS ASSOCIATED WITH CORPORATE CUSTOMERS

It may not always be particularly obvious why a corporate customer may, in some cases, be at higher risk of money laundering than a private customer. Identification verification in the form of due diligence is important in the case of corporate customers for a number of reasons, not least of which are the local regulations promulgated within each jurisdiction.

There are things which, again, should suggest that a company is a higher risk than normal, and therefore enhanced due diligence procedures should be conducted. One of these is the issue of businesses with particularly complex structures or ownership. In the case of the major fraud at Enron, it was through taking advantage of accounting rules and operating complex structures that the losses of the firm were hidden for so long. In this case, the audit could not be relied upon to identify the fraud, indeed it is important to remember that external auditors are not seeking to identify fraud in the design of their work. Instead, their work is designed to see that the results of the firm provide a true and fair view as set out by the arcane accounting standards upon which the accounts are built.

The existence of a particularly complex business structure may mean that the financial institution must undertake additional measures to be reasonably satisfied of the identities of those that control their business customers. The very existence of a complex structure will, in itself, also need to be investigated, since this could be used to hide inappropriate activity, including, potentially, tax evasion. Again, it is not just the money-laundering concern that worries the firm; rather it is the losses that would occur were the company found actually to be conducting a fraud, resulting in, for example, loans not being repaid.

Firms must be satisfied that there is an obvious legitimate commercial purpose for a corporate customer's business structure. If firms are unable to demonstrate such a legitimate purpose, then the financial institution should be alerted to the increased risk of potential money laundering or terrorist financing and again conduct enhanced due diligence. In this case, this would involve investigating the structures of the group and identifying the controlling relationships that are of greatest importance.

Another factor of concern when dealing with corporate customers is the extent of control given to individuals through a direct shareholding. Shareholders can exercise significant control over a company through their decision-making powers. They may have the power to make decisions regarding the management of funds and transactions without requiring specific additional authority. Therefore, shareholders are, in some cases, able to override internal procedures and controls. A lack of internal control and regulations is typically the type of condition which a money launderer would exploit for his own illegitimate purposes.

However, a firm would not assume that in all cases where shareholders exercise a significant level of control that they may be using the firm's corporate structure to disguise money-laundering activity. A high level of shareholder control is merely a situation which firms must investigate further on a risk-sensitive basis. Levels of control within corporate entities may depend on the nature of the company, the distribution of shareholdings and the nature and extent of any business or family connections between the beneficial owners.

16.3 BENEFICIAL OWNERS

In order to conduct thorough due diligence on a corporate customer, firms will need to identify key individuals within the corporate structure. Typically, such a figure is one that:

- Ultimately owns or controls (whether through direct or indirect ownership or control, including through bearer shareholdings) more than 25% of the shares or voting rights in the body; or
- Otherwise exercises control over the management of the body.

You will note that directors do not necessarily fall within this definition, unless the director is a beneficial owner or has a controlling influence. Directors are excluded if they do not have an ownership interest in the body, nor do they control voting rights or exercise control over management in the sense that enables them to manipulate voting and composition of the board of directors.

However, in other cases there will not be a dominant shareholder nor an external controller and the directors will be the key people that the firm would seek to identify. The question then is the extent of verification that is required and whether the full, retail-style identification procedures should be conducted.

Of course, a firm may still wish to identify signatories to the accounts of the customer, if only to make sure that they are passing some of the risk back to the customer. Signature verification will again need to have some form of document, possibly produced by the legal function or company secretary. No additional work is normally required to be undertaken in such cases.

16.4 STANDARD EVIDENCE FOR CORPORATE ENTITIES

Firms must start by asking corporate customers to produce evidence of the existence of the corporate structure that they are claiming to be. This will usually include:

- Confirmation of the company's listing (if relevant);
- A search of the relevant companies registry;
- A copy of the company's Certificate of Incorporation;
- A copy of the documents forming the entity (for trusts, partnerships and similar structures);
- The memorandum and articles of association (even though these are both standard and easily available).

The standard identification evidence which all corporate customers must provide is generally as follows:

- Full name
- Registered number
- Registered office in country of incorporation
- Business address.

Private and unlisted companies will usually also be required to provide:

- Names of all directors (or equivalent);
- Names of individuals who own or control over 25% of their shares or voting rights;
- Names of any individual(s) who otherwise exercise control over the management of the company.

The final requirement here is a particularly interesting one. The suggestion that companies should disclose the names of seemingly unconnected individuals who control a company through a third party is a great idea in theory. In practice, however, it is completely impractical. In terms of company registration, there is no requirement to disclose who controls a company, assuming they are not a shareholder. Furthermore, even if this was a legal requirement, it would be impossible to enforce. The problems which would arise when trying to prove that a company is actually being influenced by somebody who is seemingly unconnected with it would be insurmountable, rendering this requirement idealistic and ineffective.

One of the important factors to notice is that we are stating that the information needs to be provided, not verified. While there is no specific requirement to obtain additional evidence to support the information provided by the corporate customer, we would always recommend that, where possible, a firm should obtain such information. Given the existence of the internet, trade journals and registration bodies, additional information to confirm data provided by the corporate customer is generally available. Again, the telephone book may be a source of evidence, together with accounts filed at a central registry.

Just as for a personal or retail customer, in the case of a corporate customer there is rarely a requirement to confirm the source of funds. The limit of such verification is normally checking a credit rating agency and the company registry in the country, together with obtaining the accounts. This work is not normally done with money-laundering deterrence in mind, but for other reasons. In some countries, there is a requirement to obtain the memorandum and articles of association of the company, but these are generally all standard documents and actually provide very little true evidence.

The firm needs to undertake sufficient work to ensure that the company is the firm that it believes it is and to identify those persons that will be acting on the account. As such, they will need to look at a variety of sources of information including information that is not obtained directly from the firm itself, but is obtained from third party agencies or public sources. If all of the information is received directly from the company, then it is not independent and this clearly limits its use in terms of verification procedures.

16.5 PRIVATE AND UNLISTED COMPANIES

Private and unlisted companies are subject to a lower level of public disclosure than publicly quoted companies. The structure, ownership, purpose and activities of private companies will also tend to be clearer and easier for a firm to understand. Furthermore, private companies may be long-established, reputable organisations with long histories of public information, although others will be young, developing businesses, many of which will fail in their first three years.

The regulations generally applied state that standard information may be sufficient evidence to meet the firm's obligations. It is also worth searching the company's registry to check that a firm is not in the process of being dissolved, struck off or wound up, but again this is not specifically conducted to identify money laundering. Firms should make search enquiries of the registry in the country of incorporation for the relevant firm. The documentation obtained from such searches can be checked as part of the due diligence process. The accessibility of such documentation will vary considerably between different countries, and firms should pay particular care when faced with obstacles when verifying company identification. This should raise additional concerns.

In countries where there is less transparency, less of an industry profile or fewer independent means of verifying the client identity, there is a higher risk of money laundering or terrorist financing. In such cases, in addition to the standard identification procedures set out above, firms should verify the identity of shareholders and controllers and conduct such additional procedures as they consider appropriate in the circumstances. A visit to the place of business may also help to confirm the existence and activities of the entity, as well as other business associations which may influence the firm's operations, although the office may just have been set up to convey the appearance of a business to satisfy the financial institution. One thing to look for is the appearance that everything is very new or that people are not really working. Perhaps undertake a surprise, unannounced visit and see if the company looks the same as when the formal arranged meeting took place.

While the rule is generally that directors of companies need not be investigated unless they are also beneficial owners of a company, this is unlikely to be sensible in the case of smaller or private family businesses, trusts or charities. In such cases, firms should consider whether the retail identification procedures should, in fact, be applied to significant individuals within the structure. Any failure to comply with such a request should alert the firm to the enhanced risk that clearly then exists.

The firm should undertake a risk assessment of a firm's money-laundering risk to identify which person's identity it is necessary to identify. Verification will normally be appropriate for those officers that have authority to operate an account or to give the firm instructions concerning the use or transfer of funds or assets, but might be waived for other directors.

As is the case with public companies, firms also wish, as part of a risk-based approach, to take adequate measures to verify the identity of beneficial owners (those controlling 25% or more of the company's shares of voting rights), as well as individual signatories. Signatories may also be identified as part of a risk-based approach, due to their power to give instructions concerning the movement of funds or assets, as well as their power to authorise directors to make decisions.

16.6 ENHANCED DUE DILIGENCE

Additional enhanced due diligence measures should be undertaken if the nature of the customer, its business, location and product or delivery channel is assessed under a risk-based approach as needing additional verification. Such measures may include requesting additional identity information.

If a firm is linked in some way to a politically exposed person (PEP), then they are higher risk and should be subject to enhanced due diligence. This is addressed in Chapter 17. On the other hand, if the firm is itself regulated by an active regulator, then this could mean that some form of simplified process is appropriate if this is permitted by local rules.

Extra care must also be taken when dealing with companies with capital in the form of bearer shares, because it will inevitably be difficult to identify the beneficial owners. Companies that issue bearer bonds will also typically be incorporated in higher risk jurisdictions, since, in most countries, the practice has died out. Therefore, firms should implement procedures to establish the identities of the holders and material beneficial owners of such shares, in particular to ensure they are notified of any change in ownership.

As a minimum precaution, firms should obtain an undertaking in writing from the beneficial owner which states that immediate notification will be given to the firm if shares are transferred to another party. Depending on the risk assessment of the customer, it may be appropriate to have this undertaking certified by an accountant or lawyer, or require shares to be held by a custodian, with an undertaking on the custodian to notify the firm of any changes.

16.7 CHARITIES AND TRUSTS

These both represent areas with an enhanced risk of money laundering and terrorist financing, and therefore, generally, additional work will need to be undertaken. Here the deeds that formed the organisation will need to be obtained and the objectives verified. As part of the ongoing monitoring of activity, the firm should seek to ensure that there is no evidence that the organisation's income and expenditure structure is inconsistent with the stated objectives of the organisation.

The firm should also seek to verify the controllers of these organisations, since in such cases there is rarely a beneficial owner and the original settlers are of relatively limited interest. They may have died centuries earlier.

The UK Charities Commission provides a "compliance toolkit", which was last updated in December 2012. This advice and guidance is relevant to any firm in this space, and may be found at: http://www.charity-commission.gov.uk/About_us/pogs/g410a001.aspx

The Commission emphasises that it would not register an organisation that had support of terrorism as an object. It also states that the use of an existing charity's assets for support of terrorist activity is not a proper use of those assets, and any links or alleged links between a charity and terrorism are corrosive to public confidence in the integrity of charity. The Commission highlights that raising awareness in the sector to build on charities' existing safeguards is of primary importance. It also emphasises the importance of proactive oversight and supervision: proactive monitoring of the sector, analysing trends and profiling risks and vulnerabilities.

All charities must, at a minimum:

- Have some form of appropriate internal financial controls in place to ensure that all the charity's funds are fully accounted for and are spent in a manner that is consistent with the purpose of the charity. What those controls and measures are and what is appropriate will depend on the risks apparent to a particular charity based on its type, size and activities.
- Keep proper and adequate financial records for both the receipt and use of all funds, together with audit trails of decisions made and funds spent. Records of both domestic and international transactions must be sufficiently detailed to verify that funds have been spent properly as intended and in a manner consistent with the purpose and objectives of the organisation.
- Give careful consideration to what other practical measures they may need to put in place to ensure they take reasonable steps to protect the charity's funds and so meet their legal duties.
- Give careful consideration to what due diligence, monitoring and verification of use of funds they need to carry out to meet their legal duties.
- Deal responsibly with incidents when they occur, including prompt reporting to the Commission and any other relevant authorities, and ensuring the charity's funds are secure.

You can never tell how money laundering will be conducted in practice; all a firm can do is to have reasonable policies and procedures to act as a deterrent. It is also not possible to identify the firm that will always be a money launderer. There are always legitimate businesses operating in any market and likewise the unscrupulous. A recent reported case in Nicaragua highlighted the issue. A group of 18 Mexicans masquerading as a television crew were, in fact, trying to transport $9.2 million of illegal funds cross-border. The cash was concealed in six vans displaying the logos of a local television company. The detainees are facing a maximum 30-year sentence.

This case highlights that just because someone says they are from a firm does not mean they are actually from the firm. The financial institution needs to be careful. If the identity of the legitimate business is stolen by the money launderer, then the financial institution could be wasting a lot of time identifying the legitimate firm. The money launderer, of course, will have nothing to do with it. The financial institution needs to link the person they are dealing with directly to the firm they actually purport to be from by obtaining independent evidence to support the connection.

17 POLITICALLY EXPOSED PERSONS

17.1 WHAT IS A POLITICALLY EXPOSED PERSON?

Politically exposed persons (PEPs) are, quite simply, a high-risk category of individuals that have been identified internationally as requiring enhanced due diligence to be conducted. The general concern is that persons that hold high-profile political positions and those related or associated with them will pose a higher money-laundering risk to firms, as their position makes them vulnerable to corruption. The obvious risks are that the politically exposed person may take some form of facilitation payment to enable a third party to win a contract with government, receive some form of inappropriate commission, abscond with government funds or receive funds to bias legislation in favour of third parties. In the United Kingdom, the Bribery Act brings this into clear focus.

Of course, the majority of PEPs will not actually be conducting illegal activity. All that the requirements ask is that any relevant firm that identifies a customer or potential customer as a PEP should undertake additional procedures commensurate with the level of risk that the relationship poses to the firm. The next issue is what work a firm should do to identify PEPs, and, as we shall discuss, we would recommend that firms take a broad definition of such relationships. The only risk that is posed to a firm through undertaking analysis on more relationships than the minimum requirements is that some element of unnecessary due diligence will have been conducted. This would not appear to represent a significant waste of resources, since, in such cases, enhanced due diligence would normally be required anyway. It may result in the reputation of the firm being additionally protected.

From the point of view of the financial institution, it is clear that being involved with a politically exposed person will inevitably result in a higher level of potential public scrutiny and a consequent increased risk of possible adverse publicity if inappropriate activity is reported or investigated by journalists or authorities. This would result from public disclosure through newspapers or electronic media of a firm or person having obtained an illegal advantage through biasing a PEP which had been, or should have been, identified by a financial institution.

The question as to who really is a politically exposed person is a significant issue for any regulated firm. Someone may suddenly become a politically exposed person having been a client of the firm for many years through deciding to stand in, and then winning, an election. In many countries, independents have risen to public office from roles which would not have previously resulted in their being identified as PEPs. This means that a firm must continually review existing relationships to see if anyone has become a PEP and therefore requires a higher level of ongoing due diligence monitoring.

Others may be in power and operating entirely legally for many years, only having the opportunity to act illegally at some later stage. They have actually been politically exposed throughout the period, but have only undertaken inappropriate activity when the opportunity presented itself, perhaps just before they leave office. This highlights the importance of continuing to monitor such relationships throughout the period after a customer has first been identified as a PEP.

Remember that a customer having PEP status does not incriminate the individual in itself; the status does, however, put such customers into a high-risk category. The Third EC Directive, as well as the JMLSG's Guidance notes, particularly identifies PEPs as an area of concern in the fight against money laundering. Accordingly, regulated firms should have both a clear definition as to who is a PEP and have clearly documented the additional procedures that should be undertaken on PEP transactions and relationships. It is incumbent on the firm to be able to demonstrate to its regulators that appropriate and consistent procedures have been conducted, with adequate documentation of these additional procedures being maintained.

17.2 THE DEFINITION OF A POLITICALLY EXPOSED PERSON (PEP)

The UK's money-laundering regulations define a PEP as:

> *"an individual who is or has, at any time in the preceding year, been entrusted with prominently public functions and an immediate family member, or a known close associate, of such a person."*

The UK's definition also applies to those holding such a position in a state outside the UK, or in a community institution or an international body. This is actually quite a limited statement. It means, for example, that someone who stands for public office but loses in an election is not a PEP within the definition of the term. However, many firms will actually use a wider definition, which we would recommend. This bases itself on the firm's ability to know who can significantly influence functions of importance, regardless of whether or not they are entrusted with a public function. It is often the person with influence who can be most easily bribed.

There is also a limitation in the UK definition, in that an individual ceases to be recognised as a PEP after they have left office for one year. There is clearly an argument that such a time limit is far too short, since the individual will clearly remain high profile even if they are no longer a public official. Consider the position of former US Presidents or UK Prime Ministers, for example. The way that the UK rules operate to deal with this is, in part, by encouraging the implementation of a risk-based approach. This is a series of policies and procedures implemented in the firm that enables the firm to identify what might be considered higher risk relationships, regardless of whether they are or are not with PEPs. All relationships with PEPs are, by definition, higher risk relationships, but not all higher risk relationships are with PEPs. All higher risk relationships will require enhanced due diligence and continual monitoring, and we would recommend that former officials should be regularly reviewed until such time as their ability to influence has waned to such an extent that it is inconceivable that they might be undertaking illegal, or at best inappropriate, activity.

An example of this is the recent case of the Duchess of York, the former wife of Prince Andrew, who was recorded by a newspaper offering access to Prince Andrew in exchange for a cash payment. She claimed that any payment to her would be repaid tenfold through access to her ex-husband, who works as a UK trade envoy. Prince Andrew was not, in any way, implicated by the disclosure. This highlights that someone who, in this case, is divorced from a person holding a high-profile position remains in a position of influence regardless of the rules, and in this case clearly requires enhanced due diligence.

It would make little sense from a risk point of view for a firm to cease conducting additional enhanced monitoring of transactions or activity at the end of an additional one-year period. The main consideration that the firm should take into account is whether the risks associated with an individual's previous position have adequately abated, or whether they do, in fact, continue. This may need to be considered on a case-by-case basis, as opposed to one generic approach. The idea is that, regardless of the rules that apply locally, the firm would wish to know that the account it is maintaining is not being operated inappropriately such that at some time in the future its reputation could be impacted.

17.3 AT WHAT LEVEL IS SOMEONE A PEP?

It is generally recognised that public functions exercised at a lower than national level should not normally be considered to be prominent. However, there can be cases where persons that hold such positions may experience political exposure which is comparable to that of persons with similar positions at national level. An example of this could well be the Mayor of a large city such as London or Paris. In moving towards local politicians of lesser importance, the firm will need to judge whether they could be involved in inappropriate activity and whether such activity could be of such importance that the person should have been considered a PEP and subject to enhanced monitoring procedures.

Given the number of cases where inappropriate, or at best dubious, payments have been made to officials involved in local planning decisions, the firm may well choose to include all such officials in the enhanced due diligence regime. Of course, fraud does not need to be conducted at the most senior level. In a 2009 case in Toronto, Canada, nine city staff were removed from office after it was discovered that over half a million dollars may have been fraudulently claimed by employees and contractors. Examples of abuse included an employee who claimed $50,000 worth of unwarranted overtime, another who cancelled parking tickets for friends and family and a pair of staff who used counterfeit passes to take advantage of $550 worth of recreational programming.

This highlights that fraud can clearly operate at all levels of public functions, but for a really high-level case to result in adverse publicity, the culprit would need to be at a senior level. In this example, the issues were identified by the financial institution acting as administrator, which shows that they at least were undertaking due diligence on all such cases.

Once again, the key requirement will be for firms to implement a risk-based approach, using some form of consistent modelling and criteria to establish whether persons exercising those public functions should be considered PEPs. We would recommend that a standard scoring system be implemented which sets key attributes for the identification of a PEP, with weighted scoring then applied. This will enable consistent application of relevant due diligence approaches to be undertaken and provide the necessary supporting evidence to justify the approach adopted. Of course, a scoring system will not replace judgment, instead it provides a structure within which judgment can be consistently applied, justified and adequately documented.

17.4 PROMINENT PUBLIC FUNCTIONS

The UK regulations state that prominent public functions include:

- Heads of State, heads of government, ministers and deputy or assistant ministers;
- Members of Parliament;
- Members of supreme courts, of constitutional courts or other higher level judicial bodies;
- Members of courts of auditors or of the boards of central banks;
- Ambassadors, chargés d'affaires and high-ranking officers in the armed forces;
- Members of the administrative, management or supervisory boards of State-owned enterprises.

As such, these are pretty typical of the rules that are implemented globally.

Take, as an example, a 2009 case from South Africa, in which 923 government officials were caught undertaking fraud. In this case, 40,000 houses across the country were demolished or rectified because of poor workmanship. Two of these collapsed, causing the deaths of a 13-year-old youth and a woman. Those involved included 800 national officials, 123 local government officials and five people from the legal profession. This highlights that what is completely unacceptable behaviour may become normal in a group which has perhaps different ethical standards to those which might have been expected. The situation followed from questionable contracts and building standards approved by government officials and implemented by the private sector.

This case clearly illustrates that local and provincial government officials can all be involved in inappropriate activity through the receiving of inappropriate payments (or graft). The laundering of such proceeds through bank accounts without the bank having considered whether they were legally earned could potentially lay the banks open to the risk of being caught within a money-laundering investigation.

It is therefore clear that, regardless of the actual rules that have been implemented, in cases where the relationship results in additional levels of risk, the bank should undertake procedures which are commensurate with this potential risk. What this is likely to mean in practice is that the bank will analyse its relationships in four distinct groups:

- PEP accounts as defined by the local rules and regulations;
- Accounts which represent an enhanced risk of inappropriate activity;

- Other accounts, considered as standard risk;
- Accounts considered by the local rules and regulations as being low risk.

In these terms, a low-risk account could, for example, be an account set up by an employer purely for the salary of an employee.

Of course, not all inappropriate conduct will be identifiable by a financial institution. With public officials, relatively small amounts of inappropriate activity can result in adverse publicity for the person involved. The series of revelations regarding UK MPs' expenses in 2009 represents a clear case of such items. For example, a five-foot-tall floating duck house was claimed from the public purse by Tory grandee Sir Peter Viggers. The £1,645 pond feature, modelled on an 18th century Swedish building by a firm selling elaborate garden follies, sits in the pond at the Gosport MP's Hampshire home. Clearly, a single payment of £1,645 would be unlikely to be identified by a financial institution. Other claims by other MPs included submissions for jellied eels, fluffy dusters and horse manure. It would be unreasonable to expect all cases of inappropriate conduct by government officials to be identified by financial institutions.

17.5 THE IMMEDIATE FAMILY RULES

Generally, the rules applied will require that the immediate family members of a PEP are also included with the PEP in the additional monitoring regime. In the UK this is required, but in other countries it may be difficult or legally impossible to consider such connections. The issue is again clear, it may well be that the PEP transfers the inappropriate funds to a family member rather than taking them directly, or that the family member is able to exert undue influence on the PEP. There could, of course, be cases where the PEP undertakes inappropriate conduct but asks for the facilitation payment to be made to their spouse or children. In such cases, it will only be picked up through monitoring the spouse or child's account.

When it is possible to undertake such monitoring, the definition of immediate family members generally includes:

- A spouse
- A partner (including a person who is considered by his national law as equivalent to a spouse)
- Children and their spouses and partners
- Parents.

What the requirements do not generally include is brothers and sisters, nor any more remote members of the same family. Whether a firm would wish to extend the definition of family to people beyond this list is, of course, purely a matter for the individual firm to consider through the application of the risk-based approach. By complying with the local requirements, they will have met the regulators' expectations. However, they may choose to undertake additional procedures on a wider group of people due to the risks that they pose to the institution itself.

17.6 THE ASSOCIATE RULES

It is normally also important to include the associate of a PEP with the PEP when considering enhanced money-laundering-deterrence procedures. These requirements are intended to identify people with a close business relationship with a PEP that might potentially also be involved in inappropriate activity due to their relationship with, for example, a local official. A firm will need to define clearly what constitutes an associate, using a definition that includes anything that is within the local regulatory definition. Such definitions will typically include the following:

- Any individual who is known to have joint beneficial ownership of a legal entity, or any other close business relations with a person who is a PEP.
- Any individual who has sole beneficial ownership of a legal entity which is known to have been set up for the benefit of a person who is a PEP.

In determining whether a person is an associate of a PEP, the firm generally only needs to consider any information which is in its possession, or which is publicly known. It does not have to go out of its way to find out additional non-public information. Therefore, the obligation of having to obtain knowledge of such a relationship does not presuppose that active research should be conducted by the firm.

Again, the firm should implement a risk-based approach in determining associates of PEPs, and the enhanced due diligence measures which should then be conducted. If there is a known associate who is not actually a joint owner of anything with the PEP, then it would still be wise for the firm to consider them as an associate. It is to such relationships that the PEP might turn to undertake illegal activity, or for them to receive illicit funds on their behalf and therefore disguise their original source.

A recent example of the involvement of three businessmen in an official's fraudulent activities is a February 2010 UK case. This represented a complex fraud which left Yorkshire council tax payers with a bill of £13.6 million. A high-profile council employee who was an international expert in metrology, the science of calibrating weighing equipment, set up agreements with three businessmen to supply falsely inflated invoices relating to the supply of calibration equipment. He paid the invoices from company funds then conspired with the businessmen for them to pay an invoice for non-existent "calibration work".

Here it is clear that the business associates were instrumental in the fraudulent activity and therefore should clearly have been identified and monitored were it clear to the financial institution that they were actually associates of the official. It is the difficulty in knowing the total extent of an official's associates which lies at the heart of the problems that a firm is likely to face in practice. All that a firm can do is conduct a standard set of documented procedures which attempt to undertake the investigations that a relatively diligent institution would be expected to conduct, and to maintain sufficient records to justify any decisions taken.

17.7 WHAT IS THE RISK-BASED APPROACH?

There is no single definition of what constitutes the risk-based approach, and firms will need to consider their own local circumstances in developing appropriate criteria to apply in practice. Actual identified cases of PEPs being involved with local money laundering or terrorist financing can be used to back test any criteria that have been developed. This is done by taking cases of known money laundering and then applying the criteria adopted within the firm's documented enhanced due diligence procedures. They should be able to see if the case would have been identified by their systems as one requiring enhanced monitoring.

Generally, the requirement here is for the firm to develop a series of policies and procedures to ensure that the firm:

- Has appropriate risk-based procedures to determine whether a customer is a PEP;
- Obtains appropriate senior management approval for establishing a business relationship with a customer;
- Takes adequate measures to establish the source of wealth and source of funds which are involved in the business relationship or occasional transaction;
- Conducts enhanced ongoing monitoring of the business relationship.

17.8 THE RISK-BASED APPROACH TO DETERMINING PEPS

The extent to which PEPs themselves affect a firm's money-laundering obligations will depend on the nature and scope of the firm's business and whether the PEP would have a significant impact on the public perception or reputation of the firm were a case of money laundering or terrorist financing to be identified.

When applying a risk-based approach, it would be appropriate for the firm's resources to be focussed on particular products or transactions which are characterised by a high risk of money laundering. This will be determined through knowledge of money-laundering transactions that are generally conducted within the local jurisdiction and would typically, for example, focus on cash-based and non-face-to-face transactions.

A firm will first have to identify whether a PEP exists as part of its customer base. When applying specific checks, firms may be able to rely on an internet search engine, or consult relevant reports and databases regarding public officials. There are also corruption risk indices published by specialised national, international, non-governmental and commercial organisations. The Transparency International Corruption Perceptions Index, for example, ranks approximately 150 countries according to their perceived level of corruption. Clearly, such an index helps firms in assessing risk, since a politician from a high-risk country would clearly need to receive enhanced monitoring procedures.

It is also important to remember that whilst new and existing customers may not meet the definition of a PEP, they may subsequently become one during the course of the business relationship. In this respect, firms must, as far as is practically possible, be alert to public information regarding the possible changes in the status of its customers with regard to political exposure. In practice, this will mean conducting reviews on a regular basis to see if the PEPs identified are, in fact, a complete population of such accounts, or whether an existing customer has become a PEP and should now be subject to enhanced monitoring. After an election for office it is clear that an additional review should be conducted to identify newly elected PEPs who will now require additional monitoring.

The identification of the PEP, family member or associate is only the first stage in the process. Once a PEP has been identified, firms must then be clear as to the enhanced due diligence procedures that they should conduct in order to minimise, where possible, their risk of being involved with an account which actually constitutes money laundering or terrorist financing.

17.9 TRANSPARENCY INTERNATIONAL

Transparency International is an international organisation that works to fight against corruption and produces an annual global corruption report, The Transparency International Corruption Perceptions Index. The 2011 Corruption Perceptions Index measures the perceived levels of public sector corruption in 183 countries and territories around the world. The current list is included as an appendix to this book.

Transparency International provides a series of clear definitions that should prove of assistance to people drafting money-laundering-deterrence or terrorist-financing policies. Within these definitions, Transparency International specifically defines political corruption, and the problems involved with it are explained in depth. Political corruption is defined as the abuse of entrusted power by political leaders for private gain, with the objective of increasing power or wealth. It does not need to involve money changing hands; it may take the form of "trading in influence" or granting favours for the intention of receiving benefit. In any country where there is a high perceived risk of corruption, you would expect a firm to conduct a higher level of enhanced due diligence on any PEPs that have been identified.

Political corruption involves a wide range of crimes and illicit acts committed by political leaders before, during and after leaving office. It is distinct from petty or bureaucratic corruption insofar as it is perpetrated by political leaders or elected officials who have been vested with public authority and who bear the responsibility of representing the public interest. There is also a supply side to political corruption – the bribes paid to politicians – that must be addressed.

Businesspeople also sense the effects of political corruption. A survey by the World Economic Forum shows that businesspeople believe that legal donations have a high impact on politics, that bribery does feature as a regular means of achieving policy goals in about 20% of countries surveyed and that illegal political contributions are standard practice in nearly half of all countries surveyed. Political corruption points to a lack of transparency, but also to related concerns about equity and justice: corruption feeds the wrongs that deny human rights and prevent human needs from being met.

Transparency International also publishes a bribe payers' index. The 2011 Bribe Payers' Index ranks the likelihood of companies from 28 leading economies to win business abroad by paying bribes. Reproduced with the kind permission of Transparency International, the 2011 Bribe Payers' Index is shown in Table 17.1.

Countries are scored on a scale of 0–10, where a maximum score of 10 corresponds with the view that companies from that country *never* bribe abroad and a 0 corresponds with the view that they *always* do.

Table 17.1 The 2011 Transparency International Bribe Payers' Index

Rank	*Country/Territory*	*Score*	*Number of Observations*	*Standard Deviation*	*90% Confidence Interval*	
					Lower Bound	*Upper Bound*
1	Netherlands	8.8	273	2.0	8.6	9.0
1	Switzerland	8.8	244	2.2	8.5	9.0
3	Belgium	8.7	221	2.0	8.5	9.0
4	Germany	8.6	576	2.2	8.5	8.8
4	Japan	8.6	319	2.4	8.4	8.9
6	Australia	8.5	168	2.2	8.2	8.8
6	Canada	8.5	209	2.3	8.2	8.8
8	Singapore	8.3	256	2.3	8.1	8.6
8	United Kingdom	8.3	414	2.5	8.1	8.5
10	United States	8.1	651	2.7	7.9	8.3
11	France	8.0	435	2.6	7.8	8.2
11	Spain	8.0	326	2.6	7.7	8.2
13	South Korea	7.9	152	2.8	7.5	8.2
14	Brazil	7.7	163	3.0	7.3	8.1
15	Hong Kong	7.6	208	2.9	7.3	7.9
15	Italy	7.6	397	2.8	7.4	7.8
15	Malaysia	7.6	148	2.9	7.2	8.0
15	South Africa	7.6	191	2.8	7.2	7.9
19	Taiwan	7.5	193	3.0	7.2	7.9
19	India	7.5	168	3.0	7.1	7.9
19	Turkey	7.5	139	2.7	7.2	7.9
22	Saudi Arabia	7.4	138	3.0	7.0	7.8
23	Argentina	7.3	115	3.0	6.8	7.7
23	United Arab Emirates	7.3	156	2.9	6.9	7.7
25	Indonesia	7.1	153	3.4	6.6	7.5
26	Mexico	7.0	121	3.2	6.6	7.5
27	China	6.5	608	3.5	6.3	6.7
28	Russia	6.1	172	3.6	5.7	6.6
	Average	7.8				

Reproduced with the kind permission of Transparency International, the 2011 Bribe Payers Index appears above.

Again, this list may be of benefit to firms in developing risk-based criteria. As you can see, the bribes are paid by people in countries which you might consider as being relatively well regulated. It is the countries that are poorly regulated which are the recipients of such funds.

17.10 THE GLOBAL NATURE OF CORRUPTION

Many of the cases we have referred to in this chapter have taken place in the UK or USA. This is purely due to the level of publicity that such cases make in these countries, rendering the cases publicly available. However, no country can be certain that it will not have an unscrupulous PEP. Consider the following recent Chinese case.

In September 2012, a township official in Beijing appropriated over 38 million yuan ($6.03 million) from a demolition compensation fund set up for two highway construction projects. He lent more than 178 million yuan of public money to several property developers, and abused his political power to help two companies get business contracts and land. In return, he was gifted access to 80,000 yuan as well as goods to almost twice that value.

People in public office sometimes appear to think that they can get away with it, or that they are in some way entitled to take advantage of their position. The concern for the financial institution is that they do need to do sufficient investigation and ongoing monitoring (see Chapter 22) to enable them to provide their regulators or enforcement authorities with sufficient evidence that they undertook adequate due diligence. If they have done what was expected, then they should not receive any sanction from the regulators. Accordingly, enhanced due diligence is clearly what is required to be conducted in such cases.

18 NON-FACE-TO-FACE CUSTOMERS

18.1 WHO ARE NON-FACE-TO-FACE CUSTOMERS?

A non-face-to-face transaction is where a transaction occurs without a customer having to be physically present. Examples of this type of activity include internet banking, telephone banking, credit cards and online share dealing. Non-face-to-face business is becoming increasingly popular in the financial services industry due to increased customer demand, the high costs of maintaining personal customer contact services and the ability to transact from a distance, which has been facilitated by developments in technology and telecommunications.

It is generally agreed that non-face-to-face transactions are more risky than face-to-face transactions, since the primary identification measures which must be carried out cannot include matching the face of the customer with a document. To overcome this, in some countries it is commonplace for there to be requirements for the customer to visit a branch to have their identity confirmed. However, in other countries this is not the case and the financial institution will need to assess the level of risk that the relationship poses to the firm in deciding which procedures to adopt.

Clearly, it is still possible, even with a customer-facing transaction, for identification fraud to be perpetrated. Much of the identification work is designed to link the person that is in front of the firm's employee with some form of official identification documentation which includes the customer's face. This does not actually prove that the customer is as expected, rather only that the person appearing for identification is the same as the person in the picture that appears on the official document, which might itself be forged.

However, non-face-to-face transactions aggravate the risks involved in financial transactions in a number of ways. Firstly, the financial institution actually will never have met the customer. Not only would they not know what the customer looked like, but they would also not generally have received official documents that confirm the picture of the customer and link this to the address, date of birth and other relevant details. This is due to the unwillingness of customers to part with such high-risk documents by sending them to a remote location.

The following factors all contribute to the additional risks that are involved in a firm undertaking business with customers on a non-face-to-face basis:

- The ease by which the customer will have access to the facility, regardless of time and location, with a minimum of controls in operation.
- The ease of making multiple fictitious applications without the customer incurring extra costs or there being a significant risk of detection by the firm.

- The absence of physical documents. This is not only the absence of any identification documents, but also the absence of signed contractual documentation; although some firms do request that documents should be signed and posted back. The firm, of course, has no way of verifying the signature!
- The speed at which electronic transactions are undertaken also renders it difficult to verify data prior to a transaction being committed to. Controls generally only operate in arrears and would have the effect of recording the inappropriate transaction.

18.2 ADDITIONAL MEASURES FOR NON-FACE-TO-FACE CUSTOMERS

Any firm that is engaged in non-face-to-face business activity will need to develop a series of appropriate risk-based policies and procedures to ensure that adequate controls are actually applied in practice. The nature of such additional procedures required will, of course, vary depending on the nature and scope of the non-face-to-face activities. The type of issues that a firm should consider will include the following:

- The firm still needs to think about how it will identify the customer. This may involve receiving some form of documentation or taking additional steps seeking independent data for verification. At the very least, if taking a deposit they will need to think how they would be able to provide the funds back to the customer in the absence of robust identification procedures having been conducted.
- The nature of supplementary measures to verify or certify the documents supplied or requiring confirmatory certification will also vary depending on the jurisdiction. There may be independent data that serve this purpose, for example electoral roll data or credit reference agency search information. It is the combination of data from various sources which potentially provides the required level of additional assurance.
- The firm will undertake work to consider the nature of the payment profile of the customer. Typically, they will require the first payment resulting from the operation of the account to be carried out through an account opened in the customer's name with a prime bank. The non-face-to-face firm is, therefore, trying to gain some level of assurance from the work conducted by a firm that does maintain a face-to-face relationship with the client. In doing this, the bank will need to assess whether it is satisfied with the quality of the bank in which the account is placed, and many restrict such activity to a bank based in their own jurisdiction which is known to maintain high-quality controls.

18.3 RISK-BASED APPROACH TO NON-FACE-TO-FACE CUSTOMERS

The extent to which additional money-laundering-deterrence measures need to be carried out should be judged through the application of the risk-based approach. The extent of verification that will actually be conducted will, therefore, depend on the nature and characteristics of the product or service requested and the firm's assessment of the money-laundering risk presented by the customer.

While we have so far concentrated on retail customers, you do need to recognise that in some parts of the industry it is normal for the customer not to be present – in wholesale markets, for example. In such cases, the focus needs to be on identifying that the financial institution is the firm that it purports to be and that the officer has the authority to bind the firm. Again, it is necessary to ensure that the named subsidiary of a bank is actually known by the holding company, since this has been abused in a number of cases. Whilst additional procedures are implemented, such circumstances do not, in themselves, increase the risk of money laundering in a transaction. Therefore, firms need to be able to judge for themselves which transactions appear to represent a higher risk of money laundering or terrorist financing and develop appropriate systems and procedures to enable them to do this.

One particular additional area of concern is customers that appear to be deliberately avoiding face-to-face contact. If such a scenario were to occur, it would be advisable for firms to have a clear and appropriate policy to deal with such circumstances, particularly systems and procedures as mentioned above. We would generally recommend that any such cases should be rejected and the customer potentially reported to the relevant authority.

18.4 THE PROBLEMS OF BUYING ONLINE

Sir Tim Berners-Lee, inventor of the internet, was reported as having been conned online when he bought a Christmas present from an online shop which failed to arrive. After telephoning the number from the website, he found that the number did not exist and the company was, in fact, a fake. Around one in four internet users in the UK have fallen victim to online phishing scams that attempt to steal people's financial details, while one in six have fallen victim to other types of online fraud.

Clearly, if you are dealing online with a firm you have not heard of, conducting basic due diligence is required, and this might well include calling the number on a website or seeing if there is any evidence that people have had problems with the firm. Sometimes, things you acquire may not be what you expect and e-auction sites enable such activity to continue. There is always a limit to the level of due diligence that appears appropriate given the size of a transaction, but it is this fact that the unscrupulous use to extract monies illegally.

This, again, highlights that, just by doing some basic due diligence procedures on attempting to really know your customer, you may be able to identify an illegal transaction. In this case, some financial institution would have been banking and transferring the sums resulting from the fraudulent site, which would clearly be caught by the regulations. Consequently, it is also incumbent upon firms to take care in monitoring the activity of any company which undertakes a high level of online trading in case it is also operating illegally.

18.5 FATF GUIDANCE

In October 2010 the FATF published a report on *Money Laundering using New Payment Methods* (http://www.fatf-gafi.org/media/fatf/documents/reports/ML%20using%20New%20Payment%20Methods.pdf). This highlighted some cases of recent concern, including the following:

Case 1

In 2007, two defendants were prosecuted for purchasing closed-loop prepaid gift cards with stolen credit card account information. The defendants used the gift cards to purchase merchandise, which they then returned to the store in exchange for new gift cards, or they sold the merchandise for cash. Because the new prepaid cards were not linked to the stolen credit card account numbers, they were not affected when the theft of the credit card information was discovered. The defendants were convicted and ordered to pay US$82,000 in restitution. One defendant was convicted of conspiracy and fraud and sentenced to 45 months' imprisonment and three years' supervised release. The other defendant was convicted of conspiracy and money laundering and sentenced to five months' imprisonment and three years' supervised release.

Source: United States.

Case 2

Law-enforcement information indicated that the owner of a prepaid phone card company was suspected of money laundering and having links to a terrorist organisation. The owner made many large cash deposits into personal and business bank accounts and, when questioned, would indicate that prepaid phone cards were sold to retailers and convenience stores, and cash payments were received instead of cheques. This was apparently due to the fact that the owner was not confident that cheques would be honoured.

Some of the deposits were also made into accounts held by prepaid phone card suppliers. Electronic funds transfers were also ordered by the owner to the benefit of individuals in Europe and the Middle East, sometimes through accounts which previously had not seen much activity. The owner was also the beneficiary of funds ordered by the same individuals.

Source: Canada.

The FATF categorised non-face-to-face internet payment methods into three groups:

- Online banking, where credit institutions offer online access to traditional banking services based on an account held at the credit institution in the customer's name. Online banking was outside the scope of the FATF document.
- Prepaid internet payment products, where firms which may not be credit institutions allow customers to send or receive funds through a virtual, prepaid account, accessed via the internet.
- Digital currencies, where customers typically purchase units of digital currencies or precious metals which can either be exchanged between account holders of the same service or exchanged against real currencies and withdrawn.

This report provides an analysis of many of the problems faced in practice, with guidance provided where appropriate or available. The importance of monitoring is highlighted, since the paper states that monitoring systems can be a very effective tool to mitigate financial crime risk.

To be effective, such systems must, at a minimum, allow the provider to identify:

- Discrepancies, for example between submitted customer information and the IP address;
- Unusual or suspicious transactions;
- Cases where the same account is used by multiple users;
- Cases where the same user opens multiple accounts;
- Cases where several products are funded by the same source.

Where products benefit from customer due diligence exemptions, systems should detect where a customer approaches a limit (on one product/transaction or cumulatively) beyond which full customer due diligence has to be applied.

The report recognises that value and transaction limits can also be a very powerful risk mitigant as they render a product less attractive to money launderers, especially when coupled with effective monitoring systems and procedures that prevent multiple purchases of low-value cards or multiple low-value accounts for a single customer. For example, the restrictive value limits implemented by most mobile payment service providers are thought to be one of the main reasons that so few money-laundering case studies involving mobile payments have been detected so far. Of course, the fact that they have not been detected does not mean that they are not happening.

The paper indicated a number of red flags, particularly when operating cross-border. Red flags are indicators of suspicious activity where a product's actual use deviates from its intended use or does not make economic sense. For example, cash withdrawals in foreign jurisdictions will be expected where the product is a prepaid traveller card, but unusual where the product is marketed to minors. Red flags should, therefore, not be applied unthinkingly, but tailored to the product's characteristics.

The following are examples identified in the paper:

- Discrepancies between the information submitted by the customer and information detected by monitoring systems.
- Individuals who hold an unusual volume of internet accounts with the same provider.
- A large and diverse source of funds (i.e. bank transfers, credit card and cash funding from different locations) used to fund the same account(s).
- Multiple reference bank accounts from banks located in various cities used to fund the same account.
- Loading or funding of account always done by third parties.

- Numerous cash loadings, just under the reporting threshold of US$10,000 (i.e. structured loading of prepaid cards), of the same prepaid card(s), conducted by the same individual(s) on a number of occasions.
- Multiple third party funding activities of an account, followed by the immediate transfer of funds to unrelated bank account(s).
- Multiple loading or funding of the same accounts, followed by ATM withdrawals shortly afterwards, over a short period of time.
- Multiple withdrawals conducted at different ATMs (sometimes located in various countries different from the jurisdiction where the account was funded).
- Internet payment account only used for withdrawals, and not for online purchases.
- Atypical use of the payment product (including unexpected and frequent cross-border access or transactions).
- Large number of bank accounts held by the same prepaid card company (sometimes in different countries) apparently used as flow-through accounts (may be indicative of layering activity).
- Prepaid card company located in one country but holding accounts in other countries (unexplained business rationale which could be suspicious).
- Back and forth movement of funds between bank accounts held by different prepaid card companies located in different countries (may be indicative of layering activity as it does not fit the business model).
- The volume and frequency of cash transactions (sometimes structured below the reporting threshold) conducted by the owner of a prepaid card company do not make economic sense.

As always with any such list there could be legitimate reasons for the transactions to be conducted. The red flag will require the firm to conduct investigation, and should not, in itself, create a suspicion.

Among the various issues considered in the paper were exemption from verification. The paper concludes that the overall risks of a product or service can also be mitigated by other means, such as applying account and transaction limits. Imposing very restrictive limits on the transactions or other functionalities may have an even more deterring effect to would-be launderers than the prospect of being verified. Furthermore, intensive monitoring can help mitigate the money-laundering risk of products as well.

In some jurisdictions, verification of the customer's identity may be difficult to accomplish, especially where identification documentation or other reliable documentation is not available for a great part of the population. Verification can also prove to be a financial burden for institutions or customers (e.g. where customers must travel a long distance to the bank or vice versa to be verified), deterring customers and institutions alike, and potentially endangering the economic success of the service provider.

The paper reported that case studies indicated that criminals were able to launder money even where verification had taken place, e.g. by using stolen or fake identities, or strawmen.

When considering the exemption from identification issues, the paper stated that, unlike verification, identification does not seem to cause a lot of cost or effort; the service provider simply needs to ask the customer's name.

19 SUSPICIOUS CONDUCT AND TRANSACTIONS

19.1 INTRODUCTION

What is suspicious activity? The problem is that while it might be easy to see with hindsight, the question is whether there are signals which can be identified in advance. Both society at large and regulators are increasingly expecting a firm to have adequate procedures to detect suspicious activity, both when taking on an account and also when operating client activity. Many regulators actually publish lists of transactions that they consider are such that they should result in a firm becoming suspicious, but these can only ever be a subset of the type of transactions that are likely to be of concern in practice. The problem is that the expectation that is being placed on financial institutions may well exceed their ability to identify suspicious transactions, since the nature of suspicion itself is such a difficult concept to apply in practice.

Of course, a transaction that might appear suspicious to one person may appear commonplace to another. For many people, derivatives transactions, for example, appear suspicious, yet to others they are commonplace. The wealthy may borrow monies when they actually have assets available, for convenience. Such behaviour might appear bizarre to someone without such assets. Indeed, employees of the firm being familiar with the nature of business being conducted may have the effect of reducing the likelihood of a suspicion being identified.

Identifying, investigating and documenting a suspicion is always likely to be a problem for a bank. If an employee becomes suspicious regarding a particular transaction, then the firm is clearly under an obligation to undertake an additional review to establish whether there are actually grounds for true suspicion and that consequent suspicious activity (SAR) reporting is necessary. The process adopted needs to be formally documented, with the reasons for reporting, or not reporting, the transaction being clearly set out.

Reporting may be required to provide protection to the bank against future potential legal actions or against claims from a regulator that they have failed to do what was required of them. The investigation undertaken by the firm needs to be conducted without the customer becoming aware that a potential review into a possible case of money laundering is being undertaken, since this would fall within the definition of tipping off (see Chapter 23).

If there is an obvious case where there definitely is a suspicion, then the position could be even worse. Nothing can be done by either the MLRO or the firm that would, in any way, cause the customer to consider that they might be the subject of a SAR, since this again would represent tipping off, which is a criminal offence in most countries.

However, there is also an obligation under most regulations to make full and complete disclosure. Accordingly, great care needs to be taken by both the MLRO and the firm to make sure that all actions are appropriate and consistent with the legislation. This is normally best achieved by having a robust series of policies and procedures that are applied rigorously, with clear audit trails being maintained to document the actions and decisions taken in practice.

19.2 WHAT IS A SUSPICIOUS TRANSACTION?

The following are examples of potentially suspicious activities that might raise initial concerns. They would, therefore, indicate that the transactions are worthy of further investigation to determine whether the transactions or activities reflect illicit activities rather than legitimate business activities and whether a SAR should be filed. A transaction meeting the requirements stated below will not definitely be either money laundering or terrorist financing, rather the transaction will have the symptoms of what might be considered a high-risk transaction that warrants additional investigation. Just meeting the requirements below will not, in itself, result in a suspicion; additional work still needs to be conducted.

- A customer opens a greater number of different accounts than would be expected for the type of business they are purportedly conducting and/or frequently transfers funds among those accounts.
- A customer's corporate account(s) has deposits or withdrawals primarily in cash rather than cheques or other types of transfer.
- When a bank expects a customer to want cash given the nature of their activity and the customer fails to make such a request, then this will also cause concerns. For example, the owner of both a retail business and a cheque-cashing service that does not ask for cash when depositing cheques will possibly indicate the availability of another source of cash, which could, of course, be illegitimate.
- Any unusual pattern of cash transactions will alert the bank to potential concerns. If the customer engages in unusual activity in cash purchases of traveller's cheques, money orders or cashier's cheques, then this is likely to be an area requiring investigation.
- Activity that is inconsistent with the bank's understanding of the customer will always be a cause for concern. For example, if a customer deposits a large volume of cashier's cheques, money orders and/or wire transfers into an account when the nature of the account holder's business would not appear to justify such activity, then further reviews would be required.
- Generally, if a customer frequently makes large dollar transactions (such as deposits, withdrawals or purchases of monetary instruments) without an explanation as to how they will be used in the business, or the purchases allegedly are for a business that generally does not deal in large amounts of cash, then investigation will be required.
- If there is a business account history that shows little or no regular, periodic activity, or the account appears to be used primarily as a temporary repository for funds that

are transferred abroad, then this will be considered high risk. For example, if the account has numerous deposits of cash which are then followed by a single lump-sum wire transfer overseas, this could be disguising drug trafficking.

- The bank should always wonder why the account has been brought to it. Accordingly, if a customer's place of business or residence is outside the financial institution's normal service area, this is likely to raise concerns and require enhanced due diligence to be conducted.

- Understanding your customer is paramount and there cannot be any replacement for such analysis. What is unusual will need to be judged against the nature of the activity conducted. For many firms, a corporate customer that frequently makes large cash deposits and maintains high balances, but does not use other banking services would alert the firm to the need to carry out additional investigation.

- Similarly, a retail business that routinely makes numerous deposits of cheques, but rarely makes cash withdrawals for daily operations would appear to be unusual activity. Likewise, a retail business that has dramatically different patterns of cash deposits from similar businesses in the same general location might indicate that matters are not quite what they seem.

- In terms of layering of money laundering this may arise from an international transfer in an unusual currency. Generally, if the currency transaction patterns of a business experience a sudden and inconsistent change from normal activities, it would be expected that this would be identified by the firm and reviews conducted.

- For customers where there is a high level of knowledge, it may be possible that even greater levels of identification could be undertaken. For example, if the amount and frequency of cash deposits are inconsistent with those observed at the customer's place of business, this might alert the firm to some concern. Similarly, if the business frequently deposits large amounts of cash, but cheques or other debits drawn against the account are inconsistent with the customer's retail business, this should be checked out.

- If a business that does not normally generate overseas currency suddenly starts to make numerous currency transactions (i.e. a sanitation company that makes numerous deposits of cash), then this should be identified and reviewed.

- Sometimes criminals will try to identify a weakness in a control environment which they are able to exploit to disguise their activities. Accordingly, financial transactions involving monetary instruments that are either incomplete or contain fictitious payees, remitters, etc., if known, will be of particular concern.

- Generally, transactions which do not appear to have a commercial basis will be a cause for concern. For example, unusual transfers of funds among related accounts or accounts that involve the same principal or related principals should be investigated.

- If a business owner, such as an owner who has only one store, makes several deposits the same day using different bank branches, then this will be highly unusual. However, if the same customer uses accounts at a number of different banks, then they would be unlikely to be identified.

19.3 AVOIDING A NATIONAL REPORTING OR RECORD-KEEPING REQUIREMENT

If transactions look like they are being organised to try to avoid a record-keeping or reporting requirement, then this should also be a cause for potential concern. Even though there may be good commercial reasons for such activity, a higher level of investigation will be required. These requirements may be national, regulatory or generated by the policies and procedures of the institution concerned. All that is required is that they have been brought to the attention of the potential criminal.

Typical examples of transactions that might cause concern and warrant additional investigation include the following:

- Any business or new customer that asks to be exempted from policies or procedures, which are generally known in the market or are required by rules and regulations, would clearly provide reasons for investigation.
- A customer that intentionally appears to withhold part of a currency deposit or withdrawal to keep the transaction under the reporting threshold should be identified by software designed for this purpose. It suggests that the customer is aware of a reporting threshold and is attempting to avoid detection by acting below it.
- If a customer is reluctant to provide the information needed to file any form of mandatory report, to have the report filed or to proceed with a transaction after being informed that the report must be filed, then there is unlikely to be an innocent reason for this. Accordingly, such accounts should be investigated.
- Similarly, if a customer or group tries to coerce a bank employee into not filing any required record-keeping or reporting forms, then this would immediately ring alarm bells and would require investigation.
- The customer may try to avoid face-to-face contact to avoid detection. Consequently, if a customer uses an automatic teller machine or machines (ATMs) to make several bank deposits or withdrawals just below a specified threshold, then this would be cause for concern.
- Failure to provide identification documents that should be easily available will also raise concern. For example, a customer that is reluctant to furnish identification when purchasing negotiable instruments in significant amounts would obviously represent an account worthy of investigation.

This is, of course, just a small subset of the type of transactions that might give rise to concerns, and each firm needs to produce a list to set out what might be appropriate in their specific circumstances. This needs to be tailored to the specific needs of the business and to be as relevant as possible, such that staff both understand the issue and know what to do.

19.4 WIRE OR FUND TRANSFERS

Any transaction that reduces the level of review that can be undertaken prior to a transaction actually taking place and funds being transferred must be a cause for additional concern to a financial institution. Clearly, wire or fund transfers fall into this category due to the speed with which such funds can be transferred to a third party and moved around the system. Increasingly, regulators have become concerned with such transactions, which form part of the layering process within the money-laundering landscape.

In this area, examples of transactions that might create concerns and warrant additional investigation include the following:

- Wire transfer activity to/from financial secrecy haven countries without an apparent business reason or when it is inconsistent with the customer's business or history. Recognise that such havens may be used legitimately as part of taxation or estate planning and therefore it is important to understand the nature of the customer's business in such cases.
- Periodic wire transfers from a personal account(s) to bank secrecy haven countries may also be indicative of inappropriate conduct, with taxation evasion perhaps being a prime cause. However, again, estate and legitimate taxation planning could also be involved, so not all such cases will actually result in confirmed suspicions.
- Large incoming wire transfers on behalf of a foreign client with little or no explicit reason will need investigation. Diligent clients notify their bank in advance if any such case occurs, but many will fail to do so. Attempting to obtain necessary information may prove difficult in such cases and the risk of tipping off is enhanced.
- Large, round transaction amounts, for example $1 million or £500,000, may also be a concern unless it is known that the client regularly does business in such amounts.
- Funds transferred in and out of an account on the same day or within a relatively short period of time (say five working days) should be reported by relevant software systems. It might suggest that money-laundering layering is taking place, although it may also suggest that the customer is using another bank for other purposes.
- Payments or receipts with no apparent links to legitimate contracts, goods or services would obviously be a concern. For example, if a UK retailer suddenly made a large deposit in rands, you would expect suspicions to arise.
- Transfers routed through multiple foreign or domestic banks without any obvious reason would again suggest that money-laundering layering was being conducted.
- Likewise, unexplained repetitive or unusual patterns of activity should be investigated, again without alerting the client to the nature of the investigation. Using customer relationship management techniques may elicit the required information, suggesting that the fees may have been unduly high and enabling greater information to be obtained.
- Depositing of funds into several accounts, usually in relatively small but regular amounts, which are consolidated subsequently into one master account and transferred, often outside of the country, should alert the firm to suspicion. There could be legitimate reasons, for example a newspaper vendor with family overseas seeking to remit funds home. However, this could also be retail drug vending with money-laundering layering following, which would warrant investigation.
- Instructions to a financial institution to wire or transfer funds abroad and to expect an incoming wire or transfer of funds (in an equal amount) from other sources again might be warning the firm of layering. It could also be that inappropriate payments

are being made to third parties and being reimbursed, which at the very least might represent reputational risk.

- Regular deposits or withdrawals of large amounts of cash, using wire transfers to, from or through countries that either are known sources of narcotics or whose laws are ineffective in controlling the laundering of money would obviously need to be investigated.

19.5 INSUFFICIENT OR SUSPICIOUS INFORMATION BY A CUSTOMER

It may well be that the customer, in providing the data requested by the financial institution, inadvertently creates a form of suspicion. This may result, for example, from the customer providing the firm with data which makes little or no apparent sense given the nature of the activity conducted by the customer. Alternatively, there may be reluctance on the part of the customer to provide certain information.

The firm must recognise that the customer's reluctance may be natural concern that the data are unnecessary for the bank's purpose and might lead to more marketing activity, rather than criminal activity. Furthermore, it also needs to be recognised that a high-quality money launderer always has the best quality documentation, so absence of documentation rarely catches professional money laundering.

However, there are signs that might give rise to concern and should be identified by the financial institution, leading to further investigation being conducted. These include the following:

- The reluctance of a business that is establishing a new account to provide complete information about the purpose of business, its prior banking relationships, names of its officers and directors and information about the location of the business.
- A customer's refusal to provide the usual information necessary to qualify for credit or other banking services.
- A spike in the customer's activity with little or no explanation.
- A customer's desire to open an account without providing references, a local address or adequate identification as required by market practice or local legislation or regulation; or a refusal to provide any other information the financial institution requires to open an account.
- Unusual or suspicious identification documents that the financial institution cannot readily verify.
- The discovery that a customer's home/business phone is disconnected.
- No record of past or present employment for a customer on a loan application.
- A customer makes frequent or large transactions and has no record of past or present employment experience that would be consistent with such activity.
- The customer's background is at variance with his or her business activities.
- The customer's financial statements differ from those of similar businesses.

Of course, each of these may actually occur for a legitimate reason and alone will not be sufficient to raise a suspicion requiring reporting. However, collectively, after investigation or in combination given the nature of the customer's business or activity, they may provide causes for greater investigation to be undertaken.

19.6 OTHER SUSPICIOUS CUSTOMER ACTIVITY

Suspicion is always difficult to define. Effectively, the institution will generally know it when it happens, but the following is a summary list of issues which might at least provide sufficient evidence to warrant some additional level of investigation:

- Substantial deposit(s) of high denomination paper money.
- Mailing address outside the normal jurisdiction or business area of the institution.
- Frequent exchanges of small currency amounts for larger denominations.
- Certificate(s) of deposit or other investment vehicle used as loan collateral.
- A large loan is suddenly paid down with no reasonable explanation of the source of funds.
- Frequent deposits of large amounts of currency wrapped in currency straps that have been stamped by other banks.
- Frequent deposits of currency wrapped in currency straps or currency wrapped in rubber bands that are disorganised and do not balance when counted.
- Frequent deposits of musty or extremely dirty bills.
- A customer who purchases cashier's cheques, money orders and other monetary instruments with large amounts of cash.
- A professional service provider, such as a lawyer, accountant or broker, who makes substantial deposits of cash into client accounts or in-house company accounts, such as trust accounts and escrow accounts.
- A customer insists on meeting bank personnel at a location other than their place of business.
- Domestic bank accounts opened in the name of a *casa de cambio* (money exchange house), followed by suspicious wire transfers and/or structured deposits (under a specified threshold) into these accounts.
- Suspicious movements of funds from one bank into another bank and back into the first bank.
- Offshore companies, especially those located in bank secrecy haven countries, asking for a loan from a domestic bank, or for a loan secured by obligations of offshore banks.
- Use of loan proceeds in a manner inconsistent with the stated loan purpose.
- A person or business that does not hold an account and that purchases a monetary instrument with large denominated bills.

- A customer who purchases a number of cashier's cheques, money orders or traveller's cheques for large amounts under a specified threshold, or without apparent reason.
- Couriers, rather than personal account customers, make the deposits into the account.
- Money orders deposited by mail, which are numbered sequentially or have unusual symbols or stamps on them.

Of course, again, there could easily be a legitimate reason for each of the transactions. We are not suggesting that they amount to money laundering, rather that they could be money laundering. This would always mean that additional review processes should be conducted.

Clearly, these can only represent a small sample of the type of transactions that might provide a financial institution with cause for concern. What is important is for the firm to make sure that its staff is aware of the type of things they should look out for and for them then to know the actions to be taken in such circumstances. There is clearly a requirement for consistency throughout the banking business, regardless of the nature of activity being conducted. There is little point in a financial institution effectively moving the money launderer from an area where there are high levels of control operating to another area where the controls are perhaps of a lower quality.

There is also the requirement that adequate documentation should be maintained by the firm at such a level as is consistent with the local rules and regulations, together with any group rules. This is both to meet the supervisory requirements and also to support any future investigation that may be conducted.

Generally, financial institutions will make use of some form of software to provide the analysis that they require. Typical software will select a number of these potential transactions and then codify them into specific scenarios that can be applied generally. Accordingly, the codification of the scenario needs to be sufficiently detailed to ensure that the correct transactions are identified and the minimum number of transactions selected for investigation, which eventually are found not to create a suspicion (so-called false positives). A suite of scenarios is therefore required which will need to be back-tested to see if, had they been in existence at that time, they would have actually identified true cases of money laundering of which the institution is aware. In many countries, specific regulators provide reports on the types of transactions which are currently being encountered. Any such material should be included in local training programmes and promptly disseminated to relevant front-line staff.

There needs to be a regular review of all such scenarios to see that they are complete and continue to meet the ongoing needs of the business. It needs to be recognised that money launderers tend to be highly sophisticated and will take advantage of new products that may provide opportunities for money laundering prior to the institution instigating additional money-laundering controls in such areas. The skills of the quality money launderer should never be underestimated; therefore, a regular and at least annual review of the adequacy of scenarios does need to take place.

19.7 THE ROLE OF INTERNAL AUDIT

The programme of money-laundering deterrence implemented by the firm should be subject to review by internal audit. Such work should seek to establish that the firm has sufficient controls in place to ensure that the requirements of the jurisdiction are complied with. Accordingly, the audit should commence with a review of the policies and procedures adopted.

The auditor will be seeking to establish that there has been an adequate legal or compliance review conducted to ensure that such procedures are up to date and accurate, complying with local requirements. Where appropriate, international requirements should also be reviewed by an individual with the necessary skills to identify problems. The auditor will be seeking evidence that such an investigation and review has been conducted, but will rarely check such legislation themselves, due to a general lack of the specialist skills required.

The next stage of the work will be to assess the monitoring procedures conducted by the firm. Such work will be incorporated into a number of audits conducted by the firm, and therefore the internal auditor will need to ensure that sufficient work is conducted in all such assignments at the planning stage of the work.

Another piece of work will need to consider the procedures leading to the identification of suspicious transactions. If software is used by the firm to identify suspicions, the auditor will need to ensure that the software has been applied against the complete population of relevant transactions. Failure to do this completeness testing could result in a set of transactions or processes being ignored and not reviewed by the software.

Next, the auditor will need to understand the algorithms within the software to establish that the right population is actually being reported. Just because the procedural documentation states that a particular algorithm is being applied, does not mean that in practice it is being applied. Accordingly, the auditor will need to undertake a level of reperformance here to ensure that the programmed software complies with the documentation provided.

Another piece of work will be on the suspicious activity reporting programme. The auditor will seek to establish that all suspicious transactions identified were reviewed prior to being reported to the relevant authority and that all such work is properly recorded. Any cases where the transaction was not reported should be clearly explained to ensure that nothing is being hidden by the firm.

The auditor will also need to assess the adequacy of the staff training conducted by the firm. Such training should be seen to be relevant to the audience and a record maintained which seeks to document that learning objectives have been achieved.

20 UNUSUAL TRANSACTIONS

20.1 THE IDENTIFICATION OF UNUSUAL TRANSACTIONS

Regulations make it clear that staff will be held accountable if they fail to recognise an unusual transaction or arrangement where they have reasonable grounds to know or suspect money-laundering activity. This means that there will always need to be clarity and training for staff to enable them both to understand their obligations and also to make sure that they conduct the procedures expected of them in an appropriate way.

Each firm will need to provide clear guidance to all of its employees to enable them to detect those unusual transactions which they are required to identify, or which pose a reputational risk to the firm. Again, it is important to recognise that the identification of an unusual transaction will not, in itself, necessarily mean that money laundering or terrorist financing has actually been detected. There may, indeed, be an innocent explanation for the activity. The identification of an unusual transaction should, however, alert the employee to the need to conduct some form of additional procedure, potentially leading to the identification and reporting of an actual suspicion.

The investigation procedures to be adopted are discussed in the next chapter, but these can only follow from alert monitoring, whether conducted by using software solutions or through attentive employee engagement. In this chapter we focus on the role of the employee in identification of suspicions.

To ensure that employees are fully aware of what actually represents unusual activity, a clear series of policies needs to be developed, supported by appropriate procedures and systems. Training needs to be implemented which enables employees to appreciate what might be the type of unusual transaction that they are most likely to encounter in the ordinary course of their business. This training needs to be as relevant as possible to the nature of the business that the employee actually undertakes. The employee needs to be able to receive information from a customer without reacting in such a way that the customer would immediately recognise that they were being considered a money launderer or terrorist financer. This needs real training, including role plays, to provide the employee with the experience that they require. More on this later.

20.2 THE DEVELOPMENT OF POLICY

The unusual transaction policy will need to be easily understood by all employees, so it needs to be written in a language that they are able to relate to. Jargon must be avoided at all costs and the policy needs to be relevant as well as being consistent with the requirements of relevant authorities.

The policy will also need to include sufficient information to make it clear to the employee exactly what the requirements that are to be complied with consist of. The following is what you might expect to find in a typical example of a relatively short, high-level money-laundering-deterrence policy:

- Local compliance or the respective country AML officers, where applicable, should ensure that ongoing account and transaction monitoring is conducted to detect unusual or suspicious activities.
- Each business line should be responsible for monitoring all its customers and their financial behaviour. The business lines' management therefore should be aware of significant transactions and any increased activity in the accounts of their customers. Irregular behaviour (especially unusual or suspicious activities) by a customer should be recognised immediately by the relevant business line. In order to increase the efficiency of customer monitoring, all legal means available to the business unit should be utilised, where possible.
- An unusual or a suspicious activity is defined as a transaction which cannot be explained in any logical way (whether objectively or by the customer). Unusual or suspicious activities may include:
  - undertaking account transactions or other activities which are not consistent with the profile of the customer or its group members;
  - conducting transactions over a certain specified amount, as set out in business unit processes and procedures;
  - evidence of breaking up amounts before transfer or receipt without a logical explanation or clear business purpose;
  - the transfer of company funds to private accounts or vice versa;
  - the offering or acceptance of irregular transaction conditions; and
  - the occurrence of any prevailing indicators of unusual or suspicious activities which have been set out by the home or host country authorities.

What this simplified policy combines is the obligations that exist on specific employees, together with information that they may require to enable them to know precisely what this means. We would expect this to be supplemented by a series of real-life examples which highlight the specific actions that a particular firm should be required to take. This should be sufficient to enable the employee to judge whether additional investigation is actually required in the circumstances envisaged.

20.3 MONEY-LAUNDERING CONTROL

Most institutions also have a public statement that they make to highlight the importance they place on financial crime deterrence and to show that they wholeheartedly support international measures to deter financial crime. A typical statement would appear as follows:

> *"Legislation across the group pertaining to money-laundering and terrorist-financing control imposes significant requirements in terms of customer*

identification, record-keeping and training, as well as obligations to detect, prevent and report money laundering and terrorist financing. The group is committed to continually improving its control measures. The group's money-laundering and terrorist-financing control policy is being amended to accommodate Financial Action Task Force and other best practice requirements.

Global financial crime remains a concern for financial regulators and the bank will continue to update and amend its financial crime deterrence processes and procedures to ensure that they sit at the forefront of international best practice in this regard."

20.4 COMPLIANCE RISK MANAGEMENT TRAINING

Most firms also make a public statement regarding the importance that they place on training their staff to understand both the importance of imposing appropriate systems of control to deter financial crime and being able to identify transactions which might require further investigation. Such a statement might appear as follows:

"Through ongoing training and internal publications, staff are made aware of their responsibilities in terms of legislative and regulatory requirements and developments. These cover topics as diverse as treating customers fairly, money laundering and terrorist financing, market conduct and health and safety requirements, among others."

The issues to be addressed here are the same for firms in all countries. No financial institution will wish to be involved directly in assisting money laundering or terrorist financing. The investigation costs that can result as a consequence of regulatory action, together with the loss of reputation, all serve to raise the importance of the issue of suspicion identification.

Staff will need to know how to deal with difficult customers or transactions and often how to buy themselves the time that they require to obtain such information as is needed. If a customer laughs when asked a question and says "Why are you asking me such a question – do you think I am a money launderer?" the employee must know the response to be provided. Generally, such a response will state that this is a procedure that is carried out by the firm in respect of all customers and that there is nothing that the customer should take from the question being asked. Standard policies and procedures are the key items that will assist the employee in such cases.

If the customer makes a statement which is clearly incorrect, then the employee must not react. They should record the information, only checking that the customer has not made a mistake by repeating the information back to them. Employees need to be able to remain straight-faced and, again, this requires training.

20.5 THE TYPES OF EVENTS THAT MIGHT CAUSE SUSPICION

There is no definitive list of all the types of transaction that could represent an "unusual transaction". The following is based upon a list prepared for the UK market by the Joint Money Laundering Steering Group but cannot be considered exhaustive. It does, however, provide an analysis of matters that should be considered and potentially included within the guidance provided to employees of a financial institution.

The type of things to look out for which may be unusual or could potentially give rise to knowledge or suspicion could include the following:

- Transactions which have no apparent purpose, or which make no obvious economic sense, including where a person makes a loss against tax.
- Transactions which appear to be unnecessarily complex given what is intended.
- The use of non-resident accounts, companies or structures in circumstances where the customer's needs do not appear to support such economic requirements.
- Where the transaction being requested by the customer, or the size or pattern of the transaction, is, without reasonable explanation, out of the ordinary range of services normally requested or is inconsistent with the experience of the firm in relation to the particular customer.
- Where the business unit is dealing with customers that would not normally be expected in that part of the business, either due to location or the nature of the activity conducted.
- Transfers to and from high-risk jurisdictions, without reasonable explanation, which are not consistent with the customer's known foreign business dealings or interests.
- Where a series of transactions appears to be structured just below a regulatory threshold with the intention of avoiding internal or regulatory reporting requirements.
- Where a customer who has entered into a business relationship with the firm only uses the relationship for a single transaction, or uses the facilities for only a very short period of time.
- The routing of funds through third party accounts without any obvious legitimate economic purpose.
- The customer undertaking unusual investment transactions without an apparently discernible profitable motive.

Of course, it will always be necessary to make these examples relevant to the reader of the policy, aligning the specific risk to the nature of the business activity undertaken. These examples could either be incorporated into the policy manual or the information could be provided through the medium of a tailored workshop. Without such tailoring, the employee will have little understanding of the relevance of the issue to the business that they are undertaking, with a consequence that the necessary monitoring will not be undertaken and the inappropriate activity will not be identified promptly, as required.

20.6 THE PROBLEMS OF CUSTOMER IDENTIFICATION

Employees must also be vigilant when looking at customer identification, as there are various scenarios which may highlight unusual behaviour and possible money-laundering activity. The customer identification process may raise specific concerns, and the type of things employees should consider will include the following:

- Has the customer refused, or appeared particularly reluctant, to provide the information requested without reasonable explanation?
- Do you understand the legal and corporate structure of the client entity, and its ownership and control, and does the structure appear to make sense?
- Are staff members aware of any inconsistencies between locations and other information provided?
- Is the area of residence given with other profile details, such as employment?
- Does an address appear vague or unusual – e.g. an accommodation agency, a professional registered office or a trading address?
- Does it make sense for the customer to be opening the account or relationship in the jurisdiction he is asking for?
- Is the information that the customer has provided consistent with the banking or other services or facilities that he is seeking?
- Does the supporting documentation add validity to the other information provided by the customer?
- Does the customer have other banking or financial relationships with the firm? Does the collected information on all these relationships appear consistent?
- Does the client want to conclude arrangements unusually urgently, against a promise to provide information at a later stage, which is not satisfactorily explained?
- Has the customer suggested changes to a proposed arrangement in order to avoid providing certain information?

Employees maintaining natural scepticism is key to a successful money-laundering-deterrence programme being effective. The type of customer that is likely to be a money launderer or involved with terrorist financing could easily be one of the best or most profitable customers that the business has. They could be using all of the services that the firm provides and not seem particularly concerned about the price. They are also likely to have perfect documents, indeed documents that might be considered as too perfect. So, it is not just the unusual that is an issue, the employee needs to have an awareness that there could be problems hidden inside even well-documented accounts.

The type of customer that does not have great documents is probably someone just like you. Someone that does not prepare for the meeting with the bank properly or did not have the time to find the right document, thinking that something that was to hand might just do.

20.7 WHAT MIGHT HIGHLIGHT TERRORIST ACTIVITY?

As we have seen, money laundering and terrorist financing are closely connected. Accordingly, staff must also be given guidance and examples of activities which suggest potential terrorist-financing activity, which might include the following:

- The presence of round sum deposits, followed by the same amount being transferred away as a wire transfer;
- Frequent international ATM activity;
- The absence of any known source of income;
- The use of wire transfers and the internet to move funds to and from high-risk countries and geographic locations;
- Frequent address changes;
- Purchases of military items or technology;
- Media reports on suspected, arrested terrorists or groups.

Of course, no such list can, in itself, ever be complete and address all issues. What is needed is for the MLRO, or another suitably experienced and independent unit, to look closely at the processes and procedures that are maintained by the firm to identify those areas of activity which are most susceptible to inappropriate activity. The attention of employees needs to be directed towards such areas which are inherently, therefore, more risky for the bank.

Whilst software solutions may enable a firm to identify the transactions that could potentially relate to money laundering or terrorist financing once they have been undertaken, the objective is, where possible, to avoid the firm undertaking such transactions. Accordingly, the first line of defence is the front-of-house staff of the firm, and therefore vigilance and training are always paramount.

Once a case is actually prosecuted and the name of the bank is included in reporting, there is rarely a caveat highlighting that the firm reported the transaction in accordance with the rules of the country. We know this as a firm from experience. I know it is not fair that when a firm undertakes all of the procedures that it should have conducted, that it is still included in an article including the name of the criminal, but that is, with regret, just life. That the firm undertook the required procedures is hardly newsworthy, while that it actually assisted the money launderer is. Accordingly, it is always better to avoid such relationships if that is possible.

21 INVESTIGATING SUSPICIONS

21.1 THE INVESTIGATION PROCESS

As discussed in the two previous chapters, the first stage of the process of identifying suspicions is the initial identification of a transaction. Following approved company policies, the staff member will then need to make a report to an appropriate officer of the firm. Once this initial report has been made to the appropriate officer, the next stage is for an initial investigation to be undertaken by the firm itself. The objective of this stage of the investigation process is to see whether there are actually sufficient suspicions to require this transaction or relationship to be reported to the relevant external reporting body as a suspicious activity report (SAR).

There are, therefore, a number of different parties that will become involved at different stages of the process. Initially, it is the responsibility of the firm's own staff and its appointed officer to determine whether there are reasonable grounds for having knowledge or suspicion of inappropriate activity. This means the firm needs to have clearly defined what constitutes an actual suspicion, as well as the procedures that need to be followed internally to ensure that all required local reporting obligations are also met.

Once internal processes have been completed, firms must then submit the required external reports, generally known as suspicious activity reports (SARs), to the relevant reporting agency. Generally, the requirement is that, subsequent to such a report having been made, firms must then work with that agency before proceeding further.

The agency may just receive the report and state that no action is to be taken, allowing the firm to continue to act normally on the account. However, in other cases the reporting agency may either request additional information or require that action be taken on the account, which could include requiring that the customer's funds be frozen. The legal methods to achieve this do vary between jurisdictions.

There can be problems in practice in some jurisdictions. What the firm clearly requires is a prompt response to state that it can either continue to act or needs to take some specific action. In practice, there can be significant delays in receiving a response, which significantly impacts the ability of the firm to avoid tipping off a customer.

If a bank has taken on a new customer with a single suspicious deposit which has been reported, what should the firm do while it is waiting for a response from the relevant authority? What if the customer requests his/her funds (or part thereof) to be returned prior to the bank receiving any communication from the authority? They may be able to argue that the repayment requires additional approvals, but again only a set amount of delay can be achieved. We would recommend that the firm documents that it is making such a repayment to ensure that the customer is not tipped off regarding inappropriate activity and that failing to make the payment would, in effect, have tipped the customer off. Of course, the additional information should generally also be provided to the relevant authority to enable them to make such decisions as they require.

21.2 CONDUCTING AN INVESTIGATION

When you are intending to conduct an investigation into a suspicious transaction it is important to recognise that this is a project and therefore project management skills should be implemented. The goal of the initial investigation is to establish whether or not a true suspicion does exist. The next objective is to obtain sufficient information to enable the relevant report to be made to the FIU. The final objective is to maintain sufficient evidence to support the conclusions reached and provide any necessary defence required by the firm to subsequent legal or regulatory action.

Investigations need to be conducted with the greatest of care. It is not correct for the investigator to assume that staff are honest and reliable for such purposes. Indeed, they might be involved with the illegal activity. Accordingly, the greatest care needs to be taken both to ensure the safety of the investigator and to ensure that a tipping-off offence is not committed.

Initially, all internal documents and information should be obtained and these should be supported by information from relevant reputable external sources. The synthesis of this information may well lead to the conclusion that the activity can be explained and consequently there is no longer a suspicion. To finalise this, it may be necessary to obtain additional information, but again this needs to be done without tipping off the client. To do this, the first approach is to consider whether the person you require more information on is the potential perpetrator or the potential victim.

If they are the potential victim then contacting them will clearly not represent tipping off. This is the approach that you will probably have experienced when your credit card company, for example, calls you to verify that the transactions on your account are valid and appropriate. In such cases, the analytical work conducted by the bank's own systems has identified a pattern of behaviour which could suggest your card details have been obtained by a third party, leading to inappropriate transactions being carried out. Contacting you, the customer, will either confirm or reject the concern and is a low-risk and appropriate approach to adopt.

However, if the person on whom more information is required is the potential perpetrator, a different and more cautious approach needs to be adopted. In such cases, the first question is whether the investigator believes that there is also an internal staff member involved. If this is not the case then the relationship manager connected to the account can be approached for information. However, if there is concern that they may be involved, then this will need to be a witnessed investigation and consideration will need to be given to a suspension of the employee pending further investigation. In such cases, a discussion with the Human Resources function will have preceded the enquiry being pursued. Of course, if there are no concerns over the relationship manager then they should be interviewed and requested to obtain additional information.

To obtain information without raising concerns also needs the greatest of care. One approach is to adopt what might be considered a customer relationship management approach, whereby the bank's relationship manager seeks to obtain information from the customer while actually asking a series of questions, which, in combination, would solve the concerns expressed. In the course of obtaining the information, the relationship manager will be seeking to establish that the right product is being offered to the customer but that, to confirm this, additional information is required. If done well, the client will not be alerted to the financial crime concern but will provide information in the hope that better-priced or more suitable products might be provided to them.

Then there are the other cases – the real cases. This is where the investigator earns their stripes. To conduct a true forensic investigation, the investigator needs to know how far they are intending to go. It is one thing to obtain sufficient information to complete the relevant transaction report to an FIU and quite another to follow up every lead. In reality, the bank's investigator is not trying to obtain sufficient evidence for a prosecution. Rather, they are seeking to establish the facts as best they can. This generally does not require the investigator to visit the client or meet them in person, since that would clearly represent tipping off. Again, they seek to establish such facts as are available to them and keep detailed records. You need to record what you have found, where you have found it and any concerns that you may have. As concerns are cleared, document the source of the information you have relied upon to eliminate the concern – this will also be required to justify your decision making.

The closer you get to true criminal activity the more cautious you are required to be. Nobody is asking you to get killed for the bank. If you are reaching areas such as organised crime or drug trafficking, you may be considering people whose moral code is different to yours. Be careful at all times.

One area where you may choose to undertake more detailed work is where there has been staff involvement in inappropriate activity. Here you will need to consider with care the information you can and cannot rely on. One suggestion here is for the area where the transaction of concern is being conducted to be subject to a normal internal audit by your internal auditors and for the investigation unit to embed one of its team into the audit. As the auditors ask their normal questions, it would be totally appropriate for this to be reviewed by the investigator embedded within the team. Internal auditors ask all sorts of questions – they might as well ask some for the investigator. However, always be careful and remember that if someone is cornered they might strike out.

Here, documentation needs to be separated carefully from the internal audit files. The information relevant to the investigation does not appear in the audit files and only appears in the investigation files. It is important that no reference to the specific named accounts appears in the audit files at any time.

You are probably wondering how far you should go. This depends on your own risk appetite and, to an extent, your nerve. If you truly want to undertake forensic work, be properly trained to do so and this includes being trained in self-defence. Always know where the exits are and never put yourself in a compromising position. You learn this from bitter experience. If you are investigating a company, then it is the confidential waste that you are looking for. If you are investigating your own staff, then cameras and recording devices may be required. This is a different game and going undercover here is fraught with problems. This is not the job of a money-laundering-deterrence professional. Just because you have seen investigations conducted on television does not make you an expert. People do get killed. Don't become a statistic.

21.3 SEEKING CONSENT FOR FINANCIAL TRANSACTIONS IN THE UK

So, a plea, then, for authorities to provide responses to SARs as quickly as possible. In the UK, the National Crime Agency (NCA) on its website (http://www.nationalcrimeagency.gov.uk/about-us/what-we-do/specialist-capabilities/ukfiu/seeking-consent-for-financial-transactions) includes the following information:

An authorised disclosure (Section 338 of POCA) is made:

- Before a person carries out the act prohibited by Sections 327–329;
- While a person is carrying out the act prohibited by Sections 327–329, the act having begun at a point when the discloser did not know or suspect that the property is the proceeds of crime and the disclosure is made on the discloser's own initiative as soon as is practicable after s/he first knew or suspected that the property is the proceeds of crime; or
- After the act prohibited by Sections 327–329 and is made on the discloser's own initiative as soon as practicable after the act, and there is good reason for failure to make the disclosure before the act.

As a result of consent requests, SOCA can often identify asset recovery or asset denial opportunities for itself and partner agencies. Decisions are made by the Consent Team of the UKFIU on behalf of SOCA, who work in close cooperation with Law Enforcement Agencies (LEAs) and other partners when arriving at a decision as to whether or not to grant consent.

Where consent is granted, the reporter may proceed with the specified transaction, if they choose to do so, and will have a defence against the three principal money-laundering offences relating to that activity.

Consent for the purposes of Part 7 of POCA does not:

- Oblige or mandate a reporter to undertake the proposed act;
- Imply SOCA approval of the proposed act;
- Provide a criminal defence against other criminal offences pertaining to the proposed act;
- Provide derogation from professional duties of conduct or regulatory requirements;
- Override the private law rights of any person who may be entitled to the property specified in the disclosure.

All consent requests are treated as a priority within SOCA. The aim is to provide the quickest possible response to a reporter, but some decisions to consent requests will take longer than others. As soon as a decision is made it is relayed to the reporter without delay. SOCA always makes the final decision in relation to granting or refusing consent.

Readers should note that, although this appears on the National Crime Agency website, the narrative continues to refer to its predecessor organisation, the Serious Organised Crime Agency (SOCA).

21.3.1 Timeframe

The UKFIU is required to reach a decision within strict timescales set down in legislation, within the agreed NCA policy, and within the requirements of the Home Office Circular on Consent (029/2008).

The "Notice Period" (Seven Working Days)

The law specifies consent decisions must be made within seven working days (the "notice period") from the day after receipt of the consent request (excluding Bank Holidays and weekends). The purpose of the seven days is to allow the NCA and its law-enforcement partners time to risk assess, analyse, research and undertake further enquiries relating to the disclosed information in order to determine the best response to the consent request. The reporter runs the risk of committing a money-laundering offence if they proceed prior to receiving a decision from the NCA.

If nothing is heard within that time, the reporter may proceed with the specified transaction or activity and will have a defence to any potential money-laundering offences relating to that activity.

The "Moratorium Period" (31 Calendar Days)

If consent is refused within the seven working days, law enforcement has a further 31 calendar days (the "moratorium period") – from the day of refusal – to continue the investigation into the reported matter and take further action, e.g. restrain or seize funds. The 31 days includes weekends and public holidays. The reporter runs the risk of committing a money-laundering offence if they proceed during the moratorium period whilst consent is still refused.

If no restraint or seizure action occurs after the end of the 31-day period, the reporter can proceed with the transaction or activity and will have a defence to any potential money-laundering offences relating to that activity. Consent does not extend to any acts/criminal property not detailed in the initial disclosure or agreed with the NCA.

21.3.2 Notification of Consent

In the first instance, a consent decision will usually be communicated to the reporter by telephone in order to provide the quickest possible response. The NCA will also send a letter by post recording the decision, but there is no requirement to wait for this letter to proceed with the prohibited act if consent has been granted verbally.

The NCA is mindful of the sensitivity of SARs – even within the same organisation – and endeavours to communicate only with persons whose details are verifiable by the NCA. Reporters may wish to appoint a specified deputy to deal with decisions relating to the consent request in their absence to avoid delays.

Details of reporters/Money Laundering Reporting Officers (MLROs) and their deputies, including direct telephone numbers, should be registered with the NCA. Registration is available through SAR Online or by downloading forms from the following link: http://www.nationalcrimeagency.gov.uk/about-us/what-we-do/specialist-capabilities/ukfiu/how-to-report-sars

21.3.3 Submitting a Request for Consent

Reporters are encouraged to make consent requests using SAR Online, the free, secure and efficient means of submitting SARs to the NCA. SAR Online contains useful information on making a disclosure and has links to relevant legislation. You will receive an automatic acknowledgment of your SAR and the NCA financial database unique reference number for the report. The Consent Unit will also be able to start processing SAR Online submissions quicker than those submitted manually.

21.3.4 Making a Report

Regulated firms are generally required to make a report to the relevant authorities in respect of information that comes to them in the normal course of business in the regulated sector that is likely to be of interest to the enforcement authorities in their attempts to detect money laundering and the financing of terrorism. This may occur:

- Where a firm knows, or
- Where a firm suspects, or
- Where it has reasonable grounds for knowing or suspecting that a person may be engaged in money laundering or terrorist financing.

Before a suspicious report can be raised, there is an obligation on the firm to undertake its own investigations to confirm that there actually is a suspicion, as set out in its own internal procedures. Each firm must then ensure that all members of staff report to the firm's nominated officer or MLRO when they have reasonable grounds for knowledge or suspicion that a person or customer is engaged in money laundering or terrorist financing. It is then for the nominated officer or MLRO to consider the report made by employees of a firm and to consider whether they believe there are actually sufficient grounds for knowledge or suspicion. For such an internal process to work effectively, firms must ensure that staff are adequately trained (Chapter 14) in making reports to nominated officers and MLROs. MLROs must also have received adequate training to enable them to perform their investigating and reporting obligations adequately.

21.3.5 Internal Reporting

Who Should Report Suspicions?

All relevant employees of a regulated firm are obliged to report to the nominated officer when they have grounds for knowledge or suspicion of money laundering. Therefore, this must be made clear to all employees so that they know who they should report to and the impact on their and the firm's liabilities of failing to do so. Firms may suggest that employees should consult with line managers before sending reports to the nominated officer, but clearly this can only be undertaken if the employee believes that the line manager is not personally involved with the potential inappropriate activity. In such cases, there will be additional responsibilities specified concerning the actions that should be taken by the line manager, since this additional stage must not delay the firm from making SAR reports.

The nominated officer is then normally under an obligation to report as soon as is reasonably practical. In this respect, firms must ensure that internal procedures do not prevent or delay reports from reaching nominated officers. They will also need to have procedures agreed with their relevant agencies as to what would constitute an appropriate maximum time for investigation prior to reporting to the relevant agency – indeed, it is often delaying such reporting which results in the money launderer succeeding in evading detection. The officer needs to recognise that the piece of information that they are holding may only be part of a much wider story that would only be obvious to the relevant agency, and that delaying provision of information could result in necessary linkages not being made and the criminal avoiding detection.

What Should a Bank Consider When Seeking to Establish the Existence of a Reportable Suspicion?

It is important to remember that local rules and regulations generally place employees under a legal obligation to decide whether to report a potential suspicion to the nominated officer or not.

Once an employee has made a report to the nominated officer or another officer to whom the nominated officer has delegated responsibility, the employee's statutory obligation will normally have been satisfied and they will be protected by legislation from any regulatory action. In doing this, employees should not be unnecessarily influenced by colleagues or allow such a colleague to decide for them whether reporting is appropriate. This is because the colleague could, of course, be involved in the inappropriate activity, but also because their advice will not change the employee's individual responsibility. The general requirement is that each employee must decide whether to make a report based on the merits of the specific case and their personal knowledge and experience.

Clearly, staff training and awareness on the type of factors to look out for becomes vitally important. In order to ensure maximum efficiency in the reporting process, short reporting lines, with a minimum number of people between the person with the knowledge or suspicion and the nominated officer, are recommended, as they will ensure speed, confidentiality and swift access to the nominated officer.

In terms of the initial investigation by the employee, they need to look dispassionately at the information available to them and then consider whether there could either be evidence of money laundering or an indication of terrorist financing. They need to avoid reporting just because they "do not like the look of someone" and ensure that there is really some evidence. Some people may appear to be "shifty" or "creepy", but this does not mean that they are actually criminals. Comments like this do not have any place in the investigation documentation and could prejudice later actions, since they presuppose inappropriate conduct using a judgment formed on an inappropriate basis.

The employee should promptly obtain all of the information available to them and then make their initial judgment based on the facts that then present themselves. Of course, if there is any doubt, they should report.

How Should Reports be Made?

It is clearly important that reports of suspicions made to the nominated officer are appropriately documented, with a combination of physical and electronic recording normally being required. What needs to be included in a report made by an employee to a reporting officer is normally specified in the relevant firm's rules and regulations. The MLRO would want such reports to include full details of the transaction or relationship which gives rise to the knowledge or suspicion together with details of the customer who is the subject of the report. Without this information, the MLRO will be unable to identify whether a suspicion actually exists and will only then be required to request such information from the relevant employee.

All internal enquiries subsequently made by the MLRO should also be documented. The documentation produced by the MLRO and maintained by the firm should meet a number of objectives. Firstly, it should enable the MLRO to provide additional information to the relevant authorities in case of additional requests for information being made. Secondly, it should provide evidence that the MLRO has followed best practice and undertaken the work that the regulations require, leading to the suspicion being confirmed or disapproved. In this way, the MLRO is also protected in being able to produce evidence that they have been diligent in conducting their investigations.

It is also best practice for all subsequent transactions or activity concerning a customer that is the subject of a report to be reported to the MLRO as they arise, until a report is received from the responsible agency that the customer is no longer under any form of suspicion. It will be for the MLRO to judge whether additional information should be passed on to the relevant authorities, and this will often be based on communications that pass between the MLRO and the agency concerned.

21.3.6 External Referrals

Once an internal report has been made by a firm, which the MLRO or nominated officer believes to give rise to grounds for knowledge or suspicion, they must report the matter to the relevant agency set up locally to receive such reports, for example, as discussed above, the National Crime Agency (formerly the Serious Organised Crime Agency) in the UK.

As we have discussed, a referral from the nominated officer or MLRO of suspicious activity must be made as soon as it is practical, if the officer has sufficient grounds for suspicion. One of the many problems in this area is that the actual rules implemented locally may not be very clear as to the actual obligations that are placed on the MLRO in terms of either investigating or the timetable for reporting. In practice, it may actually be difficult to know at which point it is reasonably practical to report to the relevant agency, particularly where it seems the timeframe has been ambiguously defined. What is clear is that the MLRO does not need to have found out everything prior to making a report. The key question is this: at what point have they really become suspicious?

Once they are, then they should report. They can always send additional information later and indeed many regulators have specifically defined an additional information-reporting process for precisely this purpose.

Generally, a prompt transferral to the relevant agency is required once an internal report has been made. Employees need to be aware that once a report has been referred, they are then under an obligation not to inform the customer that a report has been made, hence the offence of tipping off (see Chapter 23). Indeed, they should avoid discussing the case with anyone to the maximum extent possible, including colleagues.

What is Meant by "Knowledge" and "Suspicion"?

These two concepts are clearly of paramount importance, yet their actual meaning can be unclear. Neither is a precise term and both can be subject to different interpretations. Generally, having knowledge means actually knowing something to be true. An individual must actually know that a person was engaged in money-laundering or terrorist-financing activity. It is recognised that knowledge can also be inferred from surrounding circumstances. It can also be inferred from a scenario where the existence of money laundering should have been obvious to any reasonable and adequately trained employee. However, normally there is a recognition that knowledge must only come to the firm in the course of business or as a consequence of making a relevant disclosure to the appropriate agency. If information comes to a firm in any other way, it must be disregarded and employees will not be under an obligation to submit a report.

In practice, this means that information received as a newspaper report, through electronic media or even as an unsubstantiated phone call must be disregarded as far as is possible. We would emphasise that blogs and reports on the internet are, by their nature, extremely unreliable and should not be used, including ones from so-called reputable electronic sources. There may be little substantive evidence to support the claims made.

The term "suspicion" is even more subjective and must be proven by the firm, which must produce evidence that there really is a suspicion if this is required by the relevant authority. This is to ensure that the reporting agency is not swamped by a high level of unnecessary and unhelpful information. Suspicion is typically defined by the courts as being something which has a foundation but which is beyond mere speculation. So, suspicion is not about guesswork, rather there does need to be something concrete to support the concerns.

It is also worth mentioning that an unusual transaction will not necessarily be a suspicious transaction. Customers may have perfectly rational reasons to explain unusual patterns of transactions or account activity. The existence of an unusual pattern should initiate further investigation within the firm, but will not alone result in outright suspicion. It is important to document the investigation of suspicious patterns, since they may later support a suspicion and an obligation to report will then arise. However, if an appropriate explanation is received to suggest that the unusual pattern is, in fact, normal activity, then no additional suspicion exists – although the explanation should still be recorded. This, again, protects both the firm and its officers in demonstrating that they have acted in accordance with best practice.

What is Meant by "Reasonable Grounds" to Know or Suspect?

As we have seen, employees are under an obligation to report to a nominated officer when they have suspicions or actual knowledge of money laundering/terrorist financing. Failure to do this can generally result in a criminal offence having been committed by the employee. Therefore, it is essential for the bank to know when reasonable grounds exist for knowing or suspecting that a person is engaged in money laundering and/or terrorist financing.

Generally, firms develop an objective test of suspicion based on guidance provided to them by their relevant authority. The test will be met when it can be demonstrated by a known member of staff that facts or circumstances exist from which a reasonable person engaged in a business subject to money-laundering regulations would have inferred knowledge, or formed the suspicion, that another person was engaged in money laundering or terrorist financing.

The test will always operate on the balance of probability. Put at its simplest, any transaction could be money laundering or terrorist financing, but most are not. Consequently, the information required and its assessment will vary on a case-by-case basis. Problems particularly occur in cases of complex transactions and unusual circumstances where it will prove to be particularly difficult to establish that there really is evidence of a suspicion.

Unless it is particularly obvious, employees will not always be able to spot when reasonable grounds to know or suspect money laundering exist. However, employees must be able to defend themselves against a charge that they failed to meet the objective test for suspicion. They can do this by demonstrating that they took reasonable steps in the particular circumstances, in the context of a risk-based approach, to know the customer and the rationale for the transaction, activity or instruction. Therefore, effective customer due diligence becomes vitally important.

21.3.7 The Investigation by the Nominated Officer

After a report has been made to the nominated officer, they will need to conduct a higher level of investigation leading to an assessment of the suspicion and, if necessary, the preparation and issuance of a money-laundering report.

The first obligation for the firm's nominated officer is that they must receive and consider all reports forwarded to them by employees. It is then for the nominated officer to determine whether the reports give rise to knowledge or suspicion, or reasonable grounds of suspicion. In order for the nominated officer to carry out this role effectively, they must have access to any information that they consider necessary to enable them to conduct their role, particularly the firm's Know Your Customer information.

The nominated officer may also wish to gain further information from an intermediary who may have introduced the customer to the firm or, if necessary, obtain information directly from the customer. Obtaining information from the customer must only be considered in exceptional circumstances, as such an approach may alert the customer that money-laundering-deterrence disclosure is being considered. The nominated advisor may find it easier for a customer-facing employee to obtain such information, as the nominated officer, by their very role, is likely to alert customers, and is also more at risk of tipping off the customer.

There are a number of factors which a nominated officer must address when considering an internal suspicion report. There will inevitably be a balance to be struck between the risk posed by the transaction or activity being addressed and the time it may take to make a relevant disclosure to the appropriate authorities. As discussed above, time delays are likely to occur as consent is sought and searches are made of unlinked systems and records that might hold relevant information.

An extensive review may entail looking at known connected accounts or relationships which will need to be examined. Considering the time constraints involved when reporting, nominated officers may wish to make an initial report prior to completing a full review of linked and connected relationships. It may be worthwhile to document this stage as much as possible, as any delays in reporting suspicions may be interpreted as the suspicion not being reported "as soon as is reasonably practical". This will be particularly important in the event that the nominated officer decides not to make a full report. In such a scenario, the nominated officer should keep all activity clearly documented, or recorded electronically and retained with the internal suspicion report.

21.3.8 Reporting in the UK

The UK rules on reporting are typical of those adopted elsewhere and can be considered to represent international best practice in this regard.

Reporting to the National Crime Agency (NCA)

In the UK, the nominated officer must report to the NCA (formerly SOCA) any transaction or activity which they reasonably suspect may be linked to money laundering. A suspicious activity report (or SAR) must be submitted as soon as is reasonably practical after the information becomes available.

Firms should include in each SAR as much relevant information about the customer, transaction or activity that they have in their records. In particular, law-enforcement agencies have indicated that details of an individual's occupation/company's business and National Insurance number are valuable in enabling them to access other relevant information about the customer. As there is no obligation to collect this information, a firm may not hold these details for all its customers. However, where it has obtained this information, it would be helpful to include it as part of a SAR made by a firm.

When is There No Obligation to Report?

In circumstances where neither the identity of the fraudster nor the location of the criminal property is known or likely to be discovered, there will generally not be an obligation to report, since there is limited useable information available for disclosure. For example, when a person loses a cheque book or debit card, this can lead to multiple low-value fraudulent transactions over a period of time of relatively little importance to the reporting agency.

Generally speaking, there will be no obligation to make a report, where none of the following is known or suspected:

- The identity of the person who is engaged in money laundering;
- The whereabouts of any of the laundered property;
- Any available information that would assist in identifying that person, or the whereabouts of the laundered property.

21.4 SANCTIONS AND PENALTIES FOR FAILING TO COMPLY

The regulations in each country will specify the sanctions or penalties for failing to comply with a reporting regime.

Normally, where a person fails to make disclosures to a nominated officer and/or the nominated officer fails to make a report to the relevant agency as soon as is practical, firms, employees and nominated officers, as appropriate, will be subject to criminal prosecution or regulatory censure. In the UK, a criminal prosecution can result in the penalty of imprisonment of up to five years and/or a fine.

22 ONGOING MONITORING

22.1 THE IMPORTANCE OF ONGOING MONITORING

In Chapter 13 we discussed the Know Your Customer obligations which are one of the main money-laundering-deterrence measures that every firm is required to implement. Such due diligence enables a firm to really understand its clients and therefore potentially to identify that they are undertaking inappropriate activity. Such an identification requirement should apply regardless of locally implemented regulation. It serves not only to ensure that the firm meets the regulatory requirements, but also to ensure that the reputation of the firm is not impacted by involvement with individuals or organisations which are found to be inappropriate.

Undertaking primary investigation into the business intentions and credibility of a customer is fundamental when distinguishing between a legitimate business interest and a business that is, in fact, a facade used for furthering criminal intentions. However, initial identification work is only the starting point in the money-laundering and terrorist-financing monitoring process that a regulated firm is required to implement. The initial due diligence conducted needs subsequently and continually to be supplemented by appropriate and sensible ongoing continuous customer and transaction monitoring.

Any money launderer or terrorist financer will obviously have expected initial customer due diligence to have been carried out by a firm. Indeed, they would be aware if the nature of their relationship with the firm were such that the firm would be required to conduct enhanced due diligence. Accordingly, the money launderer or terrorist financer would have developed documents and solutions in order to comply with such local regulations as would be likely to be reflected in the firm's systems and controls. This would be conducted to avoid creating suspicion at this stage. It would ensure that the money launderer or terrorist financer would get past the initial stage of working with the regulated firm either to initially place or layer illegal proceeds. It is during the subsequent layering and integration phases where the firm probably has the best opportunity to identify inappropriate activity, and it is the work required to be conducted by the regulated firm at this stage that we refer to as ongoing monitoring.

If we consider a business case, a money launderer will often register what appears to be a legitimate business and will then initially conduct activity that is consistent with the firm's expectations for such a business. At this stage, the firm will not consider that the account is operating inappropriately and no likelihood of identifying a suspicion would take place. Subsequently, the money launderer will start to introduce illicit funds into the account, using small amounts at first and large amounts later. It is at this point where analysis of the behaviour of the customer is necessary. What the firm is seeking to identify is customer activity that appears inconsistent with the firm's understanding of the customer and the nature of business being conducted.

If the money launderer is careful, they should be capable of developing a pattern of activity that appears to be legitimate. However, they often get either careless or lazy, which enables their activity to be identified.

If ongoing customer activity is closely monitored, it is possible for a firm to highlight unusual patterns of activity, which can alert the firm to the possibility of the account being used for money laundering. However, for this to be done consistently normally requires the implementation of money-laundering-deterrence software which identifies trends in customer behaviour that appear to warrant additional investigation. Clearly, initial due diligence alone cannot adequately predict how a customer relationship will develop. Therefore, ongoing monitoring is required to supplement the initial due diligence and alert the firm to any suspicious circumstances or activity which may subsequently arise.

22.2 THE LINK TO CUSTOMER RELATIONSHIP MANAGEMENT

So, the objective of ongoing monitoring of the business relationship is to help identify unusual activity. There is a clear link to customer relationship management which needs to be explored. Customer relationship management has the objective of considering a customer relationship and identifying that a specific type and nature of customer would have a predilection to acquire certain products based upon historic experience. It is of benefit to a firm to highlight potential sales of additional products to existing customers, since customer relationship management would indicate that a customer with this specific profile would normally be expected to acquire the following products. Such targeted marketing is more likely to be effective than general marketing of all products to the general business community.

Clearly, the ongoing money-laundering-deterrence monitoring obligation is really just the inverse of this. It takes the normal nature of customer relationships, potentially parameterised, and identifies transactions which are unusual for this type of customer. What this means in practice is that software solutions and approaches that are used for customer relationship management may potentially also be used in their inverse to identify unusual patterns of customer activity that may represent inappropriate activity.

An effective financial-crime-deterrence monitoring system should flag up transactions and activities warranting further examination, based on a probabilistic assessment of the nature of the activity conducted. These reports should be reviewed promptly by the appropriate person, and necessary action must be taken in response to the findings, or further examination undertaken. All of this needs to be carefully recorded, documenting clearly the decisions taken, to meet local regulatory requirements.

22.3 WHAT DOES ONGOING MONITORING INVOLVE?

There is no single way in which such monitoring should be conducted, and approaches vary considerably. The ongoing monitoring will typically include:

- Scrutiny of transactions undertaken throughout the course of the relationship (including, where necessary, the source of funds), to ensure that the transactions are consistent with the firm's knowledge of the customer, their business and risk profile.

- Ensuring that the documents, data or information held by the firm are kept up to date, since without current information it will not be possible to identify what is currently expected for this customer.

However, the firm will be aware that in some parts of its business, up-to-date, verified customer information may not be available. This may be due to local considerations or requirements including the impact of data secrecy or protection requirements. Such cases should be identified by the firm and additional procedures implemented to provide the necessary level of protection. Again, marketing approaches may be used to update information, offering new products or services to existing customers while also updating static information.

Customer transactions will need to be monitored over different periods of time to identify trends within the activity. Such monitoring should be conducted both across the business cycle and within cycles. Where possible, it would be advantageous for transactions to be monitored in real time, where transactions are reviewed as they take place or are about to take place. This will enable prompt action to take place and the funds to be identified swiftly, and reported if required.

22.4 ENHANCED ONGOING MONITORING

Certain customer relationships and transactions will require ongoing monitoring as a result of their very nature. Circumstances which may attract such enhanced ongoing monitoring will typically include:

Specific types of transactions: This can include high-risk transactions, however defined by the firm itself or required by local regulatory requirements. These could include transactions that involve transfers of large amounts of funds, such as the acquisition or disposal of commercial property. Cross-currency transactions and cross-border transactions may also be highlighted for additional review where these do not appear in the normal course of business.

The profile of the customer: A customer may, by their nature, represent a particularly high risk in light of their personal background, for example, customers who are PEPs or businesses that have a large volume of cash transactions, for example casinos. Again, a customer that has not historically had significant cash transactions and then starts to increase the incidence of such activity should be identified and become subject to additional investigation. This may take the form of individual customer contact to see if there are additional services that the customer requires, resulting from the changing nature of the business activity.

Such analysis will need to be documented, since the customer contact will serve a dual purpose. There may well be additional services that are required by such a customer given the changing nature of their activity. However, during the communication with the customer, additional information will be received which may either allay any concerns or confirm that there is, indeed, a true suspicion that requires additional investigation and potential reporting to the appropriate authority.

The parties concerned: If a payment has been made to a person or business which appears on a sanctions list, this would clearly make the payee account high risk. As discussed, since sanctions do change, a customer may be identified for the first time when new sanctions are implemented and will then require action to be taken by the firm. This is further discussed in Chapter 10.

Comparison of the activity of the customer with the profile of a similar customer: Accounts of certain businesses may show income which is higher than is normally expected from a business in the same industry sector. A comparison of the level of profits made by a similar business in the same industry sector or trade may raise awareness to the possibility of money laundering. Major frauds may be identified when a customer has a percentage of a market or level of profitability that is inconsistent with a firm's understanding of the customer.

Unusual transactions: A transaction may appear abnormal due to its very nature. It might be of an abnormal size, for example larger than transactions that are normally conducted by this specific client or the market in general. On the other hand, it might be a transaction which is unusual by its nature, in that transactions of such a type are not normally conducted by this firm, or are not normally conducted by this type of business.

There can also be transactions that are unusual due to their frequency. For example, a firm may normally make five international payments a month. If this suddenly increases to 50 transactions a month, this should trigger initial concerns warranting additional investigation.

The nature of a series of transactions: The types of things that tend to give concern here include companies that appear to issue large volumes of credit notes or make regular invoicing adjustments. It is often only when a series of transactions is looked at in the collective that the unusual pattern of behaviour can be identified by a firm.

Geographic area: The destination or origin of payments may involve a high-risk country, such as one appearing towards the lower reaches of the Transparency International list shown in the appendix. Such countries may well be considered to represent an increased risk of inappropriate activity, and therefore accounts involving these countries will require a higher level of ongoing monitoring.

Product risk: Some products may represent higher than normal risk for an institution and therefore require enhanced monitoring. There is no prescriptive list of such products, but cash collection accounts and complex savings products could, for example, fall into this category.

It is always for the firm to identify what would be considered high risk in its specific circumstances. A type of business that would be considered normal for one type of firm could, for example, appear completely abnormal for another. If you consider an institution that works in a local area providing finance for property and taking deposits, then an overseas corporate account might appear unusual and therefore high risk. Indeed, for a local savings institution, a customer from outside its normal market, even within its own jurisdiction, could be considered as warranting additional monitoring and be identified as high risk.

Transactions that, for an internationally active bank, would be considered routine may be unusual for a bank without an international presence. Therefore, each firm needs to undertake some form of risk assessment to develop the criteria to be used to define what might be considered unusual, and then to implement such systems and controls as are necessary to ensure that such transactions are promptly identified and reviewed.

One concern is where a local firm hires staff that have been working in an international bank, since they may not identify a customer or transaction as being high risk due to their familiarity with the nature of business conducted. It will be important that induction training for such employees ensures that adequate processes and procedures are consistently implemented by such hires.

Another area of higher risk is customers where there is no regular face-to-face contact. This can often be the position with firms that provide credit cards or internet banking services through some form of distance-selling process. If regular contact is expected, but does not occur, then this also could be a warning that the customer relationship represents a higher-than-expected risk. Again, the firm will seek to rely on systems-based controls to manage such risks, making greater use of external data sources as appropriate.

22.5 THE RISK OF DORMANT ACCOUNTS

One specific area that represents a particularly high risk is that of dormant accounts. A dormant account is one where there has been no customer transaction for a specific period of time. Charges posted to the account by the firm or interest payments would not serve to delay an account being classified by the firm as being dormant. There is no global rule as to what is considered dormant, and practice does vary considerably. However, an account that has no customer contacts for six months may be generally considered as being high risk for financial crime deterrence purposes.

In these cases, the key concern that the firm will typically have is that the account may be abused by employees of the firm, with funds being diverted for personal use in some way.

Any movement in a dormant account is likely to be a concern, and the maintenance of background information on dormant accounts may also prove useful. A clear definition of what might be considered as being dormant needs to have been implemented consistently by the firm. This should include looking for any form of approach that could be used by an employee to prevent an account from being classed as dormant.

The firm should also be aware of transactions that are entered into by staff which appear to have the sole objective of ensuring that the account is not classified as dormant. Such transactions will normally be in the form of some type of adjustment to the account, perhaps 10–15 days before the account would normally have been classified as becoming dormant.

A typical case was reported in November 2009 in the UK, when a former policeman and employee of a bank attempted to defraud the bank. The banker used his position to access funds from dormant or untraceable accounts, and the policeman then laundered it by pretending to be a high-flying businessman. They were caught by police after conducting a £1.1 million transaction.

This type of event highlights the problem, in that it is the staff of the firm that have the best idea of how to take advantage of the systems that are applied by the firm and therefore to exploit loopholes. Accordingly, enhanced due diligence on staff activity and their personal accounts may well also be considered appropriate.

Firms normally do apply some confidence to the fact that information on a customer account is sent to the customer. However, since there is no customer activity on a dormant account, the reliance that can normally be placed upon the customer monitoring their account cannot take place. The same type of enhanced risk can also exist for any account where the customer is distant from the bank or reliant upon a bank employee for the receipt of customer information.

Therefore, dormant and similar distant accounts which are recognised as being high risk, as well as customers who are considered high risk, may require enhanced monitoring to effectively deal with the high-risk nature of the business relationship.

22.6 WHAT TYPE OF ENHANCED MONITORING IS REQUIRED?

Monitoring customers and transactions need not necessarily be a complex and sophisticated process. The scope and complexity of a monitoring system must be determined by taking into account the firm's business activities and the size of the firm. While monitoring of transactions and customer activity can be done using either manual or automated systems, the use of software significantly assists the process.

Key elements of any monitoring system should include having up-to-date customer information, which will enable the firm to have the opportunity to spot the unusual, and ask pertinent questions to elicit an explanation or the reason for unusual transactions or activities. The aim for such a process is to be able to judge circumstances which may appear suspicious, leading to further investigation being conducted to identify or disprove a suspicion.

So, the next time your credit card does not work when you are in an overseas jurisdiction, do have some sympathy for the card issuer. It is implementing money-laundering and fraud-detection procedures which have the objective of protecting you.

22.7 AUTOMATED VS. MANUAL SYSTEMS OF MONITORING

A review of a transaction database by an employee can result in a manual report of transactions that need to be investigated, but it is very hard just from such a cursory review to identify unusual trends in individual accounts. Similarly, reports may also be generated based on analytical software applications on a standard periodic basis. The chosen system of monitoring will depend on the size and nature of the firm, as a firm that has major issues of volume may need to implement a more sophisticated automated system programmed to pick up certain factors which appear to make a transaction suspicious.

The automated transaction-monitoring systems available on the market use a variety of techniques to detect and report unusual/uncharacteristic activity. The techniques used range from artificial intelligence to simple rules. The nature of the systems available is further described in Chapter 26. Further investigation and analyses from the output from such systems may lead to a valid suspicion of money laundering. However, such systems may also be difficult to implement and maintain due to their reliance on customer reference and transaction data, and they may also have what is referred to as a high incidence of false positives. That is, the software identifies a large amount of activity that is actually legitimate business activity, wasting significant amounts of precious staff time.

There is a danger when using an automated system that customers and transactions are not monitored on a personalised basis, but on a standard, characterised basis. Consequently, some form of continued personal review to supplement such monitoring is still likely to be required.

22.8 ISSUES TO CONSIDER WHEN IMPLEMENTING A MONITORING SYSTEM

Automated and manual systems vary in the approach they take to monitoring customer transactions, as discussed above. Firms must essentially evaluate their own objectives, in terms of what they wish to achieve from their monitoring system in order to assess which systems best suit their business needs. The kind of questions which firms should address when selecting a monitoring system which meets their needs include the following:

- How does the solution enable the firm to implement a risk-based approach to assessing the risk inherent in transactions conducted with customers and third parties?
- How do the system's parameters assist with the risk-based approach and lead to a reasonable correlation between transaction alerts and the incidence of money laundering or terrorist financing?
- What are the levels of investigation that the firm is capable of undertaking and will the system produce a high level of false positives which impact the deliverance of an effective programme of monitoring?
- What are the different types of money laundering and terrorist financing that are addressed by the system and are these consistent with the activities conducted by the firm?
- What are the data requirements of the system and has the firm recorded the data necessary to support the required analysis?

Firms can, of course, always use back-testing to see if money-laundering-detection software is effective. By looking at historic data within the firm, known cases of historic money laundering should be identified whereas transactions which are known to be legitimate should not be selected for additional review.

22.9 STAFF TRAINING

Apart from a computerised monitoring system which produces reports, firms should also recognise the importance of staff awareness, as discussed in Chapter 14. Providing adequate training to staff is a direct and cost-effective method of raising the importance of staff continuously monitoring customers and transactions.

The importance of employees' experience and intuition should also not be ignored. Such knowledge can add considerably to a firm's ability to meet its ongoing monitoring obligations, as a result of the following factors:

- Staff intuition is important, as employees with experience are able to spot suspicious activity through their personal knowledge of the nature of the customer, identifying patterns and concerns which would go undetected with a computerised reporting method.
- Customer-facing employees benefit from direct exposure to a customer face-to-face, so they are able to witness changes in the customer's physical behaviour which could give rise to suspicion.
- Customer-facing employees also benefit from telephone conversations with customers, and will be able to analyse the tone of voice and language used by customers, which could potentially arouse suspicion.
- They also have practical experience of dealing with previous customers with similar backgrounds, which enables such employees to recognise differences which may give rise to suspicion.

23 TIPPING OFF

23.1 INTRODUCTION

It is easy for books on money-laundering deterrence and terrorist financing to focus almost entirely on the steps taken to identify, monitor and investigate criminal activity. However, there are other obligations which are also important. Tipping off is one area where specific additional attention must also be given to the direction of a firm's employees and also those who work internally within a firm. Such obligations extend to contractors, interim staff and also outsourced service providers.

So, what is tipping off? It is letting the customer know that they are, or might be, the subject of a suspicion. The objective of making tipping off illegal is clear: it is to ensure that nothing is conducted which might hamper an investigation. If a money launderer is tipped off, they are often able to hide their tracks and disappear before the appropriate investigations can be conducted. Clearly, this severely inhibits the objectives of money-laundering deterrence and consequently the sanctions for getting this wrong can be draconian, but vary between jurisdictions.

Money-laundering deterrence is also dependent on the discretion of those who investigate and report suspicions of money laundering. The prevention of money laundering would be severely undermined if money launderers were alerted by the staff of the firm as soon as a suspicion arose, since the funds would most likely disappear to another jurisdiction. So, tipping off could occur at the stage of initial contact with the customer, during the processing of transactions or obtaining information, when investigations are being conducted on a suspicion or even after reporting to an appropriate agency.

23.2 LETTING THE CUSTOMER KNOW

Letting the money launderer find out that they are under suspicion is generally referred to as tipping off. Generally, once an internal or external suspicion report has been made, it is a criminal offence for anyone to release information which is likely to prejudice an investigation. Persons entrusted with investigating and reporting duties must essentially conduct customer enquiries in a tactful manner regarding the background to a transaction or activity that is inconsistent with the normal pattern of activity, and carry out enhanced customer due diligence measures in a way which does not give rise to the customer being aware that they are under suspicion.

Typically, the offence of tipping off is defined as follows:

A person commits an offence if:

(a) He knows or suspects that a disclosure has been made, and
(b) He makes a disclosure which is likely to prejudice any investigation which might be conducted following the disclosure referred to above.

A person does not normally commit an offence if he did not know or suspect that the disclosure was likely to be prejudicial. However, perhaps we should add that in court the requirement would generally be whether a reasonable person might judge that the employee did not know or suspect. Remember that in a court there is always a measure of hindsight to take into account, so the employee will need to be in a position to justify the actions taken.

It is normally an offence for a person to make a disclosure to a customer or associate that was likely to prejudice any investigation that might be brought following making a suspicious activity report (SAR) to the relevant reporting agency, when that person knew or suspected that a SAR had been made. An offence would not be committed unless a SAR had been filed, since, in the absence of reporting, there is no actual confirmed suspicion.

What this means is that all members of staff at a financial institution need to be fully aware of their personal obligations under tipping-off legislation. They need to know what to say to a customer and what to do to avoid alerting them to the concerns that they may actually be harbouring. This needs training and role play to enable staff to better appreciate the issues that may arise in practice.

23.3 THE PROBLEMS IN PRACTICE

One of the concerns is what an employee should actually do when they need to conduct investigations to confirm a potential case of money laundering or terrorist financing. Naturally, they will wish to obtain further information and to undertake enhanced due diligence, but they need to do this in such a way as to ensure that the customer does not become unduly suspicious. Often, they will fall back on standard comments such as "our standard procedures require me to ask the following question" or "this is one of the general compliance things we have to deal with". By attempting to make the due diligence processes appear standard, the employee will attempt to obtain relevant information without unnecessarily alerting the customer. An employee should never say that "we are doing this as part of our money-laundering-deterrence checks", since this could take the conversation along a line that might become uncomfortable.

If a customer is undertaking inappropriate activity, it is often junior staff that are the first to speak to the customer. Even moving responsibility unusually up the line of command could potentially alert the customer to concerns and potentially be considered tipping off. Therefore, front-line staff need to be extremely vigilant in what they do and be fully aware of the processes and procedures that are to be undertaken. They may be provided with a script which they should follow in such cases, although showing the script to the customer would also clearly be tipping off.

To illustrate how difficult matters can get, consider the following example:

If a bank manager learns from the bank's MLRO that the relevant regulatory body is contemplating making an investigation into a customer's transactions and no report has yet been made by the firm, the bank manager shall normally commit an offence if they disclose the fact that a report is even being contemplated in light of the customer's transactions. In such a case, a SAR will not have been issued, yet the bank manager is still at risk.

If a customer turns up with cash funds and laughingly says, "Do you think I am laundering money?", then the bank employee has a problem. Clearly, they must fall back on the procedures that they are required to conduct and should state that these are normal procedures, trying to show that no additional procedures are being conducted. Indeed, the same approach should be taken when additional procedures are, in fact, being undertaken. Saying that everything is being conducted in line with regulation and is the same in all cases is the normal defence used to defray awkward questions.

23.4 PENALTIES FOR TIPPING OFF

There are normally major penalties on individual employees for tipping off, since this could prevent the criminal funds being seized. If the customer is tipped off, they will continue to launder their funds through another medium and typically from another place. Five years' imprisonment and unlimited fines are quite normal penalties to have imposed for tipping off, so all employees do need to take their responsibilities seriously. However, it should be noted that cases where tipping off has actually been penalised are few and far between.

23.5 COMMUNICATIONS WITH CUSTOMERS UNDER INVESTIGATION

Once a suspicion has been notified through the submission of a SAR to the relevant agency, the condition of the tipping-off offence continues. Firms cannot tell the customer the real reason why their transaction is being delayed, as informing the customer that a report is awaiting consent from the relevant agency would obviously give rise to the offence of tipping off. The issue is clear. If the bank has received instructions from its relevant authority to freeze an account, then it cannot tell the customer why the account is frozen. As you would expect, it would run out of excuses relatively quickly and the customer would then become suspicious. For how long can you blame the bank's IT systems for failing to process a transaction or transfer? While the customer may, at that stage, disappear, at least the frozen funds will be available for the enforcement officers to investigate.

The harder case is where a report has been made but there has been no response from the relevant agency. Normally, if the bank or financial institution is acting in good faith and failing to conduct a transaction would have the effect of tipping off the customer, then regulations will normally specify that the firm should undertake the transaction; even though the effect of this may be moving the funds to another jurisdiction.

In all cases, the MLRO should be involved to ensure that the actions taken by the bank or financial institution are in accordance with the regulations applying in the relevant jurisdiction.

24 CORRESPONDENT BANKING

The Financial Action Task Force (FATF), Joint Money Laundering Steering Group (JMLSG) in the UK and the Wolfsberg Group, amongst others, have highlighted the importance of being diligent when conducting correspondent banking and have produced specific guidance to be applied by such firms. The JMLSG guidance provides the source of information for this chapter, and is reproduced with the kind permission of the Joint Money Laundering Steering Group.

Correspondent banking is defined as the provision of banking-related services by one bank (correspondent) to an overseas bank (respondent) to enable the respondent to provide its own customers with cross-border products and services that it cannot provide them with itself. This is typically due to a lack of the respondent having an international network.

Correspondent banking activity can include establishing accounts, exchanging methods of authentication of instructions (e.g. by exchanging SWIFT or telex test keys and/or authorised signatures) and providing payment or other clearing-related services. A correspondent relationship can be based solely on the exchange of test keys, with cover for direct payment instructions being arranged through a third bank for credit to the correspondent's or respondent's own account in another jurisdiction. Activity can also encompass trade-related business and treasury or money market activities, for which the transactions can be settled through the correspondent relationship.

The scope of a relationship and the extent of products and services supplied will vary according to the needs of the respondent, and the correspondent's ability and willingness to supply them. Credit, operational and reputational risks also need to be considered by both the respondent and the correspondent.

A correspondent is effectively an agent (intermediary) for the respondent and executes or processes payments or other transactions for customers of the respondent. The underlying customers may be individuals, corporates or even other financial services firms. The beneficiaries of the transactions can be customers of the correspondent, the respondent itself or, in many cases, customers of other banks.

24.1 WHAT ARE THE MONEY-LAUNDERING RISKS IN CORRESPONDENT BANKING?

The correspondent often has no direct relationship with the underlying parties to a transaction and is therefore not in a position to verify their identities. Correspondents often have limited information regarding the nature or purpose of the underlying transactions, particularly when processing electronic payments or clearing cheques. For these reasons, correspondent banking is, in the main, non-face-to-face business and must be regarded as high risk from a money-laundering and/or terrorist-financing perspective. In such cases, firms undertaking such business are generally required by local regulations to apply, on a risk-sensitive basis, enhanced customer due diligence measures.

Correspondent banking relationships, if poorly controlled, can allow other financial services firms with inadequate systems and controls, and customers of those firms, direct access to international banking systems. This can undermine the objectives of the money-laundering-deterrence and counter-terrorist-financing regime implemented globally.

Any correspondent bank which handles transactions representing the proceeds of criminal activity or terrorist financing risks regulatory fines and/or damage to its reputation.

24.2 HOW TO ASSESS THE ELEMENTS OF RISK IN CORRESPONDENT BANKING

For any correspondent bank, the highest risk respondents are those that:

- Are offshore banks that are limited to conducting business with non-residents or in non-local currency, and are not subject to robust supervision of their money-laundering-deterrence or counter-terrorist-financing controls; or
- Are domiciled in jurisdictions with weak regulatory controls or where there exist other significant reputational risk factors, e.g. rampant institutionalised corruption.

Correspondent banks must not maintain relationships with respondents that are shell banks (i.e. banks that have no legitimate purpose) nor any respondent which provides banking services to such shell banks.

Enhanced customer due diligence must be undertaken on respondents (and/or third parties authorised exceptionally to provide instructions to the correspondent, for example other entities within a respondent group) using a risk-based approach. The following risk indicators should be considered both when initiating a relationship and on a continuing basis thereafter, to determine the levels of risk-based due diligence that should be undertaken:

The respondent's domicile: The jurisdiction where the respondent is based and/or where its ultimate parent is headquartered may present greater risk or may mitigate the risk, depending on the circumstances.

Certain jurisdictions are recognised internationally as having inadequate anti-money-laundering standards, insufficient regulatory supervision or presenting greater risk for crime, corruption or terrorist financing. Other jurisdictions, however, such as many members of the Financial Action Task Force (FATF), have more robust regulatory environments and may, therefore, be considered to represent lower risks. Correspondent banks should review pronouncements from regulatory agencies and international bodies such as the FATF, to evaluate the degree of risk presented by the jurisdiction in which the respondent and/or its parent is based.

The respondent's ownership and management structures: The location of owners, their corporate legal form and/or a lack of transparency of the ultimate beneficial ownership are all indicative that the respondent may present enhanced risk.

Account should be taken of whether the respondent is publicly or privately owned. If the respondent's equity is publicly held, whether its shares are traded on a recognised market or some form of exchange in a jurisdiction with a satisfactory regulatory regime, then it will have been required to comply with the rules of the exchange. This clearly provides the correspondent bank with information and evidence to reduce the level of risk perceived as being posed by the relationship.

Clearly, for a privately or family-owned institution, additional procedures should be conducted to establish the identity of any beneficial owners and controllers. Similarly, the location and experience of management may indicate additional concerns, as would unduly frequent management turnover. The involvement of PEPs in the management or ownership of certain respondents will also increase the risk, and will alone result in the respondent being subject to enhanced due diligence.

The respondent's business and customer base: The type of business the respondent engages in, as well as the type of markets it serves, is indicative to the correspondent as to the risk that the respondent presents. Involvement in certain business segments that are recognised internationally as particularly vulnerable to money laundering, corruption or terrorist financing may also present additional concerns.

Consequently, a respondent that derives a substantial part of its business income from higher-risk customers may present greater risk and require the correspondent to conduct enhanced due diligence on all business conducted. Higher-risk customers are those customers that may be involved in activities, or are connected to jurisdictions, that are identified by credible sources as activities or countries being especially susceptible to money laundering, terrorist financing or corruption.

Downstream correspondent clearing: A downstream correspondent clearer is a respondent that receives correspondent banking services from a correspondent and itself provides correspondent banking services to other financial institutions in the same currency as the account it maintains with its correspondent. When these services are offered to a respondent that is itself a downstream correspondent clearer, a correspondent should, on a risk-based approach, take reasonable steps to understand the types and risks of financial institutions to which the respondent offers such services.

Special care should be taken to ensure there are no shell bank customers, and also the correspondent should consider the degree to which the respondent examines the anti-money-laundering and terrorist-financing controls of those financial institutions.

Generally, all correspondent banking clients shall be subjected to appropriate due diligence that will seek to ensure that an institution is comfortable conducting business with a particular client given the client's risk profile. It may be appropriate for an institution to consider the fact that a correspondent banking client (as opposed to the respondent) appears to operate in, or is subjected to, a regulatory environment that is internationally recognised as adequate in the fight against money laundering. In these instances, an institution may also rely on publicly available information obtained either from the respondent or from reliable third parties (regulators, exchanges, etc.) to satisfy its due diligence requirements.

24.3 CLIENT VISIT

Unless other measures suffice, a representative of the institution should visit the respondent at their premises prior to, or within a reasonable period of time after, establishing a relationship, amongst other things to confirm that the respondent is not itself a shell bank.

24.4 ENHANCED DUE DILIGENCE

In addition to due diligence, each institution will also subject those respondents that present greater risks to enhanced due diligence.

The enhanced due diligence process will involve further consideration of the following elements, designed to ensure that the institution has secured a greater level of understanding.

Ownership and management: For all significant controlling interests, the owners' sources of wealth and background, including their reputation in the marketplace, as well as recent material ownership changes (e.g. in the last five years). Similarly, a more detailed understanding of the experience of each member of the executive management as well as recent material changes in the executive management structure (e.g. within the last two years).

PEP involvement: If a PEP appears to have an interest or management role in a respondent, then the institution shall ensure it has an understanding of that person's role in the respondent and consider the implications on the due diligence to be conducted on an ongoing basis.

Correspondent banking clients' anti-money-laundering controls: The extent of the work which an institution will require to be conducted will depend upon the risks presented. Additionally, the institution may speak with representatives of the respondent to obtain assurance that its senior management recognises the importance of anti-money-laundering controls.

Central banks and supranational organisations: The concerns regarding correspondent banking generally do not apply to relationships with central banks and monetary authorities of FATF-member countries or supranational, regional development or trade banks (e.g. European Bank for Reconstruction and Development, International Monetary Fund, the World Bank), at least insofar as the relationship with that entity involves the provision of products and services that are in keeping with that entity's primary activities.

Branches, subsidiaries and affiliates: The determination of the level and scope of due diligence that is required on a respondent should be made after considering the relationship between the respondent and its ultimate parent (if any).

In general, in situations involving branches, subsidiaries or affiliates, the parent of the respondent should be considered in determining the extent of required due diligence. In instances when the respondent is an affiliate that is not substantively and effectively controlled by the parent, then both the parent and respondent banking client should generally be reviewed. However, certain facts unique to the branch, subsidiary or affiliate may dictate that enhanced due diligence may still be required to be performed.

Application to client base: Where an institution has not applied these concepts to respondents previously, it should undertake a risk-based review of its existing respondent base to determine whether additional due diligence is necessary to achieve the level of due diligence required.

Updating client files: The institution's policies and procedures shall require that the respondent's information is reviewed and updated on a periodic basis or when a material change in the risk profile of the respondent occurs. A periodic review of the respondent should be conducted on a risk-assessed basis.

25 RECORD-KEEPING

25.1 THE PURPOSE OF RECORD-KEEPING

Record-keeping is an essential feature of money-laundering-deterrence legislation in most countries. There is generally an obligation on firms to maintain appropriate money-laundering-deterrence records and controls in relation to the firm's business, with the idea being that maintaining an adequate audit trail is an essential component of combating money laundering. Typically, there will be a requirement to retain records concerning customer identification and transactions as evidence of work that the firm has conducted in complying with its local legal and regulatory obligations. Such information may also be used by the firm as evidence in the event that an investigation is subsequently conducted by a law-enforcement agency. Not only must records exist, but generally firms must take reasonable care to keep adequate records appropriate to the scale, nature and complexity of the business and to have them available as required by local regulation.

They are also generally under obligation to keep such records up to date. This requires the firm to contact the customer in some way to ensure that the documents contain current and valid information. Of course, this is not easy for former customers, but it is not even straightforward in respect of current customers. There may be opportunities for a firm to contact a customer in the course of relationship management activities, and during this process update their records. There can also be opportunities resulting from security activities relating to online or telephone activity with the customer. In the course of such interaction, it is incumbent on the firm to obtain such information as it requires to update its records. Using customer relationship management activity as the basis for obtaining such information is, of course, completely legitimate. The firm is seeking to know its customer to ensure that they are being provided with the services that are suitable to their needs and with the increasing emphasis on treating customers fairly, this is ever-more important.

If a call is required to be made to a customer to update these records, then starting with a statement that the firm may have accounts or services that might be to the advantage of the customer, but questions need to be asked of the customer in order to confirm that this is the case, is completely appropriate. It obtains the information that is required while at the same time giving the customer the perception that they are being assisted and treated fairly by the firm. Normally, the call ends with confirmation that the customer actually does have the right accounts, although this is not always the case.

25.2 WHAT RECORDS HAVE TO BE KEPT?

The exact details of which records a firm is required to maintain will vary between jurisdictions. The general objective of such rules is to ensure that the firm is able to provide details of the identification and monitoring audit trail in the event that the firm's customer is being investigated. The types of records required to be maintained usually include the following:

- Customer information;
- Transactions;
- Internal and external suspicion reports;
- Investigation records;
- MLRO annual reports;
- Information not acted on;
- Actions taken resulting from agency requests;
- Training and compliance monitoring;
- Information about the effectiveness of training.

In most countries these records can now be maintained in electronic form, so long as it is easy for them to be obtained. The same rule generally applies if the records are not kept at the primary site of the firm. In such cases, so long as the documents being overseas does not serve to inhibit the actions that might be taken by law-enforcement agencies, this is also probably appropriate.

In all cases it will be important to verify the specific laws applying in an individual jurisdiction. While this book provides both general and specific advice, the rules do change and are subject to interpretation. Consequently, reference to the specific detailed rules and regulations, together with their interpretation, may be required.

25.2.1 Customer Identification

It would generally be expected that a firm would keep a copy of references and other evidence of a customer's identity, which has been obtained during the process of customer due diligence. Copies of identification certificates should also generally be kept. Additional information which has been obtained as a result of enhanced due diligence should also be maintained for the purposes of ongoing monitoring.

Where a financial institution is not able to produce the necessary evidence of identity, it will generally be required to provide enough evidence to enable the document to be re-obtained from the original issuance source. The information needed to achieve these objectives will normally include information on the type of document, its number, date and place of issue. There will be requirements as to the period for which customer identification information must be kept, with a period of up to five years after the relationship with the customer has ended being frequently used. The end of the relationship is, in the case of an occasional transaction, the date which is the last in a series of transactions. In the case of a longer-term business relationship ending, the termination date is generally the date when the account was closed.

It is always surprising how much information that is readily available to a firm is not maintained. In the case of the passport, for example, the firm normally photocopies the page that includes the customer's face. However, a passport often includes other information which either assists the firm in understanding the customer or provides additional verification data. Visas which include a picture of the customer clearly add additional evidence. Travelling to countries where it is known that money laundering or terrorist financing are conducted should also lead to the firm undertaking enhanced due diligence. However, in practice no notice is taken of this information. Indeed, even the classic forged passports will be photocopied and placed on the file. In too many cases the form of the regulations is complied with, rather than the substance.

The requirement is for the original document to be sighted but only a copy kept on the file. Consequently, if an employee is failing in their duty and accepts a photocopy rather than seeing the original, the only evidence maintained might be that the paper on which the document has been copied is non-standard.

25.2.2 *Transactions*

Regulations normally require that transactions which are carried out throughout the duration of the business relationship must be kept as part of the firm's records. Records of transactions can be in numerous forms such as credit and debit slips, cheques and correspondence. Firms need to ensure that they are maintained in a form where a satisfactory audit trail may be compiled and a financial profile established for any suspect account or customer.

Again, the length of time for which such records will need to be maintained will be specified in local regulation, with a period of up to five years from the date on which the transaction is completed being quite normal. However, if the transaction relates to an asset where a claim against the firm could exist in excess of five years, then it may well be appropriate for the firm to implement a longer retention period than that which is specifically required by local money-laundering-deterrence regulation to adequately protect the firm. Journalists are more likely to state that records have been destroyed by a firm without adding that this is in accordance with local rules and regulations, since the clarification renders the matter less newsworthy.

25.2.3 *Internal and External Reports*

It is normally a requirement that firms should make and retain records of all actions taken under the internal and external reporting requirements. As part of this, firms should also keep records of when the nominated officer (or MLRO) has considered information or other material concerning possible money laundering, but has not made a report to the relevant authority.

Obviously, copies of any suspicious activity reports actually made should also be retained. Again, local regulations will specify the retention period, but generally all external and internal reports should be retained for a period of up to five years from the date when the report was made.

It may also prove useful to a firm to retain records of the following:

- Procedures undertaken prior to hiring staff to ensure that they are fit and proper;
- Details of staff that have received anti-money-laundering induction training on joining the firm;

- Dates of when anti-money-laundering training was given;
- The nature of the training;
- The names of staff who received the training;
- The results of any tests undertaken by staff to show that they really understood the training;
- Reports made by the MLRO to senior management;
- Records of consideration of those reports and of any action taken as a consequence;
- Internal audit reports relating to money-laundering-deterrence policies, processes and procedures.

25.3 IN WHAT FORM SHOULD RECORDS BE KEPT?

The form in which firms will retain reports will take into account the objective of reducing the volume and density of records, while still complying with local regulatory records and retention rules. The extent to which this is permitted within a particular jurisdiction will vary, with some requiring that only, and all, original documents should be retained. The following are the options that may be considered in terms of recording information:

- By way of original documentation;
- By way of photocopies of original documents;
- On microfiche;
- In scanned form;
- In computerised or electronic form.

It is important to recognise that the record retention periods and rules are normally unaffected by the format in which the records are kept. Aside from its money-laundering obligations, records should be accessible and readily retrievable when rationalising computer systems and physical storage arrangements for firms involved in mergers and takeovers. There are generally no locations specified by regulations as to where records should be kept, simply a requirement that they should be retrievable without undue delay.

Firms have a responsibility to ensure that records held outside their country also meet the same record-keeping requirements. No secrecy or data protection legislation should be allowed to restrict access to records either by the firm and its officers, or by the home country law-enforcement agencies under court order or relevant mutual assistance procedures. If such restrictions do exist, copies of the underlying records of identity should be sought where possible, and retained in the home country. Firms which operate internationally will need to take into account the anti-money-laundering and counter-terrorist-financing legislation in all countries in which they operate and make sure that the record-keeping requirements of such countries are compatible with home country legislation.

Once records have been requested by relevant law-enforcement agencies and are subject to ongoing investigations, the records should be retained until the firm is informed by the relevant authority that the case has been closed. However, if a firm has not been advised of an ongoing investigation continuing within five years of a disclosure having been made, the records may generally be destroyed in compliance with the normal local jurisdictional record-keeping procedures; although the rules of the local jurisdiction could vary this requirement. When a firm is deciding upon its retention policy, financial sector businesses must weigh the statutory requirements against the needs of the investigating authorities in the light of normal commercial considerations.

25.4 FAILURE TO KEEP RECORDS

If a firm fails to comply with the record-keeping obligations, then the firm or the individual involved can be subject to prosecution, which can include imprisonment for up to a year and/or a fine, or regulatory censure. Consequently, record-keeping does need to be taken seriously by both the firm and its appointed officers.

26 MONEY-LAUNDERING-DETERRENCE SOFTWARE

26.1 WHAT IS MONEY-LAUNDERING-DETERRENCE SOFTWARE?

As part of a firm's obligations to combat money laundering, they often decide to invest in the use of anti-money-laundering software. Anti-money-laundering software is essentially a computer program designed to analyse and record customer data, and detect suspicious transactions. Some of the main providers of anti-money-laundering software (highlighting their owners, where relevant) include Actimize (NICE), Ambit (Sungard), Mantas (Oracle), Fiserv (formerly NetEconomy), Fortent (formerly Searchspace, also NICE), Norkom and SAS.

There is no single approach to the way in which such software operates, although the products do fall into two broad categories. The first is the scenario-modelling approach and the second the inference-based approach.

Of course, there is no specific requirement for a firm to implement money-laundering-deterrence software; the regulations are not that specific. If a firm has a limited number of clients and already knows its clients well, then there may be little requirement leading to such investment. However, the problem with the due diligence conducted by an individual is that it could either be biased or poorly documented. Money-laundering-deterrence software serves to provide the firm with an audit trail that can demonstrate that it has taken the actions expected of it. So, while it is not a requirement, it is clearly in the interests of a firm to consider how it meets these increasingly onerous requirements.

26.2 THE SCENARIO APPROACH

In the scenario-modelling approach, the software house will have considered the attributes that might identify money laundering or terrorist financing. It will then have designed a series of scenarios which it considers may represent identifiers of potential cases of money laundering. The firm then uses the software to run against a file of transactions and balances, with the software then reporting all transactions that fit the set criteria. Clearly, if the criteria do not seek to review a particular attribute, then no such transactions will be identified.

The following are the types of things that might be identified:

- Accounts where there has been a level of deposit which exceeds previous average deposits by 30%;
- Accounts where the level of activity has increased by 50%;
- Accounts where the level of overseas payments has increased by 40%;

- Accounts where there has been a new pattern of activity;
- Accounts with cash receipts which represent a change from previous activity;
- Accounts connected with persons appearing on a sanctions list.

Of course, this is just a subset of the types of analysis that such software conducts and the percentages shown are purely illustrative. In practice, such software will normally include 50+ scenarios which a firm could choose to implement. It also normally checks against lists of known money launderers and terrorist financers as well as the sanctions regime in addition to other specific reviews. We will discuss this in more detail later. The problem, of course, is that the more analysis a firm conducts, the more accounts requiring additional investigation the firm will identify. This takes up a significant amount of time and effort and leads to work being conducted on what might be referred to as false positives – transactions that appear unusual but, in fact, are legitimate.

There is always a balance to be struck between conducting additional, potentially expensive and onerous systems-led investigation and relying on the due diligence conducted by staff. This balance has now shifted in favour of software due to the current climate of concern.

26.3 THE INFERENCE APPROACH

The alternative solution is inference-based products, which seek to identify what might be considered potentially high-risk transactions through viewing the likelihood of them representing money laundering or terrorist financing based on historic data sets. These products seek to parameterise the customer and transaction profiles such that transactions and relationships which appear to diverge from normality are identified.

26.4 THE CHOICE IS YOURS!

Both solutions have their place and both have advantages and disadvantages. While the scenario modeller will identify specific transactions to review, it is difficult in such products to pick up unusual transactions related to the nature of the customer.

On the other hand, the inference modellers will require a much higher level of data to enable the inference system to work effectively. When such products fail to deliver, it is usually due either to the inability of the firm to efficiently and cost-effectively access the information it requires, or to the problem of false positives. The inference modeller effectively reports every transaction that the firm undertakes, ranking each in terms of its likelihood of being money laundering. This can result in the reporting of false positives, requiring investigation to be conducted into legitimate transactions. Accordingly, even if a firm has an inference-based system, it may well also need a scenario modeller to deal with the level of false reporting.

Firms will need to decide for themselves which type of solution is best suited to their purpose and business practice. Generally, it is the larger firms that would choose to implement inference software, although we are seeing increasingly smaller institutions starting to implement increasingly sophisticated solutions.

26.5 THE EFFECTIVENESS OF MONEY-LAUNDERING-DETERRENCE SOFTWARE

The effectiveness of anti-money-laundering software is often debated. All money-laundering-deterrence software is based on programs that are dependent on data input. They then classify transactions or accounts according to the perceived level of suspicion and inspect the data for anomalies, whether based on statistical inference or scenario. The type of anomalies picked up will include any sudden and substantial increase in funds or a large withdrawal. Clearly, the effectiveness of such a system is dependent on the level of knowledge with which the system is programmed and the data availability within the firm's systems. Any other variables, of which the program is unaware, will go undetected. However, the clear benefit of money-laundering-deterrence software is its ability to analyse large volumes of data continuously.

If you consider the position that would exist without the use of software you will see the problem. If a bank has a large number of accounts in a number of different locations, even trying to make sure that financial sanctions legislation is complied with will become time-consuming. While a manual process can easily focus on the customer acquisition process, if an error is made in this work, there will be little in terms of control procedures to identify that the customer is inappropriate. Further, changes to the list will need a reassessment of the customer base on a regular basis. Remember, financial sanctions must be complied with, while a firm always wishes to avoid doing business with a money launderer or terrorist financer. The use of software consequently serves two purposes:

1. It provides a back-up control to ensure that cases of inappropriate activity are identified and reviewed.
2. It also provides a defence for the firm against the claim that it should have undertaken more review procedures.

In the presence of large volumes of data and multiple locations it would be difficult for the MLRO to operate effectively in the absence of such monitoring procedures, and the resulting personal risks can be significant.

26.6 TRANSACTION MONITORING

In Chapter 22 we discussed the ongoing responsibility to monitor transactions. Clearly, to enable a firm to effectively monitor customer behaviour, it is important for it to maintain adequate and up-to-date transactions documentation and customer information. This is the time when firms most benefit from the use of transaction-monitoring systems, although we are not aware of any jurisdiction that explicitly requires such software to be acquired.

To have an effective transaction-monitoring system, generally a firm should:

- Analyse system performance at a sufficiently detailed level, for example on a rule-by-rule basis, to understand the real underlying drivers of the performance results.
- Set systems so they do not generate fewer alerts simply to improve performance statistics. There is a risk of "artificially" increasing the proportion of alerts that are

ultimately reported as suspicious activity reports without generating an improvement in the quality and quantity of the alerts being generated.

- Deploy analytical tools to identify suspicious activity that is currently not being flagged by existing rules or profile-based monitoring.
- Allocate adequate resources to analysing and assessing system performance, in particular how to define how success is measured, and produce robust objective data to analyse performance against these measures.
- Consistently monitor from one period to another, rather than an intermittent basis, to ensure that performance data are not distorted by, for example, ad hoc decisions to run particular rules at different times.
- Measure performance as far as possible against like-for-like comparators, e.g. peers operating in similar markets and using similar profiling and rules.

26.7 WHAT TYPES OF ACTIONS WILL BE MONITORED BY THE SOFTWARE?

The software will monitor different things, and in some cases the firm is able to add specific additional matters which it wishes to have reported in addition to those routinely provided by the software. The types of things that are likely to be reviewed include the following:

- Transaction monitoring by products, customer, value or whatever a firm decides to use as a factor;
- Dormant accounts that become active;
- Customer transaction volumes that change by more than a set percentage;
- Know Your Customer information which is inconsistent with customer activity using some form of statistical technique;
- The accounts that need to be subject to enhanced due diligence and the nature of such work;
- Customers where there is a gap in identification verification;
- Country, or business risk ratings based on external information;
- Politically exposed persons (PEPs) based usually on some form of external database being input into the system;
- Financial sanctions monitoring, again using some form of external database;
- Identification of disqualified directors or individuals where the regulator has taken action, using external information sources;
- Customer activity that changes by nature or appears to follow the structure of known historic money-laundering cases.

This is only a subset of the types of issue that will be monitored in practice, with each software product including a variety of different approaches within the single modelling approach.

26.8 THE PERCEIVED BENEFITS OF ANTI-MONEY-LAUNDERING SOFTWARE

1. AML software enables firms to easily document that they meet some of the regulatory requirements which they are obliged to do under various anti-money-laundering legislation. Programs can assist firms with ongoing monitoring, record-keeping and detecting unusual transactions.
2. The use of software can provide a defence against fines and reputational damage in cases where a firm is identified as being involved with a money launderer.
3. There should be an increase in the number of cases referred to the investigation authorities, as more focussed investigations enable information to be analysed thoroughly, accurately and quickly. This increases the chances that suspicious activity reports will be promptly submitted.
4. Operational costs are reduced, as computer software programs streamline the investigation process with less human input being required. This potentially releases resources and employees to invest in other areas of a firm's business.
5. The use of software can improve efficiency and business control, as relevant employees are given a complete view of risks which affect the business.

26.9 WHAT TYPE OF SOFTWARE IS CURRENTLY ON THE MARKET?

26.9.1 Transaction-monitoring Software

Transaction-monitoring software essentially concentrates on monitoring individual transactions for the prevention and detection of money laundering. It is particularly useful for handling large volumes of complex data within financial institutions, including retail and correspondent banks. Software currently on the market generally uses comprehensive analytical techniques to scrutinise all accounts and all transactions to produce alerts most likely to result in legitimate money-laundering cases. The software does this by:

- Analysing the risk ratings of customer type, product, service and geographical area;
- Detecting matches against published watchlists such as PEP lists and OFAC;
- Detecting hidden relationships between family members, beneficiaries and counterparties;
- Matching account activity against known money-laundering scenarios;
- Analysing transaction data based on type, combinations with other transactions and dollar amounts, to identify potentially suspicious activity.

Such software really falls into two main types – the scenario approach products (e.g. Oracle, Actimize) and the inference products (e.g. SAS and Fortent).

26.9.2 Electronic Identification Software

Anti-money-laundering software which verifies electronic ID is valuable, as it enables firms to verify key documents, which clients may have physically presented but which may be forged. Such software will use sophisticated software to find numerous ways of electronically authenticating the identity of customers. This may also involve using independent data sources to verify sources of information. Certain software on the market, such as Experian, can provide a score or index value to indicate the degree of confidence that an individual's identity and address are correct. Other similar identification software on the market includes both Complinet and Norkom.

26.9.3 Sanctions and PEP-screening Software

As part of a firm's Know Your Customer obligations, the firm must be aware if it is dealing with known fraudsters, terrorists or money launderers. The effect of not having sufficient systems in place is not just the threat of penalties from regulatory authorities, or the threat to national security, but also reputational damage to the firm. Sanctions and PEP-screening software frequently and closely screen the firm's customer list for individuals identified on national and international sanctions lists, to ensure that the firm is not unknowingly assisting the financing of terrorist activities.

Most sanctions and PEP-screening solutions will minimise "false positives" (potential matches requiring additional manual assessment) which can usually result from automated screening solutions. Most systems will also provide a full audit trail of sanctions and PEP-screening activity for compliance reporting.

26.10 SELECTING YOUR SOFTWARE

In many cases, failed software implementations are due to a lack of appreciation of the differences between types of software. These differences are not always obvious from the company websites, so meetings with the different vendors and discussions with successful users will be required.

One of the key stages in the selection process is the construction of the long list – that is, the list of firms that will be considered for selection, regardless of the method chosen for the ultimate selection. In many cases, failed selection processes result from an incomplete long list of potential suppliers that omits key product vendors.

Some of the capabilities firms may consider are as follows:

- **Transaction monitoring:** Detects and profiles customer and transaction activity across all products and channels.
- **Automated risk assessment:** Evaluates geography, product and business type, coupled with an evaluation of transactions, behaviour and static information.
- **Know Your Customer (KYC)/Customer due diligence (CDD):** Manages the customer onboarding process through a defined sequence of steps in a due diligence workflow.
- **Link analysis:** Discovers hidden relationships among transactions, customers, accounts, alerts, cases, products and channels.
- **Integration with legacy systems and databases:** Built-in connectors accelerate integration with disparate existing systems and data sources.

- **AML investigative management:** Automatically triages AML alerts and provides investigative tools to manage alerts through predefined workflows.
- **Sanctions and PEP screening:** Matches names and addresses to a range of internal and external lists using Norkom's Watch List Management technology.
- **Payment and transaction filtering:** Identifies financial transactions throughout an organisation involving persons or entities contained on watch lists.
- **e-Filing of regulatory reports:** Automates the creation, population and filing of reports in many national and international regulatory formats.

26.11 WHAT ABOUT THE SMALLER FIRM?

For smaller firms it is unrealistic to acquire money-laundering-deterrence software – it is likely to be too expensive and also the firm is unlikely to maintain sufficient data to enable the software to operate effectively. Such firms will need to implement a manual form of monitoring process and procedure to ensure that the requirements within the local jurisdiction are complied with. This would normally include a review of customer databases to ensure that sanctions and watch lists are complied with, combined with employee training to ensure that all staff are aware of their responsibilities.

By making staff aware of all of the requirements and obligations, together with the intention for such regulation, a higher level of monitoring is achievable. This, however, needs to be clearly documented and sufficient to enable the management of the firm to have assurance that the firm will not be a target for money launderers and terrorist financers.

27 COUNTRY PROFILES

There now follows a series of country profiles which provide details of the key rules and regulations that apply in a variety of specific jurisdictions. As you will note, each profile essentially follows the same format to enable readers to promptly obtain the key information that they require. Of course, rules and regulations do change over time and therefore reference should always be made to the specific rules and regulations of the specific jurisdiction to ensure that accurate and up-to-date information is obtained. However, these profiles do highlight both the similarity in the regimes applied internationally and specific issues relevant to individual jurisdictions.

The common content of the jurisdictional regulations is due to the FATF Recommendations having been implemented in the majority of countries. There is still, however, some space for variation and this is, where appropriate, dealt with in this text.

Throughout these sections we have sought to identify examples where action has been taken within the local jurisdiction against money launderers or terrorist financers. Where reference has been made to completed cases, the information has been sourced from publicly available texts which are referenced in the section. The cases will not provide all of the relevant information regarding any specific case, and names have been removed where practicable. These cases are provided to enable the reader to assess how financial crime can work in practice and the actions taken within specific jurisdictions to deal with such issues.

We have not included every European country within the country profiles that follow, since the impact of EU legislation is that the rules applied are almost identical in many cases.

As far as possible the information is considered fully up to date at the date of publication of this text. However, as stated above, rules do change. You should always have reference to the original texts, where possible, if seeking to understand the detailed implementation of local rules, although you may, of course, also contact the author through the publishers.

27.1 COUNTRY PROFILE: ALBANIA

27.1.1 Overview

The problems of financial crime in Albania have been well documented. Perhaps the collapse of the series of pyramid schemes in 1997 specifically highlights the key concerns. These financial schemes, believed to be a means of laundering money, were allegedly linked to Kosovo drug gangs and the Italian mafia. The schemes became so popular that even the poorest members of the population became embroiled. They were attracted by the interest rates offered, which were an impossibly high 44% per month. The total amount of money invested in these schemes was almost 50% of the GDP of the country ($2 billion). The collapse of the schemes in early 1997 led to nationwide riots and the deaths of over 2,000 people.

Albania still has a large informal financial services sector, which, when combined with a cash economy, provides an environment in which financial crime can thrive. That the authorities have sought to address these concerns means that most of the key international requirements have now been implemented. Albania's most significant sources of money laundering still are thought to originate from corruption and organised crime. The European Commission's 2008 Progress Report stated that drug trafficking, organised crime and money laundering remained "serious concerns" and that Albania has made limited progress in its fight against money laundering.

The General Directorate for the Prevention of Money Laundering (GDPML) (*Drejtoria e Bashkerendimit te Luftes Kunder Pastrimit te Parave,* DBLKPP) operates as the Albanian national financial intelligence unit (FIU). It is the national centre for collecting, analysing and distributing information relating to potential money-laundering activities.

27.1.2 Key Legislation

Money laundering is criminalised by Article 287 and 287a of the Albanian Criminal Code. Instruction No. 28, dated 31st December, 2012, *On The Reporting Methods, Procedures And The Preventive Measures Taken By The Subjects Of Law No. 9917, dated 19th May, 2008, On The Prevention Of Money Laundering And Terrorism Financing* provides the compliance regime, while Law No. 157, dated 10th October, 2013, *On The Measures Against Terrorism Financing* provides the counter-terrorism financing regime – the third piece of legislation in this area since 2008. Regulation 44 *On Measures Against Terrorism Financing* provides additional guidance applicable to banks.

27.1.3 Legislative History

In 2006, the Council of Europe's Committee of Experts on the Evaluation of Anti-Money Laundering Measures and the Financing of Terrorism (MONEYVAL) conducted a mutual evaluation of Albania's anti-money-laundering/counter-terrorist-financing regime. The deficiencies identified by MONEYVAL, in May 2008, were addressed by the Albanian Parliament, which passed Law No. 9917, *On Money Laundering and Terrorist Financing*. The law entered into force in September 2008.

The law consolidated all previous legislation, which includes the Criminal Code of the Republic of Albania, 1995; Criminal Procedure Code of the Republic of Albania, 1995; Law No. 8610, 2000, *On the Prevention of Money Laundering* amended by Law No. 9084, 2003 entitled *For Some Additional and Amendment in Law No. 8610, 2000, On the Prevention of Money Laundering* (OPML) (now repealed) and also by Law No. 9258, 2004 *On Measures for the Suppression of Terrorism Financing*.

Law No. 8610 established an administrative FIU, and the General Directorate for the Prevention of Money Laundering to coordinate the detection and prevention of money-laundering activity in Albania. Under Law No. 9084, the financial intelligence unit became a quasi-independent agency within the Ministry of Finance.

27.1.4 FATF Assessment

The 2013 follow-up report stated that, although Albania has made considerable progress to tackle money laundering and the financing of terrorism, the risk of money laundering remains high. Albania has a history of organised crime, with clan-based and hierarchically organised networks that are allegedly involved in drug trafficking. The relative size of the cash-based informal economy facilitates the laundering and integration of proceeds of crime. There are a number of sectors identified with illegal practices, including illegal gambling establishments and exchange bureaux, as well as the vulnerabilities that relate to cross-border transportation of currency, which also put Albania at risk for money-laundering activity.

Additionally, the FATF stated that, "In June 2012, Albania made a high-level political commitment to work with the FATF and MONEYVAL to address its strategic money laundering deterrence and counter terrorist financing deficiencies. Albania has taken steps towards improving its regime. However, the FATF has determined that strategic money laundering deterrence and counter terrorist financing deficiencies remain."

27.1.5 The Primary AML Investigation/Regulatory Authorities

The Bank of Albania

The Bank of Albania, with the attribute of being the monetary and supervisory authority of the country, has the following functions:

- It compiles, approves and implements the monetary policy of the country, and employs the appropriate monetary instruments to achieve monetary policy targets;
- It has the exclusive right to issue and circulate the national banknote and currency;
- It keeps and manages the foreign reserve of the Republic of Albania;
- It compiles, adopts and implements the foreign exchange regime and the exchange rate policy;
- It licenses or revokes a licence on exercising banking activity and supervises banking activity to ensure banking system stability;

- It acts as banker, advisor and fiscal agent to the government of the Republic of Albania;
- It serves as the bank of banks;
- It prompts the normal functioning of payment systems.

The General Directorate for the Prevention of Money Laundering

A part of the Ministry of Finance, The General Directorate for the Prevention of Money Laundering (GDPML) is the Albanian financial intelligence unit empowered by the money-laundering-deterrence and counter-terrorist-financing legislation to collect, manage and analyse reports filed by obligors in order to prevent and combat money laundering and the financing of terrorism.

The GDPML disseminates information to Albanian law-enforcement authorities if there are grounds to suspect that money-laundering or financing of terrorism offences have been, or are currently being, committed. It also cooperates closely with other financial intelligence units around the world.

The GDPML also has a supervisory role whereby it oversees obligors' compliance with the requirements of AML/CFT law and in that regard it cooperates with all the supervisory authorities and, in particular, with the Bank of Albania and the Financial Supervisory Authority.

Article 21 of the amended AML law provides the GDPML with its powers. It provides that "The General Directorate for the Prevention of Money Laundering exercises the functions of the responsible authority as an institution subordinate to the Minister of Finances. This directorate, within its scope of activity, is empowered to determine the manner of pursuing and resolving cases related to potential money laundering and financing of potential terrorist activities."

Furthermore, Article 21 specifies that "The General Directorate for the Prevention of Money Laundering acts as a specialised financial unit for the prevention and fight against money laundering and terrorism financing. Moreover, this directorate functions as the national centre in charge of the collection, analysis and dissemination to law enforcement agencies of data regarding the potential money laundering and terrorism financing activities."

As an administrative FIU, the GDPML does not have law-enforcement capabilities. The GDPML receives reports from obligated entities, i.e. the Ministry of Justice or the Ministry of Finance, analyses them and distributes the results of its analysis to the Prosecutor's Office. In reality, the role of the GDPML is limited by its capacity, and coordination and cooperation with the Prosecutor's Office is problematic, as the number of actual prosecutions made remains low.

Albanian Financial Supervisory Authority

The Albanian Financial Supervisory Authority (AFSA), established in 2006, is a public independent institution. The AFSA is responsible for the regulation and supervision of non-banking financial systems and the operators in the sector. The AFSA reports to the Albanian Parliament.

The main areas of activity of the AFSA are regulation and supervision:

- Of the insurance market and its operators;
- Of the securities market and its operators;
- Of the private supplementary pensions market and its operators;
- Of other, non-banking financial activities.

The AFSA's primary goals are the protection of consumers' interests and the promotion of sustainability, transparency and reliability in the areas of insurance, securities and private supplementary pensions.

27.1.6 Outline of Specific Money-laundering Offences

Money laundering was originally criminalised through Article 287 of the Albanian Criminal Code of 1995. Article 287 states that: "Disposing, transferring, concealing, obscuring the nature, source, or ownership of property derived from criminal activity" is an offence. Furthermore, Article 287a provides that "commission of financial transactions or other economical transactions for the purpose of money laundering, which are known to stem from criminal activity, and their recirculation and production for entrepreneurial or economic activity of any kind" is an offence.

The latest AML legislation, Law No. 10 391, provides that "Laundering of criminal offence proceeds" has the same meaning as provided by Article 287 of the Criminal Code.

Article 15 is the tipping off prohibition which prohibits employees of the subject from informing the customer, or any other person, about the verification procedures regarding suspicious cases, as well as any reporting made to the responsible authority.

Article 14 is the legal liability exemption for subjects or supervisory authorities, directors, officials or employees who are reporting criminal activity in good faith to the competent authority. This provision states that these entities shall be exempt from penal, civil or administrative liability arising from disclosure of professional or banking secrecy.

27.1.7 Penalties

Violation of Article 287 is punishable by three to ten years of imprisonment. Breach of Article 287a is punished by five to ten years of imprisonment, and if committed in collusion with others or repeatedly, is punished by seven to 15 years of imprisonment. If it has caused serious consequences, it is punishable by not less than 15 years of imprisonment.

For tipping off, natural persons shall be fined 2,500,000 Lek, and legal persons shall be fined 5,000,000 Lek.

27.1.8 Scope

Law No. 10 391 applies to a variety of financial institutions, including:

- Banking entities, and any other entity licensed or supervised by the Bank of Albania;
- Non-bank financial entities;
- Companies involved in life insurance or re-insurance, agents and their intermediaries as well as retirement funds; and
- Any other natural or legal person, in addition to the aforementioned ones, engaged in the administration of third parties' assets/managing the activities related to them.

27.1.9 Risk-based Approach

Albania adopted a risk-based approach to its anti-money-laundering policies and procedures with the enactment of Law No. 9917 *On the Prevention of Money Laundering and Terrorism Financing* (OPMLTF).

27.1.10 Role of the MLRO/Nominated Officer

By virtue of Article 10 of Law No. 10 391, reporting entities are obliged to nominate a responsible person and a deputy for the prevention of money laundering, at the administrative/management level in the central office and in every representative office, branch, subsidiary or agency, to which all employees shall report all suspicious facts, which may comprise a suspicion related to money laundering or terrorism financing. Compliance persons have ongoing access to all data kept in compliance with the AML legislation.

Furthermore, Regulation 44 provides that subjects shall assign one of their executive directors as the person responsible for accomplishing the duties related to the prevention of money laundering and terrorist financing.

27.1.11 Due Diligence

The AML legislation provides that entities should identify their customers and verify their identities by means of identification documents:

- Before establishing a business relationship.
- Where no business relationship has been established but the customer carries out, or is willing to carry out, the following:
  - a direct transfer inside or outside the country in an amount equal to or greater than 100,000 Lek or its equivalent in foreign currencies.
  - a transaction in an amount equal to:
    - not less than 200,000 Lek or its equivalent in foreign currencies to exchange offices or casinos.
    - not less that 1,500,000 Lek or its equivalent in foreign currency in the case of a sole transaction or several transactions linked to each other. If the amount

of the transaction is unknown at the time it is executed, the identification shall be made as soon as the amount is made known and the aforementioned limit is reached.

- When there are doubts about the veracity of the identification data previously collected.
- In all cases when there is reasonable doubt for money laundering or terrorism financing.

Entities must identify and verify the identity of the beneficial owner.

Law No. 9917 strengthened customer due diligence by requiring the identification of all customers regardless of the size of their transactions. It is mandatory for reporting subjects to maintain ongoing due diligence of customers according to the KYC (Know Your Customer) procedures. Subjects must undertake enhanced due diligence on a risk-sensitive basis.

There is also a better definition of client, which includes any natural or legal person.

Personal Client Due Diligence

Article 5 states that, for the purposes of identification and confirmation of the identity of clients, subjects must register and keep the following information:

- First name
- Father's name
- Last name
- Date of birth
- Place of birth
- Place of permanent residence and of temporary residence
- Employment
- Type and number of identification document, as well as the issuing authority and all changes made at the moment of execution of the financial transaction.

Furthermore, in the case of natural persons who carry out for-profit activity, entities must record:

- First name
- Last name
- Number and date of registration with the National Registration Centre
- Documents certifying the scope of activity
- Taxpayer Identification Number (TIN)
- Address
- All changes made in the moment of execution of the financial transaction.

Corporate Customer Due Diligence

In the case of legal persons that carry out for-profit activity, entities must ascertain:

- Name;
- Date of registration with the National Registration Centre;
- Document certifying the object of activity;
- Taxpayer Identification Number (TIN);
- Address;
- All changes made in the moment of execution of the financial transaction.

In the case of legal entities that do not carry out for-profit activity, entities must ascertain:

- Name, number and date of court decision related to registration as a legal person;
- Statute and the act of foundation;
- Number and date of the issuance of the licence by tax authorities;
- Permanent location;
- The type of activity.

The recent instructions specify that, in the case of legal persons and other legal arrangements, the measures taken should include the understanding of the ownership and the structure of their control; the collection of information on the purpose and intended nature of the business relationship; and the conduct of ongoing monitoring of the business relationship and the ongoing scrutiny of transactions, to ensure that these transactions are conducted consistent with the customer's business and risk profiles, including, where necessary, even the source of funds.

Third Party Customer Due Diligence

In the case of legal representatives of a customer, entities must ascertain:

- First name
- Last name
- Date of birth
- Place of birth
- Permanent and temporary residence
- Type and number of identification document, as well as the issuing authority and copy of the affidavit.

Enhanced Customer Due Diligence

The AML legislation requires entities to identify, in addition to those specified within the legislation, categories of customers which present a high risk of money laundering.

Furthermore, in order to implement the enhanced due diligence, the entities should require the physical presence of customers and their representatives:

- Prior to establishing a business relationship with the customer; and
- Prior to executing transactions on their behalf.

Politically Exposed Persons

Banking entities, in addition to the enhanced due diligence procedures for the customer, should:

- Design and implement effective systems of risk management to determine whether an existing or potential customer or a beneficial owner is a politically exposed person.
- Obtain the senior managers' approval for establishing business relationships with politically exposed persons.
- Request and receive the approval of senior managers to continue the business relationship in cases when the business relationship with the customer is established and the entity finds out that the customer or the beneficial owner has subsequently become a politically exposed person.
- Take reasonable measures to understand the source of wealth and funds of customers and beneficial owners identified as politically exposed persons.

In addition, they are obliged under the 2013 guidance to search information in available resources such as the updated national list of politically exposed persons, specific databases (Worldcheck, Factiva, etc.) as well as open sources of information for foreign persons.

In cases where entities have business relationships with politically exposed persons, they must monitor such relationships with enhanced diligence.

Anonymous Accounts

Entities shall be prohibited from starting or maintaining business relations with anonymous customers or customers using fake names. Entities shall not be allowed to open or maintain accounts that may be identified only based on the account number.

Correspondent Banking

Financial institutions are required to obtain the approval of the higher levels of administration/management, and document, for each institution, the relevant responsibilities with respect to prevention of money laundering and financing of terrorism prior to establishing a business relationship for banking correspondent services.

27.1.12 *Ongoing Monitoring*

Entities must carry out continuous monitoring of business relationships with their customers, in order to make sure that they are in conformity with the entity's information about the customers, the scope of their activity and their classification according to the level of risk they represent.

Entities must periodically update customer data in accordance with paragraph 1 of this Article and immediately when they have reason to suspect that the conditions and the actual situation of the customer have changed.

Entities are obliged to draft and apply internal regulations and guidelines that take into account the money-laundering and terrorism-financing risk, which can originate from customers or businesses, including, but not limited to:

- A customer's acceptance policy, and
- A policy for the application of procedures of enhanced due diligence in the case of high-risk customers and transactions.

27.1.13 Staff Training

Under Article 11, subjects have an obligation to train their employees on the prevention of money laundering and terrorism financing and organise periodic training programmes for their employees. Law No. 10 391 does not outline any specific training requirements, while the recent guidance specifies that subjects should periodically train their employees on the prevention of money laundering and terrorism financing, based on an annual plan of training, including acquaintance with the legal changes in this field.

27.1.14 Record-keeping

Entities must maintain documentation concerning identification, accounts and correspondence with the customer for five years from the date of closing the account or termination of the business relationship between the customer and the entity. At the request of the responsible authority, the documentation may be maintained for more than five years.

Entities must keep data registers, reports and documents related to financial transactions, national or international, regardless of whether the transaction has been executed in the name of the customer or of third parties, together with all supporting documentation, including account files and business correspondence, for five years from the date of the execution of the financial transaction. At the request of the responsible authority, the information may be kept for longer than five years, even if the account or the business relationship has been terminated.

Entities must maintain the data relating to transactions, including those specified in Article 10, with all the necessary details to allow the reestablishing of the entire cycle of transactions, with the aim of providing information to the responsible authority in accordance with this law and the sub-legal acts pursuant to it. This information shall be stored for five years from the date when the last financial transaction has been carried out. This information shall, upon a request from the responsible authority, be stored for longer than five years.

Entities must make sure that all customer and transaction data, as well as the information kept according to this article, shall immediately be made available upon request from the responsible authority.

27.1.15 Investigation and Reporting Requirements

Article 12 of Law No. 10 391 details the circumstances when subjects should report to the competent authority.

Entities submit a report to the responsible authority when they know or suspect that laundering of the proceeds of crime or terrorism financing is being committed, was committed or is being attempted. The report should be submitted immediately and not later than the period specified in any secondary legislation.

When the entity has been asked by a customer to carry out a transaction, and suspects that the transaction may be related to money laundering or terrorism financing, it should immediately report the case to the responsible authority and ask for instructions as to whether it should execute the transaction or not. The responsible authority shall be obliged to provide a response within 48 hours.

Entities are required to report to the responsible authority within the time limits set forth in any secondary legislation all cash transactions, equal to or greater than 1,500,000 Lek or its equivalent in other currencies, executed as a single transaction or as a series of linked transactions.

Banks and non-banking financial entities should report to the responsible authority in accordance with the time limits set forth in any secondary legislation all non-cash transactions, equal to or greater than 6,000,000 Lek or its equivalent in other currencies executed as a single transaction or as a series of linked transactions.

27.1.16 Penalties

The penalty for failing to apply customer due diligence measures is:

- For natural persons: from 100,000 Lek up to 500,000 Lek;
- For legal persons: from 500,000 Lek up to 1,500,000 Lek.

For failing to apply enhanced CDD measures, entities shall be fined:

- Natural persons: from 500,000 Lek up to 2,000,000 Lek;
- Legal persons: from 2,000,000 Lek up to 5,000,000 Lek.

In cases of failing to implement adequate internal controls, the fine is:

- Natural persons: from 300,000 Lek up to 1,500,000 Lek;
- Legal persons: from 1,000,000 Lek up to 3,000,000 Lek.

For failing to meet the reporting obligations, entities shall be fined:

- Natural persons: from 300,000 Lek up to 1,500,000 Lek;
- Legal persons: from 1,000,000 Lek up to 5,000,000 Lek.

In addition to the above penalties, when the entity is a legal person and the administrative violation is committed by:

- An employee or non-administrator of the entity, the person who has committed the violation shall be fined from 60,000 Lek up to 300,000 Lek;
- An administrator or a manager of the entity, the person who has committed the violation shall be fined from 100,000 Lek up to 500,000 Lek.

27.1.17 Case Studies

There have now been a number of cases reported and acted upon in Albania. The following is typical of the activity identified and acted upon.

The General Directorate for the Prevention of Money Laundering received a report that a politically exposed person (PEP) had signed a contract to buy an apartment for EUR 80,000. The financial investigation unit conducted further enquires, and identified the following:

- The PEP had made a transfer to another citizen with no apparent connection, who then bought an apartment on the same day as the PEP using the same notary.
- The PEP's brother had purchased a flat worth EUR 52,000 shortly before the PEP's purchase.
- The PEP had established a company shortly after the expiration of his mandate, as a sole partner, doing similar work to his work as a PEP. This company was a shareholder in another company located in a tax haven, which invested in Albania.

Further investigations showed that the PEP and the citizen to whom he apparently had no connection had previously lived together, the PEP had been charged with corruption and the two flats purchased were in the same building with identical contracts. Both contracts stated that 20% of the price was to be paid in cash, with the remainder to be paid through a bank loan. The market value of the property was actually 50% higher than the value paid, and besides the PEP, nobody involved had business activities.

The following conclusions were reached upon the processing of the additional information received from banks:

- Neither the PEP, his associate nor their families had received bank loans for property purchases;
- Their banking transactions were minimal in comparison to the assets purchased;

- In previous years, the PEP had made several transfers (in small amounts) in favour of his associate (an indicator that leads to the conclusion that they had known each other for several years);
- Before becoming a PEP, he had a job (from which he resigned) providing him with a salary higher than the one he received as a PEP (this indicator shows that he may have become a PEP in order to acquire money from corruption);
- The seller of the apartment purchased by the PEP's brother had paid EUR 92,000 in cash, although the sale value of the apartment was EUR 52,000.

Based on the above information, and taking into consideration the PEP's previous job, the grounded suspicion that the money invested in different ways really belonged to him and that the function held by the PEP provided numerous opportunities for corruption, the case was disseminated to the law-enforcement authorities.

27.2 COUNTRY PROFILE: ARGENTINA

27.2.1 Overview

Argentina is described by the USA State Department as a "major money-laundering country". While it is making progress in developing its AML legal framework, it is still considered to be largely out of touch with international standards.

27.2.2 Key Legislation

The key Argentine money-laundering-deterrence and counter-terrorist-financing legislation is:

- Anti-money-laundering: Law No. 25.246, which has recently been amended by Law No. 26.683.
- Counter-terrorist financing: Law No. 26.268.

Resolution 228/2007, passed by the Financial Intelligence Unit, sets out the compliance requirements.

27.2.3 Legislative History

Money laundering was first criminalised in Argentina in 1989 under Article 25 of the Narcotics Law 23.737. Law No. 25.246 was enacted and came into force in 2000, and has since been amended four times. Supplementary rules and regulations have been implemented in order to bring alignment between Argentina and the global money-laundering standards together with the regulatory framework within South America.

On 11th September, 2007, the Argentine government enacted, through Decree 1225/2007, the National Anti-Money-Laundering and Counter-Terrorism Finance Agenda (the National Agenda) to serve as a roadmap for implementing money-laundering-deterrence and counter-terrorist-financing laws and regulations. This agenda provides the structure for the government of Argentina to improve existing legislation and regulation, and enhance inter-agency coordination.

On 17th June, 2011, the legislature of Argentina passed Law 26.683 ("The AML Act") to amend the Criminal Code in order to update the criminal treatment of money laundering. The new law was adopted in response to pressure from the Financial Action Task Force.

27.2.4 FATF Assessment

Since February 2012, Argentina has taken substantial steps towards improving its money-laundering-deterrence and counter-terrorist-financing (AML/CFT) regime, including issuing a Presidential Decree creating a framework for freezing terrorist-related assets and issuing further FIU resolutions to reporting parties.

The FATF also welcomed Argentina's updated action plan on measures and milestones to assess Argentina's effective implementation of its money-laundering offence, but determined in June 2013 that certain strategic AML/CFT deficiencies remain. The Financial Action Task Force's third-round mutual evaluation report of Argentina found the country partially compliant or non-compliant with 46 of the 49 FATF Recommendations. Argentina is subject to an enhanced follow-up procedure during which the country is expected to immediately address deficiencies relating to its criminalisation of both money laundering and terrorist financing. The country is currently on the grey list, indicating that there is a lot of work still to do.

27.2.5 The Primary AML Investigation/Regulatory Authorities

The Financial Intelligence Unit

The FIU was created in May 2000 to prevent and deter money laundering. Its mandate was extended in 2007 to include the prevention of terrorism financing, and its role was most recently updated in 2011. The 2011 AML Act provides that the Financial Intelligence Unit (FIU) should work with autonomy and financial independence within the Ministry of Justice and Human Rights Office. The FIU is responsible for analysing, processing and transmission of information for the purposes of preventing and deterring money laundering and financial crime, and is supported by liaison officers appointed by the heads of many other government ministries listed in the Act.

The FIU is empowered to:

- Request reports, documents, records and any other item deemed relevant for the fulfilment of its functions from any public body, national, provincial or municipal, and natural or legal persons, public or private, all of which will be required to provide them within a period of time fixed by law.
- Receive voluntary statements, which cannot be anonymous.
- Require the cooperation of all government information services, which are required to provide such cooperation under the terms of the current procedural rules.
- Require the suspension of any suspicious transaction.
- Require the implementation of internal control systems for obligated entities, and monitor, supervise and inspect sites to check compliance.
- Apply the sanctions provided for in the Act, guaranteeing the due process.
- Issue directives and instructions which must be complied with by law.

The FIU is in charge of the analysis, use and communication of information for prevention of financial crimes. Federal courts have jurisdiction over those crimes.

Banco Central de la República Argentina

Banco Central de la República Argentina (BCRA) acts as the central bank, and operates in a supervisory capacity for the financial services sector within Argentina. It has the dual responsibility of monitoring and regulating financial crime as well as banking regulation.

The central bank's role is to monitor the appropriate operation of the financial market and implement the Law on Financial Institutions and other regulations. Furthermore, it supervises the financial and foreign exchange activity by means of the Superintendency of Foreign Exchange and Financial Institutions.

On 6th April, 2012 the new Central Bank Charter of Argentina (Law 26.739) came into force. This gives the BCRA a dual role:

1. To ensure the stability of the currency.
2. To use the financial system to benefit society.

Furthermore, the bank has been given additional powers:

- To regulate the amount of money and interest rates, and direct credit policies.
- To regulate payment systems, liquidating and clearing houses, fund remittance entities and transportation of value companies.
- To protect the rights of consumers of financial services and fair competition within the financial system.

27.2.6 *Outline of Specific Money-laundering Offences*

The Argentinian definition of money laundering, translated from Spanish, is:

> *"Anyone who converts, transfers, administers, sells, manages, disguises or through any means puts in market circulation assets from a criminal offence, with the possible consequence that goods appear to have a legal origin, when its value exceeds the sum of three hundred thousand pesos, whether in a single act or repeated acts by various interlinked, shall be punished..."*

In summary, the offence is converting, transferring, administering, selling, managing, disguising or, through any means, putting into market circulation assets derived from a crime involving a sum of over 300,000 pesos (approximately £42,000), therefore hiding its true origin and giving it a legitimate appearance.

27.2.7 *Penalties*

For money laundering as defined above, the penalty is imprisonment of three to ten years and a fine of two to ten times the amount of the transaction. However, this can be altered by one third of the maximum and half of the minimum in the following cases:

- When the offence is committed frequently;
- When the offence is committed by a member of a criminal gang;
- Where the offender is a public official who committed the offence in the course of duty (this can also result in a disqualification of three to ten years);

- Where the offender is acting in the course of an occupation requiring special authorisation (this can also result in a disqualification of three to ten years);
- Where the offender is assisting another criminal in laundering money, evading the authorities or hiding evidence (this carries a penalty of between six months' and three years' imprisonment);
- Where the value is less than 300,000 pesos (penalty between six months' and three years' imprisonment).

Judges can now make orders such as seizure of money-laundering-related assets (to compensate victims) before a conviction is obtained, provided the illegal origin has been proven. They can also order confidentiality regarding the identity of criminals and witnesses involved, to provide protection and encourage other people to come forward. Revealing the identity of a witness or accused after a judge has ordered anonymity carries a penalty of one to four years' imprisonment and a fine of 50,000 pesos.

It is also important to note that:

1. Previously, only someone who aided the criminal after the fact in hiding the origins of the money could be guilty of money laundering. Money laundering is now an autonomous crime, and you can be convicted for laundering your own money ("self-money laundering"). This legislative change closes a loophole by making money laundering a crime in itself, and not requiring it to be related to another offence.
2. The required threshold has been raised. Before this amendment came into force, only transactions (or a series of related transactions) exceeding 50,000 pesos could constitute money laundering. Transactions below 50,000 pesos could constitute only concealment, which was a lesser offence. Now, although the transaction must exceed 300,000 pesos, six times more than before, to receive the highest classification of severity, transactions involving lesser values are still punished as money laundering.

27.2.8 *The Financing of Terrorism*

The offence of the financing of terrorism is committed by anyone who collects goods or funds, either directly or indirectly, with the intention or knowledge that such goods or funds will be used to finance terror-related crime, either by a criminal organisation or by an individual. This offence is punishable by both imprisonment and a fine.

27.2.9 *Scope*

Twenty-three categories of organisation are bound by the requirements of the AML Act, including financial institutions, intermediaries, insurance companies and trustees.

Entities may establish operating procedures and appoint Compliance Officers to prevent money laundering and terrorism financing.

27.2.10 Risk-based Approach

Argentina has implemented the risk-based system as envisaged by the Financial Action Task Force, and in particular in relation to the required customer due diligence process. This is evidenced by the requirement for the systematic use of the risk matrix within financial institutions.

27.2.11 Role of the MLRO/Nominated Officer

Regulated entities must appoint a Compliance Officer, who is responsible for ensuring compliance and implementation of procedures to fulfil any legal obligations. They are also responsible for liaising with the FIU. The entity must notify the FIU in writing of the following information pertaining to the appointed Compliance Officer:

- Name
- ID
- Position
- Date of appointment
- CUID number
- Phone number
- Fax
- Email address
- Workplace.

The Compliance Officer must be completely independent and autonomous, as well as having unrestricted access to all the information required for performing their role. A deputy may be appointed to assist them.

The Compliance Officer will have the following obligations:

- To ensure compliance with policies established by the senior management to prevent, detect and report transactions that may be linked to money laundering and terrorism financing.
- To develop and implement procedures and controls to prevent, detect and report transactions that may be linked to the offences of money laundering and terrorism financing.
- To design and implement continuous training policies for officials and employees regarding their AML/CFT obligations.
- To analyse operations to detect any suspicious transactions.
- To develop systematic reporting of suspicious transactions.
- To maintain records of risk analysis and management of detected unusual transactions (regardless of whether they are reported to the FIU).
- To comply with the requirements made by the FIU.

- To monitor compliance with current regulations on the prevention of money laundering and terrorism financing.
- To ensure proper maintenance and storage of documentation.
- To pay special attention to the risk involved in trading relationships and related transactions with countries or territories which do not comply with the FATF regulations.

To fulfil the obligations outlined above, the Compliance Officer may be assisted by a Committee of Control and Prevention of Money Laundering and Terrorism Financing.

27.2.12 Due Diligence

CDD must be carried out for all "customers", who are defined as all individuals or legal entities that establish, on a casual or permanent basis, a financial, economic or commercial contractual relationship. The minimum CDD requirements are detailed below.

Personal Client Due Diligence

Information must be gathered relating to the customer's:

- Full name
- Date and place of birth
- Nationality
- Sex
- Marital status
- Original ID (national identity card, enrollment book, notebook civic card ID, passport)
- CUIT (tax ID number)/CUIL (employment number)/CDI (identification number)
- Address
- Telephone number
- Employment.

The same treatment is given to an attorney, guardian, agent or guarantor. Entities will also require an affidavit on the origin and legality of the funds, or appropriate supporting documentation as stipulated by the FIU.

Corporate Customer Due Diligence

The following information must be collected:

- Company name
- Date and number of registration
- Tax registration number
- Date of incorporation
- Copy of current bylaws, subject to the screening of the original address

- Phone number of the registered office
- Main activity performed
- Personal details of the directors authorised to act on behalf of the firm.

The CDD must be carried out for any corporation, regardless of legal status. In addition to this information, entities will also require an affidavit on the origin and legality of the funds, or appropriate supporting documentation as specified by the FIU.

Customer Profile

Entities are required to follow the Know Your Customer policy. The KYC policy should include criteria, measures and procedures that include, at least:

- The determination of the profile of each customer;
- Monitoring of operations performed by clients;
- The identification of transactions that deviate from the profile of each customer.

However, a distinction is made between regular and occasional customers. Regular customers are those:

- With which it engages in a permanent relationship, and
- Who engage in transactions worth at least 60,000 pesos per year.

Occasional customers are those:

- With whom a permanent relationship is not entered into, and
- Whose annual transactions do not exceed 60,000 pesos.

For regular customers only, entities must create a customer profile based on information collated during CDD. Regulated entities should estimate the annual amount of operations per calendar year for each regular customer and use this to monitor any suspicious transactions or unusual activity. This should be recorded in writing.

Enhanced Customer Due Diligence

If there is doubt regarding whether a client is acting on their own (or where it is certain that they are not), entities must take reasonable additional steps in order to obtain information about the true identity of the agent and beneficiary. They should pay special attention to individuals who use companies as fronts for their operations, and have procedures in place which:

- Reveal the structure of the company;
- Determine the source of its funds; and
- Identify the owners, beneficiaries and those who exercise the real control of the corporation.

Non-face-to-face Customer Due Diligence

Entities should also take specific and adequate measures to reduce the risk of money laundering and terrorist financing when they have not met their customers face to face.

Politically Exposed Persons

PEPs should be given particular attention, especially if they enter into transactions which appear unconnected with their profile and usual activity.

27.2.13 *Staff Training*

The MLRO is required to implement a formal staff-training programme.

27.2.14 *Record-keeping*

Obligated parties are obliged to keep the following documentation in such a manner that a transaction can be reconstructed:

- CDD and any supplementary information must be kept for ten years from the end of the customer relationship.
- The original documents (or certified copies) relating to transactions or operations must be kept for ten years from the completion of the transactions or operations.
- The record of the analysis leading to a suspicious activity report must be kept for a period of ten years.
- Electronic documents and the requisite software related to transactions or operations shall be kept for a period of ten years (for the purpose of reconstruction of the operation).
- The information collected as a result of the preventative procedures shall be retained for at least five years, in such a manner that it allows the information and transactions to be reconstructed.

27.2.15 *Investigation and Reporting Requirements*

Reporting entities must report any suspicious conduct or activities relating to money laundering or terrorist financing to the FIU as soon as they find out about the suspicious conduct, by submitting a suspicious activity report (SAR). The FIU determines the reporting procedure, and the Compliance Officer is responsible for submitting the report.

Indicators of suspicion include, but are not exclusive to:

- An unusually high amount, complexity or an unusual pattern of transactions;
- A transaction structured to avoid reporting requirements;

- When the client shows an unusual disregard of the risks assumed and/or transaction costs involved with the transaction, particularly if they are unfamiliar;
- When transactions involve countries or jurisdictions considered "tax havens" or identified as non-cooperative by the Financial Action Task Force;
- Where complex corporate structures are employed for no apparent reason.

Regulated entities must retain all documentation supporting a SAR, and submit it to the FIU within 48 hours of being requested. The deadline to report potential money laundering shall be 150 days after the suspicious transaction was performed or attempted. The deadline to report potential financing of terrorism is 48 hours after the suspicious transaction was performed or attempted.

27.2.16 *Purchase of Currency*

On 7th June, 2010 the BCRA passed a law to prevent money laundering and tax avoidance. This law applies to local residents accessing the exchange market and places new restrictions on foreign currency savings and/or the acquisition of foreign assets.

Under these regulations, individuals or entities purchasing more than US$ 250,000 in aggregate per year must file a detailed asset justification report to the BCRA, and the financial entity involved in the sale of foreign currency shall also be required to verify that the amount of dollars purchased is consistent with the assets declared to the relevant tax authorities. However, the obligation to report does not apply if the purchases of foreign currency do not exceed US$ 5,000 per month.

In addition to this, any local resident purchasing more than US$ 20,000 of foreign currency per calendar month must do so through a bank transfer, an electronic payment or by cheque. The maximum threshold for purchases of foreign currency by local residents for foreign currency savings and/or the acquisition of foreign assets is US$ 2,000,000 per calendar month for both entities and individuals.

27.2.17 *Penalties*

Anyone acting in charge of a body which breaches these provisions can be fined an amount between one and ten times the total value of the property or transaction to which the infringement relates, unless the act constitutes a more serious crime. This penalty will also apply to the company itself. If it is not possible to establish the value of the property, the fine shall be between ten thousand dollars and one hundred thousand dollars. The offence is subject to a five-year limitation period, after which no charges can be brought.

27.2.18 *Case Studies*

In one case, two Mexican citizens were convicted of money laundering in Argentina, and given three-year suspended sentences. They flew from Mexico into Elegize Airport, Argentina, in October 2005, carrying suitcases with false bottoms.

Customs agents searching the suitcases found $648,000, which it later transpired did not belong to either of the men. The money was confiscated, and the pair were banned from engaging in business in Argentina. This case illustrates that, despite the current age of technology and sophisticated measures, systems and structures modern criminals use, money laundering can still be done in the most simple of ways and it pays to be vigilant about smuggling.

In another case, Argentina's Anti-Money-Laundering Office fined the local unit of HSBC Holdings plc 64 million pesos ($14 million) for failing to report suspicious company transactions in August 2012. The transactions, worth about 31.7 million pesos, took place from September to December 2007 and involved a company that said it had neither employees nor installations. The UIF based the penalty on the failure to comply with the "obligation to inform" established by Law 25.246. This case highlights the severity of the penalties which firms can incur if they fail to comply with their AML obligations.

27.3 COUNTRY PROFILE: AUSTRALIA

27.3.1 Overview

A report prepared as part of a $3.2 million programme of research into money laundering and financing of terrorism in Australia found the country to have a robust money-laundering-deterrence framework, but noted that there is still work to do. Despite the regime, the number of prosecutions for money laundering in Australia has been relatively low, although prosecutions have increased considerably from five charges in 2003–04 to over 100 in 2010–11.

27.3.2 Key Legislation

The Anti-Money Laundering and Counter-Terrorism Financing Act 2006 (the AML/CTF Act), and subsequent amendments, provides the Australian AML/CFT legal framework. This is supplemented by Anti-Money Laundering and Counter-Terrorism Financing Rules Instrument 2007 (No. 1) ("The Rules"), which were last updated in June 2012.

27.3.3 Legislative History

The Anti-Money Laundering and Counter-Terrorism Financing Act 2006 (the AML/CTF Act) is the current AML legislation in Australia, which came into force on 12th December, 2006. The Act was the first tranche of legislation which Australia adopted to reform its money-laundering-deterrence and counter-terrorist-financing regulatory regime. One of the main aims of this is to bring Australia in line with international standards, including standards set by the Financial Action Task Force (FATF). The Act is supplemented by The Rules.

Additional legislative provisions were developed in August 2007 to amend the Act. The provisions specify what "designated services" will trigger obligations under the Act. Further reforms were made in 2009 and 2012 following the review by the FATF. The Australian government is currently reviewing a further tranche of legislation, which had not been implemented at the time of this book going to print.

The Act implements a risk-based approach to regulation. This requires that reporting entities will use a risk-based approach to determine the way in which they meet their obligations based on their assessment of risk. When determining and putting in place appropriate risk-based systems and controls, the reporting entity must have regard to the nature, size and complexity of its business and the type of AML/CFT risk that it might reasonably face, considering its customer types, including any politically exposed persons, the types of designated services it provides, the methods by which it delivers designated services and the foreign jurisdictions with which it deals.

27.3.4 FATF Assessment

Australia was last reviewed in 2005, where it was found to be compliant with approximately half of the FATF Recommendations. However, this review was carried out before the implementation of the current AML law, which strengthened the regime. The process for the next review will likely commence in 2014.

27.3.5 The Primary AML Investigation/Regulatory Authorities

Australian Transaction Reports and Analysis Centre

The Australian Transaction Reports and Analysis Centre (AUSTRAC) is Australia's anti-money-laundering and counter-terrorism-financing regulator and specialist financial intelligence unit. The organisation contributes to investigative and law-enforcement work to combat financial crime and prosecute criminals in Australia and overseas. AUSTRAC's purpose is to protect the integrity of Australia's financial system and contribute to the administration of justice through its expertise in countering money laundering and the financing of terrorism.

AUSTRAC has two important roles:

1. Overseeing the compliance of Australian businesses, defined as "reporting entities", with their money-laundering-deterrence requirements.
2. Providing financial information to state, territory and Australian law-enforcement, security, social justice and revenue agencies, and certain international counterparts.

The Criminal Justice Division of the Attorney General's Department

The Criminal Justice Division of the Attorney General's Department has a policy role with respect to the Act, together with any associated regulations. The First Assistant Secretary of the Criminal Justice Division takes the lead role in Australia's delegation to the FATF.

27.3.6 Outline of Specific Money-laundering Offences

It is an offence in Australia to deal with money or property that is either the proceeds of, or may become an instrument of, crime. A person deals with money or other property if they:

- Receive, possess, conceal or dispose of money or other property;
- Import into or export from Australia money or property; or
- Engage in banking transactions relating to money or other property.

It is also an offence to:

- Produce false or misleading information;
- Produce a false or misleading document;
- Forge a document for use in an applicable customer identification procedure;
- Provide or receive a designated service using a false customer name or customer anonymity;
- Structure a transaction to avoid a reporting obligation under this Act;
- Disclose information regarding a suspicious transaction report to anybody other than AUSTRAC.

"Proceeds of crime" is defined as any money or other property that is wholly or partly derived or realised, directly or indirectly, by any person from the commission of an offence against a law of the Commonwealth, a State, a Territory or a foreign country that may be dealt with as an indictable offence (even if it may, in some circumstances, be dealt with as a summary offence).

The prosecution does not have to prove what the underlying offence was, or who committed it, in order to obtain a money-laundering conviction.

In addition to the above, persons that:

- Aid, abet, counsel, procure the commission of a money-laundering offence; or
- Urge the commission of a money-laundering offence; or
- Conspire to commit a money-laundering offence

will be guilty of the principal money-laundering offence.

27.3.7 Penalties

Sections 400.3–400.8 of the Criminal Code set out a sliding scale of six money-laundering offences structured according to the value of the money or property involved. Section 400.3 applies where the value of the money or property is worth $1 million or more. At the bottom end of the scale, Section 400.8 applies to offences where the money or property is of any value.

Each section is further structured according to the element of fault involved. The most serious offence is committed where the money or property is, and the person believes it to be, the proceeds of crime, or intends that it will become an instrument of crime. The mid-level offence is committed in circumstances where the money or property is the proceeds of crime or there is a risk that it will become an instrument of crime and the person is reckless as to those facts. The lowest level offence is committed where the person is negligent as to the facts.

Penalties are on a sliding scale according to the value of the money or property and the seriousness of the fault element. The maximum penalty is 25 years' imprisonment or a fine of AUD 165,000, or both.

27.3.8 AML/CFT Programme

A reporting entity must put in place and maintain an AML/CFT programme. Generally, an AML/CFT programme must be divided into two distinct parts: Parts A and B.

Part A: The General Programme

The primary purpose of Part A of a standard AML/CFT programme is to identify, manage and mitigate any money-laundering or terrorism-financing risk a reporting entity may reasonably face. Some of the requirements specified in these rules may be complied with by a reporting entity putting in place appropriate risk-based systems or controls, which should be implemented with regard to the nature, size and complexity of its business and the type of AML/CFT risk that it might reasonably face.

Part A must be designed to enable the reporting entity to:

- Identify significant changes in AML/CFT risk for the purposes of its Part A and Part B programmes;
- Recognise such changes in AML/CFT risk for the purposes of the requirements of its Part A and Part B programmes; and
- Assess the AML/CFT risk posed by all new designated services, methods and technologies prior to introducing them to the market.

Part B: Customer Identification Procedures

The sole or primary purpose of Part B is to set out the reporting entity's customer identification procedures.

Some of the requirements may be complied with by a reporting entity putting in place appropriate risk-based systems and controls, which, as above, should be implemented with regard to the nature, size and complexity of its business and the type of AML/CFT risk that it might reasonably face.

Part B of an AML/CFT programme sets out a reporting entity's customer identification procedures:

- The programme must have appropriate risk-based systems and controls so that the reporting entity can be reasonably sure the customer is who they claim to be.
- Whether any further Know Your Customer (KYC) information is required or verified will depend on the AML/CFT risk relevant to the provision of the designated service (and the KYC information itself will vary depending on the type of customer).
- The programme must be able to respond (on a risk basis) to any discrepancies in information that arise, so the reporting entity can be reasonably satisfied the customer is who they claim to be.
- Verification can be from reliable and independent documentation, electronic data or a combination of both.

In carrying out customer due diligence, the reporting entity may request information from a customer. If the reporting entity has provided a designated service and has reasonable grounds to believe that a customer has information that is likely to assist the reporting entity, the reporting entity may, by giving written notice, request such information from the customer within a specified period. The notice must also set out the reporting entity's power to discontinue, restrict or limit the provision of designated services if the customer refuses to comply with the request for information.

27.3.9 Role of the MLRO/Nominated Officer

Part A must provide for the reporting entity to designate a person as the "AML/CTF Compliance Officer" at the management level. The AML/CTF Compliance Officer may have other duties in addition to their role as Compliance Officer.

27.3.10 Due Diligence

The Rules provide that different CDD requirements apply for different types of customer.

Personal Client Due Diligence

The entity should include appropriate risk-based systems and controls that are designed to enable the reporting entity to be reasonably satisfied that the customer is the individual that he or she claims to be.

Part B must include a procedure for the reporting entity to collect and verify, at a minimum, the following KYC information from an individual (other than a sole trader):

- The customer's full name;
- The customer's date of birth; and
- The customer's residential address.

For a sole trader, they must ascertain:

- The customer's full name;
- The customer's date of birth;
- The full business name (if any) under which the customer carries on his or her business;
- The full address of the customer's principal place of business (if any) or the customer's residential address; and
- Any ABN issued to the customer.

Part B must also verify the information based on:

- Reliable and independent documentation;
- Reliable and independent electronic data; or
- A combination of the above.

Part B must be able to respond to any discrepancy that arises in the course of verifying CDD so that it can be reasonably satisfied that the customer is the person that he or she claims to be.

Corporate Customer Due Diligence

Part B must include appropriate risk-based systems and controls to enable the reporting entity to be reasonably satisfied that:

- The company exists; and
- In respect of certain companies, the name and address of any beneficial owner of the company has been provided.

The reporting entity must collect and verify, at a minimum, the following information:

In the case of a domestic company:

- The full name of the company as registered by ASIC;
- The full address of the company's registered office;
- The full address of the company's principal place of business, if any;
- The ACN issued to the company;
- Whether the company is registered by ASIC as a proprietary or public company; and
- If the company is registered as a proprietary company, the name of each director of the company.

In the case of a registered foreign company:

- The full name of the company as registered by ASIC;
- The full address of the company's registered office in Australia;
- The full address of the company's principal place of business in Australia (if any) or the full name and address of the company's local agent in Australia (if any);
- The ARBN issued to the company;
- The country in which the company was formed, incorporated or registered;
- Whether the company is registered by the relevant foreign registration body and if so whether it is registered as a private or public company or some other type of company; and
- If the company is registered as a private company by the relevant foreign registration body, the name of each director of the company.

In the case of an unregistered foreign company:

- The full name of the company;
- The country in which the company was formed, incorporated or registered;
- Whether the company is registered by the relevant foreign registration body and, if so, any identification number issued to the company upon formation, the full address of the company and whether it is registered as a private, public or other type of company by the relevant foreign registration body;
- If the company is registered as a private company by the relevant foreign registration body, the name of each director of the company; and
- If the company is not registered by the relevant foreign registration body, the full address of the principal place of business of the company in its country of formation or incorporation.

In addition to this, the entity must be able to determine whether any other KYC information collected in respect of the company should be verified, with regard to the AML/CFT risk.

Beneficial Ownership

Part B must include a procedure for the reporting entity to collect the name and address of each beneficial owner (if any) of a proprietary or private company, and be able to ascertain whether or not it needs to verify this information.

Verification of information about a company should be based, as far as possible, on reliable and independent sources, which would include a disclosure certificate that verifies information about the beneficial ownership of a company (other than a foreign company).

The reporting entity must be able to respond to any discrepancy that arises in the course of verifying information about a company, and determine whether it is reasonably satisfied about the matters referred to above.

There are similar rules for trustees, partners, agents and customers other than individuals.

If the reporting entity suspects a customer is not who they say they are, or has other suspicions about its customers, it must, within 14 days:

- Collect any KYC information in respect of the customer, and/or
- Verify, from a reliable and independent source, certain KYC information that has been obtained in respect of the customer.

Simplified Customer Due Diligence

Where the reporting entity determines that the relationship with an individual customer is of medium or lower risk, they may complete the following as CDD:

- Collect the KYC information described above from a customer;
- Verify that any document produced by the customer has not expired (other than in the case of a passport issued by the Commonwealth that expired within the preceding two years); and
- Verify the customer's name and either the customer's residential address or date of birth, or both, from:
  - an original or certified copy of a primary photographic identification document; or
  - both an original or certified copy of a primary non-photographic identification document and an original or certified copy of a secondary identification document.

Alternatively, a reporting entity may use electronic procedures to complete reduced CDD for a medium or lower-risk customer. If so, it should collect the KYC information described above from a customer, and verify the customer's name and the customer's residential address using reliable and independent electronic data from at least two separate data sources, and either:

- The customer's date of birth using reliable and independent electronic data from at least one data source; or
- That the customer has a transaction history for at least the past three years.

For simplified corporate CDD, if the company is:

- A domestic listed public company;
- A majority owned subsidiary of a domestic listed public company; or
- Licensed and subject to the regulatory oversight of a Commonwealth, State or Territory statutory regulator in relation to its activities as a company,

CDD can be completed by obtaining and verifying one or a combination of the following:

- A search of the relevant domestic stock exchange;
- A public document issued by the relevant company;
- A search of the relevant ASIC database;
- A search of the licence or other records of the relevant regulator.

Enhanced Customer Due Diligence

A reporting entity must include an enhanced customer due diligence programme in Part A of its AML/CFT programme. The reporting entity must apply the enhanced customer due diligence programme when:

- It determines under its risk-based systems and controls that the AML/CFT risk is high; or
- A suspicion has arisen for the purposes of Section 41 of the AML/CTF Act; or
- The reporting entity is entering into, or proposing to enter into, a transaction and a party to the transaction is physically present in, or is a corporation incorporated in, a prescribed foreign country.

The enhanced customer due diligence programme should require the entity to do one or more of the following:

- Seek information from the customer or from third party sources in order to undertake one or more of the following:
  - clarify or update KYC information already collected from the customer;
  - obtain any further KYC information, including, where appropriate, taking reasonable measures to identify:
    - the source of the customer's wealth;
    - the source of the customer's funds; and
    - the ultimate beneficial ownership of the customer (if a non-individual).

- Clarify the nature of the customer's ongoing business with the reporting entity.
- Consider any suspicion that may have arisen.

It may verify or re-verify KYC information in accordance with the customer identification programme, or undertake more detailed analysis and monitoring of the customer's transactions – both past and future, including, but not limited to:

- The purpose or nature of specific transactions; or
- The expected nature and level of transaction behaviour.

It could seek senior management approval for:

- Establishing, or continuing with, a business relationship with a customer;
- Whether a transaction on an account should be processed; or
- Whether the designated service should commence to be provided or continue to be provided to the customer.

It may also lodge a suspicious matter report, if required.

Correspondent Banking

A financial institution (the first financial institution) must carry out, to the extent warranted by the risk identified, an assessment of the following matters:

- The nature of the other financial institution's business, including its product and customer base;
- The domicile of the other financial institution;
- The domicile of any parent company of the other financial institution;
- The existence and quality of any anti-money-laundering and counter-terrorism-financing regulation in the other financial institution's country of domicile;
- The existence and quality of any anti-money-laundering and counter-terrorism-financing regulation in the country of domicile of any parent company of the other financial institution – where the parent company has group-wide controls and where the other financial institution operates within the requirements of those controls;
- The adequacy of the other financial institution's controls and internal compliance practices in relation to anti-money laundering and counter-terrorism financing;
- The ownership, control and management structures of the other financial institution and any parent company, including whether a politically exposed person has ownership or control of the other financial institution or any parent company;
- The other financial institution's financial position;
- The reputation and history of the other financial institution;
- The reputation and history of any parent company of the other financial institution;
- Whether the other financial institution has been the subject of an investigation, or any criminal or civil proceedings relating to money laundering or terrorism financing.

27.3.11 Ongoing Monitoring

Part A must be subject to regular independent review. The review may be carried out by either an internal or external party. The purpose of the review should be to:

- Assess the effectiveness of the Part A programme having regard to the ML/TF risk of the reporting entity;
- Assess whether the Part A programme complies with these Rules;
- Assess whether the Part A programme has been effectively implemented; and
- Assess whether the reporting entity has complied with its Part A programme.

The result of the review, including any report prepared, must be provided to the governing board and senior management.

A reporting entity must be able to determine whether any further KYC information should be collected in respect of customers for ongoing customer due diligence purposes, and whether and in what circumstances KYC information should be updated or verified for ongoing CDD purposes.

A reporting entity must also include a transaction-monitoring programme in Part A of its AML/CFT programme to identify, having regard to ML/TF risk, any transaction that appears to be suspicious. The transaction-monitoring programme should have regard to complex, unusual, large transactions and unusual patterns of transactions, which have no apparent economic or visible lawful purpose.

27.3.12 Staff Training

Part A must include an ML/TF risk awareness training programme. The ML/TF risk awareness training programme must be designed so that the reporting entity gives its employees appropriate training at appropriate intervals, having regard to the ML/TF risks it may reasonably face. It must be designed to enable employees to understand:

- The obligations of the reporting entity under the AML/CTF Act and Rules;
- The consequences of non-compliance with the AML/CTF Act and Rules;
- The type of ML/TF risk that the reporting entity might face and the potential consequences of such risk; and
- Those processes and procedures provided by the reporting entity's AML/CFT programme that are relevant to the work carried out by the employee.

Employees must be subject to an appropriate due diligence screening programme.

27.3.13 Record-keeping

A reporting entity must make a record of a designated service and related documentation, and keep these for seven years. It must also retain a record of an applicable customer identification procedure for seven years after the end of the reporting entity's relationship with the relevant customer. A reporting entity must retain a copy of its anti-money-laundering and counter-terrorism-financing programme.

27.3.14 Reporting Requirements

Reporting entities are required to enrol with AUSTRAC and to keep enrolment details up to date. A reporting entity must submit to AUSTRAC a report relating to the reporting entity's compliance with this Act, the regulations and the AML/CFT Rules during the reporting period. The report must cover the calendar year and be submitted by 31st March of the following year.

27.3.15 Suspicious Transaction Reporting

Part A of a reporting entity's AML/CFT programme must include:

- The obligations that apply to the reporting; and
- Appropriate systems and controls of the reporting entity designed to ensure compliance with the reporting obligations of the reporting entity.

A reporting entity must submit a suspicious transaction report to AUSTRAC if:

- It suspects a customer is not who they say they are;
- It suspects evasion of any taxation, money laundering or other law;
- It suspects involvement in terrorism financing.

The report should be submitted within 24 hours for any terrorism suspicions, and three business days for other issues.

A reporting entity must report a transaction that involves the transfer of physical or e-currency amounting to not less than AU$10,000 ("a threshold transaction") to AUSTRAC within ten business days of it occurring.

27.3.16 Penalties

Pecuniary penalties are payable for contravention of civil penalty provisions. Authorised officers, customs officers and police officers may issue infringement notices for unreported cross-border movements of physical currency and bearer negotiable instruments.

In determining the pecuniary penalty, the Federal Court must have regard to all relevant matters, including:

- The nature and extent of the contravention;
- The nature and extent of any loss or damage suffered as a result of the contravention;
- The circumstances in which the contravention took place;

- Whether the person has previously been found by the Federal Court in proceedings under this Act to have engaged in any similar conduct;
- If the Federal Court considers that it is appropriate to do so, whether the person has previously been found by a court in proceedings under a law of a State or Territory to have engaged in any similar conduct;
- If the Federal Court considers that it is appropriate to do so, whether the person has previously been found by a court in a foreign country to have engaged in any similar conduct; and
- If the Federal Court considers that it is appropriate to do so, whether the person has previously been found by a court in proceedings under the Financial Transaction Reports Act 1988 to have engaged in any similar conduct.

The pecuniary penalty payable by a body corporate must not exceed 100,000 penalty units ($11,000,000). The pecuniary penalty payable by a person other than a body corporate must not exceed 20,000 penalty units ($2,200,000).

The AUSTRAC CEO is to monitor compliance by reporting entities with their obligations under this Act. The AUSTRAC CEO may give a remedial direction to a reporting entity that has contravened a civil penalty provision. The Federal Court may grant injunctions in relation to contraventions of civil penalty provisions.

27.3.17 Changes to AML/CFT Rules

Australian AML/CFT regulations are in the process of change as this book is going to print, a full description of which can be found at http://www.austrac.gov.au/draft-amlctf-rules.html.

Statutory Review of Australia's Anti-money-laundering and Counter-terrorism-financing Regime

The Australian government is conducting a public consultation on the operation of Australia's anti-money-laundering and counter-terrorism-financing regime as part of the statutory review of the country's AML/CFT regime.

The review encompasses the operation of the *Anti-Money Laundering and Counter-Terrorism Financing Act (Cth) 2006* and the associated AML/CFT rules and regulations.

Public submissions closed on Friday 28th March, 2014.

Enhancements to the Requirements for Customer Due Diligence

Submissions on the consultation on possible enhancements to the requirements for customer due diligence paper closed on 30th September, 2013 and are being considered.

At this stage it is not possible to know for certain how the regulations in Australia will change as a result of these consultations.

27.3.18 Case Studies

As stated above, the Australian authorities have been active in taking action against money laundering and terrorist financing. The following two cases illustrate the type of transactions that have been identified in practice.

In a recent case, AUSTRAC information assisted authorities with an investigation into a company suspected of a multi-million-dollar duty-free fraud. The investigation resulted in the company and its two directors being convicted of fraud-related charges.

The investigation revealed that, over a three-year period, a complex arrangement was set up where the directors of the company, which traded as a duty-free store, sold large quantities of "underbond" cigarettes (cigarettes on which excise duty had not been paid).

The directors sold the cigarettes and profited by avoiding paying the required customs and excise duty. In total, authorities believe that the suspects evaded more than AUD 2.5 million in tax.

In accordance with AML/CFT reporting requirements, reporting entities submitted a range of financial transaction reports indicating suspicious activity by the company and its directors, involving currency exchange business and casinos. Authorities believe the suspects undertook a range of activities to launder and hide the substantial proceeds of the cigarette sales.

One of the directors travelled regularly to Cambodia and would visit currency exchange businesses in Australia to convert funds to US dollars before each trip. When converting currency amounts worth more than AUD 10,000, the two directors regularly refused to complete significant cash transaction reports (SCTRs), instead opting to structure the cash into smaller amounts to avoid the SCTR-reporting requirement.

This structuring activity led to a total of 44 suspect transaction reports (SUSTRs) being submitted about the two directors, with the majority coming from a currency exchange business. It was also reported that the suspects had asked reporting entities whether or not their transactions would be recorded and reported to the Australian Taxation Office (ATO), a further indication that they were involved in illegal activity and were concerned about attracting the attention of authorities.

AUSTRAC also received SUSTRs from a casino, highlighting one suspect's continued use of a casino account to deposit and withdraw funds, despite undertaking limited gambling activity. The reports indicated the suspect was a regular patron at the casino. While the suspect's gambling activity remained limited, the amounts gambled had increased substantially over an eight-year period. It was also reported that the suspect had collaborated with a number of third parties while depositing and withdrawing funds at the casino.

In all, AUSTRAC information showed that the two directors and associates made cash deposits worth more than AUD 20 million into their business banking account.

The company and its directors were convicted and ordered to repay the AUD 2.5 million in tax they had evaded. In addition, they were ordered to pay penalties of more than AUD 600,000, as well as the Commonwealth's legal costs of AUD 140,000. The convictions finalised a long-running and complex investigation.

In another case, an Australian-based mining company initiated an internal investigation after it was suspected an employee had stolen more than AUD 1.1 million over a three-year period. The company identified the suspect through internal audit processes and the matter was referred to law-enforcement authorities for further investigation.

The law-enforcement investigation revealed that the suspect, an accountant employed by the company, had abused his position of trust by systematically making a series of unauthorised international transfers over a three-year period. The transfers were made from a company account to a number of offshore accounts held in the suspect's name and a number of his family members' names.

A suspect transaction report (SUSTR) submitted by a bank suggested that an outgoing international funds transfer instruction (IFTI) of AUD 27,500 from the suspect's personal account appeared to be sourced from company funds. The suspect was the beneficiary of the IFTI and bank staff noticed that four days prior to the IFTI, the exact amount of AUD 27,500 was transferred into the suspect's account from a company account.

AUSTRAC analysis found a number of transaction reports linked to the suspect. These supported the allegation of theft and identified the significant extent of the financial activity undertaken by the suspect.

AUSTRAC information revealed that the suspect was the beneficiary of 17 outgoing IFTIs to India in amounts of between AUD 2,400 and AUD 33,400. Funds were sent from either the suspect's personal Australian-based bank account or from the company's account. In total, approximately AUD 300,000 was transferred, all believed to be the proceeds of the theft.

Law-enforcement officers contacted the suspect while he was overseas. The suspect surrendered to authorities on his return to Australia. The suspect was charged with ten counts of stealing and sentenced to seven years' imprisonment. After serving four years, the suspect was deported from Australia.

27.4 COUNTRY PROFILE: BAHAMAS

27.4.1 *Overview*

The location of the Bahamas as an offshore financial centre means that it attracts drug trafficking more than it does money laundering. As of 2007, 14 ML prosecutions had been instituted in the Bahamas and over $6.6 million of forfeited proceeds had been placed in the Confiscated Assets Fund.

27.4.2 *Key Legislation*

The Proceeds of Crime Act 2000 provides the main money-laundering offences, supplemented by various other statutes and the Central Bank of the Bahamas' AML guidelines. At the time of writing, the Compliance Commission Codes of Practice were being revised and no information regarding the changes had been released.

27.4.3 *Legislative History*

The first money-laundering-deterrence legislation passed related to drug trafficking. This was initially criminalised through the implementation of the Forfeiture of Proceeds of Drug Trafficking Act 1987.

The Bahamas was one of the first nations to incorporate into legislation the UN Convention Against the Illicit Trafficking of Narcotics and Psychotropic Substances. The IMF noted, in its review, that there was adherence with the FATF's "40 + 9" recommendations, which can be found in the preventative measures of the Central Bank of the Bahamas.

There are five main bodies of law that currently constitute the legal framework for money-laundering deterrence operating in the Bahamas:

- The Proceeds of Crime Act 2000;
- The Financial Intelligence Unit Act 2000;
- The Financial Transactions Reporting Act 2000, amended in 2003 by The Financial Transactions Reporting Regulations;
- The Anti Terrorism Act 2004;
- The Financial Transactions Reporting (Wire Transfers) Regulations 2009.

The Central Bank of the Bahamas issued revised AML/CFT guidelines in March 2011. The Securities Commission released its guidelines for Licensees/Registrants on the Prevention of Money Laundering and Countering Terrorist Financing.

27.4.4 *FATF Assessment*

The most recent FATF mutual assessment of the Bahamas, published in 2007, was positive, describing the regime as robust, coherent and comprehensive.

27.4.5 The Primary AML Investigation/Regulatory Authorities

Financial Intelligence Unit

The Financial Intelligence Unit (FIU) is responsible for receiving, analysing, obtaining and disseminating information that relates to, or may relate to, proceeds of crime in an effort to combat money laundering and terrorist financing. Its target audience is financial institutions as defined by the Financial Transaction Reporting Act (FTRA), the regulatory bodies for all financial institutions and the general public at large. Any individual concerned with combating proceeds of crime as dictated by the Proceeds of Crime Act, while detecting criminal activity relating to money laundering and terrorist financing can approach the FIU. The FIU has two roles:

1. In its regulatory role, the agency is responsible for receiving, analysing, obtaining and, in defined circumstances, dissemination of information, which relates to, or may relate to, the proceeds of offences specified in the Second Schedule of the Proceeds of Crime Act.
2. In its intelligence role, the agency is fully committed to the Egmont Group's *Statement of Purpose* which incorporates *Principles for Information Exchange between Financial Intelligence Units for Money Laundering and Terrorism Financing Cases*.

The Compliance Commission (Corporate Practitioners)

This is an independent statutory body established as the anti-money-laundering regulatory authority for non-traditional financial institutions, for example law firms, accounting firms, real estate brokers, credit unions, etc. Although it is an independent agency, the Compliance Commission falls within the responsibility of the Minister of Finance.

The Central Bank of the Bahamas

The central bank's role is to foster an environment of monetary stability conducive to economic development, and to ensure a stable and sound financial system.

The Securities Commission

This Commission regulates the activities of the securities and capital markets, with the aim of protecting investors while strengthening the public and institutional confidence in the integrity of those markets.

Bahamas Financial Services Board (BFSB)

The BFSB represents and promotes the development of all sectors of the industry, including banking, private banking and trust services, mutual funds, capital markets, investment advisory services, accounting and legal services, insurance and corporate and shipping registries. In addition to its coordinated programmes to increase confidence and expand knowledge of The Bahamas among international businesses and investors, the private-sector-led BFSB will continue to consult with government to develop new initiatives to meet the rapidly changing demands of international financial markets.

Inspector of Financial and Corporate Service Providers

Under the provisions of the Financial and Corporate Service Providers Act 2000 the Inspector is required to maintain a general review of financial and corporate services in The Bahamas. Annually, and when required by the relevant Minister, the Inspector must conduct on-site and off-site examinations of a licensee to ensure compliance by the licensee with the FCSPA, as well as the Financial Transactions Reporting Act and the International Business Companies Act and any other relevant law.

27.4.6 Outline of Specific Money-laundering Offences

There are three main money-laundering offences in The Bahamas.

Section 40 of the Proceeds of Crime Act provides that "a person is guilty of the offence of money laundering if he uses, transfers, sends or delivers to any person or place any property which, in whole or in part, directly or indirectly represents proceeds of criminal conduct; or disposes of, converts, alters or otherwise deals with that property in any manner and by any means with the intent to conceal or disguise such property". This offence can be committed on the basis of knowledge or reasonable grounds for suspicion that the property is the proceeds of crime.

It is also an offence for a person to assist another to retain or live off the proceeds of criminal conduct knowing, suspecting or having reasonable grounds to suspect that the other person is, or has been, engaged in, or has benefited from, criminal conduct.

A person is also guilty of an offence if he knows, suspects or has reasonable grounds to suspect that any property, in whole or in part, directly or indirectly represents another person's proceeds of criminal conduct, and he acquires or uses that property or has possession of it.

27.4.7 Defences

It is a defence for a person to prove that he or she did not know, suspect or have reasonable grounds to suspect that:

- The arrangement in question related to any person's proceeds of criminal conduct; or
- The arrangement facilitated the retention or control of any property by or on behalf of the suspected person; or
- By arrangement any property was used as mentioned above.

Furthermore, it is a defence for a person to prove that he intended to disclose to a police officer a suspicion, belief or matter that any funds or property were derived from, or used in connection with, criminal conduct, but there is a reasonable excuse for failing to do so.

27.4.8 Risk-based Approach

The guidelines prescribe the operation of a risk-based approach based on the development of a risk-rating framework which should include, as a minimum:

- Differentiation of client relationships by risk categories (such as high, moderate or low);
- Differentiation of client relationships by risk factors (such as products, client type/profession, country of domicile, complexity of ownership and legal structure, source of business, type of assets, size and volume of transactions, type of transactions, cash transactions, adherence to client activity profile);
- The Know Your Customer (KYC) documentation and due diligence information requirements appropriate for each risk category and risk factor; and
- A process for the approval of the downgrading/upgrading of risk ratings.

The risk-rating framework should provide for the periodic review of the customer relationship to allow the licensee to determine whether any adjustment should be made to the risk rating. The review of the risk rating for high-risk customers may be undertaken more frequently than for other customers, and a determination made by senior management as to whether the relationship should be continued. All decisions regarding high-risk relationships and the basis for these decisions should be documented.

Licensees should monitor both potential and existing customers.

27.4.9 *Role of the MLRO/Nominated Officer*

Licensed firms are required to appoint an MLRO. Under the March 2011 Guidelines, all licensees are required to:

- Introduce procedures for the prompt investigation of suspicions and, if appropriate, subsequent reporting to the FIU;
- Ensure that the MLRO and the Compliance Officer as well as any other persons appointed to assist them, have timely access to systems, customer records and all other relevant information which they require to discharge their duties;
- Establish close cooperation and liaise with the central bank;
- Notify the central bank of the name(s) of the MLRO and the Compliance Officer;
- Include in the notification a statement that the MLRO and the Compliance Officer are fit and proper persons;
- Notify the central bank where there are any changes to the MLRO and the Compliance Officer.

A licensee may choose to combine the functions of the Compliance Officer with that of the MLRO, depending upon the scale and nature of business. The roles might be assigned to its inspection, fraud or compliance functions.

The MLRO should be sufficiently senior to command the necessary authority. The MLRO is required to determine whether the information or other matters contained in the transaction report he or she has received gives rise to a knowledge or suspicion that a customer is engaged in money laundering or the financing of terrorism. In making this judgment, the MLRO should have timely access to all other relevant information such as customer identification data and other CDD information transaction records available for a licensee concerning the person or business to which the initial report relates. This may include a review of other transaction patterns and volumes through the account or accounts in the same name, the length of the business relationship and reference to identification records held.

If, after completing this review, the MLRO decides that the initial report gives rise to a knowledge or suspicion of money laundering or terrorist financing, then the MLRO must disclose information about the former to the FIU and about the latter to the Commissioner of Police.

It would be prudent, for the MLRO's own protection, for internal procedures to require that only written reports of suspicious transactions are submitted to the MLRO, who should record his or her determination in writing and the underlying reasons for their decisions.

27.4.10 Due Diligence

Customer identification is based on the following two important aspects of knowing your customer:

- Being satisfied that a prospective customer is who he/she claims to be and is the ultimate client; and
- Ensuring that sufficient information is obtained on the nature of the business that the customer expects to undertake, and any expected or predictable pattern of transactions.

This information should be updated as appropriate, and as opportunities arise.

Licensees should observe the following timeframes when seeking to verify the identity of their customers:

- In the case of prospective customers, licensees must verify customer identity before permitting such customers to become facility holders.
- Whenever the amount of cash involved in an occasional transaction exceeds $15,000, the identity of the person who conducts the transaction should be verified before the transaction is conducted.
- Whenever the amount of cash involved in an occasional transaction exceeds $15,000 and it appears that the person is conducting the transaction on behalf of another person, the identities of the third parties must be verified before the transaction is conducted.
- Whenever it appears that two or more (occasional) transactions are, or have been, deliberately structured to avoid lawful verification and the aggregate amount of cash involved in the transaction(s) exceeds $15,000, verification should be conducted as soon as practicable after the licensee becomes aware of the foregoing circumstances.
- Whenever a licensee knows, suspects or has reasonable grounds to suspect that a customer is conducting or proposes to conduct a transaction which involves the proceeds of criminal conduct; or is an attempt to avoid the enforcement of the POCA,

verification should take place as soon as practicable after the licensee has knowledge or suspicion in respect of the relevant transaction.

- Whenever a licensee has reasonable grounds to suspect that financial services are related to, or are to be used to facilitate, an offence under the Anti-Terrorism Act, verification should take place as soon as practicable after such suspicions arise.

Where satisfactory evidence of identity is required, no transaction should be conducted over the facility pending receipt of identification evidence and information. Documents of title should not be issued, nor income remitted (though it may be re-invested) in the absence of evidence of identity.

Personal Client Due Diligence

A licensee must obtain and document the following information when seeking to verify identity:

- Full and correct name/names used;
- Correct permanent address including postcode (if appropriate);
- Date and place of birth;
- The purpose of the account and the nature of the business relationship.

The following information may also be required:

- Nationality;
- Occupation and name of employer (if self-employed, the nature of the self-employment);
- Estimated level of account activity including:
  - size, in the case of investment and custody accounts;
  - balance ranges, in the case of current and deposit accounts;
  - an indication of the expected transaction volume of the account;
  - the source of funds.

In circumstances where the licensee's customer is considered a high-risk client, the licensee is also required to confirm the customer's source of wealth.

To confirm an address, the licensee should:

- Check the Register of Electors;
- Examine a recent utility bill, tax assessment or bank or credit union statement containing details of the address (it is strongly recommended that original documents are examined);
- Check the telephone directory; and
- Undertake a home visit.

The information obtained should demonstrate that a person of that name exists at the address given, and that the facility holder is that person.

Identification documents, either originals or certified copies, should be pre-signed and bear a discernable photograph of the applicant, for example:

- Current valid passport;
- Armed forces ID card;
- Driving licence bearing the photograph and signature of the applicant;
- Voter's card;
- National identity card;
- Such other documentary evidence as is reasonably capable of establishing the identity of the individual customer.

Corporate Customer Due Diligence

Licensees must obtain the following documents and information when seeking to verify the identity of corporate clients:

- The original or a certified copy of the Certificate of Incorporation or equivalent document.
- A copy of the board resolution authorising the opening of the account or other facility and the signatories authorised to sign on the account.
- Satisfactory evidence of the identity of all account signatories, details of their relationship with the company and, if they are not employees, an explanation of the relationship. All signatories must be verified in accordance with the principles outlined above.
- Satisfactory evidence of the identity of each of the natural person(s) with a controlling interest in the corporate entity (over 10% shareholding or otherwise exercising control).
- Confirmation before a business relationship is established that the applicant company is solvent, through a current Certificate of Good Standing or equivalent document or a set of consolidated financial statements that have been audited by a reliable firm of auditors.

In addition, the guidelines strongly recommend that licensees obtain the following information and documents when seeking to verify the identity of corporate clients:

- A certified copy of the memorandum and articles of association;
- A description of the nature of the corporate entity's business, including:
  - date of commencement of business;
  - products or services provided;
  - location of principal business; and

  - name and location of the registered office and registered agent of the corporate entity, where appropriate;
- The reason for establishing the business relationship;
- The potential parameters of the account including, where applicable, size, balance ranges, an indication of the expected transaction volume of the account; the source of wealth, the source of funds and a copy of the last available financial statements, where appropriate;
- Copies of Powers of Attorney, or any other authority, affecting the operation of the account given by the directors in relation to the company and supported by a copy of the respective board resolution;
- Copies of the list/register of directors and officers of the corporate entity including their names and addresses;
- Written confirmation that all credits to the account are, and will be, beneficially owned by the facility holder except in circumstances where the account is being operated by an intermediary for the purpose of holding funds in his professional capacity;
- Satisfactory evidence of identity must be established for at least two directors, one of whom should, if applicable, be an executive director where different from account signatories; and
- Such other official documentary and other information as is reasonably capable of establishing the structural information of the corporate entity.

Simplified Customer Due Diligence

Verification of identity is not normally needed in the case of a single occasional transaction when payment by, or to, the customer is less than $15,000. Irrespective of the size of a transaction, however, any suspicions of money laundering must be reported in accordance with the FIU's Suspicious Transactions Reporting Guidelines. There are also a number of bodies subject to simplified CDD, including government bodies, superannuation schemes and employment pension schemes.

Enhanced Customer Due Diligence

Licensees should apply enhanced CDD measures on a risk-sensitive basis for such categories of customer, business relations or transactions as the licensee may assess to present a higher risk for money laundering or terrorist financing. The extent of additional monitoring and information sought will depend on the money-laundering or terrorist-financing risk involved. A licensee should hold a fuller set of information in respect of those customers.

Non-face-to-face Customer Due Diligence

The extent of verification in respect of non-face-to-face customers will depend on the nature and characteristics of the product or service provided and the assessed money-laundering and terrorist-financing risk presented by the customer. A licensee should take specific and adequate measures to compensate for the higher risk, most notably for forgery and fraud, for example, by applying one or more of the following measures:

- Requiring the customer's first payment or transaction to be carried out through an account in the customer's name with a Bahamian financial institution or a financial institution located in a country listed in the First Schedule to the FTRA.
- Seeking verification of identity from a financial institution referred to above.
- Requiring additional documents to complement those required for face-to-face customers.
- Making telephone contact with the customer on a home or business number which has been verified prior to opening an account or conducting a transaction.
- Communicating with the customer at an address that has been verified.
- Internet sign-on following verification procedures where the customer uses security codes, tokens and/or other passwords which have been set up during account opening and provided by mail (or secure delivery) to the named individual at an independently verified address.
- Requiring copy documents to be certified by a suitable certifier.

Politically Exposed Persons

Politically exposed persons (PEPs) are defined as "individuals who hold or have held, in the preceding year, important public positions". An individual ceases to be a PEP after he has left office for one year. However, licensees are encouraged to apply a risk-based approach in determining whether they should cease carrying out appropriately enhanced monitoring of a PEP's transactions and activity at the end of this period. A longer period might be appropriate, in order to ensure that the higher risks associated with the individual's previous position have adequately abated.

Correspondent Banking

Licensees should obtain senior management approval before establishing new correspondent relationships, and a review of the correspondent banking relationship should be conducted at least annually.

Transactions conducted through correspondent relationships need to be monitored according to perceived risk. Where the respondent bank or counterparty is not regulated by a country listed in the First Schedule of the FTRA, additional due diligence should be carried out to ascertain and assess whether its AML/CFT controls are in accordance with standards which are at least equivalent to those required under Bahamian law.

Additionally, licensees must gather sufficient information about the respondent's business to understand fully the nature of the respondent's business and determine, from publicly available information, the reputation of the respondent and the quality of supervision, including whether it has been subject to a money-laundering or terrorist-financing investigation or regulatory action.

Licensees should document the responsibilities of each institution in relation to KYC measures. Staff dealing with correspondent banking accounts should be trained to recognise high-risk circumstances, and be prepared to challenge respondents over irregular activity, whether isolated transactions or trends, submitting an STR where appropriate.

Licensees should guard against passing funds through accounts without taking reasonable steps to satisfy themselves that sufficient due diligence has been undertaken by the remitting bank on the underlying client and the origin of funds. In these circumstances, the licensee must be satisfied that the respondent institution is able to provide KYC documentation on the underlying customer, upon request.

Licensees should consider terminating the accounts of respondents who fail to provide satisfactory answers to reasonable enquiries including, where appropriate, confirming the identity of customers involved in unusual or suspicious transactions.

27.4.11 *Ongoing Monitoring*

Licensees are required to make arrangements to verify, on a regular basis, compliance with internal policies, procedures and controls relating to money-laundering and terrorist-financing activities, in order to satisfy management that the requirements under the law and in these guidelines, to maintain such procedures, have been discharged. Larger licensees should assign this role to their Internal Audit Department. Smaller licensees may wish to introduce a regular review by the board of directors or their external auditors.

Licensees should monitor the conduct of the relationship/account to ensure that it is consistent with the nature of business stated when the relationship/account was opened, the extent of which will depend on the risk associated with the customer. They should be aware of any significant changes or inconsistencies compared to the original stated purpose of the account. Possible areas to monitor could be:

- Transaction type
- Frequency
- Amount
- Geographical origin/destination
- Account signatories.

27.4.12 *Staff Training*

Licensees should also establish and implement appropriate policies and procedures to ensure high standards are being followed when hiring employees. To this end, licensees should have in place screening procedures, which should involve making diligent and appropriate enquiries about the personal history of the potential employee and taking up appropriate references on the individual.

Licensees must take appropriate measures to make employees aware of:

- Policies and procedures put in place to detect and prevent money laundering and to counter the financing of terrorism, including those for identification, record-keeping, the detection of unusual and suspicious transactions and internal reporting; and

- The relevant legislation pertaining to AML/CFT, and to provide relevant employees with training in the recognition and handling of suspicious transactions.

At least once per year, financial institutions shall provide relevant employees with appropriate training in the recognition and handling of transactions carried out by persons who may be engaged in money laundering. The following is recommended:

New Employees

General information on the background to money laundering and terrorist financing, and the subsequent need for reporting of any suspicious transactions to the MLRO should be provided to all new employees who will be dealing with customers or their transactions, irrespective of the level of seniority, within the first month of their employment. They should be made aware of the importance placed on the reporting of suspicions by the organisation, that there is a legal requirement to report and that there is a personal statutory obligation in this respect. They should also be provided with a copy of the written policies and procedures in place in the financial institution for the reporting of suspicious transactions.

Cashiers/Foreign Exchange Operators/Advisory Staff

All front-line staff should be made aware of the business policy for dealing with occasional customers, particularly where large cash transactions, money transfers, negotiable instruments, certificates of deposit or letters of credit and other guarantees, etc. are involved, and of the need for extra vigilance in these cases. Training should be provided on factors that may give rise to suspicions and on the procedures to be adopted when a transaction is deemed to be suspicious.

Branch staff should be trained to recognise that criminal money may not only be paid in or drawn out across branch counters but may be transferred by other means. Staff should be encouraged to take note of credit and debit transactions from other sources, e.g. credit transfers, wire transfers and ATM transactions.

Account/Facility Opening Personnel

Those members of staff responsible for account/facility opening and acceptance of new customers must receive the basic training given to cashiers or tellers in the above section. In addition, further training should be provided in respect of the need to verify a customer's identity and on the business's own account opening and customer/client verification procedures. They should also be familiarised with the business's suspicious transaction reporting procedures.

Administration/Operations Supervisors and Managers

A higher level of instruction covering all aspects of AML/CFT procedures should be provided to those with the responsibility for supervising or managing staff. This will include the offences and penalties arising from the POCA and the FTRA for non-reporting and for assisting money launderers; procedures relating to the service of production and restraint orders; internal reporting procedures; and the requirements for verification of identity, the retention of records and disclosure of suspicious transaction reports under the FIUA 2000.

27.4.13 Record-keeping

Financial institutions are required to retain records concerning customer identification and transactions for use as evidence in any investigation into money laundering or terrorist financing. The records prepared and maintained by a licensee on its customer relationships and transactions should be such that:

- The requirements of legislation are fully met;
- Competent third parties will be able to assess the licensee's observance of AML/CFT policies and procedures;
- Any transactions effected via the licensee can be reconstructed; and
- The licensee can satisfy court orders or enquiries from the appropriate authorities.

Regarding CDD, licensees must keep such records as are reasonably necessary to enable the nature of the evidence used for the purposes of that verification to be readily identified by the FIU. Records relating to the verification of the identity of facility holders must be retained for at least five years from the date a person ceases to be a facility holder, i.e. the end of the business relationship or the date of the last transaction.

Transaction records must be kept for a minimum period of five years after the transaction has been completed. The investigating authorities need to be able to compile a satisfactory audit trail for suspected laundered money or terrorist financing and to be able to establish a financial profile of any suspect account/facility.

At a minimum, the records relating to transactions which must be kept must include the following information:

- The nature of the transaction;
- Details of the transaction including the amount of the transaction, and the currency in which it was denominated;
- The date on which the transaction was conducted;
- Details of the parties to the transaction; and
- Where applicable, the facility through which the transaction was conducted, and any other facilities directly involved in the transaction.

Records of suspicions which were raised internally with the MLRO but not disclosed to the authorities should be retained for at least five years from the date of the transaction. Records of suspicions which the authorities have advised are of no interest should be retained for a similar period. Likewise, records of a licensee's findings of its enquiries into unusual activity should also be retained for a minimum of five years.

27.4.14 Suspicious Transaction Reporting

Where a transaction is inconsistent in amount, origin, destination or type with a client's known, legitimate business or personal activities, or has no apparent economic or visible lawful purpose, the transaction must be considered unusual, and the staff member put "on enquiry" as to whether the business relationship is being used for money-laundering purposes or to finance terrorism.

Where the staff member conducts enquiries and obtains what he considers to be a satisfactory explanation of the unusual transaction, or unusual pattern of transactions, he may conclude that there are no grounds for suspicion, and therefore take no further action as he is satisfied with matters. However, where the enquiries conducted by the staff member do not provide a satisfactory explanation of the transaction, he may conclude that there are grounds for suspicion requiring the filing of an STR to the FIU.

27.4.15 Penalties

Licensees should be aware that there are a number of offences which arise from failing to comply with certain obligations imposed under the AML Law and supplementary regulations, and criminal prosecution and/or penalties can be imposed. In particular, under the FIUA and The Financial Intelligence (Transactions Reporting) Regulations, where a financial institution fails to comply with the requirements of guidelines issued by the FIU or the central bank, these penalties can range from a fine of $10,000 on summary conviction or $50,000 for a first offence and $100,000 for any subsequent offence on conviction in the Supreme Court. Licensees should also be aware that the central bank also has authority under the Financial Transactions Reporting (Wire Transfers) Regulations to impose civil penalties of up to $2,000 for non-compliance with those laws and with the guidelines.

27.4.16 Case Studies

According to the US State Department Money Laundering Report 2012, there were no prosecutions or convictions for money laundering in the Bahamas in 2011.

27.5 COUNTRY PROFILE: BARBADOS

27.5.1 Overview

Barbados had previously appeared on the list of countries that caused concern for a lack of compliance when assessed by the FATF. It has recently been deemed mostly compliant by both the FATF and the regional body the CFATF. The Caribbean Financial Action Task Force (CFATF) is an organisation of states and territories of the Caribbean basin which has agreed to implement common countermeasures against money laundering. The CFATF originated in early 1990 and holds observer status with the FATF.

The 2008 FATF assessment noted that, generally, serious crime in Barbados has been on the decline. With the advent of more stringent controls in financial institutions, there have been increased attempts at structuring transactions to avoid reporting thresholds, but these have been mitigated by financial institutions risk profiling their client bases.

27.5.2 Key Legislation

The Money Laundering and Financing of Terrorism (Prevention and Control) Act 2011-23 is the primary AML legislation. The Revised Central Bank AMLA Guidelines provide further money-laundering-deterrence guidance for banks.

27.5.3 Legislative History

Money laundering in Barbados was first criminalised in 1990 through the implementation of the Proceeds of Crime Act, CAP 143 (POCA). A more focussed treatment on money-laundering-deterrence legislation was introduced by the implementation of the Money Laundering (Prevention and Control) Act (CAP 129), 1998-38 (MLPCA).

In 2000, the Anti-Money Laundering Authority and the financial intelligence unit (FIU) were established to supervise the financial sector.

The key regulations operating in Barbados arise from the implementation of the following legislation:

- Money Laundering and Financing of Terrorism (Prevention and Control) Act 2002;
- Money Laundering and Financing of Terrorism (Prevention and Control) Act, 2011;
- Money Laundering (Prevention and Control) Act 1998;
- Anti-Terrorism Act 2000;
- Proceeds of Crime Act 1990;
- Drug Abuse (Prevention and Control) Act 1990;
- Mutual Assistance Criminal Matters Act 1992.

27.5.4 FATF Assessment

The 2008 evaluation found Barbados to be partially compliant or not compliant with 27 of the 40+9 recommendations. However, the 2012 Progress Report noted that most of the recommendations have been complied with within the new AML legislation. In addition to this, further legislation and guidelines are being considered.

27.5.5 The Primary AML Investigation/Regulatory Authorities

Anti-Money Laundering Authority

The Anti-Money Laundering Authority is the FIU of Barbados. Its goal is to prevent or control money laundering and the financing of terrorism through the collection and analysis of financial intelligence and the facilitation of all legitimate and appropriate anti-money-laundering and anti-terrorism-funding efforts.

The FIU outlines and pursues a number of objectives that were intended to facilitate the attainment of this goal, which are to:

- Establish close working relationships with financial institutions and other relevant local and international agencies in order to combat and prevent money laundering and the financing of terrorism.
- Provide relevant feedback to the FIU's constituents where appropriate.
- Develop and maintain intelligence-sharing structures and systems.
- Effectively supervise the anti-money-laundering and prevention of terrorism efforts of financial institutions.
- Encourage compliance with the guidelines for financial institutions as issued by the Anti-Money Laundering Authority.
- Educate special interest groups and the general public about the prevention of money laundering and terrorist financing.
- Cooperate with international agencies and countries to prevent money laundering and terrorist financing.

The Central Bank of Barbados

The Central Bank of Barbados is responsible for promoting monetary stability, promoting a sound financial structure, fostering development of the money and capital markets, channelling commercial bank credit into productive activities and fostering credit and exchange conditions conducive to the orderly and sustained economic development of Barbados. Consistent with this, its mission statement is to foster a sound economic and financial environment which promotes the development of stakeholders and encourages a culture of excellence and leadership.

Major regulators in Barbados have signed a Memorandum of Understanding for the exchange of information, cooperation and consultation. Signatories to the Memorandum are:

- The central bank;
- The FIU;
- The Supervisor of Insurance and Pensions;

- The Ministry of Industry and International Business (now replaced by the Ministry of Economic Affairs and Development);
- The Securities Commission, Registry of Cooperatives and Friendly Services;
- The Registrar of Corporate Affairs and Intellectual Property.

Each agency licenses and supervises its constituents in accordance with various statutes, regulations and guidelines.

Royal Barbados Police Force
Responsibility for the investigation and prosecution of money-laundering and terrorist-financing-related offences rests with the Royal Barbados Police Force's (RBPF) Financial Crimes Investigation Unit (FCIU) and the Office of the Director of Public Prosecutions. The FCIU has responsibility for completing investigations into all money-laundering and terrorist-financing-related reports forwarded by the FIU.

27.5.6 Outline of Specific Money-laundering Offences

Under the Money Laundering and Financing Of Terrorism (Prevention And Control) Act, Section 5, a person engages in money laundering where:

- The person engages, directly or indirectly, in a transaction that involves money or other property or a benefit that is proceeds of crime; or
- The person receives, possesses, conceals, disposes of or brings into, or sends out of, Barbados any money or other property or a benefit that is proceeds of crime.

Furthermore, a person engages in money laundering where he knows, or has reasonable grounds to suspect, that the property or benefit is derived or realised, directly or indirectly, from some form of unlawful activity or, where the person is:

- An individual other than a person referred to below, where he fails, without reasonable excuse, to take reasonable steps to ascertain whether or not the property or benefit is derived or realised, directly or indirectly, from some form of unlawful activity; or
- A financial institution or a non-financial business entity or professional, where the financial institution or non-financial business entity or professional fails to take reasonable steps to implement or apply procedures to control or combat money laundering.

27.5.7 Penalties

A person who engages in money laundering is guilty of an offence and is liable on:

- Summary conviction, to a fine of \$200,000 or to imprisonment;
- Conviction on indictment, to a fine of \$2,000,000 or to imprisonment for 25 years or to both.

A person who aids, abets, counsels or procures, the commission of, or conspires to commit, the offence of money laundering is guilty of an offence and is liable on:

- Summary conviction, to a fine of $150,000 or to imprisonment for four years or to both; or
- Conviction on indictment, to a fine of $1,500,000 or to imprisonment for 15 years or to both.

27.5.8 Scope

The AML Act applies to "financial institutions", which means a person who conducts, as a business:

- Acceptance of deposits and other repayable funds from the public, including private banking.
- Lending, including consumer credit, mortgage credit, factoring (with or without recourse) and financing of commercial transactions, including forfeiting.
- Financial leasing other than with respect to arrangements relating to consumer products.
- Money or value transmission services.
- Issuing and managing means of payment, including credit and debit cards, travellers' cheques, money orders and bankers' drafts, and electronic money.
- Issuing financial guarantees and commitments.
- and various other financial institutions defined in the Act.

27.5.9 Risk-based Approach

Barbados has implemented a risk-based approach in line with the CFATF guidelines.

CBB and AMLA have together produced risk-based approach guidelines. AMLA oversees the national regulatory framework and makes the final decision on revisions to laws and guidelines.

It has also incorporated provisions for risk-based supervision. The licensees are themselves required to undergo risk profiling by the regulators. Similarly to the risk-based approach, there are advisory and obligatory requirements. The first allows financial institutions to find an equivalent measure in its origination, with comparable results.

27.5.10 Role of the MLRO/Nominated Officer

A financial institution shall:

- Identify a person to whom an employee is to report any information that comes to the attention of the employee in the course of his employment and gives rise to knowledge or suspicion by the employee that another person is engaged in money laundering or the financing of terrorism; and

- Enable the person identified in accordance with the above to have reasonable access to information that may be relevant to determining whether a sufficient basis exists to report the matter in accordance with the AML Act.

A report may be made by letter, facsimile or mechanical or electronic means.

The AMLA Guidelines expand on the role of the Compliance Officer. All licensees should designate a suitably qualified person with the appropriate level of authority, seniority and independence as Compliance Officer. The Compliance Officer should be independent of the receipt, transfer or payment of funds, or management of customer assets and should have timely and uninhibited access to customer identification, transaction records and other relevant information. The powers and reporting structure of the officer should be conducive to the effective and independent exercise of duties.

The Compliance Officer should:

- Undertake responsibility for developing compliance policies;
- Develop a programme to communicate policies and procedures within the entity;
- Monitor compliance with the licensee's internal AML programme;
- Receive internal reports and consider all such reports;
- Issue, in his/her own discretion, external reports to the authority as soon as practicable after determining that a transaction warrants reporting;
- Monitor the accounts of persons for whom a suspicious report has been made;
- Establish and maintain ongoing awareness and training programmes for staff at all levels;
- Establish standards for the frequency and means of training;
- Report at least annually to the board of directors (or relevant oversight body in the case of branch operations) on the operations and effectiveness of the systems and controls to combat money laundering and the financing of terrorism;
- Review compliance policies and procedures to reflect changes in legislation or international developments;
- Participate in the approval process for high-risk business lines and new products, including those involving new technologies; and
- Be available to discuss with the bank or the FIU matters pertaining to the AML/CFT function.

27.5.11 *Due Diligence*

Under the AML legislation, financial institutions are obliged to take reasonable measures to:

- Establish the true identity of a customer; and
- Verify the identity of a customer by means of reliable documents, data or information from an independent source, where:

- the customer requests the institution to enter into a business arrangement or conduct an occasional transaction with the customer;
- doubt exists about the veracity or adequacy of customer identification data previously obtained in respect of the customer; or
- there is a suspicion of money laundering or financing of terrorism in connection with the customer.

The guidelines add that as part of their due diligence process, licensees should:

- Establish procedures for obtaining identification information on new customers so as to be satisfied that a prospective customer is who he claims to be.
- Use reasonable measures to verify and adequately document the identity of the customer or account holder at the outset of a business relationship. This process should include, where appropriate:
  - taking reasonable measures to understand the ownership and control structure of the customer;
  - obtaining reliable data or information from an independent source on the purpose and intended nature of the business relationship, the source of funds and source of wealth, where applicable; and
  - discontinuing the transaction if customer documentation information is not forthcoming at the outset of the relationship.
- Employ enhanced due diligence procedures for high-risk customers or transactions.
- Update identification records, on a risk-focussed basis, to ensure that all existing customer records are current and valid and conform to any new requirements.
- Monitor account activity throughout the life of the business relationship in accordance with Section 16 of the MLFTA.
- Review the existing records if there is a material change in how the account is operated or if there are doubts about previously obtained customer identification data.

Generally, licensees should not accept funds from prospective customers unless the necessary verification has been completed. In exceptional circumstances, where it would be essential not to interrupt the normal conduct of business (e.g. non-face-to-face business and securities transactions), verification may be completed after establishment of the business relationship. Should this be determined to be an acceptable risk, licensees should adopt risk-management procedures with respect to the conditions under which a customer may utilise the business relationship prior to verification. If the requirements are not met, and it is determined that the circumstances give rise to suspicion, the licensee should make a report to the authority.

Personal Client Due Diligence

A licensee should obtain relevant information on the identity of its customer and seek to verify some of the information on a risk basis, through the use of reliable, independent source documents, data or information to prove to its satisfaction that the individual is who that individual claims to be. The basic information should include:

- True name and permanent residential address;
- Valid photo-bearing identification, with unique identifier (e.g. passport, national identification card, driving licence);
- Date and place of birth and nationality (if dual, this should be indicated);
- Occupation and business or principal activity;
- Contact details, e.g. telephone number, fax number and email address;
- Purpose of the account; and
- Signature.

In addition, the licensee may obtain any other information deemed appropriate and relevant, e.g. source of funds and estimated account turnover.

The licensee should determine the degree of verification to be undertaken on a risk basis. In some instances, verification may be satisfied by maintaining current photo-bearing identification with a unique identifier (e.g. passport, national identification card).

Corporate Customer Due Diligence

To satisfy itself as to the identity of the customer, the licensee should obtain:

- Name of the corporate entity.
- Principal place of business and registered office.
- Mailing address.
- Contact telephone and fax numbers.
- Identity information on the beneficial owners of the entity. This information should extend to identifying those who ultimately own and control the company and should include anyone who is giving instructions to the licensee to act on behalf of the company.
- Identity information on directors and officers who exercise effective control over the business and are in a position to override internal procedures/control mechanisms and, in the case of bank accounts, the signatories to the account.
- Description and nature of business.
- Purpose of the account, source of funds and the estimated account activity.
- Certified copy of the Certificate of Incorporation, Organisation, Registration or Continuance, as the case may be, or any other certificate that is evidence of the creation, registration or continuance of the body corporate, society or other legal person as such, officially authenticated where the body corporate, society or other legal person was created in another country.
- By-laws and any other relevant documents, and any amendments thereto, filed with the Registrar of Corporate Affairs and Intellectual Property, the Registrar of Co-operatives or the Registrar of Friendly Societies, as the case may be.

- Board resolution authorising the opening of the account and conferring authority on signatories to the account.
- Recent financial information or audited statements.

It should be noted that if the company is publicly listed on a recognised stock exchange and not subject to effective control by a small group of individuals, identification of shareholders is not required. Furthermore, if the company is a private company, identities should be sought for persons with a minimum of 10% shareholding.

In addition to the above, the licensee may obtain any other information deemed appropriate. For example, where it is deemed necessary, a licensee may also request the financial statements of parent or affiliate companies, or seek evidence that the entity is not in the process of being dissolved or wound up. It should request this information, particularly for non-resident companies, where the corporate customer has no known track record or it relies on established affiliates for funding.

Beneficial Ownership

Where a customer of a financial institution is not an individual, the institution shall take reasonable measures to:

- Establish the true identity of the individual who is the beneficial owner of the customer; and
- Verify the identity of the individual by means of reliable documents, data or information from an independent source.

Third Party Customer Due Diligence

The AML Act provides that a financial institution shall take reasonable measures to establish whether a customer is acting on behalf of another person. Where it appears to a financial institution that a customer is acting on behalf of another person, the institution shall take reasonable measures to:

- Establish the true identity not only of the customer but also of the person on whose behalf or for whose ultimate benefit the customer may be acting.
- Verify the identity of both the customer and the person on whose behalf or for whose ultimate benefit the customer may be acting by means of reliable documents, data or information from an independent source.
- Establish whether the customer is authorised to act on behalf of the person in the capacity and in the proposed business arrangement or occasional transaction in which he acts or seeks to act.

Simplified Customer Due Diligence

The licensee's policy document should clearly define the risk categories/approach adopted and associated due diligence, monitoring and other requirements. A licensee may apply reduced due diligence to a customer provided it satisfies itself that the customer is of such a risk level that qualifies for this treatment.

Enhanced Customer Due Diligence

In determining what constitutes reasonable measures with respect to establishing and verifying the identity of a person for the purposes of this section, regard shall be had to all the circumstances of the case and in particular to:

- Whether the person is a person based or incorporated in a country in which there are in force provisions applicable to the person to prevent the use of the financial system for the purpose of money laundering and the financing of terrorism; and
- Such relevant custom and practice as may be current in the relevant business.

Non-face-to-face Customer Due Diligence

The rapid growth of financial business by electronic means increases the scope for non-face-to-face business and increases the risk of criminal access to the financial system. Customers may use the internet, the mail service or alternative means because of their convenience or because they wish to avoid face-to-face contact. Consequently, licensees should pay special attention to risks associated with new and developing technologies. Customers may complete applications but licensees should satisfy the requirements in this section before establishing a business relationship.

When accepting business from non-face-to-face customers, in order to prove to its satisfaction that the individual is who that individual claims to be, the licensee should:

- Obtain documents certified by approved persons (listed in Appendix 5 of the guidelines);
- Ensure that all company documents are signed by the Company Secretary;
- Request additional documents to complement those which are required for face-to-face customers, including more than one form of photo-bearing ID;
- Make independent contact with the customer, for example by telephone on a listed business or other number; and
- Request third party introduction, e.g. by an introducer.

In addition, the licensee may:

- Carry out employment checks (where applicable) with the customer's consent through a job letter or verbal confirmation on a listed business or other number;
- Require the first payment to be carried out through an account in the customer's name with another bank subject to equivalent customer due diligence standards; and
- Obtain any other information deemed appropriate.

Where initial checks fail to identify the customer, the licensee should independently confirm and record additional checks. If the prospective customer is required to attend a branch to conduct the first transaction, or to collect account documentation or credit/debit cards, then valid photo-bearing identification should be obtained at that time.

Politically Exposed Persons

Concerns about the abuse of power by public officials for their own enrichment and the associated reputation and legal risks which licensees may face have led to calls for enhanced due diligence on such persons. A licensee should:

- Develop policies, procedures and processes such as the use of electronic databases to assess whether a customer is, or has become, a PEP;
- Take reasonable measures to establish the source of wealth and the source of funds of PEPs;
- Exercise greater scrutiny and monitoring of all PEP accounts; and
- Require senior management to determine whether to continue the relationship where an existing customer subsequently becomes, or is found to be, a PEP.

In addition to the identity information normally requested for personal customers, the licensee should gather the following information on a PEP:

- Estimated net worth, including financial statements;
- Information on immediate family members or close associates having transaction authority over the account; and
- References or other information to confirm the reputation of the client.

Anonymous Accounts

The AMLA guidelines provide that licensees should avoid the acceptance of anonymous accounts or accounts in fictitious names.

27.5.12 Ongoing Monitoring

A financial institution shall exercise ongoing due diligence with respect to every business arrangement and closely examine the transactions conducted in the course of such an arrangement to determine whether the transactions are consistent with its knowledge of the relevant customer, his commercial activities, if any, and risk profile and, where required, the source of his funds.

27.5.13 Staff Training

A financial institution shall:

- Take appropriate measures for the purpose of making employees aware of the laws of Barbados relating to money laundering and the financing of terrorism, and the procedures and related policies established and maintained by the institution pursuant to this Part; and
- Provide employees with appropriate training in the recognition and handling of transactions involving money laundering or the financing of terrorism.

Regarding the overall training programme, a licensee should cover topics pertinent to its operations and should be informed by developments in international AML/CFT standards. Training should be general as well as specific to the area in which the trainees operate. As staff members move between jobs, their training needs for AML/CFT may change.

In order to provide evidence of compliance with the AML Act, at a minimum, a licensee should maintain the following information:

- Details and contents of the training programme provided to staff members;
- Names of staff receiving the training;
- Dates that training sessions were held;
- Test results carried out to measure staff understanding of money-laundering and terrorist-financing requirements; and
- An ongoing training plan.

27.5.14 Record-keeping

A financial institution shall establish and maintain business transaction records of all business transactions, and where evidence of the identity of a person is obtained, a record that indicates the nature of the evidence obtained and comprises either a copy of the evidence or such information as would enable a copy of the evidence to be obtained.

Records of business transactions shall be kept for a period of no less than five years from the termination of the business arrangement, the transaction, where the transaction is an occasional transaction, or such longer period as the authority may, in any specific case, direct.

Identity records shall be kept:

- Where evidence of the identity of a person is obtained pursuant to a business arrangement or the conduct of an occasional transaction, for as long as the records established in respect of the business arrangement or occasional transaction are kept; or
- In any other case, for a period of no less than five years from the making of the record.

The guidelines provide that licensees should maintain records related to unusual and suspicious business transactions for no less than five years. These should include:

- All reports made by staff to the Compliance Officer.
- The internal written findings of transactions investigated. This applies irrespective of whether a suspicious report was made.
- Consideration of those reports and of any action taken.
- Reports by the Compliance Officer to senior management and the board of directors.

27.5.15 *Internal Reporting*

To facilitate the detection of suspicious transactions, a licensee should:

- Require customers to declare the source and/or purpose of funds for business transactions in excess of threshold limits, or such lower amount as the licensee determines, to reasonably ascertain that funds are not the proceeds of criminal activity. Appendix 8 of the guidelines indicates a specimen of a Declaration Source of Funds (DSOF) form. Where electronic reports are employed instead of the form, they should capture the information included in the appendix and should be signed by the customer.
- Develop written policies, procedures and processes to provide guidance on the reporting chain and the procedures to follow when identifying and researching unusual transactions and reporting suspicious activities.
- Identify a suitably qualified and experienced person to whom unusual and suspicious reports are channelled. The person should have direct access to the appropriate records to determine the basis for reporting the matter to the authority.
- Require its staff to document in writing their suspicion about a transaction.
- Require documentation of internal enquiries.

27.5.16 *Suspicious Transaction Reporting*

A financial institution shall monitor and report to the Reports Director:

- Any business transaction where the identity of the person involved, the transaction or any other circumstance concerning the transaction gives the institution or any officer or employee of the institution reasonable grounds to suspect that the transaction:
  - involves proceeds of crime;
  - involves the financing of terrorism; or
  - is of a suspicious or an unusual nature.
- Any exchange of currency or instruction for the transfer of international funds, whether by telegraph or wire, into and out of Barbados, where the transaction appears to be of a suspicious or an unusual nature.

Subject to certain exceptions, where:

- A person transfers Barbadian currency or foreign currency into or out of Barbados; and
- The currency is more than $10, 000 in value,

the person shall make a report in respect of the transfer in accordance with this section unless permission for the transfer is obtained under the Exchange cap 71 Control Act.

27.5.17 Internal Policies

A financial institution shall:

- Develop and implement internal policies, procedures and controls to combat money laundering and the financing of terrorism;
- Develop audit functions to evaluate such policies, procedures and terrorism controls; and
- Develop a procedure to audit compliance with this Act.

27.5.18 Penalties

A financial institution or a non-financial business entity or professional who does not maintain business transaction records is guilty of an offence and is liable on conviction on indictment to a fine of $100,000.

A person who contravenes the reporting requirements is guilty of an offence and is liable:

- On summary conviction, to a fine of $10,000 or to imprisonment for two years;
- On conviction on indictment, to a fine of $200,000 or to imprisonment for five years.

A financial institution or a non-financial business entity or professional who does not make a suspicious transaction report as required under the Act, and in the case of a non-financial business entity or professional, by virtue of Section 4, is guilty of an offence and is liable on conviction on indictment to a fine of $100,000.

For other breaches of the AML Act and regulations, the financial institution can be fined $5,000 plus $500 per day the breach remains unremedied.

27.5.19 Case Studies

In December 2011, a Barbados-born baggage handler at JFK airport was convicted of drug trafficking and financial crimes. He targeted a daily flight from Barbados, and utilised secret panels inside planes and passengers' luggage to remove narcotics from the jurisdiction.

In May 2013, a pregnant woman was sentenced to 12 months in prison after she passed out 17 parcels of marijuana weighing half a pound at a Barbados hospital. She had arrived in Barbados from Trinidad, cleared immigration and was then interviewed by the police, arrested and taken to the hospital to be examined by a doctor. She said that she was pregnant and this was confirmed by ultrasound. The young woman also admitted that she had ingested drugs and tests revealed contraband in her digestive system.

She admitted in court that she was smuggling the ganja to support her family and pleaded guilty to possession of cannabis, possession with intent to supply, trafficking in the drug and importing the drug, having been paid $5,000 to do so.

27.6 COUNTRY PROFILE: BRAZIL

27.6.1 Overview

According to the FATF, the money-laundering risks in Brazil are higher in relation to the border areas and the informal economy. The banking sector is perceived to face greater money-laundering risk in the business areas of foreign exchange and private banking.

Money-laundering risk has also been detected in the securities sector through the use of brokers to deposit funds and the conduct of stock market transactions. In the insurance sector, accumulation, life and pension/retirement products are perceived as being the most vulnerable to money laundering.

Some cases of illicit drugs being exchanged for precious stones have been detected, although this is uncommon, as profit margins for precious stones sold on the open market are relatively low because most of the precious stone trade conducted in Brazil is carried out on the wholesale export market and the retail market is residual. No money-laundering cases have been detected in the closed pension funds sector.

27.6.2 Key Legislation

The primary AML legislation in Brazil is Law 12,683 of 9th July, 2012, which provides substantial amendments to Law 9,613 of 1st March, 1998, but does not completely replace it. Therefore, a number of sections of Law 9,613 remain in force. Supplementary regulations can be found in various resolutions passed by COAF, which are highlighted in the relevant sections of this profile.

27.6.3 Legislative History

The previous anti-money-laundering legislation in Brazil was Law 9,613 of 1st March, 1998. However, this legislation had fundamental flaws for which Brazil has been widely criticised, in particular for the country's lack of speed in amending it! Ironically, on this point, despite passing the new legislation in July 2012, the date for it coming into force was postponed to the following year.

Under the old legislation, money laundering was only a criminal offence if it involved the proceeds of one of the following offences:

- Illicit trafficking in narcotic substances or similar drugs;
- Terrorism and its financing;
- Smuggling or trafficking in weapons, munitions or materials used for their production;
- Extortion through kidnapping;
- Acts against the public administration, including direct or indirect demands of benefits on behalf of oneself or others, as a condition or price for the performance or the omission of any administrative act;
- Acts against the Brazilian financial system;
- Acts committed by a criminal organisation; or
- Acts committed by an individual against a foreign public administration.

This meant that the proceeds of any of the offences not listed above could not be the subject of a money-laundering conviction, rendering the law grossly ineffective.

27.6.4 FATF Assessment

The most recent mutual evaluation of Brazil assessed the legislation which was in place in 2009. It found that the government of Brazil has been working on various initiatives to mitigate the risk of terrorist financing in its territory, although preventative measures against financial crime were much less robust outside of the banking (including money remittance and foreign exchange), securities and insurance sectors. While it was complementary of the progress Brazil had made, it did recognise that there were areas of deficiency, which is consistent with the present strengthening of the money-laundering legislation.

27.6.5 The Primary AML Investigation/Regulatory Authorities

Council for Financial Activities Control

The Council for Financial Activities Control (COAF) was created by Law 9,613, of 1st March, 1998, under the jurisdiction of the Ministry of Finance, for the purpose of regulating, applying administrative sanctions, receiving pertinent information and examining and identifying suspicious occurrences of illicit activities related to money laundering.

The principles that conduct its organisation and structure are expressed in various by-laws. For example, Annex to the Decree No. 2799, of 8th October, 1998 states that the COAF is a collegiate decision-making body whose jurisdiction includes the whole Brazilian territory. The COAF is an integral part of the Ministry of Finance, with headquarters in the Federal District. Its purpose is to discipline, apply administrative penalties, receive, examine and identify the suspicions of illicit activities referred to in the law that created it, with no prejudice to the competence of other offices and entities.

Brazilian law attributes to the COAF responsibility for the identification of customers and maintenance of registers of all operations and for the communication of suspicious operations, subjecting it to administrative penalties for the disregard of its obligations.

The Ministry of Finance

The Ministry of Finance is responsible for the formulation and implementation of economic policy in Brazil. The COAF was created under the jurisdiction of the Ministry of Finance.

27.6.6 Outline of Specific Money-laundering Offences

Law 12,683 makes it an offence to conceal or disguise the nature, source, location, disposition, movement or ownership of property, rights or values derived, directly or indirectly, from a criminal offence. It is also an offence to conceal or disguise the use of property, rights or values derived from a criminal offence, or to use, in economic or financial activity, assets, rights or valuables resulting from a criminal offence.

27.6.7 Penalties

The penalty for the offences outlined above is imprisonment for three to ten years and a fine. The penalty shall be increased by one- to two-thirds if the crimes are committed repeatedly or through a criminal organisation, but can be reduced by two-thirds or served in an open or semi-open prison if the participant spontaneously collaborates with the authorities, providing explanations that lead to the investigation of criminal offences, the identification of other participants or the location of the assets, rights and values of the crime involved.

27.6.8 Scope

The AML framework applies to individuals and entities who have, on a permanent or casual basis, together or separately, as principal or accessory activity any of the following:

- The reception, brokerage and investment of third parties' funds in Brazilian or foreign currency;
- The purchase and sale of foreign currency or gold as a financial asset;
- The custody, issuance, distribution, clearing, negotiation, brokerage or management of securities.

The framework also applies to the following individuals and entities:

- Stock exchanges, commodity exchanges and futures trading systems and the organised OTC market;
- Insurance companies, insurance brokers and institutions involved with private pension plans or social security;
- Payment or credit card administrators and "consórcios" (consumer funds commonly held and managed for the acquisition of consumer goods);
- Administrators or companies that use cards or any other electronic, magnetic or similar means, that allow fund transfers;
- Companies that engage in leasing and factoring activities;
- Companies that distribute any kind of property (including cash, real estate and goods) or services, or give discounts for the acquisition of such property or services by means of lotteries or similar methods;
- Branches or representatives of foreign entities that engage in any of the activities referred to in this article, which take place in Brazil, even if occasionally;
- All other legal entities engaged in the performance of activities that are dependent upon an authorisation from the agencies that regulate the stock exchange, financial and insurance markets;
- Any and all Brazilian or foreign individuals or entities which operate in Brazil in the capacity of agents, managers, representatives or proxies, commission agents, or represent in any other way the interests of foreign legal entities that engage in any of the activities referred to in this article;

- Individuals or entities engaged in real estate development activities or the sale of property;
- Individuals or companies that sell luxury or high-value goods, act as an intermediary or exercise commercialisation activities involving large amounts of resources in kind;
- The boards of trade and public records;
- Individuals or entities that provide, even if eventually advisory, services, consulting, bookkeeping, audit, advice or assistance of any kind, in operations involving:
  - the purchase and sale of real estate, commercial or industrial establishments or equity interests of any nature;
  - the management of funds, securities or other assets;
  - the opening or management of banks, savings, investments or securities;
  - the creation, operation or management of companies of any nature, foundations, trusts or similar structures;
  - corporate or real estate; and
  - the transfer or vesting procurement activities related to sports or arts professionals;
- Individuals or entities acting on promotion, brokerage, marketing, brokering or trading rights transfer for athletes, artists or fairs, exhibitions or similar events;
- Transport companies and custody services;
- Individuals or companies who sell goods with high value of a rural or animal nature, or who assist with their marketing; and
- Foreign branches of the entities mentioned above, through their parent companies in Brazil, for residents in the country.

These entities are obliged to:

- Adopt policies, procedures and internal controls consistent with their size and volume of transactions, enabling them to meet the provisions of this article in a disciplined manner.
- Register and keep their registration current in the supervisory and regulatory body or, failing this, the Council for Financial Activities Control (COAF), in the manner and under the conditions set by them.
- Comply with requests made by the COAF in frequency, form and conditions established by it, and preserve, under the law, the confidentiality of information provided.

27.6.9 *Role of the MLRO/Nominated Officer*

The institutions and entities mentioned in Article 1 shall inform the Central Bank of Brazil of the director or manager, as the case may be, who will be responsible for the implementation of, and compliance with, the provisions set forth in this Circular, as well as for the reports mentioned in Article 4.

27.6.10 Due Diligence

Instruction No. 301 of 16th April, 1999 provides various due diligence measures for securities companies, and there are alternative resolutions issued by the COAF for entities such as gambling companies and debt-collection companies. Circular No. 3098 of 11th June, 2003 was issued by the Central Bank of Brazil to address deposit records, cash withdrawals and orders of provision for withdrawals equal to or exceeding R$ 100,000 (one hundred thousand reals), and Circular No. 2852 of 3rd December, 1998 was issued to set forth the procedures to be followed in preventing and fighting activities related to the crimes defined in the money-laundering legislation.

Personal Client Due Diligence

The following information should be collected:

- Name and Taxpayer Identification Number (CPF) or Employer Identification Number (CNPJ), depending on the situation, of the owner or beneficial owner of the money and name and Taxpayer Identification Number (CPF) or Employer Identification Number (CNPJ), depending on the situation, of the person conducting a deposit, withdrawal or order of provision for withdrawal.
- Number of the institution, branch, cash deposit current or savings account into which the money will be deposited or from which the money will be withdrawn, depending on the situation.
- Name and Taxpayer Identification Number (CPF) or Employer Identification Number (CNPJ), depending on the situation, of holders of accounts referred to above, if they belong to the same institution.
- Date and value of the deposit, withdrawal or provision.

Corporate Customer Due Diligence

If the customer is a legal entity, the identification shall include the individuals who are legally authorised to represent it, as well as its owners.

Politically Exposed Persons

Resolution 016 of 28th March, 2007 provides the PEP regulation. Concerning foreign politically exposed persons, obligated persons may adopt the following procedures:

- Request a written declaration from customers to declare their identity;
- Access publicly available information;
- Access commercial electronic databases of politically exposed persons.

Furthermore, the internal procedures adopted shall:

- Be structured so as to facilitate the identification of politically exposed persons;
- Be employed to determine the source of funds used in transactions conducted by individuals and beneficial owners identified as politically exposed persons, the compatibility between the transaction value and the equity stated in the declaration forms being checked.

Establishment or resumption of business relationships with politically exposed persons requires prior approval of the person responsible for the obligated company or prior approval of the manager or owner of an obligated entity, in compliance with regulations issued by the COAF.

Obligated persons shall conduct enhanced ongoing monitoring of business relationships with politically exposed persons. They shall also pay special close attention to proposed business relationships and transactions with politically exposed persons of countries with which Brazil has close trade and economic relations, common boundaries or ethnic, political and linguistic proximity.

27.6.11 Ongoing Monitoring

Institutions subject to the AML regulations must keep up-to-date records of all transactions, in Brazilian and foreign currency, involving securities, bonds, credit instruments, metals or any asset that may be converted into cash that exceeds the amount set forth by the competent authorities, and which shall be in accordance with the instructions issued by the relevant authorities. In addition to this, they must pay special attention to any transaction that, in view of the provisions set forth by the competent authorities, may represent serious indications of, or be related to, financial crime.

27.6.12 Record-keeping

Records of all transactions, in Brazilian and foreign currency, involving securities, bonds, credit instruments, metals or any asset that may be converted into cash that exceeds the amount set forth by the competent authorities shall also be made whenever an individual or legal entity, or their associates, executes, during the same calendar month, transactions with the same individual, legal entity, conglomerate or group that exceed, in the aggregate, the limits set forth by the competent authorities.

The CDD records and records of the transactions referred to in the previous paragraph shall be kept for a minimum period of five years, beginning on the date the account is closed or the date the transaction is concluded. However, the competent authorities may decide, at their own discretion, to extend this period.

The central bank will keep centralised registries forming a general database of current account holders and financial institution clients, as well as their representatives.

27.6.13 Suspicious Transaction Reporting

Obligated persons shall report to the COAF, within 24 hours, the proposal or completion of:

- All high-value transactions, accompanied by the identification required; and
- Transactions which appear to be connected to a crime.

They must notify the regulator or the body responsible for oversight of their activity or, failing that, the COAF, in frequency, form and conditions set by them, of the non-occurrence of proposed transactions or operations that should have been provided as above.

27.6.14 Penalties

There are various penalties for failure to comply with the above provisions, including:

- A warning.
- A variable monetary fine not exceeding:
  - twice the amount of the transaction;
  - twice the actual profit obtained or that would presumably be obtained by performing the operation; or
  - the amount of R$ 20,000,000 (twenty million reals).
- A temporary prohibition for up to ten years on holding any management position in a legal entity.
- The termination or suspension of authorisation for activity, operation or functioning.

27.6.15 Case Studies

In a recent case, a number of senior members of the Brazilian parliament were convicted of diverting public funds to buy political support for the government when it came to power. The scheme involved making monthly payments to politicians in exchange for their votes in Congress. Additionally, legislators, bank executives and business intermediaries were convicted of fraud, money laundering or conspiracy, as the high-profile case involved a wide range of individuals.

The politicians that were convicted of receiving the funds denied that they were selling their votes and said the money went to pay off campaign debts. However, it was found that illegal payments were made to buy political support.

This case highlighted major progress in Brazil, but also illustrates an important lesson for financial institutions. It is vital, when a potentially suspicious transaction is given a potentially legitimate explanation, that the institution conducts a thorough investigation into the relevant circumstances. It would have been easy to have taken the politicians' explanations at face value, and financial institutions need to exercise care when they apply a risk-based approach.

In another case, a high-flying Brazilian banker was sentenced to ten years in prison for attempting to bribe a police officer. He was under investigation for money laundering and tax evasion regarding the major corruption scandal outlined above, when he offered a police officer $1 million to drop the investigation. He was sentenced to ten years in prison, and to pay R$13.4 million ($5.6 million) in fines and compensation.

As part of the investigation, Brazil froze more than $2 billion in accounts outside the country. About $500 million in funds were blocked with the cooperation of the US government, highlighting the importance of international cooperation in the fight against money laundering.

27.7 COUNTRY PROFILE: BRITISH VIRGIN ISLANDS

27.7.1 Overview

Similarly to the Bahamas, the BVI's location makes it a gateway into the USA for drug trafficking. The USA has been critical of the BVI's money-laundering-deterrence regime, although this regime has been strengthened in recent years. The FATF has been generally supportive of the BVI's approach to AML law.

27.7.2 Key Legislation

The Proceeds of Criminal Conduct Act (PCCA) 1997, with numerous subsequent amendments, is the key statute with regards to money laundering. It is supplemented by the Anti-Money Laundering Regulations and the Anti-Money Laundering and Terrorist Financing Codes of Practice, which provide the compliance requirements.

27.7.3 Legislative History

The PCCA was aimed at improving the British Virgin Islands' legal systems and mechanisms to counter money laundering and other criminal activity. The specified regulatory framework pertaining to money laundering is found in the Anti-Money Laundering Regulations (AMLR) 2008 and the Anti-Money Laundering Financing Code of Practice 2008. Further amendments were made in 2009, 2010 and 2012.

The AMLR applies to people carrying on relevant business, which includes many entities providing banking, trust, insurance and legal services. These are also codified in the Anti-Money Laundering and Terrorist Financing Code of Practice 2008 which applies to every entity and professional, charity, non-profit-making institution, association or organisation. The MLRO provisions were amended in 2010.

27.7.4 FATF Assessment

The most recent assessment, published in 2008, noted that, although most of the competent authorities have adequate resources to carry out their functions, the Financial Services Commission (FSC) and the Anti-Drug and Violent Crimes Task Force have quantitatively inadequate human resources. On a more positive note, it also highlighted that, as a result of increased due diligence exercised by the banks and the financial services industry generally, the risks of money-laundering activity in the British Virgin Islands have decreased considerably. This proactive vigilance has, in effect, discouraged launderers from using these institutions to transfer illegal proceeds.

27.7.5 The Primary AML Investigation/Regulatory Authorities

The Financial Services Commission (FSC)

The Commission oversees all regulatory responsibilities previously handled by the government through the Financial Services Department. The Commission has also been tasked with new responsibilities including promoting public understanding of the financial system and its products, policing the perimeter of regulated activity, reducing financial crime and preventing market abuse. The FSC describes its mission as:

- Protecting the interests of the general public and market participants;
- Ensuring industry compliance with the highest international regulatory standards and best business practices;
- Ensuring that the BVI plays its part in the fight against cross-border, white-collar crime, while safeguarding the privacy and confidentiality of legitimate business transactions.

Financial Investigation Agency

The BVI Financial Investigation Agency (FIA), launched in 2004, is the law-enforcement agency responsible for white-collar and serious financial crime, and acts as the specialist investigative law-enforcement arm of government. The main function of the FIA is to receive, obtain, investigate, analyse and disseminate information which relates, or may relate, to a financial offence or the proceeds of a financial offence or a request for legal assistance from an authority in a foreign jurisdiction which appears to the FIA to have the function of making such requests.

27.7.6 Outline of Specific Money-laundering Offences

Under the PCCA, five primary money-laundering offences are defined:

1. **Acquisition, possession or use of proceeds of criminal conduct.** A person commits an offence if he acquires, transfers or uses any property or has possession of it which, in whole or in part, directly or indirectly represents the proceeds of his own criminal conduct. It is also an offence for a person who, knowing or suspecting that any property is the proceeds of someone else's criminal conduct, acquires, transfers or uses that property or has possession of it.
2. **Assisting.** A person commits an offence if he enters into, or is otherwise concerned in, an arrangement which he knows or suspects facilitates, whether by concealment, removal from BVI, transfer to nominees or other means, the acquiring, retention, use or control of proceeds of criminal conduct.
3. **Concealing.** A person commits an offence if, knowing or having reasonable grounds to suspect that, any property, in whole or in part, directly or indirectly, represents another person's proceeds of criminal conduct, he conceals or disguises that property or converts or transfers that property or removes it from BVI.
4. **Tipping off.** A person commits an offence if he knows or suspects that an investigation is being, or is about to be, conducted into money laundering and he discloses information to any other person which is likely to prejudice that investigation. It is also an offence if a person knows or suspects that a disclosure of suspicion has been made and he leaks information likely to prejudice any investigation which might be conducted following the disclosure. This offence extends to disclosures which would prejudice a confiscation investigation as well as a money-laundering investigation.

Separate offences exist for interfering with documents and other materials relevant to an investigation.

5. **Failure to disclose.** A person commits an offence if he knows or suspects, or has reasonable grounds for knowing or suspecting, that another person is engaged in money laundering if:
   - the information on which the suspicion is based came to his attention in the course of his trade, profession, business or employment; and
   - he does not disclose his suspicion as required by the law as soon as it is reasonably practicable after it comes to his attention.

27.7.7 Defences

Those who obtained information about money laundering in privileged circumstances are protected by law. It is also a defence in such cases where it is another person's benefit in question that one intended to report the activity but had not yet done so with reasonable excuse.

27.7.8 Penalties

On conviction, a person can be liable for imprisonment and/or a fine of up to forty thousand dollars depending on the nature and severity of the offence committed. This figure has been increased from five thousand dollars in 2006, showing a massive increase and highlighting the British Virgin Islands' commitment to cracking down on money laundering.

27.7.9 Risk-based Approach

The BVI is keen to promote the use of an appropriate and proportionate risk-based approach to the detection and prevention of money laundering and terrorist financing, especially in relation to ensuring:

- Adequate customer due diligence;
- That measures adopted to effectively deal with such activities are commensurate with the risks identified; and
- A more efficient and effective use of resources to minimise burdens on customers.

The nature, form and extent of money-laundering deterrence and counter-terrorist-financing (AML/CFT) compliance controls will invariably depend on several factors, considering the status and circumstances of the entity or professional.

In developing a system of internal controls, an entity should adopt a holistic approach that takes the above factors into account. The factors operate as guidelines and adherence thereto will assist an entity or a professional in properly and effectively developing and establishing a strong AML/CFT regime that keeps the entity's or professional's name intact and insulates it or him against unwarranted criminal activity.

In assessing risks that may be associated with a customer, the following non-exhaustive considerations should be taken into account:

- Customers with complex structures where the nature of the "entity" or relationship sought makes it difficult to identify the actual beneficial owner or the person or persons with controlling interests.
- Customers who conduct their business relationships or transactions in unusual circumstances, such as where a significant and unexplained distance exists between the location of the customer and the entity, and/or frequent and unexplained movement of accounts to different entities or of funds between entities in different jurisdictions.
- Where there is insufficient commercial rationale for the transaction or business relationship.
- Where there is a request to associate undue levels of secrecy with a transaction or relationship, or a reluctance to provide information regarding the beneficial owners or controllers.
- Where intermediaries who are not subject to adequate AML/CFT compliance measures are used and in respect of whom there is inadequate supervision.

27.7.10 Role of the MLRO/Nominated Officer

The MLRO is a prescribed term within the AMLR and has specific responsibilities; there is also a requirement to appoint a senior person to the role. The requirement of seniority has been amended by the Anti-Money Laundering (Amendment) Regulations to mean:

> *"A relevant person shall appoint a Money Laundering Reporting Officer who shall ... be of sufficient seniority to perform the functions reposed on a Money Laundering Reporting Officer under the Code and these Regulations."*

To be appointed as Money Laundering Reporting Officer, a person must possess the following qualifications:

- They must, at a minimum, hold a diploma and have post-qualification experience of not less than three years;
- They must be fit and proper;
- They must have a broad knowledge of AML/CFT matters, including the relevant regional and international treaties (including United Nations Resolutions);
- They must have a good appreciation and understanding of British Virgin Islands' laws relating to money laundering and terrorist financing; and
- They must possess the ability to make independent and analytical decisions and not be easily susceptible to undue influence.

The 2010 amendment also inserted the requirement that an MLRO must:

- Be a natural person; and
- Have access to all relevant information and material of the relevant person to enable him to perform the functions reposed in him under the Code and these Regulations.

A relevant person shall, within 14 days of appointing a Money Laundering Reporting Officer, notify the agency and the Commission in writing of that fact, specifying the date of his appointment, and this requirement shall apply in every new appointment of a Money Laundering Reporting Officer.

The appointment of an MLRO may relate to an individual who:

- Is an employee of the relevant person;
- Is not an employee of the relevant person, but who is resident in the British Virgin Islands and meets the requirements to perform the functions of an MLRO; or
- May or may not be an employee of the relevant person, but who meets the requirements of this regulation and is resident in a jurisdiction that is recognised pursuant to the provisions of the Code.

The Money Laundering Reporting Officer shall be responsible for ensuring compliance by staff of the relevant person with:

- The provisions of all law relating to money laundering and terrorist financing;
- The provisions of any internal reporting procedures and manual of compliance relating to money laundering and terrorist financing; and
- Any additional reporting and related obligations provided in the Code.

The Money Laundering Reporting Officer shall, in addition, act as the liaison between the relevant person and the agency in matters relating to AML compliance.

27.7.11 Due Diligence

Every entity or professional shall engage in customer due diligence in its or his dealings with an applicant for business, irrespective of the nature or form of the business. A customer due diligence process requires an entity or a professional to:

- Enquire into and identify the applicant for business, or the intended customer, and verify their identity;
- Obtain information on the purpose and intended nature of the business relationship;
- Use reliable evidence through such inquiry as is necessary to verify the identity of the applicant for business or intended customer;
- Utilise such measures as are necessary to understand the circumstances and business of the applicant for business or the intended customer, including obtaining information on the source of wealth and funds, size and volume of the business and expected nature and level of the transaction sought;

- Conduct, where a business relationship exists, ongoing monitoring of that relationship and the transactions undertaken for purposes of making an assessment regarding consistency between the transactions undertaken by the customer and the circumstances and business of the customer; and
- Enquire into and identify that a person who purports to act on behalf of an applicant for business or a customer, which is a legal person or a partnership, trust or other legal arrangement, is so authorised, and verify the person's identity.

A relevant person shall establish and maintain identification procedures which require, as soon as is reasonably practical after first contact (including one-off transactions):

- The production by the applicant for business of satisfactory evidence of identity; or
- The taking by the relevant person of such measures as are specified in the identification procedures as will produce satisfactory evidence of the identity of the applicant for business.

The identification procedures shall also:

- Require that, where satisfactory evidence of identity is not obtained by the relevant person, the business relationship or one-off transaction shall not proceed any further until such evidence is obtained.
- Require that, where the business relationship or one-off transaction subsists, the applicant for business appears to be acting for a third party in respect of that business relationship, that satisfactory evidence of the identity of the third party will be obtained, failing which the business relationship will be terminated.
- Include the full name (including any other names and aliases) and physical address of the applicant for business and, where they are acting for a third party, the full name (including any other names and aliases) and physical address of the third party.
- Provide for the assessment by the relevant person of the risk that any business relationship or one-off transaction may involve money laundering and shall be appropriate to the circumstances, having regard to the degree of risk assessed.
- Take into account the greater risk of money laundering which arises when the applicant for business is not engaged in a face-to-face relationship.

Satisfactory evidence of identity is defined as evidence which is reasonably capable of establishing, and, to the satisfaction of the person who obtains the evidence, does establish, that the applicant for business is the person he claims to be.

When satisfactory verification of evidence of identity is not obtained or produced, the business relationship and transactions shall not proceed any further. There are, however, exemptions available within the legislation where a relevant person assesses the applicant for business to be of normal or low risk and he has reasonable grounds for believing that the applicant for business is:

- A regulated person (national or foreign); or
- A legal practitioner or an accountant belonging to a professional body with adequate requirements.

A person carrying on relevant business is generally, in relation to a one-off transaction, not required to obtain evidence of the identity of an applicant for business where the amount to be paid by, or to, the applicant for business is less than ten thousand dollars or the equivalent amount in another currency.

Personal Client Due Diligence

For the purposes of the identification and verification of an individual, an entity or a professional shall obtain information regarding the individual's:

- Full legal name (including any former name, other current name or aliases used)
- Gender
- Principal residential address
- Date of birth.

Corporate Customer Due Diligence

For the purposes of the identification and verification of a legal person, an entity or a professional shall obtain information regarding:

- The full name of the legal person;
- The official registration or other identification number of the legal person;
- The date and place of incorporation, registration or formation of the legal person;
- The address of the registered office in the country of incorporation of the legal person and its mailing address, if different;
- Where applicable, the address of the registered agent of the legal person to whom correspondence may be sent and the mailing address of the registered agent, if different;
- The legal person's principal place of business and the type of business engaged in; and
- The identity of each director of the legal person, including each individual who owns at least ten or more percent of the legal person.

For the purposes of verification in relation to a legal person that is a company, the following documents shall be required from the company:

- Memorandum and articles of association or equivalent governing constitution;
- Resolution, bank mandate, signed application form or any valid account-opening authority, including full names of all directors and their specimen signatures, signed by no fewer than the number of directors required to make a quorum;
- Copies of powers of attorney or other authorities given by the directors in relation to the company;
- A signed director's statement as to the nature of the company's business; and
- Such other additional documentation that the company considers essential to the verification process.

For the purposes of verification in relation to a legal person that is a partnership, the following information shall be required from the partnership:

- The partnership agreement.
- The full name and current residential address of each partner and manager relevant to the application for business, including:
  - in the case of the opening of an account, the postcode and any address printed on a personal account cheque tendered to open the account; and
  - as much information as is relevant to the partner as the entity or professional may consider necessary.
- The date, place of birth, nationality, telephone number, facsimile number, occupation, employer and specimen signature of each partner or other senior officer who has the ability to give directions, sign cheques or otherwise act on behalf of the partnership.

Simplified Customer Due Diligence

Where an entity or a professional assesses a legal person who is an applicant for business to be of low risk, it or he may verify the applicant's identity by relying on any two of the following:

- The legal person's Certificate of Incorporation, together with its memorandum and articles of association or equivalent document or, in the case of a partnership, the partnership agreement or equivalent document.
- The legal person's latest audited financial statements, provided they are not older than one year prior to the establishment of the business relationship.
- Information acquired from an independent data source or a third party organisation that the entity or professional considers is reasonably acceptable.
- A search of the relevant registry or office with which the legal person is registered.
- Wire transfer information, where a subscription or redemption payment is effected through a wire transfer from a specific account in a financial institution that is regulated in a jurisdiction which is recognised pursuant to Section 52 and the account is operated in the name of the applicant.

In cases where a business relationship is assessed to present normal or low risk, an entity or a professional with whom the relationship exists shall review and keep up to date the customer due diligence information in respect of that customer at least once every three years.

Enhanced Customer Due Diligence

An entity or a professional shall adopt such additional measures with respect to higher risk business relationships or transactions as are necessary:

- To increase the level of awareness of applicants for business or customers who, or transactions which, present a higher risk;

- To increase the level of knowledge of an applicant for business or a customer with whom it or he deals or a transaction it or he processes;
- To escalate the level of internal approval for the opening of accounts or establishment of other relationships; and
- To increase the level of ongoing controls and frequency of reviews of established business relationships.

Where an entity or a professional makes a determination that a business relationship presents a higher risk, it shall review and keep up to date the customer due diligence information in respect of the relevant customer at least once every year.

Following the Anti-Money Laundering and Terrorist Financing (Amendment) Code of Practice 2012, "Where an entity or a professional makes a determination from its or his risk assessment that a relationship with a trust or the product or service channels in relation to the trust presents a normal or a higher level of risk, the entity or professional shall perform customer due diligence or enhanced customer due diligence, as may be warranted by the circumstances, and obtain and verify the identities of all the beneficiaries with a vested right in the trust at the time of or before distribution of any trust property or income and such other additional information as the entity or professional considers relevant."

Non-face-to-face Customer Due Diligence

Where an entity or a professional enters into a business relationship with an applicant for business or a customer whose presence is not possible, the entity or professional shall adopt the measures outlined in this Code and such additional measures as it or he may consider relevant, having regard to appropriate risk assessments, to identify and verify the applicant for business or customer. The provisions of the Code relating to identification and verification shall apply with respect to non-face-to-face business relationships.

Politically Exposed Persons

Politically exposed persons are defined as individuals who are, or have been, entrusted with prominent public functions, together with members of their immediate family, or persons who are known to be close associates of such individuals.

An entity or a professional shall:

- Have, as part of its or his internal control systems, appropriate risk-based policies, processes and procedures for determining whether an applicant for business or a customer is a politically exposed person;
- In dealings with a politically exposed person, take such reasonable measures as are necessary to establish the source of funds or wealth respecting such person;
- Ensure that senior management approval is sought for establishing or maintaining a business relationship with a politically exposed person;
- Ensure a process of regular monitoring of the business relationship with a politically exposed person;

- In circumstances where junior staff deal with politically exposed persons, ensure that there is in place adequate supervisory oversight in that regard; and
- Ensure that the above applies in relation to a customer who becomes a politically exposed person during the course of an existing business relationship.

A customer who ceases to qualify as a PEP by virtue of no longer holding the post or relationship that qualified him as a PEP, ceases to be a PEP after two years following the day on which he ceased to qualify as a PEP.

However, even though the customer has ceased to be a PEP, an entity may consider it appropriate to guard against any potential risks that may be associated with the customer and continue to treat the customer as a PEP for such period as the entity considers relevant during the currency of the relationship, but in any case not longer than ten years from the date the customer ceased to qualify as a PEP.

27.7.12 Staff Training

There is a requirement that a relevant person shall provide education and training for all of its directors or, as the case may be, partners, all other persons involved in its management and all key staff, to ensure that they are aware of the money-laundering regulations and terrorist-financing obligations together with personal reporting obligations. The definition of "key staff" was changed by the 2010 Regulations to "an employee of a relevant person who deals with customers or clients and their transactions". Staff should also be made aware of:

- The manual of compliance procedures or internal control systems and other requirements established pursuant to these Regulations and the Code;
- Their personal liability for failure to report information or suspicions in accordance with the requirements of these Regulations, the Code and any other enactment, including any established internal procedures.

Training should be provided at least once a year.

27.7.13 Record-keeping

A record must be maintained in the BVI which:

- Indicates the nature of the evidence obtained;
- Comprises a copy of the evidence or, where this is not reasonably practicable, contains such information as would enable a copy of the evidence to be obtained;
- Includes all transactions carried out by, or on behalf of, that person (such as records sufficient to identify the source and recipient of payments from which investigating authorities will be able to compile an audit trail for suspected money laundering);
- Includes all reports made by it to the agency and all inquiries relating to money laundering received by it from the agency.

The requirement is that records should be kept for at least five years after the ending of a customer relationship, defined in Regulation 10 and amended by the 2010 Regulations as:

- When all transactions relating to a one-off transaction or a series of linked transactions were completed; or
- When the business relationship was formally ended.

27.7.14 *Reporting Requirements*

The requirements are that each record of a report to the FIU should contain:

- The date of the report;
- The person who made the report;
- Any person to whom the report was forwarded;
- A reference by which any supporting evidence is identifiable; and
- Receipt of acknowledgment from the agency.

27.7.15 *Suspicious Transaction Reporting*

A relevant person shall establish written internal reporting procedures which, in relation to its relevant business, will:

- Enable its directors, or as the case may be, partners, all other persons involved in its management and all key staff, to know to whom they should report knowledge or suspicions of money laundering;
- Ensure that there is a clear reporting chain under which suspicions of money laundering will be passed to the Money Laundering Reporting Officer;
- Ensure that the Money Laundering Reporting Officer has reasonable access to all relevant information which may be of assistance to him and which is available to the relevant person; and
- Ensure full compliance with the requirements of the Code.

27.7.16 *Penalties*

A person on summary conviction, will be subject to a fine not exceeding 10,000 dollars (increased from 5,000 dollars by the 2010 amendment); and on conviction on indictment, to a fine not exceeding fifteen thousand dollars. In proceedings against a person for an offence under these Regulations, it shall be a defence for the person to prove that he took all reasonable steps and exercised due diligence to comply with the requirements of these Regulations.

By virtue of Section 27 of the PCCA, where a person fails to comply with or contravenes a provision of a Code of Practice, he commits an offence and is liable, on summary conviction, to a fine of up to 25,000 dollars – increased from 7,000 dollars in 2006.

Where an entity or a professional fails to comply with the PEP requirements outlined above, it or he commits an offence and is liable to be prosecuted under Section 27(4) of the Proceeds of Criminal Conduct Act 1997.

27.7.17 Case Studies

In a recent case a businessman was found guilty of a £400,000 tax evasion which was conducted through a BVI bank account. He declared an income of £35,000 to the UK authorities, although through a trust in Guernsey he set up a trust in the British Virgin Islands.

Customers paid into the trust while he instructed the trust to pay money into Jersey bank accounts. Also, large cash sums were drawn by him from British branches of the bank. This complex structure allowed him to hide money for eight years before the structure was exposed.

This case highlights how organisations need to be particularly wary of complex and seemingly unnecessary financial structures, particularly when they involve tax havens.

The British Virgin Islands Financial Intelligence Unit publishes quarterly reports on enforcement actions it has taken. In quarter four of 2012, it issued almost $40,000 in administrative fines, five cease and desist orders, two warning letters and an order for a fund to revalue its assets independently. By making this information public, the BVI FIU appears to be seeking prevention and deterrence as much as it is ordering punishment.

27.8 COUNTRY PROFILE: CANADA

27.8.1 Overview

There are a variety of proposed changes to the AML law in Canada, which are outlined at the end of this section. The changes are extensive and would represent a major expansion to the Canadian AML regime.

27.8.2 Key Legislation

Money laundering is criminalised under the Canadian Criminal Code. The Proceeds of Crime (Money Laundering) and Terrorist Financing Act 2000, which has been subsequently amended (most recently in 2011), provides the key compliance requirements. These are further supplemented by the regulations provided for under this statute. This legislation is to be changed in the short term to make the legislation consistent with the current FATF regulations.

27.8.3 Legislative History

The current key legislation is the Proceeds of Crime (Money Laundering) and Terrorist Financing Act (PCMLTFA) 2000, which was amended by the Proceeds of Crime Act 2006. This amendment enhanced the client identification, record-keeping and reporting measures applicable to financial institutions and intermediaries.

Furthermore, there are five sets of regulations under the PCMLTFA:

- The Proceeds of Crime (Money Laundering) and Terrorist Financing Suspicious Transaction Reporting Regulations;
- The Proceeds of Crime (Money Laundering) and Terrorist Financing Regulations;
- The Cross-Border Currency and Monetary Instruments Reporting Regulations;
- The Proceeds of Crime (Money Laundering) and Terrorist Financing Registration Regulations;
- The Proceeds of Crime (Money Laundering) and Terrorist Financing Administrative Monetary Penalties Regulations.

27.8.4 FATF Assessment

The most recent FATF assessment, published in 2008, was largely complimentary. It praised the strength and actions of the law-enforcement agencies, but noted that further steps could be taken to enhance the AML law and preventative measures, resulting in the changes described above. In relation to international cooperation in money-laundering deterrence and counter-terrorist-financing (AML/CFT) matters, Canada is broadly in line with the international standards.

27.8.5 The Primary AML Investigation/Regulatory Authorities

Financial Transactions and Reports Analysis Centre

The Financial Transactions and Reports Analysis Centre of Canada (FINTRAC), Canada's financial intelligence unit, was created in 2000. It is an independent agency, reporting to the Minister of Finance, who is accountable to Parliament for the activities of the Centre. It was established and operates within the ambit of the Proceeds of Crime (Money Laundering) and Terrorist Financing Act (PCMLTFA) and its Regulations.

FINTRAC's mandate is to facilitate the detection, prevention and deterrence of money laundering and terrorist activity financing, while ensuring the protection of personal information under its control. The Centre fulfils its mandate through the following activities:

- Receiving financial transaction reports in accordance with the legislation and regulations and safeguarding personal information under its control;
- Ensuring compliance of reporting entities with the legislation and regulations;
- Producing financial intelligence on suspected money laundering, terrorist activity financing and other threats to the security of Canada;
- Researching and analysing data from a variety of information sources that shed light on trends and patterns in financial crime;
- Enhancing public awareness and understanding of money laundering and terrorist activity financing.

The Royal Canadian Mounted Police (RCMP)

The RCMP Anti-Money Laundering Program provides an investigative assessment on money-laundering intelligence, and monitors national and international money-laundering trends and topologies.

27.8.6 Outline of Specific Money-laundering Offences

Canadian AML legislation comprehensively covers the three stages of the money-laundering offence – placement, layering and integration. The burden of proof rests with the prosecution in any criminal proceedings. It must prove that wilful blindness or recklessness has taken place. The prosecution does not, however, have to prove that the perpetrator had actual knowledge of the exact origin of the illicit funds in question.

Under Section 462 of the Criminal Code:

> Everyone commits an offence who uses, transfers the possession of, sends or delivers to any person or place, transports, transmits, alters, disposes of or otherwise deals with, in any manner and by any means, any property or any proceeds of any property with intent to conceal or convert that property or those proceeds, knowing or believing that all or a part of that property or of those proceeds was obtained or derived directly or indirectly as a result of:
>
> - The commission in Canada of a designated offence; or
> - An act or omission anywhere that, if it had occurred in Canada, would have constituted a designated offence.

The Attorney General has the power to issue search warrants or freezing orders to enforce the AML law.

27.8.7 *Penalties*

Everyone who commits an offence as outlined above is guilty of an indictable offence and liable to imprisonment for a term not exceeding ten years; or is guilty of an offence punishable on summary conviction.

"Proceeds of crime" means any property, benefit or advantage, within or outside Canada, obtained or derived directly or indirectly as a result of:

- The commission in Canada of a designated offence; or
- An act or omission anywhere that, if it had occurred in Canada, would have constituted a designated offence.

It should be noted that Alberta, British Columbia and Quebec have all enacted their own regional sector legislation.

27.8.8 *Scope*

Reporting entities must report suspicious and certain other transactions to the Financial Transactions and Reports Analysis Centre of Canada (FINTRAC). This includes the following types of business:

- Financial entities such as banks or authorised foreign banks with respect to their operations in Canada, credit unions, caisses populaires, financial services cooperatives, credit union centrals (when they offer financial services to anyone other than a member entity of the credit union central), trust companies, loan companies and agents of the Crown that accept deposit liabilities);
- Life insurance companies, brokers and agents;
- Securities dealers;
- Money service businesses;
- Agents of the Crown that sell money orders;
- Accountants and accounting firms (when carrying out certain activities on behalf of their clients);
- Real estate brokers, sales representatives and developers (when carrying out certain activities);
- Casinos;
- Dealers in precious metals and stones;
- Public notaries and notary corporations of British Columbia (when carrying out certain activities on behalf of their clients); and
- For the purposes of suspicious transactions, employees of these reporting entities.

27.8.9 Compliance Regime

The implementation of a compliance regime is a legislative requirement and a good business practice for anyone subject to the Act and its regulations. A compliance regime will have to be tailored to fit the entity's individual needs. It should reflect the nature, size and complexity of the operations, and has to include the following:

- The appointment of a Compliance Officer.
- The development and application of compliance policies and procedures. These policies and procedures have to be in a written form and also need to be kept up to date. For any entity, they also have to be approved by a senior officer.
- An assessment and documentation of risks related to money laundering and terrorist financing needs to be conducted, as well as documenting and implementing mitigation measures to deal with those risks.
- If a firm has employees or agents or any other individuals authorised to act on its behalf, an ongoing compliance training programme needs to be implemented for them. The training programme has to be in writing and maintained (see Chapter 14).
- A review of the compliance policies and procedures needs to be conducted to test their effectiveness. The review has to cover the policies and procedures, the assessment of risks related to money laundering and terrorist financing and the training programme. The review has to be completed at least every two years.

27.8.10 Risk-based Approach

In Canada the required compliance regime has to include an assessment of the risks related to money laundering and terrorist financing in a manner that is appropriate to the nature and complexity of the firm concerned. This must be documented in writing. Such an assessment and documentation is in addition to the general client identification, record-keeping and reporting requirements, since it should focus on where the firm is most vulnerable to money laundering and terrorist financing.

In designing their control systems, institutions should consider internal controls such as:

- Focussing on the firm's specific operations (products, services, clients and geographic locations) that are more vulnerable to abuse by money launderers and criminals;
- Informing senior management of compliance initiatives, identified compliance deficiencies, corrective action taken and suspicious transaction reports filed;
- Providing for programme continuity despite changes in management, employees or structure that might occur;
- Focussing on meeting all regulatory record-keeping and reporting requirements, recommendations for anti-money-laundering and anti-terrorist-financing compliance and providing for timely updates in response to changes in requirements;

- Enabling the timely identification of reportable transactions and ensuring the accurate filing of required reports;
- Incorporating anti-money-laundering and anti-terrorist-financing compliance into job descriptions and performance evaluations of appropriate personnel; and
- Providing for adequate supervision of employees that handle currency transactions, provision of complete reports, monitoring for suspicious transactions or engaging in any other activity that forms part of the anti-money-laundering and anti-terrorist-financing programme.

27.8.11 *Role of the MLRO/Nominated Officer*

The individual appointed will be responsible for the implementation of the compliance regime. The Compliance Officer should have the authority and the resources necessary to discharge his or her responsibilities effectively. Depending on the type of business, the Compliance Officer should report, on a regular basis, to the board of directors or senior management, or to the owner or chief operator.

For a small business, the appointed officer could be a senior manager or the owner or operator of the business. An individual can be their own Compliance Officer or they may choose to appoint another individual to help implement a compliance regime.

In the case of a large business, the Compliance Officer should be from a senior level and have direct access to senior management and the board of directors. Furthermore, as a good governance practice, the appointed Compliance Officer in a large business should not be directly involved in the receipt, transfer or payment of funds.

For consistency and ongoing attention to the compliance regime, the appointed Compliance Officer may choose to delegate certain duties to other employees. For example, the officer may delegate to an individual in a local office or branch to ensure that compliance procedures are properly implemented at that location. However, where such delegation is made, the Compliance Officer retains responsibility for the implementation of the compliance regime.

27.8.12 *Due Diligence*

An entity must take the measures outlined below to identify individuals or entities, subject to the general exceptions. If the identity of an individual or an entity when they open an account cannot be established, then, in Canada, it is not possible for an institution to open the account.

The completion of a client risk assessment should be conducted where there is an ongoing relationship. An ongoing relationship is one where a client opens an account or undertakes multiple transactions over a time period with the firm, regardless of whether the transactions are related to each other. Where the firm's dealings with a client are limited to a single transaction, this is not considered to be an ongoing relationship. However, if the transaction seems suspicious, the money service or other relevant business still has to report it to FINTRAC.

General Exceptions

As a general rule, there is no need to re-identify clients if there is no reason to suspect any wrongdoing. However, if any suspicion does arise, CDD should be completed again. There are also exceptions for certain types of accounts and large public bodies.

Personal Client Due Diligence

To identify an individual, firms should refer to one of the following:

- The individual's birth certificate
- Driving licence
- Passport
- Record of landing
- Permanent resident card, or other similar document
- The individual's provincial health card, as long as it is not prohibited by provincial or territorial legislation.

For a document to be acceptable for identification purposes, it must have a unique identifier number. Also, the document must have been issued by a provincial, territorial or federal government. The document has to be a valid one and cannot have expired.

Corporate Customer Due Diligence

In the case of a corporation, in addition to confirming its existence, the reporting entity also has to determine the corporation's name, address and the names of its directors. To confirm the existence of a corporation as well as the corporation's name and address, the following documents should be referred to:

- The corporation's certificate of corporate status;
- A record that has to be filed annually under provincial securities legislation;
- Any other record that confirms the corporation's existence, such as:
  - the corporation's published annual report signed by an independent audit firm; or
  - a letter or a notice of assessment for the corporation from a municipal, provincial, territorial or federal government.

The names of the corporation's directors also have to be determined. To do this, the reporting entity may need to see the list of the corporation's directors submitted with the application for incorporation and you would expect this to be verified against the statutory records.

In the case of an entity other than a corporation, the firm should refer to a partnership agreement, articles of association or any other similar record that confirms the entity's existence.

Beneficial Ownership

If the reporting entity has to confirm the existence of a corporation or other entity at the opening of an account, it should take reasonable measures to obtain information about the entity's beneficial ownership. If obtained, a record of the following should be kept:

If the entity is a corporation:

- The name and occupation of all directors of the corporation; and
- The name, address and occupation of all individuals who, directly or indirectly, own or control 25% or more of the shares of the corporation.

If the entity is other than a corporation:

- The name, address and occupation of all individuals who, directly or indirectly, own or control 25% or more of the entity.

If this information cannot be obtained, a record explaining why beneficial ownership could not be determined should be kept.

Third Party Customer Due Diligence

Situations where a firm facilitates a transaction for which a client is acting on behalf of a third party but does not know anything about the third party may lead the firm to consider that client as being a higher risk. Similarly, a client acting on behalf of an entity who is not aware of the entity's beneficial owners (such as the names of the entity's directors or the individuals controlling the entity, for example) may also lead to the firm considering that client as being higher risk. In such cases, enhanced customer due diligence (EDD) is required.

Enhanced Customer Due Diligence

The robustness of the EDD programme should be determined based on the resources and requirements of the reporting entity, and set at a level which enables the entity to be reasonably satisfied that the necessary risks have been adequately dealt with.

Non-face-to-face Customer Due Diligence

In Canadian regulation a number of options are available to a firm to enable it to confirm the identity of an individual who is not present, referred to as a non-face-to-face customer. In such cases, firms may:

- Obtain the individual's name, address and date of birth;
- Confirm that another appropriately regulated financial entity operating in a suitably regulated country has identified the individual by referring to an original identification document; then
- Verify that the individual's name, address and date of birth provided to the firm correspond with the information kept in the records of that other entity.

Alternatively, the firm can use a combination of an oath, a reliable credit information product or a confirmation that a cheque has been cleared.

Politically Exposed Persons

If a firm knows that its client is a politically exposed foreign person (even when it is not required to make the determination or keep related records), it should consider that client as posing a higher risk.

Firms should also consider unusual circumstances, cash-intensive businesses and other indicators as also posing potentially higher risks. If a firm determines that an individual is a politically exposed foreign person for a new or an existing account, then it has to do the following:

- Get senior management's approval to keep the account open within 14 days of the new account being activated, or within 14 days of the firm determining that the existing account holder is a politically exposed foreign person.
- Take reasonable measures to establish the source of funds that have been, will be or are expected to be deposited in that account. Once the firm has determined the source of funds for the account, it is not required to do so again for future deposits, unless ongoing monitoring triggers the need to do so.
- Perform enhanced ongoing monitoring of activities for that account to detect suspicious transactions.

Note that the firm has to make the determination and get senior management approval within a single period of 14 days. For example, if it takes a firm five days after the new account is activated to make the determination that it is, in fact, dealing with a politically exposed foreign person, it now has only nine days left to get senior management approval to keep the account open.

Correspondent Banking

Specific regulations have been issued in Canada with respect to correspondent banking. These mirror those in the FATF standards. They require that institutions should take the following measures before entering into a correspondent banking relationship with a prescribed foreign entity:

- Obtain prescribed information about the foreign entity and its activities;
- Ensure that the foreign entity is not a shell bank, as defined in the regulations;
- Obtain the approval of senior management;
- Set out in writing their obligations and those of the foreign entity in respect of the correspondent banking services; and
- Take any other prescribed measures.

Shell Banking

In Canada, no person or entity is allowed to enter into a correspondent banking relationship with a shell bank, as defined in the regulations.

27.8.13 Ongoing Monitoring

A reporting entity has to take reasonable measures to keep client identification information up to date. The frequency with which client identification information is to be updated will vary in accordance with the context in which transactions occur, and therefore could differ from one situation to the next. However, for high-risk situations, the frequency of keeping client identification information updated should be at least every two years.

A review of a firm's compliance policies and procedures should be carried out every two years. This is intended to help the firm to evaluate the need to modify existing policies and procedures or to implement new ones. The review, to be conducted by an internal or external auditor, could include:

- Interviews with those handling transactions and with their supervisors to determine their knowledge of the legislative requirements and the firm's policies and procedures.
- A review of the criteria and process for identifying and reporting suspicious transactions.
- A sampling of large cash transactions followed by a review of the reporting of such transactions.
- A sampling of international electronic funds transfers (if those are reportable by the reporting entity in question) followed by a review of the reporting of such transactions.
- A test of the validity and reasonableness of any exceptions to large cash transaction reports including the required annual report to FINTRAC (this is applicable only for financial entities which choose the alternative to large cash transactions for certain business clients).
- A test of the record-keeping system for compliance with the legislation.
- A test of the client identification procedures for compliance with the legislation.
- A review of the risk assessment.

The review process and its results have to be documented, along with corrective measures and follow-up actions. Within 30 days of the review, the MLRO or Compliance Officer is required to report the following in writing to one of the firm's senior officers:

- The findings of the above review;
- Any updates that were made to the policies and procedures during the review period;
- The status of implementation of the policies and procedures updates;
- A request for a response indicating corrective actions and a timeline for implementing such actions.

If the firm does not have an internal or external auditor, then it could conduct a "self-review". If feasible, this self-review should be conducted by an individual who is independent of the reporting, record-keeping and compliance-monitoring functions. This could be an employee or an outside consultant. In other cases where such reviews are required in the absence of either an internal or external auditor, a peer conducts such a review.

27.8.14 *Staff Training*

As mentioned earlier, if a firm has employees, agents or other individuals authorised to act on behalf of the financial entity, the compliance regime has to include training. The training programme has to be in writing, kept up to date, and employees should be informed of any changes to AML policy. The training programme should be adjusted in a timely manner to reflect the entity's needs, and should be reviewed every two years.

The method of training may vary greatly depending on the size of the firm's business and the complexity of the subject matter. When assessing actual training needs, a firm should consider the following elements:

- Requirements under the AML Act and the penalties for non-compliance.
- Policies and procedures – are the employees aware of these?
- Background information on money laundering and terrorist financing.

27.8.15 *Record-keeping*

As a financial entity, the requirement is to keep the following records:

- Large cash transaction records;
- Account-opening records;
- Certain records about credit card accounts;
- Certain records created in the normal course of business;
- Certain records about the operation of an account;
- Foreign currency exchange transaction tickets;
- Certain records about transactions of $3,000 or more;
- Records about electronic funds transfers;
- Trust-related records (trust companies); and
- Suspicious transaction report records.

There are a few exceptions to the above for low-risk accounts.

Large Cash Transaction Records

This is a requirement to record every amount of cash of $10,000 or more that a firm receives from a client in a single transaction, or combination of transactions within 24 hours. In addition to this record, a large cash transaction will also require a report to FINTRAC. For any large cash transaction, the information that a firm has to keep in a large cash transaction record includes, but is not exclusive to, the following:

- The amount and currency of the cash received;
- The date of the transaction;

- The purpose, details and type of transaction (for example, the cash was deposited, or the cash was used to buy traveller's cheques, etc.) including whether any other individuals or entities were involved in the transaction.

Account-opening Records

For every account that a firm opens, it has to keep a record about the account's intended use.

In respect of certain transactions of $3,000 or more:

- If a firm receives $3,000 or more for the issuance of traveller's cheques, money orders or other similar negotiable instruments (except from another financial entity), it is required to keep a record of the date, the amount received and the name and address of the individual who gave the firm the amount, and the form in which the money was received.
- If a firm redeems $3,000 or more in money orders, whether it is one money order or two or more taken together, it is required to keep a record of the date as well as the name and address of the individual redeeming them. These records also must indicate the name of the issuer of each money order.

A firm is also required to keep the following records in respect of a PEP:

- The office or position of the individual who is a politically exposed foreign person;
- The source of the funds, if known, that are, or are expected to be, deposited in the account or used for the transaction;
- The date the firm determined that the individual was, in fact, a politically exposed foreign person;
- The name of the member of senior management who approved the account to be kept open or reviewed the transaction; and
- The date the account was approved to be kept open or the date the transaction was reviewed.

In the case of the following personal account records:

- Signature cards;
- Account-operating agreements;
- Client credit files, credit card applications;
- Records setting out the intended use of the account;
- Politically exposed foreign person records regarding an account or a credit card account

these records have to be kept for five years from the day of closing of the account to which they relate.

In the case of records to confirm the existence of an entity (including a corporation), such as:

- Beneficial ownership records;
- Politically exposed foreign person records regarding transactions; and
- Records about a corresponding banking relationship

these must be kept by the firm for five years from the day the last business transaction was conducted.

In the case of a copy of a suspicious transaction report, the record has to be kept for a period of at least five years following the date the report was made.

In the case of all other records, the records must be kept for a period of at least five years following the date they were created.

27.8.16 Reporting Requirements

The following scenarios all have to be reported to FINTRAC:

- **Suspicious transactions:** Reporting entities have to report completed or attempted transactions if there are reasonable grounds to suspect that the transactions are related to the commission or attempted commission of a money-laundering offence or a terrorist-activity-financing offence.
- **Large cash transactions:** Reporting entities have to send large cash transaction reports to FINTRAC when they receive an amount of $10,000 or more in cash in the course of a single transaction.
- **Electronic funds transfers (EFTs):** Financial entities, money services businesses and casinos have to report incoming and outgoing international EFTs of $10,000 or more in a single transaction.
- **Terrorist property:** Reporting entities have to report to FINTRAC if they have property in their possession or control that they know is owned or controlled by, or on behalf of, a terrorist group within the meaning of the Criminal Code, or if they have property in their possession or control that they believe is owned or controlled by, or on behalf of, a person listed under the Regulations Implementing the United Nations Resolutions on the Suppression of Terrorism.

This information also has to be disclosed to the RCMP and CSIS.

- **Casino disbursements:** Casinos have to report disbursements of $10,000 or more, whether paid in cash or not, in the course of a single transaction.

27.8.17 Suspicious Transaction Reporting

The FINTRAC guidelines state that:

> *"Suspicious transactions are financial transactions [which a firm has] reasonable grounds to suspect are related to the commission of a money laundering (or a terrorist financing) offence. This includes transactions that you have reasonable grounds to suspect are related to the attempted commission of a money laundering (or a terrorist financing) offence. Furthermore, 'Reasonable grounds to suspect' is determined by what is reasonable in [the specific] circumstances, including normal business practices and systems within your industry."*

The FINTRAC guidelines provide an extensive, although not exhaustive, list of potentially suspicious behaviour, which includes scenarios such as the following:

- The client does not want correspondence sent to their home address.
- The client shows uncommon curiosity about a firm's internal systems, controls and policies.
- The client attempts to develop close rapport with staff.
- The client performs two or more cash transactions of less than $10,000 each just outside of 24 hours apart, seemingly to avoid the 24-hour rule connecting such transactions.
- The client alters the transaction after being asked for identity documents.
- The client asks the firm to hold or transmit large sums of money or other assets when this type of activity is unusual for this type of client.
- The transaction conducted is unnecessarily complex for its stated purpose.
- Where multiple transactions are carried out on the same day at the same branch but with an apparent attempt to use different tellers.

The STR requirement applies to both attempted transactions and transactions which have been completed. STRs must be sent to FINTRAC within 30 days of detection, and the contents of a report must not be disclosed to anybody. A report can be submitted electronically or in paper format.

27.8.18 Penalties

Failure to comply with Canadian legislative requirements can lead to criminal charges against a firm that is a reporting entity. The following are some of the penalties:

- Failure to report a suspicious transaction or failure to make a terrorist property report – conviction of this could lead to up to five years' imprisonment, to a fine of $2,000,000, or both.
- Failure to report a large cash transaction or an electronic funds transfer – conviction of this could lead to a fine of $500,000 for a first offence and $1,000,000 for each subsequent offence.

- Failure to retain records – conviction of this could lead to up to five years' imprisonment, to a fine of $500,000, or both.
- Failure to implement a compliance regime – conviction of this could lead to up to five years' imprisonment, to a fine of $500,000, or both.

Failure to comply with the relevant legislative requirements can lead to the following administrative monetary penalties against a reporting entity:

- Failure to implement any of the five elements of the compliance regime described in Section 3 could lead to an administrative monetary penalty of up to $100,000 for each one.
- Failure by an entity to report the required information to senior management within 30 days after the review of its compliance programme could lead to an administrative monetary penalty of up to $100,000.
- Failure to identify clients, keep records, monitor financial transactions and take mitigating measures in situations where risk of money laundering or terrorist financing is high could lead to an administrative monetary penalty of up to $100,000.

27.8.19 Changes to AML/CFT Rules

At the time of writing, the Department of Finance Canada is undertaking a consultation on extensive changes to Canadian anti-money-laundering law. The consultation opened in December 2011, and the deadline for comments on the proposed changes was 1st March, 2012. At present, the Department of Finance has published the comments received, but the legislation is not listed as being currently before parliament.

The proposed amendments include the following:

1. Requiring banks and casinos to keep identification records of persons authorised to sign for business accounts so that in the event of reasonable grounds to suspect that a transaction is related to a money-laundering or terrorist-financing offence, the bank or casino can also report to FINTRAC information as to those persons authorised to sign business accounts.
2. Expanding the identification and record-keeping requirements of introduced business relationships (i.e. between banks and securities brokers).
3. Increasing security requirements in connection with the receipt by customers of electronic bank statements (although this has nothing to do with AML/CFT).
4. Tightening non-face-to-face identification methods for credit and charge card companies.
5. Reviewing the requirement for reporting entities to keep evidence of client signatures when accounts are opened.
6. Expanding the definition of politically exposed persons (PEPs) to include close associates of the person. In Canada, the Proceeds of Crime (Money Laundering) and Terrorist Financing Act varies the international definition of a PEP by limiting it to just foreign PEPs, whereas the FATF Recommendations do not include such a limitation.

7. Requiring life insurance companies to determine if clients are PEPs.
8. Requiring banks and securities dealers to determine if clients are PEPs.
9. Eliminating the reporting requirement for financial transactions between public issuers and reporting entities if the reporting issuer has assets of $75 million or more.
10. Requiring that corporate documents be current.
11. Changing the definition of "third party" to "instructing party" on the basis that reporting entities apparently do not comprehend what a third party means.
12. Eliminating the reporting monetary amount for international electronic fund transfers from $1,000 to $1. This is one of the most significant proposals, impacting not only the regulatory burden on reporting entities but also the privacy interests of Canadians.
13. Adopting the US definition of "prepaid access" for prepaid card and other such products and implementing prepaid access identification requirements for reporting entities and for cross-border currency reporting purposes. With respect to the latter, the definition of "monetary instrument" will be amended to include prepaid access products.
14. Expanding the identification and record-keeping requirements for life insurance companies and increasing the reporting requirements for life insurance companies.
15. Eliminating certain transactions from reporting for dealers in precious metals and stones and accountants.
16. Expanding what the 24-hour rule means to capture more transactions that are reportable by reporting entities.
17. Simplifying registration requirements for money services businesses.
18. Giving FINTRAC greater powers to require reporting entities to file required reports and increasing the administrative penalties for failures by reporting entities to do so.
19. Requiring reporting entities to document and keep records of each instance in which they undertook reasonable measures in client ID steps.
20. Allowing CBSA officers to question passengers departing from, or arriving in, Canada with respect to the importation and exportation of currency and other monetary instruments.
21. Expanding the information sharing among agencies, particularly for national security purposes.
22. Expanding the application of the AML regime to charities.
23. Implementing regulations to allow the Minister of Finance to issue directives in respect of AML issues.
24. Changing the law as it relates to what triggers a reportable suspicious transaction to broaden it by including activities (whether financial or not) that may be taken for a financial transaction, and it appears the change may also include eliminating

the requirement that the person reporting must have reasonable grounds to suspect that the transaction is related to a money-laundering or terrorist-financing offence as defined in the Criminal Code.

25. Allowing the sharing of information to the CBSA from FINTRAC for offences under the Immigration and Refugee Protection Act, for example in situations of immigration fraud, misrepresentation as to permanent residence or other immigration-related offences.

In addition to these changes, a consultation open between November and December 2011 explored expanding the circumstances in which client identification is required and also expanding the reporting requirements for reporting entities. The proposals, if implemented, would apply to all reporting entities in Canada and not just financial institutions. As a result, all of the following would be affected: money services businesses, casinos, financial institutions, real estate brokers, notaries, accountants, lawyers (unless otherwise exempt), life insurance brokers, securities brokers and dealers in precious stones and metals.

The proposals would expand reporting requirements to include the reporting of "business relationships", defined as any relationship between a reporting entity and a client whereby the reporting entity provides services in which there are financial activities or financial transactions. Under the proposals, the obligations will apply to business relationships irrespective of whether the reporting entity has an account with a client or has conducted a reportable transaction.

The proposals also eliminate the reporting exemption for known clients, expand the requirement to obtain beneficial ownership information and require more due diligence for high-risk clients and/or activities.

27.8.20 Case Studies

As stated earlier, Canada does take money-laundering deterrence seriously, and there have been cases reported locally of action being taken.

In Canada, there is no requirement for there to be intent to commit an act before a person can be convicted of a failure to report under the PCMLTFA. For example, in 2004, a truck driver was driving across Canada and mistakenly exited to the US border in the middle of the night in his truck. He had $70,000 in cash with him.

He turned around before reaching the US checkpoint and upon re-entering Canada, his funds were seized and forfeited to the Crown because he had failed to complete a report with the CBSA. The Federal Court of Canada decided that, based on numerous previous cases, there is no requirement to establish intent for the offence to be proven. It is also irrelevant who legally owns the currency or monetary instrument – the person in possession of the currency or monetary instrument is the person who is subject to the PCMLTFA reporting obligations.

With respect to a conveyance, the person who controls the conveyance is the responsible party for the purposes of reporting. Several recent cases have dealt with private jets entering Canada with unreported currency. The funds are routinely seized and the controller of the jet, usually the captain, is unwittingly implicated in an unreported importation of currency into Canada.

A recent Canadian case highlighted how transactions can be structured to avoid AML reporting requirements. Over two months, the criminal involved regularly travelled over 70 miles from the USA to Canada to conduct currency exchanges at a particular bank and money services business. The transactions never exceeded $10,000, to avoid the Canadian reporting threshold. However, given the frequency (sometimes twice a day) of the transactions and the fact a US citizen was travelling to Canada to do this, both the bank and the money services business filed suspicious transaction reports.

It later emerged that the individual had previous convictions for drug offences and was laundering the proceeds of crime.

This case highlights the need for constant vigilance, and that the reporting thresholds should be used as a rule of thumb and not applied rigidly.

27.9 COUNTRY PROFILE: CAYMAN ISLANDS

27.9.1 Overview

The Cayman Islands has a strong cooperative AML regime, with agreements with both domestic and international bodies. The FATF and IMF reports, in 2007 and 2009 respectively, praised the Cayman Islands, although there is still seen to be room for improvement. Since 2010, the Cayman Islands has signed twelve information exchange agreements (including with Canada, Mexico, Japan, India and South Africa), bringing the total number of exchange agreements to 31, 19 of which are already in force. In November 2013, the most recent agreement – with the United Kingdom – was signed. More recently, under pressure from overseas, it appears to be surrendering much of its data secrecy mantle.

27.9.2 Key Legislation

In the Cayman Islands, the principal regulations and statutes are:

- The Proceeds of Crime Law 2008;
- The Money Laundering Regulations 2009; and
- The Guidance Notes on the Prevention and Detection of Money Laundering and Terrorist Financing in the Cayman Islands, issued in March 2010 and last updated in November 2011, which outline the compliance requirements.

27.9.3 Legislative History

The Proceeds of Crime Law 2008, was brought into force on 30th September, 2008 and repealed the Proceeds of Criminal Conduct Law and the money laundering sections of the Misuse of Drugs Law. These acts were, prior to the Proceeds of Crime Law, the main AML legislation. This Act, therefore, brings together in one place the anti-money-laundering legislative provisions for the Cayman Islands.

The Money Laundering Regulations (MLR) were originally issued in September 2000 under the Proceeds of Criminal Conduct Law (which has now been replaced by the Proceeds of Crime Law). The MLR place additional legal and administrative requirements on entities conducting "relevant financial business".

The guidance notes are produced by The Guidance Notes Committee (GNC), which is the consultative body responsible for the review and updating of the Guidance Notes on the Prevention and Detection of Money Laundering and Terrorist Financing in the Cayman Islands. It is comprised of industry association representatives, government representatives and representatives from the Cayman Islands Monetary Authority. The guidance notes date back to 2001, and are frequently amended – the most recent guidance notes, which were released in March 2010, were updated in November 2011.

27.9.4 FATF Assessment

The most recent FATF assessment praised the Cayman Islands' AML regime. It noted that the Financial Reporting Authority is effective, and a focal point of the AML/CFT regime. Furthermore, it highlighted that there is a strong compliance culture in the

Cayman Islands and that supervision is comprehensive, although it did note that there are some constraints posed by an inadequate quantity of human resources.

27.9.5 The Primary AML Investigation/Regulatory Authorities

Cayman Islands Monetary Authority

The Cayman Islands Monetary Authority has a central role in the fight against money laundering and the preservation of financial stability. Through the prevention and detection of money laundering, the Authority is able to assist in preserving the integrity of the Cayman Islands' financial services industry whilst protecting the interests of stakeholders and maintaining the competitiveness of the Cayman Islands as a leading world financial centre.

Section 6(1)(b)(ii) of the Monetary Authority Law (2010 Revision) gives the Authority legal responsibility, as part of its regulatory function, "to monitor compliance with the money-laundering regulations".

27.9.6 Outline of Specific Money-laundering Offences

The money-laundering offences in the Cayman Islands are, in summary:

- Providing assistance to another in an arrangement which helps them to retain or control benefits of their criminal conduct. This may be by concealment, removal from the jurisdiction, transfer to nominees or otherwise. For a person to be convicted of this offence, they must know or suspect, or have reasonable grounds for knowing or suspecting, that the other person is someone who is, or has been, engaged in criminal conduct.
- The acquisition, possession or use (*even temporarily*) of property knowing that it represents the proceeds of criminal conduct.
- Concealing or disguising property which is the proceeds of criminal conduct, or converting or transferring that property or removing it from the jurisdiction. The section applies to a person's own proceeds of criminal conduct or where they know, or have reasonable grounds to suspect, that the property they are dealing with represents the proceeds of another's criminal conduct. A person commits an offence if they

  > *"enter into or become concerned in an arrangement that facilitates the retention or control by or on behalf of another person of terrorist property by concealment, by removal from the jurisdiction or by transfer to nominees".*

- Tipping off the target or a third party about an investigation or proposed investigation into money laundering, any matter which is likely to prejudice such an investigation or a report to the reporting authority.
- Failure to make a disclosure to the reporting authority as soon as reasonably practicable after knowledge or suspicion of money laundering comes to a person's attention in the course of their trade, profession, business or employment.

It is not necessary for the original offence from which the proceeds stem to have been committed in the Cayman Islands if the conduct would also constitute an indictable offence had it taken place within the Islands, i.e. an offence which is sufficiently serious to be tried in the Grand Court.

Criminal property is defined as the benefit from criminal conduct. Benefit can be in whole or part, direct or indirect, and can include financial benefit or an interest in property. The term "criminal conduct" has now been expanded to cover all criminal offences, whereas previously, the offence of money laundering arose out of conduct that was limited to only indictable or serious criminal acts. Simply put, any person who benefits in some way from criminal activity may now be subject to a money-laundering prosecution.

Section 136(5) of the Proceeds of Crime Law 2008 states that the authorities can take the guidelines into account when assessing whether an offence has been committed.

No duty is imposed on a financial services provider to inquire into the criminal law of another country in which the conduct may have occurred. The question is whether the conduct amounts to an indictable offence in the Cayman Islands or would if it took place in the Cayman Islands. A financial services provider is not expected to know the exact nature of the criminal activity concerned or that the particular funds in question are definitely those which flow from the crime.

27.9.7 Defences

A defendant must prove that they did not suspect that an arrangement related to the proceeds of criminal conduct or that it facilitated the retention or control of the proceeds by the criminal.

Additionally:

- If a disclosure of the arrangement is made before the action in question, or volunteered as soon as it reasonably might be after the action, no offence is committed.
- A person making a report may continue the action without consent from the authorities. Whether or not it will be appropriate for the financial services provider to stop the relevant transaction must depend on the circumstances.
- An employee who makes a report to his employer in accordance with established internal procedures is specifically protected.
- Financial services providers are permitted to report their suspicions to the reporting authority but continue the business relationship or transaction. In carrying out transactions where an institution is considering making a suspicious activity report, the institution should consider duties owed to third parties, such as in the case of a constructive trustee. In such cases, it is recommended that independent legal advice is sought.
- If the person charged had a reasonable excuse for not disclosing the information or other matter in question, they cannot be convicted of failing to disclose.

A report of a suspicious activity made to the reporting authority does not give rise to any civil liability to the client or others and does not constitute, under Cayman Islands' law, a breach of a duty of confidentiality. There are statutory safeguards governing the use of information received by the reporting authority.

27.9.8 *Penalties*

Tipping off carries a maximum of five years' imprisonment and an unlimited fine. Failure to disclose knowledge or suspicion of money laundering carries a maximum penalty of two years' imprisonment and an unlimited fine. The other offences carry a maximum penalty of 14 years' imprisonment and an unlimited fine.

27.9.9 *Scope*

The definitions of relevant financial businesses are detailed in Regulation 4(1) of the MLR. These are:

- Banking or trust business carried on by a person who is a licensee under the Banks and Trust Companies Law;
- Building societies licensed under the Building Societies Law;
- Cooperatives licensed under the Cooperative Societies Law;
- Insurance business and the business of an insurance manager, an insurance agent, an insurance sub-agent or an insurance broker within the meaning of the Insurance Law;
- Mutual fund administration or the business of a regulated mutual fund regulated under the Mutual Funds Law;
- Company management as defined in the Companies Management Law; and
- Any of the activities set out in the Second Schedule of the Regulations.

27.9.10 *Risk-based Approach*

In applying the risk-based approach, entities in the Cayman Islands are required to look into the nature of the risk of the activity conducted. The highest risk category relates to those products or services where unlimited third party funds can be freely received, or where funds can be regularly paid to, or received from, third parties without evidence of identity of the third parties being taken.

Some of the lowest risk products are those in which funds can only be received from a named investor by means of a payment from an account held in the name of the investor, and where the funds can only be returned to the named investor. No third party funding or payments are possible. However, despite their apparent low risk, they are not immune from money laundering.

The geographical location of a financial services provider's customer base will also affect the money-laundering risk and terrorist-financing analysis. Such firms will need to ensure that additional Know Your Customer (KYC) and/or monitoring procedures are in place to manage the enhanced risks of money laundering that such relationships present.

27.9.11 Role of the MLRO/Nominated Officer

The "Appropriate Person" as defined in the legislation is generally referred to as the Money Laundering Reporting Officer (MLRO). Vigilance systems should enable staff to react effectively to suspicious circumstances by reporting them to the relevant MLRO within the organisation.

The MLRO should be a member of staff at management level who acts as the main point of contact with the reporting authority and who has the authority to ensure internal compliance with the regulations.

The requirement is that each firm should designate a suitably qualified and experienced person as MLRO at management level, to whom suspicious activity reports must be made by staff. It is generally expected that the MLRO would be carrying out a Compliance, Audit or Legal role within the financial services provider's business. It is also recommended that financial services providers identify a deputy, who should be a staff member of similar status and experience to the MLRO.

The MLRO should be well versed in the different types of transaction which the institution handles and which may give rise to opportunities for money laundering.

Where a financial services provider has no employees in the Cayman Islands, it may not be possible for a senior member of staff to be the MLRO. In these circumstances, the financial services provider may identify someone else as the appropriate person to whom a report should be made, provided that that person has the following characteristics:

- Is a natural person;
- Is autonomous (meaning the MLRO is the final decision maker as to whether to file an SAR);
- Is independent (meaning no vested interest in the underlying activity); and
- Has, and shall have, access to all relevant material in order to make an assessment as to whether the activity is or is not suspicious.

The MLRO should:

- Receive reports of any information or other matter which comes to the attention of a person handling relevant financial business and which gives rise to actual knowledge or a suspicion of money laundering;
- Consider and investigate such reports in light of relevant information in order to determine if the information or other matter does give rise to such knowledge or suspicion;
- Have reasonable access to other information which may assist in considering such a report;
- Make prompt disclosures to the FRA on the standard form (see Appendix J of the Guidance Notes);
- If, after considering a report, there is knowledge or a suspicion of money laundering, establish and maintain a register of money-laundering reports made by staff and maintain a register of reports to the FRA.

27.9.12 Due Diligence

Financial services providers may evidence that they are undertaking necessary due diligence by ensuring that the following systems are in place:

- Training of key staff (where a financial services provider has any staff);
- Procedures for the determination and confirmation of the true identity of customers requesting their services and the nature of business that the customer expects to conduct;
- Ongoing monitoring of business relationships;
- The recognition and reporting of suspicious activities to the reporting authority;
- Maintenance of records for the prescribed period of time;
- Close liaison with the reporting authority in relation to suspicious activity reporting and with the monetary authority on matters concerning vigilance policy and systems; and
- Ensuring that internal auditing and compliance departments regularly monitor and make recommendations for the update of vigilance systems.

The Regulations require that relevant persons should not form business relationships or carry out one-off transactions with, or for, another person unless they:

- Maintain procedures which establish the identity of the applicant for business;
- Maintain record-keeping procedures;
- Adopt appropriate internal controls and communication procedures;
- Comply with the identification and record-keeping requirements;
- Adopt appropriate measures to ensure that employees are aware of and comply with the procedures in place, and the enactments of money laundering;
- Provide appropriate training for employees;
- Establish internal reporting procedures.

There are two general important aspects of knowing your customer set out in Cayman guidance, which are to:

- Be satisfied that a prospective customer is who he/she claims to be, and is the ultimate client; and
- Ensure that sufficient information is obtained on the nature of the business that the customer expects to undertake, and any expected, or predictable, pattern of transactions.

Personal Client Due Diligence

It will normally be necessary to obtain the following documented information concerning direct personal customers:

- Full name/names used;
- Correct permanent address including postcode (if appropriate);
- Date and place of birth;

- Nationality;
- Occupation;
- The purpose of the account;
- Estimated level of turnover expected for the account; and
- The source of funds (i.e. generated from what transaction or business).

In the case of non-resident prospective clients, identification documents of the same sort which bear a photograph and are pre-signed by the client should normally be obtained. This evidence should, where possible, be supplemented by a bank reference with which the client maintains a current relationship or other appropriate reference. A social insurance number is also considered useful.

Information about a person's residency and/or nationality is also considered useful in assessing whether a customer is resident in a high-risk country. Financial services providers should also take appropriate steps to verify the name and address of applicants by one or more methods, such as:

- Obtaining a reference from a "respected professional" who knows the applicant;
- Checking the register of electors;
- Making a credit reference agency search;
- Checking a local telephone directory;
- Requesting sight of a recent rates or utility bill. Care must be taken that the document is an original and not a copy; or
- Conducting a personal visit to the home of the applicant, where possible.

Identification documents, either originals or certified copies, should be pre-signed and bear a photograph of the applicant, such as:

- Current valid passport;
- Armed Forces ID card;
- A Cayman Islands' employer ID card bearing the photograph and signature of the applicant; or
- Provisional or full driving licence bearing the photograph and signature of the applicant.

Corporate Customer Due Diligence

It will normally be necessary to obtain the following documented information concerning corporate clients:

- Certificate of Incorporation or equivalent, details of the registered office and place of business.
- Explanation of the nature of the applicant's business, the reason for the relationship being established, an indication of the expected turnover, the source of funds and a copy of the last available financial statements where appropriate.

- Satisfactory evidence of the identity of each of the principal beneficial owners, these being any person holding 10% interest or more or with principal control over the company's assets and any person (or persons) on whose instructions the signatories on the account are to act or may act where such persons are not full-time employees, officers or directors of the company.
- In the case of a bank account, satisfactory evidence of the identity of the account signatories, details of their relationship with the company and, if they are not employees, an explanation of the relationship. Subsequent changes to signatories must be verified.
- Evidence of the authority to enter into the business relationship (for example, a copy of the board resolution authorising the account signatories in the case of a bank account).
- Copies of Powers of Attorney, or any other authority, affecting the operation of the account given by the directors in relation to the company.
- Copies of the list/register of directors.
- Satisfactory evidence of identity must be established for two directors, one of whom should, if applicable, be an executive director where different from account signatories.

Consideration should also be given to whether it is desirable to obtain a copy of the memorandum and articles of association, or by-laws of the client.

Non-face-to-face Customer Due Diligence

Financial services providers are also required to put into place policies and procedures that appropriately address the risks posed by non-face-to-face contact for customers, either at the opening of the business relationship or through the operation of that relationship.

Where identity is verified electronically or copy documents are used, a financial services provider should apply additional verification checks. For example, where it is impractical or impossible to obtain sight of original documents, a copy should only be accepted where it has been certified by a suitable certifier as being a true copy of the original document and that the photo is a true likeness of the applicant for business.

Politically Exposed Persons

Relevant firms are encouraged to be vigilant in relation to PEPs from all jurisdictions, and in particular from high-risk countries, who are seeking to establish business relationships. They should, in relation to politically exposed persons, in addition to performing normal due diligence measures:

- Have appropriate risk-management systems to determine whether the customer is a politically exposed person;
- Obtain senior management approval for establishing business relationships with such customers;
- Take reasonable measures to establish the source of wealth and source of funds;
- Conduct enhanced ongoing monitoring of the business relationship.

They should also obtain senior management approval to continue a business relationship once a customer or beneficial owner is found to be, or subsequently becomes, a PEP.

Correspondent Banking

Financial services providers should, in relation to cross-border correspondent banking and other similar relationships, in addition to performing normal due diligence measures:

- Gather sufficient information about a respondent institution to understand fully the nature of the respondent's business and to determine from publicly available information the reputation of the institution and the quality of supervision, including whether it has been subject to a money-laundering or terrorist-financing investigation or regulatory action.
- Assess the respondent institution's anti-money-laundering and terrorist-financing controls.
- Obtain approval from senior management before establishing new correspondent relationships.
- Document the respective responsibilities of each institution.
- With respect to "payable-through accounts", be satisfied that the respondent bank has verified the identity of, and performed ongoing due diligence on, the customers having direct access to accounts of the correspondent and that it is able to provide relevant customer identification data upon request to the correspondent bank.

Shell Banking

Financial services providers should not enter into, or continue, a correspondent relationship with a "shell bank"; and should take appropriate measures to ensure that they do not enter into, or continue, a correspondent banking relationship with a bank which is known to permit its accounts to be used by a shell bank. Neither should financial services providers set up anonymous accounts or anonymous passbooks for new or existing customers.

Financial services providers should satisfy themselves that the respondent financial institutions in foreign countries do not permit their accounts to be used by shell banks.

27.9.13 Ongoing Monitoring

Once the identification procedures have been completed and the client relationship is established, there remains a requirement to monitor the conduct of the relationship/account to ensure that it is consistent with the nature of business stated when the relationship/account was opened.

Firms are required to develop and apply written policies and procedures for taking reasonable measures to ensure that documents, data or information collected during the identification process are kept up to date and relevant by undertaking routine reviews of existing records. This does not mean that there needs to be automatic renewal of expired identification where there is sufficient information to indicate that the identification of the customer can readily be verified by other means.

Monitoring to identify unusual transactions is required to spot inconsistency with the stated original purpose of the accounts. Possible areas to monitor could be:

- Transaction type
- Frequency
- Amount
- Geographical origin/destination
- Account signatories.

There is a specific requirement that, on a regular basis, a firm should conduct an AML/CFT audit to:

- Attest to the overall integrity and effectiveness of the AML/CFT systems and controls;
- Assess its risks and exposures with respect to size, business lines, customer base and geographic locations;
- Assess the adequacy of internal policies and procedures, including customer identification and verification, record-keeping and retention, reliance relationships and supporting documentation, and transaction monitoring;
- Test compliance with the relevant laws and regulations;
- Test transactions in all areas with emphasis on high-risk areas, products and services;
- Assess employees' knowledge of the laws, regulations, guidance and policies and procedures;
- Assess the adequacy, accuracy and completeness of training programmes; and
- Assess the adequacy of the procedures for identifying suspicious activity.

27.9.14 Staff Training

Staff should be adequately trained to enable them to identify such activity and be trained in the internal reporting systems required for compliance with the regulations. Staff training should be documented and will be subject to regulatory review. It is good practice for all institutions to maintain and regularly review their instruction manual for all employees relating to entry, verification and recording of customer information and reporting procedures.

27.9.15 Suspicious Transaction Reporting

Where a staff member conducts enquiries and obtains what he considers to be a satisfactory explanation of a complex or unusual large transaction, or unusual pattern of transactions, he may conclude that there are no grounds for suspicion, and therefore take no further action as he is satisfied with matters. However, where the enquiries conducted by the staff member do not provide a satisfactory explanation of the activity, he may conclude that there are grounds for "suspicion" requiring disclosure.

Previously, financial services providers had been required to make a report relating to suspicious activity based on knowledge or suspicion that a person was involved in money laundering. The requirement to report now arises if a person knows or suspects, or has reasonable grounds for knowing or suspecting, that another person is engaged in criminal conduct. As such, those in the regulated sector have an obligation to report all breaches of law, no matter their severity or even whether they are related to money laundering.

Indicators of potentially suspicious transactions include:

- Any unusual financial activity of the customer in the context of his own usual activities;
- Any unusually linked transactions;
- Any unusual method of settlement;
- Any unwillingness to provide the information requested.

If the MLRO decides that a disclosure should be made, a report, in standard form, should be sent to the reporting authority. The form should be completed in its entirety and any fields that are not applicable should be so indicated. It is important that the MLRO fills in the form to the fullest extent possible, providing as much relevant information and detail as they have available. This will provide more assurance that the information provided is of benefit to the FRA.

It is important to note that SARs must be filed with the Financial Reporting Authority (FRA) on a suspicious transaction even if the transaction did not proceed.

27.9.16 Penalties

The monetary authority will be examining the extent to which institutions are following the procedures during the course of on-site inspections and may take appropriate action as authorised by the regulatory laws, where warranted. In determining what action to take, the monetary authority will take into account the overall circumstances including the seriousness of the non-compliance, the number of instances of non-compliance and the failure to respond to any previous recommendations or warnings given by the monetary authority.

A person who breaches the AML compliance requirements can be liable, on summary conviction, to a fine of five thousand dollars, or on conviction on indictment, to a fine and to imprisonment for two years.

27.9.17 Case Studies

The Cayman Islands was recently used as a base for a half-a-billion-dollar international pyramid scheme, with a Cayman Islands resident cooperating with two US citizens to defraud almost 2,000 investors. The "Cash4Titles" plan involved lending money to borrowers who put up titles of their motor vehicles as security, but by the time it was closed down, old investors were being paid off by the income from new investors, essentially a standard Ponzi scheme.

Offshore companies were formed by the criminals to launder the illegal finances, which highlights the importance of corporate due diligence and ascertaining the exact purpose of a corporate client. This also highlights the Cayman Islands government's commitment to combating money laundering.

27.10 COUNTRY PROFILE: CHINA

27.10.1 Overview

The People's Republic of China has recently sought to bring its AML provisions into alignment with other Asian jurisdictions with robust financial crime deterrence legislation and procedures, such as those that have been implemented in Singapore.

The position of China both geographically and economically has highlighted the need for stringency. Moreover, the strength of the money-laundering-deterrence regimes in its neighbouring jurisdictions has prompted an urgent response from China. In China, money laundering most commonly arises through the following channels:

- Cash smuggling;
- The use of legitimate banking systems – various deposit accounts;
- Underpriced export/counterfeit goods;
- Underground banking systems.

In recent years, there has been an increase in more technologically based crime due to the emergence of e-banking and e-currency.

27.10.2 Key Legislation

The relevant AML laws in China are:

- Anti-Money Laundering Law of the People's Republic of China 2006.
- The People's Bank of China Decree No.1 [2006] – The Rules for Anti-money Laundering by Financial Institutions.

Together, the AML laws and rules provide a procedural reference guide for financial institutions. The money-laundering offences are also found in the 1997 revision of the 1979 Penal Code under Articles 191, 312 and 349.

27.10.3 FATF Assessment

China was placed on an enhanced follow-up process as a result of partially compliant and non-compliant ratings in certain of the Core and Key Recommendations in its mutual evaluation report of 2007. However, it was removed from the enhanced follow-up measures in 2012 following progress in the AML regime.

27.10.4 The Primary AML Investigation/Regulatory Authorities

The People's Bank of China

The State Council appointed The People's Bank of China as the designated central bank in September 1983. In accordance with this status, The People's Bank of China (PBC) is the administrative authority for money-laundering-deterrence legislation. The Rules for Anti-money Laundering by Financial Institutions, formed in accordance with the law of the People's Republic of China on anti-money laundering, set out the functions of the PBC.

The Rules establish the PBC as the competent authority and the supervisory authority for China's banking system, whose responsibilities have been consolidated to confer certain duties to the appropriate financial institutions. Article 5 of the AML Rules lays down the PBC's supervisory responsibilities and duties pertinent to money laundering:

- To stipulate anti-money-laundering regulations for financial institutions solely or jointly with the China Banking Regulatory Commission, the China Securities Regulatory Commission and the China Insurance Regulatory Commission;
- To monitor fund flow in both RMB and foreign currencies for anti-money-laundering purposes;
- To supervise and inspect the fulfilling of anti-money-laundering obligations by financial institutions;
- To investigate suspicious transactions within its competence;
- To report transactions suspected of being involved with money-laundering crime to law-enforcement agencies;
- To exchange information and documents relevant to money laundering with overseas anti-money-laundering institutions in line with relevant laws and administrative regulations;
- Other responsibilities as defined by the State Council.

The Financial Intelligence Unit

The Financial Intelligence Unit is housed within PBC with two separate operational units:

1. The Anti Money Laundering Bureau
2. The China Anti Money Laundering Monitoring and Analysis Centre.

The Anti Money Laundering Bureau

The Anti Money Laundering Bureau (AMLB) organises and coordinates China's AML affairs, conducting administrative investigations, dissemination and providing policy oversight. Decisions about whether to carry out an administrative investigation into a suspicious transaction report (STR) or to disseminate an STR to the Ministry of Public Security or other law-enforcement agencies are made under AML law.

The China Anti Money Laundering Monitoring and Analysis Centre

The China Anti Money Laundering Monitoring and Analysis Centre (CAMLMAC) specialises in data collection, processing and analysis. It also has an extensive range of legally documented duties to perform within the realm of suspicious transaction reporting. CAMLMAC was established by the People's Bank of China, and is required to undertake the following responsibilities:

- To receive and analyse reports of large-value transactions and suspicious transactions both in RMB and foreign currencies;
- To establish a national anti-money-laundering database and properly store large-value and suspicious transaction reports submitted by financial institutions;
- To report analysis results to the People's Bank of China;
- To require financial institutions to promptly supplement and revise reports of large-value transactions and suspicious transactions in RMB and foreign currencies;
- To exchange relevant information and materials with foreign institutions with the authorisation of the People's Bank of China;
- Other responsibilities as specified by the People's Bank of China.

The Regulatory Commissions

The China Banking Regulatory Commission, China Securities Regulatory Commission and China Insurance Regulatory Commission shall each undertake anti-money-laundering supervision and management responsibilities within its competence.

27.10.5 Outline of Specific Money-laundering Offences

The money-laundering offences are contained in the Chinese Penal Code.

Article 191 contains the drug and gang proceeds offence. An offence is conducted by whoever, while clearly knowing that the funds are proceeds illegally obtained from drug-related or gang-related crimes, commits any of the following acts in order to cover up or conceal the source or nature of the funds:

- Providing fund accounts;
- Helping to exchange property into cash or any financial negotiable instruments;
- Helping to transfer capital through transferring accounts or any other form of settlement;
- Helping to remit funds to any other country; or
- Covering up or concealing by any other means the nature or source of the illegally obtained proceeds and the gains derived therefrom.

Article 312 provides that whoever knowingly conceals, transfers, purchases or helps to sell illegally acquired goods commits an offence.

Article 349 contains a further drug-related offence. This makes it an offence for anyone to shield offenders engaged in smuggling, trafficking, transporting or manufacturing narcotic drugs or to harbour, transfer or cover up for such offenders, narcotic drugs or their pecuniary and other gains from such criminal activities.

27.10.6 *Penalties*

For committing the drug or gang proceeds offence, in addition to the confiscation of the proceeds and gains, the perpetrator can be sentenced to imprisonment of up to five years and/or be fined between 5 and 20% of the amount of money laundered. If the circumstances are serious, the imprisonment will be between five and ten years and they will still have to pay the fine.

Where a company commits the offence, it shall be fined, and the persons who are directly in charge and the other persons who are directly responsible for the crime shall be sentenced to up to five years' imprisonment.

Knowingly concealing, transferring, purchasing or helping to sell goods is punishable by up to three years' imprisonment, criminal detention or public surveillance and possibly a fine.

A violation of Article 349 is punishable by imprisonment, criminal detention or public surveillance of up to three years. In more serious cases, this can be increased to up to ten years. Any conspirators to the crime are treated as joint offenders.

27.10.7 *Scope*

The Rules apply to:

- Commercial banks, city credit cooperatives, rural credit cooperatives, postal savings institutions and policy banks;
- Securities companies, future brokerage companies and fund-management companies;
- Insurance companies and insurance asset management companies;
- Trust and investment companies, financial asset management companies, finance companies, financial leasing companies, auto finance companies and money brokerage companies;
- Other financial institutions specified and announced by the People's Bank of China.

27.10.8 *AML Regime*

Under Article 15 of the AML Law, each financial institution is required to establish and implement an anti-money-laundering internal control programme. Persons in charge of the financial institution are required to take responsibility for the effective implementation of the internal control programme, and each financial institution is also required to establish a specialised unit or designate a unit to be responsible for anti-money-laundering tasks.

27.10.9 *Role of the MLRO/Nominated Officer*

Financial institutions and their branch offices are required to:

- Establish a sound anti-money-laundering internal control system;
- Establish a specialised unit or designate a unit to be responsible for anti-money-laundering tasks;

- Formulate internal operational procedures and control measures for anti-money-laundering tasks;
- Carry out staff training on anti-money laundering so as to strengthen their working capacities.

Responsible persons of financial institutions and their branch offices shall take responsibility in effective operation of the anti-money-laundering internal control system.

27.10.10 Due Diligence

Financial institutions shall establish and implement a customer identification system according to rules and regulations. The object of this system is:

- To identify a customer who wishes to establish business relations or requires occasional financial services above the prescribed amount, by requiring the customer to present an authentic and valid identity card or other identity documents, by verifying and registering such documents and by updating, in a timely manner, any change in a customer's identity information;
- To understand the purpose and nature of a customer's transaction and effectively identify beneficiaries of the transaction in line with relevant rules and regulations;
- To re-identify a customer when detecting any abnormal phenomenon in the process of business operation or suspecting the authenticity, validity or integrity of a customer's identity documents obtained previously;
- To make sure that an overseas financial institution with which it has a correspondent or similar relationship effectively conducts customer identification, and that it can obtain a customer's identity information from such overseas financial institutions.

Personal Client Due Diligence

According to the AML Law, the documents required to conduct CDD are authentic and valid personal identification certificates or other personal identification documents.

Beneficiary Due Diligence

In the case of developing life insurance, trust and other business relations with a client, where the beneficiary of the contract signed is not the client himself or herself, the financial institution shall conduct verification and registration of the ID or other personal identification documents of the beneficiary.

Anonymous Accounts

Financial institutions shall not provide services to, or conduct transactions for, clients for whom the identity is not clear, or open an anonymous account or account with fake names for the client.

Correspondent Banking

Financial institutions are required to make sure that an overseas financial institution with which they have a correspondent or similar relationship effectively conducts customer identification, and that they can obtain a customer's identity information from such overseas financial institutions.

27.10.11 Ongoing Monitoring

In cases where financial institutions have questions regarding the authenticity, validity or completeness of the ID of clients obtained previously, they shall re-establish the identification of clients. During the course of business relations, when changes are made to client ID information, updates to the records shall be completed without delay.

27.10.12 Staff Training

Financial institutions should conduct anti-money-laundering training in line with the requirements of prevention and monitoring of money laundering. As staff are bound by the AML requirements, the training must inform them of their obligations and the penalties for non-compliance.

27.10.13 Record-keeping

Financial institutions shall keep customers' identity records and transaction information such as a transaction's statistics, vouchers and accounting materials. Financial institutions and their staff shall keep confidential customer identity material and transaction information acquired when fulfilling their anti-money-laundering obligations, and shall provide such material and information to other institutions or individuals in strict accordance with relevant laws.

Financial institutions shall develop a system to keep information on client ID and trading records, as requested. Upon the completion of business relations, or the conclusion of trading, the client ID information and the trading records shall be kept for at least five years. When financial institutions go bankrupt and are dissolved, they shall transfer the information on client ID and trading records of clients to the agencies designated by the related department of the State Council.

27.10.14 Suspicious Transaction Reporting

Financial institutions shall report any large-value (denominated either in RMB or foreign currencies) and suspicious transactions to the China Anti-Money Laundering Monitoring and Analysis Centre. These reports will be confidential. In addition, when any suspicion of crime arises while carrying out its anti-money-laundering responsibilities, a financial institution shall promptly report, in a written form, to the local branch office of the People's Bank of China and the public security agency.

Financial institutions and their staff shall keep information of their anti-money-laundering work, such as reporting of suspicious transactions or cooperation with the

People's Bank of China, confidential, and should not provide such information to their customers or other individuals, since this would be in violation of regulations.

When the People's Bank of China or any of its provincial branch offices finds that a suspicious transaction needs further investigation or verification, it can request from the financial institution information on the customer account(s) involved in the transaction, records of the transaction and other related material. The financial institution must cooperate with any requests made.

Furthermore, financial institutions must implement a system to enable the reporting of large-value trading and suspicious trading. In cases where the value of a single transaction or the accumulated value of transactions within a specified period of time exceeds the specified amount or suspicious transactions are spotted by financial institutions, the financial institutions should report to the information centre of the anti-money-laundering authority without delay.

27.10.15 Auditing Requirements

Financial institutions shall submit, in accordance with regulations issued by the People's Bank of China, anti-money-laundering statistical reports, information and material, and the anti-money-laundering-related content in their audit report.

27.10.16 Penalties

In cases where the staff of the anti-money-laundering authority and other departments and agencies that are responsible for regulating anti-money laundering are found to have committed any of the following acts, they will be subject to administrative sanctions:

- Investigating, inspecting or taking temporary freezing measures in violation of regulations;
- Disclosing national or commercial secrets or personal private details known to them in the course of work related to anti-money-laundering;
- Imposing administrative sanctions on related institutions and individuals in violation of regulations;
- Other acts of violation of regulations.

In cases where a financial institution is found to be guilty of any of the following acts, the anti-money-laundering authority shall request said financial institution to rectify the situation within a specified period of time:

- Failing to set up an internal control system for anti-money laundering, as requested;
- Failing to set up a special unit for anti-money laundering or to appoint an internal unit to be responsible for anti-money laundering, as requested;
- Failing to conduct anti-money-laundering training for its employees.

In cases where the violations are serious, recommendations will be given to the related financial regulatory authorities to request that disciplinary punishments be imposed on directors and senior managers that are directly responsible and other staff that are directly involved.

In cases where a financial institution is found to be guilty of any of the following acts, the anti-money-laundering authority shall request said financial institution to rectify the situation within a specified period of time:

- Failing to implement the duties relating to client identification, as requested;
- Failing to keep client ID information and trading records, as requested;
- Failing to report large-value trading or suspicious trading, as requested;
- Conducting trading for clients whose ID is not clear, or opening an anonymous account or account with fake names for a client;
- Disclosing related information in violation of the regulations on confidentiality;
- Refusing to aid, or hindering, an anti-money-laundering investigation or inspections;
- Refusing to provide investigation materials or providing false documents intentionally.

In cases where the wrongdoings are serious, a fine of between RMB 200,000 and RMB 500,000 shall be imposed, and the directors and senior managers that are directly responsible, and other working staff that are directly involved, shall be fined between RMB 10,000 and RMB 50,000.

In cases where the above-mentioned acts by a financial institution have resulted in money laundering occurring, a fine of between RMB 500,000 and RMB 5 million shall be imposed on the financial institution and the directors and senior managers that are directly responsible; other working staff that are directly involved will be fined between RMB 50,000 and RMB 500,000. In cases where the violation and consequences are serious, the anti-money-laundering authority may recommend to the related financial regulatory bodies that the financial institution involved should cease trading and undergo re-consolidation, or have its licence to conduct financial business suspended.

For directors, senior managers and other staff members of financial institutions that are directly involved in the acts mentioned in the previous two paragraphs, the anti-money-laundering authority may recommend to the related financial regulatory bodies that the financial institutions concerned impose on them disciplinary punishments, or it may recommend the cancellation of their post-assumption qualifications according to law, or prevent them from engaging in related financial business.

Additionally, under the rules the PBC can:

- Order the financial institution to suspend business and take remedial actions or revoke its business licence;
- Disqualify directors, senior executives and other employees held immediately accountable for the misconduct from holding any positions and ban them from working in the financial industry;
- Order financial institutions to issue a disciplinary warning to directors, senior executives and other employees held immediately accountable for the misconduct.

Violations of the provisions of this law which constitute crimes shall be subject to criminal liability investigation according to law.

27.10.17 Case Studies

The booming art market in China is suspected to be hiding millions of dollars of illicit funds, although this can be difficult to prove. Experts say that "show bidding", which involves deliberately overpaying for poor art to inflate its resale value, is a technique used to launder criminal proceeds, and is successful because of the subjective nature of the value of art. Sometimes bribes are thought to pass through art transactions, so a percentage (if not all) of the value of the price of the artwork may actually be a bribe to the seller. The buyer and the seller may have an entirely different illicit relationship, but to an outside observer it would be impossible to prove that the pair had ever met.

Financial institutions need to be aware of this criminal activity, and transactions of this nature should be treated with extreme caution. In one high-profile incident, a Chinese businessman had a fake ancient jade burial suit made up. After getting a group of appraisers to verify its authenticity and value it at $375 million, he used the suit as security on a $100 million bank loan. A loan of this size with a worthless security could cripple a financial institution, so stringent, independent checks were carried out on every aspect of the situation. For this and a number of other, similar frauds, the businessman received a life sentence.

Another illicit financial market was uncovered recently in Hunan province. A simple internet search led the police to a billion-dollar illegal banking market, cutting out legitimate financial institutions altogether. This highlights the need for financial institutions to thoroughly investigate the source of wealth of their clients, and be aware that the assets clients declare may not truly reflect the assets they have to their name.

27.11 COUNTRY PROFILE: DENMARK

27.11.1 Overview

Denmark has made significant progress in its AML programme over recent years. The FATF, despite being critical in the past, has recognised that the changes Denmark has made have brought the country in line with the international AML standards.

27.11.2 Key Legislation

The Act on Measures to Prevent Money Laundering and Financing of Terrorism, passed in April 2012 as a consolidation of the 2011 version, is the current AML law.

27.11.3 Legislative History

The Third EC Directive on Money Laundering was implemented in Denmark by Danish Act No. 117 of 27th February, 2006 through the enactment of Measures to Prevent Money Laundering and Terrorist Financing, which entered into force on 1st March, 2006. The Act was later amended and consolidated by Danish Act No. 442 of 11th May, 2007.

Denmark has adopted a risk-based approach to AML, and the 2007 consolidated Act addressed areas such as enhanced customer due diligence and beneficial ownership. There are no strict guidelines which indicate signs of criminal activity at financial firms. Danish regulators are obliged to correct any misapprehensions that firms might have. In 2006, the Danish prosecutor's office published a non-exhaustive report indicating matters that might be indicative of money laundering or terrorist financing.

Denmark passed a new law in April 2012 – the Act on Measures to Prevent Money Laundering and Financing of Terrorism – which consolidated the Danish Act on Measures to Prevent Money Laundering and Financing of Terrorism of 15th April, 2011.

27.11.4 FATF Assessment

The 2006 assessment found Denmark to be partially compliant with the required AML standards. However, in October 2010 after a follow-up report, the FATF recognised that Denmark had made significant progress in addressing deficiencies identified in the previous report and removed the country from the regular follow-up process. The FATF agreed that Denmark should now report on any further improvements to its anti-money-laundering/combating the financing of terrorism (AML/CFT) system on a biennial basis.

However, the FATF did highlight in its follow-up report that doubts remain regarding the effectiveness of the STR reporting regime, and there are deficiencies in the process for identifying low-risk customers. Despite these issues, though, Denmark is described as, on the whole, largely compliant.

27.11.5 The Primary AML Investigation/Regulatory Authorities

Finanstilsynet

The primary investigating and reporting body for financial crime in Denmark is Finanstilsynet (the Danish FSA) which attends to financial regulation in Denmark. The main purpose of the body is to oversee the financial legal compliance of financial companies and of issuers and investors in the securities market, to contribute to the development of financial legislation and to collect and spread knowledge about the financial sector.

The Public Prosecutor for Serious Economic Crime

The Prosecution Service is governed by the Minister of Justice, who supervises public prosecutions. Every firm not overseen by the Danish FSA has to register with, and send reports to, the Public Prosecutor for Serious Economic Crime. The Public Prosecutor for Serious Economic Crime attends to cases involving serious financial crime on a national basis. The Public Prosecutor for Serious Economic Crime is responsible for prosecuting major financial crime. The Special International Crimes Office attends to crimes, including financial crime, committed by foreigners outside Denmark.

The money-laundering secretariat produces an annual report detailing information on money-laundering activity in Denmark.

27.11.6 Outline of Specific Money-laundering Offences

Money laundering is criminalised under Article 290 of the Criminal Code. Furthermore, Section 4 of the AML Act defines what constitutes "money laundering" under the Act. Money laundering shall mean:

- Unlawfully accepting or acquiring for oneself or others a share in profits, which are obtained by a punishable violation of the law (which also covers actions carried out by the person who committed the punishable violation of the law from which the profits originate);
- Unlawfully concealing, keeping, transporting, assisting in disposal or in a similar manner subsequently serving to ensure, for the benefit of another person, the profits of a punishable violation of the law; or
- Attempting or participating in such actions.

27.11.7 Financing of Terrorism

The Act and the Criminal Code define "financing of terrorism" as contributing "by instigation, advice or action to furthering the criminal activity or the common purpose of the group of persons or an association, which commits one or more of the offences as stated in s.114 which is directly or indirectly granting financial support to, provides or collects funds, or makes money available to a person, group or association that commits or intends to commit terrorist acts". This carries a penalty of imprisonment for any term not exceeding six years.

Section 2 describes the ban against cash transactions. Retailers and auctioneers may not receive cash payments of DKK 100,000 or more irrespective of whether payment is effected in one instance or as several payments that seem to be mutually connected.

Section 27(1) is similar to the tipping-off offence which exists in common with all other countries that have implemented the EU Directive and FATF Recommendations. It is a prohibition which states that all undertakings, employees and all other persons shall be obliged to keep secret the fact that a notification or suspicion has been passed to the State Prosecutor for Serious Economic Crime. Once information has been reported, it may be passed on by virtue of Section 27(2–7) to:

- The authorities and organisations that supervise compliance with the Act.
- Undertakings belonging to the same group as defined by Article 2(12) of Directive 2002/87/EC ("a group of undertakings, which consists of a parent undertaking, its subsidiaries and the entities in which the parent undertaking or its subsidiaries hold a participation, as well as undertakings linked to each other by a relationship within the meaning of Article 12(1) of Directive 83/349/EEC").
- Lawyers providing assistance in the planning or execution of transactions for their clients concerning purchase and sale of real property or undertakings, managing their clients' money, securities or other assets, opening or managing bank accounts, savings accounts or securities accounts, raising the necessary capital for establishment, operation or management of undertakings, or establishing, operating or managing undertakings, or who carry out a financial transaction or a transaction concerning real property, and State-authorised public accountants and registered public accountants if both the person divulging the information and the person receiving the information carry out their activities within the same legal unit or network.
- Persons or undertakings covered by Section 1(1), nos. 1–14 (which includes banks, mortgage-credit institutions, investment companies and investment management companies) provided:
  - that the information relates to an undertaking or person that is a customer of both the undertaking or person divulging the information and the undertaking or person receiving the information, and that the information relates to a transaction involving both parties;
  - that the undertaking or person divulging the information and the undertaking or person receiving the information have the same occupation;
  - that the undertaking or person divulging the information and the undertaking or person receiving the information are subject to uniform requirements as regards duty of confidentiality and protection of personal data; and
  - that the information exchanged is only applied for prevention of money laundering and financing of terrorism.

27.11.8 Penalties

Money laundering is punishable, under Article 290 of the Criminal Code, by 18 months' imprisonment, which can be increased to six years for serious or organised crimes.

Section 26 states that undertakings and persons subject to the Act shall provide information in good faith and shall not incur liability. Disclosure on information under the Act shall not be considered a breach of any duty of confidentiality.

27.11.9 Scope

The Act applies to various financial institutions including, but not exclusive to, banks, mortgage-credit institutions, investment companies, investment management companies, life assurance companies and lateral pension funds.

27.11.10 Role of the MLRO/Nominated Officer

Undertakings and persons have an obligation under Section 25(2) of the Act to appoint a person at management level to ensure that undertakings comply with their obligations under the Act and any subsequent regulations or directives. They must have access to customer information and other relevant information in order to ensure that the undertakings and persons comply with the obligations stipulated in this Act, under Section 25(3).

Employees should be informed by the person appointed under the sections above that their duties and obligations are stipulated under the Act. If there is no person able to perform the role, the duty falls on the employer.

27.11.11 Due Diligence

Part 4 of the Act details the customer due diligence requirements which relevant undertakings must carry out in order to identify the clients when they suspect money-laundering activity. Undertakings and persons under this Act are required to have knowledge of their customers; this will require customers to provide proof of identity when establishing a business relationship or when opening an account.

When a firm conducts single transactions or business with occasional customers, undertakings and persons covered by the Act must carry out due diligence, including proof of identity for each transaction of an amount corresponding to DKK 100,000 or more. The requirements concerning proof of identity apply irrespective of whether the transaction is completed in one or more related operations if these appear to be connected.

Personal Client Due Diligence

Customers that are natural persons must provide proof of identity which will include:

- Name
- Address
- National registration number (CPR number) or similar documentation if the person does not have a CPR number.

Information shall also be obtained about the business relationship in terms of the customer's business objectives and intent.

The customer relationship and transactions conducted throughout the course of the business relationship should be closely monitored on a regular basis to ensure that conduct is consistent with the undertaking's knowledge of the customer, its business and risk profile as well as the source of funds. Documents obtained, relevant data and other information should also be kept up to date by the firm.

If there are any doubts as to the credibility of customer identification documents, then new proof of identity will be required. Undertakings and persons under the Act may decide to carry out identification procedures on the basis of a risk assessment conducted, depending on the risk related to each individual customer, product or transaction. The undertaking or person must, however, be able to prove to the authorities that the extent of its investigation is adequate in relation to the risk of money laundering and the financing of terrorism.

For customer relationships established before entry into force of the Act (April 2012) and where the information mentioned above does not exist, proof of identity and collection of information should still be carried out by a firm at a suitable time and on the basis of a risk assessment.

A relevant firm should conduct identification procedures establishing a customer relationship before a transaction is undertaken. However, a customer transaction may be completed in immediate continuation of the establishment of the customer relationship on the basis of a documented risk assessment in order not to interrupt the normal conduct of business. If proof of identity cannot be carried out so as not to interrupt the normal conduct of business, then it should be completed as soon as is practical after initial contact with the customer.

If proof of identity cannot be provided, a business relationship should not be established and the transaction should not be carried out. At the same time, a notification may need to be sent to the State Prosecutor for Serious Economic Crime.

Corporate Customer Due Diligence

For customers which are undertakings, the proof of identity shall include:

- Name
- Address
- Business registration number (CVR number) or similar documentation which does not have a CVR number.

In addition to this, the ownership and control structure of the undertaking will need to be clarified and the beneficial owners of the undertaking are also required to provide proof of identity.

However, proof of identity will not be required when the beneficial owner has funds in a client account of a notary or lawyer, if the notary or lawyer is subject to regulations under the Act. It should be noted that it is a condition that information about the identity of the beneficial owner is made available to the account-holding institution when the institution requests this.

Beneficiary Customer Due Diligence

If an undertaking or person covered under this Act has knowledge or the presumption that a person other than the one they are in contact with is the beneficial customer, the undertaking or persons covered under the Act may demand to be informed of the identity procedures conducted on the actual beneficial customer. The identity of the immediate customer should be clarified on the basis of a risk assessment.

Non-face-to-face Customer Due Diligence

When a customer has not been physically present for identification purposes, the undertaking should take one or more of the following measures:

- Ensure that the customer's identity is established by additional documentation;
- Check or verify the documents supplied, or require confirmatory certification by one of the undertakings mentioned in s. 1 of the Act (banks, mortgage-credit institutions, investment companies, etc.);
- Require that the first payment in connection with the transaction is carried out through an account opened in the customer's name with a bank or a similar undertaking established in a country within the European Union, a country with which the Union has entered into an agreement for the financial area or a third country which is subject to requirements to prevent money laundering and financing of terrorism which correspond to the requirements in this Act and compliance with said requirements is being checked.

Politically Exposed Persons

PEPs are subject to enhanced due diligence requirements. Undertakings and persons covered under this Act shall:

- Have adequate procedures to determine whether the customer is a PEP who is a resident of another country;
- Have senior daily management approval for establishing business relationships with such customers;
- Take reasonable measures to gather information about the sources of income and funds that are involved in the business relationship or transaction; and
- Continuously monitor the business relationship.

Anonymous Accounts

The Act covers the enhanced due diligence obligations for anonymous products and transactions. Undertakings and persons covered by the Act must be particularly aware of any money-laundering and financing-of-terrorism threats that may arise from products or transactions that might favour anonymity, and take measures, if needed, to prevent the products or transactions being used for money laundering or the financing of terrorism.

Correspondent Banking

For cross-frontier correspondent banking relationships with banks and institutions from countries outside the European Union with which the Union has not entered into an agreement for the financial area, the banks, mortgage-credit institutions, payment institutions and e-money institutions covered by this Act shall, before establishing new correspondent banking relationships:

- Obtain sufficient information about the relevant institution to understand fully the nature of the correspondent's business and to determine from publicly available information the reputation of the institution and the quality of supervision, including information on the extent to which the institution is subject to an authority investigation or has previously received sanctions from public authorities for infringement of regulations on preventing money laundering and financing of terrorism;
- Obtain sufficient information to ensure that the relevant institution has adequate and effective control procedures in order to ensure compliance with regulations on preventing money laundering and financing of terrorism;
- Obtain approval from senior daily management to establish correspondent relationships;
- Ensure that the respondent bank has checked the identity of the customers and is regularly assessing relevant information about the customers having direct access to the account of the correspondent bank with a person or undertaking covered by this Act, and ensure that the respondent bank is able to supply relevant customer information at the request of the account holder; and
- Document the stipulation of the division of responsibilities between the institution and the correspondent bank.

Shell Banking

Banks, mortgage-credit institutions, payment institutions and e-money institutions may not enter into or continue a correspondent banking relationship with a shell bank, and they shall take reasonable measures to avoid a connection with a credit institution which is known to permit shell banks to use its accounts.

High-risk Countries

The Danish FSA may, when acting on the recommendations of the FATF, common positions or Regulations adopted by the European Union, lay down more specific regulations on the duty applying to undertakings and persons specified in Section 1 requiring them to systematically submit information to the Public Prosecutor for Serious Economic Crime concerning financial transactions with non-cooperative countries in connection with combating money laundering or the financing of terrorism. The Danish FSA may stipulate that notification is to be carried out systematically in all cases even though no suspicion has arisen.

High-risk Entities

Undertakings and persons covered by the Act shall, on the basis of a risk assessment, make further requirements of proof of identity for customers which, by their nature, can represent a higher risk of money laundering and financing of terrorism. This means that, at a minimum, they should meet the requirements for non-face-to-face customers and PEPs, as stated above.

27.11.12 Ongoing Monitoring

There is a requirement for customer relationships to be monitored on a regular basis. Specifically, transactions undertaken throughout the course of the relationship should be monitored to ensure that the transactions being conducted are consistent with the undertaking's or person's knowledge of the customer and the customer's business and risk profile, including, where necessary, the source of funds.

Documents, data and other information about the customer should be kept up to date. The enhanced due diligence requirements also highlight the obligation to continuously monitor business relationships.

27.11.13 Staff Training

Undertakings and persons under the Act must prepare adequate written internal rules about customer due diligence, reporting, record-keeping, internal control, risk assessment, risk management, management controls and communication as well as training and instruction programmes for their employees in order to forestall and prevent money laundering and the financing of terrorism. Adequate written internal rules shall also be prepared on compliance with the Regulation of the European Parliament and of the Council on information on the payer accompanying transfers of funds, where this is relevant, and regulations containing rules on financial sanctions against countries, persons, groups, legal entities or bodies. This obligation rests with the employer, unless a person at management level has been appointed to ensure compliance with the Act.

Undertakings must appoint a person at management level to ensure that the undertaking complies with its obligations under the Act. Furthermore, employees should be informed that their duties and obligations are stipulated under the Act.

27.11.14 Record-keeping

Undertakings and all persons subject to the Act must store identity information for no more than five years after the customer relationship has ceased. Documents and records concerning transactions must also be stored so that they can be located for at least five years after performance of the transactions.

If an undertaking ceases activities, the last acting management shall ensure that identity information continues to be stored. In the case of bankruptcy, the court may decide the persons who may store identity information.

27.11.15 Suspicious Transaction Reporting

Undertakings and persons under the Act are required to pay special attention to customers' activities which, by their nature, can be associated with money laundering or the financing of terrorism. Special attention must be given to transactions which are particularly large and/or complex, unusual patterns of transactions for the customer and transactions which have connection to countries or territories where, pursuant to declarations from the Financial Action Task Force, there is deemed to be a special risk of money laundering or financing of terrorism. Any suspicion that a customer's transaction is associated with money laundering must be investigated, recorded and kept. Such suspicions must also be notified to members of the Danish Bar and Law Society, who will assess whether the suspicion is subject to reporting obligations and will immediately forward notification to the State Prosecutor for Serious Economic Crime.

If the suspicion relates to offences punishable by imprisonment for more than one year and the suspicion cannot be disproved, the State Prosecutor for Serious Economic Crime should be informed immediately.

If the suspicion is related to money laundering and the transaction has not already been carried out, the transaction shall be suspended until notification has been given to the State Prosecutor. If effectuation of the transaction cannot be avoided, or if it may harm the investigation, notification can be given immediately after effectuation.

If the suspicion is related to the financing of terrorism, transactions from the account or transactions from the person in question may only be carried out with the consent of the State Prosecutor for Serious Economic Crime. The Prosecutor shall decide, as soon as possible and no later than the end of the banking day following receipt of the notification, whether seizure is to be effected.

The police have authority under the Administration of Justice Act to demand any information necessary for investigation of the case from undertakings and other persons under this Act.

If the Danish FSA or Danish Commerce and Companies Agency learns of circumstances that are presumed to be associated with money laundering or the financing of terrorism, these authorities are under an obligation to notify the State Prosecutor of Serious Economic Crime.

The Danish FSA, when acting on the recommendations of the Financial Action Task Force, has set out specific regulations on the duties which apply to undertakings, requiring them to systematically submit information to the State Prosecutor concerning financial transactions with non-cooperative countries in connection with combating money laundering.

27.11.16 Penalties

Intentional or grossly negligent breaches of the above requirements will mean that undertakings and persons under the Act shall be subject to a fine. Intentional or grossly negligent violation of Section 35(2), which prohibits unlawfully divulging information to others, shall subject the undertakings or persons to a fine, unless more severe punishment is incurred under the regulations of the Criminal Code.

For particularly gross or extensive intentional violations regarding the ban against receiving cash payments of DKK 100,000 or more, breaches of reporting and investigating obligations and due diligence requirements which relate to proof of identity for regular customer relationships, occasional customers and transactions for a third party and record-keeping obligations, the penalty may be increased to imprisonment for up to six months.

In cases involving the failure to supply the Danish Commerce and Companies Agency and/or the Danish FSA with all information necessary for supervision and compliance with the Act, these bodies will be entitled, as a coercive measure, to impose daily or weekly fines on the person or undertaking responsible.

An intentional or grossly negligent violation of the record-keeping requirements will mean that undertakings shall be subject to a fine, unless more severe punishment is incurred under the regulations of the Danish Criminal Code.

Companies may incur criminal liability according to regulations in Chapter 5 of the Criminal Code.

27.11.17 Case Studies

Suspicious transaction reports have been used to good effect on a number of occasions in Denmark. In one case, an account was actually being used by the customer's husband to conduct various fraudulent activities: hiring out fictitious holiday homes and selling shares under various names, for example.

The alarm was raised when another customer, who had only ever made one previous transaction to the account, made 120 transfers in one week. Ongoing monitoring of the account's activity was key to securing a conviction here, as well as avoiding financial and reputational damage to the financial institution.

Reports have also been used to highlight overseas scams. In various cases, victims had transferred around DKK 200,000 to people they had never met, some of them believing they were starting a relationship with the recipient. Dating websites and other social media had been used to make contact, and often the victims did not realise they were the victims of fraud. Financial institutions should be aware that these situations do occur, and enhance the due diligence and monitoring procedures when large amounts of money are being transferred to foreign jurisdictions for no apparent reason.

Phishing is another criminal practice which has been reported in Denmark. Phishing is when a criminal accesses a customer's bank account without their knowledge or permission, and transfers money from there to another "interim account". The owner of the interim account, or "mule", is told that they will be paid to transfer the money to the recipient, but is actually facilitating the money-laundering process. In one case, the mule was recruited via an email about an extra job; he responded by registering his details on a website belonging to a company which, judging by its name, was engaged in fast money transfers. He was called and told that money from German car contracts had been deposited in his account. He then received an email with instructions, but when he wanted to withdraw the money from his account in order to follow them, the bank had frozen the money. He was later found guilty of attempted money laundering.

27.12 COUNTRY PROFILE: FINLAND

27.12.1 Overview

The existence of money-laundering activity in Finland is limited; however, it is still monitored, with Finland having effective legislation in place in accordance with its international obligations. In 2007, the FATF noted that there have been few convictions for money laundering, that the number of prosecutions for offences is low and that the number of sentences provided for money-laundering convictions in Finland is also low.

27.12.2 Key Legislation

The Act on Preventing and Clearing Money Laundering and Terrorist Financing 2008 provides the AML legislative framework.

27.12.3 Legislative History

The main anti-money-laundering legislation in Finland is the Act on Preventing and Clearing Money Laundering and Terrorist Financing (503/2008), (AMLA). The Act came into force on 1st August, 2008 and incorporates the Third EC Directive into national law. According to the Finnish Financial Supervisory Authority, the Act is supplemented by Government Decree 616/2008, supplemented by Government Decree 1204/2011, Decision by the Ministry of the Interior 156/2010 and Government Decision 1022/2010. However, only Government Decree 616/2008 is listed on the official website of government decrees. Standard 2.4 of the 2010 FIN-FSA Code of Conduct provides guidance on the customer due diligence (CDD) and reporting requirements.

27.12.4 FATF Assessment

The 2007 mutual assessment noted that Finland has a good legal structure to combat money laundering and terrorist financing, and that the related offences are quite broad. The due diligence requirements were, however, lacking, for example with regard to PEPs and beneficial owners, but in June 2013, the FATF removed Finland from the regular follow-up process to which it had previously been subject.

27.12.5 The Primary AML Investigation/Regulatory Authorities

Money Laundering Clearing House

The financial intelligence unit, in connection with the National Bureau of Investigation, deals with reports submitted to it on suspicious transactions. Finland's FIU, known as the Money Laundering Clearing House, is a part of the National Bureau of Investigation and has a number of key duties under AMLA, such as:

- Preventing and clearing money laundering and terrorist financing;
- Promoting cooperation between authorities in the fight against money laundering and terrorist financing;
- Cooperation and exchange of information with the authorities of a foreign state and international organisations that are responsible for preventing and clearing money laundering and terrorist financing;

- Cooperation with parties subject to the reporting obligation;
- Giving feedback on the effects of reports;
- Keeping statistics on the number of reports received and the number of transactions suspended.

The Money Laundering Clearing House is also responsible for reporting to the Ministry of the Interior.

Financial Supervisory Authority
The Financial Supervisory Authority is responsible for ensuring that the procedures, risk management and internal control of supervised entities meet statutory requirements. It is the Financial Supervisory Authority's duty to ensure that the operating procedures, risk management and internal control of supervised entities are in compliance with existing legislation.

Ministry of the Interior
The Ministry of the Interior is responsible for internal security and migration. It is also responsible for the development of anti-money-laundering legislation.

27.12.6 Outline of Specific Money-laundering Offences

The definition of money laundering under the Act refers to Chapter 32, Sections 6–10 of the Penal Code (39/1889). Money laundering is defined in Section 6 of the Penal Code as the action of a person who:

- Receives
- Converts
- Conveys
- Transfers or
- Transmits property acquired through:
  - an offence;
  - the proceeds of crime; or
  - property replacing such property in order to:
    - conceal,
    - obliterate the illegal origin of such proceeds of property in order to assist the offender in evading the legal consequences of the offence, or
    - conceal or obliterate the true nature, origin, location or disposition of, or rights to, property acquired through an offence, the proceeds of an offence or property replacing such property, or assist another in such concealment or obliteration.

27.12.7 Penalties

The penalty for being found guilty of money laundering could be in the form of a fine or imprisonment for up to two years. The Code also states that even an attempt to undertake money laundering is punishable. The scope of the Act is addressed in the next section.

In cases of aggravated money laundering, where the property acquired has been very valuable or the offence is committed in a deliberate manner, the offender may face imprisonment for at least four, and up to six, years (Section 7 of the Penal Code).

Section 8 of the Penal Code states that a person who agrees with another on the commission of aggravated money laundering directed at the proceeds of bribery, the acceptance of a bribe or aggravated tax fraud or aggregated subsidy fraud or a property replacing such fraud shall be sentenced for conspiracy for the commission of aggravated money laundering to a fine or imprisonment for up to a year.

If the money laundering referred to in any of the above offences is considered to be petty when assessing the consideration of the value of money as a whole, the offender shall be sentenced solely to a fine for a money-laundering violation.

27.12.8 Scope

The AMLA applies to 24 different varieties of financial institution, including:

- Credit institutions;
- Branches of foreign credit and financial institutions;
- Investment firms;
- Branches of foreign investment firms;
- Limited liability companies or cooperatives engaged in restricted credit institution activities;
- Insurance companies and pension insurance companies;
- Gaming operators;
- Real estate businesses and apartment rental agencies;
- Auditors;
- Businesses or professions providing tax advice in particular;
- Businesses or professions providing money transmission or remittance services other than general payment transmission services;
- Businesses or professions performing external accounting functions;
- Businesses or professions dealing in goods, to the extent that payments are made in cash in an amount of EUR 15,000 or more, whether the transaction is executed in a single operation or in several operations which are linked.

27.12.9 Risk-based Approach

Finland has adopted a risk-based approach. Entities are under an obligation to assess the risks of money laundering and funding of terrorism, by taking into account the risks specifically related to their business, products, services, technological development and their clients' businesses and business activities.

Additionally, AMLA requires that supervised entities assess the adequacy of their CDD procedures on the basis of a documented risk analysis. Supervised entities should have adequate risk-management systems for assessing risk exposures to customers in their activities. Due diligence procedures and risk management for prevention of fraud, such as money laundering, need not be organised in a unit separated from the rest of the risk-management or business operations. Therefore, in Finland the unit may be integrated with the supervised entity's general risk-management and internal control functions. However, even though this is allowed, we would still expect firms to consider having the unit segregated from such functions and perhaps aligning it more closely to the legal, compliance and fraud investigation units.

27.12.10 Role of the MLRO/Nominated Officer

The 2010 Code of Practice introduced the concept of an MLRO, by providing that:

> *"The organisational structure of the supervised entity shall include the appointment of a contact person responsible for the prevention of money laundering and terrorist financing. The position and duties of the supervised entity's contact person may vary according to the organisational structure of the entity. The contact person must be in an independent, preferably non-business, position with the powers and capacity to act in such practical matters related to the prevention of money laundering and terrorist financing as require immediate action, such as reporting suspicious transactions or responding to enquiries from authorities."*

27.12.11 Due Diligence

On the basis of a risk-based assessment, entities should identify whether to apply normal, reduced or enhanced CDD. In customer relationships where supervised entities, on good grounds, have come to the conclusion that the business conducted has only minor or no money-laundering and/or terrorist-financing risks, normal due diligence is sufficient. In certain situations, the AMLA allows simplified customer due diligence.

Parties subject to the reporting obligation are required to obtain information on their customers' transactions, the nature and extent of the customers' business and the grounds for the use of a service or product. Parties subject to the reporting obligation should pay particular attention to transactions which are unusual in respect of their structure or extent or the size or office of the parties subject to the reporting obligation. The same also applies if transactions have no apparent economic purpose or if they are inconsistent with the parties' experience or knowledge of the customers. If necessary, measures should be taken to establish the source of funds involved in a transaction.

Parties subject to the reporting obligation are required to identify a customer's identity when they:

- Establish a customer relationship with a new customer (regular customer relationship);
- Suspect that a previously identified regular customer's identification and verification data are not sufficient or reliable;
- Without establishing a customer relationship, carry out a single transaction that individually or as the sum of interrelated transactions amounts to at least EUR 15,000;
- Detect a suspicious transaction or suspect that funds included in the transaction are being used for terrorist financing; or
- Perform a transfer of funds exceeding EUR 1,000 in cash.

Personal Client Due Diligence

The identity of a natural person should be verified with a document obtained from a reliable and independent source based on a valid official identification document. Under AMLA, the following are required to be recorded to complete the CDD process:

- The name, date of birth and personal identity code;
- The name of the document used to verify identity, the number of the document or other identification data and the body that issued the document or a copy of the document;
- Information regarding the customer, such as information on the customer's transactions, the nature and extent of the customer's business, his or her financial status, the grounds for the use of transactions or services and the source of funds;
- If the customer is a foreigner without a Finnish identity code, records shall be kept of the customer's citizenship and travel documents.

The Code notes that valid versions of the following documents issued by Finnish authorities are commonly used for identity verification in Finland:

- Driving licence
- Identification card
- Passport
- Diplomatic passport
- Alien's passport and refugee travel documents
- SII card containing photo.

Supervised entities may also verify a natural person's identity using valid documents granted by foreign authorities, such as:

- National passport
- Identification card acceptable as a travel document.

Corporate Customer Due Diligence

To complete CDD for a legal person (i.e. a company), the following should be ascertained:

- The legal person's full name, registration number, date of registration and registration authority;
- The full name, date of birth and citizenship of the members of the board of directors or a corresponding decision-making body of the legal person;
- The type of business the legal person carries out;
- The representative's name, date of birth and personal identity code;
- The beneficial owner's name, date of birth and personal identity code.

If the customer is a company or corporation whose securities are admitted to public trading, then simplified customer due diligence procedures may be undertaken, since the firm is considered to be required to provide public information as a consequence of its listed status.

Beneficial Ownership

A person representing a legal person should be identified and, if necessary, the identity should be verified (according to a risk-based approach). If necessary, the scope of authority of a legal person's representative should be confirmed via a separate power of attorney or an extract from the minutes of a decision-making body of the legal person. Information on the identity of the beneficial owners can be obtained from a limited company's list of shareholders, minutes, contracts or other documents on the company's ownership and control structures.

The supervised entity can perform an identity verification of the beneficial owners based on risk-based consideration. In addition to identification and contact information, the following information should be obtained from the customer (depending on the customer relationship):

- Information on the customer's transactions, nature and extent of the customer's business and grounds for the use of a service or product;
- Information on the customer's representatives, beneficial owners, ownership structure, financial status and on the source of funds.

Third Party Customer Due Diligence

A representative acting on behalf of a legal or natural person should be identified and the identity verified, if necessary – Section 7(3) AMLA.

Simplified Customer Due Diligence

Simplified customer due diligence procedures may be applied (according to the following exhaustive list), if the customer is:

- A Finnish authority or a comparable party, such as a municipality, the Social Insurance Institution or the Bank of Finland;
- A credit institution, insurance company, financial institution, investment firm, fund management company or payment institution that is duly authorised in an EEA State;
- A credit institution, insurance company, financial institution, investment firm or fund management company duly authorised in a non-EEA State and subject to obligations equivalent to those laid down in the Finnish Anti-Money Laundering Act and supervised for compliance with these obligations;
- A branch located in an EEA State of a credit institution, insurance company, financial institution, investment firm or fund management company duly authorised in a non-EEA State;
- A company whose securities are admitted to public trading according to the Securities Markets Act and which is subject to disclosure requirements similar to those in the Markets in Financial Instruments Directive.

Enhanced Customer Due Diligence

Supervised entities should employ enhanced due diligence to such customer relationships, transactions and services where they assess increased risk of abuse to be involved, such as money-laundering or terrorist-financing risks. The AMLA contains examples of customer relationships requiring enhanced customer due diligence:

- If a customer relationship is established without the customer being physically present, customer identification and identity verification should be performed with enhanced care;
- Customer relationships with politically exposed persons or with a family member or a close associate of such a person;
- On the basis of its own risk assessment, the supervised entity considers that a certain customer relationship, product, distribution channel or transaction requires the application of enhanced procedures.

Non-face-to-face Customer Due Diligence

If the customer is not physically present for the CDD process, the party subject to the reporting obligation shall take the following measures to mitigate the risk of money laundering and terrorist financing:

- Verify the customer's identity on the basis of additional documents or information obtained from a reliable source;

- Ensure that the payment of the transaction is made from the credit institution's account or to an account that was opened earlier in the customer's name;
- Verify the customer's identity by means of a qualified certificate, as referred to in the Identification Act, or some other electronic identification that ensures information security and is verifiable; and
- Record information on the procedure or sources that were used to verify the customer's identity in accordance with the standard individual CDD requirements.

Politically Exposed Persons

In Finland, enhanced due diligence requirements apply when dealing with PEPs (examples of PEPs are listed in Government Decree 616/2008). Parties subject to the reporting obligation must have the appropriate risk-based procedures to determine whether the customer is holding, or has held, an important public position in another state.

Supervised entities shall create procedures and internal instructions for establishing and maintaining customer relationships with politically exposed persons, their family members and close associates. To comply with this requirement:

- The senior management of the parties subject to reporting obligations should give their approval before establishing a customer relationship with such a person;
- Parties subject to the reporting obligations are also required to establish the source of wealth and funds that are involved in the customer relationship or transaction where a PEP is involved; and
- Parties subject to the reporting obligations should conduct enhanced ongoing monitoring of the customer relationship.

The legislation states that a person is no longer considered a politically exposed person when he or she has not held an important public position for at least one year. However, the operation of the risk-based approach might still result in additional, ongoing monitoring of the relationship.

Anonymous Accounts

Supervised entities should not have unidentified (anonymous) customers, and have the right to refuse customers that do not give information on themselves or their operations or whose size, place of business or nature of operations is in conflict with the business strategy of the entity.

Correspondent Banking

Enhanced CDD should be applied if a correspondent banking or equivalent business relationship is concerned. Commencement of a correspondent banking or equivalent business relationship requires the obtaining of sufficient information on the counterparty and approval from senior management. The relationship also needs to be monitored and reviewed regularly.

27.12.12 Ongoing Monitoring

Customer relationships must be continuously reviewed so as to monitor adequately the nature, extent and risks of the customers' transactions in order to ensure that the transactions conducted are consistent with parties' experience or knowledge of their customers and business. Such monitoring must be ongoing to ensure that parties subject to the reporting obligation detect any exceptional or unusual patterns or transactions.

The risk assessments must be updated regularly, taking into account any changes occurring in the services provided by the supervised entity and/or the activities of the customer (for example, introduction of new products, system changes and changes in customer ownership structure and business activities). The supervised entities shall be able to demonstrate to FIN-FSA that their customer due diligence and risk-management procedures are sufficient in relation to the existing risks and that the money-laundering and terrorist-financing risks related to the entity's nature of operations, customer relationships, products, services and to technical developments have been assessed.

Supervised entities should arrange adequate monitoring in light of the nature, extent and risks of customer operations. The ongoing monitoring shall be systematic and comprehensive, considering the scope of operations and the risks in customer relationships. The supervised entity shall have internal instructions for using ongoing monitoring procedures as well as adequate resources and internal control.

27.12.13 Staff Training

Supervised entities shall see to it that their employees are given proper training in order to ensure compliance with the provisions on preventing money laundering and terrorist financing. Regular, comprehensive training of employees should be arranged at all levels of the organisation, particularly for such groups of employees as are involved in customer relations, product development, clearing, safe-keeping and payment and/or settlement systems. All training should be recorded in a separate training register.

The obligation of protecting employees as referred to in the AMLA means that the employer should have adequate and appropriate procedures for protecting employees who report suspicious transactions to the financial intelligence unit. The obligation of protecting employees can be fulfilled through, among other things, instructions and internal training of employees, and ensuring that the identities of employees who undertake such reporting are not disclosed to customers.

Supervised entities shall also have internal instructions on customer due diligence procedures to be conducted and procedures adopted to ensure compliance with the obligation of obtaining information and reporting suspicious transactions to prevent money laundering and terrorist financing. The instructions shall be adapted to their own operations and services. The instructions should take into account, among other things, internal processes, distribution channels and products as well as outsourced activities and agent relationships. The instructions should also consider product and system developments and expansion of operations into new markets.

27.12.14 Record-keeping

Identification, identity verification and customer due diligence information should be documented and retained so that the supervised entity can later show the authorities how each customer was identified, which documents or what information was used as proof of identity and who carried out the customer identification. In addition, for customer due diligence and risk management of the customer relationship, the supervised entity should retain sufficient and essential information on the customer, its representatives, ownership structure and beneficial owners as well as members of a legal person's board of directors or corresponding decision-making body. The retention duty also applies to information on the nature of customer activities, the legal person's ordinary industry sector, the scope of operations and the services provided by the supervised entity and the use thereof.

Records must be kept of all customer due diligence data in a secure manner for a period of up to five years following the end of regular customer relationships. The data must be kept separate from the customer register, and must be removed five years after making a report, unless it is necessary to keep records of the data for a longer period (such as for the purpose of criminal investigation pending judicial proceedings). The need to keep records of data shall be reviewed no later than three years after the previous occasion on which it was reviewed.

When an occasional transaction amounts to over EUR 15,000 or to EUR 3,000 or more in cases of gaming activities, records must be kept of customer due diligence data for a period of five years following the carrying out of a transaction.

27.12.15 Suspicious Transaction Reporting

Compliance with the obligation to obtain information as referred to in the AMLA requires that supervised entities have adequate knowledge of their customers' activities so that they can detect unusual orders or transactions and report them. Parties that are subject to reporting obligations shall obtain information on their customers' transactions, the nature and extent of the customers' business and grounds for the use of a service or product. Monitoring should be arranged in view of the nature, extent and risks of the customer's transactions in order to ensure that the transaction being conducted is consistent with parties' experience and knowledge of the customers and their business.

Having detected an unusual transaction, a supervised entity is obliged, within reasonable means available, to examine the background of the transaction as well as the origin and purpose of funds included. Information may be obtained from, for example, official registers or the supervised entities' own registers or by requesting more detailed information on the transaction from the customer, such as contracts or other documents supporting the transaction. Supervised entities are also entitled to check customers' credit information.

Having fulfilled obligations to obtain information, parties subject to the reporting obligation shall immediately report a suspicious transaction or suspicion of terrorist financing to the financial intelligence unit. The report should generally be made electronically.

It is only if there is a special reason preventing electronic delivery that the report may also be submitted in some other manner. Parties subject to the reporting obligation shall give the financial intelligence unit, free of charge, all the necessary information and documents that could be significant in clearing the suspicion.

Supervised entities should act without delay so that funds or other assets related to a suspicious transaction are not transferred beyond authority access. If their suspicions are aroused, supervised entities may, at their own discretion, take the following courses of action:

- Suspend a transaction for enquiries;
- Reject a transaction if, for example, the customer's identity cannot be reliably established;
- Execute a transaction if the supervised entity cannot leave the transaction unexecuted or suspension or rejection of the transaction would be likely to hinder discovery of the beneficiary of the transaction.

Supervised entities should inform the financial intelligence unit if:

- A transaction is suspicious even after enquiries have been made to fulfil the obligation to obtain information;
- A customer is unwilling to provide the requested information;
- The supervised entity considers the provided information unreliable;
- The supervised entity rejects the execution of a suspicious transaction;
- The supervised entity executes a suspicious transaction;
- The supervised entity, after execution of the transaction, obtains information that renders the transaction suspicious.

There are additional obligations where the suspicious transaction originates from a high-risk country.

When a suspicious transaction is reported to the financial intelligence unit, the report is not a report of an offence (investigation request). It is a report based on a supervised entity's detection of an unusual transaction or order in the financial market. No minimum amount (in money) has been specified for such a report. The supervised entity need not know or evaluate what kind of criminal offence may have been committed.

A commanding police officer working at the financial intelligence unit may give parties subject to the reporting obligation an order that they should refrain from conducting transactions with a customer for no more than five working days, if such a suspension is considered necessary to prevent what is clearly money laundering or terrorist financing from being conducted.

The financial intelligence unit may also give such an order at the request of a foreign authority responsible for preventing money laundering and terrorist financing.

27.12.16 Reporting Thresholds

The reporting and due diligence threshold is when the sum of a transaction amounts to EUR 15,000, whether the transaction is carried out in a single operation or several operations which are linked to each other. The threshold is EUR 3,000 for amounts which relate to the proceeds from gaming activities.

27.12.17 Penalties

Penalties can be imposed on those subject to reporting obligations for breaching provisions of the Act. Parties subject to reporting obligations are liable for the financial loss sustained by their customers as a result of clearing a transaction, reporting a suspicious transaction or suspending or refusing to conduct a transaction, only if the parties have failed to carry out such customer due diligence measures as can reasonably be required of them, considering the circumstances.

Parties who deliberately or through negligence fail to fulfil the obligation to conduct customer due diligence or the obligations to keep records of due diligence data shall be sentenced for violation of customer due diligence to a fine, unless a more severe punishment for the act is provided elsewhere in the law.

Anyone who deliberately or through negligence fails to make a report, discloses reporting to those subject to suspicion or fails to obtain relevant information under provisions under the Act shall be sentenced for violation of the obligation to report money laundering to a fine.

27.12.18 Case Studies

While we started this chapter stating that Finland was not a major centre for money laundering, cases can still occur. One of the largest criminal cases in Finnish legal history actually involved money laundering and various other financial crimes. After investigating over 200 suspects, nearly 100 people were prosecuted and ordered to repay over EUR 5.5 million in unpaid taxes. The crime stemmed from the construction industry, where a large criminal gang had maintained an extensive business with forged receipts, and by employing undocumented workers. The business was used as a cover for criminal proceeds, and the case led to 44 custodial prison sentences.

27.13 COUNTRY PROFILE: FRANCE

27.13.1 Overview

The 2012 US Department of State report on France notes that the country remains an attractive venue for money laundering because of "its sizable economy, political stability and sophisticated financial system". As a consequence, the country has put in place comprehensive and effective systems of financial controls and is at the forefront of reform domestically and internationally to fight money laundering and terrorist financing.

27.13.2 Key Legislation

The money-laundering offence is contained within the French Penal Code. Furthermore, the Monetary and Financial Code (CMF, "The Code") details obligations on regulated entities with regard to AML procedures, and the ACP guidelines provide further guidance.

27.13.3 Legislative History

France is a European Union (EU) country, and therefore is obliged to implement all three EU money-laundering directives. The First EU Money Laundering Directive (91/308/EEC) was transposed into French law in 2004 and the Second Directive (2001/97/EC) in 2006, with Decree No. 2006-736. According to the International Bar Association Anti-Money Laundering Forum, the Third EU Money Laundering Directive was transposed into French law via Ordinance No. 2009-104 issued on 30th January, 2009. Decree No. 2009-874 was enacted on 16th July, 2009 and Decree No. 2009-1087 on 2nd September, 2009 "in order to make the Third EU Directive effective".

27.13.4 FATF Assessment

The third mutual evaluation of France, conducted in 2010, noted a variety of changes which strengthened the AML regime. However, although the suspicious transaction reporting (STR) and customer due diligence (CDD) requirements for financial institutions were largely compliant with FATF regulations, it also stated that a "considerable effort" was required with regards to non-financial institutions to achieve the same level of coverage.

27.13.5 The Primary AML Investigation/Regulatory Authorities

Traitement du Renseignement et Action Contre les Circuits Financiers Clandestins (TRACFIN)

The central authority for reporting is called TRACFIN, and is placed under the sponsorship of two ministers: the Minister of Economy and the Minister of Budget. The authority processes financial information regarding suspicious transaction reports, and has considerable autonomy and operational independence to carry out its functions. TRACFIN has signed bilateral cooperation treaties with 51 countries, most recently Saudi Arabia, Fiji, Serbia, Algeria and the Ivory Coast.

Prudential Control Authority (ACP)

The ACP is responsible for licensing and supervision of banks and insurance agencies. Its main mission is to ensure the preservation of financial stability and protection of bank customers, policyholders and beneficiaries of insurance contracts. The status of the ACP is codified in Articles L.612-1 et seq of the Monetary and Financial Code.

In September 2011, the Prudential Control Authority (ACP) took several measures to improve its ability to fight money laundering and terrorist financing. The ACP has provided guidelines to help financial institutions define and research "the effective beneficiary" of money laundering or the financing of terrorism. The ACP also has defined new reporting obligations for money exchangers. The latest ACP guidelines were released in 2012, and concern the occasional customer and due diligence requirements.

27.13.6 *Outline of Specific Money-laundering Offences*

By virtue of 324-1 of the French Penal Code, money laundering is defined as (translated from French):

> *"The facilitation, by any means, of the false justification of the origin of property or income of the perpetrator of a crime or an offence which has brought it a direct or indirect benefit."*

Money laundering also covers the provision of assistance to an investment transaction, concealment or conversion from direct or indirect proceeds of crime or misdemeanour.

27.13.7 *Penalties*

Money laundering is punishable by five years' imprisonment and a fine of EUR 375,000. Aggravated money laundering, which involves organisations, repeat offenders or those in breach of professional obligations, is punishable by ten years' imprisonment and a fine of EUR 750,000.

Both of the fines mentioned above can be increased to half the value of the property or funds involved in money-laundering operations. Attempts carry the same penalty as completed offences.

27.13.8 *Risk-based Approach*

Entities should collect information related to the knowledge of the business relationship on the basis of a risk-based approach. The information gathered should be proportionate to the risk of money laundering and financing of terrorism presented by the customer. Relevant firms should establish a classification of the risks of their activities, depending on the degree of exposure to money laundering and terrorist financing judged by the particular nature of the products or services offered, the proposed transactions, distribution channels used and the characteristics of clients.

Compliance with these provisions should allow firms to make, if necessary, a further examination of the client's circumstances or a declaration to the authorities.

The implementation of the obligations of identification and verification of customer identity, Know Your Customer, the purpose and nature of the business relationship and constant vigilance is based on the distinction between a customer relationship and a casual business customer.

Financial institutions collect and analyse information related to their knowledge of customer business relationships. The information collected should be appropriate and proportionate to the risk of money laundering and terrorist financing presented by the customer and operations.

Financial institutions establish procedures for the implementation of the CDD measures on customers. These procedures must be adapted and updated regularly to detect cases in which an occasional customer becomes a business customer. Financial institutions must create a risk profile and take into account any evidence to change the risk profile of the business relationship and accordingly update this profile, in order to detect anomalies that could give rise to a strengthened review.

27.13.9 Role of the MLRO/Nominated Officer

The 2012 ACP guidelines state that "The financial service provider must ensure, within the framework of its internal control, compliance with the AML-CFT, including measures regarding the analysis, monitoring and control of the risks of money laundering and financing terrorism operations transmitting funds". While it is not stated expressly, an MLRO could perform this role.

27.13.10 Due Diligence

The due diligence requirements differ depending on whether a customer is engaged in a business relationship. A business relationship is formed when a regulated person undertakes a professional or commercial relationship which is intended to last a certain duration, or when, in the absence of a contract, a customer receives financial services on a regular basis.

Conversely, an occasional customer is any person who addresses a regulated entity for the exclusive purpose of preparing or carrying out a specific operation or assists in the planning or execution of such an operation, whether it is performed in a single operation or several operations which appear to be linked.

In all cases, the duration is a key element of the business relationship. The concept of time is also found in the absence of a contract, with terms related to the intervention of a financial institution, such as "regularly" or "an operation with a continuing character", mentioned in the CMF.

Where an entity is not able to identify its client or to obtain information on the purpose and nature of the business relationship, it should not perform any operation, regardless of the terms, and it should not engage in, or continue, a business relationship.

Before entering into a business relationship with a client or assisting in the planning or execution of a transaction, regulated entities must identify their clients and, where applicable, the beneficial owner of the business relationship by appropriate means and verify this identification upon presentation of any other documentary proof.

They should also apply the same conditions to their occasional customers and, where applicable, the beneficial owner of a customer where they suspect that the transaction might involve money laundering or terrorist financing or, under conditions set by Order in Council of State, if the operations are of a certain nature or exceed a certain amount.

Regulated entities must verify the identity of the customer and, where appropriate, the identity and powers of persons acting on behalf thereof, under the following conditions.

Personal Client Due Diligence

When the client is an individual, the entity should examine a valid official document with a photograph. This should indicate:

- The full name;
- Date and place of birth of the person;
- The nature, date and place of issuance;
- The name and title of the authority or the person who issued the document; and
- Where appropriate, how it was authenticated.

Corporate Customer Due Diligence

When the client is a corporation, the reporting entity should examine the original or a copy of any deed or extract from an official register (which is no more than three months old) stating:

- The name
- The legal form
- The address of head office
- The identity of partners and directors.

CDD should also be carried out on any individual representing the company.

Beneficial Ownership and Occasional Customers

Before carrying out or assisting with a transaction, regulated entities are required, regardless of suspicion, to identify an occasional customer and, where applicable, the beneficial owner of the company involved. They should carry out CDD in the following cases:

- Where the amount of the transaction or related transactions exceeds EUR 15,000, for persons other than money changers, legal representatives or gambling authorities;

- Where the amount of the operation or operations exceeds EUR 8,000, for money changers;
- Notwithstanding the above and regardless of the amount of the transaction, when they effect a transfer of funds or provide services custody facilities;
- Notwithstanding the above and regardless of the amount of the transaction, for any transactions involving high-risk countries.

Simplified Customer Due Diligence

When the risk of money laundering and terrorist financing seems low, reporting entities may reduce CDD. In this case, they should justify to the supervisory authority the manner in which the extent of the measures is appropriate to those risks.

Enhanced Customer Due Diligence

Reporting entities should apply additional due diligence measures in respect of their client if:

- The client or his legal representative is not physically present for identification purposes;
- The client is a PEP;
- The product or transaction is one for which it is easy to retain anonymity;
- The transaction is a transaction for the client's own account or for third parties made with natural or legal persons, including their subsidiaries or establishments, domiciled, registered or established in a designated high-risk country;
- There are any other reasons to suggest a risk of money laundering or terrorist financing.

Reporting entities should carry out an enhanced review of any operation which is particularly complex, unusually large or which does not appear to have any economic justification or lawful purpose. In such cases, entities should ascertain from the customer information on the source and destination of the funds, the subject of the transaction and the identity of the beneficiary.

Anonymous Accounts

The opening of anonymous accounts is prohibited.

27.13.11 Ongoing Monitoring

The financial institution needs to ensure, as part of its internal control, that it complies with the CDD requirements, that it has knowledge of purpose, nature and circumstances of its business relationships and that it is constantly vigilant regarding potential money laundering by implementing procedures and adequate internal controls. Financial institutions must be able to justify the measures taken to the CPA.

The PSP shall have in place systems for monitoring and analysing their business relationships, based on knowledge of their customers, especially to detect transactions that are anomalous with respect to the profile of the business relationship and which may warrant further examination. This monitoring and analysis must consider the risks identified by the risk classification.

In practice, the PSP should set predetermined limits at which it seeks additional information on individual or multiple operations regarding the same business relationship, when they involve cross-border transactions. There should also be an upper limit at which the PSP should refuse to facilitate a transaction.

The ACP may review the transactions falling into these categories.

27.13.12 Staff Training

Entities should provide regular training and information to their personnel in respect of the obligations within the AML framework.

27.13.13 Record-keeping

Reporting entities should retain all documents relating to CDD for five years, starting from the termination of the business relationship or closure of the account. Enhanced CDD documents should be kept for longer. They should also keep any documents relating to transactions made by customers for five years, starting from the date of the transaction.

27.13.14 Reporting Requirements

Firms are required to declare any deposits or transactions involving sums which they know, suspect or have reasonable grounds to suspect come from an offence punishable by imprisonment exceeding one year or form part of terrorist financing or involve tax evasion to TRACFIN.

They are also required to report any transaction for which the identity of the customer or the beneficial owner remains uncertain despite the CDD requirements being carried out. Entities are required to refrain from conducting any operation which they suspect to be related to money laundering or terrorist financing until they have made the requisite declaration.

When an operation which should be the subject of a declaration has already been carried out, either because it was impossible to delay it or because a delay would have hindered the subsequent investigation, or if it appears after the transaction has been completed that it should be reported, the PSP shall inform the authorities as soon as possible.

27.13.15 Penalties

The National Commission may impose one of the following administrative penalties:

- A warning;
- A reprimand;

- A temporary ban on performing activity for a period not exceeding five years;
- The cancellation of registration or of the business card.

A temporary ban may include a suspension. If, within five years of the imposition of a sanction, the sanctioned person commits an offence or perpetrates misconduct resulting in the imposition of new sanctions, these new sanctions shall be more severe than those imposed previously.

The committee may decide, either instead of or in addition to these penalties, to impose a financial penalty depending on the severity of the breaches committed. This penalty cannot exceed five million euros, and is collected by the Treasury. The committee may also recover costs from the person sanctioned.

The committee may decide to publish the sanction, at the expense of the person penalised, in any relevant newspapers or publications.

27.13.16 Case Studies

The "Franceafrique" cases are a source of ongoing speculation about large-scale money laundering and financial crime. There are various unanswered questions regarding France's relationship with its former African colonies, and the extent of the finances involved from comparatively poor jurisdictions raises questions about the legitimacy of the funds involved. For example, French judges recently revealed that:

- The family of Congolese President Denis Sassou-Nguesso has 112 French bank accounts, often worth hundreds of thousands of euros each, and which allegedly paid for 91 suits from a single tailor.
- The Bongo clan of Gabon owns real estate totalling some 21 million euros, most of it in the ritzy Golden Triangle section of Paris.
- The Obiang family from the tiny West African nation of Equatorial Guinea recently had 5 million euros' worth of cars seized.

There have been charges brought against former government aides, suggesting that this scandal could go high into the French government. At the time of writing investigations were ongoing, but the outcome will be received with interest.

The small regional French bank Société Marseillaise de Crédit was found guilty of money laundering, along with the National Bank of Pakistan, in December 2008. The crimes took place in the late nineties and involved stolen or fraudulent cheques shuttled between France and Israel and via various bank accounts. The French bank was fined EUR 100,000, and one of its directors received an eight-month suspended prison sentence.

The French regulator has identified a number of case studies to provide practical guidance for financial institutions. For example:

- Customers identified as "casual" have made over 20 fund transmissions within a year. The relationship between the bank and the customer should have been classified as a business relationship.
- Over a period of two years, a customer made 28 transfers worth a total of almost one million euros. In addition to this, some of these transfers were made on consecutive days. The regulator advised that the customer should have been considered a business customer.
- Where a financial institution issues a loyalty card which is used numerous times by the customer, procedures should be in place to ascertain whether or not a business relationship exists.

27.14 COUNTRY PROFILE: GERMANY

27.14.1 Overview

Germany has generated a relatively large number of prosecutions for money laundering and also orders to confiscate assets, although the recent FATF review identified that its money-laundering-deterrence regime did have shortfalls. However, having recently introduced a new financial crime deterrence regime, Germany looks likely to become a strong country with regards to AML.

27.14.2 Key Legislation

Geldwäschereigesetz, or the Money Laundering Act, is the main AML-compliance legislation. The money-laundering offence is contained in the Penal Code.

27.14.3 Legislative History

Germany successfully implemented the Third EU Money Laundering Directive on 13th August, 2008 through the Gesetz zur Ergänzung der Bekämpfung der Geldwäsche und der Terrorismusfinanzierung (Geldwäschebekämpfungsergänzungsgesetz – GwBekErgG). The Act came into force on 21st August, 2008. However, German AML law saw a major overhaul in financial crime regulation in December 2011, with the introduction of GwG (the AML Act).

A further revision will be required to fully comply with the revised EU Money Laundering Directive (see Chapter 4).

27.14.4 FATF Assessment

The 2009 FATF assessment noted that the anti-money-laundering and counter-terrorist-financing framework operating in Germany was not fully in line with the then current FATF Recommendations, which have themselves subsequently been revised.

The FATF identified weaknesses in the legal framework and in sanctioning for non-compliance with the FATF anti-money-laundering and counter-terrorist-financing recommendations. It further highlighted a number of factors specific to Germany, such as its large economy and financial centre and 400–560 billion euro informal (cash) sector, which make the country susceptible to money laundering. However, it also highlighted that Germany's strong legal tradition, the rule of law, its political environment and having an effective single financial regulator all reduce the risk of the German financial system being used for money laundering or terrorist financing.

27.14.5 The Primary AML Investigation/Regulatory Authorities

Federal Department of the Interior

In Germany, the fight against money laundering and adherence to the Money Laundering Act is the responsibility, primarily, of the Federal Department of the Interior.

Financial Intelligence Unit

The Federal Criminal Police Office incorporates the financial intelligence unit (FIU). The German FIU releases annual reports on money laundering, which include statistics and information. The FIU is also responsible for enforcing anti-money-laundering rules. The Bundesrechtsanwaltskammer is obliged to transmit the information including its own comments to the public prosecutor and also to a special anti-money-laundering office of the German Federal Police (Bundeskriminalamt).

The FIU has certain specific responsibilities identified under the AML Act:

- To collect and analyse reports transmitted, and to compare the reports with other relevant data;
- To inform the relevant law-enforcement agencies immediately of any relevant information regarding potential crime;
- To collect statistics regarding German AML;
- To publish an annual report analysing the reports referred to above; and
- To keep entities regularly informed about new methods of money laundering and terrorism financing.

Bundesanstalt für Finanzdienstleistungsaufsicht (BaFin) (Federal Financial Supervisory Authority)

The Federal Financial Supervisory Authority (BaFin) brings together under one roof the supervision of banks and financial services providers, insurance undertakings and securities trading. It is an autonomous public-law institution and is subject to the legal and technical oversight of the Federal Ministry of Finance. It is funded by fees and contributions from the institutions and undertakings under its supervision.

27.14.6 Outline of Specific Money-laundering Offences

According to Section 261 of the Penal Code, money laundering is committed by anybody who "hides an object which is a proceed of an unlawful act, conceals its origin or obstructs or endangers the investigation of its origin, its being found, its confiscation, its deprivation or its being officially secured". Any third party or assistant can also be punished, as can anyone who attempts this.

27.14.7 Penalties

The penalty for money laundering is imprisonment from three months to five years. In especially serious cases the punishment shall be imprisonment from six months to ten years. An especially serious case exists, as a rule, if the perpetrator acts professionally or as a member of a gang which has been formed for the continued commission of money laundering.

Anyone who recklessly does not recognise that the subject derives from an unlawful act shall be punished with imprisonment not exceeding two years or a fine.

27.14.8 Scope

The AML Act applies to a large number of institutions, including, but not exclusive to:

- Banks
- Financial services institutions
- Insurance companies
- Lawyers
- Trustees
- Real estate agents.

27.14.9 Risk-based Approach

Firms are required to be able to demonstrate to the authorities that the extent of the measures adopted by them is appropriate in view of the risks of money laundering and terrorist financing.

27.14.10 Role of the MLRO/Nominated Officer

The new AML law re-introduced the requirement for the appointment of an MLRO. The MLRO must be a senior member of the company, and acts as the contact for the law-enforcement agencies and other authorities. A deputy should be appointed to take responsibility whenever the MLRO is absent.

The Money Laundering Reporting Officer shall have unrestricted access to all information, data, records and systems which may be required to perform their duties. The extent of the use of data and information by the MLRO shall only be to the extent that is necessary to enable the MLRO to perform their tasks. The MLRO must also be granted sufficient powers to enable them to carry out their functions.

27.14.11 Due Diligence

German due diligence consists of four parts:

1. The identification of the contractor or customer.
2. The gathering of information on the purpose and intended nature of the business relationship.
3. Investigation as to whether the customer has a beneficial owner. If this is the case, then the requirements under German law are to identify the ownership and control structure of the customer.
4. Continuous monitoring of the business relationship, including monitoring the transactions carried out to ensure that they are coherent with the existing information about the customer and, if there is a beneficial owner, that it is in accordance with the business and customer profile. This information should be updated at reasonable intervals.

These provisions must be met:

- In the case of establishing a business relationship.
- In the case of an existing business relationship, for a transaction valued at EUR 15,000 or more, or which, if multiple transactions are carried out, when aggregated represents an amount worth EUR 15,000 or more, provided that there is evidence that they are linked.
- When a transfer of funds is made outside of a business relationship with an amount valued at EUR 1,000 or more.
- When there is evidence that the funds, regardless of the amount, are involved in money laundering or terrorist financing.
- If there is doubt following the CDD process.

If these requirements are not met, the business relationship has not been established and no transaction should be performed by the firm. If a business relationship already exists, the requirement is that it must be terminated. How this would then be achieved without tipping off the customer is a matter open to debate!

In fulfilling the CDD requirements, the entity should have regard to the risk posed by the customer, relationship or proposed transaction. The entity should be able to demonstrate, on request, that the scope of the measures taken by it regarding the risks of money laundering and terrorist financing is reasonable.

Personal Client Due Diligence

If the customer is a natural person, the following information should be ascertained:

- Name
- Place of birth
- Date of birth
- Nationality
- Address.

This should be verified by a valid official identification document containing a photograph of the holder and a passport and ID card. The passport and ID card should be German.

Corporate Customer Due Diligence

For a company, the following information should be ascertained:

- Any company name;
- Legal form;
- Registration number;

- Address of registered office or principal place of business;
- Names of members of the representative body or the legal representative, if it is a member of a representative body.

For any other legal person or a partnership:

- Their company name;
- Legal form;
- Registration number if available;
- Address of registered office or headquarters.

This information should be verified based on an extract from the trade register or a cooperative or a comparable official register or list, by the founding documents or equivalent probative documents, or by inspection of the relevant register.

Beneficial Ownership

Obligators must always make reasonable efforts to ensure the identity of the beneficial owners is ascertained.

Simplified Customer Due Diligence

Obligators can carry out simplified CDD if they identify a low risk of money laundering. Low-risk entities include:

- Publicly traded companies;
- Transactions on behalf of national authorities;
- Clients who have already been subject to CDD by, for example, their lawyers.

Non-face-to-face Customer Due Diligence

If the customer is not physically present, a valid official identification document containing a photograph of the holder and a passport and ID card are required, or a certified copy of each.

Any other suspicious transactions must be monitored.

This, again, is an easy requirement to state in regulation but clearly impacts the online development of German banks. There are other means available to the firm to obtain confirmation and the use of the risk-based approach does provide a limited safe harbour in this respect. However, any firm that is wilfully failing to obtain the information required will clearly be taking a level of additional risk which might be considered unacceptable.

Politically Exposed Persons

Where the customer or the beneficial owner is a PEP, the following shall apply:

- The establishment of a business relationship must depend on the consent of a senior member of the reporting entity;

- There must be appropriate measures in place to establish the source of the assets which are to be used as part of the business relationship or transaction; and
- The business relationship must continue to undergo enhanced ongoing monitoring.

27.14.12 *Ongoing Monitoring*

Firms are obliged to incorporate internal safeguards, such as:

- Appointing an MLRO, as discussed above;
- Developing and updating appropriate business and customer-related security systems and controls that serve to prevent money laundering and terrorist financing, and ensuring they combat the latest ML technology;
- Staff training;
- Employing appropriate risk-based measures to verify the reliability of the workforce.

This final requirement is perhaps more stringent than applies in other jurisdictions and would normally rely on work conducted either by the risk-management function or the internal audit function. Given that the internal audit requirements globally have been extended to also incorporate reliability, these financial crime requirements might be considered to fit within such a framework.

27.14.13 *Staff Training*

Regulated entities are required to implement procedures and programmes to inform the employees about:

- Current developments and methods of money laundering and terrorist financing;
- Techniques used to prevent money laundering and terrorist financing;
- Existing obligations under the AML law.

The above should be implemented through appropriate measures. Generally, we would recommend that any such training includes a short examination to ensure that staff have achieved the learning objectives set.

27.14.14 *Record-keeping*

Records of all identification documentation and other documents used to complete CDD must be kept.

The records can be stored as reproductions on an image carrier or on other media. The data stored should not be altered during the retention period, and should be available in a readable format within a reasonable period.

The records referred to above and other evidence of business relationships and transactions should be kept for at least five years. The retention period in the case of establishing a business relationship begins at the end of the calendar year in which the business relationship ends. In other cases (e.g. one-off transactions), the period begins at the end of the calendar year in which the transaction occurred.

27.14.15 Suspicious Transaction Reporting

If there is any reason for suspicion that the assets involved in a transaction or business relationship have been acquired through money laundering or terrorist financing, the reporting entity must, regardless of the value of the assets involved, report this to the FIU. This report should be made immediately, by telephone, fax or electronic transmission.

The transaction should not be commenced or continued without permission from the authorities, unless two business days have passed since the submission of the report. If the transaction cannot be postponed before a report is submitted, the report must be submitted as soon as possible.

27.14.16 Penalties

Breach of the AML requirements is punishable by a fine of up to one hundred thousand euros.

27.14.17 Case Studies

A recent German case reached an anti-climatic conclusion when the statute of limitations time barred a six-year investigation into a $150 million money-laundering case. The case involved four German banking executives and a Danish lawyer who had been assisting a former Russian government minister selling assets which he was alleged to have control of through offshore companies, thereby concealing the identity of the true owner.

The assets were held by the bank in trust for the lawyer, but German prosecutors alleged that the true owner was the former Russian minister, through a complicated corporate structure designed to conceal a transfer from State to private ownership.

Prosecutors offered to resolve the case by accepting payments ranging from EUR 5,000 to EUR 40,000 from four of the defendants, who all maintained their innocence, because the investigation was soon to be time-barred by the statute of limitations. When you consider that it is suspected that $150 million was laundered over a number of years, the settlements seem relatively generous.

Despite the outcome of the investigation, this case highlights the need for financial institutions to investigate thoroughly the beneficial owner of assets, particularly when complex corporate structures are employed. Additionally, it also illustrates how vital international cooperation is to successful AML investigations, particularly when funds are being moved cross-border. There has been some speculation as to whether a lack of coherence between German and Russian authorities may have caused the delays which ultimately scuppered this investigation, so it is important for financial institutions to consider their relationships with the other countries involved when assessing the risk attributed to their clients.

27.15 COUNTRY PROFILE: GUERNSEY

27.15.1 Overview

The scope of the Guernsey money-laundering-deterrence programme is wide – rather than specifying particular businesses or industries, it applies to "all financial services businesses". The Bailiwick of Guernsey has a strong money-laundering-deterrence regime, although at times it has been criticised for relying too much on foreign law-enforcement agencies.

27.15.2 Key Legislation

It is always worth remembering that Guernsey, just like Jersey, Alderney and Sark, is not a member of the EU and therefore does not have to comply with European legislation.

The primary money-laundering legislation in Guernsey is the Criminal Justice (Proceeds of Crime) (Bailiwick of Guernsey) Law 1999. The compliance legislation is found in the Criminal Justice (Proceeds of Crime) (Financial Services Businesses) (Bailiwick of Guernsey) Regulations 2007, which were last updated in 2010, and the supplementary *AML Handbook*. The latest version of the handbook was released in April 2013.

27.15.3 Legislative History

Several major revisions have been made to the AML framework in Guernsey as it attempts to move forward with the rest of the world's integrated financial structures and confirm its commitment to legislating in line with current developments.

The full list of relevant legislation referred to in the Guernsey *AML Handbook* is as follows:

- The Criminal Justice (Proceeds of Crime) (Bailiwick of Guernsey) Law 1999, as amended;
- The Drug Trafficking (Bailiwick of Guernsey) Law 2000, as amended;
- The Terrorism and Crime (Bailiwick of Guernsey) Law 2002, as amended;
- The Transfer of Funds (Guernsey) Ordinance 2007;
- The Transfer of Funds (Alderney) Ordinance 2007;
- The Transfer of Funds (Sark) Ordinance 2007;
- The Disclosure (Bailiwick of Guernsey) Law 2007, as amended;
- The Disclosure (Bailiwick of Guernsey) Regulations 2007, as amended;
- The Terrorism and Crime (Bailiwick of Guernsey) Regulations 2007, as amended;
- The Registration of Non-Regulated Financial Services Businesses (Bailiwick of Guernsey) Law 2008, as amended;
- The Terrorist Asset-Freezing (Bailiwick of Guernsey) Law 2011;
- The Al-Qaida and Taliban (Freezing of Funds) (Guernsey) Ordinance 2011.

The Commission has written to the managing directors of all financial services businesses, seeking comments on proposed changes to the AML framework, including a substantial amount of the AML legislation and regulations. These consultations closed in July 2012, but the outcome had not been announced at the time of finalisation of this text.

27.15.4 FATF Assessment

Guernsey is not a member of the FATF. However, it is a member of the Group of International Finance Centre Supervisors (GIFCS), a body that is an observer to the FATF. The GIFCS conducts evaluations of its members' anti-money-laundering and counter-terrorist-financing systems.

The IMF conducted an assessment of Guernsey's compliance with the FATF AML standards in 2010. It found that:

> *"Guernsey's comprehensive AML/CFT legal framework provides a sound basis for an effective AML/CFT regime. Most shortcomings identified during the assessment are technical in nature. Some of these deficiencies were addressed by the authorities immediately after the onsite visit. Money laundering and the financing of terrorism are criminalized fully in line with the FATF standard and the legal framework provides an ability to freeze and confiscate assets in appropriate circumstances. As of the assessment date [2010], there had been no prosecutions or convictions for terrorist financing."*

27.15.5 The Primary AML Investigation/Regulatory Authorities

The Guernsey Financial Services Commission (GFSC)

The primary regulator is the Guernsey Financial Services Commission (GFSC). The GFSC supervises financial entities and publishes reports on AML in Guernsey. The IMF noted in 2010 that the GFSC has adequate authority and powers to supervise financial institutions, including money transfer systems, with respect to compliance with existing AML/CFT laws, regulations and rules.

However, powers to sanction financial institutions for non-compliance, particularly the regime for applying discretionary financial penalties, could be enhanced to ensure that the penalties are dissuasive and proportionate to the severity of the violation or level of non-compliance.

27.15.6 Outline of Specific Money-laundering Offences

The following are recognised as criminal offences in Guernsey:

- Facilitating the retention or control of the proceeds of crime (i.e. if the factual matrix had occurred in Guernsey it would have constituted a criminal offence in Guernsey which is capable of being prosecuted on indictment).

- Acquiring, possessing or using the proceeds of crime directly or indirectly to secure funds or investments.
- Concealing or transferring out of Guernsey property representing the proceeds of crime for the purpose of assisting a person either to avoid prosecution or the making of a confiscation order.
- Failure to disclose information gathered in the course of business that another person is engaged in money laundering.
- Disclosure to a person of information that is likely to prejudice an investigation into money laundering, knowing or suspecting that the investigation is being, or is about to be, conducted – "tipping off".

27.15.7 Penalties

The penalty for any of the first three offences in the above list is a maximum of 14 years' imprisonment and/or an unlimited fine. The penalty for either of the final two offences is five years' imprisonment and/or a fine.

27.15.8 Scope

Guernsey's anti-money-laundering and countering the financing of terrorism (AML/CFT) legislation (and, by extension, the handbook) applies to all financial services businesses conducting financial services business in Guernsey. This includes Guernsey-based branches and offices of companies incorporated outside Guernsey conducting financial services business in Guernsey.

27.15.9 Risk-based Approach

On direction from the relevant authorities, Guernsey has adopted a risk-based approach. A financial services business must:

- Carry out a suitable and sufficient business risk assessment as soon as reasonably practicable;
- Regularly review its business risk assessment so as to keep it up to date and, where, as a result of that review, changes to the business risk assessment are required, it must make those changes;
- Prior to the establishment of a business relationship or the carrying out of an occasional transaction, undertake a risk assessment of that proposed business relationship or occasional transaction;
- Regularly review any risk assessment carried out so as to keep it up to date and, where changes to that risk assessment are required, it must make those changes; and
- Ensure that its policies, procedures and controls on forestalling, preventing and detecting money laundering and terrorist financing are appropriate and effective, having regard to the assessed risk.

27.15.10 Role of the MLRO/Nominated Officer

The requirements for a Money Laundering Reporting Officer (MLRO) are set out under The Criminal Justice (Proceeds of Crime) (Financial Services Businesses) (Bailiwick of Guernsey) Regulations. An MLRO is defined as a manager, partner or director who is:

- Appointed by a financial services business to have responsibility for compliance with policies, procedures and controls to forestall, prevent and detect money laundering and terrorist financing; and
- Nominated by a financial services business to receive disclosures under Part I of the Disclosure Law and Section 15 of the Terrorism Law.

In addition to this, the MLRO must:

- Be employed by the financial services business. In the case of managed or administered businesses, it is acceptable for an employee of the manager or administrator of the business to be appointed as the MLRO/deputy MLRO.
- Be resident in Guernsey.
- Be the main point of contact with the Financial Intelligence Service (FIS) in the handling of disclosures.
- Have sufficient resources to perform their duties.
- Have access to the CDD records.
- Be available on a day-to-day basis.
- Receive full cooperation from all staff.
- Report directly to the board.
- Have regular contact with the board to ensure that the board is able to satisfy itself that all statutory obligations and provisions in the handbook are being met and that the financial services business is taking sufficiently robust measures to protect itself against the potential risk of being used for money laundering and/or terrorist financing.
- Be fully aware of both their obligations and those of the financial services business under the Regulations, the relevant enactments and the *AML Handbook*.

The obligation on the firm is to appoint a person of at least management level as the Money Laundering Reporting Officer and to provide the name and title of that person to the Commission and the Financial Intelligence Service as soon as is reasonably practicable. In any event, reporting must be within 14 days starting from the date of that person's appointment.

They are also required to nominate another person ("nominated officer") to receive disclosures in the absence of the Money Laundering Reporting Officer, and ensure that any relevant employee is aware of the name of that nominated officer.

Firms must ensure that where a relevant employee is required to make a disclosure, that this is done by way of a report to the Money Laundering Reporting Officer, or, in their absence, to a nominated officer.

Firms must also ensure that the Money Laundering Reporting Officer, or in their absence a nominated officer, in determining whether or not he is required to make a report to the authorities, takes into account all relevant information. The MLRO or nominated officer must be given prompt access to any other information which may be of assistance to them in considering any report.

Finally, there is a requirement for the firm to ensure that it establishes and maintains such other appropriate and effective procedures and controls as are necessary to ensure compliance with requirements to make disclosures.

27.15.11 Due Diligence

The purpose of the CDD programme is to establish that any customer, beneficial owner or underlying principal is the person that he claims to be. This has two elements – the entity must be satisfied that:

- A person exists, which must be concluded on the basis of appropriate identification data; and
- The customer, beneficial owner or underlying principal is that person. This should be achieved through verifying, from identification data, satisfactory confirmatory evidence of appropriate components of their identity.

CDD should be carried out when:

- Establishing a business relationship;
- Carrying out an occasional transaction;
- Where the financial services business knows or suspects, or has reasonable grounds for knowing or suspecting, that any party to a business relationship is engaged in money laundering or terrorist financing or is carrying out a transaction on behalf of somebody who is;
- Where the financial services business has doubts about the veracity or adequacy of previously obtained identification data.

The procedures required to be conducted are as follows:

- The customer shall be identified and their identity verified using identification data;
- Any person purporting to act on behalf of the customer shall be identified and their identity and their authority to so act shall be verified;
- The beneficial owner and underlying principal shall be identified and reasonable measures shall be taken to verify such identity using identification data and such measures shall include, in the case of a legal person or legal arrangement, measures to understand the ownership and control structure of the customer;
- A determination shall be made as to whether the customer is acting on behalf of another person and, if the customer is so acting, reasonable measures shall be taken to obtain sufficient identification data to identify and verify the identity of that other person;

- Information shall be obtained on the purpose and intended nature of each business relationship;
- A determination shall be made as to whether the customer, beneficial owner and any underlying principal is a politically exposed person.

Generally, there is an obligation on a financial services business to have regard to any relevant rules and guidance in the handbook in determining what constitutes reasonable measures.

Personal Client Due Diligence

A financial services business must collect relevant identification data on an individual, which includes:

- Legal name, any former names (such as maiden name) and any other names used;
- Principal residential address;
- Date and place of birth;
- Nationality;
- Any occupation, public position held and, where appropriate, the name of the employer; and
- An official personal identification number or other unique identifier contained in an unexpired official document (for example, passport, identification card, residence permit, social security records, driving licence) that bears a photograph of the customer.

In order to verify the legal name, address, date and place of birth, nationality and official personal identification number of the individual, the following documents are considered to be the most reliable, in descending order of acceptability:

- Current passport (providing photographic evidence of identity);
- Current national identity card (providing photographic evidence of identity);
- Armed forces identity card.

The examples quoted above are not the only possibilities.

Corporate Customer Due Diligence

One or more of the following is considered acceptable to verify the identity of a company:

- A copy of the Certificate of Incorporation (or equivalent) if applicable;
- A company registry search, if applicable, including confirmation that the legal body has not been, and is not in the process of being, dissolved, struck off, wound up or terminated;
- A copy of the latest audited financial statements;
- A copy of the memorandum and articles of association;

- A copy of the Directors' Register;
- A copy of the Shareholders' Register;
- Independent information sources, including electronic sources, for example, business information services;
- A copy of the board resolution authorising the opening of the account and recording account signatories; and
- A personal visit to the principal place of business.

Simplified Customer Due Diligence

If a financial services provider identifies a client as low risk, it may apply simplified CDD. A financial services business must obtain, at a minimum, the following information in relation to an individual customer:

- Legal name;
- Any former names (such as maiden name) and any other names used;
- Principal residential address; and
- Date, place of birth and nationality.

Enhanced Customer Due Diligence

Where a financial services business is required to carry out customer due diligence, it must also carry out enhanced customer due diligence in relation to the following business relationships or occasional transactions:

- Politically exposed persons;
- Correspondent banking relationships or similar;
- Where the customer is established or situated in a country or territory that does not apply or insufficiently applies the FATF Recommendations on money laundering, or which the financial services business considers to be a high-risk relationship;
- A business relationship or an occasional transaction which has been assessed as being a high-risk relationship.

Enhanced CDD includes:

- Obtaining senior management approval for establishing a business relationship or undertaking an occasional transaction;
- Obtaining senior management approval for, in the case of an existing business relationship with a PEP, continuing that relationship;
- Taking reasonable measures to establish the source of any funds and of the wealth of the customer and beneficial owner and underlying principal;
- Carrying out more frequent and more extensive ongoing monitoring; and

- Taking one or more of the following steps as would be appropriate to the particular business relationship or occasional transaction:
  - obtaining additional identification data;
  - verifying additional aspects of the customer's identity;
  - obtaining additional information to understand the purpose and intended nature of each business relationship.

A financial services business must ensure that it takes adequate measures which include one or more of the following:

- Requiring additional documents to complement those which are required for face-to-face customers;
- Development of independent contact with the customer and other third parties responsible for the source of funds or company registrations, etc.;
- Third party introduction;
- Requiring the first payment to be carried out through an account in the customer's name with a bank situated in a country or territory listed in Appendix C to the handbook.

Correspondent Banking

In relation to correspondent relationships for banking and those established for securities transactions or funds transfers, whether for the financial services business as principal or for its customers, a financial services business must take additional steps in relation to CDD. A firm must:

- Gather sufficient information about a respondent institution to understand fully the nature of the respondent's business;
- Determine, from publicly available information, the reputation of the institution and the quality of supervision, including whether it has been subject to a money-laundering or terrorist-financing investigation or regulatory action;
- Assess the respondent institution's AML/CFT policies, procedures and controls, and ascertain that they are adequate, appropriate and effective;
- Obtain board or senior management approval, i.e. sign off before establishing new correspondent relationships; and
- Document the respective AML/CFT responsibilities of each institution.

Where a correspondent relationship involves the maintenance of "payable-through accounts", a financial services business must also take steps so that it is satisfied that:

- Its customer (the "respondent financial services business") has performed all the required CDD obligations set out in the Regulations and *AML Handbook* on those of its customers that have direct access to the accounts of the correspondent financial services business; and
- The respondent financial services business is able to provide relevant customer identification data upon request to the correspondent financial services business.

Financial services businesses must ensure that appropriate and effective policies, procedures and controls are in place when establishing correspondent relationships with foreign banks and other institutions.

Shell Banking

A financial services business must:

- Not enter into, or continue, a correspondent banking relationship with a shell bank;
- Take appropriate measures to ensure that it does not enter into, or continue, a correspondent banking relationship where the respondent bank is known to permit its accounts to be used by a shell bank.

27.15.12 *Ongoing Monitoring*

Reporting entities are required to ensure a detailed approach that does not omit data that could prove useful for future transactions or reference. The requirements are as follows:

- To review identification data to ensure they are kept up to date and relevant, in particular for high-risk relationships or customers in respect of whom there is a high risk.
- To scrutinise any transactions or other activity, paying particular attention to all:
  - complex transactions;
  - transactions which are both large and unusual; and
  - unusual patterns of transactions, which have no apparent economic purpose or no apparent lawful purpose.
- To ensure that the way in which identification data are recorded and stored is such as to facilitate the ongoing monitoring of each business relationship.

The extent of any monitoring carried out under this regulation and the frequency at which it is carried out shall be determined on a risk-sensitive basis including whether or not the business relationship is a high-risk relationship.

The requirement to conduct ongoing CDD ensures that a financial services business is aware of any changes in the development of the business relationship. The extent of the ongoing CDD measures must be determined on a risk-sensitive basis, but a financial services business must bear in mind that as the business relationship develops, the risk of money laundering or terrorist financing may change.

27.15.13 *Staff Training*

The Regulations provide that a financial services business is required to maintain appropriate and effective procedures, when hiring employees, for the purpose of ensuring high standards of employee probity and competence.

A financial services business is also required to ensure that relevant employees receive comprehensive ongoing training in:

- The relevant enactments, regulations and the handbook;
- The personal obligations of employees and their potential criminal liability under the regulations and the relevant enactments;
- The implications of non-compliance by employees with any rules or guidance made for the purposes of the Regulations; and
- Its policies, procedures and controls for the purposes of forestalling, preventing and detecting money laundering and terrorist financing.

In addition, a financial services business must, in ensuring that relevant employees receive the ongoing training required under the Regulations, in particular ensure that they are kept informed of:

- The CDD requirements and the requirements for the internal and external reporting of suspicion;
- The criminal and regulatory sanctions in place for failing to report information in accordance with policies, procedures and controls;
- The identity and responsibilities of the MLRO;
- The principal vulnerabilities of the products and services offered by the financial services business; and
- New developments, including information on current money-laundering and terrorist-financing techniques, methods, trends and typologies.

A financial services business must, in providing the training required under the Regulations:

- Provide appropriate training to enable relevant employees adequately and responsibly to assess the information that is required for them to judge whether an activity or business relationship is suspicious in the circumstances;
- Provide relevant employees with a document outlining their own obligations and potential criminal liability and those of the financial services business under the relevant enactments and the Regulations;
- Prepare and provide relevant employees with a copy, in any format, of the financial services business's policies, procedures and controls manual for AML/CFT; and
- Ensure that its employees are fully aware of legislative requirements.

The board and senior management are responsible for the effectiveness and appropriateness of the financial services business policies, procedures and controls to counter money laundering and terrorist financing. In addition to the general training provided to relevant employees, a detailed level of additional training must be provided to the board and senior management to provide a clear explanation and understanding of:

- The relevant enactments and the Regulations and information on the offences and the related penalties, including potential director and shareholder liability;

- The CDD and record-keeping requirements; and
- The internal and external suspicion reporting procedures.

The frequency of training should be determined on a risk-based approach, with those employees with responsibility for the handling of business relationships or transactions receiving more frequent training.

27.15.14 Record-keeping

Customer Due Diligence Information

An entity must maintain:

- Copies of the identification data obtained to verify the identity of all customers, beneficial owners and underlying principals;
- Copies of any customer files, account files, business correspondence and information relating to the business relationship or occasional transaction;
- Information as to where copies of the CDD information may be obtained.

Transaction Information

All transactions carried out on behalf of, or with, a customer in the course of business, both domestic and international, must be recorded by the financial services business. In every case, sufficient information must be recorded to enable the reconstruction of individual transactions so as to provide, if necessary, evidence for prosecution of criminal activity. For transactions, documentation is maintained which must include:

- The name and address of the customer, beneficial owner and underlying principal;
- If a monetary transaction, the currency and amount of the transaction;
- Account name and number or other information by which it can be identified;
- Details of the counterparty, including account details;
- The nature of the transaction; and
- The date of the transaction.

Internal and External Suspicion Reports

A financial services business must maintain:

- The internal suspicion report;
- Records of actions taken under the internal and external reporting requirements;
- When the MLRO has considered information or other material concerning possible money laundering, but has not made a disclosure of suspicion to the FIS, a record of the other material that was considered and the reason for the decision; and
- Copies of any disclosures made to the FIS.

Training Information

Training records must include:

- The dates AML/CFT training was provided;
- The nature of the training;
- The names of the employees who received training reports by the MLRO to the board and senior management;
- Records of consideration of those reports and of any action taken as a consequence; and
- Any records made within the financial services business or by other parties in respect of compliance of the financial services business with the Regulations and the handbook.

These records must be kept for five years starting from:

- In the case of a report or a disclosure in relation to a business relationship, the date the business relationship ceased;
- In the case of a report or a disclosure in relation to an occasional transaction, the date that transaction was completed;
- In the case of training, the date the training was carried out;
- For any policies, procedures and controls which the entity was required to maintain, from the date they ceased to be operative;
- For any other documents prepared, from the date they were created.

Documents and customer due diligence information, including any copies thereof, kept under this regulation may be kept in any manner or form, provided that they are readily retrievable, and must be made available promptly to any police officer, the Financial Intelligence Service, the Commission or any other person where such documents or customer due diligence information are requested pursuant to these Regulations or any relevant enactment.

27.15.15 Internal Requirements

A financial services business must, in addition to complying with the preceding requirements of these Regulations:

- Establish such other policies, procedures and controls as may be appropriate and effective for the purposes of forestalling, preventing and detecting money laundering and terrorist financing.
- Establish and maintain an effective policy, for which responsibility must be taken by the board, for the review of its compliance with the requirements of these Regulations, and such policy shall include provision as to the extent and frequency of such reviews.
- Ensure that a review of its compliance with these Regulations is discussed and minuted at a meeting of the board at appropriate intervals, and in considering what is

appropriate, a financial services business must have regard to the risk, taking into account the size, nature and complexity of the financial services business, its customers, products and services, and the ways in which it provides those products and services.

- Ensure that any of its branch offices and, where it is a body corporate, any body corporate of which it is the majority shareholder, which, in either case, is a financial services business in any country or territory outside the Bailiwick, complies there with the requirements of these Regulations, and any requirements under the law applicable in that country or territory which are consistent with the Financial Action Task Force Recommendations on Money Laundering.

A financial services business must also ensure that there are appropriate and effective policies, procedures and controls in place which provide for the board to meet its obligations relating to compliance review, in particular the board must:

- Ensure that the compliance review policy takes into account the size, nature and complexity of the business and includes a requirement for sample testing of the effectiveness and adequacy of the policies, procedures and controls.
- Consider whether it would be appropriate to maintain a separate audit function to assess the adequacy and effectiveness of the area of compliance.
- Ensure that when a review of compliance is discussed by the board at appropriate intervals the necessary action is taken to remedy any identified deficiencies.
- Ensure that the financial services business is meeting its obligation that its branches and subsidiaries operating outside the Bailiwick comply with the Regulations and applicable local law which is consistent with the FATF Recommendations.
- Provide adequate resources from within the financial services business, within the group or externally to ensure that the AML/CFT policies, procedures and controls of the financial services business are subject to regular monitoring and testing as required by the Regulations.
- Provide adequate resources to enable the MLRO to perform their duties; and take appropriate measures to keep abreast of and guard against the use of technological developments and new methodologies in money-laundering and terrorist-financing schemes.

The board may delegate some or all of its duties but must retain responsibility for the review of overall compliance with AML/CFT requirements.

27.15.16 Suspicious Transaction Reporting

Monitoring of the activity of a business relationship must be carried out on the basis of a risk-based approach, with high-risk relationships being subjected to an appropriate frequency of scrutiny, which must be greater than may be appropriate for low-risk relationships. Scrutiny of transactions and activity must be undertaken throughout the course of the business relationship to ensure that the transactions and activity being conducted are consistent with the financial services business's knowledge of the customer, their business, source of funds and source of wealth. When monitoring complex, unusual and large transactions or unusual patterns of transactions, a financial services business must examine the background and purpose of such transactions and record such findings in writing.

Information contained in internal reports made to an MLRO must be disclosed to the FIS where the MLRO knows or suspects, or has reasonable grounds for knowing or suspecting as a result of the report, that a person is engaged in money laundering or terrorist financing.

It is a criminal offence for anyone employed by a financial services business to fail to report, where they have knowledge, suspicion or reasonable grounds for knowledge or suspicion, that another person is laundering the proceeds of any criminal conduct or is carrying out terrorist financing.

What may constitute reasonable grounds for knowledge or suspicion will be determined from facts or circumstances from which an honest and reasonable person engaged in a financial services business would have inferred knowledge or formed the suspicion that another was engaged in money laundering or terrorist financing.

27.15.17 Penalties

Any person who contravenes any requirement of the Regulations shall be guilty of an offence and liable:

- On conviction on indictment, to imprisonment not exceeding a term of five years or a fine, or both;
- On summary conviction, to imprisonment for a term not exceeding six months or a fine not exceeding £10,000, or both.

The same penalties apply to anybody who makes a dishonest or misleading statement in purported compliance with the Regulations.

27.15.18 Case Studies

It emerged during investigations into another criminal, "X", that some of the proceeds of a $12 million fraud had been laundered through the defendant's bank account. The defendant initially denied all knowledge of any criminal proceeds. He said that the relationship between X and himself was purely professional, and that although he had deposited money from X into his bank account, these transfers involved legitimate commission X had earned and the defendant made no money out of this. He also, in a somewhat contradictory manner, admitted to receiving a large personal loan from X. The police advised him to distance himself from X, as X was believed to be a criminal. The defendant was also warned that he was in danger of being prosecuted himself.

However, this warning fell on deaf ears. Immediately afterwards, the defendant attempted to open another account in Switzerland through one of his companies, with X as the signatory. He then made various payments to himself and X over the following years, including through an account in Jersey after his Guernsey account was frozen.

During this time, he maintained contact with X, as well as attempting to unfreeze the Guernsey account for X's benefit.

X was convicted of 33 counts of criminal deception in February 2006. The defendant, however, was not arrested until December 2009, when he claimed that the payments to himself and X were reimbursements of legitimate expenses incurred at X's request, payments at X's own request or repayments on the large loan X had granted him. However, he did admit, after seeing the police's evidence, that he suspected X was involved in fraud.

Following numerous years of investigation and confiscation proceedings, the defendant was charged with money laundering in November 2009. He was convicted and sentenced to two and a half years' imprisonment.

This case illustrates the need for constant monitoring of customer relationships by financial institutions, particularly between clients with seemingly legitimate professional relationships. It would have been easy for a bank to take its eye off the ball when the police investigation had started, but in this case the transactions which ultimately led to the conviction actually occurred after the police had warned the defendant of the trouble he was getting himself into. Ongoing monitoring is therefore essential to a bank's AML policy.

27.16 COUNTRY PROFILE: HONG KONG

27.16.1 Overview

Hong Kong has recently implemented specific money-laundering-deterrence legislation, prior to which the AML requirements were contained in various articles incorporated within drug-trafficking legislation. Having also submitted two progress reports since the last Financial Action Task Force (FATF) assessment, Hong Kong is committed to bringing its AML regime into line with worldwide standards.

27.16.2 Key Legislation

The current law operating in Hong Kong is Cap 615 – Anti-Money Laundering And Counter-Terrorist Financing (Financial Institutions) Ordinance. This is supplemented by guidelines which were last updated in July 2012.

27.16.3 Legislative History

The Drug Trafficking (Recovery of Proceeds) Ordinance Cap 405 (DTROP) came into force in 1989, followed by the Drug Trafficking and Organised Crime (Amendment) Ordinance 2002. 1994 saw the enactment of the Organised Serious Crime Ordinance Cap 455 (OSCO).

In 2002, United Nations (Anti Terrorism Measures) Ordinance Cap 575 (UNATMO) was brought into force in accordance with the mandatory requirements of UN S/RES/1373 (2001).

On 22nd February, 2012, the Hong Kong government introduced the UNATMO Bill into the Hong Kong Legislative Committee for its first reading. Specifically, the UNATMO Bill aimed to amend Hong Kong's existing United Nations (Anti-Terrorism) Ordinance Cap 575 (UNATMO) by:

- Repealing the definition of "funds" and replacing it with the broader term "property" so as to criminalise all assets and not simply funds;
- Expanding the definition of "terrorist act" to cover the intended coercion of international organisations;
- Criminalising the collection (in addition to the provision or making available) of funds for terrorists and terrorist organisations to cover the collection of property or the solicitation of financial (or related) services for such persons and organisations; and
- Making consequential amendments to the AMLO and Rules of the High Court.

The Anti-Money Laundering and Counter-Terrorist Financing (Financial Institutions) Ordinance Cap 615 was introduced on 1st April, 2012 and represented a major overhaul of AML law in Hong Kong. The latest guidelines were introduced in July 2012.

The 2012 guidelines reiterate that the four main pieces of legislation in Hong Kong that are concerned with ML/TF are the AMLO, the Drug Trafficking (Recovery of Proceeds)

Ordinance (the DTROP), the Organised and Serious Crimes Ordinance (the OSCO) and the United Nations (Anti-Terrorism Measures) Ordinance (the UNATMO).

27.16.4 FATF Assessment

The 2008 mutual evaluation found that Hong Kong has a good legal structure to combat money laundering (ML) and terrorist financing (TF), and that the ML offence is broad and almost fully meets the FATF requirements. However, there were some weaknesses in the compliance provisions, such as the PEP provisions for certain financial institutions.

Since the 2008 report on Hong Kong, Hong Kong has submitted two progress reports to the FATF on improvement actions taken or planned by Hong Kong to implement the FATF's earlier recommendations. In October 2012, the FATF recognised that Hong Kong had made significant progress in addressing the deficiencies identified in the 2008 Mutual Evaluation Report. The FATF agreed that Hong Kong, China should now report on any further improvements to its anti-money-laundering/combating the financing of terrorism (AML/CFT) system on a biennial update basis, essentially removing it from the regular follow-up process based on updated procedures agreed by the FATF in October 2009.

The next review should be conducted in 2014 to assess how effectively Hong Kong has implemented the Recommendations (including the latest changes).

27.16.5 The Primary AML Investigation/Regulatory Authorities

Hong Kong Monetary Authority

The HKMA is the government authority in Hong Kong responsible for maintaining monetary and banking stability. Its main functions are:

- Maintaining currency stability within the framework of the Linked Exchange Rate system;
- Promoting the stability and integrity of the financial system, including the banking system;
- Helping to maintain Hong Kong's status as an international financial centre, including the maintenance and development of Hong Kong's financial infrastructure;
- Managing the Exchange Fund.

The Securities and Futures Commission

This commission (the SFC) has a variety of regulatory functions, including monitoring and enforcing the law against criminal conduct in the securities market.

Pursuant to the Anti-Money Laundering and Counter-Terrorist Financing (Financial Institutions) Ordinance, which came into force on 1st April, 2012, the SFC, the HKMA and the new Insurance Authority and the Customs and Excise Department will be the designated authorities to supervise financial institutions' compliance with the new statutory customer due diligence and record-keeping requirements.

The Independent Commission Against Corruption

This Commission is the principal agency responsible for investigating and preventing corruption in Hong Kong. It has three departments:

- The Operations Department receives, considers and investigates alleged corruption offences.
- The Corruption Prevention Department examines practices and procedures of government departments and public bodies to reduce corruption opportunities and offers free and confidential corruption prevention advice to private organisations upon request.
- The Community Relations Department educates the public about the evils of corruption and enlists public support in combating corruption.

The Hong Kong Police Force

The Narcotics Bureau, the Organised Crime and Triad Bureau of the Police and the Customs Drug Investigation Bureau of the Hong Kong Customs and Excise Department, which are all departments of the Hong Kong Police Force, investigate money-laundering offences under the Drug Trafficking (Recovery of Proceeds) Ordinance (DTROP) and the Organised and Serious Crimes Ordinance (OSCO).

27.16.6 Outline of Specific Money-laundering Offences

The term "money laundering" is defined in Section 1 of Part 1 of Schedule 1 to the Anti-Money Laundering and Counter-Terrorist Financing (Financial Institutions) Ordinance, Cap. 615 (the AMLO), and means an act intended to have the effect of making any property:

- That is the proceeds obtained from the commission of an indictable offence under the laws of Hong Kong, or of any conduct which if it had occurred in Hong Kong would constitute an indictable offence under the laws of Hong Kong; or
- That in whole or in part, directly or indirectly, represents such proceeds

appear not to represent such proceeds.

27.16.7 Financing of Terrorism

The definition of terrorist financing was amended in 2012.

The term "terrorist financing" is defined in Section 1 of Part 1 of Schedule 1 to the AMLO and means:

(a) The provision or collection, by any means, directly or indirectly, of any property:

  (i) with the intention that the property be used; or

  (ii) knowing that the property will be used, in whole or in part, to commit one or more terrorist acts (whether or not the property is actually so used); or

(b) The making available of any property or financial (or related) services, by any means, directly or indirectly, to or for the benefit of a person knowing that, or being reckless as to whether, the person is a terrorist or terrorist associate; or

(c) The collection of property or solicitation of financial (or related) services, by any means, directly or indirectly, for the benefit of a person knowing that, or being reckless as to whether, the person is a terrorist or terrorist associate.

The key change in this section from previous legislation is that the word "property" has been used to replace the word "funds", consequently expanding the scope of the legislation.

27.16.8 *Defences*

A safe harbour defence arises for those submitting suspicious transaction reports to the JFIU. A person may deal with suspected proceeds, whether before or after making a suspicious transaction report, where a suspicious transaction report is made, providing that:

- The transaction or transactions subsequently occurs with the consent of an authorised officer; or
- A suspicious transaction report was made after the transaction, on the person's initiative, or as soon as it was reasonable for the person to make it.

If no suspicious transaction report has been made, it will be a defence if the accused can show:

- He/she intended to disclose knowledge/suspicions;
- There is a reasonable excuse for his/her failure to do so.

27.16.9 *Scope*

The guidelines apply to financial institutions.

27.16.10 *Risk-based Approach*

Financial institutions should determine the extent of customer due diligence (CDD) measures and ongoing monitoring, using a risk-based approach, depending upon the background of the customer and the product, transaction or service used by that customer. This will ensure that the preventive or mitigating measures are commensurate with the risks identified. The measures must, however, comply with the legal requirements of the AMLO.

This approach will enable financial institutions to subject customers to proportionate controls and oversight by determining:

- The extent of the due diligence to be performed on the direct customer; the extent of the measures to be undertaken to verify the identity of any beneficial owner and any person purporting to act on behalf of the customer;

- The level of ongoing monitoring to be applied to the relationship; and
- Measures to mitigate any risks identified.

27.16.11 Role of the MLRO/Nominated Officer

Financial institutions are required to appoint a Compliance Officer (CO) and a Money Laundering Reporting Officer (MLRO). These functions can be performed by the same person.

In order that the CO and MLRO can discharge their responsibilities effectively, senior management should, as far as practicable, ensure that the CO and MLRO are:

- Independent of all operational and business functions (subject to size and resources of the financial institution);
- Normally based in Hong Kong;
- Of a sufficient level of seniority and authority within the financial institution;
- Provided with regular contact with, and when required, direct access to, senior management to ensure that senior management is able to satisfy itself that the statutory obligations are being met and that the business is taking sufficiently robust measures to protect itself against the risks of ML/TF;
- Fully conversant in the financial institution's statutory and regulatory requirements and the ML/TF risks arising from the financial institution's business;
- Capable of accessing, on a timely basis, all available information (both from internal sources such as CDD records and external sources such as circulars from RAs); and
- Equipped with sufficient resources, including staff and appropriate cover for the absence of the CO and MLRO (i.e. an alternate or deputy CO and MLRO who should, where practicable, have the same status).

The principal function of the CO is to act as the focal point within a financial institution for the oversight of all activities relating to the prevention and detection of ML/TF and providing support and guidance to the senior management to ensure that ML/TF risks are adequately managed. In particular, the CO should assume responsibility for:

- Developing and/or continuously reviewing the financial institution's AML/CFT systems to ensure they remain up to date and meet current statutory and regulatory requirements; and
- The oversight of all aspects of the financial institution's AML/CFT systems, which include monitoring effectiveness and enhancing the controls and procedures where necessary.

The MLRO should play an active role in the identification and reporting of suspicious transactions. Principal functions performed are expected to include:

- Reviewing all internal disclosures and exception reports and, in light of all available relevant information, determining whether or not it is necessary to make a report to the JFIU;
- Maintaining all records related to such internal reviews;
- Providing guidance on how to avoid "tipping off" if any disclosure is made; and
- Acting as the main point of contact with the JFIU, law enforcement, and any other competent authorities in relation to ML/TF prevention and detection, investigation or compliance.

It is the responsibility of the MLRO to consider all internal disclosures he receives in the light of full access to all relevant documentation and other parties. However, the MLRO should not simply be a passive recipient of ad hoc reports of suspicious transactions. Rather, the MLRO should play an active role in the identification and reporting of suspicious transactions.

27.16.12 Due Diligence

CDD must be carried out:

- Before establishing a business relationship with the customer;
- Before carrying out for the customer an occasional transaction involving an amount equal to or above $120,000 or an equivalent amount in any other currency, whether the transaction is carried out in a single operation or in several operations that appear to the financial institution to be linked;
- In addition to the above, before carrying out for the customer an occasional transaction that is a wire transfer involving an amount equal to or above $8,000 or an equivalent amount in any other currency, whether the transaction is carried out in a single operation or in several operations that appear to the financial institution to be linked;
- When the financial institution suspects that the customer or the customer's account is involved in money laundering or terrorist financing;
- When the financial institution doubts the veracity or adequacy of any information previously obtained for the purpose of identifying the customer or for the purpose of verifying the customer's identity.

A financial institution may verify the identity of a customer and any beneficial owner of the customer after establishing a business relationship with the customer if:

- This is necessary not to interrupt the normal conduct of business with regard to the customer; and
- Any risk of money laundering or terrorist financing that may be caused by carrying out the verification after establishing the business relationship is effectively managed.

A financial institution must complete the verification as soon as reasonably practicable after establishing the business relationship.

If a financial institution cannot comply with the CDD requirements, it:

- Must not establish a business relationship or carry out any occasional transaction with that customer; or
- If it has already established a business relationship with that customer, must terminate the business relationship as soon as reasonably practicable, taking into account tipping-off requirements and obligations.

Personal Client Due Diligence

Financial institutions should collect the following identification information in respect of personal customers who need to be identified:

- Full name
- Date of birth
- Nationality
- Identity document type and number.

A customer's identity should be verified on the basis of documents, data or information provided by:

- A governmental body;
- The relevant authority or any other relevant authority;
- An authority in a place outside Hong Kong that performs functions similar to those of the relevant authority or any other relevant authority; or
- Any other reliable and independent source that is recognised by the relevant authority.

If a business relationship is to be established, information on the purpose and intended nature of the business relationship with the financial institution must be obtained, unless the purpose and intended nature are obvious.

Corporate Customer Due Diligence

A financial institution should obtain and verify the following information in relation to a customer which is a corporation:

- Full name;
- Date and place of incorporation;
- Registration or incorporation number;
- Registered office address in the place of incorporation;
- A copy of the Certificate of Incorporation and business registration (where applicable);

- A copy of the company's memorandum and articles of association which evidence the powers that regulate and bind the company; and
- Details of the ownership and control structure of the company, e.g. an ownership chart.

A financial institution should record the names of all directors and verify the identity of directors on a risk-based approach. Additionally, it should:

- Confirm the company is still registered and has not been dissolved, wound up, suspended or struck off;
- Independently identify and verify the names of the directors and shareholders recorded in the company registry in the place of incorporation; and
- Verify the company's registered office address in the place of incorporation.

This should be verified by a search of files at the Hong Kong Company Registry and the firm obtaining a company report.

Beneficial Ownership

If there is a beneficial owner in relation to the customer, the entity should take reasonable measures to verify the beneficial owner's identity so that the financial institution is satisfied that it knows who the beneficial owner is, and, where the customer is a legal person or trust, that it understands the ownership and control structure of the legal person or trust.

Except for high-risk customers, if an individual is a beneficial owner of a customer, the financial institution is not required to verify the identity of the individual unless the individual has 25% of the ownership, voting rights or control of the customer.

Third Party Customer Due Diligence

If a person purports to act on behalf of the customer, the entity should identify the person and take reasonable measures to verify the person's identity on the basis of documents, data or information provided by:

- A governmental body;
- The relevant authority or any other relevant authority;
- An authority in a place outside Hong Kong that performs functions similar to those of the relevant authority or any other relevant authority; or
- Any other reliable and independent source that is recognised by the relevant authority.

It should also verify the person's authority to act on behalf of the customer.

Simplified Due Diligence

If a customer is a specified low-risk customer under the AMLO, an entity may carry out a reduced level of CDD. This only requires identifying the customer on the basis of documents, data or information as listed above, without requiring the verification of the documents.

Enhanced Customer Due Diligence

If:

- A customer of a financial institution has not been physically present for identification purposes;
- A customer, or a beneficial owner of a customer, of a financial institution is known to the financial institution, from publicly known information or information in its possession, to be a politically exposed person; or
- A customer, or a beneficial owner of a customer, of a financial institution is involved in any other situation that, by its nature, may present a high risk of money laundering or terrorist financing

the financial institution must, in monitoring its business relationship with the customer under this section, take additional measures to compensate for any risk of money laundering or terrorist financing.

Non-face-to–face Customer Due Diligence

If a customer has not been physically present for identification purposes, a financial institution must carry out at least one of the following measures:

- Further verification of the customer's identity on the basis of CDD documents, data or information which have not been previously used for the purposes of verification of the customer's identity under that section;
- Undertake supplementary work to verify all the information provided by the customer;
- Ensure that the payment or, if there is more than one payment, the first payment made in relation to the customer's account is carried out through an account opened in the customer's name with:
  - an authorised institution; or
  - an institution that:
    - is incorporated or established in an equivalent jurisdiction;
    - carries on a business similar to that carried on by an authorised institution;
    - has measures in place to ensure compliance with requirements similar to those imposed under this Schedule; and
    - is supervised for compliance with those requirements by authorities in that jurisdiction that perform functions similar to those of the Monetary Authority.

Politically Exposed Persons

Once an entity becomes aware that a customer or a potential customer is a PEP, it should, before establishing or continuing a business relationship:

- Obtain approval from its senior management; and
- Take reasonable measures to establish the customer's or beneficial owner's source of wealth and the source of the funds that will be involved in the proposed business relationship.

Anonymous Accounts

A financial institution must not open, or maintain, any anonymous account or account in a fictitious name for any customer.

Correspondent Banking

Before establishing a correspondent banking relationship with a proposed respondent bank, the firm must:

- Collect sufficient information about the proposed respondent bank to enable it to understand fully the nature of the proposed respondent bank's business;
- Determine, from publicly available information, the reputation of the proposed respondent bank and the quality of its supervision by authorities in that place that perform functions similar to the HKMA; and
- Assess the AML/CFT controls of the proposed respondent bank.

The information to be collected should include, but is not limited to:

- The ownership and management structures of the proposed respondent bank;
- The nature of the proposed respondent bank's business;
- The domicile of the proposed respondent bank;
- The existence and quality of AML/CFT regulation and bank regulation in the proposed respondent bank's place of domicile;
- The AML/CFT efforts of the proposed respondent bank and the adequacy of its AML/CFT controls;
- The reputation and history of the proposed respondent bank; and
- The purpose of the account.

Information on the authorisation status and other details of a proposed respondent bank, including the system of bank regulation and supervision in its country, may be obtained through publicly available information. An authorised institution should consider such publicly available materials to ascertain whether the proposed respondent bank has been the subject of any ML/TF-related investigation or adverse regulatory action in the recent past.

An authorised institution must not establish a correspondent banking relationship with a proposed respondent bank unless it has obtained approval from its senior management. Providing that there is a formal delegation of authority which is properly documented, firms may use a risk-based approach to determine the appropriate level of approval within the firm that is required for establishing new correspondent banking relationships.

An authorised institution must not establish a correspondent banking relationship unless it is satisfied that the AML/CFT controls of the proposed respondent bank are adequate and effective. Authorised institutions must document their responsibilities and the responsibilities of the proposed respondent bank. This would be expected to include the responsibilities relating to AML/CFT.

Shell Banking

An authorised institution should not establish or continue a correspondent banking relationship with a shell bank, and should also take appropriate measures to ensure that it does not enter into or continue a correspondent banking relationship with a bank which is known to permit its accounts to be used by a shell bank.

27.16.13 Ongoing Monitoring

Financial institutions must continuously monitor their business relationships with customers by:

- Reviewing, from time to time, documents, data and information relating to each customer that have been obtained by the financial institution for the purpose of complying with the requirements imposed to ensure that they are up to date and relevant;
- Conducting appropriate scrutiny of transactions carried out for the customer to ensure that they are consistent with the financial institution's knowledge of the customer and the customer's business and risk profile, and with its knowledge of the source of the customer's funds; and
- Identifying transactions that:
  - are complex, unusually large in amount or of an unusual pattern; and
  - have no apparent economic or lawful purpose, and
  - examining the background and purposes of those transactions and setting out findings in writing.

27.16.14 Staff Training

Financial institutions must establish, maintain and operate appropriate procedures in order to be satisfied of the integrity of any new employees.

Financial institutions should establish and maintain procedures to ensure that:

- All staff are made aware of the identity of the MLRO and of the procedures to follow when making an internal disclosure report; and
- All disclosure reports must reach the MLRO without undue delay.

Staff should be made aware of:

- Their financial institution's and their own personal statutory obligations and the possible consequences for failure to report suspicious transactions under the DTROP, the OSCO and the UNATMO;
- Any other statutory and regulatory obligations that concern their financial institution and themselves under the DTROP, the OSCO, the UNATMO, the UNSO and the AMLO, and the possible consequences of breaches of these obligations;

- The financial institution's policies and procedures relating to AML/CFT, including suspicious transaction identification and reporting; and
- Any new and emerging techniques, methods and trends in ML/TF to the extent that such information is needed by the staff to carry out their particular roles in the financial institution with respect to AML/CFT.

Additionally, specific training could be given depending on the role of the employee. Financial institutions should monitor the effectiveness of the training by testing staff and monitoring compliance with the systems which are in place.

27.16.15 *Record-keeping*

Customer Due Diligence Information

In relation to each of its customers, a financial institution must keep:

- The original or a copy of the documents, and a record of the data and information, obtained in the course of identifying and verifying the identity of the customer in accordance with CDD; and
- The original or a copy of the files relating to the customer's account and business correspondence with the customer and any beneficial owner of the customer

throughout the continuance of the business relationship with the customer and for a period of six years beginning on the date on which the business relationship ends.

For all types of record, if the record consists of a document, either the original of the document must be kept or a copy of the document must be kept either on microfilm or in the database of a computer. If the record consists of data or information, a record of the data or information must be kept either on microfilm or in the database of a computer.

Transaction Information

A financial institution must keep the original or a copy of the documents, and a record of the data and information, obtained in connection with the transaction for a period of six years beginning on the date on which the transaction is completed, regardless of whether the business relationship ends during that period.

27.16.16 *Suspicious Transaction Reporting*

The following is a (non-exhaustive) list of examples of situations that might give rise to suspicion in certain circumstances:

- Transactions or instructions which have no apparent legitimate purpose and/or appear not to have a commercial rationale;
- Transactions, instructions or activity that involve apparently unnecessary complexity or which do not constitute the most logical, convenient or secure way to do business;

- Where the customer refuses to provide the information requested without reasonable explanation or otherwise refuses to cooperate with the CDD and/or ongoing monitoring process;
- The extensive use of trusts or offshore structures in circumstances where the customer's needs are inconsistent with the use of such services;
- Unnecessary routing of funds or other property from/to third parties or through third party accounts.

All suspicious activity should be reported to the MLRO and must be documented (in urgent cases this may follow an initial discussion by telephone). The report must include the full details of the customer and as much information as possible giving rise to the suspicion. The MLRO must acknowledge receipt of the report and at the same time provide a reminder of the obligation regarding tipping off. The tipping-off provision includes circumstances where a suspicion has been raised internally, but has not yet been reported to the JFIU. The MLRO then assesses the situation with regard to all the circumstances.

If, after completing the evaluation, the MLRO decides that there are grounds for knowledge or suspicion, he should disclose the information to the JFIU as soon as it is reasonable to do so after his evaluation is complete, together with the information on which that knowledge or suspicion is based. Providing they act in good faith in deciding not to file an STR with the JFIU, it is unlikely that there will be any criminal liability for failing to report if an MLRO concludes that there is no suspicion after taking into account all available information. It is, however, vital for MLROs to keep proper records of their deliberations and actions taken to demonstrate they have acted in a reasonable manner.

27.16.17 Penalties

Generally, if a financial institution breaches the regulations, the sanctions in Hong Kong are:

- To publicly reprimand the financial institution;
- To order the financial institution to take, by a date specified by the relevant authority, any action specified by the relevant authority for the purpose of remedying the contravention; and
- To order the financial institution to pay a pecuniary penalty not exceeding the amount that is the greater of
  - $10,000,000; or
  - three times the amount of the profit gained, or costs avoided, by the financial institution as a result of the contravention.

If a financial institution fails to comply with an order to take remedial action made under subsection (1), the relevant authority may further order the financial institution to pay a daily pecuniary penalty not exceeding $100,000 for each day on which the failure continues after the date specified in the order as being the date by which the remedial action must be taken.

If a financial institution or any of its officers knowingly breaches the CDD requirements, the financial institution commits an offence and is liable:

- On conviction on indictment, to a fine of $1,000,000 and to imprisonment for two years; or
- On summary conviction, to a fine at level 6 and to imprisonment for six months.

If a financial institution or any of its officers, with intent to defraud any relevant authority, breaches the CDD requirements, the financial institution commits an offence and is liable:

- On conviction on indictment, to a fine of $1,000,000 and to imprisonment for seven years; or
- On summary conviction, to a fine of $500,000 and to imprisonment for one year.

If a person who is an employee of a financial institution or is employed to work for a financial institution or is concerned in the management of a financial institution knowingly causes or knowingly permits the financial institution to breach the CDD requirements, the person commits an offence and is liable:

- On conviction on indictment, to a fine of $1,000,000 and to imprisonment for two years; or
- On summary conviction to a fine at level 6 and to imprisonment for six months.

If a person who is an employee of a financial institution or is employed to work for a financial institution or is concerned in the management of a financial institution, with intent to defraud the financial institution or any relevant authority, causes or permits the financial institution to breach the CDD requirements, the person commits an offence and is liable:

- On conviction on indictment, to a fine of $1,000,000 and to imprisonment for seven years; or
- On summary conviction, to a fine of $500,000 and to imprisonment for one year.

Sections 25A of the DTROP and the OSCO make it an offence to fail to disclose where a person knows or suspects that property represents the proceeds of drug trafficking or of an indictable offence respectively. Likewise, Section 12 of the UNATMO makes it an offence to fail to disclose knowledge or suspicion of terrorist property. Under the DTROP and the OSCO, failure to report knowledge or suspicion carries a maximum penalty of three months' imprisonment and a fine of $50,000.

27.16.18 Case Studies

In the early 1990s, the ICAC conducted an undercover investigation into bribery and corruption at the Television and Entertainment Licensing Authority. Following suspicions of corruption, an undercover agent joined the organisation to find evidence of corruption from the inside. After a number of months working for the TELA, the agent found himself befriending various senior members of the company, who revealed the scale of corruption within the organisation. In one instance, the agent arrived at work to find a $30,000 watch on his desk, which was indicative of the way business was being done. Bribes were being given to members of TELA to forge the requisite documents, which were then approved by the two most senior members of the organisation – who were running the whole corruption ring.

The bribes were paid through a middle man. The first half was paid when the application was submitted, with the balance being paid when it was approved. By employing a middle man, there was no need for the two leaders to ever meet the beneficiary, or even for the parties to find out each other's identities. Furthermore, because all of the bribes were settled in cash, there was never any record of them, making them virtually impossible to trace. For these reasons, it took a nine-month undercover investigation to secure convictions against the guilty parties.

Hong Kong authorities convicted 166 people of money laundering in 2012. There have been two recent court cases in which a young delivery man from Guangdong province and a 61-year-old Hong Kong public housing tenant received jail terms of about ten years for laundering billions of dollars.

In another case in September 2012, a woman was convicted of money laundering in Hong Kong. She was the accounting manager of a company which, between August 2002 and March 2004, forged the sales figures by $300 million by submitting false overseas sales invoices. She used a circulation fund of $68 million transmitted through her own account to generate false sales. This highlights the need for financial institutions to thoroughly investigate the source of funds of their clients, as well as to conduct ongoing monitoring. This may have indicated that the funds were originating from one account.

27.17 COUNTRY PROFILE: INDIA

27.17.1 Overview

As a leader among the emerging economies in Asia with a strongly growing economy and demography, India faces a range of money-laundering and terrorist-financing risks. The main sources of money laundering in India result from a range of illegal activities committed within and outside the country, mainly drug trafficking, fraud, including counterfeiting of Indian currency, transnational organised crime, human trafficking and corruption.

India is considered a drug-transit country due to its strategic location between the countries of the Golden Triangle and the Golden Crescent. India is the world's largest producer of legal opium gum for pharmaceutical preparations, but it is estimated that between 20 and 30% of the opium crop is diverted. The illicit cultivation is believed to be mainly located in the areas of Arunachal Pradesh and Himachal Pradesh in the north of India.

27.17.2 Key Legislation

The Prevention of Money Laundering Act 2002 (PMLA) forms the core of the legal framework put in place by India to combat money laundering. The PMLA and the Rules notified thereunder came into force with effect from 1st July, 2005, and there were amendments in 2009. Circular DBOD.NO.AML.BC.58/14.01.001/2004–05, dated 29th November, 2004, provides additional KYC guidance for banks.

It has been reported that further amendments were drafted in 2011 to expand the scope of the money-laundering legislation, but these were not available at the time of writing.

27.17.3 Legislative History

The AML/CFT regime in India is relatively young. The Prevention of Money Laundering Act 2002 (PMLA) came into force in 2005 and was amended in 2009. The Unlawful Activities (Prevention) Act 1967 (UAPA) was amended in 2004 to criminalise, inter alia, terrorist financing. The UAPA was further amended in December 2008 to broaden its scope and to bring the legislation more in line with the requirements of the United Nations Convention for the Suppression of the Financing of Terrorism (FT Convention).

27.17.4 FATF Assessment

From mid-2009, India has increased its focus on money laundering and the use of the ML provisions. There are some important and, in some instances, long-standing legal issues, such as the threshold condition for domestic predicate offences, that remain to be resolved. Effectiveness concerns were primarily raised by the absence of any ML convictions.

Recently, India's serious commitment to combating terrorism in all its forms was acknowledged by the FATF. From a law-enforcement perspective, this commitment is reflected in an active pursuit of the financial aspects of terrorism. At the prosecutorial level, an appropriate focus on FT can be observed. At the June 2013 Plenary meeting, the FATF decided that India had reached a satisfactory level of compliance with all of the core and key Recommendations and could be removed from the regular follow-up process.

27.17.5 The Primary AML Investigation/Regulatory Authorities

FIU – India

Financial Intelligence Unit – India (FIU–IND) was set up by the Government of India vide O.M. dated 18th November, 2004 as the central national agency responsible for receiving, processing, analysing and disseminating information relating to suspect financial transactions. FIU–IND is also responsible for coordinating and strengthening efforts of national and international intelligence, investigation and enforcement agencies in pursuing the global efforts against money laundering and related crimes. FIU–IND is an independent body reporting directly to the Economic Intelligence Council (EIC) headed by the Finance Minister.

The main function of FIU–IND is to receive cash/suspicious transaction reports, analyse them and, as appropriate, disseminate valuable financial information to intelligence/enforcement agencies and regulatory authorities. The functions of FIU–IND are:

- **Collection of information:** To act as the central reception point for receiving cash transaction reports (CTRs) and suspicious transaction reports (STRs) from various reporting entities.
- **Analysis of information:** To analyse received information in order to uncover patterns of transactions suggesting suspicion of money laundering and related crimes.
- **Sharing of information:** To share information with national intelligence/law-enforcement agencies, national regulatory authorities and foreign financial intelligence units.
- **Act as central repository:** To establish and maintain a national database on cash transactions and suspicious transactions on the basis of reports received from reporting entities.
- **Coordination:** To coordinate and strengthen collection and sharing of financial intelligence through an effective national, regional and global network to combat money laundering and related crimes.
- **Research and analysis:** To monitor and identify strategic key areas on money-laundering trends, typologies and developments.

27.17.6 Outline of Specific Money-laundering Offences

Section 3 of the Prevention of Money Laundering Act 2002 defines the offence of money laundering as:

> *"Whosoever directly or indirectly attempts to indulge or knowingly assists or knowingly is a party or is actually involved in any process or activity connected with the proceeds of crime and projecting it as untainted property shall be guilty of the offence of money laundering."*

27.17.7 Penalties

Section 4 of the Prevention of Money Laundering Act 2002 specifies punishment for money laundering as:

> *"Whoever commits the offence of money laundering shall be punishable with rigorous imprisonment for a term which shall not be less than three years but which may extend to seven years and shall also be liable to a fine which may extend to five lakh rupees."*

Where the proceeds of crime involved in money laundering relate to any of the various firearms offences, the provisions of this section shall remain the same, except that the words "which may extend to ten years", shall replace the words "which may extend to seven years".

27.17.8 Scope

The PMLA and rules apply to banking companies, financial institutions and intermediaries.

27.17.9 Risk-based Approach

Clients should be categorised by firms into low, medium or high risk depending on the characteristics of the relationship.

Banks may prepare a profile for each new customer based on risk categorisation. The customer profile may contain information relating to a customer's identity, social/financial status, nature of business activity, information about their clients' business and their location, etc. The nature and extent of due diligence will depend on the risk perceived by the bank. However, while preparing customer profiles, banks should take care to seek only such information from the customer which is relevant to the risk category and is not intrusive. The customer profile will be a confidential document and details contained therein shall not be divulged for cross selling or any other purposes.

27.17.10 Role of the MLRO/Nominated Officer

Banks may appoint a senior management officer to be designated as Principal Officer. The Principal Officer shall be located at the head/corporate office of the bank and shall be responsible for monitoring and reporting of all transactions and sharing of information as required under the law. They should maintain close liaison with enforcement agencies, banks and any other institution involved in the fight against money laundering and combating the financing of terrorism.

27.17.11 Due Diligence

Every banking company, financial institution and intermediary shall, at the time of commencement of an account-based relationship, identify its clients, verify their identity and obtain information on the purpose and intended nature of the business relationship.

In all other cases, identity should be verified while carrying out:

- A transaction of an amount equal to or exceeding fifty thousand rupees, whether conducted as a single transaction or several transactions that appear to be connected; or
- Any international money transfer operations.

A "client" shall be taken to mean a person that engages in a financial transaction or activity with a banking company, financial institution or intermediary, and includes a person on whose behalf the person that engages in the transaction or activity is acting.

Personal Client Due Diligence

Documents needed for verification are as follows:

- One certified copy of an "officially valid document" containing details of the customer's identity and address;
- One recent photograph;
- Such other documents, including in respect of the nature of business and financial status of the client, as may be required by the banking company, financial institution or intermediary.

A photograph need not be submitted by a client who does not have an account-based relationship.

An "officially valid document" means a passport, driving licence, Permanent Account Number (PAN) Card, a Voter's Identity Card issued by the Election Commission of India or any other document as may be required by the banking company, financial institution or intermediary.

Corporate Customer Due Diligence

For a company, the documents needed for verification are as follows:

- Certificate of Incorporation;
- Memorandum and articles of association;
- A resolution from the board of directors and power of attorney granted to its managers, officers or employees to transact on its behalf; and
- An officially valid document in respect of managers, officers or employees holding an attorney to transact on its behalf.

For a partnership, the documents needed for verification are as follows:

- Registration certificate;
- Partnership deed; and
- An officially valid document in respect of the person holding an attorney to transact on its behalf.

For a trust, the documents needed for verification are as follows:

- Registration certificate;
- Trust deed; and
- An officially valid document in respect of the person holding an attorney to transact on its behalf.

Beneficial Ownership

Every banking company, financial institution and intermediary, as the case may be, shall determine whether a client is acting on behalf of a beneficial owner, identify the beneficial owner and take all reasonable steps to verify their identity.

Within India, the legal definition of "beneficial owner" is the natural person who ultimately owns or controls a client and/or the person on whose behalf a transaction is being conducted, and includes a person who exercises ultimate effective control over a judicial person.

Simplified Customer Due Diligence

For the purpose of risk categorisation, individuals (other than those of high net worth) and entities whose identities and sources of wealth can be easily identified and transactions in whose accounts by and large conform to the known profile, may be categorised as low risk.

Illustrative examples of low-risk customers could be:

- Salaried employees whose salary structures are well defined;
- People belonging to lower economic strata of society whose accounts show small balances and low turnover;
- Government departments and government-owned companies;
- Regulators and statutory bodies, etc.

In such cases, the policy implemented by the firm may require that only the basic requirements of verifying the identity and location of the customer are to be met. However, under the risk-based approach, the firm should still conduct such work as is considered necessary to confirm that the reduced level of identification is considered sufficient.

Enhanced Customer Due Diligence

Customers that are likely to pose a higher-than-average risk to the bank may be categorised as medium or high risk depending on the customer's background, nature and location of activity, country of origin, sources of funds, client profile, etc.

Banks may apply enhanced due diligence measures based on a risk assessment, thereby requiring intensive "due diligence" for higher risk customers, especially those for whom the sources of funds are not clear. Examples of customers requiring higher due diligence may include:

- Non-resident customers;
- High net worth individuals;
- Trusts, charities, NGOs and organisations receiving donations;
- Companies with close family shareholdings or beneficial ownership;
- Firms with "sleeping partners";
- Politically exposed persons (PEPs) of foreign origin;
- Non-face-to-face customers;
- Those with a dubious reputation as per available public information.

Non-face-to-face Customer Due Diligence

With the introduction of telephone and electronic banking, accounts are increasingly being opened by banks for customers without the need for the customer to visit the bank branch. In the case of non-face-to-face customers, apart from applying the usual customer identification procedures, there must be specific and adequate procedures to mitigate the higher risk involved.

Certification of all the documents presented may be insisted upon and, if necessary, additional documents may be called for. In such cases, banks may also require the first payment to be effected through the customer's account with another bank which, in turn, adheres to similar Know Your Customer (KYC) standards. In the case of cross-border customers, there is the additional difficulty of matching the customer with the documentation, and the bank may have to rely on third party certification/introduction. In such cases, it must be ensured that the third party is a regulated and supervised entity and has adequate KYC systems in place.

Politically Exposed Persons

Banks should gather sufficient information on any person/customer of this category intending to establish a relationship and check all the information available on the person in the public domain.

Banks should also verify the identity of the person and seek information about the sources of funds before accepting the PEP as a customer. The decision to open an account for a PEP should be taken at a senior level, which should be clearly spelt out in Customer Acceptance policy. Banks should also subject such accounts to enhanced monitoring on an ongoing basis. The above norms may also be applied to the accounts of the family members or close relatives of PEPs.

Anonymous Accounts

Anonymous accounts are prohibited.

27.17.12 Ongoing Monitoring

Ongoing monitoring is an essential element of any firm maintaining effective Know Your Customer (KYC) procedures. Banks can effectively control and reduce their risk only if they have an understanding of the normal and reasonable activity of the customer, so that they have the means of identifying transactions that fall outside the regular pattern of activity. However, the extent of monitoring will depend on the risk sensitivity of the account.

Banks should pay special attention to all complex, unusually large transactions and all unusual patterns which have no apparent economic or visible lawful purpose. The bank may prescribe threshold limits for a particular category of accounts and pay particular attention to the transactions which exceed these limits.

Transactions that involve large amounts of cash inconsistent with the normal and expected activity of the customer should particularly attract the attention of the bank. Very high account turnover inconsistent with the size of the balance maintained may indicate to a firm that funds are being washed through the account.

High-risk accounts have to be subjected by a firm to intensified monitoring. Every bank should set key indicators for such accounts, taking note of the background of the customer, such as the country of origin, sources of funds, the type of transactions involved and other risk factors. Banks should put in place a system of periodical review of risk categorisation of accounts and the need for applying enhanced due diligence measures.

Banks should ensure that a record of transactions in the accounts is preserved and maintained as required in terms of Section 12 of the PMLA 2002. They should also ensure that transactions of a suspicious nature and/or any other type of transaction notified under Section 12 of the PMLA 2002, are reported to the appropriate law-enforcement authority.

27.17.13 Record-keeping

Every banking company, financial institution and intermediary shall maintain records of identity and current address or addresses including permanent address or addresses of its clients, the nature of business of the clients and their financial status.

The records of the identity of clients shall be maintained for a period of ten years from the date of cessation of the transactions between the client and the banking company or financial institution or intermediary.

Every banking company, financial institution and intermediary shall:

- Maintain a record of all transactions, the nature and value of which may be prescribed, whether such transactions comprise a single transaction or a series of transactions integrally connected to each other, and where such series of transactions take place within a month;
- Furnish information of transactions referred to above to the Director within such time as may be prescribed;
- Verify and maintain the records of the identity of all its clients, in such a manner as may be prescribed.

Where the Principal Officer of a banking company, financial institution or intermediary has reason to believe that a single transaction or series of transactions integrally connected to each other have been valued below the prescribed value so as to defeat the provisions of this section, such officer shall furnish information in respect of such transactions to the Director within the prescribed time.

The transaction records referred to above shall be maintained for a period of ten years from the date of said transactions between the clients and the banking company, financial institution or intermediary.

The identity records referred to above shall be maintained for a period of ten years from the date of cessation of transactions between the clients and the banking company, financial institution or intermediary.

Every banking company, financial institution or intermediary shall maintain a record of all transactions, including records of:

- All cash transactions with a value of more than ten lakh rupees, or its equivalent in foreign currency;
- All series of cash transactions integrally connected to each other which have been valued below ten lakh rupees, or its equivalent in foreign currency, where such a series of transactions has taken place within a month;
- All transactions involving receipts by non-profit organisations with a value of more than ten lakh rupees, or its equivalent in foreign currency;
- All cash transactions where forged or counterfeit currency notes or bank notes have been used as genuine or where any forgery of a valuable security or a document has taken place facilitating the transactions;
- All suspicious transactions whether or not made in cash and by way of:
  - deposits and credits, withdrawals into or from any accounts in whatsoever name they are referred to in any currency maintained by way of:
    - cheques including third party cheques, pay orders, demand drafts, cashiers' cheques or any other instrument of payment of money including electronic receipts or credits and electronic payments or debits, or
    - traveller's cheques, or
    - transfer from one account within the same banking company, financial institution or intermediary, including from or to Nostro and Vostro accounts, or
    - any other mode by whatsoever name it is referred to;
  - credits or debits into or from any non-monetary accounts such as d-mat accounts, security accounts in any currency maintained by the banking company, financial institution or intermediary;
  - money transfers or remittances in favour of the firm's own clients or non-clients from India or abroad and to third party beneficiaries in India or abroad, including transactions on its own account in any currency by any of the following:
    - payment orders,
    - cashiers' cheques,

  - demand drafts,
  - telegraphic or wire transfers or electronic remittances or transfers,
  - internet transfers,
  - Automated Clearing House remittances,
  - lock-box-driven transfers or remittances,
  - remittances for credit or loading to electronic cards, or any other mode of money transfer by whatsoever name it is called;
- loans and advances including credit or loan substitutes, investments and contingent liabilities by way of:
  - subscription to debt instruments such as commercial paper, certificates of deposit, preferential shares, debentures, securitised participation, inter-bank participation or any other investments in securities or the like in whatever form and name they are referred to,
  - purchase and negotiation of bills, cheques and other instruments,
  - foreign exchange contracts, currency, interest rate and commodity instruments and any other derivative instrument by whatsoever name it is called,
  - letters of credit, standby letters of credit, guarantees, comfort letters, solvency certificates and any other instrument for settlement and/or credit support;

- Collection services in any currency by way of collection of bills, cheques, instruments or any other mode of collection in whatsoever name it is referred to.

The records referred to above shall contain all necessary information specified by the regulator to permit reconstruction of individual transactions, including the following information:

- The nature of the transaction;
- The amount of the transaction and the currency in which it was denominated;
- The date on which the transaction was conducted; and
- The parties to the transaction.

27.17.14 Reporting Requirements

The Director may, either on their own judgment or on an application made by any authority, officer or person, call for records and may make such inquiry or cause such inquiry to be made, as he thinks fit.

27.17.15 Internal Requirements

Every banking company, financial institution and intermediary shall formulate and implement a client identification programme that it considers appropriate to enable it to determine the true identity of its clients as per the requirements under the PMLA.

27.17.16 Suspicious Transaction Reporting

Every banking company, financial institution and intermediary shall furnish to the FIU–IND information of all suspicious transactions whether or not made in cash.

A suspicious transaction means a transaction, including an attempted transaction, whether or not made in cash which, to a person acting in good faith:

- Gives rise to a reasonable ground of suspicion that it may involve proceeds of an offence specified in the Schedule to the Act, regardless of the value involved; or
- Appears to be made in circumstances of unusual or unjustified complexity; or
- Appears to have no economic rationale or bona fide purpose; or
- Gives rise to a reasonable ground of suspicion that it may involve financing of the activities relating to terrorism.

India has set out a series of broad categories that give reason for suspicion. The examples set out as being suspicious transactions in respect of a banking company are as follows:

Identity of Client

- False identification documents;
- Identification documents which could not be verified within a reasonable time;
- Accounts opened with names very close to other established business entities.

Background of Client

- Suspicious background or links with known criminals.

Multiple Accounts

- A large number of accounts having a common account holder, introducer or authorised signatory with no rationale;
- Unexplained transfers between multiple accounts with no rationale.

Activity in Accounts

- Unusual activity compared with past transactions;
- Sudden activity in dormant accounts;
- Activity inconsistent with what would be expected from declared business.

Nature of Transactions

- Unusual or unjustified complexity;
- No economic rationale or bona fide purpose;
- Frequent purchases of drafts or other negotiable instruments with cash;
- Nature of transactions inconsistent with what would be expected from declared business.

Value of Transactions

- Value just under the reporting threshold amount in an apparent attempt to avoid reporting;
- Value inconsistent with the client's apparent financial standing.

27.17.17 Penalties

If the Director, in the course of any inquiry, finds that a banking company, financial institution or an intermediary or any of its officers has failed to comply with the record-keeping provisions, then, without prejudice to any other action that may be taken under any other provisions of this Act, he may, by an order, levy a fine on such banking company or financial institution or intermediary which shall not be less than ten thousand rupees but may extend to one lakh rupees for each failure.

27.17.18 Case Studies

A major bank in India was fined Rs 5 lakh after it was found that it had inadequate KYC procedures in place. The FIU investigated the bank after a report was submitted alleging that Rs 72 lakh in cash had been deposited at the bank by a mystery customer, who then received pay orders, deposited them in multiple accounts and withdrew the cash immediately. The accounts then disappeared as soon as the cash was withdrawn. In response to this, the bank was audited, and the conclusion was reached that Know Your Customer guidelines were not being followed, resulting in the Rs 5 lakh fine.

27.18 COUNTRY PROFILE: ISLE OF MAN

27.18.1 Overview

The Isle of Man, despite not being an FATF member, has a strong money-laundering-deterrence regime which is largely compliant with international standards. It regularly updates its legislation and guidance to retain a strong reputation for AML enforcement.

27.18.2 Key Legislation

The Money Laundering and Terrorist Financing Code 2013 provides the current enforceable AML legislation in the Isle of Man. In addition to this, the *AML Handbook* provides further guidance.

27.18.3 Legislative History

The Isle of Man legislative framework for anti-money laundering and countering the financing of terrorism (AML/CFT) has been in place and effective since 1990. This legislation has been regularly updated to deal with new threats that have emerged. New legislation has strengthened the Isle of Man's defences against all crimes, money laundering and international terrorism, for example, the Criminal Justice (Money Laundering Offences) Act 1998, which amended the Criminal Justice Act 1990, the Proceeds of Crime Act, the Anti-Terrorism and Crime Act 2003 and the Terrorism (Finance) Act 2009.

The recent legislation updated the Proceeds of Crime (Money Laundering) Code 2010 (AML Code) and the Prevention of Terrorist Financing Code 2011 (CFT Code), together referred to as "the Codes".

27.18.4 FATF Assessment

Like Guernsey, the Isle of Man is not an FATF member. However, it is a member of the Group of International Finance Centre Supervisors (GIFCS), a body that is an observer to the FATF. The most recent IMF report found that the Isle of Man has brought its AML/CFT preventive measures largely into compliance with the FATF Recommendations, and that all IOM financial institutions are well supervised for AML/CFT purposes. The Financial Crime Unit (FCU), acting as the financial intelligence unit (FIU), performs its role adequately, but will require additional resources. The IOM authorities actively engage in international cooperation.

27.18.5 The Primary AML Investigation/Regulatory Authorities

The Financial Supervision Commission

The Financial Supervision Commission (FSC) is the independent statutory body whose authorisation and functions are laid out in the Financial Services Act 2008. These are as follows:

- The regulation and supervision of persons undertaking regulated activities (i.e. deposit-taking, investment business, services to collective investment schemes, fiduciary services, money transmission services) in or from the Isle of Man;

- The maintenance and development of the regulatory regime for regulated activities; and
- The oversight of directors and persons responsible for the management, administration or affairs of commercial entities.

In addition to this, the Commission's regulatory objectives are:

- To secure an appropriate degree of protection for the customers of persons carrying on a regulated activity;
- To reduce financial crime; and
- To support the island's economy and its development as an international financial centre.

Financial Crime Unit

The Financial Crime Unit is a multi-agency unit, consisting of police and customs officers, police support staff and other government departments such as Internal Audit and HM Attorney General's Chambers. The unit deals with the prevention, detection and investigation of serious financial crime, money laundering and terrorism financing. Within the unit are three distinct teams:

1. The Financial Intelligence Team which receives suspicious activity reports submitted by the financial sector or anybody in business who suspects money laundering or terrorism financing.
2. The Overseas Assistance Team which deals with all International Letters of Request or other assistance procedures provided for through Mutual Legal Assistance Treaties.
3. The Investigations Team which deals with all investigations.

27.18.6 Outline of Specific Money-laundering Offences

A person commits an offence if they enter into, or become concerned in, an arrangement which they know or suspect facilitates (by whatever means) the acquisition, retention, use or control of criminal property by, or on behalf of, another person.

In addition, a person commits an offence if they:

- Acquire criminal property;
- Use criminal property;
- Have possession of criminal property.

Tipping Off

A person commits the offence of tipping off if:

- The person discloses any matter regarding money-laundering investigation or suspicion; and

- The disclosure is likely to prejudice any investigation that might be conducted following the disclosure referred to in that subsection; and
- The information on which the disclosure is based came to the person in the course of business in the regulated sector.

It should be noted that a person also commits an offence if:

- The person discloses that an investigation into allegations that an offence under this Part has been committed, is being contemplated or is being carried out;
- The disclosure is likely to prejudice that investigation; and
- The information on which the disclosure is based came to the person in the course of business in the regulated sector.

27.18.7 *Defences*

There is a safe harbour available if that person or another person has made a disclosure:

- To a constable or customs officer serving (in either case) with the Financial Crime Unit of the Isle of Man Constabulary; or
- To a nominated officer,

of information that came to that person in the course of business in the regulated sector.

27.18.8 *Scope*

Any entity which carries out a regulated activity, as specified in the Regulated Activities Order 2011, must apply for a licence to be regulated by the FSC. This includes various financial and investment businesses. There are certain exempted businesses under the Financial Services (Exemptions) Regulations 2011.

27.18.9 *Risk-based Approach*

The Financial Supervision Commission recommends a risk-based approach which is proportionate to the scale of business operations. However, licence holders should avoid rigid internal systems of control as these can encourage the development of a "tick box" mentality that can be counter-productive. Internal systems should require employees to properly consider the risks posed by individual customers and relationships and to react appropriately. When considering how best to monitor customer transactions and behaviour, a licence holder should take into account:

- The size and complexity of its business;
- Its business risk assessment;
- The nature of its systems and controls;
- The monitoring procedures that already exist to satisfy other business needs; and
- The nature of the products and services and the means of delivery.

Methods to be considered include:

- Simple exception reports to advise supervisors/operations managers of large transactions for their review;
- More complex exception reports to advise the MLRO, or other appropriate staff, of customers and transactions matching certain predetermined criteria;
- Computerised transaction-monitoring systems.

27.18.10 Role of the MLRO/Nominated Officer

Licence holders are required to appoint an MLRO and an Officer, but the Commission expects licence holders to appoint the same individual to both of these roles. In essence, the role of the MLRO and the Officer is the same, so MLRO is used as a blanket term.

The MLRO is the person who is nominated to ultimately receive internal reports and who considers any report in the light of all other relevant information for the purpose of determining whether or not it gives rise to knowledge or a suspicion of money laundering and/or terrorist financing.

Licence holders are also required to appoint a Deputy MLRO to cover for any absence of the MLRO. The Deputy MLRO should be of similar status and experience to the MLRO. For the avoidance of doubt, the Deputy MLRO should cover all of the MLRO's responsibilities in their absence, including those under the CFT Code. MLROs and Deputy MLROs should not be placed in any situation of conflict of interest.

In order that they can carry out their responsibilities effectively, the MLRO and Deputy MLRO should:

- Normally be resident in the Isle of Man;
- Have a sufficient level of seniority, independence and authority within the business;
- Be carrying out a compliance, audit or legal role;
- Have sufficient resources, including sufficient time and support staff;
- Have regular contact with, and ready access to, the board and other members of senior management to ensure that executive management is able to satisfy itself that the statutory obligations are being met and that the business is taking sufficiently robust measures to protect itself against the risk of money laundering and terrorist financing;
- Be fully aware of both their own and their organisation's AML/CFT obligations; and
- Have access to all relevant information which may be of assistance in evaluating STRs.

Licence holders must notify the Commission of the proposed appointment and identity of the MLRO and Deputy MLRO and any subsequent changes.

The responsibilities of the MLRO will normally include:

- Undertaking the internal review of all suspicions in light of all available relevant information and determining whether or not such suspicions have substance and require disclosure to the FCU;

- Maintaining all related records;
- Giving guidance on how to avoid tipping off the customer if any disclosure is made and managing any resulting constructive trust scenarios;
- Providing support and guidance to the board and senior management to ensure that money-laundering and terrorist-financing risks are adequately managed;
- Liaising with the FCU and, if required, the Commission and participating in any other third party enquiries in relation to money-laundering or terrorist-financing prevention and detection, investigation or compliance; and
- Providing reports and other information to senior management.

27.18.11 Due Diligence

A risk-based approach to CDD is one that takes a number of discrete steps in assessing the most effective and proportionate way to manage the money-laundering and terrorist-financing risks faced by a licence holder.

The risk assessment of a particular customer will determine:

- The extent of identification information to be sought;
- Any additional information that needs to be requested;
- How that information will be verified and for whom; and
- The extent to which the relationship will be monitored.

It will also help to guard against identity theft.

Unless it is obvious from the product being provided, the following must be established:

- The purpose and intended nature of the relationship;
- The expected type, volume and value of activity;
- The expected geographical sphere of the activity;
- The activity providing the source of funds for the relationship and geographical sphere of the activity;
- Details of any existing relationships with the product/service provider.

Personal Client Due Diligence

Identification information that must be collected in respect of all personal customers and other natural persons who need to be identified comprises the following:

- Legal name, any former names (e.g. maiden name) and any other names used;
- Permanent residential address including postcode if applicable;
- Date of birth;
- Place of birth;

- Nationality;
- Gender.

For standard and higher-risk customers, an official personal identification number or other unique identifier contained in an unexpired official document must also be obtained.

Corporate Customer Due Diligence

In the case of legal persons, the following information should also be established:

- If applicable, group ownership and structure sufficient to understand the ownership and control structure;
- The nature of activities undertaken (having regard for sensitive activities and trading activities);
- The geographical sphere of the legal person's activities and assets;
- The name of the regulator, if applicable.

Information sufficient to establish the source of income or wealth should be obtained for all higher-risk relationships and all other relationships where the type of product or service being offered makes it appropriate to do so because of its risk profile. This will also include where the product or service is not consistent with information held on the customer.

Politically Exposed Persons

Licence holders can reduce risk by conducting detailed CDD at the outset of the relationship and on an ongoing basis where they know or suspect that the business relationship is with a PEP. Licence holders are required to have in place enhanced CDD measures to address PEP risk.

In particular, enhanced CDD must include:

- Appropriate procedures to determine, as far as reasonably practicable, whether an applicant for business, a customer, any natural person having power to direct the activities of an applicant for business or a customer, a beneficial owner or a known beneficiary of a legal arrangement is a PEP.
- Close scrutiny of any complex structures (e.g. involving legal persons, legal arrangements and multiple jurisdictions) so as to establish that there is a clear and legitimate reason for using such structures and a financial centre such as the Isle of Man. It should be borne in mind that most legitimate political figures would expect their personal affairs to be undertaken in a more than usually open manner, rather than the reverse.
- Every effort to establish the source of income/wealth (including the economic activity that created the wealth) as well as the source of funds involved in the relationship, establishing that these are legitimate, both at the outset of the relationship and on an ongoing basis.

- Approval of senior management before commencing the business relationship and regular review, on at least an annual basis, of the development of the relationship.
- Close scrutiny of any unusual features, such as very large transactions, the use of government or central bank accounts, particular demands for secrecy, the use of cash or bearer bonds or other instruments which break an audit trail, the use of small and unknown financial institutions in secrecy jurisdictions and regular transactions involving sums just below a typical reporting amount.

There should be full documentation of the information collected in line with the above.

Correspondent Banking

Before entering into a business relationship or one-off transaction involving correspondent banking services or other similar arrangements, licence holders must take steps additional to CDD requirements, as follows:

- Obtain sufficient information about the respondent bank to understand fully the nature of its business;
- Determine, from publicly available information, the respondent bank's reputation and quality of supervision, including whether it has been subject to a money-laundering or terrorist-financing investigation or regulatory action;
- Assess the respondent bank's AML/CFT procedures and controls, and ascertain that they are adequate and effective;
- Obtain senior management approval, i.e. sign off before establishing new correspondent banking relationships; and
- Document the respective AML/CFT responsibilities of the licence holder and the respondent bank.

Where correspondent banking services involve a payable-through account, a licence holder must be satisfied that the respondent bank:

- Has taken steps complying with the requirements formerly of Recommendation 5 (CDD and record-keeping), now FATF Recommendation 10 of the FATF Recommendations with respect to every customer having direct access to the account; and
- Will provide relevant evidence of the customer's identity on request.

Shell Banking

Licence holders must not enter into or continue correspondent banking relationships with shell banks. In addition, licence holders must be satisfied that the respondent banks with which they have correspondent banking relationships do not permit their accounts to be used by shell banks.

27.18.12 Ongoing Monitoring

Entities should have adequate systems to monitor risk on an ongoing basis. Licence holders must monitor the conduct and activities of the customer to ensure that they are consistent with the nature of business, the risk profile, source of funding and estimated turnover that was determined when the relationship was established.

Where the basis of the relationship changes significantly, licence holders must carry out further CDD procedures to ensure that the revised risk and basis of the relationship is fully understood. Ongoing monitoring procedures must take account of these changes.

Licence holders must ensure that any updated CDD information obtained through meetings, discussions or other methods of communication with the customer is recorded and retained with the customer's records. That information must be available to the MLRO.

27.18.13 Staff Training

Training should be structured to ensure compliance with all of the requirements of the applicable legislation at least annually. Each licence holder can tailor its training programmes to suit its own needs and those of its employees to whom it is delivered, depending on size, resources and the type of business it undertakes. In particular, training should cover the following.

New Employees

Irrespective of seniority, training for all new employees who will be dealing with customers, client companies or their transactions must cover:

- A general introduction to the background to money laundering and terrorist financing;
- A clear indication of the importance placed on AML/CFT issues by the organisation;
- The legal requirement to make disclosures and their personal legal obligations in this regard; and
- The procedures for reporting suspicious transactions to the MLRO.

This training must be provided prior to them becoming actively involved in day-to-day operations.

Front-line Employees

Employees who are responsible for opening new accounts, forming new client entities or dealing with new customers must receive relevant training in:

- The need to obtain satisfactory information and verification for all areas of CDD including documentary evidence of the customer's identity;
- Their obligation to make disclosures even if the transaction, activity or business relationship does not proceed, in respect of both new and existing business relationships;
- Factors that may give rise to suspicions about a customer or client entity's activities; and
- The procedures to follow when a transaction, activity or attempted transaction or activity is considered to be suspicious.

Employees should also be vigilant when dealing with occasional customers or companies established for a single purpose, especially where large cash transactions or bearer securities are involved.

Employees involved in processing deals or transactions must receive relevant training in:

- Processing and verification procedures;
- Recognising abnormal company activity, abnormal settlement, payment or delivery instructions, or any change in the normal pattern of business;
- The type of suspicious transactions or activity that may need reporting to the relevant authorities regardless of whether the transaction was completed; and
- The procedures to follow when a transaction, activity or attempted transaction or activity is considered to be suspicious.

Managerial Employees

Employees who are managerially responsible for handling customer transactions or business relationships must receive a higher level of training, covering all aspects of AML/CFT procedures including:

- Offences and penalties arising from relevant primary legislation for non-reporting or for assisting money launderers or those involved in terrorist financing;
- Procedures for dealing with Production and Restraint Orders;
- Requirements for verification of identity and retention of records; and
- In particular, the application of the licence holder's risk-based strategy and procedures.

27.18.14 Record-keeping

The records prepared and maintained by any financial services business must be such that:

- Supervisors, auditors and law-enforcement agencies will be able to assess the effectiveness of the AML/CFT policies and procedures that are maintained by a licence holder;
- Any transactions or instructions effected via the licence holder on behalf of any individual customer can be reconstructed;
- The audit trail for funds entering and leaving the Isle of Man is clear and complete;
- Any customer can be properly identified and located;
- A CDD profile can be established for all customers for whom there is a business relationship;
- All suspicions received internally, and STRs made externally, can be identified;
- The rationale for not passing on any internal suspicions to the FCU can be understood; and
- A licence holder can satisfy, within a reasonable time frame, any enquiries or court orders from the appropriate authorities as to disclosure of information.

Customer Due Diligence Information

Records relating to verification of identity must comprise the evidence itself or a copy of it or, if that is not readily available, information reasonably sufficient to obtain such a copy. Licence holders must retain CDD records, including the supporting evidence and methods used to verify identity, for at least five years after the account is closed or the business relationship ends.

Where a disclosure has been made to a constable with the FCU or a licence holder knows or believes that a matter is under investigation, the licence holder must retain the records for as long as required by the constable.

Transaction Information

Licence holders are required to maintain a record containing details of all transactions carried out with, or for, a customer in the course of their regulated business activities.

In every case, transaction records must contain:

- Details of the customer or counterparty, including account details;
- The nature of the transaction; and
- Details of the transaction.

Licence holders must ensure that a satisfactory audit trail can be established for AML/CFT purposes and that a financial profile of a suspected account or client company can be established. To satisfy this requirement, the following additional information must be sought, as appropriate, and transaction records retained of:

- The volume of funds flowing through the account/turnover of client entity;
- The origin of the funds;
- The form in which the funds were offered or withdrawn, i.e. cash, cheque, etc.;
- The identity of the person undertaking the transaction;
- The destination of the funds;
- The form of instruction and authority;
- The name and address (or identification code) of the counterparty;
- The security dealt in, including price and size;
- Whether the transaction was a purchase or a sale;
- The account details from which the funds were paid (including, in the case of cheques, bank name, sort code, account number and name of account holder);
- The form and destination of payment made by the business to the customer;
- Whether the investments were held in safe custody by the business or sent to the customer or to his/her order and, if so, to what name and address;
- Activities of the client entity; and
- Any large item/exception reports created in the course of transaction monitoring.

In order to comply with the Codes, licence holders must retain transaction records for at least five years from the date when all activities relating to the transaction were completed.

Where an STR has been made to a constable with the FCU or a licence holder knows or believes that a matter is under investigation, the licence holder must retain the records for as long as required by the constable.

Internal Suspicion Reports

Licence holders must establish and maintain a register of all money-laundering and financing of terrorism reports made to the MLRO or Deputy MLRO. The register must include details of:

- The date the report was made;
- The person who made the report;
- Whether the report was made to the MLRO or the Deputy MLRO; and
- Information to allow the papers relevant to the report to be located.

Training Information

Licence holders must maintain records which include:

- Details of the content of the training programmes provided;
- The names of staff who have received the training;
- The date on which the training was delivered; and
- The results of any testing carried out to measure staff understanding of the money-laundering requirements.

27.18.15 Suspicious Transaction Reporting

It is an offence to fail to disclose, where a person knows or suspects or has reasonable grounds for knowing or suspecting, that a terrorist-financing offence has been committed. Once knowledge or suspicion or reasonable grounds for knowledge or suspicion have been formed, the following general principles must be applied:

- In the event of suspicion of money laundering or terrorist financing, a disclosure must be made even where there has been no transaction by or through the licence holder.
- Disclosures must be made as soon as is reasonably practical after the suspicion was first identified.

It is the responsibility of the MLRO (or, if appropriate, the Deputy MLRO) to consider all internal disclosures he/she receives in light of full access to all relevant documentation and other parties. If, after completing the evaluation, the MLRO decides that there are grounds for knowledge, suspicion or reasonable grounds to suspect money laundering or terrorist financing or attempted money laundering or attempted terrorist financing, he should disclose the information to the FCU as soon as practicable after his evaluation is complete.

27.18.16 Penalties

Failure to comply with the AML Code is a criminal offence. On summary conviction, the AML Code carries a maximum custodial period of six months or a fine not exceeding £5,000 or both. On conviction on information, it carries a maximum custodial period of two years or a fine or both.

Failure to comply with the CFT Code is also a criminal offence. On summary conviction, the CFT Code carries a maximum custodial period of 12 months or a fine not exceeding £5,000 or both. On conviction on information, it carries a maximum custodial period of two years or a fine or both.

In determining whether an offence has been committed, a court may take account of any relevant supervisory or regulatory guidance which applies to that person and which is given by a competent authority. Failure to comply with the minimum requirements of the handbook may be regarded by the Commission as an indication of:

- Conduct that is not in the best economic interests or which damages the reputation of the Isle of Man;
- Lack of fitness and propriety; and/or
- A failure to comply with certain fundamental principles within the Codes.

This may, therefore, result in regulatory action at the discretion of the Commission and, in extreme cases, it may result in revocation of a licence.

27.18.17 Case Studies

A multi-millionaire was sentenced to six years in prison after being convicted of money laundering in the Isle of Man. His business interests included the Miss World competition, and he was listed in the Sunday Times Rich List. The businessman utilised complex international corporate structures to transfer funds from Switzerland to the Isle of Man, with the help of his wife. The money originated from a false accounting scheme, whereby shares in a company were sold at hugely inflated prices on the strength of falsified sales figures and records, meaning that vast sums of money were made on worthless shares. The money was then laundered through Swiss and Isle of Man bank accounts, the value of which ran into millions of pounds. This case illustrates the need for vigilance when money is being moved between jurisdictions, especially when "tax havens" are involved.

27.19 COUNTRY PROFILE: JAPAN

27.19.1 Overview

According to the US Report on Japan, although the Japanese government continues to strengthen legal institutions to permit more effective enforcement of anti-money-laundering/counter-terrorist-financing (AML/CFT) laws, Japan's compliance with international standards specific to financial institutions is notably deficient. The domestic crime rate in Japan is generally low, although, in common with other countries, the number of prosecutions regarding money-laundering cases is increasing steeply, but this still remains relatively low. The Japanese AML framework does have strengths, but on the whole there are still improvements needed to bring it up to international standards.

27.19.2 Key Legislation

The Anti-Drug Special Provisions Law and the Act on Punishment of Organised Crimes outline the money-laundering offences. The Act on Prevention of Transfer of Criminal Proceeds outlines the compliance requirements.

27.19.3 Legislative History

Japan's money-laundering legislation rested heavily on the predicate offences surrounding drug trafficking and other related offences until 1999. This emphasis stemmed from the fact that the main authority was contained in the law concerning Special Provisions for Narcotics and Psychotropic Control. 1999 saw the enactment of The Punishment of Organised Crime, Control of Crime Proceeds and Matters (Act No 136 of 1999).

The most recent legislative developments have been consolidated through the Act on the Prevention of the Transfer of Criminal Proceeds (Act No 22 of 2007). The key current legislation is:

- The Act on the Prevention of the Transfer of Criminal Proceeds (Act No 22 of 2007);
- The Punishment of Organised Crime, Control of Crime Proceeds and Matters (Act No 136 of 1999);
- The UN Convention on Terrorist Financing was incorporated through the Punishment of Financing of Offences through Public Intimidation (Law No 67 of 2002).

An additional law to prevent diversion of criminal proceeds went into full force on 1st March, 2008. Its primary purpose is to prevent money laundering. Until its implementation, the law covered mainly financial institutions. It now applies to real estate agents, precious metal dealers and jewellers as well as judicial scriveners, administrative scriveners, certified public accountants and licensed tax accountants.

In April 2011, Japan amended its basic AML law, the Criminal Proceeds Act, to improve customer due diligence (CDD) requirements. These requirements came into effect in April 2013.

Furthermore, Japan has not implemented a risk-based approach to AML/CFT, and there is currently no requirement for enhanced due diligence for higher-risk customers, business relationships and transactions. Although the April 2011 amendments to the Criminal Proceeds Act refer to a higher risk, they only require financial institutions to verify a customer's assets and income where there is a suspicion of the use of a false identity. There is no requirement to take into account any risks posed by the business itself. The current regulations also do not authorise simplified due diligence, though there are exemptions to the identification obligation on the grounds that the customer or transaction poses no or little risk of money laundering or terrorist financing.

27.19.4 FATF Assessment

The 2008 mutual evaluation found that although the ML legal provisions are sound, the CDD and STR requirements as well as the investigations carried out by JAFIC could all be significantly improved.

27.19.5 The Primary AML Investigation/Regulatory Authorities

National Public Safety Commission

The Act on Prevention of Transfer of Criminal Proceeds clarified that the National Public Safety Commission (NPSC), which controls the National Police Agency and is aided by it, is responsible for prompt and appropriate collection, arrangement and analysis of suspicious transaction reports filed from specified business operators. The Act also granted the NPSC a function related to the handling of STRs, including their dissemination to foreign FIUs as well as a function to complement supervisory measures against specified business operators. JAFIC (see below) was established within the Organised Crime Department, the Criminal Investigation Bureau of the National Police Agency, as Japan's new FIU to perform these functions.

Japan Financial Intelligence Center

The Japan Financial Intelligence Center (JAFIC) acts as the Japanese FIU. JAFIC plans and examines the legal system related to AML and provides various measures, such as "the Guideline for Promotion of the Criminal Proceeds Control". It also participates in discussion of international standards related to AML measures, and produces reports on AML within the country.

JAFIC is in charge of the following tasks provided in the Act on Prevention of Transfer of Criminal Proceeds:

- The collection, arrangement, analysis and dissemination of information on suspicious transactions to investigative authorities etc.;
- The dissemination of information to foreign FIUs;
- The provision of information and complement of supervisory measures by administrative authorities to ensure that specified business operators take required measures.

27.19.6 *Outline of Specific Money-laundering Offences*

The Anti-Drug Special Provisions Law defines the act of money laundering as a new crime, in that it has such aspects as encouraging further (drug) crimes.

The following acts are criminalised:

- The act of "disguising facts with respect to acquisition or disposition of drug crime proceeds etc.";
- The act of "concealing drug crime proceeds etc.";
- The act of "disguising facts with respect to the source of drug crime proceeds etc.";
- The act of "knowingly receiving drug crime proceeds etc".

According to the Act on Punishment of Organised Crimes, in addition to the acts of disguising, concealing and receiving stipulated in the Anti-Drug Special Provisions Law, managing an enterprise by using criminal proceeds shall be punished as another type of money-laundering crime.

The range of crimes that generate criminal proceeds is stipulated in the attachment to the Act on Punishment of Organised Crimes, to which illicit businesses such as unauthorised entertainment and amusement businesses and unlicensed banking were added in the amendment to the law enforced in July 2011.

27.19.7 *Penalties*

Any person who conceals facts concerning the acquisition or disposition of drug offence proceeds, the drug offence proceeds themselves or facts concerning the source of drug offence proceeds is liable to imprisonment for not more than five years or a fine not exceeding JPY 3,000,000, or both. Attempts are punishable by the same sanctions, and any person who intentionally prepares to commit one of these offences is liable to a term of imprisonment not exceeding two years or a fine not exceeding JPY 500,000.

Any person who knowingly receives drug offence proceeds is liable to imprisonment for not more than five years or a fine not exceeding JPY 1,000,000, or both.

A person who disguises facts with respect to acquisition or disposition of crime proceeds or the like, or who conceals crime proceeds or the like shall be imprisoned with labour for not more than five years or fined not more than JPY 3,000,000, or both. The same shall apply to any person who disguises facts with respect to the source of crime proceeds or the like. A person who, with intent to commit this offence, prepares for such offence shall be imprisoned with labour for not more than two years or fined not more than JPY 500,000.

Any person who knowingly receives crime proceeds or the like shall be imprisoned with labour for not more than three years or fined not more than JPY 1,000,000, or both; provided that this shall not apply to a person who receives any property offered for the performance of an obligation under a law or regulation or offered for the performance of an obligation under a contract (such contract shall be limited to that under which a creditor is to offer substantial property interest) at the time of the conclusion of which such person did not know that the obligation under such contract would be performed with crime proceeds or the like.

Drug crime proceeds shall be confiscated. If they cannot be confiscated because, for example, they have already been consumed or the right thereof has been transferred, collection of equivalent value will be ordered. However, the system of confiscation and collection of equivalent value provided in the Act on Punishment of Organised Crime is subject to the discretion of the court, unlike the system provided in the Anti-Drug Special Provisions Law.

At the time of the enactment of the Act on Punishment of Organised Crime, it was stipulated that so-called "crime victim property", such as proceeds obtained through crime concerning property etc., may not be confiscated in consideration of damage claims by victims. However, the law was partially revised (enforced in December 2006) to enable confiscation in certain cases where the crime is considerably organised or it would be difficult to recover the damage by civil proceedings due to money laundering or other reasons.

27.19.8 Scope

Business operators who are required to take the measures outlined in this section are called "specified business operators", the scope of which is defined in line with the FATF Recommendations as well as in consideration of business practices in Japan. Generally, financial institutions etc. had already been obliged to undertake identical measures by other Japanese legal provisions.

27.19.9 Risk-based Approach

Japan is not at present implementing an AML/CFT risk-based approach, therefore there is no provision mandating enhanced due diligence for customers that pose a higher risk within business relationships and transactions, or authorised simplified due diligence.

27.19.10 Due Diligence

Financial institutions are required to conduct CDD when a business relationship begins. In addition to this, there are certain specified transactions requiring CDD:

- The conclusion of deposit/savings contracts;
- Large cash transactions exceeding JPY 2,000,000;
- Cash remittance exceeding JPY 100,000.

Personal Client Due Diligence

Regulated entities are required to confirm:

- The name,
- Address, and
- Birth date

of the customer. In addition, identification of the person who actually carries out the transaction is required.

If they are face to face, presentation of a driving licence, health insurance certificate, etc. is sufficient. Alternatively, presentation of a copy of a certificate of residence or a government-issued document without a photo coupled with sending the documents related to the transaction to the address (which should not need forwarding) written on the personal identification document by postal mail is sufficient.

For non-face-to-face individuals, the personal identification document (or its copy) and the documents related to the transaction should be sent to the address (which should not need forwarding) written on the personal identification document by postal mail to complete CDD.

Corporate Customer Due Diligence

Regulated entities are required to confirm:

- The name of the corporation;
- The address of the headquarters or main office; and
- The person in charge of the actual transaction.

For face-to-face customers, presentation of a certificate of registered matters of the corporation, seal registration certificate, etc. combined with confirmation of the person in charge of the actual transaction is sufficient.

For non-face-to-face corporate CDD, customers must send personal identification documents such as a certificate of registered matters of the corporation, seal, registration certificate, etc., or their copies, as well as the personal identification documents of the person in charge of the actual transaction or their copies to the relevant financial institution. The entity should then send documents related to the transaction to both of the addresses (corporate and personal).

Certain Transactions

In addition to the identification information outlined above, specified business operators must confirm the following when engaging in certain transactions (generally specified within the regulations) with their customers:

- The purposes of the transaction;
- Details of the customer's occupation (if the customer is a natural person) or his/her business (if the customer is a legal person);
- The beneficial owner (if the customer is a legal person).

Further, a requirement for the confirmation of assets and income was added to the above for certain transactions exposed to a high risk of money laundering, such as those suspected of identity fraud. It should be noted that this mention of risk does not enable a Japanese entity to make a risk assessment; instead it limits the risk to a suspicion of actual fraud.

27.19.11 *Staff Training*

The amendment of the Act on Prevention of Transfer of Criminal Proceeds requires entities to develop education and training systems for employees.

27.19.12 *Record-keeping*

Entities should prepare and keep records of identification data and measures taken for CDD for seven years from the day when the transactions were completed or terminated, and prepare and keep records of the dates and details of transactions for seven years.

27.19.13 *Suspicious Transaction Reporting*

Entities are required to report transactions that are suspected of being related to criminal proceeds to the competent authority. When conducting a cross-border payment, they should notify the receiving institutions of certain items, such as the name and the account number.

Specified business operators are required to file an STR to a corresponding supervising authority when they suspect, during the course of their business, that assets they have received are criminal proceeds or that their client has committed an offence of concealment of criminal proceeds. Specified business operators are expected to judge whether the concerned transaction is a suspicious transaction with their own knowledge and experience of their industries, taking into account the form of transaction, client attributes, conditions surrounding the transaction and other factors.

27.19.14 *Penalties*

Persons who have failed to submit reports or materials, or submit false reports or materials, or who have refused on-site inspections shall be punished with imprisonment with labour for not more than one year or a fine of not more than JPY 3,000,000, or both. A person who violates an order for rectification shall be punished with imprisonment with labour for not more than two years or a fine of not more than JPY 3,000,000, or both.

Moreover, to complement the supervisory function, the National Public Safety Commission is authorised to state its opinion to competent administrative authorities (and make necessary inspections on business operators) when it detects violations.

27.19.15 *Case Studies*

One of the most prominent cases of financial crime in Japan is known as the "Furikome Fraud", which cost over 20,000 victims JPY 2.75 billion in 2008. The main financial institutions utilised were remittance transfer service providers, although banks also need to be equally vigilant to this practice.

The fraud was carried about using (usually stolen) mobile telephones, so that the victim did not suspect fraud. A phone call was made to a relative of the victim from their own phone, and the criminal spoke quickly and in generic language ("it's me" was a common opening phrase). The sense of panic in their voice, as well as background noise, created enough worry for the relative to comply with the criminal's instructions, which were to transfer funds into the criminal's bank account. The criminals usually called elderly relatives, some of whom had dementia and many of whom were unfamiliar with modern technology, to further heighten the sense of worry and the need for compliance. The reasons given included settling a parking ticket and avoiding blackmail, and once the funds were transferred, the account was usually closed down shortly afterwards.

Financial institutions have a part to play in preventing this type of fraud. The indicative signs that accounts were being closed down quickly after a transfer was made, with funds being transferred from a wide range of seemingly unconnected private personal (rather than corporate) accounts and funds being transferred from elderly people, can all be caught by ongoing monitoring of clients and their accounts, and implementing effective due diligence procedures to link the criminals to these accounts. The implementation of such procedures will enable the authorities to bring the criminals to justice.

27.20 COUNTRY PROFILE: JERSEY

27.20.1 Overview

Financial services is a key sector of Jersey's economy, accounting for approximately half of the total economic activity and a quarter of the workforce (approximately 13,400 employed). Financial services expertise and international reputation have been significant in attracting business to Jersey, as has the close working relationship with the UK financial system and the availability of favourable tax arrangements, in a developed, stable and well-regulated jurisdiction. In common with other offshore UK jurisdictions, Jersey is not a member of the EU and therefore has some advantages over other countries.

A substantial proportion (believed to be around 90% in some sectors) of customer relationships are established with non-residents. Arising from the nature of services provided and the typically non-resident, non-face-to-face nature of much of the client relationships, Jersey's financial sector is inherently exposed to the risk of money laundering, but the island has put in place a comprehensive and robust AML/CFT legal framework with a high level of compliance with almost all aspects of the FATF Recommendations.

27.20.2 Key Legislation

The Proceeds of Crime Law 1999 outlines the main money-laundering offences. The Money Laundering (Jersey) Order 2008 outlines AML requirements, which are expanded on within the *AML Handbook*. Minor amendments were made in August 2013 under the Money Laundering (Amendment No. 5) (Jersey) Order 2013.

27.20.3 Legislative History

Several overarching provisions have been implemented to combat money laundering and terrorist financing. The first enactment on the island of Jersey was made in 1988 for money laundering, and in 1990 a further Order addressed terrorist financing. These have all been updated as the money-laundering offence broadened in scope and the culpability for the offence also extended.

Primary Legislation

- Drug Trafficking Offences (Jersey) Law 1988;
- Proceeds of Crime (Jersey) 1999;
- Terrorism (Jersey) Law 2002.

Secondary Legislation

- Terrorism (United Nations Measures) (Channel Islands) Order 2001;
- Al-Qa'ida and Taliban (United Nations Measures) (Channel Islands) Order 2002;
- Money Laundering Order 2006;
- Money Laundering Order 2008;
- Proceeds of Crime (Cash Seizure) 2008.

The current Money Laundering Order supplements the previous order and preceding main body of law on the Proceeds of Crime.

27.20.4 FATF Assessment

Jersey is not an FATF member, but observes the FATF requirements through its membership of the Group of International Finance Centre Supervisors (GIFCS).

A 2010 assessment by the Financial Stability Board, in response to a call from the G20, rated Jersey as "demonstrating sufficiently strong adherence" to the relevant international standards. In 2008, the United Kingdom government publicly confirmed that it considered Jersey to have EU-equivalent AML/CFT systems.

27.20.5 The Primary AML Investigation/Regulatory Authorities

Jersey Financial Services Commission

The Jersey Financial Services Commission is responsible for the regulation, supervision and development of the financial services industry in Jersey for various financial services. Additionally, the Commission is the supervisory body for those sectors that are subject to regulatory oversight of their anti-money-laundering and countering the financing of terrorism responsibilities.

States of Jersey Police and Customs Joint Financial Crimes Unit

The Joint Financial Crimes Unit, JFCU, is divided into four sections:

- The Intelligence Wing fulfils the JFCU's role as the island's financial intelligence unit and analyses SARs;
- The Operational Wing is responsible for carrying out criminal investigations into serious and complex fraud;
- The Drugs Trafficking Confiscation Wing undertakes the specialised investigations required to confiscate the realisable assets of those who have been convicted for drug-trafficking offences;
- The Administrative Wing supports the Intelligence Wing with database maintenance and formal responses to SARs.

27.20.6 Outline of Specific Money-laundering Offences

It is an offence to assist another to retain benefit of criminal conduct. This offence is committed by someone who knows or suspects that "A" is a person who is, or has been, engaged in criminal conduct or has benefited from criminal conduct. This is quite a broad scope and so defences for such an offence are probably hard to apply. The offence rests heavily on mere suspicion of criminal conduct.

The following are also money-laundering offences:

- The acquisition, possession or use of proceeds of criminal conduct;
- Concealing or transferring proceeds of criminal conduct.

Tipping Off

There are three separate tipping-off offences:

- Knowing or suspecting that the Attorney General or the police are acting or proposing to act to investigate an alleged offence of money laundering, a person discloses to any person information that is likely to prejudice the actual or proposed investigation.
- Knowing or suspecting that a disclosure has been made to a police officer, a person discloses information that is likely to prejudice any investigation which might follow the disclosure.
- Knowing or suspecting that a disclosure of a kind (including disclosure made to Reporting Officers appointed by financial services businesses) has been made, a person discloses information that is likely to prejudice any investigation that might be conducted following the disclosure.

27.20.7 Scope

The Money Laundering (Jersey) Order 2008 applies to a person carrying on financial services business in, or from within, Jersey, and a Jersey body corporate or limited liability partnership (LLP) carrying on financial services business anywhere in the world (a "relevant person").

27.20.8 Risk-based Approach

The risk-based approach is widely adopted within the Jersey regulations. The 2010 guidelines that appear in the *Jersey Financial Services Commission Handbook* were written with the express aim of instructing financial service businesses on how they subscribe to the risk-based approach laid down by the FATF. The handbook provides excellent supplementary guidance to the statutory rules.

27.20.9 Role of the MLRO/Nominated Officer

The law requires firms to appoint both a Money Laundering Compliance Officer (MLCO) and a Money Laundering Reporting Officer (MLRO). The MLCO should ensure that the AML requirements are being complied with, whereas the MLRO should consider reports of suspicious transactions. The two roles can be performed by the same person.

The MLCO is someone who:

- Develops and maintains systems and controls (including policies and procedures) in line with evolving requirements;

- Undertakes regular reviews (including testing) of compliance with policies and procedures to counter money laundering and the financing of terrorism;
- Advises the board on anti-money-laundering and financing of terrorism compliance issues that need to be brought to its attention;
- Reports periodically, as appropriate, to the board on compliance with the business's systems and controls;
- Responds promptly to requests for information made by the Commission and the JFCU.

The MLRO should:

- Receive and consider reports;
- Have sufficient experience and skills;
- Have appropriate independence;
- Have a sufficient level of seniority and authority within the business;
- Have sufficient resources, including sufficient time, and (if appropriate) be supported by deputy MLROs;
- Be able to raise issues directly with the board; and
- Be fully aware of both his and the business's obligations.

A relevant person may designate one or more individuals (other than the reporting officer) to whom reports may be made in the first instance, for onward transmission to the reporting officer. They must be of an appropriate level of seniority and have all the necessary access to any records needed to carry out their role.

Under Paragraph 7, a relevant person must give the Commission written notice within one month after the date if:

- An appointment has been made, or
- An appointment ceases.

When an MLRO position is due to become vacant, a member from the board must be appointed on a temporary basis in order to comply with the statutory requirement that all financial businesses must have an MLRO in place at all times.

27.20.10 Due Diligence

A relevant person must apply identification measures before the establishment of a business relationship or before carrying out a one-off transaction, or as soon as reasonably practicable after the establishment of a business relationship if it is necessary not to interrupt the normal conduct of business, and there is little risk of money laundering occurring as a result of completing such identification after the establishment of that relationship. They must also apply CDD where they suspect money laundering or they have doubts about the adequacy of the documents previously obtained under CDD measures.

Personal Client Due Diligence

A relevant firm should ascertain the following for all customers:

- Legal name, any former names (such as maiden name) and any other names used;
- Principal residential address;
- Date of birth.

If the customer poses a standard or higher risk, the following additional information should be obtained:

- Place of birth;
- Nationality;
- Sex;
- Government-issued personal identification number or other government-issued unique identifier.

The information should then be verified in accordance with the following:

Lower risk – information to be verified

- Legal name, any former names (such as maiden name) and any other names used; and
- Principal residential address or date of birth.

A firm is only required to use one identification verification method in such cases.

Standard risk – information to be verified

- Legal name;
- Any former names (such as maiden name) and any other names used;
- Principal residential address;
- Date of birth;
- Place of birth;
- Nationality; and
- Sex.

In this case the firm is required to use at least two identification verification methods.

Higher risk – information to be verified

- Legal name;
- Any former names (such as maiden name) and any other names used;
- Principal residential address;
- Date of birth;

- Place of birth;
- Nationality;
- Sex; and
- Government-issued personal identification number or other government-issued unique identifier.

Again, in such cases at least two identification verification methods must be used.

This information should be verified by the following:

All customers – identification verification methods

Residential address:

- Correspondence from a central or local government department or agency (e.g. State and parish authorities).
- A letter of introduction confirming residential address from: (i) a relevant person that is regulated by the Commission; (ii) a regulated financial services business which is operating in a well-regulated jurisdiction; or (iii) a branch or subsidiary of a group headquartered in a well-regulated jurisdiction which applies group standards to subsidiaries and branches worldwide, and tests the application of, and compliance with, such standards.
- Personal visit to residential address.
- A bank statement or utility bill.
- One of the general identification information sources listed above.

Lower-risk customers

Where the above general identification information methods are not possible, identity may be verified using:

- A Jersey driving licence; or
- A birth certificate in conjunction with:
  - a bank statement or a utility bill;
  - documentation issued by a government source; or
  - a letter of introduction from a relevant person that is regulated by the Commission.

Corporate Customer Due Diligence

For all legal persons, the following information should be ascertained:

- Name of body;
- Date and country of incorporation/registration;
- Official identification number.

For standard and higher-risk customers, entities should collect this additional information:

- Registered office address;
- Principal place of business/operations (where different to registered office).

The information should then be verified. For lower-risk customers, a minimum of one verification method is sufficient, whereas for standard and higher-risk customers, a minimum of two verification methods should be employed. The methods are:

- Certificate of Incorporation (or other appropriate certificate of registration or licensing);
- Memorandum and articles of association (or equivalent);
- Company registry search, including confirmation that the body is not in the process of being dissolved, struck off, wound up or terminated;
- Latest audited financial statements;
- Independent data sources, including electronic sources, e.g. business information services;
- Personal visit to principal place of business (standard or higher risk only).

Firms should also verify the following:

All customers

- Those directors (or equivalents) who have authority to operate a relationship or to give the relevant person instructions concerning the use or transfer of funds or assets – in line with guidance for individuals.

Standard and higher-risk customers

- Individuals with ultimate effective control over the legal body's assets, including the individuals comprising the mind and management of the legal body, e.g. directors – in line with guidance for individuals.
- Individuals ultimately holding a material interest in the capital of the legal body – in line with guidance for individuals and trustees.

Enhanced Customer Due Diligence

A relevant person should apply enhanced CDD measures using a risk-based approach where:

- A customer is not physically present for identification purposes.
- The relevant person has, or proposes to have, a business relationship or proposes to carry out a one-off transaction with a person connected with a country or territory that does not apply or insufficiently applies the FATF Recommendations.

- The relevant person has, or proposes to have, a business relationship or proposes to carry out a one-off transaction with an applicant for business or a customer who is a PEP, or who is involved with or owned by a PEP.
- The nature of the situation is such that a higher risk of money laundering is likely.

Enhanced customer due diligence measures mean customer due diligence measures that involve specific and adequate measures to compensate for the higher risk of money laundering.

Enhanced due diligence measures include:

- Obtaining additional CDD information (identification information and relationship information, including further information on the source of funds and source of wealth) from either the customer or independent sources (such as the internet, public or commercially available databases);
- Taking additional steps to verify the CDD information obtained;
- Commissioning due diligence reports from independent experts to confirm the veracity of CDD information held;
- Requiring higher levels of management approval for higher-risk new customers;
- Requiring more frequent reviews of business relationships;
- Requiring the reviews of business relationships to be undertaken by the compliance function, or other employees not directly involved in managing the customer; and
- Setting lower monitoring thresholds for transactions connected with the business relationship.

Politically Exposed Persons

To carry out a transaction for a PEP, the entity must have specific and adequate measures which:

- Require any new business relationship or continuation of such a relationship or any new one-off transaction to be approved by the senior management of the relevant person; and
- Establish the source of the wealth of the PEP and the source of the funds involved in the business relationship or one-off transaction.

Correspondent Banking

Enhanced CDD must be carried out when the relevant person holds a deposit-taking licence and proposes to establish a correspondent banking relationship.

27.20.11 Ongoing Monitoring

A relevant person is required to apply ongoing monitoring during a business relationship. This means ensuring that all documents are kept up to date and relevant by undertaking reviews of existing records, including, but without prejudice to the generality of the foregoing, reviews where any inconsistency has been discovered. This should be carried out at times that are appropriate, having regard to the degree of risk of money laundering and taking into account the type of customer, business relationship, product or transaction concerned, when any suspicion arises.

A relevant person must maintain adequate procedures for monitoring and testing the effectiveness of the following actions:

- The CDD policies and procedures;
- The measures taken to prevent and detect money laundering; and
- The training provided to staff.

27.20.12 Staff Training

A relevant person must maintain appropriate policies and procedures relating to:

- Customer due diligence measures;
- Reporting in accordance with the relevant AML law;
- Record-keeping;
- Screening of employees;
- Internal control;
- Risk assessment and management; and
- The monitoring and management of compliance with, and the internal communication of, such policies and procedures in respect of that person's financial services business in order to prevent and detect money laundering.

"Appropriate policies and procedures" means policies and procedures that are appropriate having regard to the degree of risk of money laundering and taking into account the type of customers, business relationships, products or transactions with which the relevant person's business is concerned. It must also include policies and procedures for the identification and scrutiny of:

- Complex or unusually large transactions;
- Unusual patterns of transactions which have no apparent economic or visible lawful purpose; and
- Any other activity which the relevant person regards as particularly likely by its nature to be related to the risk of money laundering.

Additionally, the firm should identify:

- The requirement to take additional measures, where appropriate, to prevent the use for money laundering of products and transactions which are susceptible to anonymity, including measures to prevent the misuse of technological developments in money laundering.

- Whether a customer, a beneficial owner or controller of a customer, a third party for whom a customer is acting, a beneficial owner or controller of a third party or a person acting, or purporting to act, on behalf of a customer, is a politically exposed person.
- Whether a business relationship or transaction, or proposed business relationship or transaction, is with a person connected with a country or territory that does not apply, or insufficiently applies, the FATF Recommendations.
- Whether a business relationship or transaction, or proposed business relationship or transaction, is with a person connected with a country or territory that is subject to measures for purposes connected with the prevention and detection of money laundering, such measures being imposed by one or more countries or sanctioned by the European Union or the United Nations.

"Scrutiny" includes scrutinising the background and purpose of transactions and activities.

A relevant person must take appropriate measures from time to time for the purposes of making employees whose duties relate to the provision of financial services business aware of the following matters:

- The AML policies and procedures that are maintained by that person and relate to the business; and
- The enactments in Jersey relating to money laundering and any relevant Code of Practice.

A relevant person must provide those employees from time to time with training in the recognition and handling of:

- Transactions carried out by, or on behalf of, any person who is, or appears to be, engaged in money laundering; and
- Other conduct that indicates that a person is, or appears to be, engaged in money laundering.

Such training shall include the provision of information on current money-laundering techniques, methods and trends.

27.20.13 Record-keeping

A relevant person must keep the records specified below. A record comprises:

- A copy of the evidence of identity obtained pursuant to the application of customer due diligence measures or information that enables a copy of such evidence to be obtained;
- All the supporting documents, data or information that have been obtained in respect of a business relationship or one-off transaction following the application of customer due diligence measures;
- Details relating to each transaction carried out by the relevant person in the course of any business relationship or one-off transaction.

Records must also include sufficient information to enable the reconstruction of individual transactions, in such a manner that those records can be made available on a timely basis to the Commission, police officer or customs officer for the purposes of complying with a requirement under any enactment.

Records must contain the following details of each transaction carried out with, or for, a customer in the course of financial services business:

- The name and address of the customer;
- If a monetary transaction, the kind of currency and the amount;
- If the transaction involves a customer's account, the number, name or other identifier for the account;
- The date of the transaction;
- Details of the counterparty, including account details;
- The nature of the transaction; and
- Details of the transaction.

Adequate recording of details of transactions may be demonstrated by including (where appropriate):

- Valuation(s) and price(s);
- The form (e.g. cash, cheque, electronic transfer) in which funds are transferred;
- Memoranda of instruction(s) and authority(ies);
- Memoranda of purchase and sale;
- Custody of title documentation; and
- Other records in support of transaction records where these are necessary to enable a clear and complete audit trail of fund or asset movements to be established.

Adequate recording of details of transactions may be demonstrated by recording all transactions undertaken on behalf of a customer within that customer's records, enabling a complete transaction history for each customer to be easily constructed. For example, a customer's records should include all requests for wire transfer transactions where settlement is provided other than from funds drawn from a customer's account with the relevant person.

27.20.14 Suspicious Transaction Reporting

Financial institutions and other organisations regulated by the Jersey Financial Services Commission undertaking relevant business have an obligation to report where they have knowledge, suspicion or reasonable grounds for suspecting money laundering or terrorist financing. The format, timing and content of what the Jersey Financial Services Commission considers to be a good SAR are specified in the guidance, and should follow the basis outlined below.

If it is made to a designated person, that person must consider it, in the light of all other relevant information, for the purpose of determining whether or not the information or other matter contained in the report does give rise to knowledge, suspicion or reasonable grounds for knowledge or suspicion that another person is engaged in money laundering.

If a report is made to a designated person, the report must generally be forwarded by the designated person to the reporting officer.

If a report is made or forwarded to the reporting officer, it must be considered by the reporting officer, in the light of all other relevant information, for the purpose of determining whether or not the information or other matter contained in the report does give rise to knowledge, suspicion or reasonable grounds for knowledge or suspicion that another person is engaged in money laundering.

Any designated person through whom the report is made must have access to all other relevant information that may be of assistance to the reporting officer or that designated person, including, in particular, the records that a relevant person must keep.

If it is decided that a disclosure needs to be made, there must be procedures for the person to disclose to a designated police officer or designated customs officer as soon as is practicable, using the form set out in the Schedule to the Order.

Reports must contain the identity of the person making the report.

Section 22 considers reports that do not need to be forwarded:

- If a designated person, on considering a report, concludes that it does not give rise to knowledge, suspicion or reasonable grounds for knowledge or suspicion that another person is engaged in money laundering, the designated person need not forward it to the reporting officer.
- If a designated person, on considering a report, has concluded that it does give rise to knowledge, suspicion or reasonable grounds for knowledge or suspicion that another person is engaged in money laundering, the reporting officer need not consider whether that other person is engaged in money laundering.

27.20.15 Penalties

Failure to comply with the Money Laundering Order is a criminal offence, and in determining whether a relevant person has complied with any of the legal requirements of the Order, the court is required to take account of the guidance provided by the handbook. The sanction for failing to comply with the Money Laundering Order may be an unlimited fine or up to two years' imprisonment, or both.

Where a breach of the Money Laundering Order by a body corporate is proved to have been committed with the consent of, or to be attributable to any neglect on the part of, a director, manager or other similar officer, that individual, as well as the body corporate, shall be guilty of the offence and subject to criminal sanctions.

The consequences of non-compliance with the regulatory requirements that are set through the Supervisory Bodies Law could include an investigation by, or on behalf of, the Commission, the imposition of regulatory sanctions and criminal prosecution of the business and its employees. Regulatory sanctions include:

- Issuing a public statement;
- Imposing a direction and making this public; and
- Revocation of a licence.

In addition to this, the ability of a relevant person that is regulated by the Commission under the regulatory laws to demonstrate compliance with the regulatory requirements will be directly relevant to its regulated status and any assessment of fitness and propriety of its principals.

27.20.16 Case Studies

A lawyer in Jersey was convicted of money laundering involving assets valued at over £1 million. The funds, which were falsely represented as payment for legal services, originated from the lawyer's father – a convicted money launderer who is reported to have laundered £27 million. A transaction of this size between relatives should arouse suspicion for a financial institution, particularly when convicted financial criminals are moving funds of that size.

Jersey has been targeted as a money-laundering centre for funds originating in India and Nigeria, after a criminal was convicted of orchestrating a £28-million money-laundering scheme. The funds were laundered through the Jersey branch of the Bank of India, in a deal with a late Nigerian military dictator. This illustrates the need to conduct enhanced due diligence for PEPs, to avoid the possibility of corruption and abuse of power.

27.21 COUNTRY PROFILE: KENYA

27.21.1 *Overview*

Kenya has been slow to implement a comprehensive AML regime. As such, its attempts to comply with the international regime to combat money laundering have currently fallen short of international best practice. Its primary concern has been to focus more on the poverty that the country is affected by and to solve the further problems relating to various diseases that have been virtually wiped out in other, more developed countries.

27.21.2 *Key Legislation*

The Proceeds of Crime and Anti-Money Laundering Act 2009 provides the relevant AML law. This is supplemented by the CBK Guidelines.

27.21.3 *Legislative History*

The Proceeds of Crime and Anti-Money Laundering Act 2009 came into effect on 28th June, 2010. The Act:

- Criminalises money laundering;
- Provides for both criminal and civil restraint, seizure and forfeiture;
- Places an obligation on financial institutions to:
  - monitor and report suspected money-laundering activity,
  - verify customer identity (KYC),
  - establish and maintain customer records, and
  - establish and maintain internal reporting procedures;
- Establishes the Financial Reporting Centre (financial intelligence unit), the Asset Recovery Centre and the Criminal Assets Recovery Fund;
- Provides for procedures that facilitate international assistance with investigations and proceedings related to money-laundering offences.

Furthermore, there are various other pieces of relevant legislation:

- Prevention of Organised Crime 2007;
- Banking Act 1995 (with amendments through 2003);
- Banking (Amendment) Act 2006;
- Central Bank of Kenya Act 1966 (with amendments through 2003).

27.21.4 *FATF Assessment*

Kenya was severely criticised by the FATF in June 2012, which issued a statement saying "Despite Kenya's high-level political commitment to work with the FATF and ESAAMLG to address its strategic AML/CFT deficiencies, Kenya has not made sufficient progress in implementing its action plan, and certain strategic AML/CFT deficiencies remain." It added "Taking into account Kenya's continued lack of progress, in particular in enacting the CFT legislation, if Kenya does not take significant actions by October 2012, the FATF will call upon its members to apply countermeasures proportionate to the risks associated with Kenya."

27.21.5 The Primary AML Investigation/Regulatory Authorities

Central Bank of Kenya

The Central Bank of Kenya is the regulatory body for the financial services sector in Kenya. Non-bank financial institutions are licensed under the Banking Act and are obligated to comply with all requirements of banks subject to any qualifications stipulated for them. Currently, there are no NBFIs licensed in Kenya.

Reports in relation to money laundering and related crimes are currently made to the Central Bank of Kenya and the Criminal Investigation Department of the Kenya Police. The latest AML guidelines were issued by CBK in July 2012.

The Kenyan Ministry of Finance

The Ministry is charged with the responsibility of formulating financial and economic policies. It is also responsible for developing and maintaining sound fiscal and monetary policies that facilitate socioeconomic development, and regulating the financial sector.

Future Bodies

The FRC, Anti-Money Laundering Advisory Board and Assets Recovery Agency have been established under the Proceeds of Crime and Anti-Money Laundering Act. However, at the time of writing, these bodies were not yet operational.

27.21.6 Outline of Specific Money-laundering Offences

It is an offence for any person to enter into an agreement or engage in any arrangement or transaction with anyone in connection with property that forms part of the proceeds of crime, whether that agreement, arrangement or transaction is legally enforceable or not and whose effect is to:

- Conceal or disguise the nature, source, location, disposition, movement or ownership of the said property;
- Enable or assist any person who has committed or commits an offence, whether in Kenya or elsewhere, to avoid prosecution;
- Remove or diminish any property acquired directly, or indirectly, as a result of the commission of an offence.

Acquisition

The acquisition, use and possession of proceeds of crime, knowing that such property forms part of the proceeds, is also an offence in Kenya.

Tipping Off

It is also an offence for anyone who knows or suspects that an investigation into money laundering has been, is being, or is about to be conducted to inform someone else of that fact. The requirement that this information prejudices the investigation will be removed under the proposed amendments.

The offences above can be committed based on actual knowledge or knowledge the offender ought to have had. The Proceeds of Crime and Anti-Money Laundering (Amendment) Bill 2012, which was going through Parliament as this book was being written, introduces the offence of self-money laundering in terms of acquisition above.

Failure to Report Suspicion Regarding Proceeds of Crime

A person who wilfully fails to report a suspicion commits an offence.

Financial Promotion of an Offence

A person who knowingly transports, transmits, transfers or receives or attempts to transport, transmit, transfer or receive a monetary instrument or anything of value to another person, with intent to commit an offence, commits an offence.

Misrepresentation

A person who knowingly makes a false, fictitious or fraudulent statement or representation, or makes, or provides, any false document, knowing the same to contain any false, fictitious or fraudulent statement or entry, to a reporting institution or to a supervisory body or to the Centre commits an offence.

Malicious Reporting

Any person who wilfully gives any information to the Centre or an authorised officer knowing such information to be false commits an offence.

27.21.7 Defences

If a person is charged with committing a money-laundering offence, it is a defence that he had reported a suspicion to the authorities or, if the person is an employee of a reporting institution, in accordance with his obligations.

27.21.8 Penalties

A person found guilty of money laundering, acquisition, possession or use of criminal proceeds or financial promotion of a crime can be liable:

- In the case of a natural person, to imprisonment for a term not exceeding 14 years, or a fine not exceeding five million shillings or the amount of the value of the property involved in the offence, whichever is the higher, or to both the fine and imprisonment; and

- In the case of a body corporate, to a fine not exceeding twenty-five million shillings, or the amount of the value of the property involved in the offence, whichever is the higher.

A person who contravenes any of the provisions of sections relating to failure to report suspicion, tipping off or misuse of information is, on conviction, liable:

- In the case of a natural person, to imprisonment for a term not exceeding seven years, or a fine not exceeding two million, five hundred thousand shillings, or to both; and
- In the case of a body corporate, to a fine not exceeding ten million shillings, or the amount of the value of the property involved in the offence, whichever is the higher.

27.21.9 Risk-based Approach

Institutions should put in place effective anti-money-laundering programmes that address the risks posed by money launderers, and enhance the ability of the institution to identify, monitor and deter persons from attempting to gain access to, or make use of, the financial system. Such programmes should be documented and should establish clear responsibilities and accountabilities to ensure that policies, procedures and controls are introduced and maintained.

A programme should, amongst other things, address the following issues:

- Internal policies, procedures and controls instituted that are based upon the financial institution's money-laundering risk assessment;
- Designate an AML Compliance Officer and detail the role he/she will play in the day-to-day AML supervision of the institution;
- Provide for and document policies and procedures to perform independent testing/ audit, to measure compliance with the relevant AML laws and regulations;
- Provide for and document AML training for appropriate personnel;
- Provide for adequate screening policies and procedures to ensure high ethical and professional standards when hiring staff.

27.21.10 Internal Controls

The board of directors of an institution operating in Kenya is expected to ensure that management:

- Establishes adequate internal control measures to address potential money-laundering and terrorist-financing risks.
- Obtains, verifies and maintains proper identification of customers wishing to open accounts or make transactions, whether directly or through proxy.

- Obtains and maintains adequate records such as: copies or records of official identification documents like passports, identity cards, driving licences or similar documents; statements of accounts, account files and business correspondence including the results of any inquiries to establish the background and purpose of any complex, unusually large transactions, for a minimum of seven years, regarding the sources of funds and details of transactions in order to:
  - enable the identification of unusual or suspicious transactions, and
  - reconstruct individual transactions.
- Trains staff on a regular basis in the prevention, detection and control of money laundering and the identification of suspicious transactions.
- Monitors and reports any suspicious transactions or activities to the Central Bank of Kenya that may indicate money laundering or other attempts to conceal the true identity of customers or ownership of assets.
- Cooperates with national law-enforcement agencies by taking appropriate measures which are consistent with the law where there are reasonable grounds for suspecting money laundering.
- While taking into account the sensitive nature of extraterritorial anti-money-laundering laws and regulations, ensures that its overseas branches and subsidiaries are aware of the reporting requirements as directed by the Central Bank of Kenya with regard to suspicious transaction reporting and sanctions reporting.

27.21.11 Role of the MLRO/Nominated Officer

Procedures and responsibilities for monitoring compliance with, and effectiveness of, anti-money-laundering policies and procedures should be clearly laid down by institutions in the form of policy documents and internal procedural manuals. Institutions should appoint a Compliance Officer to undertake this function and the officer should have the necessary authority to carry out the function. Institutions should provide the Compliance Officer with the necessary access to systems and records to enable the Officer to fulfil his/her responsibilities.

The functions of the Compliance Officer shall be, amongst others:

- To receive and vet suspicious activity reports from staff;
- To file suspicious transaction reports with the Central Bank of Kenya;
- To be the central point of contact with the Central Bank of Kenya for anti-money-laundering purposes;
- To develop the institution's anti-money-laundering compliance programme;
- To ensure that the anti-money-laundering compliance programme is followed and enforced within the institution;
- To coordinate training of staff in anti-money-laundering awareness and detection methods; and
- To maintain close cooperation and liaison with the Central Bank of Kenya.

27.21.12 *Risk Assessment*

Institutions shall undertake a Money Laundering and Financing of Terrorism Risk Assessment. The Assessment should provide the means for identifying the degree of potential money laundering and financing of terrorism risks associated with specific customers and transactions, thereby allowing the institution to focus on customers and transactions that potentially pose a greater risk of money laundering and terrorism financing. Institutions should take into consideration the findings of the country's National Money Laundering and Terrorism Risk Assessment.

When preparing a risk assessment, an institution should consider factors such as:

- The number and volume of transactions per customer;
- The nature of the customer relationship; and
- Whether, for example, the institution's interaction with customers is face-to-face or non-face-to-face, such as electronic banking (for example, internet banking, mobile banking).

27.21.13 *Due Diligence*

In all circumstances, any business entity operating within the financial sector requires basic information on its customers. The nature and extent of this information will vary according to the type of business. It shall also depend on whether the business is being introduced by a financial intermediary and the type of customer involved. An institution shall take measures to satisfy itself as to the true identity of any applicant seeking to enter into a business relationship with it, or to carry out a transaction or series of transactions with it, by requiring the applicant to produce an official record for the purposes of establishing the true identity of the applicant.

Furthermore, an institution should establish, to its satisfaction, that it is dealing with a person that actually exists. It should identify those persons who are empowered to undertake the transactions, whether on their own behalf or on behalf of others. When a business relationship is being established, the nature of business that the customer expects to conduct with the institution concerned should be ascertained, so as to determine what might be expected as the customer's normal activity levels. In order to judge whether a transaction is or is not suspicious, an institution needs to have a clear understanding of the pattern of its customer's business.

Personal Client Due Diligence

An institution must identity its customers in the following circumstances:

- When establishing initial business relations;
- When undertaking occasional or one-off transactions;
- When there is cause to be suspicious;
- When there is doubt about the veracity or adequacy of previously obtained customer information.

For personal accounts or transactions, at a minimum, an entity should review and copy an original:

- Birth certificate
- Passport
- National identity card or
- Driving licence.

Additional measures that may be used to verify the identity of the customer include:

- Verifying the address of the customer's current residence utilising a referee, a utility bill, i.e. electricity or water bill, etc.;
- Verifying employment and/or source(s) of income;
- Where applicable, obtaining written confirmation from the customer's prior bank attesting to the customer's identity and history of account relationship;
- For accounts with more than one party and where one of the parties has identified the others, written confirmation must be obtained to the effect that the first party has known the other(s) personally for at least 12 months.

Corporate Customer Due Diligence

In the case of a body corporate, the following should be used to conduct CDD:

- Evidence of registration or incorporation;
- The Act establishing the body corporate;
- A corporate resolution authorising a person to act on behalf of the corporate body together with a copy of the latest annual return submitted in respect of the body corporate in accordance with the law under which it is established;
- In the case of a government department/agency, a letter from the accounting officer.

Additionally, the following should be provided at a minimum:

- Evidence of registration or incorporation through obtaining a certified copy of the Certificate of Registration or Certificate of Incorporation, and partnership deed, memorandum and articles of association or other similar documentation evidencing legal status.
- Certified copy of the board resolution stating authority to open accounts, transact business and borrow funds, and designating persons having signatory authority thereof.
- Audited financial statements, from the previous year at a minimum but preferably for the previous three years.
- In the case of a government department, a letter from the accounting officer.

Additionally, entities should verify the identity and address of the chairman of the board of directors, the Managing Director or the general partner and at least one limited partner for partnerships, or the principal owner for sole traders, etc.

Enhanced Customer Due Diligence

Enhanced due diligence measures shall be applied to persons and entities that present a higher risk to the institution. This can broadly be addressed by taking the following measures:

- Obtaining further information to establish the customer's identity;
- Applying extra measures to check documents supplied by a credit or financial institution;
- Obtaining senior management approval for the new business relationship or transaction;
- Establishing the person's/entity's source of funds;
- Carrying out ongoing monitoring of the business relationship.

An institution shall determine, based on its own criteria, whether a particular customer poses a higher risk. Certain customers and entities may pose specific risks depending on the nature of the business, the occupation of the customer or the nature of anticipated transaction activity. Some factors to consider include:

- Customers conducting their business relationship or transactions in unusual circumstances;
- Customers whose structure or nature of the entity or relationship makes it difficult to identify the true owner or controlling interests;
- Politically exposed persons (PEPs);
- Foreign corporations and domestic business entities, particularly offshore corporations such as domestic shell companies, private investment companies and international business corporations located in high-risk geographic regions;
- Cash-intensive businesses, including, for example, supermarkets, convenience stores, restaurants, retail stores, liquor stores and wholesale distributors;
- Professional service providers.

The weight assigned to each of these risk categories (individually or in combination) in assessing the overall risk of potential money laundering may vary from one institution to another, depending on their respective circumstances. Consequently, an institution will have to make its own determination as to the risk weights to assign to each different risk.

Non-face–to-face Customer Due Diligence

The procedures adopted here should confirm the identity as robustly as those adopted for face-to-face customers, and reasonable steps should be taken to avoid single or multiple fictitious applications or substitution (impersonation) fraud for the purpose of money laundering.

Some of the best means of verifying address are considered to be:

- Requesting sight of a:
  - recent utility bill,
  - local authority tax bill, or
  - institution statement;
- Checking a local telephone directory (for businesses).

In addition, satisfactory evidence of personal identity can be obtained by a number of means, some of which are set out below:

- Use of a computerised system, for internal or external application database checks, to check for any inconsistencies in the information provided – particularly those containing known fictitious application/fraud information (accommodation, addresses, aliases, etc.);
- Telephone contact with the applicant on an independently verified home or business number;
- With the customer's consent, the employer's personnel department confirms employment by verbal confirmation on a listed number;
- Salary details appearing on recent bank statements;

Care should be taken to ensure that the same supporting documentation is obtained from internet customers as for other postal/telephone/mobile banking customers.

Institutions should consider regular monitoring of accounts opened on the internet. Unusual transactions should be investigated and reported if found to be suspicious.

Politically Exposed Persons

Where a customer has been found to be a politically exposed person, institutions will be required to take the following measures:

- Obtain approval from senior management to transact/establish the relationship with that person;
- Take adequate measures to establish the source of wealth and the source of funds which are involved in the proposed business relationship or transaction;
- Obtain information on immediate family members or close associates of the PEP who may have transaction authority over the account;
- Determine the purpose of the account and the expected volume and nature of account activity; and
- Review public sources of information, for example, the internet and company registries.

Once the account has been established, institutions should conduct enhanced ongoing monitoring of the relationship.

Anonymous Accounts and Numbered Accounts

No institution shall open and/or maintain anonymous accounts or accounts in fictitious names. All numbered accounts should undergo the same identification and verification process as regular accounts.

Correspondent Banking

An institution which intends to establish a correspondent banking relationship, either as the correspondent bank or the respondent bank, shall undertake the following steps before establishing a business relationship:

- Gather sufficient information about the correspondent bank regarding the nature of its business activities;
- Determine, from available information, the reputation of the correspondent bank institution and the quality of its supervision;
- Determine the quality of anti-money-laundering regulation in the correspondent bank's jurisdiction or country of domicile;
- Assess the correspondent bank's anti-money-laundering controls;
- Obtain approval from senior management before establishing a new correspondent banking relationship;
- In respect of the correspondent bank's customers, be assured that it verifies the identity of its customers and conducts ongoing monitoring;
- Verify the ownership and management structures of the correspondent bank including whether a politically exposed person has ownership or control of the bank.

Shell Banking

Institutions should not open a foreign account with a shell bank.

27.21.14 *Ongoing Monitoring*

Institutions should verify, on a regular basis, compliance with policies, procedures and controls relating to money-laundering activities, in order to ensure that the requirement to maintain such procedures has been discharged.

Ongoing monitoring of account activity and transactions should be conducted on a risk-sensitive basis. Institutions can only effectively control and reduce their risk if they have an understanding of normal and reasonable activity of their customers. This enables them to have the means of identifying transactions which fall outside the regular pattern of an account's activity. This can be done by establishing limits for a particular class or category of accounts and paying particular attention to transactions that exceed these limits.

27.21.15 Staff Training

Each institution should institute specific "Know Your Employee" controls designed to deter internal fraud and abuse of the institution which require employees to:

- Follow a code of ethics;
- Avoid and disclose conflicts of interest;
- Maintain good credit ratings;
- Adhere to policies on rotation of duties and mandatory vacations;
- Require the use of employee identification cards for access to secure areas.

27.21.16 Investigation and Reporting Requirements

The Financial Reporting Centre was formed under the POC Act 2009. Section 24 lists its functions and provides the full ambit of its role in a very logical and sequential fashion. The list includes, but is not exclusive to, stating that the Centre:

- Shall receive and analyse reports of unusual or suspicious transactions made by reporting institutions;
- May instruct any reporting institution to take such steps as may be appropriate to facilitate any investigation undertaken or to be undertaken by the Centre, including providing documents and other relevant information;
- Shall design training requirements and may provide such training for any reporting institution in respect of transactions, record-keeping and reporting obligations in accordance with the provisions of this Act;
- Shall create and maintain a database of all reports of suspicious transactions, related government information and such other materials as the Director may, from time to time, determine to be relevant to the work of the Centre;
- Shall draft the regulations required by this Act, in consultation with the board, for submission to the Minister for his approval, prior to publication in the Gazette;
- Shall set anti-money-laundering policies in consultation with the board;
- Shall maintain proper books of accounts;
- Shall have power to compel the production of, or to obtain access to, all records, documents or information relevant to monitoring compliance outside the scope of on-site inspection (inserted by the 2012 amendment).

Suspicious Transaction Reports

If an institution becomes aware of suspicious activities or transactions which indicate possible money-laundering activities, the institution shall ensure that it is reported to the Central Bank of Kenya immediately and in any event within seven days of the date of the transaction or activity that is considered suspicious.

Sufficient information should be disclosed to indicate the nature of, and reason for, the suspicion. Where the institution has additional supporting documentation, that should also be made available.

If, following a disclosure, an institution, exercising its commercial judgment, wishes to terminate the relationship with the customer, it is recommended that before taking this step, the reporting institution should liaise with the Central Bank of Kenya to ensure that the termination does not, in any way, "tip off" the customer or prejudice possible investigation.

The suspicious transaction report shall provide sufficient details, as per the prescribed form, regarding the activities or transactions so that authorities can properly investigate and, if warranted, take appropriate action. Failure to report suspicious transactions may invite remedial action.

Cash Transaction Reports

Institutions shall file reports with the Central Bank of Kenya on all cash transactions exceeding US$ 10,000 or its equivalent in any other currency carried out by it, whether or not the transaction appears to be suspicious. The report shall be made electronically on form No. IF/10.

Tipping Off

Institutions which obtain or become aware of information which is suspicious or indicates possible money-laundering activities should not disclose such information to the customer, but should report it to the Central Bank of Kenya, as required by this guideline.

27.21.17 Penalties

It is an offence for an institution to fail to:

- Monitor and report suspected money-laundering activity;
- Verify customer identity;
- Establish and maintain customer records;
- Establish and maintain internal reporting procedures.

The penalty on conviction for any of the above is a fine not exceeding 10% of the amount of the monetary instruments involved in the offence.

The Act accords immunity or protection to institutions and officers in respect of obligations carried out under the Act in good faith, such as the reporting of suspicious transactions.

27.21.18 Case Studies

The Goldenberg scandal was a series of financial crimes in Kenya which cost the government $500 million. The perpetrator proposed to the government that he set up a formal gold and diamond exchange, to prevent the precious metals and jewellery being sold on the black market. He then charged the government 35% of the export price as commission. Despite various discrepancies, such as the invoices not matching the receipts and being provided in various currencies but from the same source, the Kenyan government paid the invoices. Shortly afterwards, the criminal set up his own commercial bank, thereby avoiding the invoice problem.

It later emerged that the criminal was buying foreign currency in the local market and representing it as foreign exchange earnings. The invoices submitted were nearly 300 times more expensive than the actual cost of gold, and, of course, were fraudulent. It later emerged that the companies the criminal was exporting to were fictitious, apart from one – which was later bought by the criminal.

Concurrent with this, the criminal was running a series of other scams. One took advantage of an export "incentive package" provided by the Kenyan government for exporters. The criminal claimed to be an exporter, and was paid hundreds of millions of dollars in pre-shipment finance, for which he then negotiated delays in repayment (and never repaid a substantial amount). He also took advantage of a scheme which allowed exporters to retain a portion of their foreign exchange earnings, by convincing the government to allow him to retain all of his earnings – the most any other business was allowed was 50%. This gained him $75 million. He also received a $210 million loan secured against an account in London, which he said he would make available to the Kenyan government, but never did.

Many of the proceeds of the scam were never recovered. However, it is known that very sophisticated financial structures were employed, involving two banks controlled by the criminal and eight separate companies. He then obtained funds from the Central Bank of Kenya using his two banks and the eight companies by overdrawing the account of the first bank at the Central Bank of Kenya and then covering the overdraft using fraudulent transfers in favour of that bank, issued by his other bank and the companies. The criminal would then carry out this fraudulent rotation of funds all over again to cover the overdraft created in the second bank.

27.22 COUNTRY PROFILE: LIECHTENSTEIN

27.22.1 Overview

Approximately 90% of Liechtenstein's financial services business is provided to non-residents. This creates a particular money-laundering risk, in response to which the authorities and the financial sector firms have developed risk-based mitigating measures. Accordingly, an increasingly stringent series of rules has been implemented.

27.22.2 Key Legislation

Money laundering is criminalised under the Criminal Code. The Due Diligence Act and the Due Diligence Ordinance provide the compliance requirements.

27.22.3 Legislative History

Liechtenstein first implemented anti-money-laundering laws in 1990, with the passage of specific EU provisions, in order to have a more integrated set of legislative arrangements. Liechtenstein also has a customs union agreement with Switzerland. Milestones in the fight against money laundering and terrorist financing include:

- Liechtenstein becoming a State Party to the Convention of the Council of Europe on Money Laundering, Search, Seizure, and Confiscation of the Proceeds from Crime (1990);
- Implementation of the First EU Money Laundering Directive (1995);
- The Due Diligence Act entering into force (1997);
- Total revision of the Liechtenstein Mutual Legal Assistance Act (2000);
- The establishment of the Liechtenstein Financial Intelligence Unit (2001);
- The Mutual Legal Assistance Treaty with the United States and adoption of the "Counterterrorism Package" (2002);
- Tightening of the Law on Professional Due Diligence in Financial Transactions (Due Diligence Act) (2004);
- The establishment of the Liechtenstein Financial Market Authority through enactment of the Financial Market Authority Act (2004);
- Implementation of the Second EU Money Laundering Directive (2005);
- Partial revision of the Mutual Legal Assistance Act (2008);
- Implementation of the Third EU Money Laundering Directive (2008);
- The signing of a Criminal Law Convention on Corruption and a Second Additional Protocol to the European Convention on Mutual Assistance in Criminal Matters (2009);
- Liechtenstein becoming a member of the Group of States against Corruption (GRECO), the monitoring body established by the Council of Europe to improve the capacity of countries to prevent and combat corruption (2010).

Money laundering is criminalised through Article 165 StGB. Article 1.6 was added in 2003, making the financing of terrorism a predicate offence. In December 2008, Parliament passed a new legislative package which includes a comprehensive review of the Due Diligence Act (DDA) as well as partial amendments to the Criminal Code including document fraud and market manipulation.

AML/CFT legal requirements are expanded and specified in the Government's Due Diligence Ordinance (DDO). This was originally introduced on 11th January, 2005, and an updated version came into force on 1st March, 2009.

27.22.4 FATF Assessment

Liechtenstein is a member of MONEYVAL. The assessment of the implementation of anti-money-laundering and counter-terrorist-financing (AML/CFT) measures in Liechtenstein was conducted by the IMF and adopted by MONEYVAL. The IMF report in 2007 noted that provisions regarding CDD are broadly in line with the international standard, but, whether conducted directly or through intermediaries, they need to be strengthened further in some areas. On the whole, Liechtenstein is making good progress (especially as it was listed as an uncooperative country until 2001), but there is still work to do.

27.22.5 The Primary AML Investigation/Regulatory Authorities

The Financial Market Authority

The FMA is an independent, integrated financial market supervisory authority operating as an autonomous institution under public law. The FMA is responsible for the supervision and execution of the special legislation, and for the regulation and the representation of the interests of Liechtenstein in international bodies (in coordination with the government).

The Financial Intelligence Unit

The FIU is the central point for collection and analysis of information which is to be used to detect money laundering, predicate offences for money laundering, organised crime and/or terrorist-financing activity.

According to Articles 4 and 5 of the FIU Act, the FIU is tasked with:

- Receiving the suspicious activity reports (SARs) submitted by the subjected (financial) entities pursuant to Articles 16 (mandatory reporting) and 17 (discretionary reporting of attempted occasional transactions) of the DDA;
- Analysing and evaluating these disclosures in the light of possible indications of money laundering, related offences, organised crime and terrorism financing;
- Reporting to the Public Prosecutor all confirmed suspicions and elements related to the relevant criminal activities resulting from the analysis;
- Creating and managing a database of relevant information collected in the course of its activities; and

- Drafting situation and strategy reports for the government which evaluate the money-laundering and terrorist-financing threat (risk analysis).

The FIU also has tracing powers to a certain extent, in that it can, on receipt of a suspicious activity report, demand additional information from the financial intermediary, who is obliged to comply immediately.

Although the FIU accepts SARs in any form, it has drafted a reporting form that reporting entities are encouraged to use (Article 23.2 Due Diligence Ordinance). Some 80% of disclosures are made this way.

27.22.6 *Outline of Specific Money-laundering Offences*

The offence of money laundering is committed by:

- Anyone who hides asset components originating from a crime, or conceals their origin, in particular by providing false information in legal transactions concerning the origin or the true nature of the ownership or other rights pertaining to the power of disposal over, the transfer of, or concerning the location of such asset components; and
- Anyone who appropriates or takes into safekeeping asset components originating from a crime committed by another person, whether with the intention merely to hold them in safekeeping, to invest them or to manage them, or who converts, realises or transfers such asset components to a third party.

Proceeds are considered criminal if they have been obtained through an offence or received for the perpetration of an offence, including assets that represent the value of the assets originally obtained or received. Therefore, both direct and converted proceeds are covered. Furthermore, "asset components" is understood in a broad sense and would include tangible as well as intangible property and all assets representing financial value, including claims and interests in such assets. The offence of money laundering, therefore, extends to any type of property, regardless of its value, that represents the proceeds of crime.

27.22.7 *Penalties*

Liechtenstein has adopted a combined approach, listing all felonies and a number of misdemeanours as predicate offences for money laundering. Felonies are intentional offences sanctioned with life imprisonment or imprisonment of more than three years, whereby the maximum sanction is the determining factor for the differentiation between felonies and misdemeanours. Misdemeanours listed as predicate offences for money laundering relate to terrorist financing, official corruption and misconduct by public officials, and offences under the Narcotics Act, including sale or procurement of narcotics, financing narcotic trafficking or the procurement of financing of narcotics.

The penalty for hiding or concealing the origin of criminal assets is imprisonment for up to three years and a fine. For anyone who appropriates or takes into safekeeping laundered assets, the penalty is two years' imprisonment and a fine. If the assets of a criminal organisation are involved, the penalty is three years' imprisonment, and for any of the above offences committed by a gang, or where the value of the assets is above CHF 75,000, the penalty is up to five years' imprisonment.

Only a few criminal offences are punished with stricter sanctions (up to ten years for counterfeiting currency, for breach of trust with particularly heavy damage, for fraud with particularly heavy damage, for fraud as a business and for fraudulent bankruptcy with particularly heavy damage). No penalties have actually been imposed by Liechtenstein courts for money laundering, and only seven prosecutions have been made.

27.22.8 Scope

The DDA applies to all financial institutions holding a licence, including, but not exclusive to:

- Banks and finance companies;
- E-money institutions;
- Asset management companies;
- Investment undertakings; and
- Insurance undertakings.

Financial transactions relevant to DDA encompass:

- Accepting or safekeeping third parties' assets;
- Assisting in the acceptance, investment or transfer of such assets; and
- Establishing, or acting as an organ of, a legal entity on the account of a third party (legal person, company, trust, association or asset entity) that does not operate commercially in the domiciliary state (holding companies excluded).

The following are considered equivalent to financial transactions:

- Transactions exceeding CHF 25,000 made by dealers in high-value goods and by auctioneers when payments are in cash, whether the transaction is operated in one or in several linked steps; and
- Granting of admission to a casino to a visitor.

27.22.9 Risk-based Approach

The prime area of vulnerability for Liechtenstein appears to occur in the layering stage of money laundering. The risk-based approach to money-laundering deterrence has been fully adopted in Liechtenstein. This means that the perception of risk within a potential customer determines the extent to which a firm considers it necessary to conduct due diligence or enhanced due diligence assessments.

A high proportion of Liechtenstein's financial service business involves private cross-border banking, which falls within the FATF's definition of "higher-risk" business.

27.22.10 Role of the MLRO/Nominated Officer

Persons subject to due diligence must appoint a contact person with the FMA, as well as Compliance and Investigating Officers (Article 22 DDA):

The Compliance Officer shall (Article 30 DDO):

- Support and advise the management in the implementation of due diligence legislation and the design of the corresponding internal organisation, but without relieving the management of its responsibility in this regard;
- Draw up internal instructions; and
- Plan and monitor the internal basic and continuing training of employees involved with business relationships.

The Investigating Officer conducts inspections in order to review records and assess completion of due diligence requirements, notably with regard to reporting obligations and responses to domestic authorities' information requests (Article 31 DDO).

The Compliance Officer and the Investigating Officer shall have a sound knowledge in matters of the prevention and combating of money laundering, predicate offences of money laundering, organised crime and terrorist financing, and be familiar with the current developments in these areas. The responsibilities of the Compliance Officer and the Investigating Officer may be transferred to suitably qualified external persons or offices.

27.22.11 Due Diligence

Financial institutions must obtain prescribed customer due diligence (CDD) information for legal persons, companies, trusts, other associations and asset entities. All information and documents required to establish and verify the identity of the contracting party and the beneficial owner shall be available, in full and in due form, at the time the business relationship is initiated. If it is necessary to maintain normal business, it may exceptionally be deemed sufficient if the information and documents required are made available as soon as possible after the business relationship has been initiated. In this event, the person or entity subject to due diligence shall ensure that no funds are transferred in the meantime.

There is no CDD requirement for low-risk, occasional transactions. Activities shall be deemed to be occasional if the individual activity does not exceed the value of CHF 1,000 and no more than 100 transactions per year are carried out.

Personal Client Due Diligence

The entity must establish and verify the identity of the contracting party by inspecting a document with probative value (original or certified copy) relating to the contracting party, to ascertain the following information:

- Last name
- First name

- Date of birth
- Address of residence
- State of residence
- Nationality.

For natural persons, documents with probative value shall include a valid official identification document with a photograph (in particular a passport, identity card or driving licence). An identification document shall be deemed to be valid if it entitles the contracting party to enter the Principality of Liechtenstein at the time when the contracting party's identity is established and verified. If the contracting party cannot provide such a document from his home country, he shall provide a confirmation of identity from the authority responsible in his domicile.

Corporate Customer Due Diligence

Reporting institutions have to establish the identity of the beneficial owner, and should use risk-based measures to verify the identity and establish the ownership and control structure of a contractor. The following are required for corporate customers:

- Name or company name;
- Legal form;
- Address of domicile;
- State of domicile;
- Date of formation;
- Place and date of entry in the public register (where applicable); and
- The names of the bodies or trustees formally acting on behalf of the legal entity in dealings with the person or entity subject to due diligence.

If the contracting party is a legal entity, the persons or entities subject to due diligence shall ensure that the person purporting to act on its behalf is authorised to do so. The persons or entities subject to due diligence shall verify the identity of such persons by inspecting a document with probative value (original or certified copy) or by confirming the authenticity of the signature. In addition:

- Documents with probative value must be original forms or certified copies; and
- Copies of these documents must be dated and signed, in order to certify that the original forms or certified copies have been verified.

A customer profile must be compiled for each long-term relationship and must include:

- The contracting party and beneficial owner;
- Authorised agents and bodies acting in dealings with the persons or entities subject to due diligence;

- The economic background and origin of the assets deposited;
- The profession and business activity of the effective depositor of the assets; and
- The intended use of the assets.

The degree of detail of the information pursuant to the above shall take account of the risk involved in the business relationship. If, in the course of the business relationship, doubts arise about the identity of the beneficial owner, the due diligence procedures must be repeated.

Beneficial Ownership

In order to establish and verify the identity of the beneficial owner, the persons or entities subject to due diligence shall collect and document the aforementioned CDD information and obtain confirmation of the accuracy of the information from the contracting party or a person authorised by the latter, by means of a signature or using a secure electronic signature.

Simplified Customer Due Diligence

Certain specified low-risk organisations, such as publicly traded companies, can be subjected to simplified due diligence.

Enhanced Customer Due Diligence

Enhanced CDD should be carried out for high-risk customers. Criteria for business relationships and transactions involving higher risks shall include, in particular:

- The registered office or place of residence of the contracting party and beneficial owner or their nationality;
- The nature and location of the contracting parties' and beneficial owner's business activity;
- The nature of the products or services requested;
- The level and type of assets deposited;
- The level of inflows and outflows of assets;
- The country of origin or destination of frequent payments.

Additional measures for transactions involving higher risks shall include, in particular:

- Verifying the identity of the contracting party using additional documents, data or information;
- Clarifying the origin of the assets deposited;
- Clarifying the intended use of assets withdrawn;
- Clarifying the professional and business activity of the contracting party and beneficial owner.

Politically Exposed Persons

For PEP CDD, an entity must:

- Add appropriate risk-based methods that determine whether the contracting party may be a PEP;
- Seek the approval of at least one member of the board before a business relationship with a PEP is commenced;
- At least annually, seek the consent of a member of the board for the continuation of business relationships with PEPs.

Anonymous Accounts

Anonymous accounts are prohibited.

Correspondent Banking

Banks and postal institutions that carry out correspondent banking services for foreign banks and postal institutions must:

- Obtain sufficient information on their respondent institutions to obtain complete clarity about their business activities. This includes information from public sources on the most important business areas of the respondent institution, its locations and the status of regulation and supervision to which the respondent institution is subject.
- Satisfy themselves that the respondent institution has taken adequate and efficient measures to guard against money laundering, organised crime and the financing of terrorism.
- Pay special attention to the risk that a correspondent account might, under certain circumstances, be used directly by a third party for its own transactions.
- Document in the due diligence files the information obtained pursuant to the above and the arrangements made. Any documents and records obtained shall also be included in the due diligence files.

27.22.12 Ongoing Monitoring

If, despite repeating the process of establishing and verifying the identity of the contracting party or beneficial owner, doubts remain as to the information provided by them, the persons or entities subject to due diligence shall discontinue the business relationship and adequately document the outflow of assets.

The business profile shall contain the following information:

- The contracting party and beneficial owner;
- Authorised agents and bodies acting in dealings with the persons or entities subject to due diligence;
- The economic background and origin of the assets deposited;

- The profession and business activity of the effective depositor of the assets; and
- The intended use of the assets.

The degree of detail of the information shall take account of the risk involved in the business relationship. Simple inquiries shall serve to assess the plausibility of circumstances or transactions that deviate from the business profile. For this reason, the person or entity subject to due diligence shall obtain, evaluate and document such information as is useful in ascertaining the background to such transactions, to identify how plausible they are.

27.22.13 Staff Training

The persons or entities subject to due diligence shall ensure that employees involved with business relationships receive up-to-date and comprehensive basic and continuing training. The knowledge imparted shall encompass the regulations on preventing and combating money laundering, predicate offences of money laundering, organised crime and terrorist financing, in particular:

- The obligations arising out of the Act and this Ordinance;
- The relevant provisions of the Criminal Code; and
- The internal instructions.

27.22.14 Record-keeping

The due diligence files shall contain the documents and records prepared and used in order to comply with the CDD provisions. They shall, in particular, include:

- The documents and records used to establish and verify the identity of the contracting party and the beneficial owner;
- The business profile;
- The records of any inquiries carried out as well as all documents and records used in this regard;
- Records describing transactions and, if applicable, the asset balance; and
- Any reports made to the FIU.

The due diligence files shall be prepared and kept in such a manner that:

- The required due diligence obligations can be complied with at any time;
- They enable third parties with sufficient expertise to form a reliable judgment of compliance with the legal requirements; and
- Requests from the responsible domestic authorities and courts, auditors and auditing offices can be fully met within a reasonable period of time.

The due diligence files may be stored in written, electronic or similar form provided that:

- They match the documents on which they are based;
- They are available at all times; and
- They can be rendered readable at any time.

The integrity and legibility of image and data storage media kept shall be checked regularly. The due diligence files shall be stored at a location within Liechtenstein that is accessible at any time.

The following information shall be added to records:

- The names of the persons entrusted with making the records;
- The nature and scope of the documents recorded;
- The place and date of recording;
- Any damage to the documents, image and data storage media identified during recording or storage.

Customer-related documents and receipts must be kept for at least ten years after the business relationship has ended or the transaction has been completed.

27.22.15 Suspicious Transaction Reporting

Where suspicion of money laundering, a predicate offence of money laundering, organised crime or terrorist financing exists, the persons subject to due diligence must immediately report, in writing, to the financial intelligence unit (FIU). Likewise, all offices of the National Administration and the FMA are subject to the obligation to report to the FIU.

The report shall contain all information required for the FIU to evaluate the matter. The FIU shall confirm, in writing, the date of receipt of the report. It may request further information after receiving the report. Such information shall be submitted without delay. The FIU may issue a standardised report form.

27.22.16 Penalties

Infringements of the DDA lead to severe punishment. Persons who do not meet their obligations and, for example, fail to carry out identification or documentation correctly may be punished by the Princely Court of Justice by up to six months' imprisonment or a fine of up to 360 daily rates. Daily rates are calculated with reference to the net income of the individual, so 360 daily rates is likely to equate to approximately a year's salary.

27.22.17 Case Studies

According to the US State Department Money Laundering Report 2012, there were seven prosecutions for money laundering from 19th October, 2010 to 31st October, 2011, but no convictions.

27.23 COUNTRY PROFILE: MALAYSIA

27.23.1 Overview

Drug trafficking is noted by the authorities as the main source of illegal proceeds in Malaysia. Authorities highlight illegal proceeds from corruption as a significant money-laundering risk in addition to a range of predicate offences that generate significant proceeds of crime. Malaysia has a significant informal remittance sector. Although elements of the AML framework in Malaysia are stringent, there is still work to be done to bring it up to international standards.

27.23.2 Key Legislation

The two main sources of anti-money-laundering legislation in place in Malaysia are the Anti-Money Laundering and Counter Financing of Terrorism Act 2001 (AMLATFA) and the Standard Guidelines on Anti-Money Laundering and Counter Financing of Terrorism.

27.23.3 Legislative History

There have been various amendments to the AMLATFA since its introduction. Furthermore, the Bank Negara Malaysia is vested with comprehensive legal powers to regulate and supervise the financial system, under various pieces of legislation including:

- Islamic Banking Act 1983;
- Banking and Financial Institutions Act 1989;
- Money-Changing Act 1998;
- Central Bank of Malaysia Act 2009;
- Money Services Business Act 2011.

In 2006 the regulatory framework was amended, making changes to AML legislation among other statutory instruments. This came into force during the following year. In March 2007, at the initiation of the NCC, Malaysia enacted amendments to five different pieces of legislation: the AMLA (now known as the AMLATFA since it now includes terrorist financing), the Penal Code, the Subordinate Courts Act, the Courts of Judicature Act and the Criminal Procedure Code. The number of predicate offences for money laundering was expanded from 219 to 223.

Moreover, the amendments impose penalties for terrorist acts, allow for the forfeiture of terrorist-related assets, allow for the prosecution of individuals who have provided material support for terrorists, expand the use of wiretaps and other surveillance of terrorist suspects and permit video testimony in terrorist cases. This enabled Malaysia to accede to the UN Convention for the Suppression of the Financing of Terrorism.

27.23.4 FATF Assessment

The APG Mutual Evaluation Report on Malaysia in 2007 noted that while the customer due diligence regime in Malaysia shows a high degree of technical compliance with FATF standards, the level of implementation of requirements to identify and verify beneficial ownership of corporate customers is unclear. While the legal provisions are in line with FATF standards, there are some concerns that implementation by the financial institutions may not yet be in compliance with the legal requirements. There were other issues regarding CDD and PEPs, although the effectiveness of the FIU was praised. It described the level of success of the Malaysian AML framework as "varied".

27.23.5 The Primary AML Investigation/Regulatory Authorities

Bank Negara Malaysia

The Bank is a statutory body wholly owned by the Government of Malaysia with the paid-up capital progressively increased, currently at RM 100 million. The Bank reports to the Minister of Finance, Malaysia and keeps the Minister informed of matters pertaining to monetary and financial sector policies.

The major role of the Bank is the conduct of monetary policy, which has seen generally low and stable inflation for decades, thereby preserving the purchasing power of the ringgit. The Bank is also responsible for bringing about financial system stability and for financial system infrastructure.

National Co-ordination Committee to Counter Money Laundering

While the Bank Negara Malaysia is the designated competent authority under the AMLA, the National Co-ordination Committee to Counter Money Laundering (NCC), consisting of 13 Ministries and government agencies, was set up in 2000 in order to achieve a coordinated approach towards ensuring the effective implementation of national AML/CFT measures. The NCC provides an integrated platform for the relevant Ministries, government agencies and supervisory authorities to ensure that Malaysia implements an effective national AML/CFT system in line with the international standards. Bank Negara Malaysia, as the Secretariat to the NCC, continues to play an instrumental role in this process by promoting a collaborative culture between the government and private sector towards achieving AML/CFT compliance.

27.23.6 Outline of Specific Money-laundering Offences

Money laundering is defined under Section 3(1) of AMLATFA as the act of a person who:

- Engages, directly or indirectly, in a transaction that involves proceeds of any unlawful activity;
- Acquires, receives, possesses, disguises, transfers, converts, exchanges, carries, disposes, uses, removes from or brings into Malaysia proceeds of any unlawful activity; or
- Conceals, disguises or impedes the establishment of the true nature, origin, location, movement, disposition, title of, rights with respect to or ownership of proceeds of any activity.

It is to be inferred from objective factual circumstances that the person knows, or has reason to believe, that property may be the proceeds from any unlawful activity. A person will also be guilty of the offence of money laundering if, without reasonable excuse, they fail to take reasonable steps to establish whether or not the property is proceeds from any unlawful activity.

The "Terrorism Financing Offence" is also defined under the same section, as any offence which essentially includes:

- Providing or collecting property for carrying out an act of terrorism;
- Providing services for terrorism purposes;
- Arranging for retention or control of terrorist property; or
- Dealing with terrorist property.

In order to find an individual to be guilty of financing terrorism, the authorities will focus on the determination of the individual's actions or the use of funds, which may have derived from legitimate sources.

27.23.7 *Penalties*

Any person who engages in, or attempts to engage in, or abets the commission of money laundering commits an offence and shall, on conviction, be liable to a fine not exceeding five million ringgit or to imprisonment for a term not exceeding five years, or to both.

Tipping off is punished by a fine of RM 1 million or a one-year jail term, or both.

The falsification, concealment and destruction of documents can be punished by a fine of RM 1 million or a one-year jail term, or both. A further fine of RM 1,000 per day will be imposed for each day during which the offence continues after conviction.

27.23.8 *Risk-based Approach*

The Standard Guidelines supplement the AMLATFA and both sources have been drawn up in accordance with international standards recommended by the Financial Action Task Force's 40 Recommendations on Money Laundering together with the nine Special Recommendations on Terrorist Financing. Collectively, the laws, policies and practices adopt a risk-based approach to combating money laundering.

27.23.9 *Role of the MLRO/Nominated Officer*

Senior management of reporting entities have a responsibility to appoint a Compliance Officer who is "fit and proper" to carry out AML/CFT responsibilities and can effectively discharge them. Similar to an MLRO, the Compliance Officer's role is to act as the reference point for AML/CFT matters, including employees' training and reporting of suspicious transactions. It is the Compliance Officer's role to submit suspicious transaction reports to the financial intelligence unit in Bank Negara Malaysia. The appointed Compliance Officer is the single point of reference for the financial intelligence unit in Bank Negara Malaysia with regards to AML/CFT matters.

It is important that the Compliance Officer who is appointed by the reporting institution has the necessary knowledge and expertise to carry out his responsibilities, which include the following:

- AML/CFT obligations required under the relevant laws and regulations;
- The latest developments in money-laundering and financing terrorism techniques;
- The AML/CFT measures undertaken in industry;
- Timely access to customer due diligence documentation and other relevant information.

Reporting institutions must inform the financial intelligence unit in Bank Negara Malaysia, in writing, if there is an appointment or change of the Compliance Officer. The name, designation, office address, office telephone number, fax and email address must all be sent to the FIU.

The role of the Compliance Officer should be clearly defined and documented. The role of the Compliance Officer is to ensure:

- The reporting institution's compliance with the AML/CFT requirements;
- Implementation of the AML/CFT policies;
- That the appropriate AML/CFT procedures, including customer acceptance policy, customer due diligence, record-keeping, ongoing monitoring, reporting of suspicious transactions and combating the financing of terrorism are implemented effectively;
- That the AML/CFT mechanism is regularly assessed to ensure that it is effective and sufficient to address any change in money-laundering and financing of terrorism trends;
- That the channel of communication from the respective employees to the branch/subsidiary Compliance Officer and subsequently to the Compliance Officer is secured and that information is kept confidential;
- That all employees are aware of the reporting institution's AML/CFT measures, including policies, control mechanisms and the channel of reporting;
- That suspicious transaction reports generated internally by the branch/subsidiary Compliance Officers are appropriately evaluated before submission to the financial intelligence unit in Bank Negara Malaysia; and
- The identification of money-laundering and financing of terrorism risks associated with new products or services or arising from the reporting institution's operational changes, including the introduction of new technology and processes.

27.23.10 Due Diligence

Customer due diligence must be carried out when:

- Establishing a business relationship with any customer;
- Carrying out cash or an occasional transaction which involves a sum in excess of the amount specified by Bank Negara Malaysia under its sectoral guidelines or relevant circular (RM 50,000 for banking transactions at the time of writing);

- There is any suspicion of money-laundering activity or the financing of terrorism;
- The institution has any reason to doubt the veracity or adequacy of previously obtained information.

The minimum customer due diligence requirement which reporting institutions must conduct includes the following:

- Identification and verification of the customer;
- Identification and verification of beneficial ownership and control of transactions;
- Collection of information on the purpose and intended nature of the business relationship/transaction;
- Ongoing due diligence and scrutiny to ensure the information provided is updated and relevant.

When dealing with customers during the customer due diligence processes, reporting institutions must pay particular attention to the behaviour of customers. The unwillingness of customers to provide certain information may be grounds for suspicion. In the event that existing customers fail to provide certain information, or indeed refuse to update certain information, business transactions and relations should cease with that customer. A suspicious transaction report should also be lodged with the financial intelligence unit at Bank Negara Malaysia.

In certain situations where the risks of money laundering and financing of terrorism are low and verification is not possible at the point of establishing a business relationship, the reporting institution may allow its customer due diligence process to be completed no later than 14 days (or the period specified in Bank Negara Malaysia's sectoral guidelines, where applicable) after the business relationship has been established to permit some flexibility for its customer to furnish the relevant documents. The risk of delaying verification is an issue which reporting institutions should address by establishing internal procedures.

Personal Client Due Diligence

When conducting customer due diligence on individual customers, the following information should be requested:

- Full name
- NIRC/Passport number
- Permanent and mailing addresses
- Date of birth
- Nationality.

This information should be substantiated by requiring the individual to furnish the original of, and make a copy of, either the NRIC for Malaysians/permanent residents or a passport for a foreigner. Customers must present copies of original documents to the reporting entity, who must also keep copies of these documents. Reporting entities are instructed to request supporting photographic identification if there is any doubt as to a customer's identity.

Corporate Customer Due Diligence

As part of customer due diligence for corporate clients, companies and businesses are required to present and produce copies of the following documents:

- Memorandum/Article/Certificate of Incorporation/Partnership (certified true copies/duly notarised copies may be accepted) or any other reliable references to verify the identity of the corporate customer.
- Identification document for directors/shareholders/partners (certified true copy/duly notarised copies or Form 24 and 49 as prescribed by the Companies Commission of Malaysia or equivalent documents for foreign incorporations may be accepted).
- Authorisation for any person to represent the company/business.
- Relevant documents to identify the person authorised to represent the company/business in its dealings with the reporting institution.

Where there is any doubt, the reporting institution should:

- Conduct a basic search or enquiry on the background of such company/business to ensure that it has not been, or is not in the process of being, dissolved or liquidated; and
- Verify the authenticity of the information provided by the company/business with the Companies Commission of Malaysia.

The reporting institution should identify the beneficial owner of the corporate customer and know the ownership and control structure of the corporate customer in order to detect any unusual circumstances concerning changes to the company/business structure or ownership or payment profile of its account. Based on the risk profiling conducted on the customer, reporting institutions should take reasonable measures to verify the beneficial owner of the corporate customer.

Simplified Corporate Customer Due Diligence

Copies of the Memorandum and Articles of Association or Certificate of Incorporation do not need to be produced and individual directors do not need to produce identification documents if the corporate customers fall into the following categories:

- Public listed companies/corporations (including foreign companies listed in exchanges recognised by Bursa Malaysia Securities Berhad) subjected to regulatory disclosure;
- Government-linked companies in Malaysia – this is typically where the government owns a controlling interest in the corporate entity, or where the government is a shareholder of a corporate entity;
- State-owned corporations or companies in Malaysia;
- Financial institutions licensed under the Islamic Banking Act 1983, the Takaful Act 1984, the Banking and Financial Institutions Act 1989, the Insurance Act 1996, the Securities Commission or the Labuan Offshore Financial Services Authority;

- Prescribed institutions under the Development Financial Institutions Act 2002 and supervised by Bank Negara Malaysia.

Beneficial Ownership

The reporting institution should conduct customer due diligence on any natural person who ultimately owns or controls the customer's transaction if it suspects a transaction is conducted on behalf of a beneficial owner and not the customer who is conducting such transaction. The customer due diligence should be as stringent as that for individual customers.

Enhanced Customer Due Diligence

For higher-risk customers, the reporting institution shall conduct enhanced customer due diligence. This should include at least:

- Obtaining more detailed information from that customer and, through publicly available information, in particular on the purpose of the transaction and source of funds; and
- Obtaining approval from the senior management of the reporting institution before establishing a business relationship with the customer.

Examples of high-risk customers include:

- High net worth individuals;
- Non-resident customers;
- Customers from locations known for their high rates of crime (e.g. drug producing, trafficking or smuggling);
- Countries or jurisdictions with inadequate AML/CFT laws and regulations as highlighted by the FATF;
- PEPs;
- Complex legal arrangements;
- Cash-based businesses; and
- Businesses/activities identified by the FATF as of higher money-laundering and financing of terrorism risk.

Non-face-to-face Customer Due Diligence

The procedures which financial institutions must have in place to limit the risks involved in non-face-to-face CDD should be just as effective as those for face-to-face customers. The Guidelines recommend the following various approaches:

- Requisition of additional documents to complement those which are required for face-to-face customers;
- Developing independent contact with the customers;
- Verification of customer information against databases maintained by the authorities.

Politically Exposed Persons

Once a PEP has been identified, the reporting institution should take reasonable and appropriate measures to establish the source of wealth and funds of the individual. The decision on whether to enter into or continue business relations with PEPs should be made by senior management of the reporting institution at the head office. In addition, the reporting institution should conduct enhanced ongoing due diligence on PEPs throughout its business relationships with such PEPs. For such purpose, the reporting institution should note that business relationships with family members or close associates of PEPs will involve similar risks to PEPs.

Correspondent Banking

When entering such a business relationship, the reporting institution should capture and assess, at the minimum, the following information on the respondent institution, to determine the reputation and quality of supervision:

- The board of directors and the management;
- Business activities and products;
- Applicable legislation, regulations and supervision; and
- AML/CFT measures and control.

The reporting institution should establish or continue a correspondent banking relationship with the respondent institution only if it is satisfied with the assessment of the information gathered.

The reporting institution should also document the responsibilities of the respective parties in relation to the correspondent banking relationship, in particular, matters in relation to customer due diligence for all products and services.

The decision and approval to establish or continue a correspondent banking relationship should be made at the senior management level.

Where a correspondent banking relationship involves the maintenance of "payable-through accounts", the reporting institution should be satisfied that:

- The respondent institution has performed all the normal obligations on its customers that have direct access to the accounts of the reporting institution; and
- The respondent institution is able to provide relevant customer identification data upon request from the reporting institution.

In addition, the reporting institution should pay special attention to correspondent banking relationships with respondent institutions from countries highlighted by the internationally recognised AML/CFT bodies such as the FATF as insufficiently implementing the internationally accepted AML/CFT measures, which would require enhanced due diligence to assess the money-laundering and financing of terrorism associated risks.

Shell Banking

The reporting institution should not establish or conduct any business relationship with shell banks. As for shell companies, for those that do not conduct any commercial activities or have any form of commercial presence in the country, extra care should be taken to verify the details of the directors, shareholders and authorised signatories.

27.23.11 Ongoing Monitoring

The reporting institution should take the necessary measures to ensure that the records of existing customers, including customer profiles, remain updated and relevant. In addition, further evidence in identifying existing customers should be obtained to ensure compliance with the reporting institution's current customer due diligence standards. The reporting institution should conduct regular reviews on existing records of customers, especially when:

- A significant transaction is to take place;
- There is a material change in the way the account is operated;
- The customer's documentation standards change substantially; or
- It discovers that the information held on the customer is insufficient.

Effective monitoring should enable reporting entities to detect money laundering or the financing of terrorism through analysing the transaction patterns or activities of the customers. Ongoing customer due diligence should examine and clarify:

- The economic background and purpose of any transaction;
- Business relationships that appear unusual;
- Business relationships that have no apparent economic purpose;
- Transactions where the legality of the transaction is not clear, especially with regards to complex and large transactions or high-risk customers.

All findings must be documented and made available to Bank Negara Malaysia and the relevant supervisory authority upon request. An effective customer due diligence process, where ongoing monitoring is carried out, should include the following:

- An accurate and updated information-management system containing customer transactions and business profiles;
- An information-management system to provide timely information to the reporting institution on suspicious activity;
- Internal criteria "red flags" to detect suspicious transactions guided by examples of suspicious transactions provided by Bank Negara Malaysia or other competent authorities and international organisations. Any "red flags" should be subjected to ongoing monitoring or enhanced due diligence;

- Ongoing due diligence and monitoring of transactions for business relationships with customers from countries highlighted by internationally recognised AML/CFT bodies such as the FATF as insufficiently implementing internationally accepted AML/CFT standards.

27.23.12 Staff Training

Reporting institutions should conduct awareness and training programmes on AML/CFT practices and measures for their employees, depending on the role of the employee. Senior management must ensure proper channels for communication are in place for all levels of employees. Employees must also be made aware that they will be held personally liable for any failure to observe the internal AML/CFT requirements.

Key training for all employees should, at a basic level, include training on the relevant guidelines on AML/CFT issued by Bank Negara Malaysia and the reporting institutions' own internal AML/CFT policies and procedures.

The Guidelines are quite thorough and highlight the type of training which should be conducted for employees appropriate to their levels of responsibility in detecting money laundering and the financing of terrorism. Particular guidance is given to the following levels of employees.

New Employees
Should be provided with a general background on AML/CFT.

"Front-line" Employees
Must be trained to conduct effective ongoing customer due diligence, detect suspicious transactions and measures that need to be taken to identify a transaction as being suspicious.

Employees Establishing Business Relationships
Should be focussed on customer identification and verification, customer due diligence, including when to conduct enhanced due diligence, reporting obligations and when there is a need to defer establishing new business relationships with new customers until due diligence is satisfactorily completed.

Supervisors and Managers
Should include a higher level of instructions covering all aspects of AML/CFT procedures, in particular the risk-based approach to customer acceptance, customer due diligence and risk profiling of customers. Other areas include the penalties for non-compliance with the AML/CFT requirements, procedures in addressing the financing of terrorism such as the Consolidated List and the list of terrorists under AMLATFA, internal suspicious transaction reporting procedures and the requirements for customer due diligence and record-keeping.

All training and awareness programmes should be conducted regularly and supplemented with refresher courses for employees. These programmes should update staff on the latest AML/CFT developments such as products or transaction modes, which are susceptible to the risk of money laundering and financing of terrorism, and remind them of their responsibilities under the AML/CFT programme.

27.23.13 *Record-keeping*

Reporting institutions are required to keep all relevant records, including any material business correspondence and documents relating to transactions, in particular those obtained during customer due diligence procedures, for at least six years after the transaction has been completed or after the business relationship with a customer has ended. Records can be retained for longer if the records are being used for ongoing investigations or prosecutions in court.

The type of documents that should be retained is those which enable an audit trail on an individual transaction. Transactions should be traceable by Bank Negara Malaysia, the relevant supervisory and law-enforcement agency. Records should be kept in a manner in which the records are secure and retrievable on request in a timely manner, and must enable the reporting institution to establish the history, circumstances and reconstruction of each transaction. The records should, at a minimum, include the following:

- The identity of the customer;
- The identity of the beneficiary;
- The identity of the person conducting the transaction, where applicable;
- The type of transaction (e.g. deposit or withdrawal);
- The form of transaction (e.g. by cheque or by cash);
- The instruction and the origin and destination of fund transfers;
- The amount and type of currency.

27.23.14 *Investigation and Reporting Requirements*

The reporting institution is required to promptly submit a suspicious transaction report to the financial intelligence unit in Bank Negara Malaysia when any of its employees suspect, or have reason to suspect, that the transaction or attempted transaction involves proceeds from an unlawful activity or the customer is involved in money laundering or the financing of terrorism. The reporting institution should provide the necessary information surrounding the suspicious transaction, as required in the suspicious transaction report form. The reporting institution must establish a reporting system for the submission of suspicious transaction reports to the financial intelligence unit in Bank Negara Malaysia.

The Compliance Officer is responsible for liaising with, and submitting reports to, Bank Negara Malaysia. Upon receiving any internal suspicious transaction report, whether from the head office, branch or subsidiary, the Compliance Officer should evaluate the grounds for suspicion and, if suspicion is confirmed, promptly submit the suspicious transaction report to the financial intelligence unit in Bank Negara Malaysia. In cases where the Compliance Officer decides that there are no reasonable grounds for suspicion, he should document his decision, ensure it is supported by the relevant documents and file the report.

The reporting institution should ensure that the suspicious transaction reporting mechanism is operated in a secure environment to maintain confidentiality and preserve secrecy. The disclosure of any information or matter which has been obtained by any person within the reporting institution, in the performance of his duties or the exercise of his functions, is an offence under the AMLATFA.

27.23.15 Reporting Thresholds

The Guidelines do not give a transaction value as a default level at which all transactions should be reported. Thus, it does not matter how high or low the value of a transaction is, a suspicious transaction report must be submitted if there is reason to suspect that the transaction involves illegal proceeds or that the customer may be involved in money laundering.

27.23.16 Penalties

Any person who contravenes any provision or regulation made, or any specification or requirement made, or any order in writing, direction, instruction or notice given, or any limit, term, condition or restriction imposed, in the exercise of any power conferred under or pursuant to any provision commits an offence and shall, on conviction, if no penalty is expressly provided for the offence or the regulation, be liable to a fine not exceeding RM 250,000.

An officer of a reporting institution must take all reasonable steps to ensure its compliance with the reporting obligation. Failure of a reporting institution to comply with any of the requirements will result in Bank Negara Malaysia taking the appropriate enforcement action, including obtaining a Court order against any or all of the officers or employees of the reporting institution on terms that the Court deems necessary to enforce compliance.

Notwithstanding any Court order, the financial intelligence unit in Bank Negara Malaysia may direct or enter into an agreement with the reporting institution to implement any action plan to ensure compliance with reporting requirements. Failure of an officer to take reasonable steps to ensure compliance, or failure of a reporting institution to implement any action plan as agreed to ensure compliance, will result in the officer or officers being personally liable to a fine not exceeding RM 100, 000 or to imprisonment for a term not exceeding six months, or to both.

In the case of a continuing offence, a further fine may be imposed on the reporting institution not exceeding RM 1,000 for each day during which the offence continues after conviction. Bank Negara Malaysia is authorised to compound, with the consent of the Public Prosecutor, any offence under the regulations by accepting from the person reasonably suspected of having committed the offence such amount not exceeding 50%

of the amount of the maximum fine for that offence, including the daily fine, if any, in the case of a continuing offence.

Any institution that fails or refuses to comply with or contravenes any direction or guidelines issued to it by the relevant regulatory or supervisory authority, or discloses a direction or guideline issued to it, commits an offence and shall, on conviction, be liable to a fine not exceeding RM 100,000.

27.23.17 Case Studies

A 62-year-old former executive director of a pharmaceutical company recently became the first person to be convicted of money laundering in Malaysia. She was charged with eight counts of money laundering involving RM 41.3 million, amongst other financial offences, and sentenced to three years' imprisonment and fined over RM 6 million.

She laundered the proceeds of unlawful activities using a joint bank account to hide the true depository. Furthermore, she used her company accounts and the accounts of five other firms, forming a complex transaction trail, to disguise the origin of the funds. In addition to this, she assisted a colleague in forging promissory notes worth RM 37 million.

This case illustrates the need to proceed cautiously, even if a customer is low-risk. A 62-year-old female would probably be identified as a low-risk customer with regards to money laundering and other financial crimes, but her position of seniority – she was an executive – suggests that she may be in an ideal position to commit a financial crime. Therefore, thorough due diligence should be conducted on any such customer, and the risk categories applied should be under continual review.

27.24 COUNTRY PROFILE: MEXICO

27.24.1 Overview

Mexico faces an unprecedented threat to its national security and stability from drug trafficking and organised crime. Powerful drug cartels, resorting to extreme violence, have extended their activities across various parts of the country, and these activities pose significant challenges to the government. In response to the financial power of these cartels, the Mexican government has instituted unprecedented measures to support law-enforcement activities against organised crime and drug trafficking. There is strong political and institutional commitment to tackle crime and money laundering in Mexico, which has driven the legislative changes.

27.24.2 Key Legislation

Article 400 Bis of the Criminal Code contains the money-laundering offence and is complemented by the Federal Law against Organised Crime. The Federal Law on the Prevention and Identification of Transactions with Proceeds of Illicit Origin passed in July 2013, and the subsequent Regulations of the Federal Law on the Prevention and Identification of Transactions with Proceeds of Illicit Origin outline the money-laundering framework.

27.24.3 Legislative History

Money laundering has been an offence in Mexico since 1989. The offence was originally set forth as a fiscal offence under Article 115 Bis of the Federal Fiscal Code. Money laundering and terrorist financing were finally criminalised in 1996, the crime relating to "Operations with Resources from Illegal Origins" under Article 400 Bis of the Federal Criminal Code. Consequently, Article 115 Bis of the Federal Fiscal Code was repealed.

Article 400 Bis of the Criminal Code introduced more procedural elements to the offence and is now complemented by Mexico's Federal Law Against Organised Crime (LFDO). The LFDO was updated in June 2012.

In May 2004, Mexican authorities issued more detailed AML/CFT regulations and extended compliance to non-bank financial institutions. The Attorney's Office has released information pertaining to its plans to map the criminal economy and the corresponding flow of illicit funds.

In April 2012, the Mexican Senate approved the latest anti-money-laundering legislation, which came into force in July 2013.

27.24.4 FATF Assessment

The 2008 mutual evaluation noted that Mexico is making good progress in developing its system for combating ML and TF and that the AML/CFT preventive measures are comprehensive, contain risk-based elements and are being implemented across principal sectors of the financial system. Nonetheless, AML/CFT regulations are still evolving and could benefit from further development.

A 2011 report by the IMF stated that Mexico has "Efficient functioning of key national AML/CFT agencies; improved compliance and enforcement; periodic reporting by national AML/CFT institutions".

27.24.5 The Primary AML Investigation/Regulatory Authorities

Banco de México

Banco de México is the central bank of Mexico. By constitutional mandate, it is autonomous in both its operations and management. Its main function is to provide domestic currency to the Mexican economy and its main priority is to ensure the stability of the domestic currency's purchasing power. Its other functions are to promote both the sound development of the financial system and the optimal functioning of the payment systems.

Secretaría de Hacienda y Crédito Público

The Ministry of Finance and Public Credit (Secretaría de Hacienda y Crédito Público – SHCP) includes the financial intelligence unit. The main tasks of the financial intelligence unit consist of implementing and monitoring mechanisms for the prevention and detection of acts, omissions and operations that could encourage, assist or provide cooperation of any kind for the offences under Articles 139 or 148 Bis of the Federal Penal Code, or that could fit the circumstances described in Article 400 Bis of the Code relating to ML/TF.

The SHCP website has, at the time of writing, a banner across the top saying "This section has initiated a process of renovation, so the information in some sections is subject to periodic changes".

Comisión Nacional Bancaria y de Valores

The National Banking and Securities Commission (CNBV, Comisión Nacional Bancaria y de Valores) is the operational supervisor for banking institutions. Its role is to safeguard the stability of the Mexican financial system and foster its efficiency and inclusive development for the benefit of society.

Subprocuraduría de Investigación Especializada en Delincuencia Organizada

SIEDO (Spanish acronym for Subprocuraduría de Investigación Especializada en Delincuencia Organizada) has primary responsibility for criminal money-laundering and terrorism-financing enforcement. The Specialised Unit for the Investigation of Operations with Resources of Illicit Origin and Forgery or Alteration of Currency (Special AML Unit) sits within the SIEDO. The Organised Crime Special Investigations, Deputy Attorney Office is also housed within SIEDO and is responsible for all federal crime prosecution, including money laundering.

27.24.6 Outline of Specific Money-laundering Offences

Money laundering is committed by anyone who, by themselves or through another person:

- Acquires;
- Disposes of;
- Manages;
- Takes custody of;
- Changes;
- Gives as security;
- Invests;
- Transports or transfers within the national territory of the latter to a foreign territory or conversely, resources, rights or property of any kind, knowing that they represent the proceeds of unlawful activity, with any of the following purposes:
  - hiding or trying to hide;
  - concealing or impeding knowledge of the origin, location, destination or ownership of such resources, rights or property; or
  - encouraging any illegal activity.

The SHCP describes money laundering as "a process to conceal or disguise the existence, origin or the use of funds generated by illegal activities to effect their integration into the economy with the appearance of legitimacy".

27.24.7 Penalties

The penalty for money laundering is five to 15 years' imprisonment and one thousand to 5,000 days of fines.

Members of a criminal gang can be punished by virtue of the fact that they have organised themselves with the intention to commit an offence. Subject to appropriate penalties for the offence or offences committed, the members of a criminal gang can be liable to the following penalties:

In cases of drug crime:

- A person having management or supervision functions within the gang, from twenty to 40 years' imprisonment and 525,000 days of fines; or
- Any other member, from ten to 20 years in prison and 250–12,500 days of fines.

These penalties shall be increased by up to one half, where:

- Any public servant is involved in carrying out the offences referred to as organised crime. In addition, such a public servant shall be removed from post and disqualified from holding any public office or commission; or
- Minors are used to commit any of the offences.

27.24.8 Risk-based Approach

The FIU indicated that it has adopted a risk-management approach to its activities that include a five-step process:

1. Identify risks.
2. Analyse risks.
3. Plan actions accordingly.
4. Track and report the evolution of the identifiable risks.
5. Control the status of risks and learn from the outcomes.

Furthermore, under the new legislation, financial institutions have various obligations:

- They must take proper measures and establish procedures to prevent and detect any acts, omissions or transactions that may involve money-laundering activity.
- They must submit to the SHCP, through the proper federal regulatory agencies authorised to oversee compliance with the above-mentioned obligations, reports on any vulnerable activities in which they engage in the event they suspect that any actions, transactions or services provided to their clients and users, or any actions undertaken by their board members, top executives, officers, employees and legal representatives may involve money-laundering activity.
- They must deliver all information and documentation relating to the actions, transactions and services mentioned above to the SHCP.
- They must preserve all information and documentation regarding the identity of their current or former clients and users, as well as the information relating to all actions, transactions and services reported as set forth above for ten years, this without prejudice to any of the provisions of all other applicable laws and regulations.

27.24.9 Role of the MLRO/Nominated Officer

If a financial institution has more than 25 members of staff, it is required to have a compliance committee, with a senior executive appointed as a Compliance Officer to lead the committee. If it has fewer than 25 members of staff, a single Compliance Officer can be appointed. The functions to be carried out by the committee or the Compliance Officer are:

- To submit the AML/CFT policies to the audit committee for approval.
- To receive the results and implement recommendations of internal auditing on their review of AML/CFT.
- To be aware of high-risk customers and transactions through the Compliance Officer.
- To establish and disseminate criteria for classification of customers based on degree of risk.
- To disseminate to appropriate staff officially recognised lists issued by international agencies or authorities from other countries of persons linked to terrorism or terrorist financing, or to other illegal activities, and the list of PEPs.

- To consider and decide whether suspicious transaction reports should be sent to the FIU.
- To approve AML/CFT training programmes.
- To inform the relevant section of the financial institution of inappropriate conduct or compliance by directors, officers, employees or agents, so that the corresponding disciplinary measures may be carried out.
- To resolve all other matters submitted to its consideration pertaining to the application of these provisions.

27.24.10 Due Diligence

Mexico has gradually applied a risk-based approach to its due diligence processes. It monitors all transactions, and reports suspicious transactions to the local financial intelligence unit, including transactions of US$ 10,000 and over. The AML/CFT regulations only require customer identification and related AML/CFT requirements when transactions are equal to or in excess of US$ 3,000.

Personal Client Due Diligence

For physical persons who are Mexican nationals, the following information should be collected:

- Name
- Address
- Date of birth
- Occupation
- Business or profession
- Telephone number
- Email address
- A national identification number (CURP) and/or federal tax identification number (RFC) and the number for the Advanced Electronic Signature.

An original personal identification document issued by an official body with a photograph and signature and, if relevant, the address should be used to verify identity. A number of alternative official documents can be presented, but it is considered by the industry that voter registration cards (which most citizens have) and passports are the most reliable.

Proof of address is required when the address given for opening the account is not the same as in the identification document, or when the identification document does not show the address. To this effect, the customer may present supporting documentation such as recent utility bills or statements. The CNBV may approve other documents for this purpose.

For non-Mexican nationals, the following should be used:

- Original passport and document showing the person's legal status in Mexico
- Full name
- Date of birth
- Nationality
- Address in country of origin
- Address in Mexico, if known
- Tax identification number
- Advanced Electronic Signature, if available.

Corporate Customer Due Diligence (Mexican)

To complete CDD for a Mexican company, an entity should use:

- Company name
- Line of business
- Tax ID number
- Advanced Electronic Signature, if available
- Address
- Telephone number
- Email address
- Date and country of incorporation
- Names of administrators
- General manager or legal representative, as applicable, who can bind the entity with respect to the financial institution.

Furthermore, the presentation and copying of the following should occur:

- Official or certified copy of the registered articles of incorporation;
- Tax identification card or Advanced Electronic Signature;
- Proof of address;
- Official or certified copy of the power of attorney;
- Personal identification for the legal representative.

For recently formed entities not yet registered in the Public Commerce Register, the financial institution shall request a legally signed document declaring that the registration will be done and undertaken to provide the necessary documentation at that time.

Corporate Customer Due Diligence (Non-Mexican)

To complete CDD for a non-Mexican company, an entity should use a legal or apostil copy of its constitution and a certified document of identity of its legal representative. When the latter is a foreigner, the documents in the previous bullet should be presented.

Simplified Customer Due Diligence

This applies to low-risk institutions, including holding companies of financial groups, investment companies, investment companies specialised in pension funds, investment management companies and investment stock-distributing companies. The following should be used to complete simplified CDD:

- Company name
- Activity or corporate purpose
- Federal tax identification number
- Advanced Electronic Signature
- Address
- Phone number
- Email address
- Names of administrators
- Director, general manager or agent (as applicable) who can bind the entity
- Official or certified copy of the power to bind the entity
- Certificate of designation as a financial institution (Article 90 of Financial Institutions Law)
- Personal identification of the legal representative.

Enhanced Customer Due Diligence

Financial institutions have been provided with the criteria which should be integral to their Know Your Customer policies. Transactional monitoring should encompass all the considerations that institutions make in investigating those customers that they deem as being potentially involved in money laundering, or at the very least involved in a suspicious pattern of transactions.

Article 24 applies to credit institutions:

- Procedures by which the institution will track the operations undertaken by its customers;
- Procedures for adequately ascertaining the transactional profile of the customer;
- Procedures to identify where the operations differ from the normal transactional profile;
- Measures for the identification of unusual operations;
- Considerations as to how and when to adapt, as needed, the degree of risk previously assigned to the customer.

This set of criteria assumes an inherent level of sophistication within the daily procedural workings of institutions. However, much concern has been raised concerning Mexico's application of regulations. The effectiveness of the law rests directly on application across the entire banking sector.

27.24.11 Ongoing Monitoring

Financial institutions are required to update customer information, including the monitoring of transaction profiles, on the basis of ML and FT risks. Some of the key provisions are described below:

- Financial institutions should have customer identification policies that, inter alia, require procedures to update customer information;
- In the case of concentration/master accounts, financial institutions should closely monitor transactions;
- Financial institutions should establish mechanisms to monitor cash transactions above a certain threshold (US$3,000);
- Financial institutions should establish more strict monitoring mechanisms with respect to customers whose line of business or activity is related to industrial, commercial or service sectors that involve large amounts of US$ cash;
- For customers classified as high risk, including PEPs, financial institutions must establish mechanisms to update customer identification files at least once a year;
- KYC policies must include, at a minimum, procedures to establish customer transaction profiles and to develop systems to monitor client transactions in order to detect inconsistencies with such transactions;
- Monitoring of customer transactions should be strengthened when there are concerns that a person is acting for another or there are doubts about information provided by a client;
- Financial institutions should have automated systems to, inter alia, detect and monitor small, structured monetary transactions below the CTR threshold (US$ 10,000).

27.24.12 Staff Training

Financial institutions are required to have training and employee dissemination programmes that must include, at a minimum, courses given at least once per year, which must be specially focussed on officers and employees who work in the areas of customer service or funds management. These courses must cover, inter alia, customer identification and Know Your Customer policies, occasional customer identification policies and criteria, measures and procedures developed by the institution for the compliance with these provisions. Financial institutions are also required to inform staff about techniques, methods and trends for the prevention, detection and reporting of unusual and suspicious transactions.

Institutions must issue participation certificates to the officers and employees that attend training courses. These participants will be tested on the knowledge acquired, and measures will be taken with respect to those that fail to achieve satisfactory results.

Officers and employees that will work in customer service or funds management areas must receive related training before assuming the position or upon beginning work.

In practice, many financial institutions have ongoing training programmes for their staff, including e-learning on AML/CFT. On average, employees get between three and ten hours of training every year.

27.24.13 Record-keeping

Financial institutions are required by the new law to keep records for at least ten years on identification of their clients, transactions undertaken and services provided.

27.24.14 Investigation and Reporting Requirements

The following reports are required.

Suspicious Transaction Reports

In 2011, the FIU described an unusual transaction as transactions, activity, conduct or behaviour of customers which is inconsistent with:

- The history or activity known by the institution or notified thereto; or
- The initial or habitual transactional profile of said customers.

This should be based on:

- The origin or destination of the funds;
- The amount;
- The frequency;
- The type or nature of the transaction in question;
- Whether there is any reasonable justification for such transaction, activity, conduct or behaviour.

It also covers any other actual or intended transaction, activity, conduct or behaviour of a customer in which, for any reason, the institution believes that the funds involved could fall under any of the money-laundering offences.

In addition to this, the 2013 legislation specifies various "vulnerable transactions", for which there are enhanced reporting measures. For financial institutions, these include the following:

- Habitual business or professional activities involving the issuance or marketing of service, credit, prepaid and all stored-value cards that are not issued or marketed by banking institutions provided that the issuer or business entity marketing them maintains a business relationship with the person who acquires them, the instruments allow for the transfer of funds, or when they are marketed only from time to time. In regard to service or credit cards, transactions must be reported when the aggregate monthly expenses charged to the account are equal to or exceed 50,000 pesos. For prepaid cards, this should be when they are marketed for an amount equal to or greater than 40,000 pesos per transaction. All other stored-value instruments shall be governed by the regulations issued under this statute. Transactions must be reported when the aggregate monthly amount charged to the card is equal to or exceeds 80,000 pesos; in the case of prepaid cards, this should be when they are marketed for amounts equal to or greater than 40,000 pesos.

- Habitual business or professional activities involving the issuance and marketing of traveller's cheques by entities other than financial institutions. Transactions for amounts equal to or in excess of 40,000 pesos must be reported.
- Habitual business or professional activities involving the granting of secured or unsecured credit and loans, and acting as surety in transactions of this kind, by persons or entities other than financial entities. Transactions involving amounts equal to or greater than 100,000 pesos must be reported.

Reports must include the following information: (i) general ID data on the person engaging in the vulnerable activity; (ii) general ID data on the client, users or controlling beneficiary and (iii) a description of the vulnerable activity being reported.

Relevant (or Currency) Transaction Reports

Transactions carried out with cash or traveller's cheques for an amount equal to or greater than the equivalent in Mexican pesos of ten thousand US dollars must be reported. Currency Exchange and Money Transfer Offices must report transactions for amounts equal to or greater than the equivalent in Mexican pesos of five thousand US dollars.

Concerning (or Worrisome) Transaction Reports

Any transactions, activity, conduct or behaviour of any of the directors, officers, employees or agents of the institution in question that, by their nature, could contravene, violate or evade the application of the provisions of the AML law, or are questionable in any other way, should be reported.

24-Hour Reports

Any unusual transaction which raises a suspicion that the resources could be used for terrorist financing and/or money laundering should be reported.

27.24.15 Penalties

For money laundering, the penalties range from a fine equal to 200 to 100,000 times the daily minimum Mexican salary, or from 10% to 100% of the value of the act or transaction. Additionally, there are fixed penalties ranging from 100,000 to 500,000 pesos, as well as between six months' and 16 years' imprisonment.

In the case of a breach of the obligations under the 2013 Act, different types of penalties ranging from administrative fines to imprisonment (from two to eight years, when committing crimes involving the presentation of false, altered or illegible information) are established.

A fine equivalent to between 200 and 2,000 days at the general minimum wage (GMW) will apply in the following cases:

- Failure to meet the requirements issued by the SHCP;
- Failure to comply with client identification and keeping of information obligations;
- Failure to submit notices on time (provided that such notice is filed within a term of 30 days following the due date);
- Submission of notices that do not meet the requirements of the Act.

A penalty from 10,000 to 65,000 days at GMW, or 10% of the value of the transaction, will be imposed for the lack of presentation of notices or for carrying out prohibited cash transactions.

27.24.16 Case Studies

In July 2012, Mexican regulators imposed the biggest fine in their history on HSBC's Mexican subsidiary, for failing to comply with AML regulations. In the same week, the chief Compliance Officer of HSBC resigned following allegations of money laundering involving the proceeds of drug trafficking in Mexico being allowed to pass through the bank. The £17.7 million fine was over half of the annual profit of the Mexican subsidiary, which said it acknowledged that it had failed to report 39 suspicious transactions and was late in reporting almost 2,000 others. The severity of this fine highlights Mexico's commitment to distancing itself from its associations with drug money, and that the country is keen to end the cycles of corruption and criminal activity carried out by gangs within the territory.

In the past decade, politics in Mexico has become entangled with money laundering and criminal organisations. A governor in Mexico throughout the nineties was arrested in 2001 and subsequently pleaded guilty to money laundering. During his time in office, areas which he governed were used as a half-way point for flights bringing cocaine from Colombia to the US–Mexico border. It is believed that the funds relating to the governor's conviction were related to the drug trafficking which blighted Mexico throughout the decade, and continues even to this day.

27.25 COUNTRY PROFILE: MONACO

27.25.1 Overview

The financial sector is dominated by private banking and fund management, although these are primarily with overseas European customers. Monaco's banking and financial system is linked to that of France, although the authorities within Monaco are responsible for enforcement. No particular trends in money laundering in the Principality were identified by the IMF in 2008, and it is believed that, like any major financial centre, Monaco has to deal with very sophisticated forms of money laundering that are mainly concerned with the second and third stages of the process: layering and integration.

27.25.2 Key Legislation

The money-laundering offence is found in Monaco's Penal Code. Act 1362 of 3rd August, 2009 on the fight against money laundering, terrorist financing and corruption and Sovereign Order 2318 of 3rd August, 2009, setting the conditions for application of the Act, provide the AML framework.

27.25.3 Legislative History

On 3rd August, 2009, the Parliament in Monaco enacted a new law – Law No. 1362 on Money Laundering, Financing of Terrorism and Corruption. This was amended in 2011.

Sovereign Order 2318 of 3rd August, 2009 sets the conditions for application of Act 1362 of 3rd August, 2009 on the fight against money laundering, terrorist financing and corruption. This was amended by Sovereign Order 3.450 of 15th September, 2011. This Order also repealed various previous Sovereign Orders from 1994 to 2004.

27.25.4 FATF Assessment

The IMF reported in 2008 on Monaco's compliance with the FATF regulations. It noted that, although the AML framework was satisfactory, it was not detailed or supported by adequate secondary legislation. However, this report was made before the introduction of the 2009 legislative changes, which highlight Monaco's commitment to maintaining international standards.

The report also noted that supervision of the financial institutions, in particular on-site supervision, needs to be significantly strengthened, as does the number of staff assigned for this purpose, as AML/CFT supervision is weak. On the whole, it considered the Monaco framework to be satisfactory but in need of expansion – which is what happened following the report.

27.25.5 The Primary AML Investigation/Regulatory Authorities

The Service d'Information et de Contrôle sur les Circuits Financiers

The Service d'Information et de Contrôle sur les Circuits Financiers (SICCFIN) is the national central authority responsible for collecting, analysing and disseminating information related to the fight against money laundering, terrorist financing and corruption. It may propose any legal or regulatory development that it considers necessary in this regard, and it is also responsible for receiving, analysing and processing AML reports.

The Association Monégasque des Activités Financières

The Association Monégasque des Activités Financières (AMAF) was founded by Sovereign Order more than 50 years ago. Its mission is to:

- Act as the professional body for authorised institutions conducting banking or financial activities in the Principality;
- Represent the Monegasque banking industry, particularly in relations with public authorities; and
- Promote the sound development of Monaco's banking sector.

With nearly one hundred members, including banks, portfolio and mutual fund-management companies, AMAF federates all of the market's financial institutions.

27.25.6 Outline of Specific Money-laundering Offences

Money laundering is committed by:

- Any person who knowingly assists in the conversion or transfer of property, with the knowledge that the property is the proceeds of crime, with the aim of dissimulating or disguising the origin of the said property or of assisting any person involved in the committing of the main offence in escaping the legal consequences of their actions;
- Any person who knowingly participates in the dissimulation or disguising of the true nature, origin, location, disposal, movement or ownership of property or rights relating to the property where the originator knows that the property is the proceeds of crime;
- Any person who has knowingly acquired, retained or used property or capital knowing, at the time when they received it, that the property was the proceeds of crime, without prejudice to legal provisions concerning the handling of stolen goods;
- Any person who has knowingly participated in one of the offences listed above or in any other association, agreement, attempt or collusion by providing assistance, help or advice with a view to committing the offence.

The intentional element of an offence may be deduced from objective factual circumstances.

Monaco law recognises as aggravating circumstances – and accordingly punishes with a heavier sentence – offenders who:

- Act as a member of a criminal organisation;
- Take part in other international organised criminal activities;

- Perform public duties which help them to commit the offence;
- Involve minors in committing the offence; or
- Have been convicted by a foreign court of a money-laundering offence.

27.25.7 Penalties

Money laundering shall be punished by imprisonment for five to ten years and a fine of EUR 18,000 to 90,000, the maximum of which may be increased tenfold. If there are aggravating circumstances, as outlined above, the penalty shall be ten to 20 years' imprisonment and a fine of EUR 18,000 to 90,000, the maximum of which may be increased twentyfold.

Attempting any of these offences will incur the same penalties as completing the offence, and it will be the same if there is an agreement or conspiracy to commit them.

The court shall order the confiscation of assets and funds of illicit origin or of goods and capital whose value matches that of the assets and funds of illicit origin. It may also order the confiscation of property or personal property acquired using these funds. The assets and funds of illicit origin can also be confiscated when they are held by a third party who knew, or should have known, of their illicit origin.

27.25.8 Scope

Organisations and persons carrying out financial activities are not subject to the provisions if the activities:

- Generate a turnover which does not exceed EUR 750,000;
- Are limited to transactions which must not exceed a maximum amount per client and per transaction of EUR 1,500 and the transaction must be carried out in a single operation or several operations appearing as related;
- Do not constitute the main activity and generate a turnover not exceeding 3% of the total turnover of the organisation or person concerned.

27.25.9 Risk-based Approach

Professionals shall decide on and implement a policy and procedures prior to initiating any business relations. These procedures must be suited to the activities that they carry out and allow them to be fully involved in the prevention of the risk of money laundering, terrorist financing and corruption. They should enable entities to become familiar with the characteristics of new clients, and to adequately examine their background, relationships and the transactions they carry out.

This policy and these procedures shall establish distinctions and requirements at different levels on the basis of objective criteria set by each professional, taking into account, in particular, the characteristics of the services and products that they offer and those of the clients targeted, so as to define an appropriate scale of risks.

27.25.10 Role of the MLRO/Nominated Officer

In Monaco, the MLRO must:

- Ensure compliance by the professional with all of its obligations with regard to the prevention of money laundering, terrorist financing and corruption;
- Have professional experience at senior level and, within the establishment employing them, the necessary power to ensure effective and independent exercising of their authority;
- Meet the conditions for good character which are required to fully exercise their authority and that their number and qualifications, as well as the means made available to them, are adapted to the activities, size and locations of the professional firm;
- Be appointed by the effective management body of each professional firm;
- Implement adequate administrative organisation and adequate internal controls;
- Have the power to propose all necessary or appropriate measures to the management of the organisation;
- Organise and implement, under their own authority, procedures for the analysis of written reports;
- Monitor the training and awareness of personnel;
- Act as the designated correspondent for the Service d'Information et de Contrôle sur les Circuits Financiers for all questions concerning the prevention of money laundering, terrorist financing and corruption;
- Establish and send an activity report to the management body of the professional firm, at least once a year, on the conditions under which the prevention of money laundering, terrorist financing and corruption have been enforced. This should include details on the adequacy of the AML provisions, as well as various other prescribed criteria. A copy of this annual activity report is to be sent to the Service d'Information et de Contrôle sur les Circuits Financiers and, if applicable, to the professional's auditors.

27.25.11 Due Diligence

Regulated entities must, when forming business relations, identify their usual clients as well as their agents and check the identities of each of them using substantiating documents of which they shall keep a copy. Said organisations or persons shall do the same for occasional clients, when:

- They wish to undertake a transfer of funds;
- They wish to undertake a transaction, the amount of which reaches or exceeds EUR 15,000, whether carried out in one or several seemingly related operations;
- They wish to perform an operation, even of an amount below the said sum, where there is a suspicion of money laundering, terrorist financing or corruption; or
- The said organisation or person has doubts as to the truth or accuracy of data identifying a client with whom it already has business relations.

Business relations are entered into when:

- A professional and a client conclude a contract under which several successive operations are carried out between them during a specific or indefinite period, or which create permanent obligations;
- A client regularly and repeatedly requests the intervention of the same professional to perform successive distinct financial operations.

Entities are also required to conduct CDD if they believe the information given is misleading.

With a view to identifying the intended purpose and nature of the business relations, professionals are to familiarise themselves with, and record, the types of operation that the client requests, as well as any information which is relevant to determine the purpose of these relations. This information, including, in particular, details on the origin of clients' assets and their business background must be supported with documents, data or reliable sources of information.

Personal Client Due Diligence

For natural persons, the surname, first name and address should be identified. They should then be verified in their presence using a valid official document bearing their photograph.

If the client's address is not mentioned on the substantiating documents presented, or in the event of doubt regarding the address mentioned, the professional is required to check this information using another document that is likely to prove their real address and of which a copy shall be retained.

Corporate Customer Due Diligence

For legal persons, legal entities and trusts, identification and verification concerns:

- The company name
- The registered office
- The list of directors
- Knowledge of the provisions governing the power to incur the liability of the legal person, legal entity or trust.

When identifying clients that are legal persons, the verification of their identity must be carried out using the following documents:

- The original, an authenticated or certified copy of a deed or extract from an official register giving the name, legal form and registered office of the legal person;
- The articles of association of the legal person;
- Any substantiating documents allowing the list of directors to be established;
- In the case of legal representation of the legal person, any document certifying the power of attorney of the company representative.

Measures should include the identification of the natural person or persons who, ultimately, own or control the client entity. If the professional considers it necessary, they should request a translation of these documents into French.

Beneficial Ownership

If the client is a legal person, the following shall be meant by beneficial owners:

- Natural persons who, ultimately, directly or indirectly own or control at least 25% of the shares or voting rights in the legal person;
- Natural persons who effectively exercise controlling power over the management of the legal person.

Professionals must take all reasonable steps to ascertain the identity of beneficial owners. The identification of beneficial owners shall include the following identifying items.

For natural persons:

- Surname
- First name
- Date of birth
- Address.

For legal persons, legal entities and trusts:

- Company name
- Registered office
- List of directors
- Knowledge of provisions governing powers to enter into binding obligations for the legal person, legal entity or trust.

If the identity of the persons described cannot be checked, professionals may neither enter into nor maintain business relations with the client concerned. They shall then determine whether the Service d'Information et de Contrôle sur les Circuits Financiers should be informed.

Enhanced Customer Due Diligence

The acceptance of clients who are likely to present particular levels of risk shall be subject to enhanced CDD. A decision to instigate this must be taken at an appropriate management level. Particular clients who should be subjected to enhanced CDD include those:

- Who request the opening of contractually designated anonymous accounts;
- Who reside or are domiciled in a country or territory qualified as an uncooperative country or territory by international institutions for cooperation and coordination that are specialised in the fight against money laundering, terrorist financing or corruption;

- Whose identification has been carried out remotely on the basis of a copy of substantiating documents;
- Who are considered likely to present a particular level of risk.

Non-face-to-face Customer Due Diligence

Professionals entering into business relations or carrying out occasional operations for a client who is a natural person that they have identified remotely, are to implement procedures which:

- Prohibit entering into business relations with, or carrying out occasional operations for, this client when there is a reason to believe that the client is trying to avoid physical contact so as to more easily dissimulate their true identity, or if they suspect the client's intention to perform operations of money laundering, terrorist financing or corruption;
- Impose, according to the risk, a verification within a reasonable time of the identity of these clients using substantiating documents;
- Aim to gradually improve knowledge of the client;
- Guarantee a first operation carried out by means of an account opened in the client's name with a credit establishment.

Politically Exposed Persons

If politically exposed persons wish to enter into business relations with professionals or contact them to perform occasional operations, the acceptance of these clients shall be subject to particular examination and must be decided at an appropriately senior level of management. Said acceptance requires the taking of all appropriate measures in order to establish the origin of their assets as well as that of funds which are, or will be, employed in the business relations or in the occasional operation contemplated.

Persons who hold, or during the last three years have held, prominent public functions in a foreign country shall be considered as politically exposed, whether they are clients, beneficial owners or proxies. The client acceptance policy must specify the criteria and methods to be used to determine whether they are politically exposed persons.

Professionals who maintain business relations with politically exposed persons are required to monitor them closely on an ongoing basis. Due diligence measures shall also apply if it later transpires that an existing client is, or becomes, a politically exposed person.

Anonymous Accounts

Anonymous accounts are prohibited. The use of numbered accounts or contractually designated accounts is only permitted in internal communications and operations, as long as:

- The identity of the client and the beneficial owner are entirely known to any appropriate person within the establishment; and
- Their identity can be communicated upon request to agents of the Service d'Information et de Contrôle sur les Circuits Financiers.

Correspondent Banking

Institutions must only authorise correspondent banking relations if:

- The purpose and nature of the relations contemplated as well as the respective responsibilities of the professional and the credit establishment or financial institution governed by foreign law within the context of these relations are agreed in writing beforehand.
- The decision to enter into business relations which, due to their purpose or nature, are likely to expose the professional to particular risks with regard to money laundering or terrorist financing shall be based on a satisfactory assessment of the controls implemented by the credit establishment or financial institution governed by foreign law with a view to the prevention of money laundering and terrorist financing.
- If payable-through accounts are opened by a credit establishment or a financial institution governed by foreign law, they must have previously guaranteed, in writing, that they have verified and implemented required due diligence measures with regard to clients having direct access to these accounts on the one hand, and that they are able to communicate without delay upon request relevant data to identify these clients on the other; the credit establishment or financial institution governed by foreign law shall undertake to communicate these data.
- Acceptance to enter into business relations or to conclude a contemplated occasional operation with the credit establishment or financial institution governed by foreign law shall be submitted to a decision-making power at an appropriate management level.

27.25.12 Ongoing Monitoring

The organisations must exercise constant due diligence with regard to business relations:

- By examining the transactions or operations concluded at any time during these relations and, if necessary, the origin of funds, so as to check that they are consistent with regard to the knowledge that the said organisations or persons have of their clients, their socioeconomic background, their commercial activities and their risk profile.
- By keeping documents, data or information held up to date through a continual and attentive examination of operations or transactions carried out. The updating of the identification data requires that new data be verified using a substantiating document, a copy of which must be kept.

The persons shall also adopt a monitoring system which allows atypical operations to be detected. The monitoring system must:

- Cover all client accounts and their operations.
- Be based on precise and relevant criteria fixed by each professional, taking into account, in particular, the characteristics of the services and products that they offer and those of the clients targeted, and should be sufficiently discriminating as to allow atypical operations to be effectively detected.

- Allow these operations to be detected rapidly.
- Produce written reports describing atypical operations which have been detected and the criteria provided for in the second point of this paragraph upon which they are based. These reports are to be sent to the MLRO.
- Be automated, except if the professional can demonstrate that the nature and volume of the operations to be monitored do not require it or that alterative means implemented do not require it. The said means must have been approved beforehand by the Service d'Information et de Contrôle sur les Circuits Financiers.
- Be subject to an initial validation procedure and a regular re-examination of its relevance with a view to adapting it, if necessary, according to developments in activities, the clientele or the environment.

When the organisations cannot fulfil these obligations, they may neither form nor maintain business relations. They shall consider whether SICCFIN should be informed.

27.25.13 *Staff Training*

The obligation to train and to raise awareness with regard to the prevention of money laundering, terrorist financing and corruption concerns members of the firm's personnel whose duties:

- Include being in contact with clients or for whom operations expose them to the risk of being faced with attempts at money laundering, terrorist financing or corruption; or
- Consist of developing procedures or computer tools or other tools that are to be applied to activities which are sensitive in view of this risk.

Training, awareness-raising and the provision of regular information to personnel have the particular aim of ensuring that they:

- Acquire knowledge and develop the critical approach necessary to detect atypical operations;
- Acquire the knowledge of procedures which is necessary to react to such operations in an adequate way;
- Include the problems of prevention of money laundering, terrorist financing and corruption in procedures or tools developed to be applied to activities which are considered as being sensitive in the light of such a risk.

27.25.14 *Record-keeping*

Regulated entities are required to:

- Keep for at least five years after ending relations with regular or occasional clients a copy of all substantiating documents which were subsequently used for identification and to check identity;

- Keep for a period of at least five years from the performance of an operation or transaction a copy of recordings, accounting books, commercial correspondence and documents concerning the operations or transactions carried out, so as to be able to precisely reconstruct them;
- Keep records in such a manner that the entity is able to meet any requests for further information from SICCFIN within the prescribed times;
- Be able to respond quickly and fully to any request for information from the Service d'Information et de Contrôle sur les Circuits Financiers for the purposes of determining whether they have, or have had, a business relationship with a given natural or legal person in the course of the last five years and the nature of these relations.

SICCFIN may request an extension to periods for storage of information where the information relates to an investigation in progress.

All information and documents concerning bureau de change operations whose total amount reaches or exceeds EUR 1,500 must be entered in a register. This information includes the client's identity, the nature of the operation, the currency or currencies involved, the amount changed and the rate applied.

All natural persons entering or leaving the territory of the Principality in possession of cash or bearer instruments whose total amount is more than EUR 10,000 must, on request from the monitoring authority, make a declaration using the form established for this purpose.

27.25.15 Suspicious Transaction Reporting

Regulated entities are required to declare to SICCFIN all sums held in their accounts and all operations which there is sufficient reason to suspect might be related to money laundering, terrorist financing or corruption. This declaration must be submitted in writing before the operation is carried out, and must give details of the facts which constitute the evidence upon which the said organisations or persons have based the declaration. It shall indicate, if applicable, the time within which the operation is to be carried out. If circumstances so require, the declaration may be made in advance by fax or appropriate electronic means.

Professionals are to implement appropriate procedures in order to carry out the analysis as soon as possible. This should be coordinated by the person responsible for the prevention of money laundering and terrorist financing, to determine whether these operations or facts should be reported to SICCFIN. The written report, its analysis and, if applicable, the declaration of suspicion to which this analysis has led are to be kept and held at the disposal of SICCFIN.

27.25.16 Penalties

Entities which breach the AML requirements can be subject to professional and criminal penalties.

Professional Penalties

Anyone who breaches these provisions is liable to a warning by SICCFIN. In a case of serious infringement of these obligations, SICCFIN may submit the case to the Minister of State in order to have one of the following penalties ordered against the party in breach:

- A reprimand;
- A pecuniary penalty which is proportional to the seriousness of the infringement and the maximum amount of which cannot exceed one and a half million euros;
- A prohibition against carrying out certain operations;
- Temporary suspension of their authorisation to exercise their profession;
- The withdrawal of this authorisation.

The fact that any of the above penalties, with the exception of the warning, has been administered may be published in the *Journal de Monaco*.

Criminal Penalties

Any person who obstructs or attempts to obstruct a SICCFIN investigation shall be punished by imprisonment for one to six months and/or by a fine of EUR 250 to 9,000.

Any person who, through disregard of their CDD obligations, fails to report a suspicion of money laundering shall be punished by a fine of EUR 9,000 to 18,000.

Any person who contravenes the record-keeping requirements shall be punished by a fine of EUR 250 to 9,000.

Directors or employees of financial organisations shall be punished by a fine of EUR 18,000 to 90,000 if they have:

- Knowingly informed the owner of the sums, the originator of one of the operations or a third party of the existence of a suspicious transaction report or declaration; or
- Disclosed to any party information concerning action taken as a result of the declaration.

Any person who, in disregard of his professional duties, assists in any transfer, investment, concealment or conversion of criminal proceeds shall be punished by imprisonment of one to five years and/or a fine of EUR 18,000 to 90,000, the maximum of which can be increased tenfold.

27.25.17 Case Studies

A lawyer based in Monaco was convicted of money laundering in July 2009, in connection with the takeover of Derby County Football Club. The lawyer received over £80,000 from one of the directors involved with the takeover, which represented a share of the commission due to the director. The lawyer then transferred it through one of his own companies, registered in the Isle of Man, back to the director. The use of various companies, registered in tax havens, was made to conceal the true path of the funds, making them look legitimate. Two other men were convicted of financial crimes during this takeover, making a total of four complicit in this money-laundering network.

Financial institutions should be aware that criminals don't work alone, particularly when funds are being transferred through a variety of accounts and countries. Furthermore, despite the fact that lawyers are bound by a strict code of conduct and are often entrusted with sensitive information, a lawyer was instrumental in laundering the money involved in this case. Therefore, financial institutions should not be overly trusting of anybody based on their profession, as corruption can spread to even seemingly unlikely places.

27.26 COUNTRY PROFILE: MOROCCO

27.26.1 *Overview*

The economy of Morocco, which is considered a free economy, is based on the sector of phosphate mines, the transactions of Moroccans who live abroad and tourism. Casablanca is considered the centre of trade and industry in Morocco, and it also includes the largest port. Morocco is considered the biggest African market in the fishing industry, and it is the biggest silver market in Africa. It ranks second internationally in exporting phosphate.

Morocco is a member of a large number of significant international and regional organisations, such as the United Nations (1956), the League of Arab States (1958) and the Group of 77 (1964). Morocco is also a founding member of the Organisation of the Islamic Conference (1969), the Arab Maghreb Union (1989), the World Trade Organisation (1995), the Mediterranean Dialogue (1995) and MENAFATF (30th November, 2004). In the framework of anti-corruption and anti-bribery efforts, Morocco has initiated a number of measures at the legislative and judicial levels to contain the problem. This initiative has come from reformist workshops whose main purpose is the eradication of corruption through a strategy that mainly aims to punish bribers and not to hesitate in activating judicial follow-ups for those involved.

27.26.2 *Key Legislation*

Article 574 of the Criminal Code provides the money-laundering offence. The AML regulations are contained in Law No. 13.10, as well as the Moroccan Commercial Code.

27.26.3 *Legislative History*

Law No. 13.10, published in the Official Gazette on 24th January, 2011, amended and supplemented certain provisions of the Penal Code, the Criminal Procedure Code and Law No. 43.05 on the fight against money laundering.

27.26.4 *FATF Assessment*

Previous FATF assessments had found that the anti-money-laundering (AML) system in Morocco was still in its comparative infancy, with the combating culture absent in financial institutions and designated non-financial businesses and professions (DNFBPs) as this concept is still recent and no direct expertise is present in this regard. However, credit institutions do have a type of culture of prudence, vigilance and caution to protect the banking system from any illicit use.

However, in October 2013 the FATF removed Morocco from its enhanced monitoring process, commending the country for establishing the legal and regulatory framework to meet its commitments in its Action Plan regarding the strategic deficiencies that the FATF had identified in February 2010.

27.26.5 The Primary AML Investigation/Regulatory Authorities

The Financial Intelligence Unit

"L'Unité de traitement du renseignement financier", or UTRF, is the financial intelligence unit of Morocco. Its statutory functions are:

- To collect, process and ask for information about acts suspected of being linked to money laundering and decide any action necessary in relation to such acts;
- To establish a database of transactions involving money laundering;
- To collaborate and participate with other services and agencies involved in the study of measures to implement the fight against money laundering;
- To ensure compliance by taxable persons with the provisions enacted by this Act, without prejudice to the tasks assigned to each of the supervisors and control provided for in Article 13.1 above;
- To ensure representation of common services and national agencies involved in the fight against money laundering;
- To propose to the government legislative reform, regulations or administrative procedures necessary in the fight against money laundering;
- To advise the government on the content of the enforcement of this chapter;
- To lay down special conditions relating to transactions that fall within the scope of the AML regulations.

The unit prepares an annual report of its activities and submits it to the Prime Minister. This report is published by the unit, and details all of its activities, including the records processed or transmitted to the judicial authorities, and an outline of its money-laundering operations.

27.26.6 Outline of Specific Money-laundering Offences

The following acts constitute money laundering, when committed intentionally and knowingly:

- The act of acquiring, holding, using, converting, transferring or transporting of goods or products for the purpose of concealing or disguising the true nature or the illicit origin of the property, in the interests of the author or others when they are the product of an offence listed below;
- The concealment or disguise of the true nature, source, location, disposition, movement or ownership of property or rights with respect to the author, knowing that they are the products of an offence listed below;
- Aiding any person involved in the commission of an offence listed below to evade the legal consequences of his actions;
- The facilitation, by any means, of false justification of the origin of goods or products of the author of any of the offences listed below, which has brought it profit directly or indirectly;

- Providing assistance or advice to an operation on the care, investment, concealment, conversion or transfer, direct or indirect, with regard to any of the offences listed below;
- The act of attempting to commit the acts listed below.

The relevant offences are:

- Illicit trafficking in narcotic drugs and psychotropic substances;
- Trafficking in human beings;
- The smuggling of migrants;
- Illicit trafficking in arms and ammunition;
- Bribery, extortion, influence peddling and embezzlement of public and private property;
- Terrorism offences;
- Counterfeiting or forgery of currency or monetary instruments of public credit or other means of payment;
- Membership of an organisation formed or established for the purpose of preparing or committing an act or acts of terrorism;
- Sexual exploitation;
- Concealment of things from a crime or misdemeanour;
- Breach of trust;
- Fraud;
- Offences relating to industrial property;
- Offences relating to copyright and neighbouring rights;
- Offences against the environment;
- Murder, violence and other assault;
- Kidnapping, illegal restraint and hostage-taking;
- Theft and extortion;
- Smuggling;
- Fraud involving goods and foodstuffs;
- Forgery and theft or improper use of functions, titles or names;
- Diversion, degradation of aircraft or ships or other means of transport, degradation of air navigation facilities, land and sea or destruction, degradation or deterioration of media;
- Using, in the exercise of a profession or function, inside information to make or knowingly permit to carry on one or more market operations.

There is also a series of penalties in Morocco contained within the data protection regulations, which readers will need to be aware of. Indeed, data integrity is taken extremely seriously in Morocco, in particular in relation to personal data.

27.26.7 Penalties

Money laundering is punishable:

- For individuals by imprisonment of between two and five years together with a fine of 20,000 to 100,000 dirhams;
- For corporate bodies by a fine of 500,000 to 3,000,000 dirhams, without prejudice to the penalties which may be imposed against their officers and agents involved in the offences.

Prison sentences and fines are doubled in the following circumstances:

- the offences are committed using facilities afforded by the exercise of a professional activity;
- the person engages habitually in money-laundering operations;
- the offence is committed by an organised gang;
- repeat offender who commits the offence had a previous conviction for a similar offence within the previous five years.

In cases where a conviction is made for an offence of money laundering, the penalty includes the total confiscation of things, objects and property used, or that might have been used, in the conduct of the offence or that are the product of the offence, or the equivalent of such things, goods or products, subject to the rights of bona fide third parties.

Those guilty of money laundering also incur one or more of the following additional penalties:

- The dissolution of the corporation;
- The publication, by all appropriate means, of convictions.

The author of the offence of money laundering may also be sentenced to temporary or permanent disqualification to exercise, directly or indirectly, one or more professions or activities during the year in which the offence was committed.

27.26.8 Scope

The following financial institutions are obliged to comply with the AML framework:

- Bank Al-Maghrib;
- Credit institutions and similar bodies;
- Banks and offshore holding companies;

- Financial companies;
- Intermediation companies in the transfer of funds;
- Exchange offices;
- Insurance companies and reinsurance intermediaries in insurance and reinsurance;
- Corporate managers of financial assets;
- Brokers;
- Auditors, external accountants and tax advisors;
- Persons who are members of an independent legal profession when participating on behalf of their client and for the account of the latter, a financial or real estate transaction, or when they assist their client in the preparation or execution of operations relating to:
  - the purchase and sale of real property or business entities;
  - the management of funds, securities or other assets belonging to the client;
  - the opening or management of bank, savings or securities accounts;
  - the organisation of contributions necessary for the creation, management or operation of companies or similar structures;
  - the creation, operation or management of trusts, companies or similar structures;
- Persons operating or managing casinos or gambling establishments, including casinos and gambling establishments on the internet;
- Real estate agents and brokers, when transactions for their clients concern the purchase or sale of real estate;
- Dealers in precious stones and metals when the transaction is in cash and the amount is greater than 150,000 dirhams, as well as people who habitually engage in the trade of antiquities and works of art;
- Service providers involved in the creation, organisation and domiciliation of companies.

27.26.9 Risk-based Approach

Financial institutions are obliged to:

- Put in place a risk-management system; and
- Establish a means of preventing the risks inherent in the use of new technologies for the purpose of money laundering.

27.26.10 Role of the MLRO/Nominated Officer

The regulations do not provide specifically for an MLRO. However, they do provide that financial institutions must provide the UTRF with the identity of directors and officers authorised to carry out suspicious transaction reports and to liaise with the said unit, and a description of the internal vigilance they implement in order to ensure compliance with the provisions of this chapter. This is not dissimilar to the role of an MLRO.

27.26.11 Due Diligence

Financial institutions are required to collect all the information to identify and verify the identity of their usual or occasional customers and beneficial owners. They must not perform operations where the identity of the persons concerned could not be verified or if said identity is incomplete or obviously fictitious.

In addition to this, financial institutions are obliged to:

- Ensure the purpose and nature of the business relationship contemplated;
- Learn about the origin of the funds;
- Neither establish nor maintain a relationship in cases where they have not been able to identify or verify the customers or beneficial owners or to obtain information on the purpose and nature of the business relationship;
- Check, before opening an account, if the applicant has other accounts on their books;
- Learn about the reasons behind the request to open a new account;
- Identify and verify the identity of persons for whom an account is opened when it appears that the people who requested the opening of the account did not act on their own behalf.

Personal Client Due Diligence

With regard to individuals, financial institutions must ascertain the home address and identity of the applicant, using the particulars given on a national identity card, a registration card for resident aliens or a passport or other identity document for foreign non-residents.

Corporate Customer Due Diligence

When the client is a corporation, institutions should check, by referring to relevant documents, the following information:

- Name
- Legal form
- Activity
- Registered office address
- Capital
- The identity of its leaders and the powers of persons authorised to represent it vis-à-vis third parties and acting on its behalf pursuant to a warrant
- Beneficial owners.

With regard to all legal persons, the following information should be obtained and verified:

- The form of the legal person
- Name
- Address of the headquarters
- The identity and authority of the person or persons entitled to physically perform operations on the account
- The registration number on the commercial register or the tax patent.

The characteristics and references of documents submitted to achieve this data confirmation should be recorded by the establishment.

Beneficial Ownership

Beneficial ownership must be ascertained, and is defined as any person on whose behalf the client is acting or, when the customer is a legal person, any person who controls said legal person.

Third Party Customer Due Diligence

Financial institutions must:

- Make sure of the identity of principals who are entitled to perform operations where the beneficiary is a third party;
- Identify and verify the identity of persons acting with the names of their clients under a mandate.

Enhanced Customer Due Diligence

Financial institutions must:

- Pay special attention to business relationships and transactions with, or for the benefit of, people from countries with a high risk of money laundering or terrorist financing;
- Apply enhanced due diligence in respect of customers, business relationships or transactions that have a high risk, especially for operations conducted by non-resident persons or on their behalf;

These should also apply to any transaction, without entering into the scope of the provisions relating to the declaration of suspicion, that appears unusual or unusually complex and appears to have no economic justification or apparent lawful purpose.

Enhanced due diligence should also be applied where a person is subject to particular scrutiny.

In all such cases, there is the obligation for the customer to confirm the origin and destination of funds as well as the beneficiaries. The characteristics of the transaction should also be recorded and stored.

In addition, there is an obligation for the persons responsible to:

- Centralise information collected on any transactions that are unusual or complex;
- Regularly inform their leaders, in writing, of the transactions of customers with a high risk profile.

Anonymous Accounts

Financial institutions must refrain from opening anonymous accounts or accounts in fictitious names.

Correspondent Banking

Financial institutions must refrain from establishing or maintaining correspondent banking relationships with shell banks, and all financial institutions should ensure that their correspondents abroad are subject to the same obligation.

27.26.12 Ongoing Monitoring

Financial institutions are obliged to:

- Ensure regular updating of client records;
- Ensure that transactions by their clients are in perfect harmony with their knowledge of these customers, their activities and their risk profiles;
- Provide special monitoring and set up a vigilance device suitable for operations with high-risk customers.

27.26.13 Record-keeping

Without prejudice to enacting more stringent requirements, every entity should retain documents relating to transactions conducted by their clients for ten years from the date of their execution. They should also maintain records for ten years on the identity of their usual or occasional customers from the date of the transaction or the termination of their relationship with them, as well as outsourcers referred to in Article 5 above and beneficial owners.

27.26.14 Internal Requirements

Financial institutions must establish and maintain effective internal vigilance, detection, monitoring and management of the risks associated with money laundering.

27.26.15 Suspicious Transaction Reporting

Financial institutions are required to make a suspicious transaction report to the unit on:

- All sums, operations or attempted execution of transactions suspected of being related to one or more of the money-laundering offences;
- Any transaction where the identity of the payer or the payee is doubtful.

Obligated persons must provide to the unit the identity of directors and officers authorised to carry out suspicious transaction reports and to liaise with the said unit, and a description of the internal vigilance they implement in order to ensure compliance with the provisions of this chapter.

Any declaration of suspicion must be made in writing. However, in an emergency, it may be made orally, subject to confirmation in writing. The FIU will acknowledge receipt of the written declaration of suspicion.

When reporting suspicion regarding a transaction that has not yet been executed, the report must indicate the period of execution of this operation, which cannot exceed two working days from the date of receipt by the unit of such declaration.

Reporting suspicions also covers operations that have already been executed when it was impossible to suspend their execution. Likewise, when it appeared, after the completion of the transaction, that the amounts in question came from money laundering.

The UTRF may oppose the execution of any transaction that is the subject of a suspicious transaction report. The execution of this transaction is deferred for a period not exceeding two working days from the date of receipt by the unit of such declaration.

27.26.16 *Penalties*

For failure to comply with these obligations, institutions may be sentenced to a fine ranging from 100,000 to 500,000 dirhams.

27.26.17 *Case Studies*

There was only one conviction for money laundering in Morocco between November 2010 and October 2011, while five prosecutions in the same time period failed to result in a conviction.

27.27 COUNTRY PROFILE: NIGERIA

27.27.1 Overview

Nigeria has been widely criticised by the FATF for its poor AML framework. The latest legislation has not yet been assessed by the FATF, so it will be noted with interest whether the organisation feels that the new law matches the political commitments made by Nigeria.

27.27.2 Key Legislation

The Money Laundering (Prohibition) Act 2011 provides the money-laundering offences and the AML framework. The Terrorism Prevention Act 2011 outlines the CFT requirements.

27.27.3 Legislative History

The Money Laundering (Prohibition) Act 2004 was repealed by the 2011 Act.

27.27.4 FATF Assessment

In February 2011, the Financial Action Task Force (FATF) expressed dissatisfaction on Nigeria's handling of its anti-money-laundering (AML) policies. It had previously delisted Nigeria from the list of non-cooperative countries in 2006.

It therefore classified the country, among others, as a high risk to the world's financial system. The FATF judged that, although Nigeria had put in place a high-level political commitment to work with the FATF and to address its strategic anti-money-laundering and combating financing of terrorism deficiencies, it was still not satisfied that Nigeria had made sufficient progress in the implementation of its action plan, and that certain deficiencies remain.

In October 2013, the FATF reviewed Nigeria's progress, welcomed the significant progress made in improving its AML/CFT regime and noted that Nigeria has established the legal and regulatory framework to meet the commitments made in 2010. As a result, Nigeria is no longer subject to the FATF's enhanced monitoring process.

27.27.5 The Primary AML Investigation/Regulatory Authorities

Central Bank of Nigeria

The CBN Act of 2007 of the Federal Republic of Nigeria charges the Bank with the overall control and administration of the monetary and financial sector policies of the federal government.

The objectives of the CBN are to:

- Ensure monetary and price stability;
- Issue legal tender currency in Nigeria;

- Maintain external reserves to safeguard the international value of the legal tender currency;
- Promote a sound financial system in Nigeria; and
- Act as banker and provide economic and financial advice to the federal government.

Economic and Financial Crimes Commission

The Economic and Financial Crimes Commission (EFCC) is responsible for combating financial and economic crimes. The Commission is empowered to prevent, investigate, prosecute and penalise economic and financial crimes and is charged with the responsibility of enforcing the provisions of other laws and regulations relating to economic and financial crimes.

National Financial Intelligence Unit

The National Financial Intelligence Unit (NFIU) is comprised of various units to develop AML strategies and investigate potential crimes.

Special Control Unit against Money Laundering

The Special Control Unit against Money Laundering (SCUML) has the mandate to monitor, supervise and regulate the activities of all designated non-financial institutions (DNFIs) in Nigeria in consonance with the country's anti-money-laundering and combating of the financing of terrorism (AML/CFT) regime. Its mission statement is "to serve as a structure for the curtailment of money laundering and terrorist financing in the DNFI sector, providing world class intelligence as regards AML/CFT issues to relevant stakeholders, and the sanitisation of the DNFI sector to create an enabling environment for the inflow of foreign direct investment".

27.27.6 *Outline of Specific Money-laundering Offences*

The money-laundering offence states that a person commits an offence if he/she:

- Conceals, removes from the jurisdiction, transfers to nominees or otherwise retains the proceeds of a crime or an illegal act on behalf of another person, while knowing or suspecting that other person to be engaged in criminal conduct or to have benefited from criminal conduct; or
- Knowing that any property, either in whole or in part, directly or indirectly represents another person's proceeds of criminal conduct, acquires or uses that property or possession of it.

The drug-trafficking offence is committed by any person who:

- Converts or transfers resources or properties derived directly from illicit traffic in narcotic drugs and psychotropic substances or participation in an organised criminal group; or
- Collaborates in concealing or disguising the genuine nature, origin, location. disposition, movement or ownership of the resources, property or right thereto derived directly or indirectly from the acts specified above.

"Tipping Off" Offence

Any person who tips off the accused, destroys records, uses a false identity, makes or accepts a payment over N 1,000 or its equivalent or fails to report a transfer of funds commits an offence.

A person who:

- Conspires with, aids, abets or counsels any other person to commit an offence;
- Attempts to commit or is an accessory to an act or offence; or
- Incites, procures or induces any other person by any means whatsoever to commit an offence, under this Act,

commits an offence and is liable, on conviction, to the same punishment as is prescribed for that offence.

Where an offence under this Act has been committed by a body corporate, any individual member of the organisation involved, as well as the body corporate, shall be guilty of that offence and shall be liable to be proceeded against and punished accordingly.

No person or body corporate shall, except in a transaction through a financial institution, make or accept cash payment of a sum exceeding:

- N 5,000,000 or its equivalent in the case of an individual; or
- N 10,000,000 in the case of a body corporate.

These figures were increased from those included in the 2004 regulations, which stated 500,000 and 2,000,000 respectively.

27.27.7 Penalties

The penalty for money laundering is imprisonment for not less than five years or a fine equivalent to five times the value of the proceeds of the criminal conduct, or both.

Anyone convicted of drug trafficking is liable for imprisonment for a term not less than five years but not more than ten years. It is irrelevant if the various acts constituting the offence were committed in different countries or places.

Depending which aspect of the tipping-off offence is committed, individuals will be liable to imprisonment for a term of not less than two years but not more than three years or to a fine of N 500,000 and not more than N 3,000,000, increasable by up to 25% of the excess for accepting a payment over the amount prescribed above. They may also be banned indefinitely or for a period of five years from practising the profession which provided the opportunity for the offence to be committed.

A financial institution or corporate body will be liable to a fine of not less than N 3,000,000 or more than N 25,000,000, as well as, if the offence was a result of an oversight or procedural flaw, disciplinary action regarding its compliance with its professional and administrative regulations. It may also be wound up and all its assets and properties forfeited to the federal government.

> ***Please Note***
>
> A circular was issued by the Central Bank of Nigeria on 28th May, 2012 stating that the KYC directive would be phased out from September 2012 and replaced by a National Identity Number scheme by January 2013, but this circular was recalled with immediate effect on 12th June by the CBN. The future of the scheme is now unclear. The remainder of this section will make reference to the original KYC directive.

27.27.8 Scope

A designated non-financial institution whose business involves cash transactions is required, before commencing business with a new customer, to submit to the Ministry a declaration of its activities. Furthermore, prior to undertaking any transaction involving a sum exceeding $1,000 or its equivalent, it is required to identify the customer by a standard data form and sight of his international passport, driving licence, national identity card or such document bearing his photograph as may be prescribed by the Federal Ministry of Commerce. Records must be kept in chronological order indicating each customer's surname, forenames and address in a register numbered and forwarded to the Federal Ministry of Commerce, and should be forwarded to the Commission by the Federal Ministry of Commerce within seven days.

"Designated non-financial institutions" include dealers in jewellery, cars and luxury goods, chartered accountants, audit firms, tax consultants, clearing and settlement companies, legal practitioners, hotels, casinos. supermarkets or such other businesses as the Federal Ministry of Commerce or appropriate regulatory authorities may, from time to time, designate.

27.27.9 Role of the MLRO/Nominated Officer

The "Know Your Customer Directive", which was circulated to all banks and financial institutions, explicitly refers to Money Laundering Reporting Officers. Banks and financial institutions are advised to have clear procedures on, and communicate to all personnel, how they can promptly report suspicious transactions to their Money Laundering Reporting Officers and/or to other competent authorities.

27.27.10 Due Diligence

The CBN is currently considering introducing a three-tiered system, so that CDD requirements are different depending on the size of the transaction. However, as consultations were still ongoing at the time of writing, they will not be further included in this book.

There is a general due diligence requirement on all financial institutions, which are required to verify a customer's identity and address before opening an account for, issuing a passbook to, entering into a fiduciary transaction with, renting a safe deposit box or establishing any other business relationship with the customer. Further due diligence requirements are stated in the Know Your Customer (KYC) Directive, which provides additional guidance for different categories of customers.

A bank customer is required to comply with the CDD requirements for any number or manner of transactions involving a sum exceeding US$ 1,000 or its equivalent. However, where a financial institution has reasonable grounds to suspect that the amount involved in a transaction is the proceeds of a crime or an illegal act, it shall require identification of the customer regardless of the amount involved.

Personal Client Due Diligence

An individual is required to provide proof of his identity by representing to the financial institution a valid original copy of an official document bearing his name and photograph. He must also verify his address by presenting to the financial institution the originals of public utility receipts issued in the previous three months.

If a mortgage is taken out, the employer of the customer needs to be informed such that the amount due can be deducted directly from salary. While this was implemented to reduce losses from loan default, this also has the effect of combating financial crime.

Corporate Customer Due Diligence

A body corporate shall be required to provide proof of its identity by presenting its Certificate of Incorporation and other valid official documents attesting to the existence of the body corporate. The manager, employees or assignee delegated by a body corporate to open the account shall be required to produce the same documentation as an individual (as above), but also proof of attorney granted to him in that behalf. The KYC Directive advises that, before a business relationship is established, measures should be taken by way of company search at the Corporate Affairs Commission (CAC) and/or other commercial enquiries to check that the applicant company has not been, or is not in the process of being, dissolved, struck off, wound up or terminated.

Beneficial Ownership

Where the customer is a body corporate, the financial institution or designated non-financial institution shall take reasonable measures to understand the ownership and control structure of the customer, and determine the natural persons who truly own or control the customer.

Non-face-to-face Customer Due Diligence

If it appears that a customer may not be acting on his own account, the financial institution shall seek from the customer by all reasonable means, information as to the true identity of the principal.

Politically Exposed Persons

Public Officers are defined as "individuals who are, or have been, entrusted with prominent public function, both within and outside Nigeria and those associated with them". The 2011 Act states that where the customer is a Public Officer, the financial institution or designated non-financial institution shall, in addition to the standard requirements:

- Put in place appropriate risk-management systems; and
- Obtain senior management approval before establishing, and during, any business relationship with the Public Officer.

The Know Your Customer Directive 2001 required financial institutions to investigate the sources of funds before accepting a PEP as a customer. The decision to open such accounts should be taken by senior management.

Anonymous Accounts

Opening or maintaining any numbered or anonymous account is prohibited under the 2011 Act.

Foreign Transfers

A transfer to or from a foreign country of funds or securities by a person or body corporate including a money service business of a sum exceeding US$ 10,000 or its equivalent, must be reported to the Central Bank of Nigeria and the Securities and Exchange Commission in writing within seven days from the date of the transaction. Transportation of cash or negotiable instruments in excess of US$ 10,000 or its equivalent by individuals in or out of the country must be declared to the Nigeria Customs Service.

27.27.11 *Ongoing Monitoring*

The Commission reserves the power to demand and receive reports directly from financial and designated non-financial institutions at any time. In this respect, the duties imposed on such financial institutions such as identification procedures are ongoing. Furthermore, the Know Your Customer Directive states that banks and financial institutions must collect sufficient information on the nature of the business that the customer intends to undertake, including the expected or predictable pattern of transactions.

27.27.12 *Staff Training*

Every financial institution must develop programmes to combat the laundering of the proceeds of a crime or other illegal acts, which will include:

- The designation of Compliance Officers at management level at its headquarters and every branch and local office;
- Regular training programmes for its employees;

- Centralisation of the information collected;
- The establishment of an internal audit unit to ensure compliance and effectiveness of the measures taken to enforce provisions of the Act.

27.27.13 *Record-keeping*

A financial institution or designated non-financial institution must preserve and keep, at the disposal of the authorities (the Central Bank of Nigeria, the Commission and the National Drug Law Enforcement Agency), the following:

- Records of a customer's identification for a period of at least five years after the closure of the account or the severance of relations with the customer;
- Records and other related information of a transaction carried out by a customer and any report provided for a period of at least five years after carrying out the transaction or the making of the report.

The director of investigation or an officer of the Commission or Agency duly authorised may demand, obtain and inspect the books and records of financial institutions to confirm compliance with the provisions of the Act.

The Know Your Customer Directive advises banks and financial institutions to maintain records of the supporting evidence and methods used to verify identity for ten years after the account is closed or the business relationship ends.

Suspicious Transaction Reports

A financial institution or designated non-financial institution must, within seven days of a suspicious transaction, draw up a written report containing all relevant information concerning the transaction including due diligence; take appropriate action to prevent the laundering of the proceeds of a crime or an illegal act; and send a copy of the report to the Commission. This process must occur whether or not the transaction is actually completed.

The Commission will acknowledge receipt of any disclosure, report or information received under this section and may demand such additional information as it may deem necessary. The acknowledgement of receipt will be sent to the financial institution or designated non-financial institution within the time allowed for transactions to be undertaken and it may be accompanied by a notice deferring the transaction for a period not exceeding 72 hours. If the acknowledgement of receipt is not accompanied by a stop notice, or the order to block the transaction is not received in time, the financial institution or non-financial institution may carry out the transaction.

If it is not possible to ascertain the origin of the funds within the period of stoppage for the transaction, the Federal High Court may, at the request of the Commission or other persons duly authorised, order that the funds, accounts or securities referred to in the report be blocked. Financial institutions and non-financial institutions which fail to carry out the above reporting obligations will be found guilty of an offence and fined up to N 1,000,000 each day the failure to report continues. The Governor of the Central Bank of Nigeria shall impose a penalty of not less than N 1,000,000 for failure to comply with reporting and investigating obligations.

The Commissioner or Agency, Central Bank of Nigeria or other regulatory authorities pursuant to an order of the Federal High Court obtained on an ex parte application supported by a sworn declaration made by the Chairman or an authorised officer of the Commission or Agency, Central Bank of Nigeria or other regulatory authorities, may, in order to identify and locate proceeds, properties, objects or other things related to the commission of an offence under the Act, have the following investigating powers:

- Place any bank account or any other account comparable to a bank account under surveillance;
- Obtain access to any suspected computer system;
- Obtain communication of any authentic instrument or private contract, together with all bank, financial and commercial records, when the account, telephone line or computer system is used by any person suspected of taking part in a transaction involving the proceeds of a financial or other crime.

The National Drug Law Enforcement Agency may also have the above investigating powers where a case relates to identifying or locating properties, objects or proceeds from narcotic drugs or psychotropic substances. When exercising such powers, the Agency must promptly make a report to the Commission.

Bank secrecy or preservation of customer confidentiality cannot be used as grounds for objection to the above investigating powers.

27.27.14 Suspicious Transaction Reporting

When a transaction:

- Involves a frequency which is unjustifiable or unreasonable; or
- Is surrounded by conditions of unusual or unjustifiable complexity; or
- Appears to have no economic justification or lawful objective; or
- In the opinion of the financial institution or designated non-financial institution involves terrorist financing; or
- Is inconsistent with the known transaction pattern of the account or business relationship,

that transaction shall be deemed to be suspicious and the financial institution involved in such transaction shall seek information from the customer as to the origin and destination of the funds, the aim of the transaction and the identity of the beneficiary.

27.27.15 Penalties

A person, including a bank employee, wilfully violating the MLPA or the AML/CFT Regulation is subject to a financial sanction not exceeding N 2,000,000, which must be published in its financial statements, and potentially imprisonment too.

The penalties for opening an anonymous account are, in the case of an individual, a term of imprisonment of not less than two years but not more than five years; or, in the case of a financial institution or corporate body, a fine of not less than N 10,000,000 but not more than N 50,000,000.

For failing to implement adequate training procedures, the Governor of the Central Bank of Nigeria may impose a penalty of not less than N 1,000,000 or the suspension of any licence issued to a financial institution.

A person who wilfully obstructs the Commission or Agency during an investigation is liable, on conviction, to a term of between two and three years' imprisonment for an individual, and in the case of a financial institution or body corporate, a fine of N 1,000,000.

27.27.16 Case Studies

A former governor of a Nigerian region was sentenced to 13 years in prison for money laundering. Nigeria has a reputation for being associated with corruption, so, although it is promising that a former governor was convicted and sentenced, it does little to mitigate this reputation. Peculiarly, the governor's defence during his trial was not that he did not launder the money, but that his crimes were mitigated by his successes as a governor, which it was argued included the construction of three Olympic and FIFA-registered stadia, an 18-hole golf course and a shooting range.

His defence counsel also called a former Wimbledon footballer as a character witness, further highlighting the bizarre nature of this case. Worryingly, although the correct verdict was reached, the conduct of this trial does suggest that amongst those in power in Nigeria, there may be a culture that corruption is acceptable, and this reputation is one which Nigeria may still find difficult to shake off in the coming years although much is being done to improve matters.

In another case, a foreign exchange dealer was sentenced to one year in prison for laundering N 300,000,000, or approximately £1,200,000. He concealed the origin of the funds with numerous accomplices, including officials and customers at the bank. Three manager's cheques were drawn in favour of a number of customers, then liquidated and moved into different accounts using the passwords belonging to two of the bank staff. As well as the one-year jail sentence, the fraudster was ordered to forfeit the N 300,000,000.

27.28 COUNTRY PROFILE: POLAND

27.28.1 Overview

The Polish authorities stated in the 2007 MONEYVAL report that the largest economic crimes within the country related to false fuel and scrap-metal dealing, resulting in lost customs and excise duties. Since new legislation has been introduced, though, the number of convictions for these crimes has increased.

Poland has been found to be deficient in regards to its AML regulation by various international bodies. However, in recent years it has introduced numerous measures to bring itself up to FATF standards.

27.28.2 Key Legislation

The AML law is contained in the Penal Code and the Act on Counteracting Money Laundering and Terrorism Financing dated 16th November, 2000, with subsequent amendments. The latest version appeared in the *Journal of Laws* in 2010. The Regulation of the Minister of Finance, dated 21st September, 2001, with subsequent amendments, provides supplementary regulation.

27.28.3 Legislative History

The Act on Counteracting Money Laundering and Terrorism Financing of 16th November, 2000 has been amended several times. Provisions regarding electronic payment were introduced in 2002, and the scope of the Act was extended in 2003 and 2004. The Third EU Anti-Money Laundering Directive was introduced in Poland by the Act of 25th July, 2009 amending the AML Act by implementing the EU Directives 2005/60/CE and 2006/70/CE.

27.28.4 FATF Assessment

The 2007 MONEYVAL report noted a large number of aspects missing from the Polish AML regime, such as the requirement to submit an STR or to terminate a relationship when CDD cannot be completed (both of which have since been rectified). Poland was rated "largely compliant" or "compliant" in just 18 of the 49 recommendations. However, the 2010 progress report noted that, since the adoption of the MER and the First Progress Report, Poland has taken the following measures with a view to addressing the deficiencies identified:

- Implementation of a new AML/CFT Law incorporating the Third EU Directive requirements;
- The creation of an autonomous offence of financing of terrorism;
- Achievement of a number of money-laundering convictions, including five autonomous convictions;

- Implementation of further outreach and training to the private sector;
- Implementation of further training to prosecutors and judges on the elements of money-laundering offences.

27.28.5 *The Primary AML Investigation/Regulatory Authorities*

Minister Responsible for Financial Institutions

Article 3 of the AML Act provides that the Minister Responsible for Financial Institutions shall be the supreme authority of financial information. The Minister of Finance, via the Ministry, controls the General Inspector of Financial Information.

General Inspectorate of Financial Information

The role of the General Inspectorate of Financial Information (GIFI) is to obtain, collect, process and analyse information in the manner prescribed in the AML Act and to take action to prevent money laundering and terrorist financing. Article 4 of the AML Act specifies further duties of the GIFI, including:

- Investigating STRs;
- Initiating and undertaking measures to prevent money laundering;
- Monitoring compliance with AML regulations.

The GIFI is bound to report the execution of its duties to the Prime Minister of Poland on a yearly basis.

Cooperating Units

The AML Act lists the National Bank of Poland, the Polish Financial Supervision Authority and the Supreme Chamber of Control as "cooperating units".

27.28.6 *Outline of Specific Money-laundering Offences*

Money laundering is defined in the Act of 16th November, 2000 on Counteracting Money Laundering and Terrorism Financing as any deliberate action such as:

- Conversion or transfer of asset values derived from criminal activity or from participation in such activity in order to conceal or disguise the illicit origin of asset values, or granting assistance to a person who participates in such activities in order to avoid legal consequences of actions undertaken by such a person.
- Concealment or disguise of the true nature of asset values or property rights associated with them, of their source, location, disposition and an event of their dislocation, being aware that these values are derived from criminal activity or participation in such activity.
- Acquisition, taking possession or use of asset values derived from criminal activity or participation in such an activity.
- Complicity, attempt to commit, aiding or abetting the above.

These definitions apply even if the activities leading to the attainment of such asset values were conducted in the territory of a country other than the Republic of Poland.

Furthermore, the Polish Penal Code Article 299 defines money laundering as:

> *"Whoever receives, transfers or transports abroad, assists in its transfer of title or possession of legal tenders, securities or other foreign currency values, property rights or real or movable property obtained from the profits of offences committed by other persons ... or takes other action which can prevent, or make significantly more difficult, determination of their criminal origin or place of deposition, detection or forfeiture."*

27.28.7 *Financing of Terrorism*

Terrorism financing is defined as an act referred to in Article 165a of the Penal Code, which contains the terrorism offences.

27.28.8 *Defences*

Where a person voluntarily discloses before a law-enforcement agency information about persons taking part in the perpetration of an offence or about the circumstances of an offence, if it prevented the perpetration of another offence, that person shall not be liable to the penalty for the offence specified in Section 1-4. If the perpetrator undertook efforts leading to the disclosure of this information and circumstances, the court may apply extraordinary mitigation of punishment.

27.28.9 *Penalties*

The penalty for money laundering is deprivation of liberty for a term of between three months and five years. The punishment shall be imposed on anyone who, being an employee of a bank, financial or credit institution, unlawfully receives, in cash, significant amounts of money or foreign currency, transfers or converts them, receives them under other circumstances arousing justifiable suspicion as to their origin, or else provides services to conceal their unlawful origin or in securing them against seizure.

If money laundering is committed as a group, or the perpetrator gains considerable material benefit, the penalty of deprivation of liberty shall be for a term of between one and ten years.

27.28.10 *Scope*

The AML Act applies to "obligated institutions", and lists 21 types of financial entity bound by the legislation.

27.28.11 Risk-based Approach

Any obligated institutions shall introduce a written internal procedure on counteracting money laundering and terrorist financing. Such an internal procedure should contain, in particular:

- The determination of how the financial security measures shall be implemented;
- Transactions registered;
- Analyses performed and risk assessed;
- Transaction information transmitted to the General Inspector;
- The suspension of transactions;
- Any account blocking and account freezing carried out;
- The manner in which the statements are received, if they are received; and
- How the information is stored.

27.28.12 Role of the MLRO/Nominated Officer

Obligated institutions must designate persons responsible for fulfilling the requirements of the AML law. The MLRO should be a board member appointed by the management board.

When the obligated institution exercises its business activity individually, a person responsible is a person performing this activity.

27.28.13 Due Diligence

CDD should be performed before entering into a contract with a client or prior to a transaction. It may be completed after having established an economic relationship only if it is necessary to ensure further business operations and where there is little risk of money laundering or terrorist financing, determined on the basis of relevant analysis performed.

Any obligated institution shall apply financial security measures for its clients. Their scope is determined on the basis of risk assessment for money laundering and terrorist financing, hereinafter referred to as "risk assessment", resulting from the analysis, taking into account, in particular, the type of client, economic relationships, products and transactions. The risk assessment should consist of:

- Client identification and verification of his identity on the basis of documents or information publicly available;
- Making attempts, with due diligence, to identify a beneficial owner and apply verification measures, dependent on appropriate risk assessment, in order to provide the obligated institution with data required on the actual identity of a beneficial owner, including determination of the ownership structure and dependence of the client;

- Obtaining information regarding the purpose and the nature of economic relationships intended by a client;
- Constant monitoring of current economic relationships with a client, therein surveying transactions carried out to ensure that such transactions are in accordance with the knowledge of the obligated institution of the client and the business profile of his operations and with the risk; and, if possible, surveying the origins of assets and constantly updating documents and information in the obligated institution's possession.

Financial security measures are applied, in particular:

- When concluding a contract with a client;
- When carrying out a transaction with a client with whom the obligated institution has not previously concluded any agreements of the equivalent of more than EUR 15,000, regardless of whether the transaction is carried out as a single operation or as several operations if the circumstances indicate that they are linked;
- When there is a suspicion of money laundering or terrorist financing regardless of the value of such a transaction, its organisational form or the type of client;
- When there are doubts raised that the previously received data referred to in Article 9 are authentic and complete.

In the event the obligated institution cannot perform these duties, it should cease business transactions and submit a report to the General Inspector.

Personal Client Due Diligence
For natural persons and their representatives, document(s) confirming the following aspects of the identity of the person should be examined:

- The first and last name;
- The nationality and address of the person performing the transaction;
- His/her PESEL number, or, if the person has no PESEL number, his/her date of birth or the number of an identity document confirming the identity of an alien, or a country code if a passport was presented.

Corporate Customer Due Diligence
For corporate entities:

- An extract of the Court Register or another document indicating the company's name and organisational form;
- Its registered office and address;
- Its tax identification number along with the first and last name and the PESEL number of the person representing this legal entity, or, in the case of a person with no PESEL number, his/her date of birth.

Occasional Customers

CDD shall also apply to parties to a transaction who are not clients. This includes the determination and recording of their (or their company's) names or the first and last name and address.

Simplified Customer Due Diligence

In certain justifiable cases, it is possible to open an account without satisfying the CDD requirements. These include transactions with specified low-risk entities and also on electronic payment devices where the maximum amount stored in the device does not exceed the equivalent of EUR 150 or an aggregate of EUR 2,500 per calendar year. In the case of a device which can be recharged, provided that the redemption amount is at least the equivalent of EUR 1,000 per calendar year in question, simplified CDD may be carried out.

Enhanced Customer Due Diligence

Any obligated institution shall apply, on the basis of risk analysis, increased security measures against a client in events which may involve a higher risk of money laundering or terrorist financing and particularly in the cases referred to below.

Non-face-to-face Customer Due Diligence

If the client is absent, the obligated institution shall apply at least one of the following measures in order to reduce the risk:

- Establish the identity of the client on the basis of additional documents or information;
- Conduct additional verification of the authenticity of the documents or attestation of their compliance with the original copies by a notary public, a government body, a local government authority or an entity providing financial services;
- Ascertain the fact that the first transaction was conducted via the client's account in the entity providing financial services.

Politically Exposed Persons

With regard to politically exposed persons, the obligated institution should:

- Implement procedures based on risk assessment to determine whether such client is a person holding a politically exposed position;
- Apply measures, adequate to the risk determined by this obligated institution, in order to establish the source of asset values introduced to trading;
- Maintain constant monitoring of transactions conducted;
- Conclude a contract with a client after having obtained the consent of the board, the designated member of the management board or a person designated by the board or a person responsible for the activities of the obligated institution.

The obligated institution may collect written statements on whether a client is a person holding a politically exposed position, for which it would be a criminal offence to give misleading answers.

Anonymous Accounts

Any obligated institution shall apply appropriate measures of financial security in order to prevent money laundering or terrorist financing, which may arise from products or transactions allowing the client to maintain anonymity.

Correspondent Banking

In terms of cross-border relations with institutional correspondents from countries other than EU Member States and equivalent countries, any obligated institutions being a provider of financial services shall:

- Collect information allowing the determination of the scope of operations, and whether a provider of financial services is supervised by the State;
- Assess measures taken by a provider of financial services which is a correspondent insofar as counteracting money laundering and terrorist financing;
- Prepare documentation defining the scope of responsibilities of each provider of financial services;
- Ascertain, with respect to payable-through accounts, that a provider of financial services, which is a correspondent, has conducted verification of identity and has taken appropriate actions under procedures on the application of financial security measures in relation with clients having direct access to such a correspondent's bank accounts, and that it is able to provide, on demand from the correspondent, any data related to the application of financial security measures in regard to a client;
- Establish cooperation, with the prior consent of a board of directors or a designated member of such a board or a person designated by such a board or an MLRO.

Shell Banking

No obligated institution, which is a provider of financial services, shall establish and maintain cooperation within correspondent banking with a shell bank.

No obligated institution shall establish and maintain cooperation within correspondent banking with any obligated institution which is a provider of financial services concluding contracts on accounts with a shell bank.

27.28.14 Ongoing Monitoring

Any obligated institution shall undertake ongoing analysis of transactions carried out. The results of such analyses should be documented in paper or electronic form.

27.28.15 Staff Training

Any obligated institution must ensure that employees who perform duties related to counteracting money laundering and terrorist financing participate in training programmes related to their duties.

27.28.16 Record-keeping

The register of suspicious transactions shall be stored for a period of five years, calculating from the first day of the year following the year in which transactions were recorded. Any information on the transactions carried out by the obligated institution and documents related to such transactions shall be stored for a period of five years, calculating from the first day of the year following the year in which the last record associated with the transaction took place.

Information obtained as a result of the application of CDD measures should be stored for a period of five years from the first day of the year following the year in which the transaction was carried out with the client. Documents and other data retained by the entity with a reporting obligation shall be destroyed within one year after expiry of the retention period.

All of the results of investigations carried out in pursuance of the ongoing monitoring requirements shall be kept for a period of five years, calculating from the first day of the year following the year in which they were conducted.

27.28.17 Investigation and Reporting Requirements

At the written request of the General Inspector, any obligated institution shall immediately disclose any information about the transactions covered by the AML law. Such a disclosure consists, in particular, of the provision of information about the parties to the transaction, the content of documents, including the balances and turnover on the account, certified copies of theirs, or a disclosure of relevant documents, to provide insight for authorised employees of the relevant authority in order to produce notes or copies.

The information shall be forwarded electronically to the General Inspector free of charge and, if the General Inspector requests.

27.28.18 Suspicious Transaction Reporting

Any obligated institution must provide information on suspicious transactions to the General Inspector. Any report must include the following information:

- Identification data of the parties to the transaction;
- The amount, currency and type of the transaction;
- Numbers of accounts used to conduct the transaction if the transactions involve such accounts;

- Substantiation, along with the place, date and manner of placing disposition, in the event of providing information on the transaction.

Any obligated institution conducting a transaction for which the circumstances may suggest that it was related to money laundering or terrorist financing is required to register such a transaction, regardless of its value and character.

In the event that the obligated institution does not accept the disposition or order to conduct a transaction, the reporting obligation shall still apply if the institution is aware of, or with due diligence should be aware of, such a transaction in regard to the contract with its client.

If it conducts a transaction exceeding the equivalent of EUR 15,000, the institution is required to register the transaction. Furthermore, if numerous transactions appear to be linked and were divided into smaller transactions to avoid the registration requirement, they must still be reported. This obligation shall not apply to, for example:

- Transfers from a deposit account to a time deposit account belonging to the same client at the same obligated institution;
- Transfers to a deposit account from a time deposit account belonging to the same client at the same obligated institution;
- Incoming transfers with the exception of bank transfers from abroad;
- Transactions related to the internal management of the obligated institutions.

Information on a transaction shall be forwarded to the General Inspector:

- In the case of transactions exceeding the threshold, within 14 days after the end of each calendar month;
- In the case of suspicious transactions, immediately.

27.28.19 Waived Registration Regulations

Article 9d item 1 of the AML Act sets forth the circumstances in which the registration obligation and financial security measures may be waived. These include:

(a) When the client is an entity providing financial services established in the territory of any of the EU Member States or equivalent countries; or

(b) In relation to:

- government bodies, local government authorities and execution bodies;
- life insurance policies, provided that a fixed annual premium does not exceed the equivalent of EUR 1,000, and that a single premium does not exceed the equivalent of EUR 2,500;
- transactions regarding insurance policies being a part of retirement insurance, provided that the terms and conditions of the policy do not include a surrender clause, and that such policy cannot be used as collateral for a loan;

- electronic money devices, within the meaning of the Polish Act of 19th August, 2011 on payment services, if the maximum amount stored in the device does not exceed:
  - EUR 250, in the case of devices that cannot be recharged; or
  - EUR 2,500 per calendar year, in the case of rechargeable devices, provided that the redemption amount is at least the equivalent of EUR 1,000 per calendar year concerned;
- transactions that can be traced back by payment service providers of the payee due to a unique reference number assigned to the transaction for the supply of goods and services with the payee, even if the amount of such a transaction does not exceed the equivalent of EUR 1,000.

27.28.20 Penalties

Any obligated institution, with the exception of the National Bank of Poland, which:

- Fails to register a transaction exceeding the threshold, fails to provide the General Inspector with the documents relating to this transaction or fails to store records of the transaction or documents relating to this transaction for the required period of time;
- Fails to carry out risk analysis essential for the application of appropriate financial security measures;
- Fails to apply financial security measures;
- Fails to store documented results of the analysis for the required period of time;
- Fails to meet the obligation to provide employees with a training programme;
- Fails to comply, in a timely manner, with the post-audit conclusions or recommendations;
- Establishes and/or maintains cooperation with a shell bank

shall be subject to pecuniary penalties. The penalty imposed shall be decided by the General Inspector, and shall not exceed 750,000 PLN. (Note that much of the legislation still refers to PLN or zloty, as opposed to euros. Our expectation is that when the Fourth Money Laundering Directive is implemented in Poland during 2016, these amounts will be changed to euros.) When determining the amount of such a pecuniary penalty, the General Inspector shall take into account the nature and the extent of violations, the previous operation of the obligated institution and its financial capacity.

Any person who acts on behalf of, or in the interest of, the obligated institution and, contrary to the provisions of the Act, fails to:

- Register a transaction, to submit documentation relating to this transaction to the General Inspector or to store a register of such transaction or documentation relating to this transaction for the required period of time;

- Maintain financial security measures, in accordance with the prescribed procedures, or to store information obtained in connection with the implementation of financial security measures;
- Notify the General Inspector about required transactions;
- Suspend a transaction or block an account;
- Introduce the internal procedures required;
- Designate an MLRO

shall be subject to the punishment of imprisonment for up to three years.

Anyone who discloses the information collected in accordance with the AML law to any unauthorised persons, any account holder or any person to whom the transaction relates, or uses this information in any other unauthorised manner shall be subject to the same punishment. If this is done unintentionally, the perpetrator shall be subject to a fine.

Anyone who, acting on behalf of or in the interest of the obligated institution:

- Refuses to submit information or documents to the General Inspector; or
- Submits false data to the General Inspector or hides real data on transactions, accounts or persons

shall be subject to the punishment of imprisonment from three months to five years.

Anyone who commits any of the above offences and, as a result, causes substantial damage, shall be subject to the punishment of imprisonment from six months to eight years.

27.28.21 *Case Studies*

In the financial year 2010–11, the Polish authorities recovered zł.60 million in laundered money, bringing the total recovered to zł.215.6 million. However, this is only a fraction of the zł.1.33 billion that was suspected of being laundered in the same financial year by 387 companies, highlighting that the authorities still have a lot to do.

One of the latest innovations by money launderers in Poland is to put laundered money on a new variety of cash card that can be bought in stores. These cards are not registered to anyone, meaning they can be thrown away without leaving a trace. Criminals often use them to make transactions online.

Money launderers are also transferring money online through non-banking institutions, such as credit unions. This makes transactions difficult to detect because the value is usually under zł.200–300, there are many of them taking place and the recipient's location could be anywhere. This highlights the need for financial institutions to adapt to changing technological advances to maintain the upper hand in the fight against money laundering.

27.29 COUNTRY PROFILE: RUSSIA

27.29.1 Overview

The Russian authorities are well aware of the money-laundering (ML) and terrorist-financing (TF) schemes used in Russia. Many ML schemes involve the misuse of (foreign) legal entities and financial institutions. Laundered money is often invested in real estate or security instruments, or used to buy luxury consumer goods. Russia has been a repeated victim of terrorism, and the authorities report the use of TF schemes involving the misuse of alternative remittance networks by foreign and North Caucasian terrorist groups.

A general impediment to the fight against ML/TF is the high level of corruption in the public and private sectors. There are no indications that the FIU is affected by corruption, but some law-enforcement bodies and private sector businesses are impacted by corruption in varying degrees. The current and previous Presidents of Russia have rightfully established eliminating corruption as a priority for the Russian government.

27.29.2 Key Legislation

The Russian Criminal Code criminalises the money-laundering offence. This is supplemented by various regulations provided by the FIU, including Ordinance No. 30, dated 23rd June, 2004, on Approval of Regulations on the Federal Financial Monitoring Service, Ordinance No. 245, dated 17th April, 2002, on Approval of the Regulation for Submitting Information to the Federal Financial Monitoring Service by Organisations Performing Operations in Monetary Funds or Other Assets and Federal Law No. 115-FZ, of 7th August, 2001, on Combating Legalisation (Laundering) of Criminally Gained Income and Financing of Terrorism. The most recent legislation, enacted in June 2013, Federal Law of 28.06.2013 No. 134-FZ "On amendments to certain legislative acts of the Russian Federation on counteraction to illegal financial transactions" made various amendments to the AML framework.

27.29.3 Legislative History

Money laundering was first criminalised in Russia in 1997.

27.29.4 FATF Assessment

The most recent mutual evaluation found that Russia has, in a short time, implemented and enhanced its AML/CFT system and has done so in less time than many other countries. It was particularly complimentary towards the FIU, Rosfinmonitoring, for performing the traditional tasks of an FIU in full compliance with the FATF standards, as well as many other tasks, including serving as the central responsible agency for AML/CFT matters. Further, the FATF praised Russia for introducing the concept of beneficial ownership into its framework, and amending and strengthening its legislation to bring the country into line with FATF standards.

27.29.5 The Primary AML Investigation/Regulatory Authorities

Federal Financial Monitoring Service

Rosfinmonitoring, The Federal Financial Monitoring Service, is a federal executive body carrying out functions on combating legalisation (laundering) of proceeds from crime and financing of terrorism, and coordinating activities of other federal executive bodies in this sphere.

Rosfinmonitoring became operational on 1st February, 2002 by order of Decree of the President of the Russian Federation No. 1263 "On the Authorised Agency for Combating Legalisation (Laundering) of Proceeds from Crime and Financing of Terrorism", which was signed on 1st November, 2001.

The Federal Financial Monitoring Service is supervised by the Government of the Russian Federation in line with the Decree of the President of the Russian Federation No. 1274 "Issue on structure of the federal executive bodies", dated 24th September, 2007.

Rosfinmonitoring is guided in its activities by the Constitution of the Russian Federation, federal constitutional laws, federal laws, acts of the President of the Russian Federation and of the Government of the Russian Federation, international agreements of the Russian Federation, normative legal acts of the Ministry of Finance of the Russian Federation and the Regulations on Rosfinmonitoring.

The Federal Financial Monitoring Service carries out its activities directly and through its territorial bodies in collaboration with other federal executive bodies, executive bodies of the constituent entities of the Russian Federation, local self-government bodies, public associations and other organisations.

The Central Bank of Russia

The Central Bank of Russia was founded in 1990. In April 2005, the Russian government and Bank of Russia adopted the Banking Sector Development Strategy for the Period up to 2008, a document which set, as the main objective of banking sector development in the medium term (2005–2008), the enhancement of the banking sector's stability and efficiency.

The principal goals of banking sector development are as follows:

- To increase the protection of interests of depositors and other creditors of banks;
- To enhance the effectiveness of the banking sector's activity in accumulating household and enterprise sector funds and transforming them into loans and investments;
- To make Russian credit institutions more competitive;
- To prevent the use of credit institutions in dishonest commercial practices and illegal activities, especially the financing of terrorism and money laundering;
- To promote the development of the competitive environment and ensure the transparency of credit institutions;
- To build up investor, creditor and depositor confidence in the banking sector.

Banking sector reform will help implement Russia's medium-term social and economic development programmes, especially its objective to end the raw materials bias of the Russian economy by rapidly diversifying it and utilising its competitive advantages. In the current stage (2009–2015), the Russian government and Bank of Russia are attaching priority to effectively positioning the Russian banking sector on international financial markets.

27.29.6 Outline of Specific Money-laundering Offences

The accomplishment of large-scale financial transactions and other deals in amounts of money or other property knowingly acquired by other persons in an illegal way (except the offences stipulated by Articles 193, 194, 198 and 199 of the present Code) for the purpose of bringing the appearance of legality to the possession, use and disposal of the said amounts of money or other property constitutes an offence.

Note: The "large-scale financial transactions and other deals in amounts of money or other property" in the present article means financial transactions and other deals in amounts of money or other property accomplished in an amount exceeding 2,000 times the minimum wage rate.

Self-money laundering is also criminalised in Russia by Article 174.1 of the Criminal Code. It is defined as the accomplishment of large-scale financial transactions and other deals in amounts of money or other property acquired by a person as the result of his/her having committed an offence (except for the offences stipulated by Articles 193, 194, 198 and 199 of the present Code) or the use of these amounts of money or other property for the pursuance of entrepreneurial or other economic activity.

The acquisition or sale of property, knowingly obtained in a criminal manner, also constitutes a criminal offence.

27.29.7 Penalties

The primary money-laundering offence shall be punishable by a fine at a rate of 500 to 700 times the minimum wage rate or in the amount of the convict's wage or other income for a period of five to seven months or imprisonment for a term of up to four years with a fine at a rate of up to 100 times the minimum wage rate or in the amount of the convict's wage or other income for a term of up to one month or without such a fine.

The same actions committed:

- By a group of persons by preliminary agreement;
- Repeatedly; or
- By a person abusing his/her position

shall be punishable by imprisonment for a term of four to eight years with the confiscation of property or without such a confiscation.

The offence, when committed by an organised group, shall be punishable by imprisonment for a term of seven to ten years with the confiscation of property or without such a confiscation.

Self-money laundering shall be punishable by a fine at a rate of 700 to 1,000 times the minimum wage rate or in the amount of the convict's wage or other income for a period of six to ten months or imprisonment for a term of up to five years with a fine at a rate of up to 100 times the minimum wage rate or in the amount of the convict's wage or other income for a term of up to one month or without such a fine.

Self-money laundering committed:

- By a group of persons by preliminary agreement;
- Repeatedly; or
- By a person abusing his/her position

shall be punishable by imprisonment for a term of five to eight years with the confiscation of property or without such a confiscation.

Self-money laundering committed by an organised group shall be punishable by imprisonment for a term of 10 to 15 years with the confiscation of property or without such a confiscation.

Acquiring criminal property shall be punishable by a fine in the amount of 50 to 100 times the minimum wage rate, or in the amount of the wage or salary or any other income of the convicted person for a period of up to one month, or by compulsory works for a term of 180 to 240 hours, or by corrective labour for a term of one to two years, or by deprivation of liberty for a term of up to two years.

When the acquisition of criminal property is made:

- By a group of persons in a preliminary conspiracy;
- In relation to a car or any other property of large value;
- By a person who was earlier tried for stealing, extortion or acquisition or sale of property, knowingly obtained in a criminal manner,

it shall be punishable by restraint of liberty for a term of up to three years, or by arrest for a term of four to six years, or by deprivation of liberty for a term of up to five years with a fine in the amount of 50 times the minimum wage rate, or in the amount of the wage or salary, or any other income of the convicted person for a period of up to one month.

The acquisition of criminal property, when committed by an organised group or a person using his official position, shall be punishable by deprivation of liberty for a term of three to seven years with a fine in the amount of 100 times the minimum wage rate, or in the amount of the wage or salary, or any other income of the convicted person for a period of up to one month.

27.29.8 Scope

For the purposes of the AML framework, the following information shall relate to organisations performing operations with monetary funds or other assets:

- Credit institutions;
- Professional participants in the securities market;
- Insurance organisations and leasing companies;
- Organisations of federal post communication;
- Pawn shops;
- Organisations involved in the purchase or buying–selling of precious metals and precious stones, jewellery made out of them and scratched items;
- Organisations arranging totalisators and bookmaker offices as well as organising and carrying out lotteries, totalisators (mutual bets) and other risk-based games, including in electronic form;
- Organisations managing investment funds or non-governmental pension funds;
- Organisations rendering intermediary services when performing operations of sale and purchase of real estate;
- Non-credit organisations accepting cash funds from physical persons in cases provided for by the legislation on banks and banking activity.

27.29.9 Risk-based Approach

The requirements for identification can differ depending on the degree (level) of risk posed by the client of operations with regard to the legalisation (laundering) of criminally gained income or the financing of terrorism.

27.29.10 Role of the MLRO/Nominated Officer

Financial institutions are required to appoint an official to oversee compliance with the relevant AML regulations. For more on this, please see "Internal Requirements" below.

27.29.11 Due Diligence

CDD does not need to be conducted on a natural person, and verification and identification of the beneficiary are not performed when organisations performing operations with funds or other assets carry out depositing operations for clients (natural persons) of the following payments if they do not exceed 30,000 roubles or an amount in foreign currency equivalent to 30,000 roubles:

- Related to settlements with budgets of all levels of the budget system of the Russian Federation (including federal, regional and local taxes and duties, as well as those fines provided for by the legislation of the Russian Federation on taxes and duties);

- Related to payment for services rendered by budget institutions managed by federal executive bodies, executive bodies of the subjects of the Russian Federation and bodies of local self-government;
- Related to payment for flats, communal services, payment for safeguarding flats and installation of safeguarding equipment, as well as payment for communication services;
- Related to payment of contributions by members of orchid, garden, summer house and non-commercial associations of citizens and garage-construction cooperatives. Payments for paid auto placements;
- Related to payments of aliments.

It is perhaps surprising that orchid and other associations are listed in this way. The general point is that since they are cooperatives the normal rules do not need to apply.

When a natural person buys or sells, in cash, foreign currency for an amount not exceeding 15,000 roubles or not exceeding the amount in foreign currency equivalent to 15,000 roubles, identification of the client and/or identification and verification of the beneficiary are not performed except in cases where an officer of the organisation performing the operation with monetary funds or other assets suspects that this operation is being carried out with the aim of legalisation (laundering) of criminal proceeds or the financing of terrorism.

Credit organisations are authorised to refuse to conclude a contract for a bank account deposit with a natural or legal person in the following cases:

- The absence in the location of the legal person of its permanent control body, other body or person who has the right to act on behalf of the legal person without a proxy;
- A person or legal entity fails to submit documents certifying the data indicated in the present Article, or if invalid documents are presented;
- There are data on the natural or legal person concerning participation in terrorist activity, received in accordance with the present Federal law.

Personal Client Due Diligence

Regarding natural persons, the following must be ascertained:

- Surname;
- A name and also a patronymic (if such does not follow from the law or national custom);
- Citizenship;
- Data from a document identifying the person;
- Migration card data;
- A document confirming the right of a foreign citizen or a person without citizenship to stay (reside) in the Russian Federation;

- The residential (registration) address or the place where a foreign citizen is staying; and
- Taxpayer's identification number (where applicable).

Corporate Customer Due Diligence

Regarding legal persons, the following must be ascertained:

- Name;
- Taxpayer's identification number or the relevant code for a foreign organisation;
- State registration number;
- Place of State registration; and
- Business address.

Beneficial Ownership

The pre-2013 legislation only obliged financial institutions to undertake measures that were reasonable and accessible in the specific circumstances for the identification of beneficiaries – people who benefit from a company. However, the 2013 law expands this to beneficial owners – anybody who owns or controls over 25% of the company. This is the first time the concept of a beneficial owner has appeared in Russian law.

Organisations performing transactions with monetary funds now must request information about ownership structure, including all individual owners. However, if these measures do not help to identify the beneficial owner(s), the authorities can declare that the company is owned by its sole executive body.

Enhanced Customer Due Diligence

The following instances are subject to enhanced CDD:

- Operations with monetary funds or other assets if the amount involved in said operation equals or exceeds 600,000 roubles or a hard currency sum equivalent to 600,000 roubles, and, by its character, said operation is one of the following:
  - A cash operation with monetary funds:
    - The withdrawal from an account or placement in an account of a legal entity cash funds which are not deemed to fit with the character of its economic activity;
    - The purchase or sale of cash foreign currency by a natural person;
    - The acquisition by a person of securities for cash;
    - Cashing a bearer's cheque that was issued by a non-resident;
    - Changing notes of one denomination for notes of another denomination;
    - Contributing cash funds to the authorised capital of an organisation.
  - The placement or remittance of monetary funds into an account involving a territory which does not participate in international cooperation in the sphere of

combating money laundering and financing of terrorism, or in which there is information on illegal production of drugs.

- An operation on a bank account (deposits):
  - The placement of monetary funds in deposit or other accounts with execution of documents certifying a bearer's deposit;
  - The opening of a deposit account in favour of a third party with the placement therein of cash funds;
  - The remittance of monetary funds abroad into a deposit account opened for an anonymous owner, and the arrival of monetary funds from abroad from a deposit account opened for an anonymous owner;
  - The placement of monetary funds into an account or the withdrawal from an account of a legal entity whose activity does not exceed three months from the date of its registration, or placement of monetary funds into an account or withdrawal from an account by a legal entity on whose accounts operations have not been performed from the date of opening thereof.
- Another operation with movable property:
  - The placement of securities, precious metals, precious stones, jewellery made out of them and scratched items or other valuables into a pawn shop;
  - The payment of an insurance indemnity to a person or receiving from him an insurance premium for life insurance or other types of accumulation insurance or pension allowance;
  - Obtaining or providing property under contract of financial leasing;
  - The remittance of monetary funds performed by non-credit institutions by client's order;
  - The purchase, buying–selling of precious metals and precious stones, jewellery items made from them and scratched items;
  - Receiving monetary funds as payment for participation in a lottery, totalisator (mutual bet) and other risk-based games, including in electronic form, and payment of monetary funds as the prize received from participation in these games;
  - Granting, by legal persons that are not credit organisations, of interest-free loans to natural persons and (or) to other legal persons, as well as the receipt of such a loan.

Anonymous Accounts

It is prohibited for a financial institution to:

- Open accounts (deposits) for anonymous owners, i.e. without the necessary identification documents being provided by the person or legal entity opening the account (deposit);
- Open accounts (deposits) for natural persons in the absence of the person opening the account (deposit) or his representative.

27.29.12 Ongoing Monitoring

Financial institutions are required to regularly update the information on clients and beneficiaries.

27.29.13 Staff Training

As outlined in the section on internal requirements below, the internal procedures must include a system for the training of staff.

27.29.14 Record-keeping

All relevant information must be documented in the following circumstances:

- Intricate or unusual deals which do not make evident economic sense or have an evident legal purpose;
- Lack of compliance of a deal with the goals of the organisation, established by the founding documents of this organisation;
- The repeated performance of operations or deals whose character makes an entity suppose that the purpose of their performance is the evasion of the obligatory control procedures, provided by this Federal law;
- Other circumstances, which give reason to suppose that deals are being performed for the purposes of legalisation (laundering) of criminally gained income or the financing of terrorism.

Documents containing information stated in this article, and the data necessary for identification of the person, shall be kept for not less than five years. The specified term is calculated from the date of the termination of relations with the client.

27.29.15 Internal Requirements

In order to prevent the legalisation (laundering) of criminally gained income and the financing of terrorism, organisations performing operations with monetary funds and other assets must develop rules of internal control and relevant programmes to ensure that these are complied with. They must appoint officials responsible for the observance of these rules and the realisation of these programmes, and take other relevant internal organisational measures.

The internal control rules of an organisation performing operations with monetary funds and other assets must include a procedure for recording the necessary information in documents, a procedure for the provision of confidentiality of information, qualification requirements in terms of the preparation and training of staff and criteria for revealing and identifying extraordinary deals where the account portrays specific features of the activity of this organisation.

In accordance with the rules of internal control, any organisation performing operations with monetary funds and other assets must document the information obtained as a result of the application of these rules and the realisation of the programme of internal control, and in doing so must preserve the confidential nature of such information.

27.29.16 Suspicious Transaction Reporting

Financial institutions are required to collate documents and submit to the FIU the following information on operations with monetary funds or other assets which are subject to obligatory control, not later than the working day following the date of undertaking the operation:

- The type of operation and the grounds for performance thereof;
- The date on which the operation with monetary funds or other assets was carried out, as well as the amount involved;
- Information necessary to identify the person who carried out the operation with monetary funds or other assets (passport or other identification card data), the data from a migration card, a document confirming the right of a foreign citizen or a person without citizenship to stay (reside) in the Russian Federation, a taxpayer identification number (if one exists) and the address of his residence or the place in which he is staying;
- In the case of a legal entity, the name, taxpayer identification number, State registration number, place of State registration and the address of the entity that performed the operation with monetary funds or other assets;
- Information necessary for the identification of a person or legal entity by whose order and on whose behalf an operation with monetary funds or other assets was performed, the data from a migration card, a document confirming the right of a foreign citizen or a person without citizenship to stay (reside) in the Russian Federation, a taxpayer identification number (if one exists), a residential address or the business address, respectively, of a person or legal entity;
- Information necessary for the identification of the representative of the natural or legal person, the attorney, the agent, the commission agent or the trustee performing the operation with monetary funds or other assets, on behalf of or in interests of or at expense of another person by virtue of power based on proxy, contract, the law or a certificate from an authorised State body or institution of local government, the data from a migration card, a document confirming the right of a foreign citizen or a person without citizenship to stay (reside) in the Russian Federation, a taxpayer identification number (if one exists) and the residential address of the representative of the natural or legal person;
- Information necessary for the identification of the addressee of the operation with monetary funds or other assets and his representative, including the data from a migration card and a document confirming the right of a foreign citizen or a person without citizenship to stay (reside) in the Russian Federation, a taxpayer identification number (if one exists) and the address of a residence or site of the addressee and his representative if it is stipulated by the rules pertaining to the performance of the corresponding operation.

Information about operations in monetary funds or other assets subject to mandatory control shall be submitted by the organisation not later than on the business day following the day on which the relevant operation was undertaken.

Information about operations in monetary funds or other assets considered by internal control to be performed with the objective of money laundering or the financing of terrorism shall be submitted by the organisation not later than on the business day following the day of identification of the relevant operation.

The information specified above with regard to the present regulation shall be submitted to the Federal Financial Monitoring Service in electronic form via communication channels or on magnetic media.

If employees of an organisation performing operations with monetary funds and other assets have any suspicions resulting from the realisation of the internal control programmes, stated in Clause 2 of this article, that some operations are being performed for the purposes of legalisation (laundering) of criminally gained income and/or the financing of terrorism, this organisation, not later than the working day following the day on which such operations are detected, must forward to the authorised body information on these operations regardless of whether they refer to operations provided by Article 6 of this Federal law or not.

27.29.17 Penalties

Infringement by organisations performing operations with monetary funds or other assets and acting with the authority of a licence may lead to the withdrawal (annulment) of the licence in accordance with the procedure provided by the legislation of the Russian Federation.

Persons guilty of infringement of this Federal law shall bear administrative, civil and criminal responsibility in accordance with the legislation of the Russian Federation. The 2013 legislation added the power to freeze assets.

27.29.18 Case Studies

A former oil tycoon, who was once Russia's richest man with $15 billion in personal wealth, was convicted of money laundering in 2005 and sentenced to a total of 14 years in prison. Along with his former partner, the tycoon was then charged again with laundering more than $20 billion and stealing over 200 million tons of oil in 2009, when he was already halfway through his first sentence. However, the conviction is currently being reviewed as part of the appeal process.

The tycoon was arrested for laundering funds through his company, as well as on tax-evasion charges. For a financial institution, despite the suspicion surrounding the background to this case, it highlights the need not to take companies at face value. The lesson from this is that even if a company has a good reputation, appropriate AML checks still clearly need to be carried out.

27.30 COUNTRY PROFILE: SINGAPORE

27.30.1 Overview

Law-enforcement agencies in Singapore keep to strict programmes of governance and protection for the country's economy. *The Global Competitiveness Report*, published by the World Economic Forum, rated Singapore the best for protecting businesses from criminals.

27.30.2 Key Legislation

The key money-laundering legislation is the Corruption, Drug Trafficking and Other Serious Crimes (Confiscation of Benefits) Act, Chapter 65A. The AML regulations in Singapore are issued by the Monetary Authority of Singapore (MAS) pursuant to Section 27B of the Monetary Authority of Singapore Act (Cap. 186). The regulations, MAS notice 626, were issued on 2nd July, 2007 and last revised on 2nd December, 2009. *The AML Compliance Handbook*, issued by the Commercial Affairs Department, provides supplementary AML information.

27.30.3 Legislative History

Singapore has criminalised the money-laundering offence in eight separate provisions of the Corruption, Drug Trafficking and Other Serious Crimes Act (CDSA), which was last updated in March 2012. Singapore's laws are largely consistent with the 2000 UN Convention against Transnational Organised Crime (the Palermo Convention). Furthermore, the Terrorism (Suppression of Financing) Act, Chapter 325 was enacted in 2002 and amended in 2003. This Act provides the legislative framework for the offence of terrorism financing and the confiscation of any property associated with the financing of terrorism.

The Mutual Assistance in Criminal Matters Act, Chapter 190A, enacted in April 2000, allows the Singapore government to provide and receive international mutual assistance with regards to money laundering and the financing of terrorism. The Act was amended in 2006.

27.30.4 FATF Assessment

The 2008 mutual evaluation of Singapore was particularly impressive, with the country scoring "compliant" or "largely compliant" with 43 of the 49 FATF Recommendations. The remaining six areas were addressed by the time of its 2011 follow-up report, although the FATF noticed that deficiencies remained regarding politically exposed persons, wire transfers, transparency and beneficial ownership of legal persons, statistics and guidance and feedback. Overall, the money-laundering offences were described as broad, the international cooperation regime as comprehensive and the Suspicious Transaction Reporting Office as generally well structured, staffed and funded.

27.30.5 The Primary AML Investigation/Regulatory Authorities

Commercial Affairs Department

The Commercial Affairs Department (CAD) is the principal white-collar crime investigation agency in Singapore. It investigates a wide spectrum of commercial and financial crimes and has its own investigative and intelligence resources in the Singapore Police Force. In addition to this, the CAD issues *The AML Compliance Handbook*.

The Financial Investigation Branch

The Financial Investigation Branch (FIB) is the branch of the CAD which investigates laundering offences under the Corruption, Drug Trafficking and Other Serious Crimes (Confiscation of Benefits) Act (CDSA).

The Proceeds of Crime Unit

The Proceeds of Crime Unit (PCU), which is a branch of the CAD, identifies and seizes proceeds of crime, and manages such assets until they are dealt with under the CDSA. Enforcement agencies that come across a possible incidence of money laundering while investigating any offence may refer the case to the PCU for a joint investigation and subsequent prosecution.

The Suspicious Transaction Reporting Office

The Suspicious Transaction Reporting Office (STRO) is Singapore's financial intelligence unit (FIU). It is the central agency in Singapore for receiving, analysing and disseminating reports of suspicious transactions, known as suspicious transaction reports (STRs). The STRO turns raw data contained in STRs into financial intelligence that could be used to detect money laundering, terrorism financing and other criminal offences. It also disseminates financial intelligence to relevant enforcement and regulatory agencies.

STRs have been very useful in combating crime. The CAD has successfully detected a wide variety of criminal activity, such as cheating, criminal breach of trust, forgery and securities trading malpractices, as well as money laundering and terrorism financing. STR information has, directly or indirectly, led to the seizure of $110 million of proceeds of crime since 2000.

The STRO conducts various outreach programmes to various industry sectors to raise anti-money-laundering and counter financing of terrorism (AML/CFT) awareness, as well as to encourage an increase in the quantity and quality of STRs.

At the international front, as Singapore's FIU, the STRO represents Singapore at international forums and regional bodies in global AML/CFT efforts. The STRO also maintains close working relationships with FIUs in other countries through the Egmont Group of FIUs.

The Cash Enforcement Branch (CEB)

This branch of the CAD investigates cross-border movements of cash valued at over SGD 30,000.

Monetary Authority of Singapore

The Monetary Authority of Singapore (MAS) is governed by the MAS Act, which confers on the MAS powers to issue legal instruments for the regulation and supervision of financial institutions. In addition, the MAS also has frameworks and guidelines in place on topics which cut across various classes of financial institutions.

27.30.6 Outline of Specific Money-laundering Offences

The key offences are as follows:

- Assisting another to retain the benefits of drug trafficking;
- Assisting another to retain benefits from criminal conduct;
- Providing an exception under the reporting procedure;
- Acquiring, possessing, using, concealing or transferring benefits of drug trafficking;
- Acquiring, possessing, using, concealing or transferring benefits of criminal conduct;
- Tipping off;
- Prejudicing an investigation.

The money-laundering offence applies to both legal and natural persons, and proof of knowledge is derived from factual objective circumstances.

In July 2013, predicate offences were extended to include serious taxation offences and additional changes are anticipated in 2014.

27.30.7 Defences

It is a defence to prove:

- That one did not know, and had no reasonable grounds to believe, that the arrangement related to any person's proceeds of drug trafficking;
- That one did not know, and had no reasonable grounds to believe, that, by the arrangement, the retention or control by, or on behalf of, the relevant person of any property was facilitated or, as the case may be, that, by the arrangement, any property was used as mentioned above;
- That:
  - one intended to disclose to an authorised officer such suspicion or belief that the proceeds of drug trafficking were involved in relation to the arrangement; and
  - there is reasonable excuse for the person's failure to make disclosure; or
- That, in the case of a person who was in employment at the time in question and he enters or is otherwise concerned in the arrangement in the course of his employment, he disclosed the suspicion or belief that proceeds of drug trafficking were involved in relation to the arrangement to the appropriate person in accordance with the procedure established by his employer for the making of such disclosures.

27.30.8 *Penalties*

Natural persons are subject to a SGD 500,000 fine or up to seven years' imprisonment. Legal persons are subject to a SGD 1,000,000 fine.

27.30.9 *Role of the MLRO/Nominated Officer*

The bank should develop appropriate compliance management arrangements including, at least, the appointment of a management-level officer as the AML/CFT Compliance Officer. The bank must ensure that the AML/CFT Compliance Officer, as well as any other persons appointed to assist him, has timely access to all customer records and other relevant information which they require to discharge their functions.

27.30.10 *Due Diligence*

The requirement is that the bank must identify each customer who applies to the bank to establish business relations. A bank is required to perform CDD measures when:

- The bank establishes business relations with any customer;
- The bank undertakes any transaction with a value exceeding SGD 20,000 for any customer who has not otherwise established business relations with the bank;
- There is a suspicion of money laundering or terrorist financing, notwithstanding that the bank would otherwise not be required to perform CDD measures; or
- The bank has doubts about the veracity or adequacy of any information previously obtained.

A bank should complete verification of the identity of the customer and beneficial owner:

- Before the bank establishes business relations; or
- Before the bank undertakes any transaction for a customer, where the customer does not have business relations with the bank.

However, a bank may establish business relations with a customer before completing the verification of the identity of the customer and beneficial owner if:

- The deferral of completion of the verification of the identity of the customer and beneficial owner is essential in order not to interrupt the normal conduct of business operations; and
- The risks of money laundering and terrorist financing can be effectively managed by the bank.

Where the bank establishes business relations before verification of the identity of the customer or beneficial owner, the bank should complete verification as soon as is reasonably practicable.

Where the bank is unable to complete CDD measures, it should terminate the business relationship and consider if the circumstances are suspicious enough to warrant the filing of a suspicious transaction report (STR).

Personal Client Due Diligence

The bank is required to obtain and record information on the customer, including, but not limited to, the following:

- Full name, including any aliases;
- Unique identification number (such as an identity card number, birth certificate number or passport number, or, where the customer is not a natural person, the incorporation number or business registration number);
- Existing residential address, registered or business address (as may be appropriate) and contact telephone number(s);
- Date of birth, incorporation or registration (as may be appropriate); and
- Nationality or place of incorporation or registration (as may be appropriate).

The requirement is that the bank must verify the identity of the customer using reliable, independent sources. The bank is then required to retain copies of all reference documents used to verify the identity of the customer.

Corporate Customer Due Diligence

Where the customer is a company, the bank is required, apart from identifying the customer, also to identify the directors of the company. Where the customer is a partnership or a limited liability partnership, the bank is also required to identify the partners.

Where the customer is any other body corporate or unincorporated vehicle, the bank is required also to identify the persons having executive authority in that body corporate or unincorporated vehicle.

Beneficial Ownership

A bank shall inquire if there exists any beneficial owner in relation to a corporate customer (unless a waiver applies – see below). Furthermore, the bank shall take reasonable measures to understand the ownership and control structure of the company. Where there is one or more beneficial owner in relation to a customer, the bank shall take reasonable measures to obtain information sufficient to identify and verify the identities of the beneficial owner(s).

Simplified Customer Due Diligence

The regulations permit a bank to perform simplified CDD measures it considers adequate to effectively identify and verify the identity of the customer, a natural person appointed to act on the customer's behalf and any beneficial owner if it is satisfied that the risks of money laundering and terrorist financing are low. However, if the jurisdiction of the client is one seen to have weak AML/CFT measures in place (as specified by regulatory authorities), or where the bank suspects that money laundering or terrorist financing is involved, then full due diligence will need to be conducted.

Where the bank performs simplified CDD measures in relation to a customer, it should document:

- The details of its risk assessment; and
- The nature of the simplified CDD measures.

A bank is not required to inquire if there is a beneficial owner in relation to various specified low-risk entities, such as government departments. However, this does not apply if the bank suspects that the transaction is connected with money laundering or terrorist financing.

Business Profile

The bank is required to obtain from the customer, when processing the application to establish business relations, information as to the purpose and intended nature of business relations.

Non-face-to-face Customer Due Diligence

In such cases, the requirement is for the bank to put in place policies and procedures to address any specific risks associated with non-face-to-face business relationships or transactions. The intention is that CDD measures should be conducted that are as stringent as those that would be required to be performed if there were face-to-face contact.

Non-account Holders

When a bank in Singapore undertakes any transaction with a value exceeding SGD 20,000 for any customer who does not otherwise have business relations with the bank, it should:

- Establish and verify the identity of the customer as if the customer had applied to the bank to establish business relations; and
- Record adequate details of the transaction so as to permit the reconstruction of the transaction, including the nature and date of the transaction, the type and amount of currency involved, the value date and the details of the payee or beneficiary.

Where a bank suspects that two or more transactions are, or may be, related, linked or the result of a deliberate restructuring of an otherwise single transaction into smaller transactions in order to evade the measures outlined above, the bank shall treat the transactions as a single transaction and aggregate their values.

Politically Exposed Persons

Where any PEP is identified, the requirement is for the bank to perform enhanced CDD measures, including, but not limited to, the following:

- Implement appropriate internal policies, procedures and controls to determine if a customer or beneficial owner is a politically exposed person;

- Obtain approval from the bank's senior management to establish or continue business relations where the customer or a beneficial owner is a politically exposed person or subsequently becomes a politically exposed person;
- Establish, by appropriate and reasonable means, the source of wealth and source of funds of the customer or beneficial owner; and
- Conduct, during the course of business relations, enhanced monitoring of business relations with the customer.

A bank shall perform enhanced CDD measures for such other categories of customers, business relations or transactions as the bank may assess to present a higher risk for money laundering and terrorist financing.

Anonymous Accounts

No bank in Singapore is allowed to open or maintain anonymous accounts or accounts in fictitious names.

27.30.11 *Ongoing Monitoring*

There is a general requirement that the bank must monitor, on an ongoing basis, its business relations with customers. To achieve this, the bank is required, during the course of business relations, to observe the conduct of the customer's account and scrutinise transactions undertaken to ensure that the transactions are consistent with the bank's knowledge of the customer, its business and risk profile and, where appropriate, the source of funds. It should pay special attention to all complex or unusually large transactions or unusual patterns of transactions that have no apparent or visible economic or lawful purpose. If any are identified, the bank should, to the extent possible, inquire into the background and purpose of the transactions and document its findings with a view to making this information available to the relevant competent authorities should the need arise. Of course, this needs to be done without tipping off the customer.

To keep materials up to date, the bank is required periodically to review the adequacy of customer identification information obtained in respect of customers and beneficial owners and ensure that the information is kept up to date, particularly for higher-risk categories of customer. This, of course, enables the bank to obtain improved and updated information based on the regulations without alerting the customer to any specific issue regarding their relationship with the bank.

27.30.12 *Staff Training*

The bank is required to take all appropriate steps to ensure that its staff (whether in Singapore or overseas) are regularly trained on:

- AML/CFT laws and regulations and, in particular, CDD measures, detecting and reporting of suspicious transactions;
- Prevailing techniques, methods and trends in money laundering and terrorist financing; and

- The bank's internal policies, procedures and controls on AML/CFT and the roles and responsibilities of staff in combating money laundering and terrorist financing.

The bank must have in place screening procedures to ensure high standards when hiring employees.

27.30.13 Record-keeping

The requirement is that the bank must prepare, maintain and retain documentation on all its business relations and transactions with its customers such that:

- All requirements imposed by law are met;
- Any transaction undertaken by the bank can be reconstructed so as to provide, if necessary, evidence for prosecution of criminal activity;
- The relevant competent authorities in Singapore and the internal and external auditors of the bank are able to review the bank's transactions and assess the level of compliance with the regulations; and
- The bank can satisfy, within a reasonable time or any more specific time period imposed by law, any enquiry or order from the relevant competent authorities in Singapore for information.

The bank must, when setting its record-retention policies, comply with the following document-retention periods:

- A period of at least five years following the termination of business relations for customer identification information and other documents relating to the establishment of business relations, as well as account files and business correspondence; and
- A period of at least five years following the completion of the transaction for records relating to a transaction, including any information needed to explain and reconstruct the transaction.

The bank may retain documents as originals or copies, in paper or electronic form or on microfilm, provided that they are admissible as evidence in a Singapore court of law.

27.30.14 Investigation and Reporting Requirements

Anyone moving SGD 30,000 or more into or out of Singapore must lodge a cash movement report (CMR). The names and identity of individuals who lodge reports are only disclosed if they have wilfully submitted false information.

The Suspicious Transaction Reporting Office (STRO) receives all suspicious transaction reports (STRs) from the relevant officer. The Singapore STRO is part of the Egmont Group. It is also a member of the Asia Pacific Group on money laundering (APG).

27.30.15 *Internal Requirements*

A bank is required to develop and implement internal policies, procedures and controls to help prevent money laundering and terrorist financing and communicate these to its employees. The policies, procedures and controls should include, amongst other things, CDD measures, record retention, the detection of unusual and/or suspicious transactions and the obligation to make suspicious transaction reports.

27.30.16 *Suspicious Transaction Reporting*

Where a person knows, or has reasonable grounds to suspect, that any property, in whole or in part, directly or indirectly, represents the proceeds of, was used in connection with or is intended to be used in connection with any act which may constitute drug trafficking or criminal conduct, as the case may be, and the information or matter on which the knowledge or suspicion is based came to his attention in the course of his trade, profession, business or employment, he shall disclose the knowledge or suspicion or the information or other matter on which that knowledge or suspicion is based to a Suspicious Transaction Reporting Officer as soon as is reasonably practicable after it comes to his attention.

Where the property referred to above is the subject of a transaction, the person referred to in that subsection shall make the disclosure referred to in that subsection regardless of whether the transaction was completed.

A bank shall implement appropriate internal policies, procedures and controls for meeting its obligations under the law, including the following:

- The establishment of a single reference point within the organisation to whom all staff are instructed to promptly refer all transactions suspected of being connected with money laundering or terrorist financing, for possible referral to the STRO via STRs; and
- The creation and storage of records of all transactions referred to the STRO, together with all internal findings and analysis done in relation to them.

A bank shall submit reports on suspicious transactions (including attempted transactions) to the STRO, and extend a copy to the authority for information.

A bank shall consider if the circumstances are suspicious so as to warrant the filing of an STR and document the basis for its determination where:

- The bank is, for any reason, unable to complete CDD measures; or
- The customer is reluctant, unable or unwilling to provide any information requested by the bank, decides to withdraw a pending application to establish business relations or a pending transaction or to terminate existing business relations.

27.30.17 *Penalties*

Any person who fails to report a suspicious transaction shall be guilty of an offence and shall be liable, on conviction, to a fine not exceeding SGD 20,000, although it is a defence that the person charged had a reasonable excuse for not disclosing the information or other matter in question, or that, if they were an employee, they disclosed it in accordance with their internal procedures.

27.30.18 Case Studies

The first money-laundering case in Singapore concerned a major airline. In this case a supervisory clerk was granted almost total control over a computer program which computed and paid out the crew's salaries and allowances by making direct credits into staff bank accounts. The clerk dishonestly misappropriated numerous amounts from the airline's bank account by causing them to be paid to bank accounts which were in his name or controlled by him. Random checks were supposed to be made. However, there was no way the supervisors could verify all the details keyed in by the clerk, and he had also falsely altered a computer-generated report printed daily which contained all the adjustments made to crew allowances for that day. He defrauded the airline of almost SGD 35 million, and at the conclusion of investigations, SGD 14 million remained unrecovered. He was sentenced to 24 years' imprisonment.

In another case, a customer-service officer in a worldwide bank stole US$ 7.2 million (SGD 12.6 million) from the bank over a period of five years. He pleaded guilty to the single money-laundering charge and the other charges of cheating (altogether there were more than 1,000 charges which took the court interpreter two hours to read) and was sentenced to 12 years' imprisonment. The clerk was a compulsive gambler, and often bet (with the stolen money) on the lottery with $500,000 per week (and struck the first prize twice, totalling $6m). When the police raided his home they found over 1,000 lottery tickets; hence the number of charges exceeding 1,000.

In 2003, the biggest fraud case in Singapore history occurred. The finance manager of a brewery was charged for 44 offences of forgery and cheating and two charges of money-laundering offences involving a total sum of SGD 117 million. He pleaded guilty to all 46 charges and was sentenced (by the same District Court judge as in case study one) to 42 years' imprisonment. The manager flew in private jets to bet in the world's leading casinos, at $400,000 per bet and lost $62.3 million. He used funds he had cheated from four major banks, which then took legal action against the brewery.

27.31 COUNTRY PROFILE: SOUTH AFRICA

27.31.1 Overview

South Africa has demonstrated a strong commitment to implementing AML/CFT systems, which has involved close cooperation and coordination between a variety of government departments and agencies. The authorities have sought to construct a system which uses as its reference the relevant United Nations Conventions and the international standards as set out by the Financial Action Task Force.

27.31.2 Key Legislation

The money-laundering offence is found in the Prevention of Organised Crime Act (POCA). The Financial Intelligence Centre Act, which was amended by the Financial Intelligence Centre Amendment Act 2008, contains the AML compliance legislation. The Money Laundering Control Regulations ("the Regulations") were issued under the Act in December 2002. These were updated in 2010.

27.31.3 Legislative History

South Africa supplemented its AML law with statutory provisions in the Drugs and Drug Trafficking Act 140 of 1992. This Act criminalised the laundering of the proceeds of specific drug-related offences and required the reporting of suspicious transactions involving the proceeds of drug-related offences. The Proceeds of Crime Act 76 of 1996 broadened the scope of the statutory laundering provisions to all types of offences. In 1999, the Proceeds of Crime Act, as well as the laundering provisions of the Drugs and Drug Trafficking Act, were repealed when POCA came into effect.

Money laundering is criminalised in Section 4 of the Prevention of Organised Crime Act 1998. The AML control measures are found in the Financial Intelligence Centre Act 2001 and subsequent regulations.

The requirements are further elaborated in guidance notes issued by the Centre and circulars issued by the South African Reserve Bank (SARB), which is the central bank of South Africa. However, neither of these is legally enforceable, and they are only intended to provide guidance.

It should also be noted that South Africa's AML/CFT framework is currently undergoing a process of transition. The FIC Act (FICA) was substantially amended by the Financial Intelligence Centre Amendment Act 2008 (FIC Amendment Act) which was gazetted on 28th August, 2008.

The FIC launched a new communication platform – a Public Compliance Communication (PCC) series – on 22nd February, 2010. The purpose of the PCC is to facilitate a better understanding of the Financial Intelligence Centre Act 2001 (Act No. 38 of 2001) (FICA) by all businesses, including accountable institutions, and to address some of the complex questions arising from the administration of FICA and its subordinate legislation. The main purpose of the PCC series is to provide guidance under Section 4(c) of FICA on the FIC's interpretation of the relevant legislation. This form of guidance will have the same legal status as the guidance notes that have been, and will continue to be, issued by the FIC.

27.31.4 FATF Assessment

The 2008 FATF mutual evaluation described the development of AML/CFT systems in South Africa as "work in progress". The country was rated "largely compliant" or "compliant" in approximately half of the 49 recommendations, which highlights that there is still work to be done to bring South Africa into line with FATF Recommendations.

27.31.5 The Primary AML Investigation/Regulatory Authorities

Financial Intelligence Centre

The Financial Intelligence Centre (the Centre) was established under FICA No. 38 of 2001, in February 2002. The Centre started receiving reports on suspicious and unusual transactions on 3rd February, 2003.

FICA also sets up a regulatory anti-money-laundering regime which is intended to break the cycle used by organised criminal groups to benefit from illegitimate profits. By doing this, the Act aims to maintain the integrity of the financial system.

South African Reserve Bank

The South African Reserve Bank is the central bank of the Republic of South Africa. The primary purpose of the Bank is to achieve and maintain price stability in the interest of balanced and sustainable economic growth in South Africa. Together with other institutions, it also plays a pivotal role in ensuring financial stability. The Bank assesses, on a continuous basis, the stability and efficiency of key components of the South African financial system.

27.31.6 Outline of Specific Money-laundering Offences

Money Laundering

Any person who knows, or ought reasonably to have known, that property is, or forms part of, the proceeds of unlawful activities and

- Enters into any agreement or engages in any arrangement or transaction with anyone in connection with that property, whether such agreement, arrangement or transaction is legally enforceable or not; or
- Performs any other act in connection with such property, whether it is performed independently or in concert with any other person,

which has, or is likely to have, the effect

- Of concealing or disguising the nature, source, location, disposition or movement of the said property or the ownership thereof or any interest which anyone may have in respect thereof;
- Of enabling or assisting any person who has committed or commits an offence, whether in the Republic or elsewhere

- to avoid prosecution; or
- to remove or diminish any property acquired directly, or indirectly, as a result of the commission of an offence,

shall be guilty of an offence.

Assisting Another to Benefit from Proceeds of Unlawful Activities

Any person who knows, or ought reasonably to have known, that another person has obtained the proceeds of unlawful activities, and who enters into any agreement with anyone or engages in any arrangement or transaction whereby

- The retention or the control by, or on behalf of, the said other person of the proceeds of unlawful activities is facilitated; or
- The said proceeds of unlawful activities are used to make funds available to the said other person or to acquire property on his or her behalf or to benefit him or her in any other way,

shall be guilty of an offence.

Acquisition, Possession or Use of Proceeds of Unlawful Activities

Any person who acquires, uses or has possession of property and who knows, or ought reasonably to have known, that it is or forms part of the proceeds of unlawful activities of another person, shall be guilty of an offence.

27.31.7 Defences

A person may raise as a defence the fact that he or she had reported a knowledge or suspicion, or, if they are an employee of a financial institution, that person may also raise as a defence the fact that he or she had:

- Complied with the applicable obligations in terms of the internal rules relating to the reporting of information of the accountable institution; or
- Reported the matter to the person charged with the responsibility of ensuring compliance by the accountable institution with its legal duties; or
- Reported a suspicion to his or her superior, if any, if:
  - the accountable institution had not appointed such a person or established such rules;
  - the accountable institution had not complied with its legal obligations in respect of that person; or
  - those rules were not applicable to that person.

27.31.8 Penalties

Any person convicted of an offence outlined above shall be liable to a fine not exceeding R 100 million, or to imprisonment for a period not exceeding 30 years.

27.31.9 Scope

The AML Act applies to 19 "accountable institutions", including banks, estate agents and various other financial services.

27.31.10 Risk-based Approach

The Act and the Regulations require accountable institutions to identify all clients with whom they do business unless an exemption applies in a given circumstance. However, institutions are not required to follow a one-size-fits-all approach in the methods they use and the levels of verification they apply to all relevant clients.

In many instances, the Regulations make reference to the fact that accountable institutions must verify certain particulars against information which can be reasonably expected to achieve such verification and is obtained by reasonably practical means, taking into account any guidance notes concerning the verification of identities which may apply.

The use of expressions in the Regulations such as "can reasonably be expected to achieve such verification" and "is obtained by reasonably practical means" implies that a risk-based approach is appropriate, and that the greater the risk, the higher the level of verification and the more secure the methods of verification used should be.

The assessment of risk factors should best be done by means of a systematic approach to determining different risk classes and identifying criteria to characterise clients and products. In order to achieve this, an accountable institution would need to document and make use of a risk framework.

As with all risk management, an institution's risk framework needs to be regularly updated and supported with documentation to enable and ensure compliance within each institution.

27.31.11 Role of the MLRO/Nominated Officer

Accountable institutions must write and implement internal rules relating to money-laundering control and appoint an officer who is responsible for ensuring compliance by the institution. The MLRO is also required to train the institution's employees to enable them to comply with their money-laundering control obligations.

Once the Compliance Officer has been appointed, they will be required to familiarise themselves with the relevant money-laundering laws and the particular guidelines and regulations. They will then need to ascertain the current level of compliance by the business and its employees with the duty to report suspicious and unusual transactions and ensure that appropriate policy documents and rules are implemented. They will be required to monitor and report to management on compliance.

27.31.12 Due Diligence

FICA prevents accountable institutions from establishing business relationships or entering into single transactions with their clients unless they have established and verified the identities of the clients concerned and of the agents and principals of their clients, as well as any authority the agent, client or principal has to act on behalf of another person.

The Act also requires institutions to verify an agent's authority to act on behalf of a principal. The Regulations provide some detail on the identification and verification of most classes of clients an institution is likely to deal with. These are, for instance, natural persons, companies and close corporations, other legal persons, partnerships and trusts.

The Regulations require institutions to obtain specific information concerning the identities of each of these categories of clients, and also indicate the manner in which the basic client identification particulars should be verified. For instance, an individual's name and identity number should be verified by reference to an identity document.

Other forms of verification are only acceptable if a person is, for a reason which is acceptable to the institution, unable to produce an identity document. Additional identification particulars, such as residential addresses, may be verified by reference to any information which can reasonably be expected to serve as verification for the particulars in question.

Personal Client Due Diligence

An accountable institution must obtain from, or in respect of, a natural person who is a citizen of, or resident in, South Africa, that person's:

- Full names
- Date of birth
- Identity number
- Income tax registration number, if such a number has been issued to that person
- Residential address.

They should verify the above by comparing the information with an identification document of that person, or, in the case where that person is, for a reason that is acceptable to the institution, unable to produce an identification document, another document which is acceptable to the institution and bears:

- A photograph of that person;
- That person's full names or initials and surname;
- That person's date of birth;
- That person's identity number;
- Any information which is obtained from any other independent source, if it is believed to be reasonably necessary to verify the identity of the individual.

An accountable institution must verify the income tax registration number by comparing this number with a document issued by the South African Revenue Service bearing such a number and the name of the natural person.

Foreign Customer Due Diligence

An accountable institution must obtain from, or in respect of, a natural person who is a citizen of another country and is not resident in the Republic, that person's:

- Full names
- Date of birth
- Nationality
- Passport number
- South African income tax registration number, if such a number has been issued to that person
- Residential address.

For foreign nationals, the information should be compared with an identification document of that person.

Corporate Customer Due Diligence

An accountable institution must obtain from the natural person acting or purporting to act on behalf of a close corporation or South African company with which it is establishing a business relationship or concluding a single transaction:

- The registered name of the close corporation or company;
- The registration number under which the close corporation or company is incorporated;
- The registered address of the close corporation or company;
- The name under which the close corporation or company conducts business;
- The address from which the close corporation or company operates, or if it operates from multiple addresses
  - the address of the office seeking to establish a business relationship or to enter into a single transaction with the accountable institution; and
  - the address of its head office;
- In the case of a company:
  - the full name, date of birth, identity number and name of the country, as may be applicable, concerning:
    - the manager of the company; and
    - each natural person who purports to be authorised to establish a business relationship or to enter into a transaction with the accountable institution on behalf of the company;

  - the full names, date of birth, identity number, registered name, registration number, registered address, trade name and business address, as may be applicable, concerning the natural or legal person, partnership or trust holding 25% or more of the voting rights at a general meeting of the company concerned;
- The income tax and value added tax registration numbers of the close corporation or company, if such numbers were issued to that close corporation or company;
- The residential address and contact particulars of
  - the manager;
  - each natural or legal person, partnership or trust holding 25% or more of the voting rights at a general meeting of the company concerned; and
  - each natural person who purports to be authorised to establish a business relationship or to enter into a transaction with the accountable institution on behalf of the company.

An accountable institution must verify the particulars obtained in respect of a close corporation or company by comparing the details with:

- In the case of a company, the most recent versions of the Certificate of Incorporation (form CM1) and Notice of Registered Office and Postal Address (form CM22), bearing the stamp of the Registrar of Companies and signed by the company secretary; or
- In the case of a close corporation, the most recent versions of the Founding Statement and Certificate of Incorporation (form CK1), and Amended Founding Statement (form CK2), if applicable, bearing the stamp of the Registrar of Close Corporations and signed by an authorised member or employee of the close corporation.

Enhanced Customer Due Diligence

If an accountable institution obtained the required information about a natural or legal person, partnership or trust without contact in person with that natural person, or with a representative of that legal person or trust, the institution must take reasonable steps to establish the existence, or to establish or verify the identity, of that natural or legal person, partnership or trust, taking into account any guidance notes concerning the verification of identities which may apply to that institution.

27.31.13 Ongoing Monitoring

An accountable institution must obtain information in respect of:

- A client who has established a business relationship or concludes a single transaction; or
- A prospective client seeking to establish a business relationship or conclude a single transaction.

An accountable institution must obtain information whenever it is reasonably necessary, taking into account any guidance notes concerning the verification of identities or the reporting of suspicious and unusual transactions, with a view to obtaining additional information:

- Concerning a business relationship or single transaction which poses a particularly high risk of facilitating money laundering activities; or
- To enable the accountable institution to identify the proceeds of unlawful activity or money-laundering activities.

The information obtained must be adequate to reasonably enable the institution to determine whether transactions involving a client are consistent with the institution's knowledge of that client and that client's business activities and must include particulars concerning:

- The source of that client's income; and
- The source of the funds which that client expects to use in concluding the single transaction or transactions in the course of the business relationship.

27.31.14 Staff Training

The MLRO is responsible for training the employees to enable them to comply with their money-laundering control obligations.

27.31.15 Reporting Thresholds

The accountable or reporting institution will be required to file a cash threshold report with the Centre when the accountable or reporting institution has knowledge of the transaction that exceeds the prescribed threshold. This knowledge will normally be acquired when the accountable or reporting institution:

- Physically receives or pays out cash exceeding R 24,999.99; or
- Peruses its bank statement or a bank deposit slip from the client reflecting a transaction that exceeds R 24,999.99.

A general 15,000 US$/EUR suspicious reporting threshold has been implemented.

According to the 2010 amendments, the report must contain full particulars of the natural or legal person making the report or other entity on whose behalf the report is made, including:

- The name of the person or entity;
- The identifying particulars of the person or entity such as identity number, registration number or practice number, for example;
- The address of the person or entity;
- The type of business or economic sector of the accountable institution and reporting institution;

- In the case of a natural person, the person's contact particulars; and
- In the case of a legal person or entity, the surname, initials and contact particulars of a contact person.

In respect of the transaction or aggregated transactions for which a report is made, the report must contain as much of the following information as is readily available:

- The date and time of the transaction, or in the case of a series of transactions, the time of the transactions in the 24-hour period;
- A description of the transaction or series of transactions;
- The amount of funds per transaction or series of transactions;
- The currency in which the funds were disposed of; and
- The purpose of the transaction or series of transactions.

In respect of each natural or legal person conducting the transaction(s) for which a report is made, the report must contain as much of the following information as is readily available:

In the case of a natural person, full particulars of:

- The person's name and surname, or initials and surname if the name is not available;
- The date of birth of the person or identification number; and
- The type of identifying document from which the above were obtained.

In the case of a legal person, full particulars of:

- The person or entity's name;
- The person or entity's identifying number;
- The names of the natural person with authority to conduct the transaction on behalf of the person or entity.

In the case of any other entity, any information which is readily available should be included.

A report must:

- Contain a full description of the amount of cash in excess of the prescribed limit which is paid out by the accountable institution and reporting institution; and
- Contain a full description of the amount of cash in excess of the prescribed limit which is received by the accountable institution and reporting institution.

A report must be sent to the Centre as soon as possible but not later than two days after a natural person or any of his or her employees, or any of the employees of officers of a legal person or other entity, has become aware of a cash transaction or series of cash transactions that has exceeded the prescribed limit.

27.31.16 Internal Requirements

The internal rules of an accountable institution concerning the establishment and verification of identities must:

- Provide for the necessary processes and working methods which will cause the required particulars concerning the identities of the parties to a business relationship or single transaction to be obtained on each occasion when a business relationship is established or a single transaction is concluded with the institution;
- Provide for steps to be taken by the relevant staff members aimed at the verification of the required particulars concerning the identities of the parties to a business relationship or single transaction;
- Provide for the responsibility of the management of the institution in respect of compliance with the Act, the regulations and the internal rules;
- Allocate responsibilities and accountability to ensure that staff duties concerning the establishment and verification of identities are complied with;
- Provide for disciplinary steps against the relevant staff members for non-compliance with the Act, the regulations and the internal rules; and
- Take into account any guidance notes concerning the verification of identities which may apply to that institution.

27.31.17 Penalties

A person convicted of:

- Failure to identify persons;
- Destroying or tampering with records;
- Failure to give assistance;
- Failure to advise the Centre of a client;
- Failure to report cash transactions;
- Failure to report suspicious or unusual transactions;
- Unauthorised disclosure;
- Failure to report conveyance of cash into or out of the Republic;
- Failure to report electronic transfers;
- Failure to comply with requests;
- Failure to comply with directions by the Centre;
- Failure to comply with a monitoring order;
- Misuse of information;
- Obstructing of an official in the performance of functions;
- Conducting transactions to avoid reporting duties;

- Unauthorised access to a computer system or an application or data;
- Unauthorised modification of the contents of a computer system

is liable to imprisonment for a period not exceeding 15 years or to a fine not exceeding R 10,000,000.

A person convicted of

- Failure to send a report to the Centre;
- Failure to formulate and implement internal rules;
- Failure to provide training or appoint a Compliance Officer

is liable to imprisonment for a period not exceeding five years or to a fine not exceeding R 1,000,000.

27.31.18 Case Studies

The FIC of South Africa has been used to perpetuate fraud, through scam letters claiming to be officially from the FIC. The FIC disassociated itself from this fraud, and urges anyone who receives a letter to report it. It is unknown whether any, or how much, money was lost as a result. The text of one of the scam letters, sent on headed paper designed to look as if it has come from the FIC, appears below.

Dear Email Owner/Fund Beneficiary,

COMPENSATION FUNDS PAYMENT ORDER VIA ATM CARD

This is to inform you that, We have been working towards the eradication of fraudsters and scam Artists in Africa with the help of the Organization of African Unity (OAU), United Nations (UN), European Union (EU) and the International Monetary Fund (IMF) and FBI. We have been able to track down so many of this scam artist in various parts of African countries which includes (Nigeria, Republic of Benin, Ghana, Cameroon and Senegal) and they are all in Government custody now, they will appear at **International Criminal Court (ICC) Hague (Netherlands)** soon for Criminal/Fraud Justice.

During the course of our investigation, we have been able to recover so much money from these scam artists. The United Nations Anti-Crime Commission and the International Monetary Fund (IMF) have ordered the money recovered from the Scammers to be shared among 100 Lucky people around the World for compensation. This Email/Letter is been directed to you because your email address was found in one of the scammer Artists file and computer hard-disk while the investigation, maybe you have been scammed. You are therefore being compensated in your local currency with the sum of **R1,200,000.00 (ZAR) (One Million Two Hundred Thousand South African Rand Only)**. We have also arrested some of those who claim that they are barristers, bank officials, Lottery Agents who has been sending you SMS on your phone that you have won a lottery which does not exist. Since your email address appeared among the lucky beneficiaries who will receive

(*continued overview*)

(continued)

a compensation funds, we have arranged your payment to be paid to you through **ATM VISA CARD**. An ATM Visa Card will be issued in your name and your **R1,200,000.00 Rands** will be loaded into it, and deliver it to your postal address with the Pin Number, as to enable you withdrawal your funds from any Bank ATM Machine in South Africa.

To issue the **ATM Visa Card,** you are therefore advised to contact the **HSBC BANK PLC LONDON UNITED KINGDOM,** this is so because the United Nations Anti-Crime Commission and the International Monetary Fund (IMF) and the Government has chosen them to payout all the compensation funds to the 100 Lucky beneficiaries, because **HSBC Bank ATM Visa Card** is a global payments technology that enables consumers, businesses, financial institutions and governments to use digital currency instead of cash and checks,. Kindly contact the **HSBC Bank ATM Visa Card Issuance Department** now with the below contact details:

Contact: DR. W. R. MARSHALL

Director ATM VISA CARD Issuance Department

(HSBC Bank Plc London UK)

Contact Email: wrmarshall_atmcard1@london.com

Direct Office lines: +44-703-174-0594

Fax Number: +44-844-774-7814

Contact him now for the delivery of your ATM Card. As soon as you establish a contact with him, an ATM card will be issued to you immediately which you can use to withdraw your funds in any Bank ATM Machine, but the maximum is R50,000 (Rands) per day because the Card has been upgrade. So if you like to receive your funds through this means you're advised to contact (DR. W. R. MARSHALL) with the following information as stated below:

1. **Your Full Name**
2. **Address Where You Want the Courier Company to Send Your ATM Card To or (P.O Box)**
3. **Your Age**
4. **Occupation**
5. **Cell/Mobile Number**

Please Be Warned, as The United Nations Anti-Crime Commission and the International Monetary Fund (IMF) does not instruct any other Bank or agent in this payment except (**DR. W. R. MARSHALL**), whom we can only give attention to, and from now, we advice you to stop all the communications you are having with any other Agent or bank officials in Europe, Asia and Africa regarding to your payment. Thanks for your understanding as you follow instructions.

The advice not to tell anybody, the email address "@london.com", the withdrawal per day limit and the poor English are just some of the many problems with the letter. A number of examples of this type of scam were sent claiming to be from the FIC.

In another case, a physiotherapist was convicted of laundering R 2,100,000 which was stolen from the government, with help from two accomplices. The funds came from a fund covering workers injured or disabled at work or for diseases sustained from the hazardous work environment, and the accomplices worked for the Department of Labour. The fraudster was working with his accomplices to siphon millions of rands of public funds by claiming money for treatment to patients that was never done and using intricate means to siphon payments into his own accounts. The laundered money was deposited into the criminal's personal account and those of his businesses. The accomplices were still on trial and the physiotherapist had not been sentenced at the time of writing.

27.32 COUNTRY PROFILE: SOUTH KOREA ("REPUBLIC OF KOREA")

27.32.1 Overview

Korea has demonstrated political commitment to improving its AML efforts since the mid-1990s. The most common money-laundering techniques involve cash transactions and accounts in other persons' names. Accordingly, the authorities have made a concerted effort to combat these over the less prevalent drug-trafficking offences. Despite some deficiencies in the AML regime, the compliance culture within Korean financial institutions is very strong.

27.32.2 Key Legislation

The Proceeds of Crime Act, last amended in 2010, contains the money-laundering offence. The Financial Transaction Reports Act, also amended in 2010 and supplemented by the KoFIU AML/CFT Regulation, provides the AML compliance requirements.

27.32.3 Legislative History

Korea first introduced AML/CFT measures in 2001 and has sought to implement a collaborative approach to the fight against money laundering and associated crimes.

27.32.4 FATF Assessment

The 2009 FATF mutual evaluation found that the money-laundering offences are largely in line with international requirements but the penalties available and applied are not sufficiently effective, proportionate or dissuasive. Furthermore, there is a lack of focus on money-laundering investigations.

Customer identification and verification represents a strength in the Korean preventive measures, but issues such as beneficial ownership, politically exposed persons and correspondent banking have yet to be addressed. The Korean AML/CFT system is heavily reliant on KoFIU's work on financial intelligence, AML/CFT supervision, training of obliged entities, policy, reform, national coordination and international cooperation.

27.32.5 The Primary AML Investigation/Regulatory Authorities

Financial Services Commission

The Financial Services Commission was established in 2008. The aim of the Financial Services Commission is to protect the integrity of Korea's financial market, by focussing on devising and updating financial policies in tune with the needs of and developments in the market.

Korea Financial Intelligence Unit

Founded in November 2001, KoFIU is the primary executive agency responsible for implementing an effective anti-money-laundering and combating the financing of terrorism (AML/CFT) regime in Korea.

KoFIU's responsibilities include:

- Collecting, analysing and disseminating suspicious transaction reports and currency transaction reports filed by financial institutions;
- Formulating and implementing effective AML/CFT policies and regulations; and
- Supervising and overseeing financial institutions' compliance with AML/CFT obligations.

KoFIU works closely with various law-enforcement agencies in Korea, including the Ministry of Justice, National Police Agency, National Tax Service, the Korea Customs Service and the Financial Supervisory Service.

KoFIU was originally within the Ministry of Finance and Economy (MOFE), but as a result of the government reorganisation in February 2008 has been transferred to the Financial Services Commission (FSC). KoFIU comprises AML/CFT experts from the FSC, Ministry of Justice (MOJ), National Police Agency (NPA), National Tax Service (NTS), Korea Customs Service (KCS) and the Financial Supervisory Service (FSS). The independence and autonomy of KoFIU is guaranteed by law. KoFIU works as an institutional link between financial institutions and law-enforcement agencies by receiving suspicious transaction report (STRs) from financial institutions, analysing the STRs and disseminating them to law-enforcement agencies for further action. KoFIU is also the primary organisation responsible for AML/CFT policy formulation and implementation, AML/CFT supervision and the education of financial institutions.

27.32.6 Outline of Specific Money-laundering Offences

Any person who commits, or attempts to commit, any of the following acts shall be guilty of money laundering:

- Disguising the acquisition or disposition of criminal proceeds and related properties;
- Disguising the origin of criminal proceeds;
- Concealing criminal proceeds and related properties for the purpose of facilitating a predicate offence or disguising illegally obtained properties as properties obtained from legitimate sources.

Furthermore, any person who knowingly accepts criminal proceeds and related properties commits an offence, unless it is in relation to fulfillment of legal obligations or obligations under a contract which he/she entered into without the knowledge that it would be fulfilled with criminal proceeds or related properties.

27.32.7 Penalties

Money laundering, or its attempt, is punishable by imprisonment not exceeding five years or a fine not exceeding 30 million won. Preparation or conspiracy to commit money laundering is punishable by imprisonment not exceeding two years or a fine not exceeding 10 million won.

Accepting criminal proceeds is punishable by imprisonment not exceeding three years or a fine not exceeding 20 million won.

If any of the offences above are committed by a legal person, both the individual responsible and the legal entity can be subjected to the relevant penalties.

27.32.8 Scope

The AML legislation applies to various financial institutions listed in Article 2(1) of the Financial Transaction Reports Act, and includes banks, investment trading companies and insurance companies.

27.32.9 Risk-based Approach

Financial institutions shall identify and assess the risks of money laundering and terrorist financing and use such information for customer due diligence. When identifying and assessing the risks of money laundering and terrorist financing, financial institutions should consider country risk, customer type and product and service risk. Financial institutions shall assess the risks of money laundering and terrorist financing of a customer based on set criteria for risk assessment factors and risk levels, so as to apply such risks to the assessment appropriately.

27.32.10 Role of the MLRO/Nominated Officer

Reporting entities are obliged to:

- Designate persons responsible for the external reporting and establishment of an internal reporting system;
- Establish and implement internal guidelines for the prevention of money laundering and the financing of offences of public intimidation; and
- Organise training and education of employees regarding the prevention of money laundering and the financing of offences of public intimidation.

Financial institutions shall assign to senior management the following roles and responsibilities:

- To design, operate and evaluate AML/CFT internal controls;
- To approve regulations on AML/CFT internal controls;
- To report to the board of directors on compliance with internal control policy and actions taken to improve weaknesses;
- To address the weaknesses identified in the process of implementing the internal control system;
- To appoint a qualified reporting officer with the expertise and independence necessary to run efficient AML/CFT activities and notify the appointment to the Commissioner of the Korea Financial Intelligence Unit (KoFIU).

The MLRO's role shall be:

- To file suspicious transaction reports (STRs) and currency transaction reports (CTRs) to the KoFIU Commissioner;
- To have general responsibility for CDD-related matters;
- To establish and operate relevant regulations and detailed business guidelines;
- To specify roles, responsibilities and reporting lines of employees with regard to AML/CFT in job descriptions or relevant regulations;
- To establish measures to deal with new patterns and techniques of money laundering and terrorist financing in response to the development of electronic financial technology and new financial products;
- To establish and operate the Know Your Employee (KYE) system;
- To provide education and training for employees;
- To keep records of documents related to AML/CFT;
- To monitor, improve and complement the operational status of AML/CFT affairs;
- To report to senior management concerning the periodic review on operational effects of the AML/CFT system/control activities and results and actions taken to improve the system;
- To assign an appropriate number of employees to the AML/CFT task in consideration of internal business conditions such as financial transaction volume;
- To handle necessary arrangements related to AML/CFT affairs;
- To take appropriate measures to facilitate inter-agency coordination and information exchange with KoFIU.

27.32.11 Due Diligence

To prevent money laundering and terrorism financing, reporting entities shall establish and apply internal guidelines:

- Verifying the customer identification information when the customer opens a new account or when the customer makes an occasional financial transaction in the amount, or in excess, of KRW 20 million for domestic currency transactions and US$10,000 for foreign currency transactions;
- Verifying whether the customer is the beneficial owner and obtaining information regarding the purpose of the transaction when it is suspected that the customer is engaged in money laundering or the financing of offences of public intimidation.

The internal guidelines shall include details regarding contents, procedures and methods of adequate measures designed to prevent money laundering and financing of offences of public intimidation according to the types of customer or types of financial transaction. Financial institutions shall include each of the following provisions in their business guidelines established and operated to implement CDD effectively:

- Targets of CDD and the timing of transactions that require CDD and the time for performing CDD;
- CDD in accordance with ML/TF risks and customer identification and verification procedures and measures;
- Procedures and measures to be taken when the customer identification and verification process is refused;
- CDD implementation for a major high-risk category;
- The ongoing monitoring of CDD;
- The establishment and operation of a transaction-monitoring system in accordance with the risks of ML/TF.

Financial institutions shall:

- Conduct CDD when customers are suspected of being involved in money laundering or terrorist financing;
- Conduct CDD where there is a suspicion that the existing customer identification information might be contrary to fact, or invalid;
- Identify the name and resident registration number of the sender and the account number of the receiver when a wire transfer transaction worth more than KRW 1 million is made;
- Identify the customer and verify the accuracy of the identity with the means of reliable documentation, data or information during a business relationship with the customer;
- Obtain information on the purpose and intended nature of the transaction during a business relationship with a customer.

Personal Client Due Diligence

Financial institutions shall obtain each of the following pieces of information for natural persons (including foreign persons):

- Name;
- Date of birth and gender (confined to foreign non-residents);
- Identification number;
- Nationality (limited to foreigners);
- Address and contact information (in the case of foreign non-residents, actual residence and contact information).

This should be verified by means of a certificate bearing the real name, such as a resident registration card or driving licence, and which also contains a photo and other essential identification information required.

Corporate Customer Due Diligence

Financial institutions shall obtain each of the following pieces of information for legal persons:

- Name of legal person (organisation);
- Identification number;
- Address and location of headquarters and offices (in the case of a foreign legal person, actual address of office and contact information);
- Information on the representative (following the identification criteria for individual customers);
- Business type (in the case of a for-profit entity) and contact number;
- Purpose of establishment (in the case of a non-profit entity).

Financial institutions shall confirm the authority of any person ("agent") who conducts financial transactions on behalf of natural and legal persons or other organisations and the identity of such agents, and shall check if legal persons or arrangements actually exist through documents that can prove the establishment of legal entities, such as a copy of the corporate register.

The above information should be verified.

Beneficial Ownership

Financial institutions shall identify the natural persons who ultimately own or control the customer (beneficial owners) by means of reliable documentation in consideration of the risks of ML/TF, and should take necessary measures to identify whether a legal person customer is the beneficial owner when there is suspicion or concern that the customer might not be the beneficial owner and might be involved in ML/TF.

Simplified Customer Due Diligence

Simplified customer due diligence may be applied to certain types of customer or products or services categorised as low risk with respect to ML/TF. This permits an exemption for some of the identification procedures and measures. However, sufficient information is still required to identify the customer, including name and address. If you choose to take advantage of this exemption, you will need to be clear why you are doing so and the risk that this poses, and judge whether it is appropriate in the circumstances. If you are unfortunate and treat a customer as low risk when this is patently not the case, you must be prepared to face regulatory sanctions.

Enhanced Customer Due Diligence

Enhanced due diligence requires additional CDD information for certain types of high-risk customer or products/services. For natural persons, financial institutions shall identify each of the following additional pieces of information for high-risk customers:

- Occupation or business type (independent business owner);
- Purpose of transaction;
- Source of funds used for transaction;
- Others deemed necessary by financial institutions for the purpose of addressing concerns about money laundering.

For legal persons, financial institutions shall identify each of the following additional pieces of information:

- Basic information on the company, such as the type of company (large enterprise, small or medium-sized enterprise, and so on);
- Listing information (stock exchange, KOSDAQ, and so on);
- Date of establishment;
- Website details (or email address);
- Purpose of transaction;
- Source of funds used for transaction;
- Others deemed necessary by financial institutions for the purpose of addressing concerns about money laundering.

Non-face-to-face Customer Due Diligence

Financial institutions shall establish policies and procedures to address the risk of ML/TF related to non-face-to-face transactions. Financial institutions shall follow the policies and procedures when they establish new business relationships with non-face-to-face customers and conduct ongoing CDD for them.

Politically Exposed Persons

Financial institutions shall establish an appropriate procedure to identify whether a customer or beneficial owner is a foreign PEP. Financial institutions shall obtain approval from senior management:

- To accept an account-opening transaction by a foreign PEP;
- To maintain a business relationship when customers (or beneficial owners) who have already opened accounts are identified as being foreign PEPs.

Financial institutions shall conduct enhanced due diligence pursuant to Article 20(3) when customers (or beneficial owners) are identified as foreign PEPs, and take due measures to identify the source of funds or assets. Such measures include identifying the following additional information:

- Identification information of family members with authority over account transactions or persons with a close relationship with foreign PEPs;
- Information on legal persons or organisations associated with foreign PEPs.

Financial institutions shall conduct ongoing monitoring to determine if the existing customer is a foreign PEP, and shall enhance transaction monitoring during any business relationship with a customer who is a politically exposed person.

Correspondent Banking

Financial institutions shall establish and operate procedures and control measures necessary for preventing and mitigating the risks of money laundering and terrorist financing related to correspondent banking services when entering into correspondent banking relationships.

The correspondent bank shall take appropriate measures to ensure the respondent bank prevents its correspondent banking account from being used by shell banks.

When entering into a correspondent banking relationship, the correspondent bank shall take the following measures with regard to the respondent bank:

- Identify the respondent bank's operational and business characteristics by collecting information on the respondent bank's governance structure, major business activity and main location (or country);
- Based on available and publicly disclosed information, evaluate the reputation of the respondent bank and level of supervision or regulation on the respondent bank, including whether it is subject to investigation into cases of money laundering and/or terrorist financing;
- Evaluate the adequacy and effectiveness of AML/CFT measures for a jurisdiction or country where the respondent bank is mainly located and of AML/CFT control measures taken by the respondent bank;
- Document AML/CFT obligations for the correspondent and respondent banks.

When the service of providing a customer with direct access to a correspondent banking account (hereinafter referred to as payable-through account) is included in the correspondent banking contract, the following measures shall also be taken:

- The respondent bank shall perform CDD on the customer who intends to conduct transactions using a payable-through account;
- Upon a request from the correspondent bank, the respondent bank shall provide customer identification information.

When entering into a new correspondent banking relationship, the correspondent bank shall obtain prior approval from senior management.

Shell Banking

The correspondent bank is prohibited from entering into or continuing correspondent banking relationships with shell banks.

27.32.12 Ongoing Monitoring

Financial institutions shall conduct ongoing due diligence on business relationships. Ongoing due diligence shall be conducted through each of the following measures:

- Scrutiny of transactions undertaken throughout the course of the relationship to ensure that the transactions being conducted are consistent with the institution's knowledge of the customer, their business, risk profile and the source of funds;
- Undertaking reviews of existing records, particularly for higher-risk categories of customers or business relationships, to ensure that documents, data and information collected under the CDD process are kept up to date and relevant.

Financial institutions shall determine how often CDD needs to be conducted in accordance with the ML/TF risk level in consideration of customer transaction activities. Financial institutions shall establish and operate an ongoing monitoring system on customers' transactions and activities, which includes each of the following:

- Measures to perform ongoing monitoring of customers' transactions;
- Analysis and reporting of monitoring results;
- Procedures to keep records of analysis undertaken.

Financial institutions shall pay special attention to all complex, unusually large transactions or unusual patterns of transactions that have no apparent economic or lawful purpose, including each of the following:

- Transactions of unusually large amount or volume;
- Excessively high account turnover compared to the size of the balance;
- Transactions which fall outside the regular pattern of the account's activity.

Financial institutions shall examine, as much as possible, the background and purpose of the transactions, and shall maintain records on their findings.

For the purpose of preventing ML/TF, financial institutions shall establish procedures to identify unusual transactions or patterns through a transaction-monitoring system which includes the following measures:

- Reviewing and comparing information on the profile of a customer or similar customer group with information on the customer's transaction history;
- Reviewing and comparing information on a customer's transaction with standardised samples from money-laundering cases in the past;
- Estimating money-laundering risks on customer transaction information and evaluating transaction records;
- Analysing financial transaction patterns by linking information on the customer, the account and the transaction.

27.32.13 *Staff Training*

Financial institutions shall develop and operate education and training programmes for their employees. The reporting officer shall provide employees with education and training more than once a year.

Financial institutions shall provide their employees with adequate and different education and training in accordance with their differing positions and responsibilities, and shall make sure education and training cover each of the following:

- Information on the AML/CFT system and relevant laws and regulations;
- Internal policies and procedures related to AML/CFT;
- Types and recent trends of suspicious transactions;
- Business procedures by customer type regarding the implementation of CDD;
- Business procedures for STRs and CTRs;
- Roles of employees regarding AML/CFT.

Once the education and training sessions have been conducted, financial institutions shall retain records on the dates, participants and content of the sessions.

A Know Your Employee (KYE) system refers to a system that enables financial institutions to check identification information of their existing and new executives and employees when hiring them, so as to prevent them from getting involved in money-laundering and terrorist-financing activity. Financial institutions shall establish procedures and measures for the implementation of a KYE system.

27.32.14 *Record-keeping*

Financial institutions shall maintain information regarding customer identification and verification records, financial transaction records, internal and external reports including STRs and other relevant documents for a minimum of five years.

Information or documents to be retained with regard to customer identification and verification include the following:

- Identification documents for customers (including agents and beneficial owners), copies of certificates of real name verification and any other information or documents acquired for customer identification and verification;
- Additional information or documents obtained to identify the purpose and characteristics of a financial transaction besides customer identification information;
- Information or documents related to internal permission for performing CDD;
- Information or documents related to account opening, such as the date of account opening and the person who opened the account.

Information or documents to be retained with regard to financial transaction records include the following:

- Electronic data that contain account numbers used for transactions, product types, transaction dates, currency types and transaction amounts;
- Transaction requests;
- Certificates of contract;
- Detailed statements;
- Copies of slips and business correspondence;
- Information or documents that prove internal approval for financial transactions.

Internal and external reports and related documents include the following:

- Suspicious transaction reports (copies of the reports or internal approval forms) and records of reported transactions;
- Records of reasonable grounds for suspicion (including documents collected from business offices, documents that reviewed reasonable grounds for suspicion or some notes in report form);
- Records or documents on the examined possibility of unreported suspicious transactions being involved in money laundering and/or terrorist financing;
- Senior management reports by the AML/CFT reporting officer.

Financial institutions shall retain the following information or documents in addition to those specified above for five years:

- Documents related to planning, managing and evaluating of internal control activities for AML/CFT;
- Records of independent supervision and actions taken thereafter;
- Records of AML/CFT training including content, date and participants of the training.

27.32.15 Suspicious Transaction Reporting

Financial institutions and casinos are required to report to the KoFIU when:

- They have a "reasonable ground" to suspect that the funds they received in relation to a financial transaction are illegal assets or that the customer is engaged in money laundering or financing of offences of public intimidation and the amount of such transaction is KRW 10 million (US$5,000 for foreign currency transactions) or above; or
- They have reported to a law-enforcement agency any funds that they have come to know are proceeds of crime or any transaction that they have come to know is involved in money laundering.

Financial institutions and casinos can file a suspicious transaction report even when the amount of the transaction is below the reporting threshold. For failures to report suspicious transactions, the Korea Financial Intelligence Unit can apply sanctions such as disciplinary action for employees of financial institutions and administrative fines for financial institutions.

27.32.16 Currency Transaction Reporting

In 2006, Korea implemented a currency transaction report (CTR) system. This obliges financial institutions to report to the KoFIU all cash transactions when the amount of cash paid or received in transactions conducted in one trading day in the same name is above the threshold, which is currently KRW 20 million.

27.32.17 Penalties

Any person who falls under any of the following shall be subject to imprisonment for a period not exceeding five years or a fine in an amount not exceeding 30 million won:

- Any person who, by abusing his/her official authority, accesses and/or makes photocopies of records kept by a reporting entity or requests the head of a reporting entity to provide such records;
- Any person who discloses specific financial transaction information obtained in the course of performing his/her duty or information or records received in accordance with the AML law, or uses such information for any purpose other than those for which such information was provided; or
- Any person who requests the provision of specific financial transaction information or information provided to the KoFIU or requests to use them for any purpose other than those for which such information was provided.

Any person who falls under any of the following shall be subject to imprisonment for a period not exceeding one year or a fine in an amount not exceeding 5 million won:

- Any person who makes a false report in relation to the reporting obligations; or
- Any person who tips off the subject of an STR.

27.32.18 Case Studies

A Korean national with multiple passports and identities admitted laundering money in Los Angeles. For three years, he illegally "structured" more than $5 million in bank deposits by parcelling them into 254 transactions averaging about $6,000 each, thereby avoiding the cross-border currency reporting threshold. He also used false South Korean and American identity documents, and opened two accounts at the same bank using different Korean passports and visas. He had not been sentenced at the time of writing.

This case highlights the need for financial institutions to consider the wider circumstances of financial transactions, and not just take them at face value. Numerous transactions by the same person must be aggregated in accordance with local laws, so that the reporting thresholds apply and appropriate action can be taken. The risk of false identities being used is also illustrated in this case, so it is not enough to see official documents – they should be verified as well.

27.33 COUNTRY PROFILE: SWITZERLAND

27.33.1 Overview

Switzerland's body of money-laundering laws has grown incrementally. It recognised itself as one of several susceptible countries, understanding the lucrative nature of the private banking business conducted in the country. It has become world renowned for enforcing the strictest anti-money-laundering codes, to the extent that many other countries have since modelled their own AML framework on Switzerland's robust programme. However, it has to be recognised that it is the desirability of having funds within Switzerland, given the stringent secrecy laws for which the country is known, that means it remains a potential target for inappropriate funds. In June 2012, an official Federal Council press release outlining an expansion of the powers of the Money Laundering Reporting Office Switzerland stated that, "The Federal Council is intent on stepping up the fight against money laundering". True to its word, in November 2013, the money laundering regulations were strengthened, and in particular the legislation allows for secrecy to be lifted and information passed on in various circumstances following suspicious transaction reports. This signals a key commitment to maintaining Switzerland's economic position, at the expense of its well-known secrecy regime.

27.33.2 Key Legislation

The money-laundering offence is contained in the Swiss Penal Code (Art. 305bis and 305ter StGB). Furthermore, the Federal Act on Combating Money Laundering and Terrorist Financing in the Financial Sector (AMLA) and a corresponding Ordinance of the Swiss Financial Market Supervisory Authority (FINMA) on the Prevention of Money Laundering and Terrorist Financing (FINMA Anti-Money Laundering Ordinance, AMLO-FINMA) contain the AML compliance regime – most recently updated in November 2013.

27.33.3 Legislative History

Switzerland's mechanisms for combating money laundering, which were established with the Agreement on Due Diligence (CDB) in 1977 and have been expanding ever since, today include provisions in the Swiss Penal Code (Art. 305bis and 305ter StGB), the Federal Act on Combating Money Laundering and Terrorist Financing in the Financial Sector (AMLA) and a corresponding Ordinance of the Swiss Financial Market Supervisory Authority (FINMA) on the Prevention of Money Laundering and Terrorist Financing (FINMA Anti-Money Laundering Ordinance, AMLO-FINMA).

27.33.4 FATF Assessment

The 2005 mutual evaluation report found Switzerland to be "largely compliant" or "compliant" with 32 of the 49 FATF regulations. The Follow-Up Report agreed by the FATF in October 2009 found that Switzerland had taken sufficient action in remedying the deficiencies that were identified in the Mutual Evaluation Report. Switzerland provided a further progress report in 2011, but this had not been analysed by the FATF at the time of writing.

The Federal Department of Finance looked into the individual criticisms of Switzerland's anti-money-laundering mechanisms within the FATF report. Subsequent AML legislation and ordinances were brought into force, bringing Switzerland largely into line with FATF requirements.

27.33.5 The Primary AML Investigation/Regulatory Authorities

The Federal Office of Police

The Federal Office of Police is required by the AML Act to manage the Money Laundering Reporting Office Switzerland.

Money Laundering Reporting Office Switzerland

The Money Laundering Reporting Office Switzerland (MROS), which is a part of the Federal Office of Police, is Switzerland's central anti-money-laundering office and functions as a relay and filtration point between financial intermediaries and the law-enforcement agencies. According to the Money Laundering Act, the MROS is responsible for receiving and analysing suspicious activity reports in connection with money laundering and, if necessary, forwarding them to the law-enforcement agencies.

The MROS is also a specialised body that publishes annual statistics on developments in the fight against money laundering, organised crime and terrorist financing in Switzerland, and identifies typologies that are useful for training the financial intermediaries. The MROS is organised as a section within the Federal Office of Police; it is not a police authority in itself, but rather an administrative unit with special tasks.

The Reporting Office is a member of the Egmont Group, which is an international association of financial intelligence units (FIUs) whose objective is to foster a safe, prompt and legally admissible exchange of information in order to combat money laundering and terrorist financing. According to a June 2012 press release, the MROS will be given extended powers to share information with foreign FIUs.

Federal Financial Market Supervisory Authority

The Swiss Financial Market Supervisory Authority (FINMA), in its role as State supervisory authority, acts as an oversight authority of banks, insurance companies, exchanges, securities dealers, collective investment schemes, distributors and insurance intermediaries. It is responsible for combating money laundering and, where necessary, conducts restructuring and bankruptcy proceedings and issues operating licences for companies in the supervised sectors. Through its supervisory activities, it ensures that supervised institutions comply with the requisite laws, ordinances, directives and regulations, and continue at all times to fulfil the licensing requirements.

FINMA imposes sanctions and provides administrative assistance to the extent permissible by law. It also supervises the disclosure of shareholdings, conducts the necessary proceedings, issues orders and, where wrongdoing is suspected, files criminal complaints with the Swiss Federal Department of Finance. FINMA also acts as a regulatory body: it participates in legislative procedures, issues its own ordinances and circulars where authorised to do so, and is responsible for the recognition of self-regulatory standards.

The Swiss Federal Banking Commission and the Anti-Money Laundering Control Authority (see below) will be integrated into FINMA.

Anti-Money-Laundering Control Authority

The AML Control Authority (AMLCA) is the supervisory authority for the non-banking sector, which is supervised only to the extent of its compliance with the AMLA. This non-banking sector includes asset managers, fiduciaries, money changers and payment services providers, as well as lawyers and notaries who offer ancillary financial services and others.

Swiss Federal Banking Commission

Amongst other financial supervisory obligations, the Swiss Federal Banking Commission monitors whether the financial intermediaries under its supervision comply with the provisions of the Anti-Money Laundering Act.

27.33.6 Outline of Specific Money-laundering Offences

Money laundering is committed by any person who carries out an act that is aimed at frustrating the identification of the origin, the tracing or the forfeiture of assets which he knows, or must believe, originate from a felony.

27.33.7 Penalties

Any person found guilty of money laundering shall be liable to a custodial sentence not exceeding three years or to a monetary penalty. In serious cases, the penalty shall be a custodial sentence not exceeding five years and/or a monetary penalty. A custodial sentence shall be combined with a monetary penalty not exceeding 500 daily penalty units [1,500,000 francs].

A serious case is, for example, where the offender:

- Acts as a member of a criminal organisation;
- Acts as a member of a group that has been formed for the purpose of the continued conduct of money-laundering activities; or
- Achieves a large turnover or substantial profit through commercial money laundering.

27.33.8 Scope

The AMLA applies to financial intermediaries, which are listed in Article 2 of the Federal Act on Combating Money Laundering and Terrorist Financing in the Financial Sector. Financial intermediaries include banks, fund managers and persons who, on a professional basis, accept or hold on deposit assets belonging to others or who assist in the investment or transfer of such assets.

27.33.9 Due Diligence

When establishing a business relationship, the financial intermediary must verify the identity of the customer on the basis of a document of evidentiary value. Where the customer is a legal entity, the financial intermediary must acknowledge the provisions regulating the power to bind the legal entity, and verify the identity of the persons who enter into the business relationship on behalf of the legal entity.

In the case of cash transactions with a customer whose identity has not yet been established, the duty to verify identity applies only if one transaction, or two or more transactions that appear to be connected, involve a considerable financial value (see below). Furthermore, if there is any suspicion of money laundering or terrorist financing, the identity of the customer must be verified even if the relevant amounts have not been reached.

The financial intermediary is required to identify the nature and purpose of the business relationship wanted by the customer. The extent of the information that must be obtained is determined by the risk represented by the customer.

The financial intermediary must clarify the economic background and the purpose of a transaction or of a business relationship if:

- It appears unusual, unless its legality is clear;
- There are indications that assets are the proceeds of a felony or are subject to the power of disposal of a criminal organisation or serve the financing of terrorism.

The DSFI shall identify the contracting party if one or more transactions, which appear to be interlinked, reach or exceed the following amount:

- CHF 5,000 for foreign exchange transactions;
- CHF 25,000 for all other cash transactions.

Personal Client Due Diligence

For natural persons as well as owners of sole proprietorships, the following should be established:

- Family name
- Given name
- Date of birth
- Place of domicile and nationality.

Upon initiation of the business relationship with a natural person or owner of a sole proprietorship, the DSFI shall identify the contracting party by inspecting an identification document of the contracting party. If the business relationship is started without a personal interview, the DSFI shall additionally review the place of domicile through postal delivery or equivalent method. All identification documents are permitted which include a photograph and which are issued by a Swiss or foreign authority.

Corporate Customer Due Diligence

For legal entities and companies, the reporting entity should ascertain:

- The company name
- The address of the registered office.

The DSFI shall also identify the person who begins the business relationship in the name of the contracting party. The DSFI shall acknowledge and document the provisions of the contracting party's power of attorney regarding this person.

Upon initiation of the business relationship with a legal entity or partnership, the DSFI shall identify the contracting party by means of one of the following documents:

- A certificate of registration issued by an officer of the commercial registry;
- A written statement from a database managed by the commercial registry authority;
- A written statement from a trustworthy, privately administered directory and database.

Legal entities and partnerships not listed in the commercial registry are to be identified by means of one of the following documents:

- The articles of association;
- The constituent instrument or the founding treaties;
- A confirmation from the auditors;
- An authoritative approval for the exercising of activities or an equivalent document;
- A written statement from a trustworthy, privately administered directory and database.

A commercial registry statement, confirmation from the auditor and a directory or database statement may be no more than twelve months old at the time of identification and must correspond with the current circumstances.

The DSFI can waive the certification of authenticity if it takes other measures that allow it to examine the identity and the address of the contracting party. The measures taken are to be documented.

If the contracting party does not have any identification documents within the sense of this Ordinance, then the identity may be determined by means of valid replacement documents as an exception. These exceptional situations should be explained in a note in the file.

Beneficial Ownership

The financial intermediary must obtain a written declaration from the customer indicating who the beneficial owner is if:

- The customer is not the beneficial owner or if there is any doubt about the matter;
- The customer is a domiciliary company;

- A cash transaction of considerable financial value in terms of Article 3 paragraph 2 is being carried out;
- A person who is not in a discernibly close relationship with the contracting party is granted a power of attorney that enables the person to withdraw assets;
- The assets, which the contracting party deposits, clearly exceed the contracting party's financial situation;
- Contact with the contracting party reveals other unusual findings;
- The business relationship commences without a personal visit.

The written declaration from the contracting party concerning the beneficial owner must include the following information for natural persons as well as owners of sole proprietorships:

- Family name
- Given name
- Date of birth
- Place of domicile
- Nationality.

For legal entities and companies, it should include the following information:

- Company name
- Address of the registered office.

The declaration can be signed by the contracting party or one of its agents. For legal entities, the declaration is to be signed by a person who is authorised to do so pursuant to the company documents. If questions remain concerning the correctness of the declaration of the contracting party and such questions cannot be resolved through further clarification, then the DSFI shall decline the business relationship or terminate it.

Simplified Customer Due Diligence

The financial intermediary may dispense with complying with the duties of due diligence if the business relationship only involves assets of low value and there is no suspicion of money laundering or terrorist financing.

Enhanced Customer Due Diligence

Financial intermediaries shall formulate criteria to identify business relationships and transactions which involve increased risks. Depending on the type of operations conducted by the financial intermediary, the following criteria may be of particular relevance:

- The registered office, permanent place of residence or nationality of the contracting party and/or beneficial owner;

- The nature and location of the business activities conducted by the contracting party and/or beneficial owner;
- The absence of personal contact with the contracting party as well as the beneficial owner;
- The type of services or products requested;
- The total of the assets deposited;
- The total of incoming and outgoing assets;
- Country of origin or destination of frequent payments;
- Complexity of the structures, in particular through the use of domiciliary companies;
- The total of incoming and outgoing assets;
- Any significant deviations from the type, volume or frequency of transactions that would be normal in the context of the business relationship;
- Any significant deviations from the type, volume or frequency of transactions that would be normal in comparable business relationships.

Business relationships with politically exposed persons are, in all cases, deemed to be business relationships with increased risk.

Transactions in which assets exceeding more than CHF 100,000 are physically deposited in a single or series of deposits at the onset of the business relationship are deemed, in all cases, to be transactions with increased risks.

Financial intermediaries shall carry out additional investigations with appropriate effort for business relationships or transactions with increased risks.

Any transaction is deemed to be of increased risk if the value exceeds CHF 5,000.

The acceptance of business relationships involving increased risk requires the approval of a senior person or body or the management. The senior executive body, or at least one of its members, shall decide on:

- The acceptance of business relationships with politically exposed persons and, on an annual basis, the continuation of such relationships;
- The planning of regular reviews of all business relationships involving higher risk and monitoring and evaluating such relationships.

Correspondent Banking
Financial institutions are obliged to treat correspondent banking relationships as high-risk relationships.

27.33.10 Ongoing Monitoring

The financial intermediary shall provide effective monitoring of business relationships and transactions, and ensure that increased risks are identified. For the monitoring of transactions, the financial intermediary shall use an IT-supported system to identify transactions with increased risks. Any transactions identified by the IT system shall be evaluated within an appropriate timeframe and, when necessary, additional clarification shall be sought.

A financial intermediary which has a low number of contracting parties and beneficial owners or transactions can waive an IT-supported transaction-monitoring system if it instructs its audit company to perform a stringent annual transaction-monitoring audit.

27.33.11 *Staff Training*

Financial intermediaries must take the measures that are required to prevent money laundering and terrorist financing in their field of business. They must, in particular, ensure that their staff receive adequate training to be able to perform their duties. Furthermore, the financial intermediary shall ensure the prudent selection of personnel as well as the regular training of all concerned staff with respect to the relevant aspects of the prevention of money laundering and the financing of terrorism.

27.33.12 *Record-keeping*

The financial intermediary must keep records of transactions carried out and other documents required in such a manner that other specially qualified persons will be able to make a reliable assessment of the transactions and business relationships and of compliance with the AML provisions. The financial intermediary must retain the records in such a manner as to be able to respond within a reasonable time to any requests made by the prosecution authorities for information or for the seizure of assets. After the termination of the business relationship or after completion of the transaction, the financial intermediary must retain the records for a minimum of ten years.

27.33.13 *Suspicious Transaction Reporting*

A financial intermediary must immediately file a report with the Money Laundering Reporting Office Switzerland ("the Reporting Office") if it knows, or has reasonable grounds to suspect, that assets involved in the business relationship:

- Are the proceeds of a felony;
- Are subject to the power of disposal of a criminal organisation; or
- Serve the financing of terrorism.

It should terminate any business relationship if any suspicion arises.

The name of the financial intermediary must appear in any report. The identity of the financial intermediary's staff who are in charge of the case may be made anonymous in the report, provided it is guaranteed that the Reporting Office and the competent prosecution authority are able to contact them without delay.

A financial intermediary must immediately freeze the assets entrusted to it that are connected with the report, and must continue to freeze the assets until it receives an order from the competent prosecution authority, but at the most for five working days from the time at which the report is filed with the Reporting Office.

The November 2013 amendments provide that if the Reporting Office requires additional information in order to analyse a report that it has received, the financial intermediary making the report must, on request, provide such information that is in its possession. If, based on this analysis, it becomes apparent that in addition to the financial intermediary making the report, other financial intermediaries are, or were, involved in a transaction or business relationship, the financial intermediaries involved must, on request, provide the Reporting Office with all related information that is in their possession.

The Reporting Office may pass on the personal data and other information that are in its possession or that it may obtain under this Act to a foreign reporting office provided that office:

- Guarantees that it will use the information solely for the purpose of analysis in the context of combating money laundering and its predicate offences, organised crime or terrorist financing;
- Guarantees that it will reciprocate on receipt of a similar request from Switzerland;
- Guarantees that official and professional secrecy will be preserved;
- Guarantees that it will not pass on the information received to third parties without the express consent of the Reporting Office; and
- Will comply with the conditions and restrictions imposed by the Reporting Office.

It may pass on the following information in particular:

- The name of the financial intermediary, provided the anonymity of the person making the report or who has complied with a duty to provide information under this Act is preserved;
- Account holders, account numbers and account balances;
- Beneficial owners;
- Details of transactions.

The Reporting Office may consent to information being passed on by the foreign reporting office to a third authority provided the latter guarantees that:

- It will use the information solely for the purpose of analysis in the context of combating money laundering and its predicate offences, organised crime or terrorist financing, or to institute criminal proceedings relating to money laundering and its predicate offences, organised crime or terrorist financing or to obtain evidence in response to a request for mutual assistance relating to such criminal proceedings;
- It will not use the information to prosecute offences that are not offences predicate to money laundering under Swiss law;
- It will not use the information in evidence; and
- It will preserve official or professional secrecy.

A request for information from a foreign reporting office shall not be granted if:

- The request has no connection with Switzerland;
- The request requires the application of procedural compulsion or other measures or acts for which Swiss law stipulates mutual assistance procedures or another procedure regulated in special legislation or an international treaty;
- National interests or public security and order will be prejudiced.

27.33.14 Penalties

Any person who, in a professional capacity, accepts, holds on deposit or assists in investing or transferring outside assets and fails to ascertain the identity of the beneficial owner of the assets in accordance with the above requirements shall be liable to a custodial sentence not exceeding one year or to a monetary penalty.

Anyone who fails to comply with the duty to report a suspicious transaction shall be liable to a fine of up to 500,000 francs. If the offender acts through negligence, he or she shall be liable to a fine of up to 150,000 francs. However, if they repeat the offence within five years of the conviction taking full legal effect, the fine shall be a minimum of 10,000 francs.

27.33.15 Case Studies

The Swiss FIU produces a number of AML case studies as part of its annual reports, some of which are reproduced below. The reports are available at: http://www.fedpol.admin.ch/content/fedpol/en/home/themen/kriminalitaet/geldwaescherei/jahresberichte.html.

In early 2011, a foreign client received a wire transfer of US$300,000 on behalf of a law firm in his home country. The compliance division asked the client advisor to obtain additional clarification regarding the economic background of this deposit. The client explained that the payment related to a contractual obligation with a well-known law firm that also represented his country in various matters. The client advisor requested more details regarding the contractual obligation between the client and the law firm. The client advisor forwarded these details to the compliance division along with the client's request that the details of the transaction remain confidential. After examining the documentation, the Compliance Officer concluded that the documentation was not detailed enough.

Additional searches of public sources revealed that the law firm in question had been involved in criminal activities such as misappropriation of public funds in the client's home country. In addition, the owner of the law firm was a close legal representative of the President of the client's home country. The client advisor contacted the client again but was still unable to determine the economic background of the incoming payment. Certain statements made by the client also indicated that some of the deposited funds might actually have been derived from influence peddling. An SAR was therefore submitted to the MROS. However, examination of police and judicial records and subsequent investigation of the persons named in the SAR did not reveal any relevant details. For motives of convenience, a decision was reached not to contact the FIU in the client's home country but rather to forward the SAR to the Office of the Attorney General of Switzerland.

In another case, a financial intermediary sent the MROS an SAR regarding a business relationship with one of its clients, a South American woman employed as a salesperson. The account balance showed tens of thousands of Swiss francs that had come from another account held by the client at a well-known lending institution. Apparently, the money in question was a loan that the client had asked to have credited to the reported account. A few days later, a travel cash card provider informed the financial intermediary that the client had recently loaded tens of thousands of Swiss francs onto her travel cash cards from the reported account.

Based on this information, the financial intermediary took a closer look at the business relationship. It turned out that the client had actually stolen the identity of the real salesperson for the purpose of opening the account. The real salesperson informed the financial intermediary that she had never opened a bank account there nor had ever received correspondence or documents relating to this account. Comparison of the ID photos of the real salesperson and the client revealed that they were, in fact, two different people. Unknown third parties had opened the account via post and had sent a copy of the fake Swiss ID card with the account application. The copy of the Swiss ID card appeared to have been certified by a notary. However, closer investigation revealed that the notary who had certified the Swiss ID card did not exist. The account documents sent via post had been removed from the salesperson's mailbox by the perpetrators of the fraud. All indications pointed to the fact that unknown third parties had used a stolen identity to open an account at a lending institution by fraudulent means, obtained a loan and then transferred the loan amount to the reported account – which had also been opened using the stolen identity. The money was immediately transferred to travel cash cards and eventually withdrawn as cash from various automatic teller machines (ATMs).

Subsequent investigation by the MROS proved unsuccessful, since the names of the persons who had stolen and misused the salesperson's name were not known. The salesperson herself has no police record. Since the reported account had been used to channel incriminated assets, the MROS forwarded the SAR to cantonal prosecution services.

In a third case, a financial intermediary detected an international wire transfer made by one of its clients to a person in an African country. The wire transfer was considered very high given the client's profile. Initial verifications uncovered other transfers that added up to a very large sum. The financial intermediary requested clarification from the client, who was unable to provide a convincing explanation. An SAR was sent to the MROS. In its analysis, the MROS began checking the various transactions carried out on the client's account. There were frequent payments of small amounts from different payers. The sum of these amounts would then be sent to the said African country. The MROS noted that the explanations provided by the client were not plausible. He had explained that the small payments had been minor loans from friends as well as income from odd jobs such as tutoring. The client was nevertheless unable to provide any proof to back his claims. He justified the transfer of these amounts to the African country by saying that it was to pay back a loan for his education. However, there were no indications that the wire transfers related to reimbursement of a loan. Finally, the client was unable to explain why the payments were for such a high amount.

The MROS was also struck by the fact that the financial intermediary had only discovered the case by accident. Since the sum of the amounts paid into this account was rather high, the financial intermediary should have realised earlier that the transactions were unusual. Analysis of the transactions revealed that they had all taken place within a period of several months and the total amount was very high. The client's profile could not possibly justify such income.

Unable to exclude a possible criminal origin of the funds, the MROS forwarded the SAR to the prosecution authorities.

27.34 COUNTRY PROFILE: UAE

27.34.1 Overview

The stability and location of the UAE, roughly half way between Asia and Europe, together with expansionist economic policies, has made it an attractive area in which to do business. The UAE has a relatively low crime rate, with the majority of financial crime and money laundering within the region being committed by criminals overseas.

27.34.2 Key Legislation

The primary AML legislation is Federal Law No. 4 of 2002 Regarding Criminalisation of Money Laundering (the AML Law), which was introduced in January 2002. There are also AML provisions in the UAE Penal Code. The *DFSA Rulebook* provides guidance on the law within the DIFC.

27.34.3 Legislative History

Some of the AML provisions in the UAE Criminal Code were introduced as early as 1987. This legislation has been supplemented by various directives from the UAE Central Bank.

27.34.4 FATF Assessment

The 2008 FATF mutual evaluation found that although a basic legal framework for combating money laundering and terrorist financing is in place in the UAE, it needs further strengthening in a number of areas, including with regard to AML legislation, the role of the FIU and STR reporting. Furthermore, the report noted that "the absence of meaningful statistics was a significant hindrance to the progress of the assessment. With only minor exceptions, the level of effectiveness of AML/CFT measures across all sectors was difficult or impossible to gauge. The development of a national strategy for AML/CFT must urgently address this issue if recent progress is to be built upon."

27.34.5 The Primary AML Investigation/Regulatory Authorities

Anti-Money Laundering and Suspicious Cases Unit

The Anti-Money Laundering and Suspicious Cases Unit (AMLSCU) is a part of the UAE Central Bank. It was created to assist the central bank's AML efforts, and acts as the FIU for the UAE.

Article 7 of Federal Law No. 4 directed the central bank to set up a financial information unit (FIU) to deal with money laundering and suspicious cases, and to provide a centre for reporting. The FIU was also directed to make the information available to law-enforcement agencies to facilitate their investigations. It was also empowered by Article 7 to facilitate the exchange of information with its counterparts in other countries, either pursuant to a convention or simply on the basis of reciprocity.

Dubai Financial Services Authority

The Dubai Financial Services Authority (DFSA) is the independent regulator of all financial and ancillary services conducted through the DIFC, a purpose-built free zone in Dubai.

The DFSA's regulatory mandate covers asset management, banking and credit services, securities, collective investment funds, custody and trust services, commodities futures trading, Islamic finance, insurance, an international equities exchange and an international commodities derivatives exchange.

The DFSA has signed 57 bilateral Memoranda of Understanding with regulators in jurisdictions across the world.

UAE Central Bank

The central bank's statutory objectives are to direct monetary, credit and banking policy and supervise their implementation in accordance with the State's general policy and in such ways as to help support the national economy and stability of the currency.

The UAE Central Bank is the predominant supervisory authority of the country's financial institutions in respect of compliance with anti-money-laundering obligations, although other public institutions also play roles in the process.

27.34.6 Outline of Specific Money-laundering Offences

Money laundering is defined as any act involving transfer, conversion or deposit of property, or concealment or disguise of the true nature of that property, which was derived from any of the following offences:

- Illicit dealing in narcotics and psychotropic substances;
- Kidnapping, piracy and terrorism;
- Violations of the law of the environment;
- Illicit dealing in firearms and ammunition;
- Bribery, embezzlement and damage to public property;
- Fraud, breach of trust and related offences;
- Any other related offences referred to in international conventions to which the UAE is a party.

Theft is likely to fall under "related offences".

Furthermore, where any person intentionally commits or assists in the commission of any of the following acts in respect of property derived from any of the offences stated above, such person shall be considered a perpetrator of the money-laundering offence:

- The conversion or transfer or deposit of proceeds, with intent to conceal or disguise the illicit origin of such proceeds;

- The concealment or disguise of the true nature, source, location, disposition, movement, rights with respect to or ownership of proceeds;
- The acquisition, possession or use of such proceeds.

"Property" is defined widely and means assets of every kind, whether tangible or intangible, moveable or immoveable, and legal documents or instruments evidencing title to those assets or any related rights.

27.34.7 *Penalties*

Money laundering shall be punished by imprisonment for a term not exceeding seven years, or by a fine of between AED 30,000 and AED 300,000. In addition to this, the proceeds of the crime, or an equivalent amount if they are no longer in existence, shall be confiscated.

Financial institutions which intentionally commit money laundering shall be punished by a fine of between AED 300,000 and AED 1,000,000, in addition to the confiscation of the proceeds of crime (or an equivalent amount) involved.

27.34.8 *Risk-based Approach*

The anti-money-laundering policies, procedures, systems and controls of an authorised firm must adequately address the money-laundering risks, taking into account any vulnerabilities of its products, services and customers. In assessing the risks in relation to money laundering, an authorised firm must have regard to the relevant provisions of AML law. An authorised firm must assess its risks in relation to money laundering and perform enhanced due diligence investigations for higher-risk products, services and customers. An authorised firm must be aware of any money-laundering risks that may arise from new or developing technologies that might favour anonymity and take measures to prevent their use for the purpose of money laundering.

27.34.9 *Role of the MLRO/Nominated Officer*

Institutions are required to appoint an individual to the licensed function of MLRO, who must be ordinarily resident in the UAE. An authorised firm must also appoint an individual to act as a deputy MLRO, who must fulfil the role of MLRO in his absence. An authorised firm should have a policy statement detailing the duties and obligations of its MLRO, and must ensure that the MLRO is of sufficient seniority within the firm to enable him to:

- Act on his own authority;
- Have direct access to the governing body and senior management;
- Have sufficient resources including, if necessary, an appropriate number of appropriately trained employees to assist in the performance of his duties in an effective, objective and independent manner;
- Have unrestricted access to information the firm has about the financial and business circumstances of a customer or any person on whose behalf the customer is, or has been, acting; and

- Have unrestricted access to relevant information about the features of the transaction which the authorised firm has entered into, or may have contemplated entering into, with or for the customer or that person.

An authorised firm must ensure that its MLRO is responsible for all of its anti-money-laundering activities carried on in, or from, the DIFC, and must ensure that its MLRO carries out, and is responsible for, the following:

- Establishing and maintaining the authorised firm's anti-money-laundering policies, procedures, systems and controls and compliance with anti-money-laundering legislation applicable in the DIFC;
- The day-to-day operations for compliance with the authorised firm's anti-money-laundering policies, procedures, systems and controls;
- Acting as the point of contact to receive internal suspicious transaction reports from the authorised firm's employees;
- Taking appropriate action following the receipt of an internal suspicious transaction report from the firm's staff;
- Making external suspicious transaction reports to the Anti Money Laundering Suspicious Cases Unit (AMLSCU) of the UAE and sending corresponding copies to the DFSA;
- Acting as the point of contact within the authorised firm for competent UAE authorities and the DFSA regarding money-laundering issues;
- Responding promptly to any request for information made by competent UAE authorities or the DFSA;
- Receiving and acting upon any relevant findings, recommendations, guidance, directives, resolutions, sanctions, notices or other conclusions; and
- Establishing and maintaining an appropriate anti-money-laundering training programme and adequate awareness arrangements.

The MLRO must report at least annually to the governing body or senior management of the authorised firm on the extent of AML compliance, including the matters referred to above, and the governing body should promptly assess and act on this report. The report provided and the records of the assessment and actions must be documented in writing, and a complete copy of each must be provided to the DFSA promptly.

27.34.10 Due Diligence

Subject to an exception, an authorised firm must establish and verify the identity of any customer with, or for, whom it acts or proposes to act. In establishing and verifying a customer's true identity, a firm must obtain sufficient and satisfactory evidence having considered:

- Its risk assessment in respect of the customer; and
- The relevant AML law.

An authorised firm must update, as appropriate, any customer identification policies, procedures, systems and controls, and should adopt a risk-based approach for the customer identification and verification process. Depending on the outcome of the authorised firm's money-laundering risk assessment of its customer, it should decide to what level of detail the customer identification and verification process will need to be performed.

An authorised firm is required to be satisfied that a prospective customer is who he claims to be and obtain evidence to prove this.

Firms should obtain the following:

- **Personal details:** An authorised firm should obtain and verify details which include the true full name or names used and the current permanent address;
- **The nature and level of business to be conducted:** An authorised firm should ensure that sufficient information is obtained regarding the nature of the business that the customer expects to undertake, and any expected or predictable pattern of transactions. This information should include the purpose and reason for opening the account or establishing the business relationship, the anticipated level and nature of the activity that is to be undertaken and the various relationships of signatories to the account and the underlying beneficial owners;
- **The origin of funds:** An authorised firm should identify how all payments were made, from where and by whom. All payments should be recorded to provide an audit trail; and
- **The source of wealth:** An authorised firm should establish a source of wealth or income, including how the funds were acquired, to assess whether the actual transaction pattern is consistent with the expected transaction pattern and whether this constitutes any grounds for suspicion of money laundering.

Any unusual facts of which an authorised firm becomes aware during the identification process may be an indication of money laundering and should prompt the firm to request supplementary information and evidence. CDD must be fulfilled before the authorised firm effects any transaction on behalf of the customer, except for low-risk customers (see below).

Personal Client Due Diligence

The authorised firm should verify that it is dealing with a true and existing person. It also should obtain evidence of verification that is sufficient to establish that the person is indeed who he claims to be. The following list, which is not meant to be exhaustive, should be considered as guidance regarding the type of information and evidence which should be obtained to establish and verify the identity of a customer:

- True full name or names used;
- Complete current permanent address, including all relevant details with regard to country of residence;
- Telephone, fax number and email address;

- Date and place of birth;
- Nationality;
- Fiscal residence;
- Occupation or profession, name of employer and location of activity;
- Information regarding the nature of the business to be conducted;
- Information regarding the origin of the funds; and
- Information regarding the source of wealth or income.

The address of a prospective customer should enable an authorised firm to physically locate the customer. If PO Box numbers are customary to a country, additional methods of physically locating the customer should be applied.

Documentary evidence of identity:

- Current, signed passport;
- Current, signed ID card; or
- Other identification documentation that is customary in the country of residence, such as a driving licence, including a clear photograph of the prospective customer.

Documentary evidence of address:

- Record of home visit;
- Confirmation from an electoral register search that a person of such a name lives at that address;
- Tenancy agreement;
- Utility bill; or
- Local authority tax bill.

Corporate Customer Due Diligence

For companies, the following should be obtained in either documentary or electronic form:

- Registered corporate name and any trading names used;
- Complete current registered address and any separate principal trading addresses, including all relevant details with regard to country of residence;
- Telephone, fax number and email address;
- Date and place of incorporation;
- Corporate registration number;
- Fiscal residence;
- Business activity;

- Regulatory body, if applicable;
- Name and address of group, if applicable;
- Legal form;
- Name of external auditor;
- Information regarding the nature and level of the business to be conducted;
- Information regarding the origin of the funds; and
- Information regarding the source of wealth/income.

Documentary evidence of identity:

- Copy of the extract of the register of the regulator or exchange, or State law or edict creating the entity, in the case of regulated, listed or State-owned companies;
- Certified copy of the articles of association or statutes;
- Certified copy of either the Certificate of Incorporation or the trade register entry and the trading licence including the renewal date;
- Latest annual report, audited and published if applicable;
- Certified copies of the list of authorised signatories specifying who is authorised to act on behalf of the customer account and of the board resolution authorising the signatories to operate the account;
- Certified copies of the identification documentation of the authorised signatories;
- Names, country of residence, nationality of directors or partners and of the members of the governing body; and
- List of the main shareholders holding more than 5% of the issued capital.

If the applying customer is not obliged to publish an audited annual report, adequate information about the financial accounts should be obtained. An authorised firm should verify that the applying customer is active and has not been, or is not in the process of being, dissolved, wound up or terminated.

For unincorporated businesses or partnerships, the following should be obtained:

- True full name or names;
- Complete current registered and trading address, including relevant details with regard to country of establishment;
- Telephone, fax number and email address;
- Fiscal residence;
- Business activity;
- Information on the nature of the business to be conducted;
- Trading licence, with renewal date;

- List of authorised signatories of the business or partnership;
- Regulatory body, if applicable;
- Information regarding the origin of funds; and
- Information regarding the source of wealth/income.

Documentary evidence of identity:

- Latest annual report and accounts, audited where applicable; and
- Certified copy of the partnership deed, to ensure that it has a legitimate purpose and to ascertain the nature of the business or partnership.

Beneficial Ownership

Whenever an authorised firm comes into contact with a customer with, or for, whom it acts or proposes to act, it must establish whether the customer is acting on his own behalf or on the behalf of another person. An authorised firm must establish and verify the identity of both the customer and any other person on whose behalf the customer is acting, including that of the beneficial owner of the relevant funds, which may be the subject of a transaction to be considered, and must obtain sufficient and satisfactory evidence of their identities.

An authorised firm should obtain a statement from a prospective customer to the effect that he is, or is not, acting on his own behalf. In cases where the customer is acting on behalf of third parties, it is recommended that the authorised firm obtain a written statement, confirming the statement made by the customer, from the parties including the beneficial owner.

Politically Exposed Persons

An authorised firm must have systems and controls to determine whether a customer is a politically exposed person, and where a customer relationship is maintained with a PEP, detailed monitoring and due diligence procedures should include:

- Analysis of any complex structures, for example involving trusts or multiple jurisdictions;
- Appropriate measures to establish the source of wealth;
- Development of a profile of expected activity for the business relationship in order to provide a basis for transaction and account monitoring;
- Senior management approval for the account opening; and
- Regular oversight of the relationship with a politically exposed person by senior management.

Correspondent Banking

An authorised firm that establishes, operates or maintains a correspondent account for a correspondent banking client must ensure that it has arrangements to:

- Conduct due diligence in respect of the opening of a correspondent account for a correspondent banking client, including measures to identify its:
  - ownership and management structure;
  - major business activities and customer base;
  - location; and
  - intended purpose of the correspondent account;
- Identify third parties that will use the correspondent account; and
- Monitor transactions processed through a correspondent account that has been opened by a correspondent banking client, in order to detect and report any suspicion of money laundering.

Shell Banking

An authorised firm must not:

- Establish a correspondent banking relationship with a shell bank;
- Establish or keep anonymous accounts or accounts in false names; or
- Maintain a nominee account which is held in the name of one person, but controlled by or held for the benefit of another person whose identity has not been disclosed to the authorised firm.

Low-risk Entities

An authorised firm does not have to fulfil the CDD obligations before effecting a transaction for a customer where it has, on reasonable grounds, established that:

- Following a preliminary risk assessment, the proposed transaction presents a low risk in relation to money laundering and terrorist financing;
- It would be prejudicial to the customer to interrupt or delay the normal course of business in respect of effecting the transaction; and
- The transaction is in respect of investment business or insurance business.

A firm can conduct reduced due diligence for certain specified low-risk customers, unless it has reasonable grounds to know or suspect that a customer, or a person on whose behalf he is acting, is engaged in money laundering.

Where the authorised firm is unable to establish and verify the identity of any customer referred to above, including, where applicable, any beneficiaries, beneficial owners or trustees, within the 30 days following receipt of the customer's instruction, it must:

- Consider the circumstances and determine whether to make an internal suspicious transaction report to the MLRO;
- Where it has determined that it is unnecessary to make such a report, return to the customer any monies associated with the transaction excluding any reasonable costs incurred by the authorised firm;

- Where the authorised firm has determined to make such a report, not return any monies or provide any investments to the customer, unless instructed to do so by the MLRO and otherwise act in accordance with instructions issued by the MLRO; and
- Not establish any further business relationship with that customer until the verification process has been completed for that customer in accordance with the AML rules.

27.34.11 Ongoing Monitoring

An authorised firm must:

- Ensure that the information and documentation concerning a customer's identity remains accurate and up to date; and
- Conduct ongoing due diligence on its business relationship with, and ongoing scrutiny of, transactions undertaken by a customer throughout the course of the relationship.

If, at any time, an authorised firm becomes aware that it lacks sufficient information or documentation concerning a customer's identification, or develops a concern about the accuracy of its current information or documentation, it must promptly obtain appropriate material to verify the customer's identity.

An authorised firm should undertake a periodic review to ensure that customer identity documentation is accurate and up to date. An authorised firm should undertake a review particularly when:

- The authorised firm changes its Know Your Customer documentation requirements;
- A significant transaction with the customer is expected to take place;
- There is a material change in the business relationship with the customer; or
- There is a material change in the nature or ownership of the customer.

If a customer account is dormant or an authorised firm has had no contact with the customer within the previous twelve months, an authorised firm should take reasonable steps to verify whether available information, documentation and evidence concerning the customer is still valid and up to date.

In addition to this, an authorised firm must review the effectiveness of its anti-money-laundering policies, procedures, systems and controls at least annually. The review process should include an assessment of the authorised firm's anti-money-laundering policies, procedures, systems and controls. This review process may be undertaken:

- Internally by the internal audit or compliance function; or
- By a competent firm of independent auditors or compliance professionals.

The review process should cover at least the following:

- A sample testing of Know Your Customer arrangements;
- An analysis of all suspicious transaction reports to highlight any area where procedures or training may need to be enhanced; and
- A review of the nature and frequency of the dialogue between the governing body or senior management and the MLRO to ensure that their responsibility for implementing and maintaining adequate controls is satisfactory.

27.34.12 Staff Training

An authorised firm must have arrangements to provide periodic information and training to all employees to ensure that they are aware of:

- The identity and responsibilities of the authorised firm's MLRO and his deputy;
- Applicable legislation relating to money laundering;
- The potential effect on the authorised firm, its employees and its customers of breaches of applicable legislation relating to money laundering;
- The authorised firm's anti-money-laundering policies, procedures, systems and controls and any changes to these;
- Money-laundering risks, trends and techniques;
- The types of activity that may constitute suspicious activity in the context of the business in which an employee is engaged that may warrant an internal suspicious transaction report;
- The authorised firm's arrangements regarding the making of an internal suspicious transaction report;
- The use of relevant findings, recommendations, guidance, directives, resolutions, sanctions, notices or other conclusions; and
- Requirements relating to customer identification and ongoing due diligence and scrutiny of transactions.

The information described above must be brought to the attention of new employees and must remain available to all employees.

An authorised firm must have arrangements to ensure that:

- Its anti-money-laundering training is up to date with money-laundering trends and techniques;
- Its anti-money-laundering training is appropriately tailored to the authorised firm's different activities, services, customers and indicates any different levels of money-laundering risk and vulnerabilities; and
- All employees receive anti-money-laundering training.

An authorised firm must conduct anti-money-laundering training sessions with sufficient frequency to ensure that within 12 months it is provided to all employees.

27.34.13 Record-keeping

All relevant CDD and ongoing monitoring documentation and correspondence must be kept for at least six years from the date on which the business relationship with a customer has ended. If the date on which the business relationship with a customer has ended remains unclear, it may be taken to have ended on the date of the completion of the last transaction.

The records maintained by an authorised firm should be kept in such a manner that:

- The DFSA or another competent third party is able to assess the authorised firm's compliance with legislation applicable in the DIFC;
- Any transaction which was processed by or through the authorised firm on behalf of a customer or other third party can be reconstructed;
- Any customer or third party can be identified;
- All internal and external suspicious transaction reports can be identified; and
- The authorised firm can satisfy, within an appropriate time, any regulatory enquiry or court order to disclose information.

All relevant details of any transaction carried out by the authorised firm with, or for, a customer must be kept for at least six years from the date on which the transaction was completed.

All relevant details of the authorised firm's anti-money-laundering training must be recorded, including:

- Dates when the training was given;
- The nature of the training; and
- The names of the employees who received the training.

These records must be kept for at least six years from the date on which the training was given. Furthermore, all relevant details of any internal and external suspicious transactions must be kept for at least six years from the date on which the report was made.

27.34.14 Suspicious Transaction Reporting

An authorised firm must have appropriate arrangements to ensure that whenever any employee, acting in the ordinary course of his employment, either knows or suspects, or has reasonable grounds for knowing or suspecting, that a person is engaged in money laundering, that the employee makes an internal suspicious transaction report to the authorised firm's MLRO. An authorised firm must have policies and procedures to ensure that disciplinary action can be taken against any employee who fails to make such a report.

The requirement for employees to make internal STRs should include situations when no business relationship was developed because the circumstances were suspicious.

If an authorised firm's MLRO receives an internal suspicious transaction report he must, without delay:

- Investigate the circumstances in relation to which the report was made;
- Determine whether a corresponding external suspicious transaction report must be made to the AMLSCU;
- If required, make such an external report to the AMLSCU; and
- Provide a copy of said external report to the DFSA.

An authorised firm may allow its employees to consult with their line managers before sending a report to the MLRO. The DFSA would expect that such consultation does not prevent making a report whenever an employee has stated that he has knowledge, suspicion or reasonable grounds for knowing or suspecting that a transaction may involve money laundering.

The failure to report suspicions of money laundering may constitute a criminal offence that is punishable under the laws of the UAE.

The MLRO must document:

- The steps taken to investigate the circumstances in relation to which an internal suspicious transaction report has been made; and
- Where no external suspicious transaction report is made to the AMLSCU, the reasons why no such report was made.

Furthermore, an authorised firm must ensure that if the MLRO decides to make an external suspicious transaction report, his decision is made independently and is not subject to the consent or approval of any other person.

Authorised firms must not carry out transactions which they know or suspect, or have reasonable grounds for knowing or suspecting, to be related to money laundering until they have informed the AMLSCU and the DFSA.

In accordance with Article 16 of the UAE Law No. 4, authorised firms or any of their employees must not tip off or inform any person that his transaction is being scrutinised for possible involvement in suspicious money-laundering operations, or that any other competent authority is investigating his possible involvement. If an authorised firm reasonably believes that performing CDD will tip off a customer or potential customer, it may choose not to pursue that process and should file a suspicious transaction report.

27.34.15 Penalties

Chairmen, directors, managers and employees of financial institutions who know of, yet fail to report to the FIU, any act that occurred within their establishments and was related to the money-laundering offence shall be punished by imprisonment or by a fine of between AED 10,000 and AED 100,000, or by both penalties.

Anyone who tips off a suspect shall be punished by imprisonment for a term not exceeding one year, or by a fine of between AED 5,000 and AED 50,000, or by both penalties.

Whoever violates any of the other provisions herein shall be punished by imprisonment or by a fine not exceeding AED 100,000 and not less than AED 10,000.

Despite the above, it will be a defence to show that any breach or report made was done in good faith. This will result in immunity from any penalty which would otherwise be imposed.

27.34.16 Case Studies

A UAE-based bank reported to the UAE Central Bank's Anti-Money Laundering and Suspicious Cases Unit about suspected transactions in a customer's account. The report noted that deposits in the customer's account had raised questions in light of his job and salary, which reached AED 6,600,000 in just over a year. These deposits were made from various locations in the country, but when the bank asked him, the man failed to present the bank with any documentation to verify the origin of such funds. As a result, the Anti-Money Laundering and Suspicious Cases Unit referred the case to the Abu Dhabi Public Prosecution.

The investigation in this case is still ongoing, but it does raise important points to note for financial institutions. Ongoing monitoring of client accounts and transactions is vital to identify and take action against suspicious transactions, and it is important that deposits of this nature do not slip under the radar.

27.35 COUNTRY PROFILE: UKRAINE

27.35.1 *Overview*

Ukraine has experienced a recent surge in its financial economy. This is partly due to its increased activity with the European markets. Commercial banks still have the largest share of the Ukrainian economy. The insurance sector is also becoming a more integral part of the economy, with a number of insurance companies emerging in recent years. There has also been a surge in technological developments as far as the banking system is concerned. The Law on Financial Services sought to bring an element of financial stability.

The current banking system in Ukraine is two-tiered, comprising the central bank of the country and commercial banks. The central bank of Ukraine is the National Bank of Ukraine (NBU); it controls the national currency, supervises the banking system and issues current banking regulations. Commercial banks operate under the authorisation and supervision of the NBU, including the State-owned export–import bank (Ukreximbank) and a specialised commercial savings bank (Oschadnybank).

27.35.2 *Key Legislation*

The Criminal Code provides the money-laundering offences. In addition to this, the primary AML law is the Law of Ukraine on the Prevention and Counteraction of the Legalisation of the Proceeds from Crime (the AML Act), which was amended on 18th May, 2010.

27.35.3 *Legislative History*

Ukraine implemented various United Nations Security Council Resolutions in 1999 and 2001. The legislation has always been enacted through the AML Act, including the most recent 2010 amendments.

27.35.4 *FATF Assessment*

The FATF identified Ukraine as having serious deficiencies in its AML framework in its mutual evaluation report in 2009. However, in its follow-up report issued in 2011, the FATF issued the following statement:

> *"The FATF welcomes Ukraine's significant progress in improving its AML/CFT regime and notes that Ukraine has largely met its commitments in its Action Plan regarding the strategic deficiencies that the FATF had identified in February 2010. Ukraine is therefore no longer subject to FATF's monitoring process under its on-going global AML/CFT compliance process. Ukraine will work with MONEYVAL as it continues to address the full range of AML/CFT issues identified in its Mutual Evaluation Report, and further strengthen its AML/CFT regime."*

27.35.5 The Primary AML Investigation/Regulatory Authorities

National Bank of Ukraine

The main function of the country's central bank is to ensure the stability of the monetary unit – the Hryvnia. To carry out this function, the National Bank fosters stability in the banking system and price stability.

Ministry of Finance of Ukraine

The Ministry of Finance is the statutory executive body responsible for forming and implementing the financial, budget, tax and customs policy of Ukraine. It is also responsible for regulating, supervising and implementing the Ukrainian AML policy.

The Ministry of Finance is also the licensing agency for the organisation of gambling activities, while the licensing agency for the organisation and maintenance of totalizators and gambling institutions is the Council of Ministers of the Autonomous Republic of Crimea, regional state administrations and the Kyiv and Sevastopol city administrations. Control over the observation by business entities of licensing terms is undertaken by the Ministry of Finance and the State Committee for Regulatory Policy and Entrepreneurship.

Ministry of Economy of Ukraine

The Ministry supports the implementation of government economic, pricing, investment and foreign economic policy regarding internal trade and interdepartmental cooperation. It also ensures coordination between Ukraine and the EU.

State Commission for Financial Services Markets Regulation of Ukraine

The State Commission for Financial Services Markets Regulation of Ukraine (hereinafter referred to as the SCFM of Ukraine) is the central agency of executive power with special status, the activity of which is directed and coordinated by the Cabinet of Ministers of Ukraine.

The SCFM of Ukraine is the specially authorised agency with executive power in the area of financial monitoring.

27.35.6 Outline of Specific Money-laundering Offences

The Criminal Code describes money laundering as:

- Effecting financial transactions and other deals involving money or other property known to be the proceeds from crime; and
- Committing acts aimed at covering up the illegal origin of such money or other property or their ownership, the rights to such money or property, their origin, location or transfer, as well as obtaining, holding or using money or other property known to be the proceeds of crime.

Furthermore, the AML Act describes money laundering as any act related to the property or proceeds of crime, directed to conceal the origin of such proceeds or property or assistance to the person who is the associate in the crime that is the origin of such proceeds or property.

27.35.7 *Penalties*

Money laundering shall be punishable by imprisonment for a term of three to six years, with a prohibition on occupying certain positions or engaging in certain activities for a term up to two years and the forfeiture of criminally obtained money and other property and forfeiture of property.

Money laundering committed repeatedly, by a group or where the amount involved exceeds 6,000 days' salary (defined in the legislation as "tax-free minimum incomes") shall be punishable by imprisonment of seven to twelve years, with a prohibition on occupying certain positions or engaging in certain activities for a term up to three years, and the forfeiture of criminally obtained money and other property and forfeiture of property.

Money laundering committed by an organised group or where the amount involved exceeds 18,000 days' salary (defined in the legislation as "tax-free minimum incomes") shall be punishable by imprisonment for a term of eight to 15 years, a prohibition on occupying certain positions or engaging in certain activities for up to three years and the confiscation of money or other illegally obtained property.

27.35.8 *Scope*

The AML Act applies to "the citizens of Ukraine, foreigners and stateless persons, as well as to the legal persons, their subsidiaries, branches and other separate divisions that ensure execution of financial transactions both in Ukraine and abroad according to the international treaties of Ukraine ratified by the Verkhovna Rada of Ukraine". This is a broad definition.

27.35.9 *Risk-based Approach*

A reporting entity shall be obliged to manage ML/TF risks considering the results of customer identification, services provided to a customer, analysis of conducted customer transactions and their correspondence to the financial conditions and nature of the client's activity. The risk assessment by a reporting entity shall be executed considering relevant criteria such as the type of customer, the geographical location (country) of customer registration and the institution through which the customer transfers (receives) assets in the form of goods and services.

To reduce any detected risks, a reporting entity shall take measures including:

- Enhanced identification and verification of the customer and beneficial owners, if necessary;
- Additional obligations on the customer while opening an account or establishing relations;
- Increasing the frequency of customer verification, including its owners;

- The collection of information on purpose, to understand the customer's activity, nature and level of transactions conducted; and
- Enhanced monitoring of customer transactions.

27.35.10 Role of the MLRO/Nominated Officer

A Compliance Officer shall be appointed at the managerial level of the reporting entity. The appointment and dismissal of the Compliance Officer shall be agreed with the National Bank of Ukraine.

The role of the Compliance Officer of a reporting entity shall include:

- Taking the decision to inform the relevant authorities of suspicious transactions where there is a reasonable suspicion that they are connected with, related to or intended for money laundering or terrorist financing;
- Monitoring the levels of compliance with the rules regarding internal financial monitoring and the execution of financial monitoring programmes by the entity and its staff;
- Access to all the premises, documents and telecommunication facilities of the reporting entity;
- Requiring any other staff to perform AML/CFT measures and inspections;
- Organising, developing, submitting for approval, introducing and implementing rules for internal financial monitoring and financial monitoring execution programmes;
- Receiving explanations from staff on the performance of financial monitoring;
- Assisting authorised representatives of the relevant State financial monitoring agencies when they inspect the reporting entity's level of compliance with Ukrainian AML/CFT legislation;
- Executing other tasks according to the legislation.

The senior manager of a reporting entity shall be obliged to assist the Compliance Officer in the execution of his functions. The Compliance Officer shall be independent in his activity, accountable only to the senior manager of the reporting entity and is obliged, at least once a month, to provide the senior manager with written information on detected financial transactions subject to financial monitoring, and measures undertaken.

The Compliance Officer should be trained at least once every three years.

27.35.11 Due Diligence

Reporting entities are obliged to perform customer due diligence and should apply individual CDD policies depending on the risk posed by the customer, and enhanced CDD should be applied for high-risk customers. CDD should be conducted on the basis of official documents or duly certified copies.

The identification and verification of activity shall be conducted when:

- Establishing business relations with clients;
- There is a suspicion that the financial transaction might be related to ML or TF;
- Executing a financial transaction subject to financial monitoring;
- Executing a single financial transaction without establishing business relations with clients, where the amount equals or exceeds UAH 150,000.

Depending on the risk of money laundering, customer identification should also be carried out when conducting a financial transaction for a client which exceeds UAH 150,000, whether it is through a single operation or as numerous operations that may be linked to each other.

In the case of any suspicion regarding the reliability or adequacy of information provided during CDD, the reporting entity should take further measures to verify and clarify the information given.

A reporting entity has the right to demand, and the customer is obliged to provide, information concerning his/her identity, nature of activity and financial condition if it is required to comply with the AML/CFT legislation. If the customer with whom the business relations were established fails to submit the necessary information on identification and verification of financial activity, the reporting entity has the right to refuse to execute further financial transactions.

Personal Client Due Diligence

For the purposes of identifying residents, reporting entities shall obtain, for natural persons:

- Surname
- Name
- Date of birth
- Series and number of passport (or other ID)
- Date of issue and issuing agency of passport.

The address and ID number shall be verified using the State register and tax information. For entrepreneurs, during the identification of the place of residence, the essential elements of the State registration certificate, the issuing authority, the bank in which the account is held and the number of the bank account (if available) shall be verified.

For the purposes of identifying non-residents, reporting entities shall obtain, for natural persons:

- Surname
- Name
- Date of birth
- Series and number of passport (or other ID)

- Date of issue and issuing agency of passport
- Citizenship.

During the identification, the data on the place of residence or temporary residence in Ukraine shall be verified.

Corporate Customer Due Diligence

For legal persons, the following shall be ascertained:

- Full title;
- Location;
- Essential elements of the State registration certificate and issuing authority;
- Information on managing bodies and their composition;
- Information on persons who have the right to manage accounts and property;
- Owners of a significant share of the legal person;
- CDD for anybody in control of the company;
- Identification number according to the Unified State Register of Entities and Organisations of Ukraine;
- Details of the bank where the account is held and the bank account number.

For a non-resident legal person:

- Full title;
- Location and essential elements of the bank where the account is held and bank account number;
- Information on managing bodies and their composition;
- Identification information on the persons who have the right to manage accounts and property;
- Data on owners of a significant share in the legal person;
- Data on controllers of the legal person.

The reporting entity should also be provided with a copy of the registration certificate from the relevant foreign authorities to verify the registration of the relevant legal person.

Third Party Customer Due Diligence

If a customer acts as a representative or in the interests of another natural person, the reporting entity doubts whether the person is acting on their own behalf or the beneficiary is another person, the reporting entity is obliged to identify the person on whose behalf, under the order of whom or in the interests of whom the financial transaction is being conducted, or who is a beneficiary. If a person acts as a representative of another person, the reporting entity should verify the relevant powers of that person as well.

The reporting entity may not establish a business relationship with a client if it cannot carry out the CDD procedures. In such a case, the reporting entity must inform the Specially Authorised Agency, either on the same or the following business day, that the customer was unwilling to comply with the CDD requirements.

The reporting entity has the right to refuse to establish a business relationship with any customer if it is not satisfied that the CDD requirements have yielded adequate results. If this happens, the entity is obliged to inform the Specially Authorised Agency no later than the following business day that it has made the refusal.

Simplified Customer Due Diligence

The reporting entity can use a simplified identification procedure in cases involving various specified customers, including government or State-owned bodies.

Politically Exposed Persons

To establish relations with politically exposed persons and their associates, the following must be adhered to:

- Permission should be given by the senior management of the reporting entity;
- Measures should be taken to establish the sources of funds of such persons;
- Any operations conducted should be monitored continually.

Correspondent Banking

Before establishing a correspondent banking relationship, institutions are obliged:

- To collect information on the nature of the financial institution's activity and its financial condition and reputation, including whether this institution has been subject to enforcement measures taken by the agency providing regulation and supervision over its activity in the AML/CFT sphere;
- To ascertain what measures are taken by the institution for the prevention and counteraction of the legalisation (laundering) of the proceeds of crime or terrorist financing;
- To ascertain, on the basis of received information, the sufficiency and efficiency of measures taken by a foreign institution to combat money laundering or terrorist financing;
- To open correspondent accounts for foreign financial institutions and in foreign financial institutions under senior manager approval.

27.35.12 Staff Training

Entities must take measures, on a continual basis, to train personnel on the detection of financial transactions subject to financial monitoring according to the current law by conducting educational and practical events.

27.35.13 Record-keeping

Entities are obliged:

- To maintain documents on the identification of persons who conducted any financial transaction which, pursuant to the current law, is subject to financial monitoring, as well as all documents connected to business relations with clients for no less than five years after the termination of business relations;
- To maintain all essential data on transactions for no less than five years after the completion of a transaction;
- To ensure, on documentary request, unimpeded access of entities of State financial monitoring and law-enforcement agencies to documents or information contained therein, according to the requirements of legislation.

27.35.14 Monitoring Thresholds

Any financial transaction shall be subject to obligatory financial monitoring if its amount equals or exceeds UAH 150,000 (UAH 13,000 for gambling), or the foreign equivalent, and it has one or more of the indicators provided below (this list is not exhaustive):

- The transfer of funds to or from an anonymous overseas account, or in a country included by the Cabinet of Ministers of Ukraine's list of offshore zones;
- Purchase or sale of cheques, travel cheques or other similar payment means for cash;
- Placement of cash funds on account and further transfer to another person on the same or the next transaction day;
- Transfer of funds abroad by a person other than in pursuance of an international contract.

In addition to this, a financial transaction shall be subject to internal financial monitoring if it has one or more of the following indicators, or if it contains other risks:

- This transaction, or an aggregate of connected financial transactions, has a complex or unusual character without any apparent economic or visible lawful purpose;
- The transaction does not fit with the character and nature of the customer's activity;
- Repeated transactions designed to evade the UAH 150,000 reporting threshold have been made;
- The reporting entity has grounds to believe that the financial transaction is connected with money laundering or terrorist financing.

The reporting entity has the right to suspend any financial transaction if such transaction contains indicators of money laundering, and should, within the same day, report it to the Specially Authorised Agency. The transaction will be suspended for up to two business days, pending a further extension by the SAA.

Furthermore, entities are obliged:

- To ensure ML/TF risks are managed and to develop risk criteria;
- To develop rules and programmes for the execution of financial monitoring;
- To conduct annual internal inspections of compliance with AML/CFT legislation requirements;
- To detect financial transactions subject to obligatory financial monitoring according to UAH 150,000;
- To verify the purpose and nature of future business relations with clients;
- To continually update information on the nature of a client's activity and financial condition.

27.35.15 Reporting Requirements

Entities are obliged to report a financial transaction which is subject to financial monitoring by the business day following its detection, and to inform the Specially Authorised Agency of:

- Any financial transactions subject to obligatory financial monitoring within three business days of the date of such transactions or attempts to conduct such transactions.
- Financial transactions subject to internal financial monitoring as a result of a reasonable suspicion of money laundering. This should ideally be done on the day the suspicions arise, but should be submitted no later than ten business days after the transaction has occurred or has been attempted.
- Financial transactions which the entity reasonably suspects are connected with, related to or intended for terrorist financing. These should be submitted on the day of detection of the attempt to conduct the transaction.

Entities must also submit any requested information to assist the SAA.

27.35.16 Detailed Rules on Penalties

Persons guilty of violating the current law shall be subject to criminal, administrative and civil liability according to the law. Such persons may also be deprived of the right to conduct certain kinds of activity pursuant to the law. Legal persons conducting ML/TF financial transactions may be liquidated by a court decision.

If a reporting entity fails to comply with the requirements of the current law and/or undertakes other AML/CFT normative-legal acts, it could be fined according to the procedure defined by the law:

- For violation of the CDD requirements: 500 days' salary for individuals and 100 days' salary for companies;
- For non-detection, late detection and violation of the reporting procedure for financial monitoring: 800 days' salary for individuals and 100 days' salary for companies;

- For non-submission, late submission, false submission or violation of the procedure for submission to the Specially Authorised Agency on financial monitoring: 2,000 days' salary for individuals and 100 days' salary for companies;
- For violation of the procedure on the suspension of financial transactions: 1,000 days' salary for individuals and 100 days' salary for companies;
- For violation of other obligations: 300 days' salary for individuals and 100 days' salary for companies;
- For repeated violation by a reporting entity within a year: 3,000 days' salary for individuals and 200 days' salary for companies.

The penalty system clearly takes action against those involved with the failure to comply with the obligations.

In addition to this, the State financial monitoring entity could restrict, terminate or cancel a licence or other special authority to conduct certain activities.

In cases of severe violation by a reporting entity, the State financial monitoring entity could enforce a suspension.

Deliberate failure, untimely submission or submission of false information on financial transactions, if such actions caused substantial damage, shall be punishable by a fine of 1,000 to 2,000 days' salary, or imprisonment for up to two years, and a restriction on the right to occupy certain positions or engage in certain activities for up to three years.

Tipping off, if it causes substantial damage, shall be punishable by a fine of 1,000 to 2,000 days' salary, or imprisonment for up to three years, and a restriction on the right to occupy certain positions or engage in certain activities for up to three years.

27.35.17 Case Studies

A former Ukrainian prime minister was convicted of laundering $21.7 million in extorted funds through US banks. He committed the fraud by requiring the victim to turn over half his profits from his agriculture and metals import and export company as a condition of doing business. He then laundered the money in a complex series of transactions that went through banks in Poland, Switzerland and Antigua and ended up in banks in San Francisco.

The former prime minister was sentenced to a total of over ten years in prison, as well as paying a $9 million fine and compensating the victim.

27.36 COUNTRY PROFILE: UNITED STATES OF AMERICA

27.36.1 Overview

The USA has a comprehensive AML programme, which has been further enhanced in response to the 11th September terrorist attacks. As the USA carries a considerable terrorism threat, the CFT programme is of primary concern to the legislature. Proposals to make bank executives personally responsible for money-laundering failures were in discussion, but not in force, at the time of going to print.

27.36.2 Key Legislation

The Bank Secrecy Act establishes the basic AML framework, and the Federal Financial Institutions Examination Council released an AML handbook under the Bank Secrecy Act in 2010. In addition to this, the USA Patriot Act provides various AML provisions for financial institutions.

27.36.3 Legislative History

The Bank Secrecy Act (BSA) was initially adopted in 1970. The USA Patriot Act was enacted by Congress in 2001 in response to the 11th September terrorist attacks. Among other things, the USA Patriot Act amended and strengthened the BSA. Various NYSE and NASD rules were then approved, and have now been incorporated into a new FINRA Rule 3310. FINRA Rule 3310 provides the minimum requirements for an AML programme.

27.36.4 FATF Assessment

The 2006 mutual evaluation stated that the USA has "implemented an effective AML/CFT system, although there are remaining concerns in relation to some of the specific requirements for undertaking customer due diligence, the availability of corporate ownership information, and the requirements applicable to certain designated non-financial businesses and professions". The AML framework was described as "comprehensive", the regulatory framework as "effective" and the USA pursues criminals involved in money laundering "vigorously".

27.36.5 The Primary AML Investigation/Regulatory Authorities

The US Department of Treasury

The BSA authorises the Secretary of the Treasury to issue regulations requiring banks and other financial institutions to take a number of precautions against financial crime, including the establishment of AML programmes and the filing of reports that have been determined to have a high degree of usefulness in criminal, tax and regulatory investigations and proceedings, and certain intelligence and counter-terrorism matters. The Secretary of the Treasury has delegated to the Director of FinCEN the authority to implement, administer and enforce compliance with the BSA and associated regulations.

Financial Crimes Enforcement Network

The Financial Crimes Enforcement Network (FinCEN) is a bureau of the US Department of the Treasury. FinCEN's mission is to enhance the integrity of financial systems by facilitating the detection and deterrence of financial crime.

FinCEN carries out its mission by receiving and maintaining financial transactions data; analysing and disseminating that data for law-enforcement purposes; and building global cooperation with counterpart organisations in other countries and with international bodies.

Financial Industry Regulatory Authority

The Financial Industry Regulatory Authority (FINRA) is the largest independent regulator for all securities firms doing business in the United States. FINRA's mission is to protect America's investors by making sure the securities industry operates fairly and honestly.

Internal Revenue Service Criminal Investigation

The Internal Revenue Service Criminal Investigation investigates potential criminal violations of the Internal Revenue Code and related financial crimes in a manner that fosters confidence in the tax system and compliance with the law.

The Office of Terrorism and Financial Intelligence

Headed by an Under Secretary, the Office of Terrorism and Financial Intelligence (TFI) marshals the Treasury Department's policy, enforcement, regulatory and intelligence functions to sever the lines of financial support to international terrorists, WMD proliferators, narcotics traffickers, money launderers and other threats to national security.

Two components of TFI are led by Assistant Secretaries. The Office of Terrorist Financing and Financial Crimes (TFFC) is the policy and outreach apparatus for TFI. The Office of Intelligence and Analysis (OIA) is responsible for TFI's intelligence functions, integrating the Treasury Department into the larger intelligence community (IC), and providing support to both Treasury leadership and the IC.

TFI also oversees several component offices and bureaus. The Office of Foreign Assets Control (OFAC) administers and enforces economic and trade sanctions. The Treasury Executive Office for Asset Forfeiture (TEOAF) administers the Treasury Forfeiture Fund (TFF), which is the receipt account for the deposit of non-tax forfeitures. Responsible for administering the Bank Secrecy Act (BSA) and other regulatory functions is one of the Treasury's bureaus, the Financial Crimes Enforcement Network (FinCEN), which supports law-enforcement investigative efforts and fosters interagency and global cooperation against domestic and international financial crimes. It also provides US policymakers with strategic analyses of domestic and worldwide trends and patterns. The director of FinCEN reports directly to the Under Secretary. TFI also works in close partnership with the IRS Criminal Investigative Division (IRS-CI) to enforce laws against terrorist financing and money laundering, including the Bank Secrecy Act.

The Drug Enforcement Agency

The Drug Enforcement Agency's objective with financial investigations is to identify and halt the use of drug proceeds that finance the continued operations of drug traffickers.

Federal Financial Institutions Examination Council

The Council is a formal inter-agency body empowered to prescribe uniform principles, standards and report forms for the federal examination of financial institutions by various government agencies, and to make recommendations to promote uniformity in the supervision of financial institutions.

27.36.6 *Outline of Specific Money-laundering Offences*

Money laundering is committed by anyone who, knowing that the property involved in a financial transaction represents the proceeds of some form of unlawful activity, conducts or attempts to conduct such a financial transaction which in fact involves the proceeds of specified unlawful activity:

- With the intent to promote the carrying on of specified unlawful activity; or
- With the intent to engage in conduct to evade tax or commit fraud; or
- Knowing that the transaction is designed, in whole or in part:
  - to conceal or disguise the nature, the location, the source, the ownership or the control of the proceeds of specified unlawful activity; or
  - to avoid a transaction reporting requirement under State or Federal law.

An offence is also committed by anyone who transports, transmits or transfers, or attempts to transport, transmit or transfer a monetary instrument or funds from a place in the United States to, or through, a place outside the United States or to a place in the United States from, or through, a place outside the United States:

- With the intent to promote the carrying on of specified unlawful activity; or
- Knowing that the monetary instrument or funds involved in the transportation, transmission or transfer represent the proceeds of some form of unlawful activity, and knowing that such transportation, transmission or transfer is designed, in whole or in part:
  - to conceal or disguise the nature, the location, the source, the ownership or the control of the proceeds of specified unlawful activity; or
  - to avoid a transaction reporting requirement under State or Federal law.

27.36.7 *Penalties*

The penalty for money laundering is a fine of not more than $500,000 or twice the value of the property involved in the transaction, whichever is greater, or imprisonment for not more than 20 years, or both.

Moving money in/out of the country as outlined above is punishable by a fine of not more than $500,000 or twice the value of the monetary instrument or funds involved in the transportation, transmission or transfer, whichever is greater, or imprisonment for not more than 20 years, or both.

Whoever, with the intent:

- To promote the carrying on of specified unlawful activity;
- To conceal or disguise the nature, location, source, ownership or control of property believed to be the proceeds of specified unlawful activity; or
- To avoid a transaction reporting requirement under State or Federal law

conducts, or attempts to conduct, a financial transaction involving property representing the proceeds of specified unlawful activity, or property used to conduct or facilitate specified unlawful activity, shall be fined or imprisoned for not more than 20 years, or both.

The term "proceeds" means any property derived from or obtained or retained, directly or indirectly, through some form of unlawful activity, including the gross receipts of such activity. Any person who conspires to commit any offence defined shall be subject to the same penalties as those prescribed for the commission of the offence which was the object of the conspiracy.

27.36.8 Risk Assessment

The board of directors, acting through senior management, is ultimately responsible for ensuring that the bank maintains an effective BSA/AML internal control structure, including suspicious activity monitoring and reporting. The board of directors and management should create a culture of compliance to ensure staff adherence to the bank's BSA/AML policies, procedures and processes. The level of sophistication of the internal controls should be commensurate with the size, structure, risks and complexity of the bank. Internal controls should:

- Identify banking operations which are more vulnerable to abuse by money launderers and criminals;
- Provide for periodic updates to the bank's risk profile;
- Provide for a BSA/AML compliance programme tailored to manage risks;
- Identify a person or persons responsible for BSA/AML compliance;
- Meet all regulatory record-keeping and reporting requirements, meet recommendations for BSA/AML compliance and provide for timely updates in response to changes in regulations;
- Implement risk-based CDD policies, procedures and processes;
- Provide sufficient controls and systems for filing CTRs and CTR exemptions;
- Provide sufficient controls and monitoring systems for timely detection and reporting of suspicious activity;

- Train employees to be aware of their responsibilities under the BSA regulations and internal policy guidelines.

The above list is not designed to be all-inclusive and should be tailored to reflect the bank's BSA/AML risk profile.

Management should structure the bank's BSA/AML compliance programme to adequately address its risk profile, as identified by the risk assessment. Management should understand the bank's BSA/AML risk exposure and develop appropriate policies, procedures and processes to monitor and control BSA/AML risks. It is sound practice for banks to periodically reassess their BSA/AML risks at least every 12 to 18 months.

27.36.9 Role of the MLRO/Nominated Officer

The bank's board of directors must designate a qualified individual to serve as the BSA Compliance Officer. The BSA Compliance Officer is responsible for coordinating and monitoring day-to-day BSA/AML compliance. The BSA Compliance Officer is also charged with managing all aspects of the BSA/AML compliance programme and with managing the bank's adherence to the BSA and its implementing regulations; however, the board of directors is ultimately responsible for the bank's BSA/AML compliance.

The Compliance Officer's level of authority and responsibility within the bank is critical. They may delegate BSA/AML duties to other employees, but the Compliance Officer should be responsible for overall BSA/AML compliance. The BSA Compliance Officer should be fully knowledgeable of the BSA and all related regulations, and should also understand the bank's products, services, customers, entities and geographic locations, and the potential money-laundering and terrorist-financing risks associated with those activities.

The line of communication should allow the BSA Compliance Officer to regularly update the board of directors and senior management on ongoing compliance with the BSA. Pertinent BSA-related information, including the reporting of SARs filed with FinCEN, should be reported to the board of directors or an appropriate board committee so that these individuals can make informed decisions about overall BSA/AML compliance.

27.36.10 Due Diligence

All banks must have a written Customer Identification Programme (CIP). The CIP is intended to enable the bank to form a reasonable belief that it knows the true identity of each customer, and must include account-opening procedures that specify the identifying information that will be obtained from each customer. It must also include reasonable and practical risk-based procedures for verifying the identity of each customer. Banks should conduct a risk assessment of their customer base and product offerings, and in determining the risks, consider:

- The types of accounts offered by the bank;
- The bank's methods of opening accounts;

- The types of identifying information available;
- The bank's size, location and customer base, including types of products and services used by customers in different geographic locations.

Personal Client Due Diligence

The CIP must contain account-opening procedures detailing the identifying information that must be obtained from each customer. At a minimum, the bank must obtain the following identifying information from each customer before opening an account:

- Name
- Date of birth for individuals
- Address
- Identification number.

Based on its risk assessment, a bank may require identifying information in addition to the items above for certain customers or product lines.

The CIP must contain risk-based procedures for verifying the identity of the customer within a reasonable period of time after the account is opened. A bank need not establish the accuracy of every element of identifying information obtained, but it must verify enough information to form a reasonable belief that it knows the true identity of the customer. The bank's procedures must describe when it will use documents, non-documentary methods or a combination of both.

A bank must have procedures that set forth the minimum acceptable documentation. This identification must provide evidence of a customer's nationality or residence and bear a photograph or similar safeguard; examples include a driving licence or passport. However, other forms of identification may be used if they enable the bank to form a reasonable belief that it knows the true identity of the customer.

Corporate Customer Due Diligence

For a legal person, the bank should obtain documents showing the legal existence of the entity, such as certified articles of incorporation, an unexpired government-issued business licence, a partnership agreement or a trust instrument.

Banks are not required to use non-documentary methods to verify a customer's identity. However, a bank using non-documentary methods to verify a customer's identity must have procedures that set forth the methods the bank will use. Non-documentary methods may include:

- Contacting a customer;
- Independently verifying the customer's identity through the comparison of information provided by the customer with information obtained from a consumer reporting agency, public database or other source;

- Checking references with other financial institutions; and
- Obtaining a financial statement.

The CIP must address situations where, based on its risk assessment of a new account opened by a company, the bank will obtain information about individuals with authority or control over the accounts, including signatories, in order to verify the customer's identity. This verification method applies only when the bank cannot verify the customer's true identity using documentary or non-documentary methods.

The CIP must also have procedures for circumstances in which the bank cannot form a reasonable belief that it knows the true identity of the customer. These procedures should describe:

- Circumstances in which the bank should not open an account;
- The terms under which a customer may use an account while the bank attempts to verify the customer's identity;
- When the bank should close an account, after attempts to verify a customer's identity have failed;
- When the bank should file a SAR in accordance with applicable law and regulations.

Enhanced Due Diligence

Higher-risk customers and their transactions should be reviewed more closely at account opening and more frequently throughout the term of their relationship with the bank. The bank may determine that a customer poses a higher risk because of the customer's business activity, ownership structure and/or the anticipated or actual volume and types of transactions, including those transactions involving higher-risk jurisdictions. If so, the bank should consider obtaining, both at account opening and throughout the relationship, the following information on the customer:

- Purpose of the account;
- Source of funds and wealth;
- Individuals with ownership or control over the account, such as beneficial owners, signatories or guarantors;
- Occupation or type of business (of customer or other individuals with ownership or control over the account);
- Financial statements;
- Banking references;
- Domicile (where the business is organised);
- Proximity of the customer's residence, place of employment or place of business to the bank;
- Description of the customer's primary trade area and whether international transactions are expected to be routine;

- Description of the business operations, the anticipated volume of currency and total sales and a list of major customers and suppliers;
- Explanations for changes in account activity.

Furthermore, for high-risk customers, the following should be scrutinised:

- Purpose of the account;
- Actual or anticipated activity in the account;
- Nature of the customer's business/occupation;
- Customer's location;
- Types of products and services used by the customer.

As due diligence is an ongoing process, a bank should take measures to ensure account profiles are current and monitoring should be risk-based. Banks should consider whether risk profiles should be adjusted or suspicious activity reported when the activity is inconsistent with the profile.

Politically Exposed Persons

Banks should establish risk-based controls and procedures that include reasonable steps to ascertain the status of an individual as a PEP and to conduct risk-based scrutiny of accounts held by these individuals. Risk will vary depending on other factors such as products and services used and size or complexity of the account relationship.

Commensurate with the identified level of risk, due diligence procedures should include, but are not necessarily limited to, the following:

- Identify the account holder and beneficial owner, including the nominal and beneficial owners of companies, trusts, partnerships, private investment companies or other legal entities that are account holders;
- Seek information directly from the account holder and beneficial owner regarding possible PEP status;
- Obtain information regarding employment, including industry and sector and the level of risk for corruption associated with the industries and sectors;
- Identify the account holder's and beneficial owner's source of wealth and funds;
- Obtain information on immediate family members or close associates either having transaction authority over the account or benefiting from transactions conducted through the account;
- Determine the purpose of the account and the expected volume and nature of account activity;
- Make reasonable efforts to review public sources of information.

Correspondent Banking

A bank that maintains a correspondent account in the United States for a foreign bank must maintain records in the United States identifying the owners of each foreign bank. A bank must also record the name and street address of a person who resides in the United States and who is authorised, and has agreed, to be an agent to accept services of legal process. A bank must produce these records within seven days upon receipt of a written request from a federal law-enforcement officer.

The regulation also contains specific provisions as to when banks must obtain the required information or close correspondent accounts. Banks must obtain certifications (or recertifications) or otherwise obtain the required information within 30 calendar days after the date an account is established and at least once every three years thereafter. If the bank is unable to obtain the required information, it must close all correspondent accounts with the foreign bank within a commercially reasonable time.

A bank should review certifications for reasonableness and accuracy. If a bank, at any time, knows, suspects or has reason to suspect that any information contained in a certification (or recertification), or that any other information it relied on, is no longer correct, the bank must request that the foreign bank verify or correct such information, or the bank must take other appropriate measures to ascertain its accuracy.

Shell Banking

A bank is prohibited from establishing, maintaining, administering or managing a correspondent account in the United States for, or on behalf of, a foreign shell bank. An exception, however, permits a bank to maintain a correspondent account for a foreign shell bank that is a regulated affiliate. A bank must also take reasonable steps to ensure that any correspondent account established, maintained, administered or managed in the United States for a foreign bank is not being used by that foreign bank to provide banking services indirectly to foreign shell banks.

27.36.11 Ongoing Monitoring

Appropriate policies, procedures and processes should be in place to monitor and identify unusual activity. The sophistication of monitoring systems should be dictated by the bank's risk profile, with particular emphasis on the composition of higher-risk products, services, customers, entities and geographies. The bank should ensure adequate staff is assigned to the identification, research and reporting of suspicious activities, taking into account the bank's overall risk profile and the volume of transactions. Monitoring systems typically include employee identification or referrals, transaction-based (manual) systems, surveillance (automated) systems or any combination of these.

27.36.12 Staff Training

Banks must ensure that appropriate personnel are trained in applicable aspects of the BSA. Training should include regulatory requirements and the bank's internal BSA/AML policies, procedures and processes. At a minimum, the bank's training programme must provide training for all personnel whose duties require knowledge of the BSA. The training should be tailored to the person's specific responsibilities. In addition, an overview of the BSA/AML requirements typically should be given to new staff during employee orientation. Training should encompass information related to applicable business lines, such as trust services, international and private banking. The BSA Compliance Officer should receive periodic training that is relevant and appropriate given changes to regulatory requirements as well as the activities and overall BSA/AML risk profile of the bank.

The board of directors and senior management should be informed of changes and new developments in the BSA, its implementing regulations and directives and the federal banking agencies' regulations. While the board of directors may not require the same degree of training as banking operations personnel, they need to understand the importance of BSA/AML regulatory requirements, the ramifications of non-compliance and the risks posed to the bank. Without a general understanding of the BSA, the board of directors cannot adequately provide BSA/AML oversight; approve BSA/AML policies, procedures and processes; or provide sufficient BSA/AML resources.

Training should be ongoing and incorporate current developments and changes to the BSA and any related regulations. Changes to internal policies, procedures, processes and monitoring systems should also be covered during training. The programme should reinforce the importance that the board and senior management place on the bank's compliance with the BSA and ensure that all employees understand their role in maintaining an effective BSA/AML compliance programme.

Examples of money-laundering activity and suspicious activity monitoring and reporting can and should be tailored to each individual audience. For example, training for tellers should focus on examples involving large currency transactions or other suspicious activities; training for the loan department should provide examples involving money laundering through lending arrangements.

Banks should document their training programmes. Training and testing materials, the dates of training sessions and attendance records should be maintained by the bank and be available for examiner review.

27.36.13 Record-keeping

A bank's CIP must include record-keeping procedures. At a minimum, the bank must retain the identifying information (name, address, date of birth for an individual, TIN and any other information required by the CIP) obtained at account opening for a period of five years after the account is closed. For credit cards, the retention period is five years after the account closes or becomes dormant. The bank must also keep a description of the following for five years after the record was made:

- Any document that was relied on to verify identity, noting the type of document, the identification number, the place of issuance and, if any, the date of issuance and expiration date;
- The method and the results of any measures undertaken to verify identity;
- The results of any substantive discrepancy discovered when verifying identity.

Funds Transfer Records

The BSA requires banks to maintain records of funds transfer in amounts of $3,000 and above.

Monetary Instrument Records

Records for monetary instrument sales are required by the BSA. Such records can assist the bank in identifying possible currency structuring through the purchase of cashier's cheques, official bank cheques, money orders or traveller's cheques in amounts of $3,000 to $10,000.

27.36.14 Reporting Requirements

When a domestic financial institution is involved in a transaction involving the movement of over $10,000, the institution shall file a report on the transaction at the time and in the way the Secretary prescribes. Entities may be exempted from this if the customer is well known or a frequent customer.

Suspicious Transaction Reports

The Secretary may require any financial institution, and any director, officer, employee or agent of any financial institution, to report any suspicious transaction relevant to a possible violation of law or regulation. Disclosure of the report is prohibited. Banks, bank holding companies and their subsidiaries are required by federal regulations to file a SAR with respect to:

- Criminal violations involving insider abuse in any amount.
- Criminal violations aggregating $5,000 or more when a suspect can be identified.
- Criminal violations aggregating $25,000 or more regardless of a potential suspect.
- Transactions conducted or attempted by, at or through the bank (or an affiliate) and aggregating $5,000 or more, if the bank or affiliate knows, suspects or has reason to suspect that the transaction:
  - may involve potential money laundering or other illegal activity (e.g. terrorism financing);
  - is designed to evade the BSA or its implementing regulations;
  - has no business or apparent lawful purpose or is not the type of transaction that the particular customer would normally be expected to engage in, and the bank knows of no reasonable explanation for the transaction after examining the available facts, including the background and possible purpose of the transaction.

Anyone who submits a SAR in good faith is exempted from prosecution.

Currency Activity Reports

Most vendors offer reports that identify all currency activity or currency activity greater than $10,000. These reports assist bankers with filing CTRs and identifying suspicious currency activity.

27.36.15 Internal Requirements

In order to guard against money laundering through financial institutions, each financial institution shall establish anti-money-laundering programmes, including, at a minimum:

- The development of internal policies, procedures and controls;
- The designation of a Compliance Officer;
- An ongoing employee training programme; and
- An independent audit function to test programmes.

Under FINRA Rule 3310, an AML programme must be in writing and include, at a minimum:

- Policies, procedures and internal controls reasonably designed to achieve compliance with the BSA and its implementing rules;
- Policies and procedures that can be reasonably expected to detect and cause the reporting of transactions and the implementing regulations thereunder;
- The designation of an AML Compliance Officer (AML Officer), including notification to the SROs;
- Ongoing AML employee training; and
- An independent test of the firm's AML programme, annually for most firms.

27.36.16 Penalties

Simple breaches of the reporting obligations are punishable by imprisonment for not more than five years, a fine of not more than $250,000, or both. Violations committed during the commission of another federal crime or as part of a pattern of illegal activity involving more than $100,000 over the course of a year are punishable by imprisonment for not more than ten years. The punishment is a fine of not more than $500,000 (not more than $1 million for a special measures violation or a violation involving a breach of CDD).

27.36.17 Case Studies

In the first case, a criminal was sentenced to 12 months and one day in prison for her role in a money-laundering conspiracy that involved proceeds from the unlawful distribution of prescription painkilling medication. She was part of a ring which unlawfully transported a powerful and addictive prescription painkiller from Las Vegas, Nevada, to Fairbanks. She then wire transferred or deposited approximately $14,000 that consisted of proceeds from the unlawful distribution of the painkillers in the Fairbanks area. Approximately $140,000 was laundered during the conspiracy. Other participants in the conspiracy received sentences of 80 months, 18 months and 12 months and a day in prison.

In another case, the president of a payphone company was sentenced to 54 months in prison for money laundering. For three years, he conspired with other senior members of the company to fraudulently collect dial-around compensation fees by programming payphones to autodial toll-free telephone numbers.

Under FCC regulations, payphone owners are paid $.494 for every toll-free call placed from their payphones. The criminal's payphones were programmed to place toll-free calls and to choose the appropriate options in the automated messaging system to stay connected long enough to ensure the payphone would collect the dial-around compensation fee. The phone would then automatically hang up. The scheme generated over $1 million in fraudulent dial-around compensation fees. The accomplices were sentenced to three months and 12 months in prison.

In a further case, a criminal was sentenced to 36 months in prison and three years of supervised release after pleading guilty to conspiring to launder monetary instruments. The son of the owner of an auto dealership sold vehicles to three individuals but put different names on the vehicle titles. The vehicles were purchased with illegal funds. He then allowed falsified information to be presented to the financial institutions to secure the loans for the vehicles.

27.37 COUNTRY PROFILE: VIETNAM

27.37.1 Overview

Vietnam is predominantly a cash economy. The ineffective AML regime had been the subject of vast criticism by the FATF, but a major overhaul of the legislative provisions in 2013 – the first since 2005 – sought to address the numerous deficiencies.

The new rules require that businesses report transactions over a certain threshold and suspicious transactions to Vietnam's financial intelligence unit (FIU). In addition:

- Jewellery sellers will have to ascertain identities for, and report, transactions of US$ 14,000 or more;
- Securities brokers, dealers and real estate vendors will have to report all transactions to the FIU regardless of the amount of the transaction;
- Banks will have to ascertain the identity of businesses and persons undertaking transactions equal to or greater than VND 300 million per day if the person or entity has not undertaken transactions in six months;
- Casinos will have to ascertain the identity of persons gambling when the bets or the wins are equal to or exceed VND 60 million per day;
- Charities will have to report the names and addresses of organisations and persons who make donations and will have to report how the funds were used.

All obliged or reporting entities will have to undertake AML risk assessments in respect of their business and implement compliance plans to mitigate those risks.

27.37.2 Key Legislation

The money-laundering offences are contained in Articles 250 and 251 of the Vietnam Penal Code. The Law on Prevention and Combat of Money Laundering (the Law) came into effect in early 2013, with the relevant AML and compliance provisions contained in Decree 116/2013/ND-CP.

27.37.3 Legislative History

Vietnam signed border control agreements with neighbouring countries in the early 1990s, to try to prevent cross-border money laundering. In addition, Vietnam ratified various UN conventions in the late nineties and 2000, and the AML Decree in 2005. The previous compliance law was Decree 74/2005/ND-CP on prevention of money laundering, supplemented by Circular No. 41/2011/TT-NHNN, which guided the identification and update of customer information on a risk basis with regard to combating money laundering.

27.37.4 FATF Assessment

In June 2012, the FATF released a statement in which it said "Vietnam has taken steps towards improving its AML/CFT regime, including by issuing an Inter-Ministerial Circular on terrorist financing and amended its AML legislation. However, despite

Vietnam's high-level political commitment to work with the FATF and APG to address its strategic AML/CFT deficiencies, Vietnam has not made sufficient progress in implementing its action plan, and certain strategic AML/CFT deficiencies remain." Vietnam has recently implemented new AML legislation to address these issues, but its effectiveness remains to be seen.

27.37.5 *The Primary AML Investigation/Regulatory Authorities*

The Ministry for Public Security

According to Article 16(3) of AML Decree 74, the Ministry for Public Security (MPS) is the lead agency responsible for investigating money laundering. The two key MPS departments are the Economic Crimes Investigation Department, which undertakes money-laundering investigations, and the Anti-Terrorism Department. The official website of the Ministry for Public Security was "under construction" at the time of writing.

State Bank of Vietnam

The duties of the State Bank of Vietnam, as listed in Decree 178/2007/ND-CP dated 3rd December, 2007 and Decree 96/ND-CP dated 26th August, 2008 by the government on functions, roles and responsibilities and the structure of Ministries and ministerial agencies, include inspecting, investigating and handling any complaints, accusations or violations of the law related to banking and finance, and to the fight against corruption.

Anti Money Laundering Information Centre

The Anti Money Laundering Information Centre was set up under the 2005 Decree to receive reports and coordinate AML compliance. It is a part of the State Bank of Vietnam.

Vietnam will not introduce an FIU as part of the 2013 overhaul. Instead, the National Assembly has decided that the functions of AML authorities will be distributed to various ministries and government agencies.

27.37.6 *Outline of Specific Money-laundering Offences*

It should be noted that suspicion is not generally recognised as a concept within Vietnamese law, and only a natural person can be convicted of a crime under the Penal Code.

Money laundering is defined in the Vietnam Penal Code as follows:

> *"Using financial and/or banking operators or other transactions to legalise money and/or property obtained through the commission of crime or using such money and/or property to conduct business activities or other economic activities."*

The harbouring offence is committed by:

> *"Those who, without prior promise, harbour or consume property with the full knowledge that it was acquired through the commission of crime by other persons."*

There is no requirement to prove possession and concealment, proof of either will be sufficient to obtain a conviction under Article 250.

The definition of money laundering includes:

- Supporting individuals and/or organisations related to criminals to avoid legal liabilities by legalising the origin of property acquired from criminal activity; and
- Possessing property which has been known to be property acquired from criminal activity at the time of receiving the property in order to legalise the origin of the property.

27.37.7 Penalties

The penalty for money laundering is a sentence of between one and five years of imprisonment. Furthermore, anyone committing the crime in one of the following circumstances shall be sentenced to between three and ten years of imprisonment:

- In an organised manner;
- Abusing positions and/or powers;
- Committing the offence more than once.

Offenders shall be sentenced to between five and 15 years of imprisonment if they commit the crime in particularly serious circumstances. The offenders may also be subject to the confiscation of property, to a fine treble the amount of money or the value of the property that has been legalised and/or to a ban from holding certain posts, practising certain occupations or doing certain jobs for one to five years.

Anyone found guilty of the harbouring offence shall be sentenced to a fine of between five million dong and fifty million dong, non-custodial reform of up to three years or a prison term of between six months and three years.

If someone is found to have committed the crime in one of the following circumstances, the offenders shall be sentenced to between two and seven years of imprisonment:

- In an organised manner;
- The crime has been committed "professionally" (i.e. by a professional money launderer);
- The property or things involved in the offence are of high value;
- The person is found to have gained a large amount of illicit profit;
- The offence constitutes a case of dangerous recidivism.

A further requirement relates to those found to have committed the crime in one of the following circumstances, where offenders shall be sentenced to between five and ten years of imprisonment:

- The property or things involved in the offence are of very high value;
- A very large amount of profit is illegally gained.

This is further extended for those committing the crime in one of the following circumstances; the offenders shall be sentenced to between seven and 15 years of imprisonment:

- The property or things involved in the offence are of particularly great value;
- A particularly great amount of profit is illegally gained.

The offender may also be subject to a fine of between three million dong and thirty million dong and/or the confiscation of part or whole of their property.

27.37.8 *Scope*

Financial organisations must apply measures to identify clients in the following cases:

- When clients open accounts or set up transactions with financial organisations;
- When clients make infrequent transactions of high value or carry out an electronic money transfer but lack information about the name, address or account number of the originator;
- When there is doubt as to whether a transaction or the parties concerned in a transaction are involved in money laundering;
- When there are doubts about the accuracy or completeness of the client's identification information collected previously;
- When clients conduct irregular transactions of high value, defined as clients possessing no account or possessing a payment account but having no transactions within six months or more and then conducting a transaction with a total value of 300,000,000 (three hundred million) dong or more in a day.

27.37.9 *Risk-based Approach*

Depending on the scale and scope of activity and the transactions carried out by customers, reporting entities shall check and classify their customers according to whether they pose a high, medium or low level of risk. For customers with a high risk level, reporting entities must apply customer identification measures at an enhanced level.

27.37.10 *Role of the MLRO/Nominated Officer*

Each reporting organisation should appoint a member of the executive board to be in charge of organising, conducting and inspecting compliance with provisions of applicable laws on the prevention and combating of money laundering at their unit (hereinafter referred to as the person in charge of money laundering prevention and combating) and register the details of this person with the Anti-Money-Laundering Office of the Banking Inspection and Supervision Agency. The details should include the name, work address, phone number, fax number and a contact email address. When the person in charge of money laundering prevention and combating, or any information relating to that person, changes, the reporting organisation shall be required to make a timely written report outlining the changes to the Anti-Money-Laundering Office of the Banking Inspection and Supervision Agency.

Depending on the scale, scope and specific features of the operation, the reporting organisation shall decide whether to establish a specialised unit (division, department) or to set up a unit at the head office to oversee all matters pertaining to the prevention and combating of money laundering. Within each operational department and branch, the reporting organisation shall appoint one or several officers to be in charge of the prevention and combating of money laundering.

27.37.11 Due Diligence

There are two objectives of the CDD requirements:

- To ensure the reliability and timeliness of information identifying customers;
- To ensure the confidentiality of information identifying customers.

Personal Client and Corporate Due Diligence

Reporting entities are responsible for setting their own CDD requirements, which must include the following elements:

- Date, month and year for opening accounts or conducting transactions;
- Full name of the person or persons representing agencies or organisations wishing to offer services, together with the passport, identity card or other personal papers, address or registered permanent residence;
- For companies, the full and abbreviated company name, business registration, tax registration number and address of the organisation, fax number, areas of operation and business, information on the founder and any representative specified;
- Name, address and proof of business registration for individuals and organisations related to the transaction;
- The form, purpose and value of the transaction;
- For legal entity clients or those acting upon the provision of an authorised agreement service, information on ownership and control structure to determine any individual or individuals with a controlling interest or that governs the operation of that legal entity.

Beneficial Ownership

Reporting entities must define beneficial owners according to the following criteria:

- **Individuals owning, in reality, an account or a transaction:** Account owners, account co-owners or any person who controls or benefits from such account or transaction;
- **Individuals who have the right to control legal entities:** Individuals holding 10% or more of the charter capital of such a legal entity; individuals holding 20% or more of the charter capital of an organisation which contributes more than 10% of the capital for such a legal entity; owners of private enterprises; other individuals controlling such a legal entity in reality;

Enhanced Customer Due Diligence

Reporting entities must draw up regulation on the classification of clients on the basis of the money-laundering risk based on the following elements:

- **Client type:** Residents or non-residents; organisations or individuals; clients on or not on any black list or warning list; fields and methods of operation and trading.
- **Types of products or services which clients use or anticipate using:** Cash or remittance services; payment services or services of money transfer or exchange; brokerage, entrustment or authorisation services; life insurance or non-life insurance services.
- **Geographical locations in which clients reside or have their head offices:** Countries on the embargo list stated in resolutions of the United Nations Security Council; countries listed by the FATF as being non-compliant or insufficiently compliant with recommendations on preventing money laundering and preventing the financing of terrorism; countries, regions or territories which are known to conduct many activities involving heroin, corruption and/or money laundering.
- **Other elements:** Reporting entities may self-define other elements, based on their particular circumstances.

Politically Exposed Persons

A reporting entity shall be responsible for identifying customers who are politically exposed persons. In the event that a customer is a politically exposed person, the reporting entity shall apply enhanced measures as follows:

- Obtain the approval of the General Director (Director) or authorised Deputy General Director (Deputy Director) before establishing the relationship or immediately after the current customer is identified as a politically exposed person;
- Take measures to find out about the source of funds and assets of the customer.

27.37.12 Ongoing Monitoring

A reporting entity must regularly update client identification information during the course of the business relationship to ensure that the transactions being conducted by clients through the reporting entity are in accordance with the information already known about the clients, about the business operation, the risks and the origins of the clients' property.

Internal regulations on the prevention and combating of money laundering should include the following contents:

- **A policy of client acceptance:** According to the extent of risk posed, levels deemed acceptable for approval and requirements about opening accounts or setting up transactions.
- **Processes by which to identify clients, verify and update information on clients:** Decentralisation of responsibility for identification, periodic updating of information and assessment of clients according to the extent of risk posed; decentralisation of access and use of general information in the system; regulations on the identification of clients with accounts or transactions at many branches in the system.
- **Guidance on the reporting process for certain transactions:** Transactions of high value; electronic remittance transactions; doubtful transactions; transactions related to money laundering with the aim of financing terrorism; transactions related to criminal activities; transactions related to the list of terrorist individuals and organisations and terrorist donors according to resolutions of the United Nations Security Council; transactions conducted by any other person on a black list or warning list.
- **Processes to review, detect and handle suspicious transactions:** Entities must review and analyse clients and transactions related to clients which appear suspicious, as prescribed in Clause 2 and Clause 8, and must report, as prescribed in Clause 1, Article 22 of the law on prevention and combat of money laundering. Entities must also define responsibilities according to each level of employment. The handling of reports on suspicious transactions must be conducted on the basis of analysing information held on the entire system. Entities must also set out the method of dealing with clients conducting suspicious transactions, so as to ensure that information is not revealed (tipping off).
- **Policies on the storage of information and the maintenance of confidentiality:** Entities should outline the method of storage, the level of storage and procedures for accessing the information.
- **Policies outlining the application of temporary measures and principles in the handling of cases involving the postponement of the implementation of a transaction:** Entities are required to provide details of specific cases when such temporary measures apply; and to specify levels of responsibility in their application and in implementing requests from functional agencies.
- **The regime for reporting and providing information to the State Bank of Vietnam and competent State agencies:** The method and process of reporting and information provision should aim to ensure that the contents of the reports and the time before submission of the reports are in accordance with requirements.
- **A training policy:** An entity must draw up a training programme; the content of the training should be tailored and scaled to suit different levels (management level, policy level and execution level), organisational sections (head office, branch or region) and operational fields. The policy should also outline the frequency of such training.
- **Internal audit and control policies to monitor compliance with policies, regulations, processes and procedures involving the prevention and combating of money laundering:** An entity should set out the structure, organisation and method of conducting

such control and internal audits. The procedures for reporting to competent State agencies and the associated reporting time limits and contents should also be clearly set out, along with regulations on handling and remedying any detected violations.

27.37.13 AML Management with Risk-based Customer Classification

Article 12 of the Law provides an additional responsibility to financial institutions and designated non-financial businesses and professions. Besides customer identification, which is already required by sub-law regulations, under the new Law, reporting entities will have to produce internal regulations on customer classification based on risk exposure by types of clients, goods/services in use and places of residence/head office.

Additional evaluations shall be applied to customers and transactions which are classified in the high-risk range. Said high-risk customers and transactions include politically exposed foreigners, agent banking operations, transactions relating to new technology, transactions with individuals and organisations from countries and territories on the warning list and introduced business.

The modern risk-based AML management approach was first applied in the banking sector in Circular 41. Under the Law, this approach is extended to other sectors. As a result, not only financial institutions but also real estate agents, real estate floors, insurance companies and stock brokers will have to establish an AML management system with risk-based customer classification to fully comply with the Law.

27.37.14 Staff Training

On an annual basis, a reporting organisation shall set up and carry out a programme of training and raising awareness of the measures for preventing and combating money laundering for all officers and staff relating to money and other asset transactions of the reporting organisation. The reporting organisation must have a policy on giving priority to the training of those staff who directly transact with the customers and officers and staff in charge of the prevention and combating of money laundering.

The reporting organisation shall, by its own decision, select the training form that best corresponds with its organisational and operational features. It shall also take the initiative in coordinating with the Banking Inspection and Supervision Agency and concerned units to organise the training for officers and staff with respect to the professional skills and operations required in the prevention and combating of money laundering.

The contents of officer and staff training must be in line with their work and the level of money-laundering risk relating to their work. It must also be relevant to their responsibility for the implementation of internal regulations on the prevention and combating of money laundering, and should include the following:

- Provisions of laws and internal regulations on the prevention and combating of money laundering; legal responsibilities in cases of failing to implement the provisions of laws on the prevention and combating of money laundering;

- Current methods and tricks used in money laundering and money-laundering trends for the foreseeable future;
- The risks of money laundering relating to the products, services and work that they are involved with.

Within a period of six months of recruiting staff to execute duties relating to monetary and other asset transactions, a reporting organisation shall provide training for the new employees to provide a basic knowledge of means of preventing and combating money laundering.

27.37.15 Record-keeping

In addition to storing and preserving information according to the current regulations, individuals and organisations mentioned in Article 6 of this Decree shall have to keep identifying information related to customer transactions for at least five years from the date of account closure or five years from the end of the transaction.

27.37.16 Reporting Requirements

The following transactions must be reported:

- One or more transactions in a day by individuals or organisations which have a total cash value of VND 200 million or more, whether it is in a foreign currency or has a gold equivalent value of this amount.

27.37.17 Suspicious Transaction Reporting

The 2013 legislation provides some basic signals for suspicious transactions to assist entities with implementing their STR programmes. Entities will also be obliged to take additional precautions and make reports where there is a suspicion of criminal activity. Under the 2005 Decree, entities could choose whether or not to do this.

Firms are required to look out for suspicious signs including:

(a) The client provides incorrect, incomplete or inconsistent client identification information;

(b) The client persuades the reporting entity not to make a report on a transaction to the competent State agencies;

(c) An inability to identify a client using the information provided by the client, or a transaction is related to a party whose identity cannot be identified;

(d) The individual or agency phone number provided by the client agencies cannot be contacted, or this phone number does not appear to exist after opening the account or carrying out the transaction;

(e) The transactions are requested by order or under the authorisation of organisations or individuals on a warning list;

(f) Transactions where, through analysis of the client identification information or through the consideration of economic and legal grounds, it can be determined that they involve criminal activities or are related to organisations and/or individuals on a warning list;

(g) Organisations and individuals involved in transactions with large amounts that are inconsistent with the income and business activities of these organisations and individuals;

(h) Clients' transactions made through the reporting entities that do not follow the proper processes and procedures as prescribed by law.

Suspicious signs in the banking area include:

(a) A sudden change in the transaction turnover on the account; money deposited into and withdrawn quickly from accounts; high transaction turnover but a very small or zero account balance;

(b) The transfer of money of small value from many different accounts to an account or vice versa in a short time; money is transferred through multiple accounts; the parties concerned are not interested in trading fees; carrying out multiple transactions, each transaction being near the large value rate that must be reported;

(c) Using letters of credit and other trade financing methods of great value, with the discount rate at a higher value than normal;

(d) Clients who open multiple accounts at foreign credit organisations, bank branches in other geographical areas different from the place where clients are residing, working or undertaking business activities;

(e) The client's account is not traded for over a year, and is suddenly traded again without plausible reasons; clients' accounts without any transactions suddenly get a cash deposit or money transfer of great value;

(f) Transfer of money from the account of an enterprise overseas after receiving a lot of small amounts of money transferred by electronic money transfer, cheques or drafts;

(g) Enterprises with foreign investment capital transfer money overseas immediately after receiving the investment capital or transfer money overseas not in accordance with the business activities; foreign enterprises transferring money overseas immediately after receiving money from abroad transferred into accounts opened at foreign credit organizations or bank branches operating in Vietnam;

(h) Clients often change money with small denominations into larger denominations;

(i) Transactions involving the deposit, withdrawal or transfer of money made by organisations or individuals associated with the crimes creating illegal property published on mass media;

(j) A client requests to borrow the maximum amount allowed based on the contracts of single-premium contracts right after the premium payment, except for a case where this is required by the credit organisation;

(k) Information about the origin of property used for financing, investment, loan, financial leasing or investment trust of clients is not clear and transparent;

(l) Information about the origin of the security property of the clients asking for a capital loan is not clear and transparent.

Suspicious signs in the area of insurance include:

(a) A client requires to purchase an insurance contract of great value or requires the package payment of the single premium for insurance products that do not apply a package payment, while the current insurance contracts of the client only have small value and periodic payments;

(b) A client requires to sign insurance contracts with periodic premiums inconsistent with the current income of the client or requires to purchase insurance contracts related to business outside the normal business activities of the client;

(c) The buyer of an insurance contract makes payment from an account that is not his account or by an instrument of transfer without a name being recorded;

(d) A client requests to change the beneficiary appointed, or this is done by a person who has an unclear relationship with the buyer of the insurance contracts;

(e) A client accepts all unfavourable conditions not related to his age and health; a client requires to buy insurance with no clear purpose and reluctantly provides a reason to participate in insurance; the conditions and value of insurance contracts are contrary to the client's needs;

(f) A client cancels the insurance contract right after taking it out and asks for a transfer of money to a third party; the client regularly participates in insurance and assigns the insurance contract to a third party;

(g) A client is an enterprise having a number of insurance contracts for employees or the premium of the single-premium contract abnormally increases;

(h) The insurance enterprise often pays the premium with a large amount to the same customer.

Suspicious signs in the area of securities include:

(a) Purchasing or selling securities with abnormal signs in one day or several days done by an organisation or an individual;

(b) The client makes a transfer of securities outside the system without any plausible reasons;

(c) The securities company transfers money not in accordance with the securities trading activities;

(d) A resident transfers a large amount from the securities trading account out of Vietnam;

(e) A client often sells his portfolio and requires the securities company to make payment by cash or cheque;

(f) A client invests abnormally in many types of securities in cash or cheques in a short period or is willing to invest in a securities portfolio that has no benefit;

(g) Following a long period of inactivity a very large investment is suddenly made in a client's securities account. This investment does not seem to accord with the client's financial means;

(h) The purchase and sale of securities with money from investment funds opened in territories that the international organisations have classified as high risk for money laundering.

Suspicious signs in games with prizes and casinos include:

(a) A customer appears to constantly lose intentionally at the casino;

(b) A client exchanges conventional currency of great value in a casino or a prize-winning gaming website place but does not play or plays with a very small amount and then converts back to cash or cheque, bank draft or transfers money to other accounts;

(c) A client requests to transfer the game winnings or prize winnings to a third party that has no clear relationship with the customer, or the third party does not reside permanently with the customer;

(d) A client adds cash or a cheque to the winning prize amount and requires the casino or the prize-winning gaming website to turn this into cheques of great value;

(e) A client, many times a day, requires a casino or a prize-winning gaming website to exchange an amount of conventional money into cash;

(f) A client, many times a day, requires a third party on his behalf to exchange an amount of conventional money with great value and asks the third party to play games for him;

(g) A client, many times a day, purchases lottery tickets and/or betting slips and exchanges conventional money near the limit for large value transactions;

(h) A client re-purchases a high value winning lottery ticket from others.

Suspicious signs in the area of real estate business include:

(a) The real estate transactions are authorised transactions but there are no legal grounds;

(b) The client does not pay attention to the price of real estate and the transaction fees to be paid;

(c) The client cannot provide information related to real estate or does not want to provide additional personal information;

(d) The price agreed between the parties to the transaction does not match the market price.

27.37.18 Penalties

Under the 2013 Law, the penalties are "those prescribed by law". The latest regulations at the time of writing can be found in the 2005 provisions, which specified that the following penalties can be administered for failing to comply with the AML provisions:

- A warning shall be given where there is no regulation on internal control or auditing, including clauses on the prevention and combating of money laundering, or for failing to appoint officials responsible for deploying anti-money-laundering measures; a warning shall also be given to an entity which does not have a customer-monitoring process or CDD procedures which comply with the legal requirements.
- A fine of VND 5,000,000 to VND 15,000,000 shall be imposed for an act of not informing or not reporting to the Information Centre or to the competent State agency; not preserving books, files or documents relating to transactions for the required time in conformity with the Law; or not informing the Information Centre or the competent State agency when a mistake has been detected in a file, document, report or books which have been previously sent to them.
- A fine of VND 10,000,000 to VND 30,000,000 shall be imposed for an act of informing parties to a transaction about the content of reports or information that has been provided; or for delaying or failing to implement the requirements of the Information Centre or other competent agency without a proper reason.
- Besides a warning or a fine, violating individuals and/or organisations may be deprived, with or without a time limit, of their operating licence or certificate of professional practice which enabled them to commit an act of violation; material evidence and any tools used to commit the violation may be confiscated in accordance with the provisions of the Law on Settlement of Administrative Violation.

27.37.19 Case Studies

According to a 2012 US government report on Vietnam, there have been no money-laundering prosecutions or convictions in the country.

APPENDIX

TRANSPARENCY INTERNATIONAL 2013 CORRUPTION PERCEPTIONS INDEX

This index ranks countries and territories based on how corrupt their public sector is perceived to be. A country or territory's score indicates the perceived level of public sector corruption on a scale of 0–100, where 0 means that a country is perceived as highly corrupt and 100 means it is perceived as very clean. A country's rank indicates its position relative to the other countries and territories included in the index. The 2013 index includes 175 countries and territories.

1	Denmark	91	7
1	New Zealand	91	7
3	Finland	89	7
3	Sweden	89	7
5	Norway	86	7
5	Singapore	86	9
7	Switzerland	85	6
8	Netherlands	83	7
9	Australia	81	8
9	Canada	81	7
11	Luxembourg	80	6
12	Germany	78	8
12	Iceland	78	6
14	United Kingdom	76	8

15	Barbados	75	3
15	Belgium	75	7
15	Hong Kong	75	8
18	Japan	74	9
19	United States of America	73	9
19	Uruguay	73	6
21	Ireland	72	6
22	The Bahamas	71	3
22	Chile	71	9
22	France	71	8
22	Saint Lucia	71	3
26	Austria	69	8
26	United Arab Emirates	69	7
28	Estonia	68	9
28	Qatar	68	6
30	Botswana	64	7
31	Bhutan	63	4
31	Cyprus	63	5
33	Portugal	62	7
33	Puerto Rico	62	3
33	Saint Vincent and the Grenadines	62	3
36	Israel	61	6
36	Taiwan	61	7
38	Brunei	60	3
38	Poland	60	10
40	Spain	59	7
41	Cape Verde	58	4
41	Dominica	58	3
43	Lithuania	57	8
43	Slovenia	57	9
45	Malta	56	5
46	South Korea	55	10
47	Hungary	54	10
47	Seychelles	54	4

49	Costa Rica	53	5
49	Latvia	53	8
49	Rwanda	53	5
52	Mauritius	52	5
53	Malaysia	50	9
53	Turkey	50	9
55	Georgia	49	6
55	Lesotho	49	5
57	Bahrain	48	5
57	Croatia	48	9
57	Czech Republic	48	10
57	Namibia	48	6
61	Oman	47	5
61	Slovakia	47	8
63	Cuba	46	4
63	Ghana	46	9
63	Saudi Arabia	46	5
66	Jordan	45	7
67	Macedonia FYR	44	6
67	Montenegro	44	4
69	Italy	43	7
69	Kuwait	43	5
69	Romania	43	9
72	Bosnia and Herzegovina	42	7
72	Brazil	42	8
72	Sao Tome and Principe	42	3
72	Serbia	42	7
72	South Africa	42	9
77	Bulgaria	41	9
77	Senegal	41	9
77	Tunisia	41	7
80	China	40	9
80	Greece	40	7
82	Swaziland	39	4

83	Burkina Faso	38	7
83	El Salvador	38	6
83	Jamaica	38	6
83	Liberia	38	7
83	Mongolia	38	7
83	Peru	38	7
83	Trinidad and Tobago	38	4
83	Zambia	38	8
91	Malawi	37	8
91	Morocco	37	8
91	Sri Lanka	37	7
94	Algeria	36	6
94	Armenia	36	6
94	Benin	36	6
94	Colombia	36	7
94	Djibouti	36	3
94	India	36	10
94	Philippines	36	9
94	Suriname	36	3
102	Ecuador	35	6
102	Moldova	35	8
102	Panama	35	6
102	Thailand	35	8
106	Argentina	34	8
106	Bolivia	34	7
106	Gabon	34	5
106	Mexico	34	9
106	Niger	34	5
111	Ethiopia	33	8
111	Kosovo	33	3
111	Tanzania	33	8
114	Egypt	32	7
114	Indonesia	32	9
116	Albania	31	7

116	Nepal	31	5
116	Vietnam	31	8
119	Mauritania	30	5
119	Mozambique	30	7
119	Sierra Leone	30	8
119	East Timor	30	3
123	Belarus	29	5
123	Dominican Republic	29	6
123	Guatemala	29	6
123	Togo	29	5
127	Azerbaijan	28	6
127	Comoros	28	3
127	Gambia	28	5
127	Lebanon	28	6
127	Madagascar	28	8
127	Mali	28	6
127	Nicaragua	28	7
127	Pakistan	28	8
127	Russia	28	9
136	Bangladesh	27	7
136	Ivory Coast	27	8
136	Guyana	27	4
136	Kenya	27	8
140	Honduras	26	6
140	Kazakhstan	26	8
140	Laos	26	4
140	Uganda	26	8
144	Cameroon	25	8
144	Central African Republic	25	4
144	Iran	25	6
144	Nigeria	25	9
144	Papua New Guinea	25	5
144	Ukraine	25	8
150	Guinea	24	7

150	Kyrgyzstan	24	6
150	Paraguay	24	5
153	Angola	23	7
154	Republic of Congo	22	6
154	Democratic Republic of the Congo	22	5
154	Tajikistan	22	5
157	Burundi	21	5
157	Myanmar	21	6
157	Zimbabwe	21	8
160	Cambodia	20	7
160	Eritrea	20	4
160	Venezuela	20	7
163	Chad	19	5
163	Equatorial Guinea	19	3
163	Guinea Bissau	19	4
163	Haiti	19	5
167	Yemen	18	6
168	Syria	17	4
168	Turkmenistan	17	3
168	Uzbekistan	17	6
171	Iraq	16	4
172	Libya	15	6
173	South Sudan	14	3
174	Sudan	11	6
175	Afghanistan	8	3
175	North Korea	8	3
175	Somalia	8	4

INDEX

Printed and bound by CPI Group (UK) Ltd, Croydon, CR0 4YY

23/04/2025

14660964-0002